Content Area Literacy
Teaching for Today and Tomorrow

Delmar Publishers' Online Services
To access Delmar on the World Wide Web, point your browser to:
http://www.delmar.com/delmar.html
To access through Gopher: gopher://gopher.delmar.com
(Delmar Online is part of "thomson.com", and Internet site with information on
more than 30 publishers of the International Thomson Publishing organization.)
For more information on our products and services:
email: info@delmar.com
or call 800-347-7707

Content Area Literacy
Teaching for Today and Tomorrow

Robin Eanes, Ph.D.
St. Edward's University
Austin, Texas

Delmar Publishers™
I⬤P An International Thomson Publishing Company

Albany • Bonn • Boston • Cincinnati • Detroit • London • Madrid • Melbourne
Mexico City • New York • Pacific Grove • Paris • San Francisco • Singapore • Tokyo
Toronto • Washington

NOTICE TO THE READER

Cover Design: Timothy J. Conners

Delmar Staff

Publisher: Diane L. McOscar
Associate Editor: Erin J. O'Connor Traylor
Project Editor : Colleen A. Corrice
Production Coordinator: James Zayicek
Art and Design Coordinator: Timothy J. Conners
Editorial Assistant: Glenna Stanfield

COPYRIGHT © 1997
By Delmar Publishers
A division of International Thomson Publishing Inc.

I(T)P The ITP logo is a trademark under license

Printed in the United States of America

For more information, contact:

Delmar Publishers
3 Columbia Circle, Box 15015
Albany, NY 12212-5015

International Thomson Publishing Europe
Bershire House 168-173
High Holborn
London, WC1V7AA
England

Thomas Nelson Australia
102 Dodd Street
South Melbourne, 3205
Victoria, Australia

Nelson Canada
1120 Birchmount Road
Scarborough, Ontario
Canada M1K 5G4

International Thomson Editors
Compos Eliseos 385, Piso 7
Col Polanco
11560 Mexico D F Mexico

International Thomson Publishing Gmbh
Königswinterer Strasse 418
53227 Bonn
Germany

International Thomson Publishing Asia
221 Henderson Road
#05-10 Henderson Building
Singapore 0315

International Thomson Publishing – Japan
Hirakawacho Kyowa Building, 3F
2-2-1 Hirakawa-cho
Chiyoda-ku, 102 Tokyo
Japan

1 2 3 4 5 6 7 8 9 10 XXX 01 00 99 98 97 96

Library of Congress Cataloging-in-Publication Data

Eanes, Robin.
    Content area literacy: teaching for today and tomorrow / Robin
Eanes.
      p. cm.
    Includes bibliographical references and index.
    ISBN 0-8273-5954-3
    1. Language arts—Correlation with content subjects—United
States. 2. Language arts teachers—Training of—United States.
3. Lesson planning—United States. I. Title.
LB1576.E16 1995
372.6044—dc20

95–19884
CIP

Contents

For Richard and Lauren

Acknowledgements

First, I want to acknowledge Jay Bonstingl for generously giving permission to include his work on Total Quality in education. The principles he has so eloquently described, I believe, are a critical component of the new paradigm of education. This new paradigm, and the principles of Total Quality in particular, provides an important foundation and context for understanding and applying the methods and strategies involved in content area reading and literacy. I recommend his 1992 book, *Schools of Quality: An Introduction to Total Quality Management in Education* (published by the Association for Supervision and Curriculum Development) as an excellent resource for teachers.

I also acknowledge Marie Carbo for giving me permission to use the learning styles checklist presented in Chapter 2. Her work involving reading and learning styles has made important contributions, in my opinion, to the new paradigm philosophy of adapting instruction to fit the child rather than remediating the child to fit the instruction. A workshop she presented in Dallas (and which I attended several years ago), served as a great inspiration for me.

For a project that spans more than three years since its inception, I would have to include an additional chapter to do justice in acknowledging everyone who made possible the completion of this book. So, although I will mention them briefly below, I would like to say to all of them that I realize and appreciate the generous amounts of time and hard work they dedicated to this project. I feel satisfaction in knowing that their devoted efforts were not done for any external reward or acknowledgment. Rather, their contributions reflect their support of me and our shared commitment to quality education.

For their hard work in researching, editing, proofreading, photocopying, faxing, mailing, word processing, and most importantly, for their cheerful and enthusiastic attitudes through it all, I gratefully acknowledge Quita Buck and Liz Ing (formerly my students and now first-rate teachers!), as well as, Paige Pozzi, Robin Blackburn and most of all, Jeanne Po. I especially want to thank Liz for setting up my research system, as well as for her excellent feedback and creative ideas. For superlative technical writing consulting, I thank my colleague, Laurie Drummond, who not only contributed her expertise in writing but also her emotional support as my good friend.

For his exceptional talents in artistic design, graphics, drawing, and photography, I thank Jeff Williams (formerly my student and now a superb teacher!); the illustrations, Graphic Organizers, charts, and photographs he contributed have made this book user friendly, particularly for visual learners. I also want to thank Jeff for his enthusiastic belief in the educational philosophies behind this project and his energetic crusade to see the concepts of content area reading and literacy at work in classrooms.

I am very grateful to Jeanne Po, Quita Buck, Liz Ing, and Suzette Thorpe-Johnson (another former student who is now a superlative teacher!) for their invaluable help and support as my teaching assistants. Their belief in me as a teacher, as well as their invaluable assistance, gave me renewed energy in times of exhaustion after spending days on end observing interns and student teachers in the schools and nights on end grading papers, planning classes, and revising chapters. In particular, Jeanne (alias Radar O'Reilly), gave me incredible help and support during the hectic final stages of production. I have great admiration and respect for her.

I especially want to thank Quita for her help with the glossary, strategy charts, sample lesson plans, and other appendices. Her voluntary and enthusiastic assistance, as deadlines drew near, not only gave me great encouragement and energy but also resulted in quality contributions to this text.

I want to thank Suzette for her almost evangelical dedication and efforts; she worked hard to spread the use of teaching methods and strategies she learned in my class among faculty in secondary and university classrooms! Her efforts led to excellent feedback and ideas for this project.

In addition to Quita and Suzette, I want to thank Don Clark (a terrific secondary science teacher!) and his students for setting up the color photo sessions; I especially want to thank Roger Buck for his exceptional photographic talents and generous donation of time. Thanks also to Jeff and his middle school students for setting up the black and white photo sessions. All their photographs bring the concepts in this book to life.

I am especially indebted to all the St. Edward's University (SEU) teacher education students who used drafts of this book as their course text from Fall 1993 through Fall 1995. From my view, their feedback and ideas based on a student's perspective have resulted in greatly enhanced quality. I acknowledge and appreciate the difficulty they experienced in reading a textbook that had no index, graphics, glossary, or other study aids. In spite of those difficulties, their patience and positive suggestions demonstrated their true commitment and willingness to make sacrifices for the betterment of education. Finally, I am deeply grateful for the truly outstanding lesson plans, study guides, and Graphic Organizers developed and submitted by SEU students. They are of such high quality that I have included many of them as examples in this text.

I feel exceptionally grateful to my colleague, Dr. Molly Minus, for her intensive and extensive support of me and this project. Her almost daily encouragement, positive feedback, and excellent suggestions have helped me, on numerous occasions, keep going beyond the point of exhaustion. Her sincere belief in the worthiness of this book was a constant source of energy for me. She is a true colleague whose friendship I value dearly.

I specifically want to thank Molly for her help in setting up the glossary, and for proofreading and editing. Finally, I am very grateful to her for using the draft as the text in her classes and channeling to me the superb feedback and sample lesson plans, study guides, and Graphic Organizers of her students. In particular, I appreciate the time and energy volunteered by Virginia Alexander, whose feedback and suggestions improved the quality of the text immensely. I also want to thank Dr. Karen Schumaker for using the draft with her classes and channeling to me the invaluable feedback of her and her students. I am deeply grateful to my colleague and dear friend, Barbara Frandsen, for generously sharing the excellent resource guides she authored, as well as her extensive private collection of books and materials. Finally, I say thanks to J. Frank Smith, Dean of the School of Education at SEU, for his continuing support and encouragement on this and other projects. His sincere appreciation and recognition of my work helps make it all worthwhile.

Although "just doing their jobs," I want to acknowledge the following people for the extensive quantity and high quality of work they contributed to this project. First, the in-depth and honest feedback and the positive suggestions offered by the professional reviewers were invaluable and greatly appreciated. Second, I owe a tremendous debt of gratitude to the classroom teachers and their students who have given the SEU interns and student teachers the opportunity to apply strategies and activities in real classroom settings. As a result of these experiences, we have all learned invaluable lessons about good practices in teaching and learning.

I am extremely grateful to Betty Cliff for her never-ending patience and superlative skills at photocopying and binding mass quantities of text drafts for use with students. I would like to acknowledge Alison Carpenter, Armando Garcia, Claudia Kweder, and the reference librarians at the Scarborough-Phillips Library for their extensive research assistance. I also want to thank Diane Calvert for her efficiency, patience, and kindness in the copyediting phase of this project. I am deeply grateful to her and her colleagues for the exceptional contributions they made to the quality of this book. Finally, I appreciate the assistance and support provided by Erin O'Connor Traylor, my associate editor, and her colleagues at Delmar.

REVIEWERS

Catherine J. Coggin   Donna J. Corlett
Stetson University   University of Portland
Deland, Florida   Portland, Oregon

Katherine L. Schlick-Noe
Seattle University
Seattle, Washington

Joan L. Thompson
The Catholic University of America
Washington, District of Columbia

M. Kay Stickle
Ball State University
Muncie, Indiana

The following acknowledgements go to my devoted family and friends who made this remarkable accomplishment possible. First, words cannot express the full extent of my gratitude to my mother, Edith Smith Farris, for her generous gift of a computer, on which this entire book has been written. Second, I also have difficulty finding words to show my gratitude to my sister, Kris, and nephews, Gifford and Jordan. Unbelievably, they have completely forgiven me for virtually dropping out of their lives for the past two years. I look forward to spending more time with them now. I'm especially grateful to Kris, a superb classroom teacher, for trying out my ideas and giving me feedback on the effectiveness of various strategies and activities.

Fortunately, I don't need to find the words to thank Quita, my best friend, because I think she already knows. Spending time with her has been a major source of relaxation and renewal for me over the past year. Even through the times when I know she was tired of hearing about this book, she was upbeat and encouraging. On many occasions, she forgot her own troubles to bolster my spirits and reinforce my conviction to finish this project while maintaining only the highest standards of quality. I thank her for being an ardent supporter and faithful friend. Most of all, though, I want to thank her for the time I have been able to spend with her daughter, and my goddaughter, Lauren.

The times I have spent and continue to spend with Lauren are some of the most valued parts of my life. The love she gives me is addictive; I can't get enough. She reminds me how to have fun and how to keep my priorities straight. Sharing my love of horses and horseback riding with her has been an awesome experience. I am extremely proud of the person she is and grateful that she chooses to spend time with me.

Thanking Richard, my husband, who is the most amazing person I've ever met, is most difficult of all. His unconditional and unending love, patience, and encouragement seem truly remarkable to me. I feel so very fortunate to be spending my life with him. He is a constant source of pleasure, strength, perspective, wisdom, and fulfillment. I am truly grateful for every minute I get to spend with Richard. His love and devotion to me are my most precious possessions.

Finally, I must include Darwin and Kudra, my cocker spaniels and surrogate children, for faithfully keeping me company those hundreds of hours at the computer. They too have given unconditional love and devotion to me. They think I'm wonderful, and I think they are too.

Preface

The intended purpose of this textbook, *Content Area Reading and Literacy: Teaching for Today and Tomorrow,* is to serve as a primary text for teacher education courses that focus on methods for developing literacy skills to enhance the learning of content area subject matter across all disciplines. Therefore, it is appropriately used in courses for elementary, middle, and high school teachers. Also, it is appropriate both in courses that require a practicum/internship experience and those that do not. Inservice K–12 classroom teachers will benefit from reading it as well.

Whether you are or intend to be an elementary, middle school, or secondary teacher, one of your primary responsibilities is or will be helping students learn content in one or more disciplines. The concept of content area literacy is based on the notion that certain abilities in reading, writing, and thinking are necessary for learning subject matter with maximal effectiveness and efficiency. Although the exact nature of these skills varies from discipline to discipline, some of them are essential to all disciplines. As a content teacher, your ultimate goal is helping students internalize content at the highest possible levels of thought. To achieve this goal with maximal success, you must make sure that your students are equipped with the requisite literacy tools. The primary purpose of this text is to equip *you* with the methodologies and strategies you will need to help your students. They, in turn, will be able to develop, employ, and integrate the necessary literacy tools for the primary goal of enhancing content learning.

The rationale behind the format of this text involves the importance of teachers becoming proficient with the very tools for learning they will be teaching their students to use. Simply reading and learning about the skills and strategies involved in content area literacy is not sufficient. For you to develop your students' literacy tools effectively during classroom instruction, it is imperative that you become proficient with those tools and use them successfully as a learner. Teachers who have not had first-hand experience with the strategies will not be able to model them effectively. Unfortunately, the "do as I say, not as I do" approach is not sufficient for students to internalize important lifelong learning and study strategies.

In support of that rationale, most of the activities to be offered in the computerized study guide (on computer disk) are designed to give teachers the opportunity to apply as learners the reading, writing, and study strategies they will be assigning during classroom instruction. So, although writing out responses in each activity may not be necessary for *you* to internalize information effectively, the *process* of doing so is crucial to your ability to apply the strategy as a teacher. As you work through the activities, ask yourself questions: "What is this experience telling me about what I will expect from my students?" and "How could I use this strategy to enhance learning?" If you can answer such questions satisfactorily, then the value and relevance of each assignment become obvious. Throughout the study guide, you will be provided opportunities for guided practice and implementation of the techniques. Further, the text will continue to reinforce these learning strategies and concepts while introducing new concepts throughout the book.

This textbook is designed to help you become a more effective teacher by first making you a better student. Therefore, the activities offered in the study guide demonstrate a student-centered approach rather than the information-based approach found in many college texts. This approach is based on the fact that students have differing learning styles. Therefore, a variety of options will be provided, so that you may select the activities best suited to your particular learning style.

TEACHER-AS-MANAGER APPROACH

This text is also designed to prepare teachers for a major paradigm shift in education. As William Glasser describes in *The Quality School*, the effective teacher of today and tomorrow will also have to be an effective manager. Glasser describes a teacher in the old paradigm of education as someone who presents information to be learned to students who are willing to learn it. He describes a teacher in the new paradigm of education as more of a teacher-manager who faces the immense challenge of persuading students to become willing participants in the learning process.

THE METACOGNITIVE APPROACH

The metacognitive approach emphasized by this text focuses on quality learning through a continual improvement paradigm. First, you will learn how to set goals and establish clear and specific purposes for reading and learning. Second, you will be instructed on how to identify options and plan strategies for achieving your objectives. Third, you will learn how to monitor and assess your own learning. Finally, you will learn how to evaluate and reflect on your learning for the purposes of formulating new goals and strategies. Because this continual improvement approach to quality in learning involves the same approach for quality in teaching, you should be better prepared to master the role of instructional decision maker.

CONTINUAL IMPROVEMENT PARADIGM

A continual improvement paradigm will also be used to help you focus on quality instruction. First, you will learn how to establish instructional objectives. Second, you will be instructed on how to select content area literacy strategies appropriate for the students' needs and the materials' demands. You will learn that the selection of strategies is not an arbitrary process. Rather, it involves a reflective process of matching pedagogies to students and materials. Once you have mastered a core set of strategies, you will be encouraged to make eclectic use of those strategies by mixing and matching them appropriately to develop adaptations and variations. Third, you will learn how to evaluate the results of instruction to formulate new objectives and revise instruction based on those results. This ongoing process of goal setting, planning, implementing, evaluating, and revising is essential to the quality-minded teacher who has been empowered to be an instructional decision maker.

COOPERATIVE LEARNING

In addition to the metacognitive, student-centered approach described, this text also emphasizes cooperative learning, problem solving, and experiential approaches. You will have opportunities to work with fellow students as colleagues in partnerships and small groups to solve problems creatively and master practical applications of instructional concepts and principles. In doing so, you will learn the value of synergy, which means that a group's collective intelligence and creativity is far greater than that of any single individual.

ACTIVITIES

Again, the rationale of having you participate in cooperative-learning activities involves the notion that teachers will use such approaches appropriately and effectively as instructional devices only if they have successfully mastered them as students. Only in the role of a student can you appreciate the importance of structuring cooperative-learning activities so that each partner or group member participates equitably, is held accountable for learning, and is given incentives to help others. Once you have become a successful participant in synergy, you will be better prepared to use cooperative-learning effectively in your own classroom. You will also be able to work effectively with fellow teachers to solve instructional dilemmas and make curricular and pedagogical decisions.

CHAPTER ORGANIZATION

Outline of Key Concepts/Graphic Organizer

At the beginning of each chapter, an introduction is provided to give you necessary background knowledge along with the "big picture" of the key concepts contained in the chapter. Also at the beginning of each chapter, you will find a Graphic Organizer that provides a visual outline of the major concepts and their relationships. You will additionally find a traditional outline of the major concepts for that chapter. Depending on your individual learning style, you will probably prefer one type over the other. Keep in mind that your students' preferences will also vary according to their learning styles. So, as a teacher, you should demonstrate and teach a *variety* of outline types for helping students organize main ideas. As you read this text, use the outlines provided at the beginnings of the chapters as models for developing variations that may work better for you. Then, show your students how to do the same.

Content Objectives

Finally, at the beginning of each chapter, you will find a set of content objectives. These objectives will not only provide you with clear purposes for reading but will also assist you in monitoring and evaluating your comprehension and learning. As you work through the chapters, you will appreciate the importance of being provided guidance in the form of clear and specific expectations. Learning is enhanced when the reader is given focus and direction.

Learning Outcomes

Just as you are given specific learning outcomes for each chapter, you will provide your students with the same type of support. At times, you will be given choices and be allowed to set your own purposes for reading and learning. In the same way, you should allow your students to participate in the decision-making process about what they are expected to learn. Ultimately, you want your students to be able to set their own purposes for reading and learning, so that they may engage in focused, goal-directed learning on their own.

VISUAL FORMATS

You will find information provided in a variety of visual formats to suit the preferences of various learning styles. Graphic aids, pictures, and photographs will be included regularly for the visual learners who rely on them. Chapter sections will be clearly defined by subheadings. Make special note of the print types that identify the relationships between subheadings. You probably take these details for granted at this stage of your career as a student, but you will find it necessary as a teacher to take the time to help your students appreciate these subtleties of textbook reading.

CRITICAL THINKING/ENRICHMENT ACTIVITIES

You will notice that responding to the objectives will require thinking at all levels. Although it will be tempting to focus on the literal-level objectives and avoid the higher-level ones, remember that if you cannot successfully apply the literal-level information in responding at higher levels, you may not understand the material as well as you thought you did. Also, taking the extra time and effort necessary to respond to the objectives that require critical thinking will help you internalize the material as you read each chapter. This investment will pay off later when the time comes to prepare for tests or other forms of assessment and, eventually, to apply the information in the classroom. Enrichment activities will also be suggested at the end of each chapter to provide you with opportunities for practical application of chapter content.

STUDY SKILLS

Please note that the chapter on study skills has been placed early in the book so that you may apply the skills, concepts, and strategies introduced in that chapter as you read the rest of the book. Each chapter will introduce two different instructional strategies for content literacy; these sections are designed to provide a handy guide to the descriptions, procedures, and uses of some of the most popular and effective strategies for content literacy. In addition to the topics almost universally found in texts on content area literacy, this text will also give attention to the following:

- special needs learners (including the limited English proficient, the gifted, and the reading and learning disabled)

- cooperative learning and cooperative group testing
- flexible grouping practices
- supplementing content area textbooks with a variety of fiction and nonfiction trade books and other materials
- instructional and media technology
- learning styles
- classroom management and positive reinforcement

PROFESSIONAL DEVELOPMENT

If you are a preservice teacher, this text will be of maximal value if you put yourself into the following scenario: You have just been hired by a school whose principal believes that reading and writing are a key component of instruction in every subject. The school district is paying to send you to an inservice course on how to use reading, writing, and thinking strategies to maximize learning in content classes (i.e., science, social studies, math, art, physical education, computer science, history, literature, and so forth). You have one semester to master the art of teaching content using literacy-based strategies. By the end of the course, you should have the basic tools you need to challenge, inspire, and guide your students to become better readers, writers, and learners. As you work through the course, collecting and organizing materials, keep in mind that you will want to refer to these materials when you are the classroom teacher, a professional.

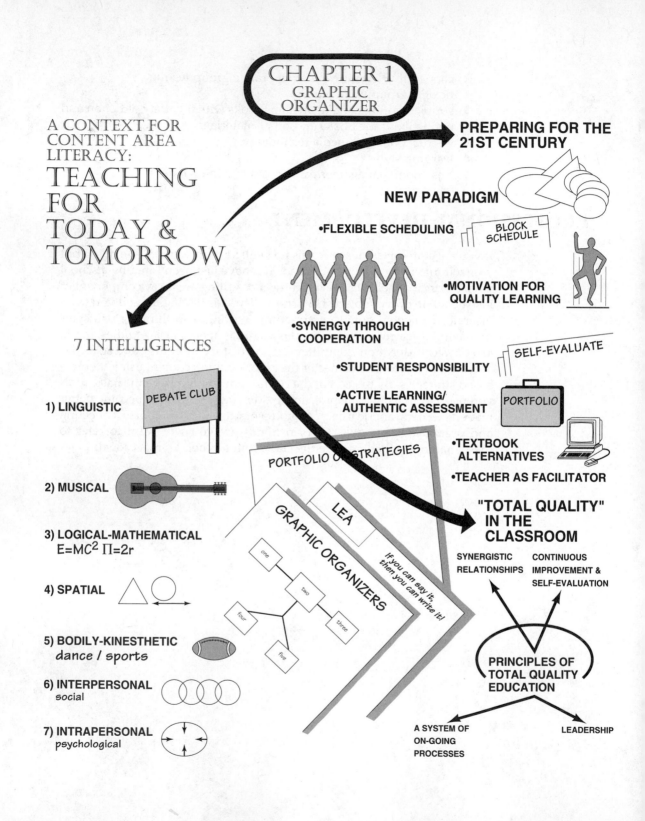

CHAPTER 1
GRAPHIC ORGANIZER

A CONTEXT FOR CONTENT AREA LITERACY:
TEACHING FOR TODAY & TOMORROW

PREPARING FOR THE 21ST CENTURY

NEW PARADIGM

• FLEXIBLE SCHEDULING

BLOCK SCHEDULE

• MOTIVATION FOR QUALITY LEARNING

• SYNERGY THROUGH COOPERATION

• STUDENT RESPONSIBILITY

SELF-EVALUATE

• ACTIVE LEARNING/ AUTHENTIC ASSESSMENT

PORTFOLIO

• TEXTBOOK ALTERNATIVES

• TEACHER AS FACILITATOR

7 INTELLIGENCES

1) LINGUISTIC

DEBATE CLUB

2) MUSICAL

3) LOGICAL-MATHEMATICAL
$E = MC^2$ $\Pi = 2r$

4) SPATIAL

5) BODILY-KINESTHETIC
dance / sports

6) INTERPERSONAL
social

7) INTRAPERSONAL
psychological

PORTFOLIO OF STRATEGIES

GRAPHIC ORGANIZERS

LEA

If you can say it, then you can write it!

one
two
three
four
five

"TOTAL QUALITY" IN THE CLASSROOM

SYNERGISTIC RELATIONSHIPS

CONTINUOUS IMPROVEMENT & SELF-EVALUATION

PRINCIPLES OF TOTAL QUALITY EDUCATION

A SYSTEM OF ON-GOING PROCESSES

LEADERSHIP

A Context for Content Area Literacy: Teaching for Today and Tomorrow

To demonstrate mastery of the content, the student will be able to do the following:

PART 1 OBJECTIVES

1. Identify the following strategy, describe its distinguishing features, and assess its significance to teaching content area literacy: Graphic Organizers.
2. Define *content area* and *content area literacy*.
3. Summarize the reforms that define a new paradigm of education emerging from the changing needs of society as we prepare students for the twenty-first century.
4. Describe the role of content area literacy in support of the new paradigm of education emerging from the reforms.

PART 2 OBJECTIVES

1. Identify the following strategy, describe its distinguishing features, and assess its significance to teaching content area literacy: LEA.
2. Define the concept of *Total Quality* and summarize four Total Quality principles that are valuable to education reform.
3. Explain how *Total Quality* principles are reflected in content area literacy instruction.
4. Create a personal mission statement for teaching that includes the following:
   ▪ The role of literacy in your content area classroom
   ▪ Your role and responsibilities as a content area teacher

PART 2 OBJECTIVES—continued

- Why you became or want to become a teacher
- What kind of teacher you are or want to be (character traits)
- Accomplishments and contributions you want to make as a teacher
- The values that guide your professional ethics and choices
- A plan for continued renewal through professional development

INTRODUCTION

Content refers to the knowledge students are expected to gain in a particular subject area. A subject area such as science, social studies, literature, math, art, or physical education is also known as a *content area*. Much of the learning that takes place in the content area classroom occurs through reading and writing.

The ultimate goal of learning in the content area classroom is to prepare students to meet their personal needs in lifelong learning. These needs are seldom limited to mastery of a particular body of content. Generally, the goal is to understand and learn the content for the purpose of identifying and solving problems, asking and answering questions, and generating and satisfying curiosities (Tierney and Pearson 1992). Therefore, along with reading and writing, critical thinking plays an important role in content area learning.

Entire books have been written on the complex processes involved in defining the term *literacy*. An inclusive definition would extend beyond reading, writing, and critical thinking as tools for learning. However, for the purposes and scope of this text, the definition of literacy will be limited to the use of reading, writing, and critical thinking as forms of communication. Therefore, *content area literacy* refers to the combined use of reading, writing, and critical thinking for the purpose of learning content in the content area classroom. An important implication of this concept is that reading and writing are complementary tasks that enhance content area learning (McKenna and Robinson 1990).

Content area literacy is a concept that enhances content area learning at all levels. In elementary school curricula, content area literacy affords students the opportunity to apply skills learned in reading and language arts instruction. Students not only gain practice in reading and writing skills but also experience the importance and practical value of those skills. Since content area learning involves real-life reading-to-learn experiences, students are empowered to fulfill natural curiosities and appetites for knowledge. Reading to learn then becomes reading for fun. As a result, positive attitudes toward reading and writing are fostered.

Literacy skills are not fully developed upon successful completion of the elementary school curriculum; in fact, these skills continue to develop throughout life to meet individual demands and desires for knowledge. In secondary school curricula, content area literacy provides students the opportunity to continue building on the foundation of literacy skills developed in elementary school. Furthermore, the literacy skills developed in elementary school are generally inadequate for the learning demands of secondary school curricula. Some secondary schools offer special classes in reading and/or language arts. However, one isolated class per day is not sufficient for students to develop the literacy skills needed to succeed in most secondary school curricula, nor to function in today's work place and society. Students' reading and writing skills, as tools for gaining desired information in a variety of settings, must be reinforced throughout the curriculum. As with elementary students, content area literacy empowers secondary students to satisfy personal interests and needs related to communicating and learning.

McKenna and Robinson (1990, p. 184) define a similar term, *content literacy,* as "the ability to use reading and writing for the acquisition of new content in a given discipline." They describe three components included in this ability: general literacy skills, content-specific literacy skills, and prior knowledge of content. The interaction of all three components help define one's content literacy, which is not the same as one's content knowledge (McKenna and Robinson 1990).

Your content knowledge (i.e., prior knowledge of content) consists of the information you have internalized and can recall about a particular subject. In order for that information to be useful you must have sufficiently developed communication skills (i.e., general literacy skills). You also must have sufficient mastery of the terminology that represents that information (i.e., content-specific literacy skills).

Content area literacy is influenced by a variety of factors, some of which are related to the subject matter itself. The demands placed on a learner vary by discipline. Therefore, an important implication of content literacy is that it is content specific. For example, literacy in social studies requires a different set of abilities and applications than does literacy in science.

However, content areas such as math, art, music, and physical education, which generally do not rely heavily on reading and writing, also require important literacy skills. These content areas have their own vocabularies, concepts, and ways of understanding, which are all important to content area literacy; reading and writing can enhance learning in all subject areas. Consequently, another important implication of content literacy is that it is relevant to all subject areas, not just those that rely heavily on printed materials (McKenna and Robinson 1990).

Content area literacy is influenced by characteristics of the textual materials. Factors such as conceptual density (which refers to the number of new or difficult concepts introduced), writing style, visual aids, and text organization all affect content area literacy. Textual demands may vary from book to book within a discipline, from chapter to chapter within a single text, and even from section to section within a chapter. Therefore, another important implication of content literacy is that it is relative to the tasks expected of students (McKenna and Robinson 1990). In short, content area literacy involves a variety of skills and strategies that enable the learner to adjust to the varying demands of content area learning.

Content area literacy is further influenced by characteristics of the learner. For example, prior knowledge, attitudes and interests, learning objectives (purposes), reading and writing experiences, learning styles, and familiarity with the subject all affect content area literacy and must be taken into consideration in its development.

Although influenced by many factors, content area literacy can be developed by teachers in all disciplines and at all levels. All the factors that influence content area literacy can be addressed through the use of specially designed lesson formats and strategies. When teachers use these tactics, they actively involve students in the literacy processes and applications that enhance learning. Moreover, teachers can generate enthusiasm for learning by helping students successfully glean exciting content from textual materials.

Students' literacy skills continue developing throughout and beyond elementary school, middle school, and high school. In fact, they continue developing beyond college and throughout life. Since literacy provides the tools for research and learning, literacy skills develop as the need arises to use them.

The first priority for elementary teachers is to teach students how to read, write, and think critically. However, equally important is teachers' responsibility for helping students learn about the world around them. In fact, the two responsibilities come together as students uncover one of the important functions of literacy skills: the discovery and learning of knowledge. Elementary teachers can help students develop a solid foundation of applying literacy skills for learning by guiding them in the strategic application of reading, writing, and critical thinking skills to learn subject matter content.

If students learn to read, write, and think critically in elementary school, one would think that they have the necessary tools for continuing their education in middle and secondary school. However, at these later stages students will learn more advanced content using more difficult reading materials. Therefore, literacy skills must continually develop in order to be effective tools for learning at higher levels.

Should schools therefore require all students to take reading classes in middle and high schools to develop the literacy skills students will need to learn content in their other classes? While reading classes can certainly be helpful in building general literacy skills, they are not enough to develop literacy skills in all content areas. Since each content area has its own vocabulary, conceptual frameworks, learning methods, and resource materials, one reading class cannot adequately prepare students for meeting the learning demands they will face in other classes.

Since adequate content area literacy skills cannot be developed in one class, should *all* middle and high school teachers become reading and writing teachers? Not necessarily. The answer lies in the application of simple, literacy-based instructional strategies designed to enhance the learning of content. Content area teachers are themselves masters of content area literacy, at least in their own areas of expertise. Literacy-based strategies allow teachers to model for their students effective ways to learn content through reading, writing, and critical thinking. Regular and consistent application of the strategies should result in the students developing content area literacy (i.e., the ability to read, write, and think the unique language of the content).

This book is designed to guide teachers at all levels through the process of learning about their own content area literacy skills and how these skills serve as tools for effectively learning content. As teachers develop awareness of their own learning through literacy processes, they also discover easy and obvious ways to guide their students through the learning process. As teachers help their students develop content area literacy, students will automatically learn the content more effectively. In other words, through literacy-based strategies in content area teaching and learning, teachers can make their jobs more efficient, while at the same time increasing their teaching effectiveness.

In this chapter, your role as a content area teacher will be placed in the overall context of the teaching profession. First, you will learn about the role of content area literacy in the new paradigm of learning that is emerging with today's public school reforms. Next, you will learn about the concept of Total Quality, its role in the new educational model, and the role of content area literacy and learning in the application of Total Quality principles to education. You will also learn about *cooperative learning* and the significant role it plays in the new education paradigm of teaching and learning. Finally, you will be introduced to the world of professional development, which will be your arena for continuous, life-long learning. Use the objectives at the beginning of this and every chapter to monitor your understanding and learning of important chapter content.

Each chapter in this textbook is divided into two parts. This structure is designed to give you the option of completing each chapter as two separate assignments. Also, each chapter will introduce you to two of the most popular and effective strategies for enhancing content area learning and literacy. In Parts 1 and 2 of each chapter, you will be introduced to an instructional strategy in content area literacy. The strategies are spaced separately to give you more time to process, reflect on, and perhaps try out each one before being introduced to the next. Trying to learn too many strategies in a short time can be an overwhelming and frustrating experience. By the time you finish this text, you will be familiar with a number of popular and effective instructional strategies for content area literacy. The two literacy-based strategies that will be introduced in this chapter are Graphic Organizers and the Language Experience Approach (LEA).

PART 1

STRATEGY: GRAPHIC ORGANIZERS

Chapter 2 will include a discussion of the importance of using different strategies for meeting the needs of various types of intelligence and individual learning styles. An important strategy for meeting the needs of visual learners, in particular, is the Graphic Organizer. This strategy provides a visual outline of vocabulary representing important concepts and the categories that relate them. You will find examples of Graphic Organizers at the beginning of each chapter in this text. Graphic Organizers provide a crucial alternative for learners who need a more visually-oriented representation of concepts.

Graphic Organizers give students an overall view of the topic, so they are especially effective as a prereading tool for introducing a reading assignment. When presented prior to reading, they can provide students with a skeletal frame on which to build during reading. Graphic Organizers summarize, in an easily recalled format, the key concepts and their relationships. By giving students an overview of the important information to be gleaned from the reading, purposes for reading are reinforced.

In addition to being an important prereading tool, Graphic Organizers can also improve students' comprehension and retention during and after reading. When students construct their own Graphic Organizers, they become actively engaged with the text. After reading, Graphic Organizers can be used to evaluate the purposes set for reading. For example, the teacher can develop a Graphic Organizer that summarizes key concepts and their relationships. The teacher could provide students with their own copies of the Graphic Organizer, on which some of the key concepts have been replaced by blanks. The Graphic Organizer with blanks can also be presented on an overhead projector. The teacher then guides the students in a discussion to elicit the key concepts, which are then added to the Graphic Organizer. Students fill in the blanks on their individual copies.

Research indicates that Graphic Organizers are effective instructional tools for content area literacy and learning (Alvermann and Swafford 1989). However, crucial to their effectiveness are the discussion components (Stahl and Vancil 1986). In order for these strategies to have maximum effectiveness, students must become actively engaged with them (Dinnel and Glover 1985). Discussion promotes cognitive interplay, and is, therefore, a vital part of the process. Therefore, cooperative learning and whole-class settings produce the best results (Darch, Carnine, and Kameenui 1986). Simply presenting Graphic Organizers to students without discussing them is an inappropriate use of strategy as an instructional tool. In addition to discussing them, many students need to learn the rationale and purpose of using them (Reinking 1986). Therefore, teachers should help their students understand how Graphic Organizers can be used for enhancing learning and literacy in the content area.

Structured Overviews

Graphic Organizers take many forms. One of the most popular was developed by Barron (1969), who originally called it the Structured Overview (see Figures 1–1 and 1–2). It is designed to provide a means of introducing the technical vocabulary of a chapter, present an "idea framework" that shows important conceptual relationships between the vocabulary, and help the teacher clarify content goals. The Structured Overview should be presented before reading to acquaint students with key terms and to activate their background knowledge related to the concepts. One way to present the Structured Overview is to display the completed version and lead a discussion of each term along with its relationship to the other terms and categories. Another way to present the Structured Overview is to construct it during the discussion; as each word is added, guide students in discussing its meaning and relationship to the other work categories.

FIGURE 1–1 Structured Overview developed for a social studies lesson on communities

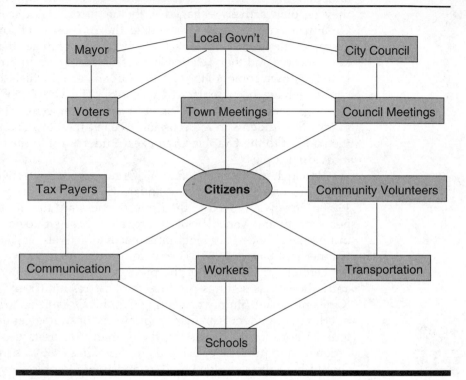

Semantic Maps

Another popular Graphic Organizer is the Semantic Map, which activates and builds on a student's prior knowledge base—schema (Heimlich and Pittelman 1986) (see Figures 1–3 and 1–4). Semantic Mapping was suggested for general vocabulary development by Johnson and Pearson (1984). The following adaptation of their model is designed to demonstrate the process for students and help them develop confidence in creating their own Semantic Maps.

1. Identify one or more key words or topics related to the reading assignment.
2. Write the words or topics on the board, overhead, or large chart tablet.
3. Individually, students brainstorm and list by categories on a sheet of paper as many words related to the key words as they can.

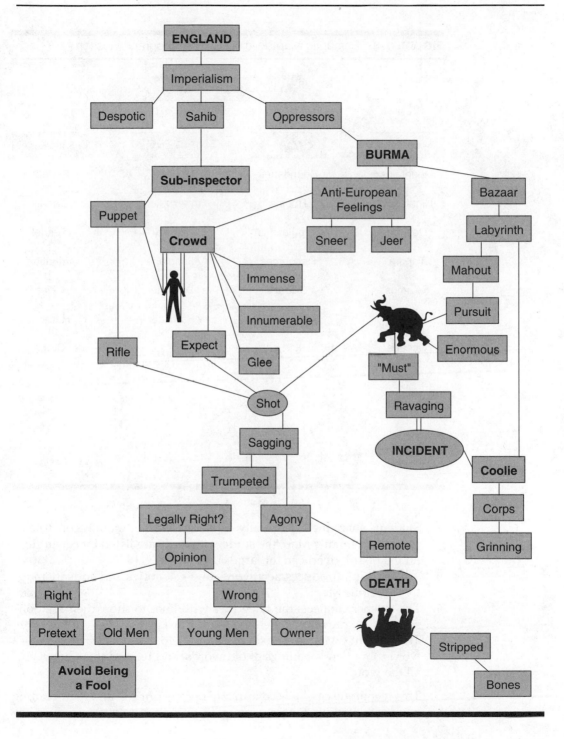

FIGURE 1–3 Semantic Map developed for a geography lesson

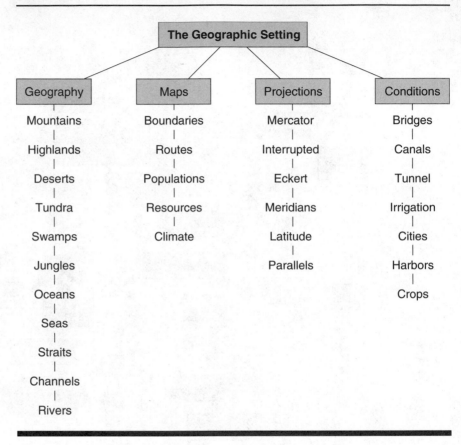

4. Students share their lists orally, while the teacher models construction of a Semantic Map; the students' words are listed by categories on the board, overhead, or large chart tablet.

5. The teacher introduces new words and categories and adds them to the Semantic Map.

6. The teacher connects the categories with lines to show their relationships to the previously identified key word.

7. The Semantic Map is then discussed to help students learn the new words, any new meanings of old words, and relationships between all the words.

This technique can be used as a tool before, during, and after reading for enhanced learning. Before reading, it serves not only to introduce key

FIGURE 1–4 Semantic Map developed for a health lesson

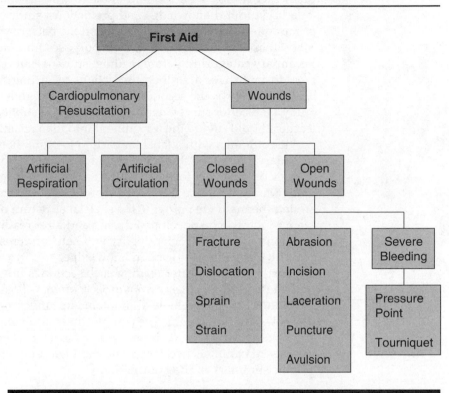

vocabulary, but also to assess and develop prior knowledge (schema) on the topic. During reading, students can add words and categories to their own copies of the Semantic Map. After reading, a discussion of the Semantic Map can emphasize and reinforce the main points students should have gleaned from their reading (Heimlich and Pittelman 1986).

When students begin to generate their own Semantic Maps during and after reading, the Semantic Mapping process becomes a valuable study tool. Hanf (1971) describes a procedure for helping students learn to use Semantic Mapping as a study strategy by developing a Study Map. Following is an adaptation of that procedure.

1. **Identification of main idea.** First, either the teacher or the student identifies the main idea, and the student writes it in the middle of a sheet of paper with a geometric shape drawn around it. This main idea forms the beginning of the Study Map. Next, students work in

pairs to think of everything they already know about the topic and predict what they expect to find in the reading assignment. From their background knowledge and predictions, students write three or four questions related to the topic on the back of their Study Maps; these questions serve as their purposes for reading.

2. **Secondary categories.** Before reading, students survey the assignment to confirm or alter their predictions regarding the content. Subheadings serve as the secondary categories and are written on their Study Maps after surveying. (If the text has no subheadings, the teacher should divide the assignment into manageable units and provide students with a label for each.) No more than six or seven secondary categories should be included on one Study Map. If more than six or seven are included in the reading assignment, more Study Maps should be developed. The secondary categories placed around the main idea provide the skeletal structure of the Study Map, which will be developed during and after reading. Placing question marks after each category will help students reinforce their purpose for reading—to obtain knowledge.

3. **Supporting details.** After reading each section, students add details from memory using their own words as often as possible. Doing so holds students immediately accountable for understanding and remembering the content. The completeness and comprehensibility of the Study Map provide immediate feedback to determine whether rereading is necessary. The completed map then provides a graphic summary of the information.

Other forms of Graphic Organizers include word maps, concept maps, webs, flowcharts, diagrams, text frames, schematic organizers, and cognitive maps. Whether presented to the students before, during, or after readings or constructed by students as study and learning devices, Graphic Organizers help students interact with and outline important textual information. For example, when Graphic Organizers are presented before reading, students read with a focus on important ideas and their relationships. When they construct their own Graphic Organizers, they become actively involved in assessing and manipulating those ideas and relationships. For visual learners who tend to rely on visual imagery as a memory device, the product itself makes the information it contains more easily recalled.

Whether you prefer the traditional outline or the Graphic Organizer, you need experience with both; as a teacher, you will be responsible for guiding a variety of learners. Even if you prefer the traditional outline, you still need the experience of developing a Graphic Organizer; many of your students who are visual learners will need your guidance and support in developing their skills.

CONTENT AREA LITERACY: PREPARING FOR THE TWENTY-FIRST CENTURY

A New Paradigm of Education

In his book, *Smart Schools, Smart Kids,* Edward Fiske (1991) argues that anything short of fundamental structural changes in the current system of public education is futile. He reaches this conclusion after analyzing the failed reforms of the 1980s, which tried to improve the current system through more testing, higher salaries, and tighter curriculums (i.e., state mandates to teachers regarding content and teaching style). He likens these attempts to increase learning potential in the current system to "trying to get the Pony Express to compete with the telegraph by breeding faster ponies" (Fiske 1991, 15). In other words, we have been trying to use a nineteenth-century institution to prepare students for life in the twenty-first century.

As we near the close of the twentieth century, our education system, for the most part, still patterns itself after an early industrial model of assembly-line production. This model has outlived its usefulness in education, as well as in the world of business and industry, which created it (Fiske 1991). Just as U.S. business and industry finally accepted the need for drastic changes to meet the challenges of the twenty-first century, educators have recently begun to accept the need for extreme reforms of our education system. Earlier in this century, our education system served a very different function; it was designed to educate the elite few who were wealthy and showed potential for leadership. Today, in order to compete in a world economy, we recognize that education only for our leaders in politics and business is not enough. We need to educate all of our citizens, because each plays a crucial role in our democratic society and global capitalistic economy. Gone are the days when the United States could rest on the laurels of its bountiful natural resources for economic success and a high standard of living. We have entered a new era marked by a global economy of competition based *not* on a nation's size, location, or availability of natural resources, but rather on the capacity of its citizens to think, learn, create, and solve problems (Fiske 1991).

Therefore, we must invest in the *human* resources we possess: the minds of our children. It follows that our education system must change to meet these new challenges. Widespread reforms are needed to prepare U.S. workers for a highly competitive global economy and marketplace. These reforms must enable U.S. schools to educate a greater percentage of the population and a more widely diverse population than previously encountered. As educators and legislators have begun to accept this need for drastic restructuring, radical reforms of every aspect of public education including school district administration, grade level structures, classroom organization, scheduling, assessment, community involvement, and accountability are in motion across the country. Many of the changes have been occurring in bits and pieces, with each district deciding for itself which blend of reforms is appropriate for its particular needs. In fact, this pattern of reform based on individual need is at the heart of the current revolution in education. Educators, legislators, parents, and citizens are concluding that the notion of a "single best system" for overhauling public schools is unrealistic (Fiske 1991).

To better understand and visualize how schools might go about planning and implementing major reforms to address their unique needs, consider the following case study. In 1989, a "vertical team" was formed by three schools existing in close proximity in an inner-city neighborhood in Austin, Texas. These schools, Travis Heights Elementary School, Fulmore Middle School, and Travis High School share a common interest: the success of their students. The elementary school is a feeder school for the middle school, and the middle school is a feeder school for the high school. Therefore, the principals and teachers at the three schools decided to collaborate in developing a set of reforms that would address the needs of their shared population of students as they progressed through the vertical team system.

In 1989, leadership for organizing the vertical team was provided by Dr. Patricia Hayes, president of St. Edward's University (SEU), a private liberal arts university located in the same neighborhood as the three vertical team schools. Dr. Hayes and an SEU School of Education faculty member, Ms. Barbara Frandsen, initiated a project called "Teachers as Agents of Change." This project was funded by a grant from Southwestern Bell and provided an opportunity for the vertical team principals and teachers to collaborate as they learned about effective and innovative reforms while designing ambitious reorganization plans.

From this collaboration, the principals organized a cohesive partnership for implementing the structuring components. This triumvirate of principals, Marilyn Butcher (Travis Heights Elementary), Vicki Baldwin (Fulmore Middle School), and Elena Vela (Travis High School) quickly put into practice an incremental series of reforms. They expanded the vertical team coalition to include partnerships with local colleges and universities, businesses, parent groups, and other community organizations. The resulting project was called IMAGE (international, multicultural, and global education).

In 1991, the three vertical team schools were selected by the National Education Association's Center for Innovation to be the sixth site in the nation for its Mastery in Learning Consortium. This national consortium provided the Austin schools with a broad system of support for their ambitious reforms. At this point, IBM Austin joined the partnership by providing the technology and expertise needed to electronically link the Austin site, via the School Renewal Network, with researchers, teachers, and others involved in educational restructuring across the country.

The vertical team's restructuring efforts resulted in a model for new paradigm education. By 1994, all three schools had been selected as mentor schools for the state of Texas. As mentor schools, the campuses were visited by hundreds of people from schools and communities across the state who came to see the innovations at work. What the visitors saw was a myriad of innovative structures and programs. Some specific examples of these innovations are described in the sections that follow.

Content Area Literacy and the New Paradigm

These reforms are drastically changing traditional classroom schedules, management, structures, curricula, pedagogies, and materials. Teacher and student roles are also changing. As a result, a new educational model is being defined. Literacy-based instruction in the content areas emerges from key components of this new paradigm.

Component 1: Flexible Scheduling and Multiage Grouping

According to Glasser (1992), students should not be penalized for taking more time than allowed by the schedule to finish their work successfully. In the new paradigm, classroom schedules accommodate differences in rates of learning. Schedules shift from fixed time slots, during which students move through an assembly line of classes to receive each component of the curriculum. Instead, scheduling emphasizes flexible blocks of time, in which students work with teams of teachers on interdisciplinary projects.

For example, at Travis High School, the traditional daily schedule of fifty-minute classes has been replaced with ninety-minute sessions. The reduction in the number of times students change classes resulted in a significant increase in instructional time given students. The block schedule also allowed students to work more intensively on instructional projects, so that course curricula could be mastered in one semester instead of two. As a result, students are better prepared for a transformation to college schedules. Also, the block schedule allows more time for the interdisciplinary projects that give students opportunities to internalize and apply learned content and developed literacy skills in meaningful ways.

Multiage grouping is another form of flexible scheduling that allows students to progress from grade level to grade level at individual rates. For example, at Travis Heights Elementary School, the rigidly defined traditional grade levels (i.e., first grade, second grade, third grade, and so on) have been abandoned in favor of multiage classes. These flexible classes allow higher-ability students to move on to more challenging curricula, while at the same time, allowing extra time for students progressing at a slower rate. For example, in a first/second grade class, students who have not yet mastered the first-grade curriculum could be given extra time to succeed without being retained. In other words, those students would remain in the first/second class another year to develop confidence with literacy skills. During that second year, their rates of progress should increase as their literacy skills improve, thereby allowing them to move on to a second/third class or third/fourth class at the end of their second year in the first/second class.

In content area literacy and learning, revised scheduling allows teachers and students the flexibility to engage in a wider variety of activities, including interdisciplinary studies, team projects, research, and writing. Flexible scheduling helps students learn to set priorities: they have more choices and fewer predetermined procedures. Setting priorities helps students develop the lifelong ability to make the best use of their time for maximum efficiency.

Again, an example can be seen at Travis Heights Elementary. Instead of fixed time slots for instruction in different subjects, the daily schedule reflects larger blocks of time for working on a variety of subjects and skills at the same time. Learning centers in which students move from project to project within the classroom are used extensively. The centers are designed around topics and activities of interest to the children and allow them to explore a variety of topics. Each center provides explicit instructions for students in a variety of hands-on activities including reading library books on the topic of study, writing summaries, composing stories, illustrating information, articulating concepts, and discussing open-ended topics. Students are given some freedom in choosing their own centers; in the course of two hours, students will have engaged in responsible decision making to participate in perhaps four or five activities. As a result, they have studied several different content areas and applied several different literacy skills for learning and communicating in meaningful and personally relevant ways.

Many teachers at Travis Heights Elementary, including Sue Gizelbach and Vickie St. Pierre, open the day with the "calendar project," an interdisciplinary set of activities based on and related to the calendar. From the following examples you can see activities involving a variety of content areas including math, social studies, science, and history. Activities might be related to days of the week, specific dates, months, years, birthdays of classmates, famous people, historical figures, times of day, the first day of the school year, special events, historical events, holidays and their significance, garden planting dates, actual growth compared with projected growth, and counting by ones, twos, fives, and tens. After a few weeks of modeling by the teacher, the children take the teacher's role in presenting the day's calendar activities.

Component 2: Motivation for Quality Learning

In the new paradigm, classroom management shifts from an emphasis on coercion, threats, and punishment to motivation, encouragement, positive reinforcement, and quality learning. The idea behind this shift is that if students are willing participants in the learning process, behavior management takes care of itself. According to Glasser (1992), schools managed by the old model are failing because they were designed to educate students who came to school ready and willing to learn. Today, a new model is required to motivate students to participate, for example, by providing quality learning experiences and by demonstrating the value of the content and the learning process. In fact, Glasser (1992) defines education as the ongoing process of discovering that learning adds to quality of life.

Glasser (1992) further describes the motivational aspects of the new paradigm in terms of *Control Theory*, which is the opposite of *Stimulus/Response Theory*. Basically, Control Theory means that regardless of the effort, it is impossible to control the actions of other people. You can control only your own actions and behaviors. Therefore, the only way you

In the new paradigm of education, students begin to take more and more responsibility for their own learning; the teacher becomes a "guide on the side," rather than a "sage on the stage."

can get students and teachers to participate in the learning process is to motivate them to do it themselves. Implementing control theory means being proactive by taking responsibility for your own actions and behaving from the conscious choices you make, rather than reacting to the actions or desires of others. As you will see, being proactive is an important ingredient in the new model of education.

An increased emphasis on motivation over coercion means an increased need to tap into students' background knowledge. By helping students understand the relevance of the learning to their own lives and experiences, the value of the learning becomes more obvious. Since literacy-based strategies are designed to activate students' background knowledge and make the content more relevant, using these strategies helps teachers motivate students. The increased need for student motivation also emphasizes the importance of helping students set their own short- and long-term goals. Motivation is increased when students see the value of what they are learning in terms of making choices that will help them reach their personally defined goals.

Examples of motivated learning can be seen throughout the classrooms at Travis Heights Elementary. Sue Gizelbach, who teaches a multiage K/first class, encourages her students to bring their own books and materials related to the topic of study. She also encourages them to bring in objects and books related to other topics of interest to them. Gizelbach

Flexible scheduling and multi-age grouping allow students the opportunity to teach and learn from each other on meaningful and enjoyable literacy-based projects.

then designs lessons around those topics, allowing the children to do research and contribute something to each lesson. She also creates learning center activities related to those topics, allowing children to share interesting information with their classmates. The important implication is that not everyone in the class must be discussing the same topic at the same time. Students should be given the freedom to choose from among a wide range of topics.

Another excellent example of motivation for quality learning can be seen at all three vertical team schools in the "YouthVue" project. A teacher/facilitator is assigned to the YouthVue board from each of the three schools: William Walls (Travis Heights), Morgan Golbarth (Fulmore), and Jacqueline Spiser (Travis). The participating students represent a heterogeneous mix of students ranging from those considered "at risk" to those identified as gifted and talented. The YouthVue students from the three schools meet weekly with professionals from KVUE 24 (the local ABC affiliate), the Austin American-Statesman (a local newspaper), and GSD&M (a large advertising firm). In these weekly board meetings, students pitch ideas for ninety-second news packages to air on KVUE 24. The story ideas are then assigned to teams of students who write, tape, and produce them. YouthVue has expanded over the last three years in include the Travis Heights TV (THTV) program at Travis Heights Elementary, and two YouthVue broadcast journalism classes at both Fulmore and Travis. The project has led to paid internships for students, as well as full-time jobs for Travis High graduates; the real-world relevance of everything the students are learning is readily apparent.

At Travis High School, social studies teacher Lyn Loeffler conducts mock legislative sessions with his government classes. The students are responsible for electing the presiding officers, assigning committees, and appointing committee chairs. Two classes participate, one as the Senate and the other as the House of Representatives. Students learn the process for introducing and seeking passage of bills by actually authoring their own bills and attempting to pass them into law. They write a bill related to a school, city, or state issue; in order to write their bills, they have to do research on the issue. Since students take ownership for the bill, they are motivated to learn as much as possible to ensure the law's passage. When the bills are introduced in committees, the students do peer evaluations, editing, and revisions. They then present their bills to the open floor for debate; they must be prepared to defend their bill, anticipate objections, and address concerns about it. Since the students can attend the committee hearings in the other chamber but are not allowed to speak there, they must lobby students in the other class to speak in favor of their bills. From the total experience with mock legislative sessions, students learn how to participate in our democratic process. They also find out why it is so important to be informed about issues related to their daily lives.

Component 3: Synergy through Cooperative Learning and Cross-Age Learning

In the new paradigm, instead of quiet structure, isolated workstations, and competition, classrooms emphasize "organized chaos," teams of workers, and cooperation. This new structure emphasizes the value of synergy, the concept that combining the talents and efforts of individuals working together can lead to greater performance than can be expected of an individual working alone. Synergy is a critical component of content area literacy instruction in which students are members of a learning community; they teach and learn from each other, develop lifelong skills for effective teamwork and problem solving, and stimulate creativity in one another.

A good example of cooperative learning in action can be seen at Fulmore Middle School. In Karen Flournoy's and Linda Goller's sixth-grade language arts classes, students study literature in cooperative learning groups. As they arrive each day, the groups receive their individually assigned roles and tasks, which have been carefully structured by the teacher to ensure equitable participation by all group members. The structure designed by the teacher also includes incentives for the group members to collaborate and help each other succeed. The cooperative learning activities require all group members to read and understand the books. Checkpoints for assessing understanding are built into the activities, as are opportunities for peer teaching and learning.

Through cooperative learning, students learn the value of synergy; for example, that "two heads are better than one."

Another example of cooperative learning in action can be seen at Travis High School. Rows of desks have been replaced with circles and semicircles. Also, desks are moved frequently within a single class; these changes in the physical arrangement of the classroom reflect major changes in instructional techniques. For example, the straight lecture and note taking format has been replaced with a variety of strategies and activities that emphasize cooperative learning. One teacher in particular, Wendy Campbell, uses cooperative learning extensively in her biology classes. For example, when learning about diseases, each group is assigned a different disease. They are then given a carefully structured set of procedures for researching their assigned disease and developing a presentation to teach it to the rest of the class. So they know how they will be assessed, students are also given rubrics that outline the specific criteria that must be demonstrated by each presentation. The students are responsible for pre- and posttesting the class to determine how much students learned about each disease. The level of learning effectiveness is one of the criteria in the grading rubric.

Travis Heights Elementary offers an excellent example of cooperative learning and cross-age learning. In their multiage classrooms, not only do younger children learn from the older ones, but quite often, the younger ones have valuable knowledge or skills to share with the older students. Many times children can more easily understand a concept explained by their peers than by an adult. The wide range of developmental levels in a multiage classroom make it possible for virtually every child to have experience both as a peer teacher and peer learner.

Component 4: More Student Responsibility for Learning

In the new paradigm, curricular emphasis shifts from test performance, isolated skills, and "being right." Instead, the learning process, critical thinking, and self-evaluation are emphasized. Through a process of ongoing self-evaluation and self-improvement, students learn that they have control over their own learning. Because of the emphasis on proactivity and responsibility for their own learning, content area literacy becomes a meaningful tool for students.

As a result, the new curriculum emphasizes the strong interrelationship between literacy and content. Students learn the importance of reading, writing, and thinking critically for effective and independent learning. They learn how to use literacy as a tool for discovering and mastering content. Literacy-based strategies support the new curriculum by emphasizing learning processes, critical thinking, and self-monitoring.

Ms. Flourney's and Ms. Goller's language art classes at Fulmore Middle School offer a good example of giving students more responsibility for their own learning. Cooperative learning groups are formed for literature study. Although the groups have limited choices for the books they read (the choices being limited by the books available to the teacher), they have a great range of freedom for selecting learning activities. At first, the teachers design the options, but eventually students are allowed to create their own activities and products. For example, one group chose to produce a critical literary review for submission to a children's magazine.

After modeling by the teacher, in addition to designing their own learning products, students design their own rubrics for grading them. For example, the students decide what criteria they must demonstrate to earn an A, B, or C. Anything less that a C is not accepted, students simply go back to the drawing board to make the necessary improvements. Interestingly, the teachers report that students typically identify more rigorous criteria in their rubrics than teachers!

Fulmore social studies teacher, Terri Hiner, gives her students more responsibility by having them produce an atlas of the United States. After being assigned states, students conduct their own research under Terri's guidance. Once they have compiled adequate data, they develop two pages for the atlas. On the first page, they summarize the information they have compiled using graphs and charts. On the second page, they design a tourism advertisement using information likely to persuade people to vacation in that state. Not only does this project give students more responsibility for their own learning, it also integrates a wide range of content areas and literacy skills. For example, students develop library research skills; they use computers to do research, compile their data, and design their atlas pages; they use persuasive writing in the advertisement; and they use math calculations to develop their charts and graphs.

Another example of giving students more responsibility for their own learning can be seen in the YouthVue program described in an earlier section. The students not only must identify topics they believe will be of interest to their viewers, they also must research and prepare a "pitch" presentation to convince the board members to select their topics. Then, they research the topics themselves, conduct interviews, write and revise the news copy, rehearse its presentation, videotape their interviews, and finally, broadcast the program. Many of the students also work behind the scenes for set decoration, lighting, sound, camera work, teleprompting, and so forth.

Component 5: Active Learning and Authentic Assessment

In the new paradigm, pedagogy shifts from an emphasis on passive learning, lecture/notetaking, memorization, and test taking. Instead, emphasis is placed on active learning, meaningful research projects, writing, discussions, and portfolios of sample work. This shift from passive to active learning creates a new role for the student in content area literacy and

Because authentic assessment is based on portfolios of student samples, it generally provides a more accurate reflection of learning than do traditional tests.

learning. Students must learn literacy skills, the tools necessary for finding and applying content information to answer questions and solve problems; they can no longer rely on teachers to complete that process for them. Students also must learn to use literacy as a tool for internalizing content in a meaningful way. Further, they must learn how to use literacy skills to demonstrate and document their mastery of content in authentic ways.

The shift in emphasis from passive to active learning again emphasizes the importance of being proactive. Students become more responsible for setting personal goals for learning. In doing so, they take a greater role in deciding what and how they are going to learn. They can then design meaningful research that is consistent with their personal learning goals.

Travis Heights Elementary provides an excellent example of a school curriculum based totally on active learning and authentic assessment. Grades are no longer given; instead, teachers write narrative reports, children do self-assessments, teachers and students collaborate to develop student work portfolios, and parents, teachers, and students have three-way conferences to report and demonstrate students' progress.

At Fulmore Middle School and Travis High School, grades are accompanied by authentic assessment rubrics to specify the demonstrated knowledge and skills represented by each grade. Rubrics allow assessment to be more descriptive and reflective of students' achievements and abilities. In addition to rubrics, teachers have implemented a "no-failure" policy. In other words, students are not allowed to accept a failing grade as the final result of their work. They are assigned a "no-grade" status until they have achieved a predetermined expected level of mastery. As a result, students have greater incentives and more opportunities to succeed. They work with the teachers to develop and implement action plans for success.

An excellent example of an interdisciplinary project based on meaningful active learning and authentic assessment is the RiverWatch program. Students from all three vertical team schools work together to monitor the water quality of local creeks, rivers, and lakes, report on their findings, and lobby for action. The accuracy of their reports and effectiveness of their lobbying efforts provide an authentic assessment of their learning not only of content but also of literacy and communication skills.

Component 6: Textbook Alternatives and Supplements

Use of instructional materials shifts from an overreliance on the textbook and teacher's manual as the ultimate authority and decision maker; emphasis also shifts from the use of workbooks and worksheets. In the new paradigm, teachers become the decision makers, using the textbook only as a resource and guide; the text is supplemented or even replaced with trade (library) books, and greater emphasis is placed on student-generated work.

The changes in instructional materials mean greater flexibility in selecting materials and planning curriculum for content area literacy and learning. Teachers can help students choose the most appropriate materials for their learning projects. Consequently, students have more opportunities to select their own materials according to their personal interests and curiosities. Teachers can plan curriculum to address specific student needs in terms of background knowledge and literacy skills. Since teachers make the instructional decisions, they can incorporate a greater use of literacy and literacy-based strategies for teaching content. Instructional materials in the new paradigm once again emphasize the importance of being proactive and goal directed. Both teachers and students are afforded greater choices in planning strategies and selecting tools for reaching their goals for content learning and literacy.

Travis Heights Elementary offers excellent examples of the use of textbook alternatives and supplements. Teachers like Betsy May and Vickie St. Pierre create classroom libraries that include a variety of literary genre; the books cover a wide range of topics, some of which deal directly or indirectly with a currently studied topic. Students use these books in activities throughout the day; for example, they use them for learning center activities, researching topics of interest, pleasure reading during free time, making in-class presentations, and sharing ideas and stories with their classmates. One teacher, Holly Brandt, orders trade books (the types of books found in libraries) for her permanent classroom library collection. She gets about six copies of each book so that students can work together in groups, as well as have a choice about which books they read. Brandt selects about four different books of varying levels of difficulty and related to a topic they are studying; she then places the books on a table and allows the students to spend time looking through them. Students then choose the books they wish to read; groups are formed, and the students work together to read the book, talk about it, and complete enrichment activities related to it. Some of the activities involve art, music, and drama presented to the rest of the class; others include writing reactions, adaptations, or sequels; still others involve reading other books by the same author or that are related to the topic in some way.

At Fulmore Middle School and Travis High School, textbooks are used as a teacher resource and student reference but do not drive the curriculum. They are supplemented and often replaced with a variety of fiction and nonfiction books, reference books, magazines, newspapers, and student-authored materials. Some courses are completely nontextual. For example, Fulmore offers a photocommunications course and a television journalism course, both of which engage students in real-life activities both on and off campus (e.g., local television stations and newspaper offices). Travis offers a multimedia course in which students develop their own software in response to real-life needs identified by community members or business leaders.

Component 7: Teacher as Facilitator and Consultant

The role of teacher shifts from all-knowing lecturer, information-giver, and final authority to consultant, guide, model, resource, and facilitator. This new role for teachers emphasizes the content area classroom as a learning community. Teachers become partners in learning with students; they provide leadership through their own experiences as effective learners.

The new role for teachers emphasizes the importance of providing leadership through modeling. As leaders in the classroom learning community, teachers model principles of interpersonal leadership by helping students identify a wide range of options for solving problems, taking positions on controversial issues, and answering difficult questions. Additionally, they model principles of empathic listening, i.e., full understanding of opposing viewpoints without agreeing or disagreeing. By actively seeking out and showing appreciation for alternate points of view, teachers can help students become empathic listeners themselves.

A good example of the changing roles of teachers can be seen at Fulmore Middle School. Instead of the traditional content-area and literacy-skills classes (e.g., social studies, science, math, and language arts) being planned and taught in isolation by individual teachers, teachers collaborate for "interdisciplinary teaming." Each member of a teaching team has specific expertise in one or more content areas and/or literacy skills. They work together to design and implement curricular projects that integrate instruction in the various content areas and literacy skills. In the classroom, the teachers provide support to the students as coaches would support a team of players. Each "coach" has a different area of expertise; they combine talents to form a well-rounded coaching staff for the students.

An example of interdisciplinary teaming can be seen in the following outline of a unit on nutrition; the science teacher could design activities for studying the chemical make-up of various foods and their relationships with the body's nutritional needs; the social studies teacher could design activities for studying the effects of malnutrition on a society as a whole; the math teacher could design activities for calculating caloric values, fat content, and vitamin and mineral content with respect to the body's metabolic needs; and of course, the language arts teacher could design activities involving research, technical writing, nonfiction reading, and oral presentations.

Travis Heights Elementary offers another example of the changing role of the teacher as a partner in learning with the students. As an option for teacher appraisal, teachers can participate in action research of their own design. They can work alone, with a partner, or with a team to develop and implement an action research plan. First, teachers identify a question, problem, challenge, or goal related to improving teaching effectiveness. They then hypothesize or propose an answer, solution, or improvement that can be tested in the classroom. After implementation, teachers evaluate the effectiveness of their hypothesis or proposal. If successful, they make changes based on the results and begin plans to address another question; if not successful, they reformulate their hypothesis or make a new proposal and test it again. Through action research, teachers demonstrate for students a model for lifelong learning. Also, the process shows students that the teacher is indeed a partner in their learning community.

Component 8: Meeting the Special Needs of Every Student

The new paradigm emphasizes the inclusion of all learners working together in the same instructional setting. In the old paradigm, the concept of "mainstreaming" moved from total segregation of students with special needs (e.g., self-contained special education classrooms) to partial integration of these students. Through mainstreaming, special needs students were assigned to regular classrooms for part of the day and spent the remainder of the day in separate classrooms with specially trained teachers (e.g., resource rooms). In the new paradigm, the concept of "inclusion" keeps learners with special needs in the regular classroom all day. The specially trained teachers work with students and teachers in the regular classroom setting to tailor instruction effectively.

In the new paradigm, emphasis is placed on tailoring instruction to the individual needs of students. In the old paradigm, students were generally blamed for failure: it was assumed they did not work hard enough, nor were they motivated, smart, or quick enough. According to this philosophy, students who were not successful were given remediation in the form of reteaching in the same way, but at a slower pace. Students were given repeated opportunities to correct the problems that caused their failures, but little consideration was given to changing the form of instruction to make it more effective. Subjecting students to repeated failure with the same instruction was like trying to force a square peg into a round hole. Some progress could be made, but it was often a difficult and painful process. Providing matching holes is proving more effective.

In the new paradigm, students who are not successful indicate a problem with the instruction, not the student. Every student is considered a special needs learner, because every student has unique learning strengths and challenges. Because adapting instruction to students' needs is so important, every chapter of this text will address ways to match instruction to the unique needs of students. Every lesson planned, every strategy applied, and every activity designed should be done with the special needs of all students in mind. Instruction should involve a process of continuous improvement based on observation and assessment of what works and what does not work.

A good example of instruction designed to meet the needs of all students can be seen at Casis Elementary School in Austin, Texas. Teachers Liz Ing and Janie Ruiz team teach a fifth grade class of forty to fifty students. They have both been trained and certified in education for the gifted and talented, and they use that training to design a challenging curriculum for all of their students. Their goal as teachers is to develop an "inclusion" classroom in which all special-needs learners are taught. In other words, students are not pulled out of the regular classroom for special instruction in the resource classroom, nor are multihandicapped children segregated into self-contained classrooms. The classroom teachers provide individual support as needed to help their students achieve the high-level objectives they have set. One of the keys to achieving their goal is the working relationships they develop with their teaching colleagues who have been specially trained to support a variety of special needs. For example, one resource teacher specializes in helping learning disabled students meet the reading and writing demands in the regular classroom. That teacher works with Liz and Janie in planning and sometimes in the classroom. The resource teacher works alongside the classroom teachers to help not only those children identified as having a learning disability, but also anyone experiencing difficulty reading or writing.

Similarly, Travis Heights Elementary has inclusion classrooms. Since they have a large population of Hispanic students, the bilingual education and English as a Second Language (ESL) teachers collaborate with the classroom teachers to modify instruction. The bilingual and ESL teachers also work in the classroom alongside the regular classroom teachers to help not only the Spanish-speaking children with their Spanish and English skills, but also the English-speaking students with their English and Spanish skills. As a result, the native Spanish speakers are learning English as a second language, and the native English speakers are learning Spanish as a second language!

Fulmore Middle School provides another excellent model for meeting the needs of all students. The Texas State School for the Deaf, only a few blocks away, sends many of its students to attend regular classes at Fulmore to learn and socialize with their hearing peers. Specially trained teachers and interpreters work with the classroom teachers to make sure the hearing-impaired students are fully integrated into all classroom activities. In fact, the teachers are offered workshops and students offered courses in American sign language.

At Travis High School, an English and journalism teacher, Claire Dodillet, has implemented a flexible system of deadlines for completed work. The effectiveness of her system relies heavily on her careful observations and perceptions of students' needs. This system tremendously benefits her students who have limited English proficiency and are likely to need more time and assistance in completing assignments. Her students who are teenage mothers also benefit from the flexibility and support afforded by her system. Once a student has requested an extension or assistance, or Dodillet has perceived that a student has a legitimate need for special consideration, she has a conference with the student. During that conference, she and the student develop a contract that specifies a new deadline along with appropriate support mechanisms including working with the librarian, the teacher after school, or other students in the class. For students who really need and would benefit from the extra time and assistance, this flexible system has tremendous results in terms of enhanced learning, self-confidence, self-esteem, and motivation.

PART 2

STRATEGY: LANGUAGE EXPERIENCE APPROACH (LEA)

Distinguishing Features and Benefits of LEA

A second strategy for teaching content area literacy is the Language Experience Approach (LEA). This strategy was made popular as an approach for teaching beginning reading by Roach Van Allen (1966). It is based on the following premises:

What I can think about, I can talk about.
What I can say, I can write (or someone can write for me).
What I can write, I can read.
I can read what others write for me to read (Allen and Allen 1966, 6).

Language is the key word in the name of this strategy. Reading materials related to the content are generated by the students who put the information into their own words. In this way, students can monitor and evaluate their own learning. By using their own wording, they also make the content meaningful by relating it to prior knowledge. The steps of the LEA include presenting content, discussing content, dictating or writing to summarize content, and reading the summaries. This strategy is particularly effective in terms of integrating reading, writing, and thinking as part of the learning process.

The first step, presentation of content, can take many forms. For example, it can be a reading assignment, a video, a guest speaker, an individual or group student presentation, a computer hypertext program, a slide presentation, a lecture, a discussion, or even a field trip. Before the content is presented, students should be provided requisite background knowledge and vocabulary, as well as specific purposes for reading, viewing, and/or listening. They should know exactly what you expect them to learn from the experience.

Once the content is presented, it should be discussed. The teacher leads the discussion with questions that require students to think at all levels. In this step, it is important to let the students do most of the talking. Remember that language is the key component of this strategy; allow ample time for students to process the information using their own words. The teacher's role is to keep the discussion focused, as well as to help students assess and fill in any apparent gaps in their understanding and learning of the content. The purpose of the discussion is to help students assess and activate schemata and internalize the content by relating it to prior knowledge.

Once students have had time to discuss the content thoroughly, and the teacher is satisfied that the level of learning is adequate, the students either dictate or write their own summaries of the information. The dictation could take place as a whole group, with the teacher serving as recorder and the students providing the information. The dictation could also take place in pairs or small groups, with one student serving as the recorder, while the others provide the information. The teacher should guide the dictation process with leading questions to make sure the summary is complete and accurate.

The most important thing to remember about taking dictation is that the information should be recorded exactly as the student says it. Recalling the Allens' premises of this approach, the concept of literacy is based on the relationship between speech and print. Therefore, the student should be able to read and hear the exact words as they were dictated. Recording the students' language without editing can be difficult, especially if the student uses inappropriate grammar or gives inaccurate information. However, these errors should be addressed *after* the information has been recorded.

Exact dictation can be made easier by following certain guidelines. First, before the dictation, the teacher should specify whether the information needs to be presented in complete sentences. Then, when a student volunteers or is called on to contribute, she or he should be allowed to formulate the phrase or sentence orally or in writing before it is recorded. Some students may need to say the information out loud or write it down before formulating the final version of the phrase or sentence they want recorded.

Errors should be dealt with in such a way as to avoid embarrassing students. If not handled properly, errors can make students reluctant to participate again. Errors can be emphasized as an important part of the learning process, and students should be given a safe place to make mistakes. The Language Experience Approach deals with errors in a constructive manner. Grammar errors are pointed out as informal English, which may be appropriate for informal environments like home, gym, or cafeteria but is not appropriate for formal learning environments and work places. Provide several appropriate standard English alternatives for stating the students' concepts and let the students select the versions they want recorded. The crucial thing to avoid is labeling students' language "wrong" or "bad." Instead, take this opportunity to teach students the important differences between informal and standard English and appropriate uses of each.

Errors in content should also be addressed gently. First say something positive about the response like, "This is a good sentence related to the topic," or "I can tell you learned something about the topic." Then suggest that the student check out the information with other students or the reading assignment while you go on to take dictation from another student. Later, inquire whether the student who made the error wishes to change anything. If not, explain which part is not accurate and provide several alternatives for restating the content accurately. Let the student choose one to be recorded. When errors are made, stick with that student, providing hints and alternatives until a correct statement is given. Avoid embarrassing the student by asking another student to "help out." Having another student correct the mistake in front of the class does not help anyone. Once you go to another student for a correct response, the original student has essentially been labeled a failure and will probably be reluctant to participate in the future. If you want another student's input, you could have the students discuss in private before allowing the original student to try again in front of the class.

Once the dictated summary is complete and accurate, students should be given opportunities to reread it silently or orally with partners or in small groups; younger students can reread it orally as a whole class. Rereading activities should be purposeful and meaningful. For example, students can read the parts that answer particular questions; listeners can be asked to restate the information read orally; students can be asked to read for the purpose of identifying key vocabulary and concepts; and students can be asked to reread the parts that they perceive as most interesting and/or important. The recorded summary should then be copied for distribution to the class. These summaries provide important study aids, especially for poor readers.

"TOTAL QUALITY" TEACHING AND LEARNING IN THE CONTENT AREA CLASSROOM

Defining Total Quality

Total Quality Management (TQM) involves a set of general principles about the fundamental culture and norms of practice of a working organization dedicated to quality (Hixson and Lovelace 1992). Many of the educational reforms being implemented today are based on this concept, which has been revolutionizing U.S. business and industry for the past decade. Only recently have leaders in education begun to adopt TQM as an operational philosophy (Bonstingl 1992b). Many educators resist the application of Total Quality principles to education, claiming that not enough parallels can be drawn between business and education to warrant widespread reforms. Nevertheless, those educational reformers who claim success with TQM maintain that many of its principles are directly applicable to quality in the classroom. They caution, however, that TQM is not necessarily a "recipe" for success; rather, it provides schools with the tools necessary for organizational restructuring.

The concept of TQM was developed by an American, W. Edwards Deming, after World War II for improving the production quality of goods and services. The concept was not taken seriously by Americans until the Japanese, who adopted it in 1950 to resurrect their postwar business and industry, used it to dominate world markets by 1980. By then, most U.S. manufacturers had finally accepted that the nineteenth-century assembly-line factory model was outdated for the modern global economic markets. They ultimately became convinced when their "bottom lines began to bleed red ink, as customers the world over registered their preference for Japanese goods over American products" (Bonstingl 1992b, 5).

Applying Total Quality Principles to Education

Many educators believe that Deming's concept of TQM provides guiding principles for needed educational reform. In his article, "The Quality Revolution in Education," John Jay Bonstingl (1992b) outlines the TQM principles he believes are most salient to education reform. He calls them the "Four Pillars of Total Quality Management."

Principle 1: Synergistic Relationships

An organization must focus, first and foremost, on its suppliers and customers. In a TQM organization, everyone is both a customer and supplier; this confusing concept emphasizes "the systemic nature of the work in which all are involved" (Bonstingl 1992b, 6). In other words, teamwork and collaboration are essential. Traditionally, education has been prone to individual and departmental isolation. However, according to Bonstingl (1992b, 6), this outdated practice no longer serves us:

> "When I close the classroom door, those kids are *mine*!" is a notion too narrow to survive in a world in which teamwork and collaboration result in high-quality benefits for the greatest number of people.

Applying the first pillar of TQM to education emphasizes the synergistic relationship between the "suppliers" and "customers" (Bonstingl 1992b). As mentioned earlier in this chapter, the concept of synergy suggests that performance and production is enhanced by pooling the talent and experience of individuals. In Bonstingl's (1992b, 6) description of teachers and students working together as suppliers and customers, you can recognize content area literacy's community spirit of learning.

In the classroom, teacher-student teams are the equivalent of industry's front-line workers. The product of their successful work together is the development of the student's capabilities, interests, and character. In one sense, the student is the teacher's customer, as the recipient of educational services provided for the student's growth and improvement. Viewed in this way, the teacher and the school are suppliers of effective learning tools, environments, and systems to the student, who is the school's *primary customer*. The school is responsible for providing for the long-term educational welfare of students by teaching them how to learn and communicate in high-quality ways, how to assess quality in their own work and in that of others, and how to invest in their own lifelong and life-*wide* learning processes by maximizing opportunities for growth in every aspect of daily life. In another sense, the student is also a worker, whose product is essentially his or her own continuous improvement and personal growth.

The notion of the student as the school's primary customer provides an important guiding principle for many of today's school reforms. In many schools, this principle can be seen in the philosophy that "We teach students, not content." This philosophy represents a major paradigm shift from process to product. When efforts to improve learning focused on rigid instructional processes and materials, the resulting emphasis was on "covering material." Many hoped that if teachers followed the approved process (curriculum guides) to the letter, students' learning would improve. As a result, instructional quality was evaluated in terms of how well teachers could document coverage of the content, regardless of how well or poorly the students learned it. However, this approach proved to be unsuccessful, and reforms have been reflecting a major shift in emphasis to the students' quality of learning.

Content area literacy instruction reflects this shift in emphasis toward learning processes by emphasizing teachers and students working together as communities of learners. Tremendous value is placed on teamwork and team building for creative problem solving. Team members work together to stimulate new ways of thinking. Synergistic team members learn to understand and appreciate alternate and sometimes opposing points of view for the purpose of expanding perspectives and reaching higher levels of knowledge. Team members learn to recognize and tap the vast resources made available by a diverse group of people working together toward the same goals. They learn to value differences by putting together the best everyone has to offer. The synergy generated in content area instruction emphasizes ownership of problems by all team members and genuine involvement of all members in the problem-solving process (Covey 1990).

Today, more and more schools are empowering teachers to make instructional decisions based on the characteristics and needs of students.

This emphasis on teaching students rather than content means that as long as the students learn the content, the instructional methods and materials are left to the discretion of the teacher. Therefore, instructional quality is now evaluated in terms of how much and how well students learn, rather than on the instructional processes and materials a teacher uses. As a result, teachers are encouraged to assess, on a regular basis, their own teaching effectiveness and make the necessary adjustments to meet the learning needs of their students. Content area literacy supports teachers in this decision-making role by providing a wide range of varied techniques and strategies to meet the wide-ranging needs of the students, as well as demands of the instructional materials.

Principle 2: Continuous Improvement and Self-Evaluation

The second pillar of TQM applied to education is that everyone in the organization must be dedicated to continuous improvement, personally and collectively (Bonstingl 1992b, 6):

> Within a Total Quality school setting, administrators work collaboratively with their customers: teachers. Gone are the vestiges of "Scientific Management" . . . whose watchwords were compliance, control, and command. The foundations for this system were fear, intimidation, and an adversarial approach to problem-solving. Today it is in our best interest to encourage everyone's potential by dedicating ourselves to the continual improvement of our own abilities and those of the people with whom we work and live. Total Quality is, essentially, a win-win philosophy that works to everyone's ultimate advantage.

One implication of this TQM principle for education involves an increased emphasis on training, "quality circles" (in which everyone involved discusses ways for improvement), research (especially classroom research) and communication (with students, parents, business leaders, community representatives, and so forth). This emphasis on training is a characteristic of what Peter Senge (1990) calls "learning organizations," in which people, processes, and systems are dedicated to continuous learning and improvement. If schools are to become true learning organizations, they must be afforded the necessary resources, especially time and money, for training, quality circles, research, and communication (Bonstingl 1992b).

According to Deming, no human being should ever evaluate another human being. Therefore, TQM emphasizes self-evaluation as part of a continuous improvement process. Glasser (1992, 180) explains the importance of self-evaluation in a quality organization:

> The main difference between happy and unhappy people is that happy people mostly evaluate their own behavior and constantly attempt to

improve what they do. Unhappy people, on the other hand, mostly evaluate the behavior of others and spend their time criticizing, complaining, and judging in an attempt to coerce them into "improving" what they do. A quality organization, therefore, will consist of many more happy than unhappy people.

A second implication of this TQM principle for education involves a change in focus from students' limitations to their innate strengths and talents (Bonstingl 1992b). Applying this principle means focusing on students' strengths, individual learning styles, and different types of intelligences. Howard Gardner (1983) has encouraged educators to acknowledge the existence of multiple intelligences and potentials (see Chapter 2) and help students appreciate and develop their full range of intelligences. Instruction is based on the commitment that every child will learn.

A third implication of the TQM principle for education involves a major change in assessment procedures. Deming goes so far as to suggest that grades (A, B, C, D, F) be abolished altogether because students tend to focus more on the grade than on the learning (Bonstingl 1992a). At the very least, educators dedicated to the continuous improvement of all students must reexamine current practices of grading and assessment. The bell-shaped curve is an example of a traditional grading system that is inconsistent with the spirit of mutual improvement. In fact, the bell curve, as well as some other grading systems, sets up win/lose situations for students (Bonstingl 1992b). In other words, grading systems such as the bell curve result in one student's success at the expense of another student's failure. These win/lose paradigms are counterproductive to the spirit of cooperation for a community of learners. Many assessment reforms are focusing on "authentic assessment," which many educators believe provides a more accurate representation of a student's learning and abilities. Authentic assessment includes actual examples of students' work presented in portfolios and exhibits.

Instruction in content area literacy reflects this second Total Quality principle in several ways. Literacy-based instruction and strategies emphasize the ongoing processes of self-reflection, goal setting, self-evaluation, and improvement. Teachers model for students the process of continually assessing effectiveness and making adjustments accordingly. Students are taught how and encouraged to monitor and evaluate their own learning on a regular basis. They are also taught self-help and survival strategies to address difficulties in comprehension and learning, once they are identified. Techniques and strategies in content area literacy provide support for this emphasis on students' self-monitoring and self-evaluation of comprehension and learning. Content area literacy supports the commitment to teaching students, not content. Literacy-based instruction is designed to help students identify their own learning styles and strengths, as well as appropriate strategies and techniques to help them capitalize on those strengths. Finally, content area literacy emphasizes authentic assessment. Literacy-based instruction provides a vehicle for documentation of student learning. Students use their reading, writing, and thinking skills to generate products that demonstrate their mastery of the content, as well as their ability to apply the content in meaningful ways.

Principle 3: A System of Ongoing Processes

The third pillar of TQM applied to education is that the organization must be viewed as a system, and the work people do within the system must be seen as ongoing processes (Bonstingl 1992b). The primary implication of this principle is that individual students and teachers are less to blame for failure than the system in which they work. Quality speaks to working on the system, which must be examined to identify and eliminate the flawed processes that allow its participants to fail. Since systems are made up of processes, the improvements made in the quality of those processes largely determine the quality of the resulting product.

In the new paradigm of learning, continual improvement of learning processes based on learning outcomes replaces the outdated "teach and test" mode. The quality of teaching/learning processes then becomes mirrored in learning outcomes. Therefore, focusing attention on results is premature, and possibly counterproductive, without prior focus given to the processes designed to bring about desired results (Bonstingl 1992b). Content area literacy supports this principle by emphasizing an ongoing process for learning that involves setting goals, monitoring progress with respect to those goals, and making changes based on self-evaluation.

Principle 4: Leadership

The fourth TQM principle applied to education is that the success of TQM is the responsibility of top management (Bonstingl 1992b). Therefore, school leaders must establish the context in which students can best achieve their potential through the continuous improvement that results from teachers and students working together. The outcomes that drive school leaders in establishing such a context are described by Bonstingl (1992b, 7–8):

> Educational leaders who create Total Quality school environments know that improving test scores and assessment symbols is less important than the progress inherent in the learning processes of students, teachers, administrators and all of the school's stakeholders.

In the same way that a school's leaders set the tone for their school's teaching culture, teachers set the tone for their classroom's learning culture. Teachers who emphasize content area literacy and principle-centered teaching provide the leadership, framework, and tools necessary for continuous improvement in the learning process.

Implementing TQM Principles in the New Paradigm

Successful implementation of TQM principles requires a great deal of patience, because TQM is not a quick fix. It can take as long as ten years to implement and produce documentable results. TQM represents a system whose rewards begin to emerge when its ideas and practices become so embedded in the culture of the organization (i.e., the day-to-day work of its people and systems) that it becomes "the way we do things around here" (Bonstingl 1992b). With patience and persistence, TQM can lead to significant cultural changes in schools by providing a valuable organizational framework for restructuring.

One success story of TQM in education involves the Detroit public schools. In their article, "Total Quality Management's Challenge to Urban Schools," Hixson and Lovelace (1992, 24) describe the accomplishments Detroit schools have enjoyed through TQM. However, they offer the following caution:

> Urban schools face some unique conditions and constraints not found in private sector environments where TQM principles have evolved and been validated.

Hixson and Lovelace (1992, 25) believe that as long as urban schools do not count on TQM for simple answers and quick fixes, TQM principles can help city schools address the following unique challenges they face.

1. Redefine the role, purpose, and responsibilities of schools.
2. Improve schools as a "way of life."
3. Plan comprehensive leadership training for educators at all levels.
4. Create staff development that addresses the attitudes and beliefs of school staff.
5. Use research- and practice-based information to guide both policy and practice.
6. Design comprehensive child-development initiatives that cut across a variety of agencies and institutions.

In addition to patience, participatory management among well-trained and educated partners is crucial to the success of TQM in education; everyone involved must understand and believe in the principles. School personnel who are committed to the principles can facilitate success with TQM. Their vision and skills in leadership, management, interpersonal communication, problem solving, and creative cooperation are important qualities for successful implementation of TQM.

In *The Quality School*, William Glasser (1992) summarizes the key ingredients to quality in education. First, treat people well by motivating them to do a good job without coercion. Second, teach people to evaluate their own work. Third, establish a warm, caring environment by eliminating fear, punishment, and threats. Fourth, make the learning useful, and more importantly, ensure that the learning is perceived as useful to the students.

TQM and Content Area Literacy: A Summary

As you have seen, many principles of TQM are reflected in content area literacy and learning. Literacy-based strategies help motivate students by making the learning relevant and valuable. They teach students to monitor and evaluate their own learning in an ongoing process of continual improvement. They emphasize synergy among a community of learners. They emphasize a variety of learning strategies to match the variety of intelligences, learning styles, and needs individual students bring to the classroom. They emphasize the integration of literacy and content in the learning process, and authentic assessment. Content area teachers committed to literacy-based instruction are key players in school cultures that emphasize TQM principles.

PROFESSIONAL DEVELOPMENT FOR CONTENT AREA TEACHERS

A first step in planning a program of professional development is to develop a mission statement that clearly defines your professional goals and roles. Begin now to ponder questions such as these: Which teachers, professors, and other mentors have served as positive role models in your life? What qualities do/did they have that you hope you will have as a teacher? What kind of teacher do you want to be? Why do you want to be a teacher? What contributions do you want to make as a teacher?

Once you have developed a Mission Statement, use it as a part of your own system of continuous quality improvement. At least once or twice a year, reflect on your teaching experiences as they relate to your Mission Statement. If you note incongruencies, make appropriate changes either in your teaching plans, your Mission Statement, or both.

Continual self-reflection and self-assessment are critical components of a teacher's professional development. One effective system for making improvements based on your own reflections and assessments is known as Action Research. In this system, you identify a topic, question, area, problem, or issue you want to investigate for a semester or year. Then, you develop a plan to try out different approaches, methodologies, strategies, activities, and so on. As you carry out your plan, compile anecdotal records and other forms of assessment data. Finally, evaluate your results and revise your plan. This system is ongoing and cyclical in that you are continually restructuring your plans, implementing experimental techniques, compiling data, evaluating the results, and using those results to further restructure.

Of course, continued renewal includes participation in required in-service teacher training programs, but renewal will be more meaningful and effective if activities are self-selected and self-determined. Creating your own program of professional development is an important activity. Since it is not necessarily considered urgent, however, professional development does not always receive top priority in a teacher's professional planning. Professional development is crucial not only to stay current in your field but also to maintain enthusiasm and excitement for teaching. You can start planning now by becoming familiar with all the professional development options open to teachers. You can even start participating now: most professional education organizations welcome participation by students and even offer special student rates.

The largest organization for reading teachers is the International Reading Association (IRA), which holds many international conferences each year, along with conferences at the national, regional, state, and local levels. Many of the conference presentations are made *by* classroom teachers *for* classroom teachers. Among other things, attending conferences allows you to network with other teachers, share ideas, examine materials at the publishers' exhibits, learn about the latest classroom research, and participate in special interest groups. You should also consider making conference presentations to share with your colleagues your own classroom research and ideas for effective use of materials, strategies, and activities.

The International Reading Association publishes four journals:

- *The Reading Teacher* (preschool/elementary)
- *The Journal of Adolescent and Adult Literacy* (formerly *The Journal of Reading*) (secondary/adult)
- *Reading Research Quarterly*
- *Lectura y Vida* (Spanish)

The Reading Teacher and *The Journal of Adolescent and Adult Literacy,* in particular, are full of short, readable, and practical articles on materials, strategies, and innovative programs. The IRA also publishes numerous books, booklets, brochures, and pamphlets each year, available at discount prices to members.

Other professional educational organizations include:

- National Education Association
- National Reading Conference

■ American Reading Forum
■ American Educational Research Association
■ National Council of Teachers of English

Other professional journals include:

■ *Educational Leadership*
■ *Language Arts*
■ *Reading World*
■ *Journal of Educational Psychology*
■ *Educational Horizons*
■ *Journal of Reading Behavior*
■ *Reading Horizons*
■ *Journal of Educational Research*
■ *Elementary School Journal*

In addition to reading selected articles from professional journals regularly, you should also consider submitting articles for publication to share your own experiences and ideas related to classroom teaching.

Aside from attending conferences and reading professional journals regularly, professional development includes other opportunities for self-renewal. For example, building and participating in a teaching culture within your school is a valuable way to stimulate and maintain enthusiasm for teaching. A teaching culture can be developed in a variety of ways. Observing other teachers in your school or community is an excellent way to gather new ideas. The wonders of videotaping make this suggestion a viable one. Also, videotaping yourself and your students is an enlightening experience for self-reflection and improvement. Another tactic is reaching out to your colleagues by offering to coordinate short but regular informal working group meetings to share experiences and ideas, brainstorm, and solve problems. Lay some ground rules to make sure such meetings are a beneficial use of time and do not degenerate into "gripe and gossip" sessions. Because they are not solution-focused, these types of sessions almost always result in the participants feeling worse than better. An example of an important ground rule for productive sessions is that anyone wanting to voice a concern or bring up a problem for group feedback must agree to refrain from "Yes, but . . ." responses to proposed ideas and solutions. Instead, listen to and take with you all proposed solutions; then decide later which ones may suit your needs. Also, it is important to remain focused on creative problem solving and positive ideas for improved instruction. Briefly prepare a preplanned agenda in which one or more people informally address specific problems or share ideas. Finally, sharing materials on a regular basis by establishing a routing system within your department or area can prove very beneficial.

SUMMARY

Content refers to the knowledge or information students are expected to learn in a particular subject area. A subject area such as science, social studies, literature, math, art, or physical education is also known as a content area. Content area literacy refers to the combined use of reading, writing, and critical thinking for the purpose of learning content in the content area classroom. Content area literacy is influenced by a variety of factors including the demands of the subject matter and the text and the characteristics of the learner. Although influenced by many factors, content area literacy can be developed by teachers in all disciplines and at all levels.

The concept of content area literacy is consistent with the model of education emerging through today's educational reforms. The goals of this model include providing the communication skills, knowledge base, and learning tools necessary for empowering twenty-first century Americans to participate in our democratic society and compete in a global economy. The reforms associated with this paradigm of education reflect drastic changes in traditional classroom schedules, management structures, curricula, pedagogies, and materials, as well as teacher and student roles. The new paradigm includes flexible scheduling, classroom management based on motivation rather than coercion, cooperative rather than competitive learning, process-oriented learning, self-monitoring and self-evaluation of learning, active learning, and authentic assessment. Content area literacy can support teachers in implementing all facets of this new paradigm of education.

Many of the educational reforms being implemented are based on the concept of Total Quality Management (TQM), a set of general principles concerning the fundamental culture and norms of practice of a working organization dedicated to quality (Hixson and Lovelace 1992). Successful implementation of TQM principles for education reform requires a great deal of patience, because TQM is not a quick fix. It can take as long as ten years to implement and produce documentable results. With patience and persistence, TQM can lead to significant cultural changes in schools by providing a valuable organizational framework for restructuring. Many of the TQM principles that have been successfully applied in educational reform are reflected in content area literacy. Content area teachers who are committed to literacy-based instruction are key players in a school whose culture is based on TQM principles.

Crucial to a teacher's ongoing professional development is composing a personal mission statement for teaching, which addresses the role literacy plays in your content area classroom, the contributions you want to make as a teacher, what kind of teacher you want to be, and a plan for ongoing renewal for professional development. Also crucial to professional development is engaging in activities for renewal to prevent burnout. Opportunities for professional development include attending conferences, presenting at conferences, reading professional journals, writing for professional journals, and self-reflection for continuous improvement. Membership in professional organizations entitles you to receive journals and attend conferences to help you keep abreast of the latest developments in teaching and exchange ideas with colleagues. Building and participating in a teaching culture within your school, through peer observations, informal working groups, networking, and sharing materials, is also a valuable part of professional development.

One of the two content area literacy strategies introduced in this chapter involves Graphic Organizers, which are visual outlines. They provide a pictorial or graphic format for summarizing key concepts, ideas, and vocabulary. Graphic Organizers can be developed by the teacher and discussed with the students as a prereading device to introduce key vocabulary and activate background knowledge. They can also be developed by the students as a notetaking or postreading activity. Graphic Organizers display the terms that represent key concepts in such ways as to illustrate the relationships among them. Semantic Maps or Semantic Webs can be developed by the teacher and students together to introduce vocabulary and activate schemata. Semantic Mapping can also serve as a study strategy when students develop their own Study Maps in the process of reading to learn.

The second content area literacy strategy introduced in this chapter is the Language Experience Approach (LEA). In this strategy, content is summarized using the students' own language. Doing so helps both students and teacher assess learning; it also helps students internalize the information better. It can be especially helpful for poor readers who have difficulty reading the assigned text. In the first step, the content is presented in almost any form—for example, reading, discussion, video, computers, lecture, field trip, and so forth. In the second step, the content is discussed extensively by the students with guidance from the teacher. In the third step, students either write or dictate summaries of the content in their own words. Finally, students reread the summaries silently or orally for specific, meaningful purposes.

ENRICHMENT ACTIVITIES

1. Choose a content area and grade level, and write a brief description of a lesson using a Graphic Organizer or LEA in teaching a topic related to the content area. Describe the specific procedures you would follow in applying the strategy.

2. Interview two parents and two students to find out what they would contribute as part of a Total Quality Management system, in which they could make suggestions for improving the effectiveness of the schools. Submit in writing an assessment of the value of their suggestions. Consider these questions in your assessment: Are they practical? Are they feasible? Are they innovative? Are they consistent with current school reforms? Do they indicate anything about whether involving parents and students in the decision-making process is a good idea?

3. Rank the seven types of intelligence/learning for yourself, with 1 being your greatest strength:

_____ **Linguistic/Verbal Intelligence**
▮ enjoys reading, writing, and speaking
▮ enjoys research and report writing
▮ easily recalls names, places, dates, and details
▮ prefers typing to writing
▮ likes to use tape recorders
▮ likes books, periodicals, recordings
▮ enjoys storytelling and oral reading to share stories
▮ likes creative writing, poetry, joke telling
▮ particularly enjoys social studies
▮ enjoys libraries and bookstores

_____ **Mathematical/Logical Intelligence**
▮ strong in math
▮ good problem-solving and reasoning skills
▮ likes to formulate and answer logical questions
▮ enjoys sorting, categorizing, and classifying
▮ likes to explore and analyze
▮ likes puzzles, mysteries, riddles
▮ enjoys conducting experiments
▮ likes working with numbers
▮ enjoys composing word problems
▮ likes computers and other forms of instructional technology

_____ **Spatial/Visual Intelligence**
▮ needs visuals to understand new concepts
▮ uses a lot of mental imagery (picturing things)
▮ likes to make and read maps, charts, and diagrams
▮ enjoys mazes and puzzles
▮ has a strong imagination
▮ good at designing, drawing, creating, and constructing
▮ likes videos, photographs, slides, filmstrips, multimedia

- likes designing and giving media presentations
- likes museums, planetariums, and so on
- likes to daydream

_____ Musical/Rhythmic Intelligence

- enjoys listening and responding to music
- easily recalls melodies and likes to sing
- notices things like pitch and rhythm
- highly aware of sounds in the environment
- loves musical instruments and recorded music
- fascinated by computerized sound systems
- easily learns information in the form of ballads or song lyrics
- can make percussion instruments out of almost anything
- learns better while listening to certain types of music
- loves concerts and music stores

_____ Bodily/Kinesthetic Intelligence

- good at physical activities
- likes to move around a lot (difficulty keeping still)
- likes to touch things
- uses lots of gestures for communicating
- likes hands-on learning, particularly crafts
- especially interested in playground and sports equipment
- has both fine and large motor coordination
- likes to communicate through drama, dance, and movement
- loves sporting events and dance performances
- fascinated with sports personalities

_____ Interpersonal/Personal Intelligence Directed toward Other Persons

- strong leadership skills
- very sociable with good interpersonal skills
- good at organizing people
- good communicator
- good mediator and listener
- solves problems by talking through them
- likes lots of discussion
- enjoys interviewing and debating
- learns best by talking to others
- enjoys cooperative learning

_____ Intrapersonal/Personal Intelligence Directed toward Oneself

- has a strong sense of self
- is very self-confident

■ prefers working alone
■ has good instincts about strengths and abilities
■ follows interests, dreams, and goals
■ seeks help if necessary to pursue goals
■ likes independent research projects
■ likes cumulative writing projects
■ likes to sit quietly, think, and dream
■ likes to pursue personal interests and hobbies

4. Consider the following in creating your own personal mission statement for teaching:
   ■ the role of literacy in your content area classroom
   ■ your role and responsibilities as a content area teacher
   ■ why you became or want to become a teacher
   ■ what kind of teacher you are or want to be (character traits)
   ■ accomplishments and contributions you want to make as a teacher
   ■ the values that guide your professional ethics and choices
   ■ a plan for continued renewal through professional development

5. Interview two or more school district administrators in charge of staff development (principals, assistant principals, curriculum supervisors, department chairs, and so on) or representatives of the Regional Education Service Center. Ask them what kinds of opportunities are currently available for professional development for teachers. Then, submit in writing a list of those opportunities, as well as other types of opportunities you personally would like to see offered.

REFERENCES

Allen, R. V., and C. Allen. (1966). *Language experiences in reading, level 1.* Chicago: Encyclopedia.

Alvermann, D. E., and J. Swafford. (1989). Do content area strategies have a research base? *Journal of Reading* 32:388–394.

Barron, R. F. (1969). The use of vocabulary as an advance organizer. In *Research in reading in the content areas: First year report.* Edited by H. L. Herber and P. L. Sanders. Syracuse, NY: Reading and Language Arts Center, Syracuse University.

Bonstingl, J. J. (1992a). The total quality classroom. *Educational Leadership* 49:66–70.

———. (1992b). The quality revolution in education. *Educational Leadership* 50:4–9.

Covey, S. R. (1990). *The seven habits of highly effective people.* New York: Fireside.

Darch, C. B., D. W. Carnine, and E. J. Kameenui. (1986). The role of graphic organizers and social structure in content area instruction. *Journal of Reading Behavior* 18:275–295.

Dinnel, D., and J. H. Glover. (1985). Advance organizers: Encoding manipulations. *Journal of Educational Psychology* 77:514–521.

Faggella, K., and J. Horowitz. (1990). Different child, different style. *Instructor* 100:49–54.

Fiske, E. B. (1991). *Smart schools, smart kids.* New York: Touchstone.

Freedman, G., and E. G. Reynolds. (1980). Enriching basal reader lessons with semantic webbing. *The Reading Teacher* 33:677–684.

Gardner, H. (1983). *Frames of mind: The theory of multiple intelligences.* New York: Basic.

————. (1993). *Frames of mind: The theory of multiple intelligences* (Tenth-Anniversary Edition). New York: Basic.

Glasser, W. (1992). *The quality school.* New York: HarperCollins.

Hanf, M. B. (1971). Mapping: A technique for translating reading into thinking. *Journal of Reading* 14:225–230, 270.

Heimlich, J. E., and S. D. Pittelman. (1986). *Semantic mapping: Classroom applications.* Newark, DE: International Reading Association.

Hixson, J., and K. Lovelace. (1992). Total quality management's challenge to urban schools. *Educational Leadership* 50:24–27.

Johnson, D. D., and P. D. Pearson. (1984). *Teaching reading vocabulary,* 2d ed. New York: Holt, Rinehart and Winston.

McKenna, M., and R. Robinson. (1990). Content literacy: A definition and implications. *Journal of Reading* 34:184–186.

Reinking, D. (1986). Integrating graphic aids into content area instruction: The graphic information lesson. *The Reading Teacher* 30:146–151.

Senge, P. (1990). *The Fifth Discipline.* New York: Doubleday.

Stahl, S. A., and S. J. Vancil. (1986). Discussion is what makes semantic maps work in vocabulary instruction. *The Reading Teacher* 40:62–67.

Tierney, R. J., and P. D. Pearson. (1992). A revisionist perspective on "Learning to learn from text: A framework for improving classroom practice." In *Reading in the content areas: Improving classroom instruction.* Edited by E. K. Dishner, T. W. Bean, J. E. Readence, and D. W. Moore. Dubuque, IA: Kendall/Hunt Publishing Company.

Tierney, R. J., J. E. Readence, and E. K. Dishner. (1990). *Reading strategies and practices: A compendium,* 3d ed. Needham Heights, MA: Allyn and Bacon.

Vacca, R. T., and J. L. Vacca. (1993). *Content Area Reading,* 4th ed. New York: HarperCollins.

CHAPTER 2
GRAPHIC
ORGANIZER

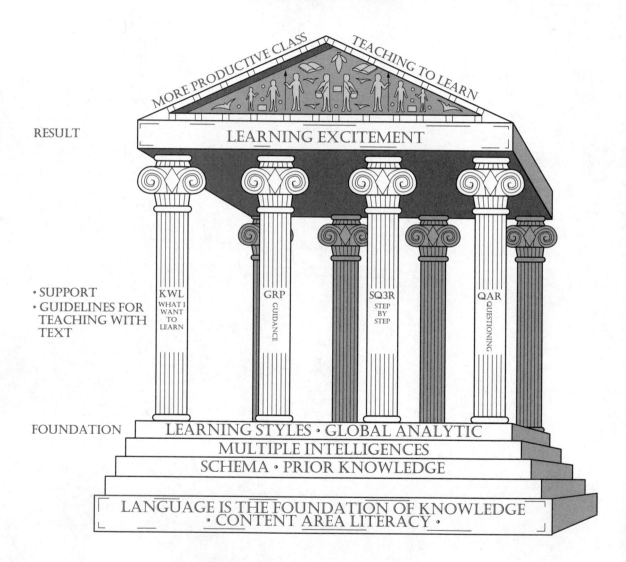

MORE PRODUCTIVE CLASS   TEACHING TO LEARN

RESULT   LEARNING EXCITEMENT

- SUPPORT
- GUIDELINES FOR
  TEACHING WITH
  TEXT

KWL
WHAT I
WANT
TO
LEARN

GRP
GUIDANCE

SQ3R
STEP
BY
STEP

QAR
QUESTIONING

FOUNDATION   LEARNING STYLES · GLOBAL ANALYTIC
MULTIPLE INTELLIGENCES
SCHEMA · PRIOR KNOWLEDGE

LANGUAGE IS THE FOUNDATION OF KNOWLEDGE
· CONTENT AREA LITERACY ·

CONTENT AREA LITERACY:
EXCITEMENT IN
LEARNING

CHAPTER 2

Content Area Literacy: Excitement in Learning

To demonstrate mastery of the content, the student will be able to do the following:

PART 1 OBJECTIVES

1. Identify the following strategy, describe its distinguishing features, and assess its significance to teaching content area literacy: KWL.
2. Describe the role of content area literacy in content area teaching and learning.
3. Assess the benefits of content area literacy for content area teachers and students.
4. Define schema and assess its role in content area teaching and learning.
5. List ways teachers can help ESL and other students build and activate schemata before, during, and after reading.

PART 2 OBJECTIVES

1. Identify the following strategy, describe its distinguishing features, and assess its significance to teaching content area literacy: GRP.
2. Identify four guidelines for teaching content with textual materials.
3. List ways teachers can help students activate schemata before, during, and after reading.
4. Distinguish the characteristics and assess the significance of the seven types of intelligence identified by Gardner.
5. Distinguish global from analytic learning style preferences.
6. Identify the type of learning style preference that is more conducive for success in the old paradigm of education and explain why.

49

PART 2 OBJECTIVES—continued

7. Assess the importance of mastering a wide variety of teaching and learning strategies for developing content area literacy.

INTRODUCTION

In this chapter, you will learn the important role content area literacy plays in support of content area learning. You will also learn the benefits of content area literacy for both teachers and students. Finally, you will be introduced to schema theory, an important principle underlying content area literacy and learning. Schema theory will help you understand why you have a more difficult time comprehending some texts than others, and how you can help your students improve their comprehension and learning with text. Research on schema theory supports the rationale behind the guidelines you will learn for effectively teaching content with textual materials.

In Chapter 1, you were introduced to the concept of content area literacy and its significance to the new paradigm of education emerging in classroom reforms. You were also introduced to the concept of Total Quality teaching and learning in the content area classroom. You will recall that literacy-based strategies reflect Total Quality principles in a variety of ways. Chapter 1 introduced you to two of those strategies for content area literacy. You will be introduced to two additional strategies in this chapter, the KWL and the Guided Reading Procedure (GRP). Each remaining chapter in this text will then introduce you to two different literacy-based strategies.

Later in this chapter, you will learn the importance of using a wide variety of strategies in content area literacy to meet the needs of all your students. Once you are confident with these strategies, or a subset of them, you will be able to mix and match them to form even more varied strategies. Also in this chapter you will learn key guidelines to follow in mixing and matching or even creating your own new strategies. The possibilities are endless.

The concepts of multiple intelligences and learning styles will help you begin to understand the varying instructional needs of your students. You will be introduced to seven types of intelligence as well as one of the many paradigms of learning styles, along with a simple checklist to help you identify the different learning styles of your students. The concept of learning styles is extremely complicated, and an in-depth discussion of the major paradigms and assessment inventories is beyond the scope of this text. Consequently, for the purpose of introducing you to the objective of matching varied learning styles with applicable instructional strategies, the paradigm introduced in this text is a simple one. It can be quite effective, however, in helping you begin to recognize and plan for learning differences.

PART 1

STRATEGY: WHAT I KNOW, WHAT I WANT TO LEARN, WHAT I LEARNED (KWL)

Another strategy for content area literacy is called "What I Know, What I Want to Learn, What I Learned" (KWL). This strategy was developed by Ogle (1986) to help teachers activate students' background knowledge and interest in a topic. It involves three basic steps that guide the students in accessing what they already know, determining what they want to learn, and recalling what they learned from reading. To facilitate the group process and emphasize the concreteness of the steps, provide each student with a KWL form, which is divided into three labeled sections, and has a section at the bottom for categories (see Figure 2–1).

The first step, What I Know (K), involves brainstorming previous knowledge of and experience with the topic, and then generating categories of information likely to be encountered in the reading. The brainstorming takes place as a whole-class discussion led by the teacher, who begins by asking a question such as, "What do you know about _____?" As the teacher writes student responses on the board, chart, or overhead, discussion is generated with follow-up questions such as, "Where did you learn about that?" or "How do you know that?" As students contribute to and participate in the brainstorming session, they record the information they already know about the topic. After brainstorming, the teacher asks students to think about what kinds of information are likely to be presented on this topic. The teacher generates examples of categories from the information gathered during brainstorming and then asks the students to think of other possible categories, which are also recorded. Until students are confident generating categories, the teacher may need to model the process for them and present many examples.

In the second step, What I Want to Learn (W), the teacher guides students in setting specific purposes for reading. From interests, curiosities, uncertainties, and knowledge gaps generated during the first step, possible questions are formulated by the teacher and written on the board. The teacher then attempts to provoke student questions by pointing out inconsistencies, conflicting information, and particularly intriguing ideas.

FIGURE 2–1 Sample KWL form

What I Know	What I Want to Learn	What I Learned

Categories of information
we expect to use:
A.
B.
C.
D.
E.
F.

Students are encouraged to write their own questions and/or select ones from the board. These questions then serve as purposes for reading.

The third step, What I Learned (L) takes place after reading as a follow-up to determine to what extent the purposes set for reading were met. Students list information they have learned and identify any questions left unanswered, and the teacher helps students develop plans for investigating these questions. In this way, emphasis is placed on reading for the purpose of fulfilling personal curiosities rather than learning only what was presented.

THE ROLE AND BENEFITS OF LITERACY IN THE CONTENT AREA CLASSROOM

The Role of Content Area Literacy

In classrooms in which content area literacy does not play a significant role in learning, students and teachers may associate the use of textbooks with boredom and drudgery. Many teachers complain that students either cannot or will not read their assignments; in turn, many students believe that the text is boring and that the same old assignments are nothing but busy work. The exciting possibilities offered by content area literacy can become a welcome reprieve to these difficulties.

Through content area literacy, teachers can empower and motivate students to read the text. They can also supplement the text with stimulating and provocative materials on related topics. Students can be given choices, which provides them with a vested interest in instructional decisions. They can also be guided in the development of problem-solving projects related to relevant controversial issues. The application of literacy-based strategies and activities in the content area classroom opens a boundless realm of inspiring possibilities. For example, through content area literacy, students can:

- become willing and eager participants in the learning process.
- strengthen their reading and writing abilities.
- cultivate their critical thinking skills.
- develop positive attitudes toward literacy and learning.
- acquire an appreciation for teamwork.
- take more responsibility for their own learning.
- experience the joys of success.
- fulfill personal goals.
- recognize their learning strengths.
- build effective systems for study.
- gain a sense of independence through learning.
- realize the power of knowledge and literacy for getting what they need and want in life.

The good news for content area teachers is that they do not have to become specialists in reading or writing instruction to incorporate literacy-based strategies and activities into content area instruction. Using reading, writing, and critical thinking as instructional tools does not mean incorporating more content into an already packed curriculum. Rather, content area literacy means teaching differently, not more. Furthermore, content area literacy does not require teachers to instruct students in the mechanics of reading and writing (McKenna and Robinson 1990). Therefore, teachers can develop content area literacy by applying easy-to-use strategies designed and proven to enhance learning, even for poor readers and writers. Simple techniques for designing homework assignments and in-class activities can empower content area teachers to help their students become more effective and independent learners.

Additionally, content area literacy means making the best use of the teacher's time and energies. Since content area literacy is based primarily on active learning approaches, the teacher's role changes: Students take more responsibility for their own learning, and teachers become facilitators of knowledge, rather than "fountains of knowledge" (Johnson, Johnson, and Holubec 1991). Through literacy-based strategies and activities, students learn how to work independently and in collaboration with one another. The teacher becomes a guide and consultant and serves as one of many learning resources. When teachers are not responsible for "spoon feeding" (or in many cases "force feeding") information to students, they have more time to observe students, identify needs, and provide feedback.

In addition to serving as a resource, teachers become partners in learning with the students. Since teachers are already literate in their content areas, they can serve as important models and guides in the learning process. Tierney and Pearson (1992) suggest a definition of the teacher's role in the content area classroom, which views teachers as senior members of a community of learners. Since teachers are more knowledgeable, experienced, and skilled at important learning processes, they have an obligation to share, model, and demonstrate the skills involved in content area literacy. As master learners, teachers can empower students by passing on the tools and skills of their trade (Tierney and Pearson 1992).

In summary, the role of content area literacy in the content area classroom is multifaceted. Content area literacy can assist the content area teacher in motivating students by making the content more relevant and valuable and by making the instruction more stimulating and successful. Teachers empower students to be more effective and independent readers and learners, and to make more efficient use of time and energy by redefining teacher and student roles.

Benefits of Content Area Literacy

The content area teacher who can empower students to become successful, independent learners is a winner in two ways. First, documentation of the teacher's instructional effectiveness is enhanced by improved learning outcomes. Second, the teacher's job becomes more exciting and rewarding as the teacher and students become partners in learning.

The good news for students is that they have many opportunities to practice and apply their reading and writing skills and strategies for learning. Content area literacy involves real-life reading. In other words, students read and write for the purposes of discovering, learning, and applying content information. At the same time, of course, they are sharpening and developing their literacy skills. For example, they develop effective reading strategies, efficient study habits, powerful vocabularies, critical thinking, and confidence in writing. As a result, content area literacy empowers students to explore, research, and enjoy content knowledge according to their own needs and interests as independent learners.

The good news for both teachers and students is that content area literacy has the potential to maximize content acquisition (McKenna and Robinson 1990). Certainly the primary role of the content area teacher is to teach the content effectively. In fulfilling that role, the content teacher whose students are effective readers, competent writers, critical thinkers, and independent learners will be at an obvious advantage. The best way to develop those abilities in students is to give them practice and guidance; therefore, using strategies in content area literacy for content area instruction provides a double bonus. The strategies not only develop students' content area literacy but also enhance their learning of content. With this outcome, both students and teachers are winners.

Although content could probably be taught successfully through direct oral instruction alone, McKenna and Robinson (1990) identify four important reasons why direct instruction should not be used exclusively. First, the products of literacy activities serve to complement oral instruction and broaden students' perspectives. Second, literacy activities provide a natural follow-up to direct instruction, allowing teachers to address individual student needs and interests. Third, current models of direct instruction include practice phases, for which literacy activities seem ideally suited. Fourth, students who have been given opportunities to develop content literacy are more likely to extend their knowledge of a discipline beyond the scope and time constraints of the course.

Since students continue developing literacy skills throughout and beyond their elementary and secondary school programs, continual opportunities for literacy development are crucial. As each content teacher, at every level, increases opportunities for reading and writing experiences, students become more content literate. As they become more content literate, they have the necessary tools to learn content more effectively and efficiently across all disciplines. Content classrooms provide ideal settings for practical application of developing literacy skills. Finally, content area literacy provides a crucial foundation for lifelong learning and literacy development.

SCHEMA THEORY: A FOUNDATION FOR CONTENT AREA LITERACY

Defining Schema

The notion of schema, or preexisting knowledge structures, was first described by Frederick C. Bartlett (1932) in his research of story retellings. He observed that, when retelling a folktale whose structure and content was not familiar, his subjects tended to paraphrase the story in a way that made it more similar to texts they were accustomed to reading. In other words, when they had no prior knowledge of a foreign folktale, they had a tendency to force the story's structure and content into their own preexisting knowledge structures, which he called schemata. Therefore, their comprehension was characterized by a reconstruction of knowledge guided by their own schemata. Bartlett's insights about the role of schema and the reconstructive nature of comprehension were incorporated into modern cognitive theories of understanding and knowing, such as Anderson's (1984) notions of schemata in reading (Weaver and Kintsch 1991).

Schemata provide the mental categories and frameworks necessary for processing and integrating new knowledge. They are the "hooks" upon which new pieces of information are hung. These hooks are part of an intricate framework of associations that connect the various stored schemata. The reading process brings the student's schemata to a conscious level, thereby making the information meaningful for that student. As the student strives to comprehend information in the context of her or his schemata, the student's individual framework of associations is tapped. The result is a deeper and more meaningful level of understanding.

The Role of Schema in Content Area Literacy

Since a reader's schemata provide the necessary background knowledge and frameworks for reconstructing meaning, it is not surprising that research has clearly confirmed the crucial role played by schemata in understanding text (Anderson 1984). New information is internalized through a process of relating it to prior knowledge; therefore, without the necessary schemata, new knowledge is in danger of being lost.

When students' background knowledge of the topic of a given content area reading assignment is limited, their understanding will almost certainly be inadequate. With this crucial piece of information, teachers can easily prevent students' failures, frustrations, deflated egos, and loss of enthusiasm resulting from limited background knowledge. By taking a little extra time to assess and develop students' prior knowledge and experience, valuable time, energy, and momentum can be saved. Limitations in prior knowledge can be overcome easily if the teacher is aware of them and takes a few simple steps to address them in preparation for the reading assignment. Techniques and strategies in content area literacy assess and build background knowledge without detracting from the presentation of content. The time spent helping students assess and activate their schemata before, during, and after reading is easily made up by the time saved in not having to reread, explain, and reteach content after reading. Specific guidelines for activating schemata will be discussed later in this chapter.

Another valuable aspect of schema is the role it plays in motivation. When students can relate new information to their own background knowledge and experiences, it becomes much more meaningful to them. Curiosity and interest in a topic can be aroused by providing examples of how the information relates to real-life experiences with which students are familiar. Students can more easily perceive the value of information when it is made directly relevant to their own lives and experiences.

Read again the description of the KWL strategy at the beginning of this chapter. Notice how this strategy is based on schema theory. The first step is designed to assess and activate each student's schema. The second step is designed to establish purposes for reading that emerge from assessing and activating background knowledge. The last step is designed to help the reader internalize the content by relating it to schema.

Building Schema: Meeting the Needs of ESL and Other Students Who Need to Develop Background Knowledge

The following activities for developing students' background knowledge were designed and recommended specifically for students for whom English is a second language (ESL). As you will see, these activities are appropriate for all students who need to develop their background knowledge. For example, Schifini (1994) recommends that activities designed to build background knowledge involve one or more of the five senses, integrate expressive communication (writing and speaking) with receptive communication (reading and listening), and be motivating. He suggests the following five prereading activities, which have those characteristics.

1. Have students work in small groups to make observations about visual stimuli (e.g., pictures and diagrams from lower-level textbooks, relevant photographs, pictures related to a theme and collected by the students). Students talk and write about their observations. They should be guided to describe what they see, speculate, or hypothesize about the pictures, and relate these observations to their own personal knowledge and experiences.

2. Use manipulatives and multimedia presentations to introduce topics or lessons. Offer concrete objects related to the topic of study for students to handle, examine, describe, and discuss. Multimedia, such as videotapes, audiotapes, filmstrips, computer programs, laser disks, and so on are also useful to introduce and stimulate discussion on the topic.

3. Have students share their own diverse experiences and prior knowledge with each other. For example, you can present and have students respond to poetry, journal entries, music, art, literary selections, newspaper articles, and magazine articles. Encourage students to share their interpretations and responses, which will be based on their prior knowledge. Use questioning to guide a discussion of their interpretations and predictions about the reading assignment.

4. Use writing activities that tap into students' background knowledge and help them build schemata. For example, before reading, have them brainstorm by writing everything they can think of about a given topic. They could also write in journals and respond to writing prompts to encourage them to think about a particular topic, what they know about it, and what personal experiences they have had in relation to it.

5. Help students link prior knowledge to new concepts and ideas using the KWL strategy.

Kang (1994) and Schifini (1994) both recommend the use of *semantic mapping* (see Chapter 1) and *semantic feature analysis* (see Chapter 8) to develop vocabulary while also building and activating background knowledge. In addition, Kang (1994) recommends the use of brainstorming, structured overviews, and other prereading activities to build and activate background knowledge. Using these activities, you can help students build bridges between what they already know and the new concepts they will encounter. Help students recognize differences between their background knowledge and the information found in the text; for example, point out contradictions, note exceptions, identify opposing examples, bring up additional considerations, and have students compare personal experiences with the textual information (Kang 1994).

Based on research by Carrell, Pharis, and Liberto (1989), *semantic mapping* is also recommended as a background-building strategy by Reyes and Molner (1991). Following is a set of procedures adapted from their recommendations for semantic mapping. Be sure to include your ESL students in all steps, even if some translation and simplification is necessary.

1. Before reading, provide students with a topic, and have them brainstorm words and phrases they associate with that topic. Record the responses for all to see.

2. Lead a discussion about the words and phrases generated and how they relate to the topic. Guide the students in organizing the information into their own semantic maps (see Chapter 1).

3. After reading, help students revise their maps to combine their background knowledge with new information gained from the reading.

A second strategy Reyes and Molner (1991) recommend for background building is Langer's (1984) *Pre-Reading Plan* (PReP) (see Chapter 9). As its name implies, the entire strategy takes place in preparation for a reading assignment. The teacher's role is observer, questioner, and recorder, not critic. In other words, you want to guide students in their own discovery and processing of what they already know about a concept. In doing so, you gain valuable information about the students' levels of background knowledge, and students benefit from listening to each other's ideas and interpretations.

Following are a set of procedures adapted from PReP (Langer 1981). Keep in mind the importance of including your ESL students in every step. Notice the similarities between PReP and semantic mapping. How do both strategies build background knowledge and relate it to the content?

1. *Initial associations with the concept.* Select one or more key concepts to present for discussion, one at a time. Present the first concept and have students brainstorm ideas they associate with that concept. Ask something such as "What comes to mind when you see or hear _____?" Record students' responses, even those that are incomplete or inaccurate.

2. *Reflections on initial associations.* Lead a discussion to allow students to reflect on and explain their initial associations. Ask such questions as "What made you think of that?" or "Where did you learn that?"

3. *Reformulation of knowledge.* Guide students in making elaborations, additions, deletions, or changes, if any, following the discussion. Ask questions such as, "Did you think of anything new you would like to add?" or "Is there anything you want to delete or change?"

PART 2

STRATEGY: GUIDED READING PROCEDURE (GRP)

Distinguishing Features and Significance of GRP

The Guided Reading Procedure was developed by Manzo (1975) to "(1) assist students' unaided recall of specific information read; (2) improve the students' abilities to generate their own (implicit) questions as they read; (3) develop the students' understanding of the importance of self-correction; and (4) improve the students' abilities to organize information" (Tierney, Readence, and Dishner, 1990, 242). Research has confirmed the effectiveness of the GRP in enhancing learning from text (Ankney and McClurg 1981; Bean and Pardi 1979). The GRP consists of six basic steps.

The teacher prepares students for reading the assignment by assessing and developing requisite background knowledge, introducing vocabulary, and setting purposes for reading. Although the purpose for reading using GRP is a general one, it is crucial to the success of the strategy. The purpose for reading, which must be communicated to students, is to remember as many details as possible. Students could also be told to "remember as much as possible" or "read to remember everything you can."

After understanding their purpose for reading, students read silently. The teacher walks around and monitors their progress, providing assistance as necessary. Students are instructed to turn the material face down on their desks as a signal that they are finished reading. When most students have finished reading, the teacher asks students to share details that they remember, an activity known as "free recall" or "unaided recall." The reading material must remain face down on their desks during this segment. As students recall information, the teacher records the information on the board or overhead; much space will be needed for recording. The teacher must write quickly, using abbreviations; neatness may be sacrificed as long as the writing is still legible.

After recording all the information the students can remember, the students return to the reading material to make corrections and add information. The teacher makes the additions and changes as they are suggested by the students. After the students have finished making corrections and adding information, the teacher directs their attention to missed information or inaccuracies, as necessary.

The teacher next assists the students in organizing the information. For example, the main ideas can be separated from the supporting details, the information can be categorized, or the information can be sequenced in some fashion. The teacher may demonstrate more than one option for organizing the information.

Then the teacher asks thought-provoking questions that require students to relate the new information to previous knowledge and think critically about it. The purpose of this transfer-of-learning segment is to help students process and apply the new information. The teacher serves as a model by asking questions that require students to synthesize information with previously learned information.

The final step is to test students on their short-term memory of the information. A short quiz is given to allow both the teacher and students to assess the students' understanding and recall of the information. The format of the quiz is not important; any type or combination of types of questions may be used. The teacher may also provide additional opportunities for the students to discuss, manipulate, and reflect on the information. The teacher may want to check recall over longer periods of time, as well.

GUIDELINES FOR TEACHING CONTENT WITH TEXTUAL MATERIALS

Structures for teaching with text were developed from extensive research on the nature of comprehension and learning with text. Tierney and Pearson (1981) summarize four guidelines for helping students learn with text. These guidelines form the basis of most instructional strategies in content area literacy. As you learn the strategies, notice that although they provide a wide variety of instructional options, all have certain shared characteristics. As the following guidelines are discussed, notice how the roles of the teacher and of schema theory work to: prepare students before reading; guide and monitor students during reading; and help students assess and apply what they have understood and learned after reading. You will recognize these carefully defined roles as running themes in the instructional strategies presented in later chapters.

Assessing Schemata and Setting Purposes before Reading

The first guideline suggested by Tierney and Pearson (1986) for helping students learn with text involves determining whether they possess the requisite schemata for understanding. Specifically, do the students' prior knowledge and purposes for reading match the intentions and expectations of the authors? If not, the teacher must make necessary adjustments; for example, the teacher may need to develop background knowledge, introduce vocabulary, revise purposes for reading, and/or alter, supplement, or replace the text.

The emphasis this guideline places on setting purposes for reading is important for a number of reasons. Setting purposes helps readers activate prior knowledge, and having specific purposes in mind helps readers maintain concentration for improved comprehension and retention. Setting purposes helps the reader establish goals for monitoring comprehension; consistently providing students with specific purposes for reading helps them learn to set their own purposes as independent readers. Finally, purposeful reading is a characteristic of active readers, who interact with the text as they read; reading for specific purposes leads to text interaction at the highest levels of thought.

Activating Schemata before, during, and after Reading

The second guideline suggested by Tierney and Pearson (1986) involves student engagement with the text. Once the teacher is satisfied that the students have the relevant schemata and appropriate purposes for reading, the next step is to take measures for activating the readers' schemata. Before, during, and after reading, the following activities help ensure activation of schemata:

▌ Review students' background knowledge and purposes for reading.
▌ Direct students' attention to the relevance and value of the learning experience.
▌ Relate the content to students' personal knowledge and experiences.
▌ Help students assess learning with respect to their purposes for reading.

Monitoring Comprehension during Reading

The third guideline suggested by Tierney and Pearson (1986) involves monitoring reader-text interactions. When readers interact with text, they integrate information with their own background knowledge. This interaction forms the basis of the readers' interpretations of the text. At this point, differences in subject matter and textual demands come into play. The teacher's role is to help students make distinctions in the different interpretations that are appropriate for different texts. Some texts demand a more text-based interpretation, while for others, a reader-based interpretation is more appropriate.

A text-based interpretation emphasizes accurate interpretation of the text through literal-level comprehension. The students' responsibility is to understand, paraphrase, summarize, and interpret the author's intended meaning. Text-based interpretations sometimes require students to make inferences and draw conclusions. When situations require a more text-based interpretation, Tierney and Pearson (1986, 98) recommend that teachers provide the following support:

> Alert the students to the need to read the material carefully; provide adjuncts (inserted questions or activities) that encourage students to monitor their developing interpretation; provide students with strategies such as outlining and notetaking for carefully reading the text; encourage students to consciously consider their purposes, their level of understanding, and ways to monitor that understanding; and have the students read the material in conjunction with carrying out some relevant activity (for example, an experiment in which successful performance is contingent upon a careful reading).

A reader-based interpretation, on the other hand, emphasizes the reader's reactions and responses to the text through higher-level thinking. The reader's responsibility includes not only the literal-level understanding required for text-based interpretations, but also critical-level interpretations. For example, the reader must not only understand and interpret the author's message but also analyze, evaluate, and apply it. As with text-based interpretations, some reader-based interpretations require students to make inferences and draw conclusions. When situations call for a more reader-based interpretation, Tierney and Pearson (1986, 98–99) suggest the following support:

> Encourage readers to relate their background of experience to what they read and alert them to the importance of their own ideas, perspective, and purpose in any communication. Minimally, the reader should be asked to discuss his or her knowledge including a perspective about a topic in conjunction with a discussion of the author's perspective and what the author assumed the reader knew and might learn. Otherwise, the facilitation might be accomplished either through adjunct questions, activities, or appropriate variations.

Evaluating Comprehension after Reading

The fourth guideline suggested by Tierney and Pearson (1986) involves assessing the readers' interpretations. The important point to remember in helping students assess their understanding of the text is that accuracy is defined according to both the author's intentions and the readers' purposes. Tierney and Pearson (1986, 100) suggest the following questions in helping teachers assess readers' interpretations of text:

> To what extent was the reader's understanding adequate for the text and purposes for reading?

> When a reader's understanding diverges from some consensual author's intention, can the reader's interpretation be justified?

Another consideration in the assessment of readers' understanding and interpretations of text is the notion of transfer, the ability to apply what has been read or learned to other situations. Tierney and Pearson (1986, 101) suggest the following questions to further assess readers' interpretations of text:

> Can readers use the new knowledge they have acquired?

> Can readers use the new strategies they have acquired when they encounter new texts on their own?

Once students' learning and applications of learning have been assessed, the teacher may need to make instructional revisions. Also, students may need guidance in revising their strategies for learning with text. Most importantly, teachers need to provide students with strategies for rereading, if necessary, to ensure that purposes are met.

Following the Guidelines through a Variety of Strategies

All four of the previously mentioned guidelines are important considerations for instructional decision making. Teachers can ensure that they follow the guidelines as closely as possible simply by using lesson formats, strategies, and activities that have been designed for content area literacy. All of the structures for teaching and learning with text presented in this chapter and in later chapters have been specially designed to follow the guidelines indicated by classroom research. The effectiveness of these lesson frameworks and strategies has also been validated through classroom research. Although they are all based on the same general guidelines, they provide a variety of alternatives for effectively teaching with text.

MULTIPLE INTELLIGENCES

Howard Gardner (1993), in his efforts to expand the traditional concept of intelligence as measured by short-answer, paper-and-pencil tests, postulated the theory of multiple intelligences. He contends that intelligence includes a much broader and more universal set of competences. Following is his definition of intelligence.

> An intelligence is the ability to solve problems, or to create products, that are valued within one or more cultural settings. (Gardner 1993, x)

From his research on biological and anthropological evidence, Gardner (1993) identified a set of criteria that he uses to define the concept of intelligence. From these criteria, he identified seven distinct intelligences: verbal/linguistic, logical/mathematical, visual/spatial, body/kinesthetic, musical/rhythmic, interpersonal, and intrapersonal.

Fagella and Horowitz (1990) outlined various learning strengths and preferences typically associated with each type of intelligence. From the following examples, you can see the importance of incorporating a wide variety of strategies, techniques, and activities to maximize learning and intellectual development for all students.

Learners with strong **verbal/linguistic** intelligence often:

- Enjoy reading, writing, and speaking
- Enjoy research and report writing
- Recall names, places, dates, and details easily

▌ Prefer typing to writing
▌ Like to use tape recorders
▌ Like books, periodicals, recordings
▌ Enjoy storytelling and oral reading to share stories
▌ Like creative writing, poetry, joke telling
▌ Enjoy social studies
▌ Enjoy libraries and bookstores

Learners with strong **logical/mathematical** intelligence often:

▌ Are strong in math
▌ Have good problem-solving and reasoning skills
▌ Like to formulate and answer logical questions
▌ Enjoy sorting, categorizing, and classifying
▌ Like to explore and analyze
▌ Like puzzles, mysteries, and riddles
▌ Enjoy conducting experiments
▌ Like working with numbers
▌ Enjoy composing word problems
▌ Like computers and other forms of instructional technology

Learners with strong **visual/spatial** intelligence often:

▌ Need visuals to understand new concepts
▌ Use a great deal of mental imagery (visualizing)
▌ Like to make and read maps, charts, and diagrams
▌ Enjoy mazes and puzzles
▌ Have strong imaginations
▌ Are good at designing, drawing, creating, and constructing
▌ Enjoy videos, photographs, slides, filmstrips, and multimedia
▌ Enjoy designing and giving media presentations
▌ Enjoy museums, planetariums, and so on
▌ Enjoy daydreaming

Learners with strong **body/kinesthetic** intelligence often:

▌ Are good at physical activities
▌ Like to move around a great deal and have difficulty keeping still
▌ Like to touch things
▌ Use lots of gestures for communicating
▌ Enjoy hands-on learning, particularly crafts
▌ Are especially interested in playground and sports equipment
▌ Have both fine- and large-motor coordination
▌ Like to communicate through drama, dance, and movement
▌ Love sporting events and dance performances
▌ Are fascinated with sports personalities

Learners with strong **musical/rhythmic** intelligence often:

▌ Enjoy listening and responding to music
▌ Recall melodies easily and like to sing
▌ Notice things like pitch and rhythm
▌ Are highly aware of sounds in the environment
▌ Love musical instruments and recorded music
▌ Are fascinated by computerized sound systems
▌ Learn information more easily in the form of ballads or song lyrics
▌ Can make percussion instruments out of most anything
▌ Learn better while listening to certain types of music
▌ Love concerts and music stores

Learners with strong **interpersonal** intelligence often:

▌ Have strong leadership skills
▌ Are very sociable and have good interpersonal skills
▌ Are good at organizing people
▌ Are good communicators
▌ Are good mediators and listeners
▌ Solve problems by talking through them
▌ Like a great deal of discussion
▌ Enjoy interviewing and debating
▌ Learn best by talking to others
▌ Enjoy cooperative learning

Learners with strong **intrapersonal** intelligence often:

▌ Have a strong sense of self
▌ Are very self-confident
▌ Prefer working alone
▌ Have good instincts about strengths and abilities
▌ Pursue their own interests, dreams, and goals
▌ Seek help if necessary to pursue or achieve their goals
▌ Like independent research projects
▌ Like cumulative writing projects
▌ Like to sit quietly, think, and daydream
▌ Like to pursue personal interests and hobbies

Understanding and accepting a wide range of intelligences is important to teachers in the process of identifying and building on the individual strengths of students. The concept of multiple intelligences is also important for helping students develop strong self-concepts and an appreciation of their own strengths. You recall from the previous chapter that the Total Quality principle of continuous improvement and self-evaluation involves helping students focus on and develop their innate talents instead of identifying and emphasizing their deficiencies. Finally, the concept of multiple intelligences is important for helping students develop a tolerance for diversity and an appreciation of differences in ability and talents. Valuing diversity is crucial to the development of synergy and synergistic relationships, one of the goals of the new paradigm of education.

LEARNING STYLES: USING A VARIETY OF STRATEGIES TO MEET THE SPECIAL NEEDS OF ALL STUDENTS

A Checklist for Learning Style Preferences

As a teacher, it is important that you understand and appreciate your own learning style factors, so that you can have greater insights into the varied relationships and levels of communication you will have with your students. Understanding the learning styles of your students is important for several reasons. First, you can help them develop an awareness of and appreciation for their own learning strengths. Second, you will be able to use the information to make decisions about instructional materials, methodologies, and strategies. Third, you can help your students develop an appreciation for learning differences among their peers by showing them how different strengths can contribute to and result in greater learning for all when students work together. The fourth and most important reason for understanding the learning style factors of your students is the realization that the ways in which *you* learn best may not be the ways in which *your students* learn best.

The concept of learning styles is a complex one. Since each student is unique, it is impossible to group students into discrete learning style categories. No one student will fit perfectly into any one category, of course. However, you can help students develop awareness of their learning style preferences by observing the students, asking them questions, and helping them characterize themselves. Several reliable instruments are available to help develop an awareness of individual learning style preferences. One such instrument is the Reading Styles Inventory, developed by Marie Carbo (1991). This inventory helps identify thirty-four style characteristics, including global and analytic inclinations, and then suggests methods and materials that accommodate or "match" the students' reading styles (i.e., learning styles for reading).

Figure 2–2 contains a short form of Carbo's (1991) Global/Analytic Reading Styles Inventory of learning style preferences. This checklist is designed to help you determine whether you are predominantly global, analytic, or a combination of both styles. Although this checklist may

---

FIGURE 2–2 Carbo's Global/Analytical Reading Styles Checklist

---

Name _____   Date _____

Are You Global? Analytic? Or Both?

To help you determine whether you are predominantly global or analytic, or a mixture of both styles, fill in the Global/Analytic Reading Styles Checklist. Parents or teachers may want to complete this checklist for children who are too young to do it themselves.

Global/Analytic Reading Styles Checklist

> **Scoring Key:**
>
> | | |
> |---|---|
> | Strongly Analytic 9–10 | Strongly Global 9–10 |
> | Moderately Analytic 6–8 | Moderately Global 6–8 |
> | Somewhat Analytic 3–5 | Somewhat Global 3–5 |
> | Slightly Analytic 0–2 | Slightly Global 0–2 |

Analytic People Often:

____ Recall what they hear
____ Make decisions based on logic, facts, and "common sense"
____ Recall facts and names
____ Are good planners
____ Like to work in a very organized environment
____ Are very punctual

____ Like to do one thing at a time
____ Are tidy and meticulous
____ Learn best when information is presented in sequential steps
____ Speak with few gestures

My Analytic Score _____

Global People Often:

____ Recall what they see, touch, feel
____ Make decisions based on their emotions and intuition
____ Recall places and faces
____ Are spontaneous
____ Like to work in a less-organized environment
____ May not be punctual, unless the event is very important
____ Like to do many things at once
____ Focus on being creative
____ Learn best when information is presented in a story with humor or emotion
____ Speak with many gestures

My Global Score _____

Scoring Directions: Add the number of checked items for each column and determine your score from the Scoring Key above.

Reprinted with permission of Marie Carbo.

provide a somewhat oversimplified view of the learning styles concept, it provides a good introduction to the idea of differing learning style preferences. Since it is based on learning and living activities in everyday life, you can more easily recognize and appreciate your own characteristics, as well as the characteristics of your close friends and family members.

As a teacher, you could observe a student and ask questions as necessary to complete the checklist, or you could let the students complete the checklist themselves as you explain and provide examples for each characteristic. Working through the checklist is an important way for students to develop awareness of their own styles of learning. As you and your students work through the checklist, place a check beside each characteristic that is most like the student most of the time, particularly in reading, study, and learning activities. If you absolutely cannot make up your mind because you believe you or they are one way sometimes and the other way the rest of the time, place a check in both categories. Then, total the number of checks for each category and use the scoring key to help you make a decision as to whether you and your students have mostly global, mostly analytic, or a balance of the two style preferences.

As you complete the checklist, keep in mind that you will probably not be totally analytic or totally global in any one category. Rather, you will fall somewhere along a continuum between the two extremes. It is important to remember and communicate to your students that *one learning style preference is no better or worse than another*. They each have their unique strengths. Once you become familiar with the preferences associated with various learning styles, you can more easily develop an appreciation for your own strengths and those of your friends, family members, and classmates, even if theirs are different from your own. Each style has its own benefits in different situations; for example, although global learners may face a greater challenge in a structured academic environment, they can often more easily tap into their creative abilities and use divergent thinking for critical reasoning and creative problem solving. The idea behind developing an awareness of learning style preferences is to appreciate your own natural abilities and the differing abilities your peers bring with them to cooperative learning situations.

As observed from the characteristics identified in the checklist, students with analytic learning style preferences often are more successful in the old paradigm of education. However, many successful students are global learners who have learned to adapt in an analytic world by developing intrinsic motivation through a realization that succeeding in school is an important step to getting what they want in life. They also recognize that sacrifices made now are investments that will pay off later when they are searching for personally and financially rewarding jobs. Many combination-style learners may have begun as global learners and eventually learned to adapt and feel comfortable with the analytic preferences that helped them achieve success in school.

Another important reason for developing an awareness of and appreciation for a variety of learning style preferences is that throughout life, students will face many diverse challenges. For example, meeting the demands of the workplace often requires a variety of approaches and strategies. Therefore, the ability to be synergistic and work with others in a team effort is crucial; working with a diversity of people affords the opportunity to learn and appreciate a variety of approaches to problem solving.

Information about your students' learning style preferences can be very useful for a variety of purposes. First, students can be grouped homogeneously for projects that would be more easily completed by students with similar global or analytic style preferences. Second, they can be grouped heterogeneously for projects that would benefit from a combination of approaches. Third, learning partners can be matched so that students learn to cooperate with others of differing global or analytic preferences. Fourth, as mentioned previously, knowing the global or analytic preferences of the students can help you make instructional decisions. Fifth, and most importantly, students can develop an appreciation for their own global or analytic preferences, as well as those of their peers.

A Variety of Strategies for a Variety of Preferences and Needs

The most important implication of the notion of learning style preferences is the need for using a wide variety of instructional strategies. As you read this book, you will learn many different strategies for teaching with text. Teachers need to be familiar with various options so that methodologies can be matched to the needs of the students and the demands of the text. The needs of the students include reading skills and levels, learning style preferences, background knowledge, motivation levels, and interest in the topic. The demands of the text include length, conceptual difficulty and density, technical vocabulary, sentence and word length, organization, text structures, graphic aids (e.g., charts, graphs, and pictures), reading aids (e.g., outlines, summaries, and margin notes) and print features (e.g., size and type of print and headings).

In addition to considering individual differences in students and textual materials, teachers must also consider their own individual teaching styles, as well as constraints of time and space. Variety is an important key to generating and maintaining interest in and enthusiasm for learning, both for the students and the teacher. Once you have a core set of strategies in your instructional repertoire, you will soon identify those you feel most comfortable using, as well as those that seem to work best for different students. You will then find yourself mixing, matching, and adapting strategies to meet instructional needs. Once you have mastered the basic guidelines and principles embodied in the strategies presented in this text, you will, with experience, become the ultimate decision maker by creating your own strategies for maximum learning in your classroom.

SUMMARY

The benefits of content area literacy are many. Students can be empowered and motivated to read the text and stimulating supplementary materials, thereby strengthening their reading, writing, and critical thinking skills. They can be given choices, which encourage a vested interest in instructional decisions. They can become willing and eager participants in the learning process and develop more positive attitudes toward literacy, learning, and teamwork. Students can become more responsible, independent, and confident learners and recognize the power of knowledge and literacy. Most importantly, they can become more effective learners of content.

The good news for teachers is that they do not need to become specialists in reading or writing instruction to incorporate literacy-based strategies and activities into content area instruction. They can develop content area literacy by applying easy-to-use strategies designed and proven to enhance learning, even for poor readers and writers. Simple techniques for designing homework assignments and in-class activities can empower content area teachers to help their students become more effective and independent learners. Content area literacy makes the best use of the teacher's time and energies. The teacher becomes a guide and consultant for active learners rather than the "fountain of knowledge" whose job it is to pour information into passive learners. Teachers become partners in learning with the students.

An important foundation for instruction in content area literacy is schema theory. Schemata are preexisting knowledge structures that determine how well or poorly one understands and internalizes new knowledge. Schemata provide the mental categories and frameworks for processing and integrating new knowledge. Activating schema makes new information meaningful. In fact, activating schema is so crucial to comprehension and learning that teachers should take time before giving a reading assignment to assess and develop background knowledge. Doing so might save students the frustration, reduced self-esteem, and loss of enthusiasm due to failure. Finally, valuable time, which might otherwise be spent rereading and reteaching will be saved.

Important guidelines for teaching content with textual materials are based on schema theory. First, teachers should assess students' prior knowledge. Second, teachers should activate schema before, during, and after reading. Third, teachers should help students make distinctions among the different interpretations that are appropriate for different texts and purposes for reading. Fourth, teachers should help students assess their understandings of the text.

The concept of learning styles is a complex one. Through observation, however, teachers and students can become aware of learning differences and learning strengths. One of the most important implications of the notion of learning styles is the need for a wide variety of strategies.

Teachers must be familiar with many different strategies so that methodologies can be matched to the needs of the student and the demands of the text. Equally important, variety is a key to generating and maintaining interest in and enthusiasm for learning, both for students and teacher. Once you have mastered a set of literacy-based strategies for teaching content, you will be able to mix and match them to create new variations, as well as your own strategies to maximize learning in the classroom.

Two strategies for content area literacy were introduced in this chapter. The first strategy, called What I Know, What I Want to Learn, What I Learned (KWL), helps students activate their background knowledge, establish personal purposes for reading, and evaluate their own learning after reading.

Another strategy for content area literacy is the Guided Reading Procedure (GRP). In this strategy, the purpose for reading is to remember everything—or at least as many details as possible. It is designed to assist students' free recall, teach them how to organize recalled information, develop their abilities to ask themselves thought-provoking questions regarding recalled information, and emphasize the importance of self-correction.

ENRICHMENT ACTIVITIES

1. Choose a content area and grade level, and write a brief description of a lesson using the KWL in teaching a topic related to the content area. Include the specific questions and instructions you would use to guide the first two steps.
2. Interview two or more K–12 teachers, asking them to assess the importance of literacy skills in learning content. Ask them to justify or support their positions. Then, submit summaries of their positions in writing along with explanations of why you agree or disagree with the positions they espouse.

3. Interview two or more college professors, and after defining schema theory for them, ask them to assess its significance for learning in their content areas. Submit summaries of their responses along with your own reaction, in terms of whether their assessments are consistent with the information presented in Chapter 2.

4. Borrow two or more content area textbook teacher's manuals from the university curriculum library or from a local school. Analyze the instructions given to teachers for teaching content with the textbook. Are they consistent with the guidelines presented in Chapter 2?

5. Administer the Learning Styles Checklist to two or more children, adolescents, or adults. Summarize your findings along with an analysis of how consistent the results were in relation to your knowledge of and experience with each person. Share with each subject, and then submit in writing, a set of suggestions for helping each one to capitalize on strengths to become a more successful learner.

REFERENCES

Anderson, R. C. (1984). Role of the reader's schema in comprehension, learning, and memory. In *Learning to read in American schools.* Edited by R. C. Anderson, J. Osborn, and R. J. Tierney. Hillsdale, NJ: Erlbaum.

Ankney, P., and P. McClurg. (1981). Testing Manzo's guided reading procedure. *The Reading Teacher* 34:681–685.

Bartlett, F. C. (1932). *Remembering: A study in experimental and social psychology.* London: Cambridge University Press.

Bean, T. W., and R. Pardi. (1979). A field test of a guided reading strategy. *Journal of Reading* 23:144–147.

Carbo, M. (1991). *Reading styles inventory.* Roslyn Heights, NY: National Reading Styles Institute.

Carrell, P. L., B. G. Pharis, and J. C. Liberto. (1989). Metacognitive strategy training for ESL reading. *TESOL Quarterly* 23:647–678.

Johnson, D., R. Johnson, and E. Holubec. (1991). *Cooperation in the classroom, revised.* Edina, MN: Interaction Book Company.

Kang, Hee-Won. (1994). Helping second language readers learn from content area text through collaboration and support. *Journal of Reading* 37:646–652.

Langer, J. A. (1981). From theory to practice: A prereading plan. *Journal of Reading* 25:152–156.

Manzo, A. V. (1975). Guided reading procedure. *Journal of Reading* 18:287–291.

McKenna, M., and R. Robinson. (1990). Content literacy: A definition and implications. *Journal of Reading* 34:184–186.

_____. (1993). *Teaching and learning through text.* White Plains, NY: Longman.

Ogle, D. (1986). K-W-L: A teaching model that develops active reading of expository text. *The Reading Teacher* 39:564–570.

Reyes, M., and L. A. Molner. (1991). Instructional strategies for second-language learners in the content areas. *Journal of Reading* 35:96–103.

Schifini, A. (1994). Language, literacy, and content instruction: Strategies for teachers. In *Kids come in all languages: Reading instruction for ESL students.* Edited by K. Spangenberg-Urbschat and R. Pritchard. Newark, DE: International Reading Association.

Tierney, R. J., and P. D. Pearson. (1981). Learning to learn from text: A framework for improving classroom practice. In *Reading in the content areas: Improving classroom instruction.* Edited by E. K. Dishner, T. W. Bean, J. E. Readence, and D. W. Moore. Dubuque, IA: Kendall/Hunt Publishing Company.

_____. (1992). A revisionist perspective on "Learning to learn from text: A framework for improving classroom practice." In *Reading in the content areas: Improving classroom instruction.* Edited by E. K. Dishner, T. W. Bean, J. E. Readence, and D. W. Moore. Dubuque, IA: Kendall/Hunt Publishing Company.

Tierney, R. J., J. E. Readence, and E. K. Dishner. (1990). *Reading strategies and practices: A compendium,* 3d ed. Needham Heights, MA: Allyn & Bacon.

Weaver, C. A., and W. Kintsch. (1991). Expository text. In *Handbook of reading research,* volume II. Edited by R. Barr, M. L. Kamil, P. Mosenthal, and P. D. Pearson. White Plains, NY: Longman.

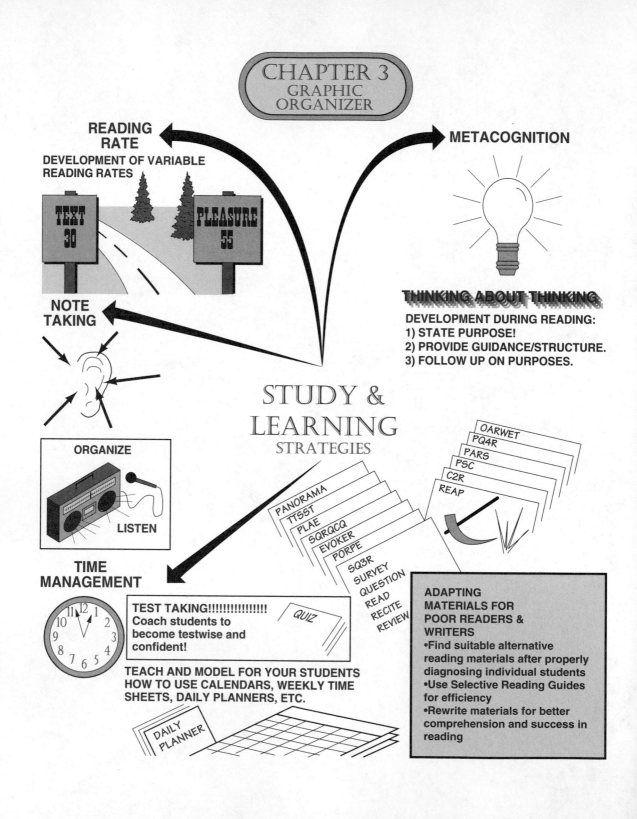

CHAPTER 3
GRAPHIC ORGANIZER

READING RATE

DEVELOPMENT OF VARIABLE READING RATES

TEXT 30

PLEASURE 55

METACOGNITION

THINKING ABOUT THINKING

DEVELOPMENT DURING READING:
1) STATE PURPOSE!
2) PROVIDE GUIDANCE/STRUCTURE.
3) FOLLOW UP ON PURPOSES.

NOTE TAKING

STUDY & LEARNING STRATEGIES

ORGANIZE

LISTEN

OARWET
PQ4R
PARS
PSC
C2R
REAP

PANORAMA
TTSST
PLAE
SQRQCQ
EVOKER
PORPE

SQ3R
SURVEY
QUESTION
READ
RECITE
REVIEW

TIME MANAGEMENT

TEST TAKING!!!!!!!!!!!!!!!!!!
Coach students to become testwise and confident!

QUIZ

TEACH AND MODEL FOR YOUR STUDENTS HOW TO USE CALENDARS, WEEKLY TIME SHEETS, DAILY PLANNERS, ETC.

DAILY PLANNER

ADAPTING MATERIALS FOR POOR READERS & WRITERS
•Find suitable alternative reading materials after properly diagnosing individual students
•Use Selective Reading Guides for efficiency
•Rewrite materials for better comprehension and success in reading

CHAPTER 3

Study and Learning Strategies

To demonstrate mastery of the content, the student will be able to do the following:

PART 1 OBJECTIVES

1. Identify the following strategy, describe its distinguishing features, and assess its significance to teaching content area literacy: SQ3R.
2. Define metacognition and assess the role of metacognitive awareness in content area teaching and learning.
3. Distinguish the metacognitive characteristics of good and poor readers.
4. Explain why SQ3R is a sound study strategy, in terms of developing metacognitive awareness.
5. Describe three ways to adapt materials for learners who have difficulty reading and writing.
6. Describe at least three variations of or alternatives to SQ3R for a selected grade level and content area.

PART 2 OBJECTIVES

1. Identify the following strategy, describe its distinguishing features, and assess its significance to teaching content area literacy: REAP.
2. Synthesize a set of general guidelines for learning (as opposed to teaching) through textual materials. (Hint: These guidelines should focus on what the student does, not the teacher, and on what effective study strategies such as SQ3R have in common.)
3. Synthesize a set of guidelines for learning with textual material in a content area of your choice.
4. Justify time spent in the content area classroom on helping students improve their reading rates and develop flexibility of rate.

PART 2 OBJECTIVES—continued

5. Create a list of ways content area teachers can help students improve their reading rates and rate flexibility.

6. Assess the importance of and identify ways to help students set goals, develop effective time management systems, and make sound educational decisions. (Hint: Consider the implications for classroom management, attitudes, motivation, and learning effectiveness.)

7. Assess the importance of and describe two strategies for improving listening and notetaking to enhance content area learning and literacy.

8. Synthesize a set of test-taking strategies and guidelines designed to help students develop confidence in demonstrating their mastery of content.

INTRODUCTION

As you begin learning about effective study and learning strategies in content area literacy, you will notice that although they are varied, they also have certain common elements. Some of the commonalities stem from the foundation provided by Schema Theory. As you recall from Chapter 2, activation of schemata plays an important role in the guidelines Tierney and Pearson (1981) summarized for helping students learn with text.

Another concept that plays a major role in those guidelines is metacognition. In this chapter, you will be introduced to this concept and its implications for effective study and learning strategies. You will see how general guidelines for learning through textual materials are solidly based in research on schema, metacognition, and the characteristics of good readers. You will also learn specific guidelines for learning through textual materials in a variety of content areas.

Also in this chapter, you will be introduced to the importance of reading rate as a tool for effective study and learning. You will learn a variety of ways content area teachers can help their students develop their reading rates and flexibility of rates. Finally, you will learn the importance of helping students learn to set goals, develop effective time management systems, and make sound educational decisions and how to implement these strategies. Students should be guided to make decisions only after identifying their options and considering the positive and negative consequences of each option. You will then learn the implications of these abilities for classroom management, attitudes, motivation, and learning effectiveness. Finally, you will be introduced to two new strategies for content area literacy: SQ3R and REAP.

Before reading this chapter, choose one or two activities for documenting content mastery from those listed at the end of the chapter. You may either use the same activity for both parts of the chapter or a different activity for each part. Follow any instructions provided for the option(s) you choose. The purposes you set for reading, the procedures you follow while reading, and the notes you take during reading will be influenced by the type of activity you select. Therefore, it is important that you consider your options *before* reading.

PART 1

STRATEGY: SURVEY, QUESTION, READ, RECITE, REVIEW (SQ3R)

Distinguishing Features of SQ3R

One of the most popular and commonly used strategies for effective study and learning is SQ3R, which stands for Survey, Question, Read, Recite, and Review. This strategy is not new; it was developed by Robinson (1961) to provide students with a systematic approach to reading for study and to promote more efficient learning through assigned readings. If used regularly and consistently, it can help students develop effective study habits by teaching them how to prepare for reading, read actively, assess their learning, and internalize content.

Two difficulties associated with strategies like SQ3R are the lack of instructional procedures for ensuring its appropriate use and the teacher's inability to convince students of its value (Tierney, Readence, and Dishner 1990). The first difficulty will be addressed, after describing the strategy, by providing a set of instructional procedures for appropriately guiding students through its steps. The second difficulty can be addressed with assignments that *require* students to follow the steps of the strategy until the habit is formed.

Simply recommending the strategy to students is not very effective in getting them to use it regularly and consistently. In fact, until habits are developed, reading assignments should be accompanied by written assignments that help students develop the habit of applying effective strategies for study and learning. You will be provided an example of such assignments.

The first two steps of SQ3R prepare the students for reading. Students **survey** or preview the assignment by reading the title, chapter objectives, introduction, subheadings, graphic aids, summary, and end-of-chapter questions. The survey is designed to give students an overview of the content in order to help them activate schema and assess their background knowledge. In surveying a chapter, students attempt to discover its content, what they already know about the topic, how interested they are in the content, how difficult the concepts are, and how the information is presented.

The second step sets purposes for reading by formulating **questions** from the subheadings. The questions give students specific ideas to look for while reading. Keeping a question in mind can help maintain concentration on the reading's focus; greater concentration can then lead to improved comprehension and efficiency. Before formulating questions from the subheadings, students should consider their general purposes by answering such questions as "Why am I reading this?" "What do I have to get out of it?" "What do I want to get out of it?" "How will my understanding and learning be assessed?"

The third and fourth steps involve active **read**ing and comprehension monitoring. As students read for answers to the questions, they underline or take notes on information related to the question, as well as other information that seems important, relevant, and/or interesting. To monitor their understanding of the material as they read, they **recite** the answers to the questions and the other important information either orally or in writing, using their own words. If they are unable to recite this information, students should reread or seek assistance.

The fifth step involves a **review** that allows students to assess and reflect on their learning for greater long-term retention. Students review their notes and responses to ensure that purposes have been met. If necessary, information is reread, questions are noted, and reflections are made. The value and usefulness of the information learned is pondered; a critical review or analysis would also be appropriate at this point.

SQ3R as an Instructional Strategy

Before students can be expected to apply SQ3R successfully and independently, teachers must model the steps for students in class by guiding them through the strategy. When using SQ3R in this way, it becomes an instructional strategy that has the characteristics of effective instructional strategies outlined in Chapter 1. The important thing to remember when using SQ3R as an instructional strategy is to avoid assuming that students can do the steps independently.

For example, do not presume that students will know what to do when you tell them to survey the chapter. You must provide specific, detailed instructions for surveying, model the procedures for them, verbalize the steps as you model them, and then give students time to complete the survey step under your guidance and supervision. Observe them carefully as they survey and offer feedback to let them know whether they are on the right track. After they survey, ask them to state out loud (to a partner or call on individuals to respond to the whole class) what they learned from the survey. From their responses, you can evaluate how well students surveyed and then reteach or move on to the next step.

Help students learn to set their own purposes for reading by having them answer questions about why they are reading and what they need or hope to get out of it. Then, demonstrate for them how to turn subheadings into questions and have them formulate their own questions. Assess the quality of students' questions in terms of setting specific purposes for reading. If their questions are appropriate, go on to the next step; if not, reteach the process until students can successfully turn subheadings into fairly specific purpose-setting questions. Have them write down their questions.

Show students how to read actively by reading to find the answers to their questions. Model the process through the following steps: State aloud the purpose-setting question for one subheading. Read aloud the first paragraph. Stop and verbalize the points that seemed interesting or important in the paragraph. Decide whether information in the paragraph addressed the stated purpose. If so, write down the relevant information; if not, continue by reading the next paragraph. Before going on, however, write down any information you found personally interesting or relevant, even if it does not address the stated purpose. Emphasize to students that reading with a specific purpose in mind helps them concentrate, so that they can understand and learn even *more* information than was identified by the purpose.

Repeat this process with the next subheading. Have students take notes as they read. After reading that section, have them state out loud the relevant information for addressing the stated purpose. Then have them identify any other information they found particularly interesting, relevant, or useful.

Teach students to stop at the end of each subheading and attempt to answer the purpose-setting questions. Show them how to answer in their own words and record their responses. If unable to answer the question, show them how to reread as necessary to locate the identified information.

Finally, model the review process by rereading all notes and restating in your own words all the responses to the purpose-setting questions. Observe students as they complete this process with a partner or small group. Demonstrate the importance of talking and writing about what was learned for greater long-term retention.

In addition to modeling SQ3R by using it as an instructional strategy, teachers should also use it to develop written assignments to accompany reading assignments. An example is provided in Figure 3–1. However, these assignments should be given as an independent activity only after you have modeled and guided students through the process in class several times.

METACOGNITION: A FOUNDATION FOR EFFECTIVE STUDY AND LEARNING

Defining Metacognition

Metacognition involves thinking about thinking. It means being aware of your own thinking and learning processes, consciously in control of those processes, and aware of that control. An important part of metacognition is the silent "self-talk" you experience while reading and learning. For example, you might think to yourself something like the following: "This assignment is extremely long and difficult. Considering that I know so little about this topic, along with my lack of interest in it, reading this assignment is going to be difficult. Maybe I should read it in short sections, stopping frequently to look up key vocabulary and paraphrase main ideas. Taking notes will probably help me, too." When you engage in such self-talk, you are not thinking about the actual content to be learned; rather, you are thinking about the strategy and processes you will use to help you learn the content. This type of thinking is *metacognition*.

Metacognitive Awareness: Distinguishing Good from Poor Readers

Metacognitive awareness provides one of the key differences between good and poor readers. Good readers approach different types of text in different ways, forming strategies appropriate for each. Poor readers often approach all types of text in the same way. Good readers invest time to prepare themselves and make plans before reading. Poor readers typically dive right in and read straight through from beginning to end without stopping. Good readers recognize problems with comprehension

---

FIGURE 3-1 SQ3R sample written assignment

Follow the steps outlined below. You will turn in your responses (which should be brief) to the questions and instructions that follow each step.

1. Survey the chapter: Read the introduction, summary, and subheadings.

   What did you discover about what will be covered in this chapter?

   What do you already know about this topic?

   How might this information be important and/or relevant to you?

2. Question: Formulate each subheading into a question and list them. These questions will serve as your purposes for reading.

3. Read the chapter, looking for the answers to these questions. As you begin each section, reread the question; keep the purposes for reading in mind as you read. Continually refer to them to help you keep your mind on what you are reading. You might want to make a few notes as you read to help you focus on information that answers each question, as well as information that you find particularly interesting or consider important.

4. From your notes, answer the questions.

   Recite the answers by summarizing them briefly in your own words.

5. Review the chapter by rereading any parts that are still unclear, those highlighted, and your notes, double-checking your answers to the purpose-setting questions, and answering (briefly) the following questions.

   How does the information you learned relate to what you already knew about this topic?

   In what ways is this information personally relevant and/or helpful to you?

---

when they arise and implement appropriate strategies to compensate for them. Poor readers generally do not recognize problems with comprehension, and when they do recognize problems, they do not have strategies for dealing with them.

Study and learning strategies for content area literacy are designed to develop the metacognitive awareness possessed by good readers. Through these strategies, teachers can help their students develop metacognition appropriate for the content area. The common threads that run through content area study and learning strategies involve the following metacognitive traits manifested by good readers.

Before reading, readers who are metacognitively aware make a conscious effort to prepare for reading by planning and forming strategies appropriate to the material. They identify requisite background knowledge and assess their own relevant schemata. If necessary, students develop background knowledge by looking up vocabulary and reading some corollary works. They also consider their purposes for reading and identify key points involved in the reading.

During reading, readers who are metacognitively aware monitor their comprehension. They ask themselves questions, answer those questions, take notes, and paraphrase information often. Through this process they are able to recognize difficulties in comprehension. Vacca and Vacca (1993, 51) suggest that readers know comprehension problems are occurring when they cannot summarize information, answer questions, or when they do not understand:

- a key word or words.
- a phrase or sentence.
- how sentences relate to one another.
- the meaning or purpose of a paragraph.
- how paragraphs, sections, or chapters relate to one another.
- the meaning or purpose of extended text.

Vacca and Vacca (1993, 52) also point out that students recognize problems with comprehension when

- text information does not agree with what the reader already knows.
- ideas do not fit together because one cannot tell to whom or what is being referred to.
- ideas don't fit together because they seem contradictory.
- information is missing or not clearly explained.

Once good readers recognize problems, they identify and implement appropriate strategies to ensure adequate understanding. For example, Cicchetti (1990, 20–21) suggests the following "fix-up" strategies for readers to apply when they recognize comprehension problems.

1. Ignore the word or phrase and read on.
2. Think of an example.
3. Think of a visual image.
4. Read ahead and connect information.
5. Reread and connect information.
6. Use text patterns, signal words, and pronouns to make connections.

After reading, readers who are metacognitively aware evaluate their comprehension, determining whether their purposes for reading have been met. If necessary, they form a plan for rereading to learn information they missed or did not understand. They also relate the information to prior learning and consider it in relation to their overall learning goals.

Conversely, readers who are *not* metacognitively aware generally do *not* prepare for reading, do *not* read actively with good concentration, do *not* recognize inadequate comprehension, and do *not* reread appropriately to ensure purposes have been met. As a result, they generally have little success reading and learning. Many students who are considered poor readers simply lack effective strategies for developing and maintaining metacognitive awareness. Even good readers can become more effective and efficient learners through the application of strategies designed to enhance metacognitive awareness.

Self-Awareness of Preferences for Strategies and Environmental Factors

In addition to understanding the demands of the task and regulating their study and learning strategies accordingly, readers who are metacognitively aware also take into account what they know about themselves as learners. For example, they make calculated decisions about what time of day to study, where they will study, how long they will study, how often they will take breaks, how much lighting they need, whether they will eat or drink something while studying, whether they study best alone or with others, and other such important yet often overlooked considerations. These environmental factors are actually very important for effective study and learning and are used by students who are metacognitively aware. Such students also take into account their learning styles or preferences in making decisions about which strategies they will use.

Good reading habits can be modeled by content area teachers through regular and consistent use of effective strategies for study and learning, such as SQ3R. Teachers must give students frequent opportunities to apply a variety of strategies. In addition, teachers need to help students identify which strategies or parts of strategies work best for them. Repeated use of a variety of study strategies is crucial for helping students develop awareness of what works and what does not work for them.

Once they are aware of their personal styles, students should be encouraged to develop individual variations of strategies such as SQ3R. Some of the more popular variations will be described later in this chapter.

Think-Aloud: A Strategy for Developing Metacognitive Awareness

This strategy was suggested by Davey (1983) as a means of helping poor readers monitor their comprehension and apply self-correction strategies. The underlying principle of the strategy is that, through teacher-modeling and guided practice, less-skilled readers can improve their reading abilities by developing the thinking processes that characterize good readers.

First, the teacher selects a fairly difficult passage that is approximately 100 to 300 words in length. Prepare your "think-aloud" comments by playing the part of a reader who is metacognitively aware. Keep in mind that you want to provide a model of what a good reader might be thinking. Davey (1983) recommends five different types of think-aloud comments:

1. For **making predictions**, the teacher might say, "From the subheading and picture, I predict that this passage will define ecosystems and explain how they work."
2. For **describing visual images**, the teacher might say, "As I read this part, I can picture a jungle with many different kinds of plants and animals. I can see some of the animals eating plants and some of them stalking other animals."
3. For **making analogies**, the teacher might say, "This is like a row of dominoes standing on end. Touching just one of them will cause all the others to fall."
4. For **describing confusion and monitoring comprehension**, the teacher might say, "This paragraph is confusing. It has some new vocabulary, and I'm not really sure what's important to remember."
5. For **demonstrating various "fix-up" strategies**, the teacher might say, "I'm going to reread this part because I'm not sure what this information has to do with an ecosystem," or "I'm going to keep reading and use context to figure out the meaning of this word."

Before presenting your prepared think-aloud comments, tell the students exactly what you are going to do (e.g., "I am going to show you what I am saying to myself while I read this passage"). Then, read the passage to the class, inserting your think-aloud comments as you go. Afterwards, encourage students to ask questions. Next, have students do their own think-alouds with partners, taking turns reading orally and thinking aloud. The listener adds thoughts and/or suggestions.

After practicing with partners, encourage students to practice paying attention to what they are thinking as they read silently. Provide them with checklists to remind them of the kinds of things they should be thinking about while they read, i.e., predicting, visualizing, comparing, identifying problems, and applying fix-up strategies. After students have experience and confidence with the think-aloud strategy, continue integrating it into content area lessons occasionally.

ADAPTING MATERIALS FOR LEARNERS WHO HAVE DIFFICULTY READING AND WRITING

If students have difficulty reading the assigned text or other materials, the first adaptation you should consider is finding or writing a simplified version of the original assignment. To locate or rewrite suitable materials, you need to know the approximate reading levels of the students you suspect are having difficulty reading assigned materials. Following are some suggestions for determining approximate reading levels:

1. Examine students' cumulative folders for standardized test results and other diagnostic information that might be available.

2. Administer a content area reading inventory (CARI) (see Chapter 9). This test serves as a screening device to identify students who may have difficulty reading the assigned text.

3. Administer an informal reading inventory (IRI) (see Chapter 9). This test is given individually to students identified by the CARI as possibly having difficulty reading assigned materials. The IRI is given individually to determine the level at which the student can successfully read with instructional support (i.e., the instructional reading level), and the level at which the student can successfully read materials independently without instructional support (i.e., the independent reading level).

4. Administer a series of cloze tests (see Chapter 9). Once you have some idea of the student's instructional and independent reading levels (either from standardized test scores or from IRI results), select what you believe will be appropriate alternate (simplified) materials. Then, verify your selections with cloze tests. Each cloze test is developed from the actual reading materials you select. The test is designed to give you a yes/no answer to the questions "Can this student read this material successfully with instructional support?" and "Can this student read this material successfully without instructional support (independently)?" On the basis of the answers to these questions, you may have to select and implement different materials until you find ones suitable for your purposes.

Finding Alternative Materials

Once you know the approximate instructional and independent reading levels of the students you suspect are having difficulty reading the assigned text, you can begin locating appropriate materials. After selecting what you believe will be appropriate materials, check their suitability with cloze tests (see Chapter 9). Following are some suggestions for locating or rewriting materials:

1. Meet with the school administrator in charge of textbooks (often an assistant principal) to find out what supplementary or alternative textbooks are available. Sometimes textbooks at the same grade level can be found that cover the same content in simpler language. You might also be able to find textbooks that cover the same content at lower grade levels.
2. Ask your school librarian or administrator in charge of curriculum funds to order one or both of the following books for your own or the school's curriculum library:

   ▪ Ryder, R. J., B. B. Graves, and M. F. Graves. 1989. *Easy Reading Book Series and Periodicals for Less Able Readers,* 2d ed. Newark, DE: International Reading Association.
   ▪ McBride, W. G. (editor) 1990. *High Interest–Easy Reading: A Booklist for Junior and Senior High School Students,* 6th ed. Urbana, IL: National Council of Teachers of English.

   Then, ask your local parent-teacher association, school librarian, or school administrator in charge of curriculum funds to help obtain books and periodicals from these bibliographies for the school library and/or your classroom library collection.
3. Collaborate with your school and community librarians to develop a bibliography of trade books (see Chapter 7) on the topics covered by the textbook. Categorize the trade books by grade level either from information provided by the publishers or from your own readability assessment (see Chapter 7). Ask your local parent-teacher association, school librarian, or school administrator in charge of curriculum funds to help obtain books from this bibliography for the school library and/or your classroom library collection.

Rewriting Materials

If you are unable to find suitable alternate materials for a particular topic, you might want to simply rewrite the content using simpler language. Although the idea of rewriting materials might sound overwhelming and time consuming, once you have rewritten something, you will have it in your files for future use. Eventually, you will have at your fingertips a substantial file of alternate materials on a variety of topics. Following are some suggestions for rewriting materials:

1. Identify and write down the key concepts you want to communicate and key vocabulary you want to introduce or reinforce. Putting this information in outline form would be helpful in the rewriting process.

2. Using the list or outline of concepts and vocabulary as a guide, write a summary of the information you have identified as important. Make sure you use short, simple sentences and commonly used word choices. For key vocabulary, provide plenty of context for understanding the concepts being introduced or reinforced. Give thorough and direct explanations of the concepts and provide as many concrete examples as possible.

3. Have competent students rewrite the materials for you. This process would be an excellent enrichment activity for students who master the content quickly or have already mastered it. You could substitute this activity for another assignment or offer it as an extra-credit opportunity or in exchange for free time or some other valued commodity. Provide student rewriters with your list or outline of concepts from which to work and give them a sample paragraph demonstrating the type of summary you want. Instruct them to write a summary of the information, using language they might use in everyday speech. Explain that although this is a writing assignment, you want the writing to be more informal, although grammatically correct.

4. Provide poor readers with their own copies of the rewritten summaries. Use the rewritten materials with appropriate content area literacy strategies, just as you would with the regular text materials. For example, introduce new, technical vocabulary, develop and activate necessary background knowledge, and set specific purposes for reading. Evaluate after reading to see that the purposes have been met and hold the students accountable for mastering the information in the summaries.

Selective Reading Guides

If you are unable to locate alternate materials or do not have time to rewrite materials, another way to simplify reading assignments is through the use of Selective Reading Guides. (See Chapter 5 for a detailed description and example of a Selective Reading Guide.) The rationale for using them with poor readers and writers is that you can edit the assigned reading materials using the guide. You can simplify the materials by instructing the reader to omit certain parts, focus specifically on others, and examine particular graphic aids (e.g., charts, diagrams, illustrations, and so forth). Using a Selective Reading Guide allows you to provide guidance and support without actually having to tutor students individually. You can significantly shorten the reading assignment, making the task reasonable for poor readers and writers. You can also provide explanations, simplified definitions, and concrete examples to make the material more comprehensible.

STUDY STRATEGIES FOR ALL LEARNERS AND CONTENT AREAS

The importance of using a variety of instructional strategies was discussed in Chapter 1. For many of the same reasons, students should be taught how to use a variety of strategies for studying and learning. The varying demands of learner, text, and content require that content area teachers introduce students to a wide variety of strategies. You will discover that although many students find SQ3R an effective study strategy, it does not work for everyone. Once SQ3R has been introduced, you will find that some students like it more than others. Because of special needs and individual differences in learning and study styles and preferences, not everyone will feel comfortable with SQ3R. Therefore, it is important to introduce students to a variety of study strategies, all similar to SQ3R in terms of developing metacognitive awareness.

As a content area teacher, you will need to demonstrate study and learning strategy alternatives appropriate for the content area, the textual demands, the task demands of the assignment, and the characteristics of the learner. Once students learn the common qualities of strategies that work for them, they can mix and match portions of them to develop original, personalized versions of the strategies. Students should be encouraged to use the parts of the strategies that work best for them and to change or adapt the other parts until they feel comfortable with them. It is important to remember that students often need help distinguishing what they like from what works for them. They may not *like* to follow all the procedures involved in SQ3R, but the strategy may still *work* for them.

A wide variety of effective study and learning strategies is presented in Appendix A and summarized in Figure 3–2. As you read about them, make note of which strategies seem particularly appropriate for various content areas, including science, social studies, math, literature, and health. Also note the features of each strategy that, in your opinion, make it especially suitable for one or more specific content areas.

FIGURE 3–2 Variations of the SQ3R Strategy

STRATEGY	RECOMMENDED CONTENT AREAS	DISTINGUISHING CHARACTERISTICS	PROCEDURES
PORPE	history, science, literature, and others that emphasize essay exams	helps prepare for essay exams; uses a process that focuses on content and its relation to students' lives; can be taught without jeopardizing time necessary for learning content	1. Predict 2. Organize 3. Rehearse 4. Practice 5. Evaluate
OARWET	all	includes an evaluation step that helps process & internalize information; uses questions about significance, implications, and relevance to students	1. Overview 2. Ask 3. Read 4. Write 5. Evaluate 6. Test
PQ4R	all	to reflect, students are guided in rereading if necessary to fulfill purposes for reading; also helps identify important and meaningful information	1. Preview 2. Question 3. Read 4. Reflect 5. Recite 6. Review
PARS	all	emphasizes the use of summarizing for self-evaluation of comprehension and for learning content	1. Preview 2. Ask questions 3. Read 4. Summarize
PSC	all	breaks material into short segments; for each segment, the 3 basic steps are completed; includes use of summaries	1. Preview 2. Study 3. Check
SQ4R	all	survey step is quick overview only; students spend more time recording, reciting, and reflecting	1. Survey 2. Question 3. Read 4. Record 5. Recite 6. Reflect
PANORAMA	history, social studies, literature, science, and others with lengthy reading assignments	students consider purposes for reading along with varied reading rates; writing to learn is emphasized with annotating and outlining on note cards; memorizing is facilitated with acronyms and mnemonic devices; finally, self-assessment is done	1. Purpose 2. Adaptability of rate 3. Need to question 4. Overview 5. Read and Relate 6. Annotate 7. Memorize 8. Assess

FIGURE 3–2 Variations of the SQ3R Strategy—continued

STRATEGY	RECOMMENDED CONTENT AREAS	DISTINGUISHING CHARACTERISTICS	PROCEDURES
TTSST	all	generates students' interest in reading; relates content to prior learning; emphasizes paraphrasing; helps students draw conclusions, identify implications, and react personally	1. Think 2. Think 3. Skim 4. Study 5. Think
C2R	all	students consider learning styles and preferences; personalized decisions are made about where, when, and with whom to study; text patterns and rate adjustments are emphasized	1. Concentrate 2. Read 3. Remember
PLAE	all	a process of helping students select appropriate strategies and evaluate the effectiveness of ones selected; presumes students have knowledge of a variety of strategies	1. Preplan 2. List 3. Activate 4. Evaluate
SQRQCQ	mathematics	designed to assist students in reading mathematics; focuses on information needed to solve problems	1. Survey 2. Question 3. Reread 4. Question 5. Compute 6. Question
PQRST	science	students raise questions related to study purposes; after reading, content is organized and summarized; students test themselves against summaries	1. Preview 2. Question 3. Read 4. Summarize 5. Test
EVOKER	literature	designed to give students a sense of the big picture of the author's message; students then read and analyze with that message in mind	1. Explore 2. Vocabulary 3. Oral reading 4. Key ideas 5. Evaluate 6. Recapitulate

PART 2

STRATEGY: READ, ENCODE, ANNOTATE, PONDER (REAP)

The REAP technique for study and learning was developed by Eanet and Manzo (1976) to help students synthesize ideas into their own words and develop their critical thinking and writing skills as tools for learning. REAP is an effective technique because it actively involves students in processing information for both text-based and reader-based interpretations. It develops students' abilities to paraphrase and evaluate critically what they read. Also, it develops students' writing abilities by using writing as a tool for processing and learning. The REAP technique consists of four steps:

1. **Read** to discover the author's ideas.
2. **Encode** the author's ideas into your own words.
3. **Annotate** those ideas in writing for yourself or to share with others.
4. **Ponder** the significance of the message through internal dialogue or discussion with others.

Types of Annotations

In the process of writing annotations, readers must discriminate and synthesize the ideas of the author, translate them into their own wording, and put them in writing. A variety of annotation types might be used, depending on the teaching and learning goals. Seven annotations are recommended by Eanet and Manzo (1976):

1. **Heuristic annotation.** A heuristic annotation is a statement, usually a sentence from the text, designed to suggest the idea of the selection and provoke a response.
2. **Summary annotation.** A summary annotation condenses the author's ideas into the reader's own words.
3. **Thesis annotation.** A thesis annotation identifies the overall theme and author's point.
4. **Question annotation.** A question annotation involves reformulating key ideas from the text into questions designed to stimulate a more critical level of thinking.
5. **Intention annotation.** An intention annotation identifies the author's reasons for writing and is based on what the author reveals in the text and what the reader knows about the author.

6. **Motivation annotation.** A motivation annotation interprets the author's motives, biases, and perspective.
7. **Critical annotation.** A critical annotation interprets the author's stance, provides the reader's reaction to the author's position, and explains a basis for the reaction. It is a personal response that consists of the reader's overall impression and reaction. Critical annotations address the extent to which the message, position, or point of view is interesting, important, valuable, questionable, viable, practical, confusing, and so on.

An Instructional Strategy for Writing Annotations

Central to the success of the REAP technique is developing the students' abilities to write annotations. Eanet and Manzo (1976) suggest a process for teaching students how to write annotations, focusing on one type of annotation at a time. The process consists of four steps:

1. **Recognizing and defining.** In this step, the teacher instructs the students to read a short selection and then provides an example of an annotation. Then, the teacher elicits from the students how the annotation relates to the selection read.
2. **Discriminating.** The teacher instructs the students to read another short selection and then provides three sample annotations. One of them is a good model of an annotation. The other two are poor examples. Through class discussion, students choose the best annotation, justifying their choice and explaining the problems with the other two options.
3. **Modeling the process.** After reading a third selection, the teacher "walks" students through the process of developing an annotation. In this step, the teacher should demonstrate the relationships between the major ideas and the annotation.
4. **Practicing.** After reading a fourth selection, each student writes an annotation. Then in pairs or groups of three or four, students use their individual annotations as a basis for developing the best annotation possible. They may refer to the passage if necessary. Then, the whole class compares, discusses, and evaluates the final group products.

Pondering Annotations

Once students can successfully write a variety of annotations, they are ready to "ponder" or process them for personal study or in-class activities. Eanet and Manzo (1976) recommend a variety of uses of annotations, a powerful tool for personal study and learning:

1. Students write short summary annotations to review material and help both teachers and students assess content mastery.
2. Students write critical annotations of books they've read to assist other students in the process of book selection.
3. Students write annotations as part of the process for more extensive writing projects.
4. Teachers use students' annotations as required readings for discussion and review by the entire class.

GUIDELINES FOR LEARNING WITH TEXTUAL MATERIALS

Research on the metacognitive awareness exhibited by good readers, along with schema theory, provide a strong foundation of support for the guidelines that define effective strategies for study and learning. A set of guidelines becomes evident by looking at the commonalities of the literacy-based strategies designed for study and learning in content areas. As you noticed from the descriptions of the many variations of SQ3R, they have several common traits.

First, they all guide students to prepare for active reading with good concentration. Usually, this preparation consists of some sort of preview and purpose setting. Second, they all provide guidance during reading by having students read for identified purposes. This guidance supports students in monitoring their comprehension as they read. Third, they all have follow-up activities after reading to help students evaluate their learning and ensure that purposes have been met.

From these common threads, the following guidelines emerge for effectively learning through textual materials. Notice how closely these guidelines mirror the guidelines presented in Chapter 1 for effectively teaching through textual materials. The guidelines are presented in three categories: before, during, and after reading.

Guidelines for Preparing to Read

1. Prepare for reading by surveying the material to gain an overview of the topic.
2. Assess your background knowledge and schemata on that topic.
3. If necessary, prepare for successful reading by building and activating requisite background knowledge and schemata.
4. Specify, in the form of written questions, clearly defined purposes for reading.

Guidelines for Reading Actively

1. Focus on your established purposes.
2. Interact with the text (e.g., by asking and answering questions).
3. Monitor your comprehension by taking notes related to your purposes.
4. Make appropriate adjustments to ensure adequate comprehension.

Guidelines for Assessing and Enhancing Learning after Reading

1. Evaluate your learning by reciting aloud or writing answers to your purpose-setting questions.
2. Reread and/or research as necessary to fulfill purposes accurately and completely.
3. Process and internalize the content by analyzing and evaluating it.
4. Personalize the content by relating it to prior knowledge and identifying its personal value and relevance.

FLEXIBILITY OF READING RATE AS A TOOL FOR LEARNING

The Role of Rate Adaptability in Metacognitive Awareness

Content area teachers can enhance their students' reading-to-learn skills by helping them develop flexibility of rate. Tonjes and Zintz (1992) call this skill adaptability of rate because adaptable seems a more accurate term for referring to the concept of adjusting rate suitably for the material and the purpose. One of the characteristics of metacognitively aware readers is knowledge of when and how to adjust reading rate for improved comprehension and learning.

Students who are not metacognitively aware read everything at the same rate, which is usually their slowest rate. Good readers, on the other hand, use their slowest rates for studying difficult material and their fastest rates for reading easy material for pleasure. They also employ a variety of rates between their fastest and slowest rates.

Many factors help determine appropriate rates. These factors include purpose for reading, level of background knowledge, interest in the topic, difficulty of the material, and the amount of time available for reading. Content area teachers can help their students improve their metacognitive awareness by helping them learn to decide how fast to read various materials for varying purposes. Teachers can model for their students how to consider the relevant factors and then decide approximately how fast they should attempt to read.

As students learn to monitor their comprehension while reading, teach them how to make adjustments in rate appropriately. Show them how to speed up and slow down to accommodate comprehension and concentration needs. Remind them that they should be understanding and remembering most, but not necessarily all, of what they read. If they lose concentration on meaning and find themselves reading the same paragraph over and over again, they should try adjusting their reading rates.

The Value of Developing a Range of Rates for Adaptability

Before students can be taught to vary their reading rates appropriately, they need to have a variety of rates at their disposal. Content area teachers can help students develop differing rates by providing a few minutes of rate practice each day. In fact, students can significantly increase their reading rates after just a few weeks of daily practice. Students who practice their fastest rates daily with easy, pleasurable reading material can automatically improve their slowest study rates. Therefore, students can not only develop a variety of rates but can also increase the entire range of their rates.

The small investment of time each day can have many worthwhile benefits. Many students enjoy the rate development process and activities, and this enjoyment translates into improved attitudes toward reading. When students practice their rates, they are also practicing their reading skills in general, so overall reading abilities can be improved. Many students avoid reading because they read very slowly, and it takes longer than they are willing to spend to read something. Therefore, if they could read something in less time by improving their rates, perhaps they would be motivated to read more. Measuring and recording improvements in reading rate enhances self-esteem and self-confidence in relation to reading. Students who read too slowly or too quickly often have difficulty maintaining concentration: if their minds wander a great deal while reading, knowing how to vary their rates appropriately could be a valuable skill. A wide range of reading rates is important for flexibility and efficiency in reading, and having varied and flexible reading rates is a skill that will enhance reading and learning on a lifelong basis. Finally, daily practice with easy, narrative materials provides students the opportunity to read a variety of materials related to the topic of study.

Helping Students Develop a Range of Rates for Adaptability

Helping students improve their rates is a relatively simple process. The following suggestions will give you an idea of the kinds of activities you can use to help your students develop a wide range of reading rates, as well as flexibility of rate.

1. Provide opportunities for daily timed readings (five to ten minutes).
2. Provide books, preferably narrative, that are easy enough for the students to read independently. Keep a small library in your class-room stocked with a wide selection of books related to the current topic of study.
3. Allow students to select their own books for rate practice.
4. Teach students how to calculate their rates in terms of words per minute.
5. Provide progress charts for daily assessment of rates and comprehension.
6. Show students how to use pacing devices such as a pointer (e.g., pen, pencil, or finger) or index card to push themselves to move their eyes gently beyond their comfort zones.
7. Since reading is a skill, the more they practice, the more students will improve; reward them for practicing outside of class.

Following is a process for calculating reading rate:

1. Calculate the average words per page in the book.
   a. Select a full page of print (e.g., not the beginning or end of a chapter).
   b. Count the number of words in three full lines of print.
   c. Divide by three to get the average number of words per line.
   d. Count the number of lines on the page.
   e. Subtract two to compensate for short lines.
   f. Multiply the number of lines by the number of words per line.
   g. Record this number, so you can reuse it each time you calculate your rate for this particular book.
2. Read for a predetermined number of minutes, usually between five and twenty.
3. Count the number of pages you read in that time.
4. Multiply the number of pages by the number of words per page (calculated in the first step).
5. Divide by the number of minutes.
6. Record your rate, along with the date, and a general rating of your level of comprehension (e.g., poor, fair, adequate, good, excellent).

While providing daily practice for improving rate, teach students the difference between slower rates for studying and fast rates for pleasure reading. Tonjes and Zintz (1992) identify five different rates:

1. Slow/study   50 to 250 words per minute
2. Average/normal   250 to 350 words per minute
3. Rapid reading   350 to 800 words per minute
4. Skimming   more than 800 words per minute
5. Scanning   more than 1,000 words per minute

The average/normal rates are similar to rates of speech. Therefore, students who consistently read everything below 350 words per minute are probably pronouncing each and every word to themselves as if they were reading orally. Since slow readers stop and fixate on each and every word, their eye movements are inefficient.

The eyes move across lines of print in short, choppy motions called *saccadic movements*. The motion of the eyes appears choppy, because they move rapidly from one focal point to the next. Using peripheral vision, the eyes can actually see more than one word per fixation. Rather than fixating on every word, fast readers fixate their eyes phrase-by-phrase, thereby reducing the number of times the eyes have to stop per line.

With practice, students can push themselves into the rapid reading ranges; this shift occurs as they learn to read phrase-by-phrase instead of word-by-word. Students who read phrase-by-phrase still see and process most words, but they do not silently pronounce all of them. This shift cannot happen through conscious effort; it will occur automatically and unconsciously after weeks of daily practice with a focus on gradually increasing the comfort zone.

Skimming and scanning are useful study skills, but should be carefully distinguished from rapid reading. Skimming is used to get a general overview of a passage. It involves only a partial reading of the passage. For example, you might read introductory and concluding paragraphs, initial and final sentences, introductions, summaries, and subheadings. Scanning is used to locate a specific piece of information. It is especially useful with reference materials and involves concentrating on a specific topic, question, or key word, usually by repeating it over and over to yourself, while your eyes move quickly over the text in search of matching information.

To assist students in developing their abilities to read at a variety of rates, content area teachers need to provide students with a variety of reading opportunities. For example, vary your assignments so that students have practice reading for a variety of purposes. Also, provide a variety of reading materials as alternatives or supplements to the text (e.g., magazines, newspapers, journals, novels, pamphlets, technical reports, instruction manuals, and so on).

GOAL SETTING, TIME MANAGEMENT, AND DECISION MAKING

Many students need help with goal setting. Therefore, spending time helping them set long-range goals is worthwhile in terms of developing internal motivation. When students can perceive how day-to-day studying and classroom learning can help them get what they want out of life, their motivation to participate can be enhanced.

Also, many students need guidance in taking responsibility for their own learning. More specifically, they need help identifying the choices available to them, along with the positive and negative consequences of each option. The decision-making process can be directly taught by providing students with a blank form that has spaces for the question to be answered or decision to be made, the options available, and the pros and cons of each option. Guide them through the process of making decisions, emphasizing their choices, and stress that by making choices, they take control of their own lives.

Many students also need help learning how to prioritize. Teach them how to manage their time wisely by identifying activities that are pressing and important, as well as those that are important but not necessarily urgent. Then, help your students develop realistic study schedules that take into account the following: the time of day they study best, work and other commitments, other homework, learning styles or preferences, and priorities.

At least two of the Total Quality principles described in Chapter 1 are applicable for helping students become more successful, independent learners, and thinkers. The concepts of continuous improvement and self-evaluation are important for helping students set goals, manage their time wisely, and make proactive decisions. Students who engage in an ongoing process of improvement through self-evaluation are more likely to be goal directed, time efficient, and proactive.

Teachers can help students develop the habit of engaging in ongoing self-assessment. Encourage them and give them opportunities to continually assess, and if appropriate, revise or refine the goals they have set for themselves. Questions such as the following might be helpful for this purpose: Are my goals realistic? Are they worthy? Are they fulfilling? Am I making satisfactory progress toward them?

Continuous improvement and self-evaluation are also important principles for successful time management. Students should constantly monitor their systems of study and evaluate their learning to assess how well their time-management system is working. Content area teachers can provide support by modeling and guiding students in the self-evaluation process.

The continuous improvement and self-evaluation processes are also closely tied to decision making. Teachers can play an important role in helping students make decisions as part of ongoing self-evaluation in several ways. Teachers can help students learn how to identify options as well as criteria for evaluating those options. They can help students learn to make decisions and take responsibility for the consequences of the choices they make. Finally, teachers can provide opportunities for students to practice the process of self-evaluation.

Opportunities for helping students learn to set goals, develop efficient time-management systems, and make sound decisions can help students become more effective and independent learners, and in turn, positively affect attitudes toward learning and studying. Teachers can provide these opportunities by integrating some of the Total Quality principles into lessons involving strategies for content area literacy. As discussed in Chapter 1, integrating these principles into content area instruction can enhance motivation and learning; in particular, these principles might be considered crucial components of effective systems for study and independent learning.

LISTENING AND NOTETAKING

Listening is a receptive literacy skill that parallels reading, and in the classroom may be as important as reading. The writing process is just as important to effective listening as it is to effective reading. Listening strategies can be useful for developing students' listening abilities and enhancing learning. Many reading strategies can become effective listening strategies by substituting listening for the reading portion of the strategy. For example, the Guided Reading Procedure (GRP) can become the Guided Listening Procedure if the passage is read aloud, and students do an unaided recall immediately afterwards. Just as in the GRP, students make corrections or additions by listening to the passage again. Then, the information is organized appropriately.

Guided Lecture Procedure

A similar strategy, the Guided Lecture Procedure (GLP), was designed by Kelly and Holmes (1979) to provide students with an effective system for listening and taking notes. The GLP is not only a procedure for taking notes, but also a teaching and studying technique. It consists of four steps.

Students **prepare** by reading and recording the lecture objectives, along with new vocabulary, to establish a purpose for listening. Next, students listen to a lecture no longer than 30 minutes; they are told to **listen** actively, but not to take notes. After the lecture, they write down, in short form, everything they can **recall** in five minutes. Next, students **organize** their notes by working collaboratively in small groups to recapitulate the lecture. Students are instructed to use the lecture objectives and vocabulary to guide their organization. During this process, students check the accuracy and completeness of their notes by comparing with classmates. Also during this process, they put the notes in proper sequence, identify major concepts and supporting details, and draw appropriate conclusions. For the last step, students **reflect** on the notes and then **write** in narrative form, without looking at their notes, the major concepts, important details, and conclusions of the lecture. This final writing activity helps students retain the information and provides an immediate self-assessment regarding areas that need to be studied in greater detail.

Cornell System for Notetaking

One of the most popular notetaking systems is the Cornell System, which was developed by Pauk (1988). This system requires paper with a wide left margin (approximately two inches), often called *legal-ruled* paper. Students can easily widen the margins on regular notebook paper by drawing a line down the page about two inches from the left side.

During class, students take notes on the right side of the paper only. After class, students record key words and phrases on the left side of the paper. These words and phrases should serve as cues for the information on the right side. Students should also formulate and record questions they can use for self-testing. Then, to review and study the notes, students cover the right side and check themselves to see how much of the information they can recall. This process helps them identify the information they need to spend more time reviewing and relearning.

TEST-TAKING STRATEGIES AND GUIDELINES

Tests, in their various forms and functions, are a fact of life in schools today. They can be effective devices for helping both teachers and students discover what has been learned well and what needs to be retaught. However, for students who experience test anxiety and are not "testwise," tests may not be a valid indicator of what and how much they know. The concept of "testwiseness" involves good test-taking skills, e.g., knowing how to select the best option in a multiple-choice question or budgeting time wisely so that no questions are left blank. Helping students become testwise and confident with various types of tests is a worthwhile investment of time, because doing so is likely to maximize the validity of the tests; in other words, the tests are more likely to be accurate measures of what the students know.

One of the most important ways to reduce test anxiety and increase confidence is to ensure that students have effective strategies to prepare for tests. Through examples, show students the different levels of understanding required by different types of tests. For example, multiple-choice tests require students to be familiar enough with the information to be able to recognize it; whereas, essay tests require students to know the information so well that they can produce it with a minimal prompt. Because of these differences, students need to learn that different preparation strategies are appropriate for different types of tests. Therefore, the first step in preparing for a test is for students to understand the test's format.

You can help your students develop effective test-preparation strategies in several ways. Teach them to ask you and other teachers what kinds of tests they can expect and model for them different ways of studying for different types of tests. Help students learn to begin preparing early to avoid the need to cram. For example, you can help them develop schedules for regular and periodic review of the material. Encourage students to collect the materials they will need for study, e.g., homework assignments, class notes, quizzes, outlines, graphic organizers, and textbook study aids (like chapter summaries and review questions). Finally, help students assess the effectiveness of their preparation strategies and make adjustments accordingly.

Being testwise involves knowing general guidelines for approaching and analyzing different types of test questions. Students who know and apply these guidelines feel more confident and experience less test anxiety. Some of these guidelines are appropriate for all types of tests. For example, one guideline is that test takers should plan their available time wisely and pace themselves to avoid running out of time. One way to manage test-taking time is to quickly review the questions and allot a maximum amount of time to be spent on each. Test takers should save a few minutes at the end of the testing period to check for careless errors and change answers if warranted from further consideration. Students should avoid spending too much time on any question, regardless of the test format. If a question is difficult and time consuming, the test taker should skip it, or better yet, put a tentative response and mark it as a reminder to return to it after the remaining questions have been answered. Students who read and follow the directions carefully and look for clues to answers in other questions or parts of the test are usually more successful. As a final general guideline, students should answer all questions, even if they have to guess (as long as there is no penalty for guessing, of course). The guidelines that follow are appropriate for specific types of test questions.

Multiple Choice

First, read all of the options. As you read the options, delete those you are sure are not correct. Then, go back and reconsider the others to select the best possible choice. Another approach is to eliminate options that do not match the stem grammatically or complete it logically. For options like *all of the above, none of the above,* or *both c and d,* restate the option in sentence form and consider it as if it were a true/false statement. Once you have narrowed your options, choose the longest one because, generally, more information is needed to make it correct. If two of the options are opposites, one of them is probably the correct answer. Finally, if you have to guess, the correct answer is least likely to be the first or last option.

True/False

Watch for absolutes like *all, none, always, never,* and *only;* they generally indicate that the statement is false. Statements that make broad generalizations tend to be true, especially if they contain qualifiers like *sometimes, rarely, often,* and *generally.* Keep in mind that longer statements tend to be true and that if any part of the statement is false, the entire statement is considered false. Finally, avoid reading too much into a statement (rare, unlikely exceptions), especially if the statement is obviously true.

Essay

Begin by reading the question carefully and underlining or jotting down verbs that give you directions for responding (e.g., explain, list, justify, assess, compare, contrast, summarize, and so forth). Make sure you know what kinds of responses are appropriate for the various types of essay directives. Then briefly outline your response, making sure it is a complete and appropriate answer to the question. You want to be sure your response answers the question completely and with sufficient elaboration. Remember to keep your answer focused on what is asked of you. Avoid giving extraneous information that does not help answer the question directly; instead, use the technical language and vocabulary in ways that clearly demonstrate your understanding of the concepts. Finally, carefully proofread your answer and edit for accuracy in content and form. You especially want to avoid careless errors in spelling, grammar, and punctuation. These seemingly trivial errors can seriously detract from your answer, even if the content is good.

Content Area Literacy: Teaching for Today and Tomorrow

As a teacher, how can you use content area literacy to motivate students?

You can guide students in developing the literacy tools they need to pursue personal interests and curiosities. When learning is of personal relevance, students' increased enthusiasm and excitement for learning are obvious. Look for the literacy-based strategies introduced in each chapter. Also, see Chapter 6 for literacy-based activities and other ideas for motivating students in the content area classroom.

Textbook Alternatives and Supplements

How can a variety of learning resources enhance learning and motivation in the content area classroom?

When textbooks are overused, content learning can be diminished, not to mention tedious and boring. You can help students renew their interest in learning by guiding their discovery and selection of alternatives. Many interesting and attractive books, periodicals, and non-print media are available for learning about our world. See Chapter 7 for ways to incorporate textbook alternatives and supplements, and Chapter 12 for ways to incorporate instructional technology into the content area classroom.

The Teacher's Role as Facilitator

How can teachers enhance learning and motivation by expanding their classroom role from lecturer and information-giver to guide, consultant, and learning-facilitator?

When teachers share the responsibility for learning with their students, the classroom becomes a community of learners. As leader of this community, the teacher models and guides students through applications of content area literacy for questioning, researching, problem-solving, and so on. See Chapter 5 for ways to expand your role as facilitator through questioning techniques, class discussions, and study guides.

$\mathscr{C}$ooperative Learning

How does cooperative learning differ from traditional "group work," and how can it enhance content area literacy and learning?

Cooperative learning is structured so that every group member contributes her/his fair share, fulfills the learning objectives, and helps her/his group members achieve success. Content area literacy and learning are enhanced through the combined knowledge, abilities, and efforts of all group members. The positive effects cooperative learning can have on learning are significant. See Chapter 4 for ways to structure cooperative learning effectively in the content area classroom.

More Student Responsibility for Learning

How can teachers help students take more responsibility for their own learning, thereby developing skills for a lifetime of learning content?

Teachers can shift emphasis from test performance, memorization of facts, and mastery of isolated skills. Instead, they can emphasize self-questioning, research, investigation, analysis, synthesis, and problem-solving. These are the kinds of critical thinking, literacy, and study skills that will endow students with a lifetime of independent learning. See Chapter 3 for ways to help students become more effective, responsible, and independent learners.

Active Learning and Authentic Assessment

How do active learning and authentic assessment use literacy to enhance and document content area learning?

Active learning and authentic assessment are interrelated. In active learning, students use literacy as a tool for learning content in meaningful ways. Then, the work students produce through literacy applications also provides an authentic assessment and documentation of their learning. See Chapters 9 and 10 for ways to design and incorporate active learning and authentic assessment into the content area classroom.

Writing Across the Curriculum

How can writing-to-learn activities enhance learning and motivation in all content areas?

As a literacy skill, writing is a crucial component of content area literacy. Just as students need a variety of reading experiences, they also need extensive and varied writing experiences across content areas. Writing is also a valuable tool for learning content; it can make knowledge meaningful and more easily retained. See Chapter 11 for a variety of ways writing activities and assignments can be used to enhance content area learning and literacy _without_ resulting in significantly more papers to grade!

Meeting the Varied Needs of Learners

How can instruction in the content area classroom meet the literacy and learning needs of a variety of learners?

The beauty of content area literacy strategies and activities is that they can be tailored to meet the varying ages, interests, and needs of learners. For example, materials can be modified to be more or less challenging; teachers can provide a great deal of guidance or very little at all; a variety of strategies and activities can be used to address the styles of a variety of learners. Because every learner has some type of special need, you will find ways to modify materials, strategies, and activities throughout this text. For example, Chapter 2 suggests ways to identify learning styles and teach to their strengths. Chapters 3, 5, and 11 offer ways to adapt materials and activities for students who have difficulty reading and writing. Chapter 4 suggests modifications for gifted and talented learners. Chapters 4, 6, 8, and 11 offer ideas specifically designed to support ESL students. Chapter 12 suggests uses of instructional technology for learners with motor, speech, learning, hearing, and vision impairments.

SUMMARY

Metacognitive awareness involves conscious planning before reading, active monitoring during reading, forming and implementing appropriate strategies, and evaluating and reviewing after reading for more effective and efficient learning. Metacognitive awareness can be developed through direct instruction and guided practice using the Think-Aloud strategy. A popular study strategy that develops metacognitive awareness is Survey, Question, Read, Recite, Review (SQ3R). It embodies the general guidelines for effective study strategies. Following the steps of SQ3R can help students develop the metacognitive awareness that characterizes good readers. Many variations of SQ3R have been developed to assist students in meeting the demands of text, task, content, and individual learning styles or preferences. Guidelines for effective study strategies include before, during, and after steps to help students prepare and set purposes for reading, monitor their comprehension, and evaluate learning with respect to established purposes.

A study strategy that follows these guidelines, while emphasizing writing and critical reflection as tools for learning, is Read, Encode, Annotate, Ponder (REAP). This strategy requires direct instruction and guided practice in writing a variety of annotations. Writing annotations helps students monitor comprehension, assess learning, internalize content, and develop critical thinking and writing skills.

Students can benefit from opportunities to improve their reading rates and develop flexibility of rate. They can also benefit from teacher modeling and guided practice in goal setting, time management, and decision making. An often overlooked yet important literacy skill involves listening and notetaking. Students can benefit from direct instruction and guided practice using such strategies as the Guided Lecture Procedure and the Cornell System for Notetaking. Students can also benefit significantly from instruction and guidance in test-taking strategies and guidelines for testwiseness.

ENRICHMENT ACTIVITIES

Do these activities with a cooperative learning group of two to four members. Divide each activity so that each person in the group is assigned a specific task or role and is held accountable for her or his assignment.

1. Select a passage, in the content area of your choice, at least 300 words in length. Prepare a think-aloud for it, making sure that you provide an ideal model for metacognitive awareness.

2. Give a reading rate pretest to two or more children, adolescents, or adults. Share with each one and then submit in writing a set of suggestions for helping them improve rate and flexibility of rate.

3. Interview two or more students (elementary, secondary, or college) about their study skills. Share with each one and then submit in writing a set of suggestions for helping them read and study with greater efficiency, concentration, comprehension, and retention.

4. Interview two or more students (elementary, secondary, or college) about their long-term goals and the relationship of school work to achieving their goals. Share with each one and then submit in writing a set of suggestions for helping them set goals, develop internal motivation in relation to those goals, improve time management skills, and become a proactive decision maker.

REFERENCES

Cicchetti, G. (1990). *Cognitive modeling and reciprocal teaching of reading and study strategies.* Watertown, CT: Cicchetti Associates.

Crawley, S. J., and L. H. Mountain. (1988). *Strategies for guiding content reading.* Needham Heights, MA: Allyn & Bacon.

Davey, B. (1983). Think-aloud modeling the cognitive processes of reading comprehension. *Journal of Reading* 27(1):44–47.

Eanet, M. G., and A. V. Manzo. (1976). REAP—A strategy for improving reading/writing/study skills. *Journal of Reading* 19:647–652.

Edwards, P. (1973). Panorama: A Study Technique. *Journal of Reading* 17:132–153.

Fay, L. (1965). Reading study skills: Math and science. In *Reading and inquiry.* Edited by J. A. Figurel. Newark, DE: International Reading Association.

Kelly, B. W., and J. Holmes. (1979). The Guided Lecture Procedure. *Journal of Reading* 22:602–604.

Maxwell, H., and E. Norman. (1980). *Successful reading,* 3d ed. New York: Holt, Rinehart and Winston.

McBride, W. G. (Ed.). (1990). *High interest-easy reading: A booklist for junior and senior high school students,* 6th ed. Urbana, IL: National Council for Teachers of English.

Moore, M. A. (1981). C2R: Concentrate, read, remember. *Journal of Reading* 24:337–339.

Orlando, V. P. (1980). Training students to use a modified version of SQ3R: An instructional strategy. *Reading World* 20:65–70.

Pauk, W. (1963). On scholarship: Advice to high school students. *The Reading Teacher* 17:73–78.

_____. (1984). The new SQ3R. *Reading World* 23:274–275.

_____. (1988). *How to study in college,* 3d ed. Boston: Houghton Mifflin.

Robinson, F. P. (1961). *Effective study.* (revised ed.) New York: Harper and Bros.

Ryder, R. J., B. B. Graves, and M. F. Graves. (1989). *Easy reading: Book series and periodicals for less able readers*, 2d ed. Newark, DE: International Reading Association.

Simpson, M. L. (1986). PORPE: A writing strategy for studying and learning in the content areas. *Journal of Reading* 29:407–414.

Simpson, M. L., and S. L. Nist. (1984). PLAE: A model for planning successful independent learning. *Journal of Reading* 28:218–223.

Smith, R., and P. G. Elliot. (1979). *Reading activities for middle and secondary schools.* New York: Holt, Rinehart and Winston.

Thomas, E. L., and H. A. Robinson. (1972). *Improving reading in every class: A sourcebook for teachers.* Boston: Allyn & Bacon.

Tierney, R. J., and P. D. Pearson. (1981). Learning to learn from text: A framework for improving classroom practice. In E. K. Dishner, T. W. Bean, J. E. Readence, and D. W. Moore (Eds.), *Reading in the Content Areas: Improving Classroom Instruction* (pp. 87–103), Dubuque, IA: Kendall/Hunt Publishing Company.

Tierney, R. J., J. E. Readence, and E. K. Dishner. (1990). *Reading strategies and practices: A compendium*, 3d ed. Needham Heights, MA: Allyn & Bacon.

Tonjes, M. J., and M. V. Zintz. (1992). *Teaching reading thinking study skills in content classrooms.* 3d ed. Dubuque, IA: Wm. C. Brown.

Vacca, R. T., and J. L. Vacca. (1993). *Content area reading,* 4th ed. New York: HarperCollins.

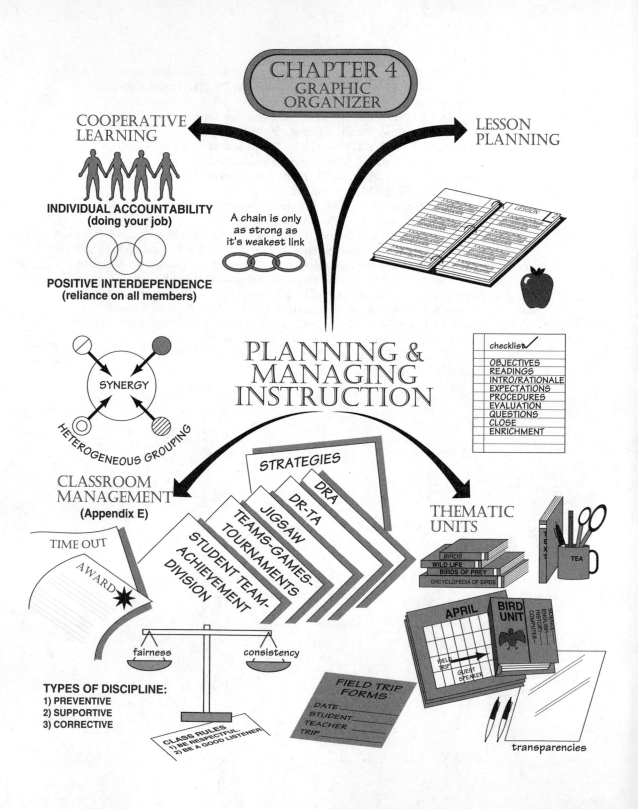

CHAPTER 4
GRAPHIC ORGANIZER

COOPERATIVE LEARNING

LESSON PLANNING

INDIVIDUAL ACCOUNTABILITY
(doing your job)

POSITIVE INTERDEPENDENCE
(reliance on all members)

A chain is only as strong as it's weakest link

SYNERGY

HETEROGENEOUS GROUPING

PLANNING & MANAGING INSTRUCTION

checklist ✓

OBJECTIVES
READINGS
INTRO/RATIONALE
EXPECTATIONS
PROCEDURES
EVALUATION
QUESTIONS
CLOSE
ENRICHMENT

STRATEGIES

DRA
DR-TA
JIGSAW
TEAMS-GAMES-TOURNAMENTS
STUDENT TEAM-ACHIEVEMENT DIVISION

CLASSROOM MANAGEMENT
(Appendix E)

THEMATIC UNITS

TIME OUT

AWARD

fairness   consistency

TYPES OF DISCIPLINE:
1) PREVENTIVE
2) SUPPORTIVE
3) CORRECTIVE

CLASS RULES
1) BE RESPECTFUL.
2) BE A GOOD LISTENER

FIELD TRIP FORMS
DATE
STUDENT
TEACHER
TRIP

BIRDS
WILD LIFE
BIRDS OF PREY
ENCYCLOPEDIA OF BIRDS

TEXT

TEA

APRIL

BIRD UNIT
SCIENCE
ENGLISH
HISTORY
COMPUTER

FIELD TRIP

GUEST SPEAKER

transparencies

LESSON

Planning and Managing Instruction and Cooperative Learning

To demonstrate mastery of the content, the student will be able to do the following:

PART 1 OBJECTIVES

1. Identify the following strategy, describe its distinguishing features, and assess its significance to teaching content area literacy: DRA.
2. Outline the components of an Instructional Framework that not only teaches content but also develops and applies content area literacy as a tool for learning.
3. Explain what it means for the teacher to "set a purpose for reading" and why the content area teacher should *always* specify a purpose for reading.
4. Assess the importance of mastering a wide variety of teaching and learning strategies for developing content area literacy.

PART 2 OBJECTIVES

1. Identify the following strategy, describe its distinguishing features, and assess its significance to teaching content area literacy: DR-TA.
2. Distinguish cooperative learning from other forms of group work.
3. Define individual accountability and positive interdependence, two conditions necessary for cooperative learning.
4. Identify examples of how lessons could be structured to ensure individual accountability and positive interdependence.
5. Assess the importance and summarize the benefits of using cooperative learning in the content area classroom on a regular basis.

5. Define the thematic unit as a framework for planning and assess its importance to planning instruction in content area learning and literacy.
6. Define "curriculum compacting" and examine its role as a structure for adapting instruction for gifted and talented students.
7. Propose five enrichment activities appropriate for gifted and talented students in a specific content area and grade level.

6. Summarize the guidelines for effective cooperative grouping.
7. Examine the role of cooperative learning, addressing both heterogeneous and homogeneous grouping, for meeting the special needs of and enhancing instruction for gifted and talented students.
8. Describe at least one cooperative learning strategy especially suited to the needs of ESL students.
9. Describe at least one additional cooperative learning strategy and explain how it could be used as part of a specific content area literacy strategy you identify.
10. Describe the role and assess the importance of cooperative grouping for individualizing instruction to meet the special needs of students.

INTRODUCTION

The content area literacy strategies you have been learning are a key component in planning and managing instruction. You will learn two more strategies in this chapter, the Directed Reading Activity (DRA) and the Directed Reading-Thinking Activity (DR-TA). You will also learn a basic lesson plan framework for content area teaching that will allow you to make instructional decisions based on the needs of your students and the demands of the material. Following this framework and applying content area literacy strategies in content area instruction will help you implement the guidelines suggested by research on effective teaching. This chapter will emphasize the importance of two of those guidelines in particular, which are setting purposes for reading and implementing a wide variety of instructional strategies.

This chapter will put the content area literacy strategies into a broader context of planning and managing content area instruction. The broader context was defined in Chapter 1 as the components of the new paradigm of education and the principles of Total Quality. This chapter will further demonstrate how content area literacy strategies fit into the new paradigm and support the principles of Total Quality.

Individual strategies and lesson plans are tied together into a larger planning framework known as the thematic unit. The concept of the thematic unit will be introduced as a format for planning that allows teachers rather than textbook teachers' manuals to make the instructional decisions. The thematic unit provides a structure for guiding teachers in planning instruction for appropriate and meaningful application of strategies.

In the old paradigm of education, students who mastered content quickly (thereby completing their work early), were often given more of the same type of work to keep them busy. This chapter will introduce an alternate planning system for adapting instruction so that these students are given *different* rather than *more* of the same type of work. This system, "curriculum compacting" (Reis and Renzulli 1992), fits into the new paradigm of education, in that it helps the teacher adapt instruction to meet the special needs of gifted and talented students, as well as others who master certain content quickly. Curriculum compacting allows teachers to offer these students more challenging, enriching, and motivating instructional options.

You will also learn more about how to capitalize on the concept of synergy through cooperative learning in this chapter. You recall from Chapter 1 that cooperative learning is one of the components of the new paradigm of education, and that synergistic relationships is one of the principles of Total Quality. This chapter will help you distinguish cooperative learning from traditional group learning. It will also emphasize the importance of using cooperative grouping to meet the individual needs of a variety of learners. You will learn about two factors that are keys to the success of cooperative learning: individual accountability and positive interdependence. You will also learn a set of guidelines that are crucial for effective cooperative learning. This chapter will describe for you a variety of cooperative learning strategies, all of which can be used as part of content area literacy strategies.

PART 1

STRATEGY: DIRECTED READING ACTIVITY (DRA)

The Directed Reading Activity was originally designed by Betts (1946) as a basal reader lesson. The steps basically follow the guidelines of preparing students before reading, guiding students during silent reading, and following the reading with a comprehension check and skills lesson. This strategy has since been adapted for use in content area instruction. For the purposes of this text, the DRA will be defined as it has been adapted for content area teaching: a general framework for planning content area lessons that emphasize reading as a medium of instruction and literacy as a tool for learning.

As a literacy-based strategy for content area instruction, the DRA provides a basic lesson format that has great flexibility and is applicable in a wide variety of content areas. It gives teachers a basic format for providing systematic instruction along with a reading assignment. It can be used with almost any lesson based primarily on a reading assignment. The DRA's main assumption is that comprehension can be increased by building background knowledge, setting specific purposes for reading, discussing, and extending understanding after reading (McKenna and Robinson 1993). The components of the strategy are divided into three phases: preparation, directed silent reading, and follow-up.

The Preparation Phase

The first phase of the DRA prepares the students for reading and has several components. First, and possibly most important, the reading assignment is introduced by relating it directly to the students' own lives, background knowledge, and experiences. You will recognize this activity as one that activates schemata. This component is important not only because it activates schemata but also because it helps stir interest in and curiosity about the topic. In short, it captures the students' attention by helping them personalize the content. Since the value and relevance of the information to the students' lives are not always obvious, they must be made explicit. The role of the teacher in this phase is to model the process for generating interest in a topic—the teacher's genuine enthusiasm and excitement for the topic is crucial to drawing students into the learning process.

The second component of the preparation phase involves relating the content to prior learning. The teacher again activates schemata by reviewing information previously learned and then demonstrating how the current topic fits into that context. This component of the preparation step is important for several reasons. First, it allows the teacher to assess requisite background knowledge and, if necessary, review, reteach, or clarify. Second, it helps students understand relationships between concepts. Third, it gives students an overall framework for processing new information.

The third component of the preparation phase involves introducing new vocabulary. The teacher selects between five and ten key words, especially those that are content specific. The words are then introduced in writing, in the context of sentences that provide clues to each word's meaning. The list of sentences, with the key words underlined, is presented using a chalkboard, overhead projector, or chart paper. The teacher then reads the sentences aloud and explains the meanings of the key words. Students are asked to explain the meanings in their own words, and possibly, to compose sentences using the words. The vocabulary discussions should be brief; remember, you are only introducing the words at this point. Elaboration will come later.

The fourth component of the preparation phase involves setting purposes for reading. You recall from Chapter 2 the importance of specifying one or more purposes for reading. Purposes help students maintain concentration for better comprehension and retention. They also provide students with a means to monitor their own comprehension. Purposes should be presented in writing so that students may continually refer to them while reading. Purposes may be presented in a variety of ways. One way would be to list specific information following this stem: "Read to find out . . ." Other ways would be to provide students with a set of questions to be answered or to frame the purposes in the form of performance objectives. For example, after reading, you will list, define, explain, assess, create, analyze, synthesize, identify, distinguish, and so on. Performance objectives should specify the activity students will use to demonstrate their mastery of the content. Purposes can also be presented in the form of reading and study guides, which provide questions and information designed to guide students in discovering the main ideas.

The Directed Silent Reading Phase

The second phase of the DRA involves directed silent reading. Students should read silently because silent reading increases comprehension, is more typical of real-life reading activities, and encourages students to practice applying study strategies independently. During this phase, the teacher should walk around the classroom, closely monitoring the students' reading. With experience, you will be able to detect problems by simply observing the students, even though they are reading silently. Readers who are comprehending well have markedly different body language from readers who are having trouble. However, even if you have poor readers who have mastered the art of pretending to understand, you can still monitor their progress. For example, stop occasionally at students' desks and ask them to retell in their own words some of the key points they have read. You could also ask them to read one or two key sentences aloud to you. Still another way to monitor progress would be to ask specific questions related to the purposes set for reading.

Monitoring students during the silent reading phase is important for several reasons. First, it encourages the teacher to guide students in applying word-attack skills to decode unknown words. It also allows the teacher to coach students on using "fix-up strategies" and applying effective study strategies when they are having trouble comprehending. Monitoring students provides the teacher the opportunity to model metacognitive awareness through "think alouds." It helps the teacher to intervene and provide guidance if a significant number of students are having trouble with the same concept or section. Finally, it allows the teacher to continually remind students to focus on their purposes for reading.

The Follow-Up Phase

The third phase of the DRA is the follow-up done after reading. The first component of this phase, done immediately after reading, is to ensure that purposes have been met. Using this component, the teacher guides students through a process of assessing their own comprehension. Text-based interpretations are appropriate at this point. The purposes for reading provide the criteria for assessment; if purposes have not been met, the teacher directs the student(s) to reread the appropriate part(s). This rereading phase can be done either silently or orally. If students are reading a brief passage aloud to identify a specific piece of information, oral reading is purposeful and appropriate. Oral rereading of selected parts can also be used to verify that purposes have been met.

The second component of the follow-up phase is to guide students in a review and reflection of the content. Reader-based interpretations are appropriate during this phase. Questions should be formulated carefully to require students to think critically about what they have just read. During this phase, students should be encouraged to discuss the content, particularly in terms of their personal reactions to it. The content will more likely be retained if students can clearly relate it to their personal lives, experiences, and opinions. They should also be encouraged to evaluate the information through a critical review of it.

The third aspect of the follow-up phase is enrichment. Students should be given a variety of enrichment activities from which to choose. These activities will foster opportunities to continue processing the content. For example, activities might involve writing about the content, researching more about the topic, discussing it further, or applying the information for creative problem solving. The most important type of follow-up activity may be further reading on the topic. A room library is essential for this type of enrichment. A shelf or cart should be restocked regularly with interesting and exciting books and periodicals related to the current topic of study. Exposing students to a variety of high-quality reading materials not only reinforces learning but also helps to improve students' attitudes toward reading and learning.

LESSON PLANNING

An Instructional Framework

An Instructional Framework (IF) was outlined by Herber (1978) as a flexible structure for planning instruction. The structure consists of three parts: preparation, guidance, and independence. The preparation component is similar to that of the DRA, with one major difference. In addition to motivating, reviewing background knowledge, setting purposes, and introducing vocabulary, the IF helps students plan a process for reading that is appropriate for their purposes and background knowledge and for the difficulty of the material. The teacher provides oral or, preferably, written directions for using a study guide that leads students through the identified process. The teacher reviews the directions with the students to make sure they understand the tasks that are essential to the successful completion of the study guide.

The guidance component generally takes the form of a study guide that provides a structure to lead students through the reading with a conscious awareness of the process and directs students to the discovery of important concepts. The guides can be individualized to meet the differing needs, background knowledge, and ability levels of the students. Consequently, the guides demonstrate for students the role of content area literacy as a tool for uncovering knowledge.

The last component is designed to promote independence in applying content area literacy as a tool for learning. Teachers reinforce the learning processes developed in the guidance component by providing students additional opportunities to apply both the literacy skills and the concepts. The teacher's role in this component is that of coach to help students recall prior learning and processes that could be applied appropriately in the new situation. Coaching the students helps them develop independence as they transfer knowledge and literacy skills to new learning opportunities. Once students can successfully transfer the process as it was originally applied, they should be encouraged to personalize it by adapting the process to suit their learning styles and needs.

Setting Purposes for Reading

As you have seen, "setting purposes" involves both the general reasons for reading and the specific information that should be gleaned from the assignment. General purposes can include the following reasons for reading: to prepare for a test, to research a paper, to participate in a class discussion, to have fun, and to learn more about something to satisfy personal curiosities. Specific purposes, whether identified by the teacher or student, tell the reader for what specific information to look while reading.

Specific purposes are usually written and can be presented in a variety of formats, including the following: a list of information, questions, performance objectives, and study guides. Students should understand that focusing on specific purposes will help them concentrate and consequently discover other information not necessarily related to the purposes. In other words, setting purposes does not mean that students should ignore information unrelated to the purposes. Rather, they should make note of all information they consider especially interesting or important, whether specified by the purposes or not. Purposeful reading helps students understand and remember more information than the specific purposes.

One of the guidelines presented in Chapter 2 for teaching with textual materials emphasized setting purposes as an important way to activate schemata. Establishing clear purposes for reading should be part of every content area lesson plan that involves a reading assignment. As you have noticed, the content area literacy strategies you have learned all set purposes, although in different ways. For example, in the KWL, students generate their own purposes by listing questions they would like to have answered by the reading. When using SQ3R as an instructional strategy, the teacher models for students the process of establishing purposes by formulating questions from the subheadings. In the DRA, the teacher specifies the purposes in writing. Even the GRP establishes a purpose, although a general one, before reading: Read to remember *everything*.

The purpose-setting component is an essential part of all content area lessons involving content area literacy. As discussed in Chapter 2, the practice of setting purposes is important for a number of reasons. Setting purposes helps the reader activate prior knowledge and establish goals for monitoring comprehension. Having specific purposes in mind encourages the reader to maintain concentration for improved comprehension and retention. Consistently providing students with specific purposes for reading helps them learn to set their own purposes as independent, active readers who interact with the text as they read. Finally, reading for specific purposes leads to text interaction at the highest levels of thought.

Using a Variety of Instructional Frameworks and Strategies

A variety of instructional frameworks and strategies should be used in content area teaching. Perhaps the most important reason for emphasizing variety is that it helps generate and maintain interest in and enthusiasm for learning. Both students and teachers need variety to enhance motivation.

Variety in lesson planning is also important for meeting the diverse needs of the students. For example, they have widely-differing reading abilities, and their attitudes toward reading and learning range from very negative to very positive. Each student has a unique set of learning-style preferences. Levels of background knowledge are widely disparate for any given topic. Motivation levels vary not only between students, but also within each student on a day-to-day basis. Topics that some students find fascinating put others to sleep. All of these different student characteristics are important considerations in planning lessons and selecting strategies. The only practical way to meet the diverse needs of students is to use many different instructional frameworks and strategies.

The demands of the reading materials must also be taken into account when planning instruction. The lengths of the assignments must be assessed and altered appropriately. The difficulty of the concepts must be evaluated, along with concept density, which refers to the number of concepts introduced within a particular section. The number and difficulty of technical vocabulary and textual factors such as word and sentence length and complexity must be considered. The way the reading is organized (e.g., chronological, cause/effect, compare/contrast, or spatial) is important in planning appropriate instruction. Graphic aids (e.g., charts, graphs, and pictures), reading aids (e.g., outlines, summaries, and marginal notes), and print features (e.g., size and type of print and headings) are other important considerations. Awareness of these factors is important in planning content area instruction, and using a variety of frameworks and strategies is the only way that so many different textual demands can be addressed.

In addition to considering individual differences in students and textual materials, teachers also must think about their own individual teaching styles, as well as constraints in time and space. Such information is important for appropriately planning instruction and selecting strategies. With experience, you will develop confidence in choosing appropriate instructional frameworks and strategies. Even as a new teacher, though, you can address the relevant factors by using a variety of instructional frameworks and strategies. Once you have mastered a core set of strategies and some basic guidelines for lesson planning, you will become the ultimate instructional decision maker by creating your own strategies to maximize learning in your classroom.

Writing Lesson Plans

The process of writing detailed lesson plans is not as important for the experienced teacher as it is for the new teacher (Peterson 1978). The process itself is crucial because it requires you to think through the lesson carefully from beginning to end. With experience, you will be able to visualize the lesson quickly and easily; for now, however, as a preservice teacher, the lesson-planning process might be rather time consuming. Keep in mind that with experience, the process gets easier and more efficient.

Content area lesson plans should be detailed at first, until the planning process becomes automatic. Appendix C provides a suggested process and format for learning to write lesson plans. Appendix D provides some sample lesson plans written using the process and format. Many variations of this process and format are widely used. Even the components can vary, so expect to encounter many different lesson plan formats used by content area teachers.

THEMATIC UNITS

A thematic unit is a set of lesson plans related to a selected topic. The length of the unit can vary from one week to as many as six weeks, depending on the grade level and specificity of the topic. Just as the Instructional Framework provides a structure for planning within the context of a single lesson, the thematic unit provides a structure for organizing instruction around a set of lessons that uses a variety of activities, reading materials, and strategies. Following is Vacca and Vacca's (1993, 77) general definition of the thematic unit:

> A planning tool that includes (1) A title reflecting the thematic or topical nature of the unit, (2) The major concepts to be learned, (3) The texts and information sources to be studied by students, (4) The unit's instructional activities, and (5) Provisions for evaluating what students have learned as a result of participating in the unit.

Significance to Content Area Literacy and Learning

Thematic units are particularly important for content area literacy because they allow the teacher to integrate literacy instruction with content instruction. Specifically, they provide a structure that helps the teacher consider the demands of the materials and identify the literacy tools necessary for successful learning of the content. Thematic units also allow the teacher to select strategies and activities appropriate for developing those literacy skills and guiding students in meeting the demands of the content materials.

In short, the thematic unit allows the teacher rather than the textbook to be the decision maker. Instead of relying solely on the recommendations for instruction provided by the textbook teacher's manual, the teacher uses these recommendations as resources and guidelines for instruction. The teacher then makes the final decisions about the content, sequence, style, and time allotment for teaching the unit.

Although the teacher is the instructional decision maker in thematic unit instruction, the textbook can provide a valuable reference source. Students should be taught how to use it as a source of information, along with other referential sources such as trade books (i.e., library books), newspapers, magazines, journals, pamphlets, reference books, computer programs, multimedia (e.g., CD-ROMs), educational television, and laser video discs (see Chapter 12 for a discussion of various forms of instructional technology).

Thematic unit instruction is an important tool in the new paradigm of teaching. It provides a format that supports all eight of the new-paradigm components (see Chapter 1). Because it structures lessons as ongoing projects related to a central theme rather than a series of discrete activities, it lends itself nicely to flexible scheduling and longer time frames for lessons. Thematic units are motivational because they offer a variety of opportunities for students to pursue topics of personal interest and relevance. Thematic units also provide cooperative learning opportunities for students to investigate topics and issues of common interest, while allowing both teachers and students the freedom and flexibility to engage in a wide variety of active learning activities (both cooperative and individualistic), the products of which provide authentic means of assessment.

Because thematic unit instruction provides a format for helping students research from a variety of sources, it helps students assume more responsibility for their own learning. When students take more responsibility for their own learning in thematic unit instruction, the teacher's role shifts from lecturer to facilitator and consultant. The thematic focus of unit planning and instruction encourages a wide variety of textbook alternatives and supplements. Finally, the many different activities and materials that characterize thematic units offer greater opportunities for teachers to meet the special needs of every student.

Developing Thematic Units

Structures and processes for organizing and developing thematic units vary greatly. One method for organizing a thematic unit is to develop a sequential set of lessons based on reading assignments from a single textbook. Although this type of organization is highly structured and even somewhat restrictive in its limited use of alternative forms of literature (Vacca and Vacca 1993), it can be a good starting point for the preservice or new teacher.

A second method for organizing a thematic unit is to plan the first few lessons around selections from a single textbook. Later lessons can be planned around multiple texts, alternate information sources, and varied instructional activities. A third method is to organize the unit entirely around individual or group inquiry and research projects. Combining single-text with multiple-text instruction and using a variety of activities including inquiry and research is another option (Vacca and Vacca 1993).

The following steps for unit development are based on the first method of organization described above, that is, developing a sequential set of lessons based on reading assignments from a single textbook. Developing a unit around this basic organization provides an important foundation for creating units using more advanced and complex forms of organization. However, the emphasis will continue to be on supplementing the text with varied forms of literature.

Step 1: Title, Goals, and Rationale

The first step in developing a thematic unit based on reading assignments from a single text is to select the **reading assignments** to be used. These selections may include entire chapters or parts of chapters and need not follow the same sequence as presented in the text. Assignments should be clearly related, however, and lend themselves to a logical sequence of lessons. After identifying the reading selections, *select a title that clearly reflects the theme or topic connecting all the reading assignments.*

The scope of the thematic unit is defined by a set of overall or general **goals** through an analysis of the selected reading assignments that identify the content to be taught. Choose a reasonable number of major concepts and understandings that students can be expected to learn in the established amount of time; then set priorities and select a realistic number of the most important ones. The number of concepts can vary anywhere from three to ten, depending on the time frame, length of the reading assignments, and difficulty of the material. Brozo and Tomlinson (1986, 289) suggest the following questions to help identify the concepts that become unit goals:

1. What are the driving human forces behind the events?
2. What patterns of behavior need to be studied?
3. What phenomena have affected or may affect ordinary people in the future?

The major concepts and understandings students should learn from the reading assignments become the goals of the thematic unit. These goals need not be phrased in behavioral/performance terms as long as the concepts are clearly identified (Vacca and Vacca 1993).

Once the goals have been established, compose a clearly stated **rationale** for teaching this particular content. The rationale can be expressed in one or more paragraphs and should answer questions such as the following:

- Why is it important for an educated person in our culture to understand this information?
- How is this information important for solving the problems of today and tomorrow?
- What is the immediate value and relevance of this information to the students' lives?
- What are the long-term payoffs of mastering this content?
- How does this information relate to future learning?

Step 2: Pre-Tests

Before planning your lessons, you need to gather some information about your students. At the very least, you need to implement a **Cloze Test** and **Content Area Reading Inventory (CARI)** (see Chapter 9). The Cloze Test will help you determine whether the materials you have tentatively selected are appropriate for your students' reading levels. The CARI will help you identify your students' strengths and skill needs with respect to the reading materials you intend to use for instruction. Both of these tests are valuable informal assessment tools that will help you in selecting materials, planning strategies, and choosing activities for your lesson plans.

Step 3: Lesson Plans

Following the format outlined in Appendix C, lesson plans should include literacy-based and other instructional strategies appropriate for the content area of the thematic unit. Activities should be appropriate for whole-class instruction, small-group collaboration, and individual learning. Make sure that you include strategies and activities suitable for a wide range of learning style preferences. For example, activities could involve listening, observing, reading, speaking, teaching, writing, demonstrating, discussing, collaborating, creating (artistically), role playing, and participating in field trips. Also, be sure to incorporate a wide variety of reading materials and other instructional resources.

Step 4: Implementation and Evaluation

Lesson plans are best written and implemented a few at a time so that you can make changes based on student performance, reaction, and response. However, you could still make adjustments and modifications as necessary, even if you have written the lesson plans in advance. The important thing to remember is that you immediately process the effectiveness of each lesson and make appropriate changes for continuous improvement. You recall from Chapter 1 the importance of self-reflection and continuous improvement to Total Quality teaching.

Students should be given the opportunity to participate in the evaluation process. They should be given time and guidance in identifying what they liked about a lesson, as well as what they would like to change. Modeling the process of self-evaluation and giving students opportunities to assess their own participation and level of learning will encourage independence. Developing metacognitive awareness is an important characteristic of self-directed, independent learners. Students should also be encouraged and given opportunities to evaluate one another by giving praise and suggestions for improved learning.

Step 5: Post-Tests and/or Authentic Assessment

Attainment of the unit goals should somehow be assessed. The means of assessment should provide both teacher and students with clear evidence of learning (or lack of learning). Goals can be assessed through traditional tests or through other authentic forms of assessment including samples of student-generated work, observation checklists (completed by teacher and peers), interviews with students, and collaborative projects (see Chapter 9). Once learning has been evaluated with respect to the goals of the thematic unit, some reteaching or review might be in order. Both students and teachers should use the information to decide where to go from there. In other words, the next thematic unit could be a spin-off from or natural follow-up to the previous one. You recall from Chapter 1 the importance of student involvement in the evaluation and planning process for Total Quality teaching.

CURRICULUM COMPACTING FOR GIFTED AND TALENTED STUDENTS

Public Law 95-561, a federal law passed by Congress in 1978, provides the following definition of gifted and talented students (Tuttle, Becker, and Sousa 1988, 31):

> The term gifted and talented children means children and whenever applicable, youth, who are identified at the preschool, elementary, or secondary level as possessing demonstrated or potential abilities that give evidence of high performance in capability in areas such as intellectual, creative, specific academic, or leadership ability, or in the performing and visual arts, and who by reason thereof require service or activities not ordinarily provided by the school.

Tuttle, Becker, and Sousa (1988, 31–32) offer the following descriptions of the areas of giftedness specified in that definition:

> *General Intellectual Ability.* This category includes individuals who demonstrate characteristics such as intellectual curiosity, exceptional powers of observation, ability to abstract, a questioning attitude, and associative thinking skills.

Academic Talent. This area encompasses the excellent students, those who achieve high grades, who score very well on tests, and who demonstrate high ability in academic pursuits. Of course, some of these gifted students do not perform well in school but develop their academic skills outside school. Many schools have already developed programs for the academically gifted, including honors classes and advanced placement courses.

Creative and Productive Thinking Skills. Students with these abilities are often those who come up with original and divergent ideas. In addition, they have the ability to elaborate and develop their original ideas, as well as to realize many different ways of perceiving a single thought or topic. Such students are often overlooked in classrooms where emphasis is on assimilating a quantity of information and repeating predetermined answers.

Leadership. While many educators discuss this ability, few have actually been able to describe it adequately for classroom use. On the one hand, it includes those students who emerge as social or academic leaders in a group. However, leadership should also encompass another trait: the willingness to accept responsibility for one's actions and to have a feeling of control over one's life and decisions. In most programs for gifted students we have found the second trait, personal leadership, to be the more important of the two. Leadership involves use of power, productive interaction with others, and self-control.

Visual and Performing Arts. This area relates to activities such as painting, sculpting, drawing, filmmaking, dancing, singing, playing instruments, and performing dramatically. Individuals with superior abilities in these fields seldom have the opportunity to demonstrate their giftedness in most academic classes because the behaviors that reflect such abilities are usually relegated to outside-of-class work and then encouraged only if academic requirements have been fulfilled. Some educators and programs, however, such as the Education Center for the Arts in New Haven (Connecticut) and the Houston (Texas) School for the Visual and Performing Arts, stress this area of giftedness.

Psychomotor Skills. Although this category was not specifically referred to in the 1978 definition, the earlier report recognized its importance. We also believe it is an area worthy of special mention. Besides encompassing athletic prowess, as reflected in many sports programs, it includes superior use of fine motor skills as found in exceptional woodworking, crafts, drafting, and mechanical abilities. In most schools, these abilities are usually developed under vocational education where superior performances by students in these areas are seldom acknowledged as gifted. In fact, referral to such programs is often considered a viable option for somewhat disabled learners.

As you can see from these descriptions, gifted and talented (GT) students represent a widely varying range of strengths. Because of these varying strengths, GT students master content at vastly different rates. Depending on their background knowledge and strengths, GT students often master content more rapidly than other students in the class.

How do you plan instruction for students who master the content and satisfactorily complete their work more quickly than other students in your class? Your first impulse might be to give them more work than the other students. After all, if they can complete it faster, then they can complete a greater amount of work in the same amount of time. However, the flaw in this reasoning is that you are rewarding efficient work with more work. Students quickly catch on to this system, realizing that they can avoid more work simply by doing their work more slowly or with poor quality. The potentially negative impact on study habits, attitudes, motivation, and learning behaviors is obvious.

How, then, can you plan instruction to meet the needs of these students more effectively?

An excellent alternative to the "rewarding efficient work with more work" model is "curriculum compacting" (Reis and Renzulli 1992). The idea behind curriculum compacting is that GT students or others with strengths or high interests in one or more content areas may have already mastered a significant part of the curriculum and can easily master the rest in a short period of time. Therefore, they can skip the parts of the curriculum they already understand, and then master the remainder in a fraction of the time needed by other students. Another potential benefit of curriculum compacting is the motivational effect it can have on bright but underachieving students. When they realize they can earn time to work on self-selected projects of personal interest, students often become motivated to complete regular assignments more efficiently.

This model emerged from an expansive study involving twenty-seven school districts and 465 classroom teachers completed at the University of Connecticut's National Research Center on the Gifted and Talented. In the study, between 40 and 50 percent of the classroom curricula was "compacted" for selected students in one or more content areas. Remarkably, these students scored the same or higher on achievement tests in math, science, social studies, and spelling than their peers in the control group, who received instruction as usual (Reis and Renzulli 1992).

The study examined strategies for modifying the curriculum according to the strengths of high-ability students and the types of alternate activities that appropriately challenge them. Three categories of replacement strategies and activities were examined: enrichment, acceleration, and other (e.g., peer tutoring, cooperative learning, grading papers, and so on). The results of the study indicated the following model for curriculum compacting.

Goals and Assessment

The first step is to identify specific learning outcomes (i.e., content objectives) for a particular unit of instruction. These objectives can usually be found in textbook teachers' guides, scope-and-sequence charts, and curriculum guides. The second step is to identify students who have already mastered the content (Reis and Renzulli 1992).

One way to assess students' mastery is to design a pretest for the classes that all the students take. A pretest is an efficient way to check students' strengths and mastery of content. It also provides concrete documentation of students' abilities and knowledge for later measuring achievement gains. A suitable alternative to designing your own test is to use the unit or chapter tests that often accompany textbooks.

You can design a summary matrix of results for the whole class, with students' names listed vertically down the left-hand side, and the content mastery objectives listed horizontally across the top. Using this matrix, you can record the pretest results to indicate what each student has mastered. This information can be quite useful in pairing and grouping for instruction and replacement activities. In addition to identifying students who have mastered the content, pretests can also help determine which students are in need of extra help with certain skills or content.

Another way to identify students who have already mastered the content is to estimate students' potentials by reviewing previous test scores, assignments, and class participation. Standardized tests can provide some useful information for estimating students' potentials, although their scores should be interpreted with caution. See Chapter 9 for a discussion of ways to avoid misinterpreting standardized test scores.

Once you have identified students you believe may have already mastered the content, give them a pretest to determine whether they have, in fact, successfully fulfilled the current objectives (Reis and Renzulli 1992). Estimating potentials and giving a pretest only to selected students can save the teacher some administrative time and the students some instructional time. However, keep in mind that by giving the pretest only to some of the students, you are potentially overlooking students who might surprise you with their knowledge of this particular content.

For content not easily measured by a pretest, a different assessment process is recommended. This process is also useful for students who have not yet mastered the content, but who you believe have the potential for understanding it quickly. Although effective, this process can be somewhat impractical because it requires a one-on-one discussion with each student you believe may have mastered the content or has the potential to master it quickly.

The first step is to discuss a selected portion of the content with the student for the purpose of ensuring the student understands the goals and procedures of compacting curriculum. The second step is to specify for the student how he or she will demonstrate mastery (e.g., answering chapter questions, writing an essay, taking an end-of-unit test). The third step is to discuss with the student the amount of time needed to complete the unit and the procedures for periodic review (e.g., progress reports, log entries, journals). The last step is to discuss potential enrichment and replacement activities that will follow the unit (Reis and Renzulli 1992).

Enrichment Alternatives

Once high-ability students have been identified, the next step is to design and select appropriate supplemental or alternate strategies, materials, activities, and projects. The primary criteria for selection should be the extent of academic challenge offered with respect to individual students' strengths and interests. Of course you also need to take into consideration criteria like available time, space, and resources.

This selection process requires creative and cooperative decision making by teachers, students, and school personnel. To identify potential strategies, materials, activities, and projects, first consult with other teachers, librarians, instructional technology specialists, content area specialists, and gifted education specialists. The compacting process offers an excellent opportunity for creative cooperation among faculty and between faculty and staff.

With the help of other teachers and staff members, select materials that include self-directed activities, materials that emphasize critical thinking, and a variety of project-oriented activities. These activities should encourage active research and investigation by students. As much as possible, research projects should have a multidisciplinary focus on current and controversial issues that require examination from multiple perspectives.

A menu of enrichment options can be developed for each content area or grade level. As content area experts themselves, teachers provide excellent enrichment resources: they can mentor students, teach seminars or mini-courses, share materials, or design research projects. In addition, older students, parents, and community members who are experts in one or more content areas or content topics can serve as potential resources (Reis and Renzulli 1992). These experts could lead special-topic seminars, offer apprenticeships in local businesses and social service agencies, conduct field trips, serve as mentors, or offer access to specialized instructional technology. Curriculum compacting encourages GT students to work on improving their study skills. For example, many GT students who have mastered the content might still benefit from working on time management, test-taking skills, reading-rate variability, skimming and scanning, self-monitoring, self-evaluating, and using appropriate strategies according to their purposes for reading. In addition, GT students could enrich their learning and study skill mastery by developing independent strategies for vocabulary concept development.

Another important area for GT enrichment involves communication skills. Expressive communication skills can be sharpened with a variety of writing assignments including creative writing, journals, research reports, and correspondence. Speaking and listening skills can be developed through drama, speeches, debates, poetry reading, discussions, and foreign language study. Broad-based reading assignments including literary study groups, analysis and interpretation of literature, reporting from nonfiction sources, and examining literary devices such as tone and point of view encourage receptive communication skills.

Study guides provide a practical vehicle for adapting instruction to meet the needs of GT students. For example, GT students may not need to read the entire assignment; perhaps they have already mastered most of the content. In that case, the teachers can guide students to read only key parts, provide them with higher-level questions, and then advance them to other tasks.

PART 2

STRATEGY: DIRECTED READING-THINKING ACTIVITY (DR-TA)

The Directed Reading-Thinking Activity (DR-TA) is a popular variation of the DRA. Like the DRA, the DR-TA was designed originally as a strategy for basal reader instruction (Stauffer 1969), and also like the DRA, the DR-TA has been adapted for use in content area instruction. As a content area strategy, it provides a basic framework for planning literacy-based content area lessons. Similar to the DRA, the DR-TA has great flexibility and can be used in a wide range of content areas for lessons that emphasize literacy tools for learning and reading as the medium of instruction.

One strength of the DR-TA is that it provides a process for helping students learn to make predictions as purposes for reading. For use with expository materials (e.g., textbooks), the concept of a "prediction" is broadly defined as any speculation about the contents of the reading material. Whereas, with narrative materials (e.g., literary fiction), the concept of a prediction involves a chronological sequence of events by speculating about future events.

Additional strengths of the DR-TA are its emphasis on reading as a thinking activity and the importance it places on helping students determine their own purposes for reading. The DR-TA also provides a form of guided problem solving (Manzo and Manzo 1990): students are led through a cycle of making predictions, reading to verify predictions, evaluating comprehension with respect to the predictions, and making new predictions based on acquired knowledge.

Stauffer (1976) based this strategy on his notion that reading is a thinking process in which the reader uses prior knowledge and experience to reconstruct the author's meaning. This course of reconstruction begins with the formulation of hypotheses (i.e., predictions) that reflect the reader's assumptions; the hypotheses/predictions then serve as purposes for reading. The process continues as the reader gathers data to test or verify the hypotheses/predictions. The strategies involved in the DRTA resemble the traditional scientific method and thus are extremely valuable in familiarizing students with that type of thinking.

According to Stauffer (1969), one of three outcomes is possible. First, the reader may find verification of the hypotheses/predictions, thus fulfilling the purposes for reading. Second, the reader may find only partial verification or implied verification. In this case, the reader either reformulates the hypotheses/predictions by setting new purposes in light of the new information or withholds judgment until more information has been gathered. Third, the reader finds no verification and declares completely new hypotheses/predictions as purposes for reading.

Manzo and Manzo (1990, 106) describe a simplified version of the DRTA that provides a useful formula for planning prereading, guided silent reading, and postreading:

Teacher actions

1. What do you think you will find in the text? *(activate thought)*
2. Why do you think so? *(agitate thought)*
3. Prove it! *(require evidence)*

Student actions

1. Predict *(set purposes)*
2. Read *(process ideas)*
3. Prove *(seek verification in text)*

The Prereading Phase

As in the DRA, assess students' background knowledge to determine whether they possess the requisite schemata to comprehend the concepts to be learned. If necessary, provide appropriate teaching to address lack of information and misconceptions (McKenna and Robinson 1993). New vocabulary words can be introduced and discussed at this point if they represent concepts that provide crucial background knowledge; otherwise, their definitions can be addressed when setting purposes for reading.

Help students identify their own purposes for reading. Begin by asking them to survey the assignment briefly by looking at the title, subheadings, graphic aids, and so on. Then ask students to predict what material they think will be covered. If they are not familiar with the concept of a prediction, many students will have difficulty with this task at first; once they develop confidence through practice, you will not have to provide as much guidance. Initially, you will need to explain and provide examples of a prediction. Try using instructions like "Take a guess about what will be covered" or "Tell us what you suspect might be covered." If students are absolutely baffled by the concept and cannot offer a prediction, you may have to provide them with several alternatives from which to choose. This procedure gives students the opportunity to see good examples modeled before they formulate their own predictions.

In the beginning, students will probably be fearful of making predictions, because they are facing a great risk of being wrong. Explain that the point of making predictions is not to guess right but rather to make an educated guess that will provide you with a hypothesis to test by reading. Remind students that without having read the material, it is impossible to be absolutely sure that a prediction will be correct—the best we can hope for is that it will be reasonable and logical in terms of the information provided thus far. You should communicate repeatedly the notion that as long as a prediction is reasonable and logical based on available data, it is a good one. To reinforce the purpose of the predictive process as learning how to make good but not necessarily correct predictions, avoid labeling predictions as wrong or incorrect when they are analyzed later. Rather, emphasize the importance of changing predictions once sufficient evidence is gathered.

The atmosphere you create during the process of predicting is critical to the success of the strategy: you must be extremely positive, supportive, and encouraging. At first, until students become comfortable with taking risks and confident in making predictions, you should accept all of their predictions as valid, no matter how far-fetched they may be. Students who take the risk of formulating predictions only to have them labeled unrealistic or incorrect will probably not be willing to take the chance again. Once students are secure that the predictions will not be judged, you can begin to teach them how to use available information to improve their hypotheses. Through discussion, you and the students who have mastered the art of educated guessing can model the process of playing detective by identifying clues and making predictions based on those clues.

The reading assignment should be divided into manageable sections. Then, the process of making predictions can be done either once for the entire reading selection or one section at a time. If predictions are made all at once for the entire selection, the hypotheses for each section should be reviewed immediately before reading that section and then analyzed before going on to the next section. The prediction for the next section might need to be changed according to evidence gathered from reading the first section.

Ask the students to write down their predictions or dictate them to you. If they record their own, ask several students to share their hypotheses with the class and record them on a chalkboard, overhead, or chart paper. Then, lead a discussion of the predictions, asking questions such as "What makes you think so?" and "Why do you think that will be covered?" Encourage students to compare predictions and explain how two conflicting predictions both can be good. If the discussion indicates some major gaps in background knowledge, continue the discussion to review key concepts.

Help students set their purposes for reading by explaining or reminding them that their purpose for reading is to verify or check their predictions. They should be looking for information that will provide clues about whether their predictions need to be changed. Just before they begin reading, students should review the predictions they made for the first section.

The Guided Silent Reading Phase

As with the DRA, monitor closely the students' silent reading. Provide individual assistance as indicated by either student requests for help or your own observations of those having trouble. Coach students on using word attack skills, the glossary, and other textbook reading aids to encourage and reinforce independent learning and problem solving in the students. Also, remind them to adjust rate appropriately, use skimming and scanning if necessary, and take a few notes on the clues they uncover in relation to the predictons they made as purposes for reading.

The Postreading Phase

After reading the first section, students should reassess their purposes for reading by analyzing their predictions in light of the information gained from the reading. Ask them to decide whether their predictions were verified, need to be changed, or should be held until additional information is obtained. As students make their decisions, have them identify specific information to support their conclusions. They should record this proof and share it with the class in a follow-up discussion. If predictions change, students should record the revised version.

Once students have enough experience and confidence verifying and changing predictions, they can go through the process individually while reading. Until then, predictions should be analyzed and discussed as a group at the end of each section before reviewing or making new predictions for the next section. In the follow-up discussions, you should ask questions such as "What do you think now?" and "Which part makes you think that?" Ask students to read aloud the parts that support their acceptance or rejection of the hypotheses, along with their revised predictions. At this point, you should ask questions that direct their attention to any key points not addressed by their predictions and revised predictions and help students relate these key points to their predictions. Finally, guide students through a discussion of the value and relevance of the information to their own lives and goals.

COOPERATIVE LEARNING AND EFFECTIVE GROUPING

Many teachers, and students as well, hear the term "cooperative learning" and conclude that it is just a fancy new term for the typical "group work" or "small-group projects" most of us have experienced at one time or another. Unfortunately, most of us have also had at least one negative experience with group work or small-group projects. The litany of problems with these unsuccessful learning groups goes something like this: One person ends up doing the lion's share of the work. The "slackers" get full credit for doing little or none of the work. Someone does not do his or her share of the project, and everyone gets penalized. The product is

Cooperative learning differs from group work or small group projects.

usually representative of what the stronger students have mastered; therefore, the weaker students get good grades even though they have not mastered the content. The more vocal and aggressive students dominate the activities and leadership roles at the expense of students who probably need the leadership experience more. The more capable students do most of the explaining, and since the amount of time spent explaining correlates highly with the amount learned, the strong get stronger and the weak get weaker (Johnson, Johnson, and Holubec 1991). The list continues, but you get the idea. You might recognize some of these characteristics and could probably add some of your own based on negative experiences with group work. Cooperative learning is a completely different concept and was specifically designed to avoid the pitfalls of traditional learning groups.

Cooperative Learning vs. Group Work

The concept of cooperative learning differs from these other forms of group work in many ways. One way they differ is that activities are structured to hold each student accountable for mastering the content and doing his or her fair share. This condition for cooperative learning is known as individual accountability (Johnson, Johnson, and Holubec 1991). Individual accountability requires structuring the activity so that each group member is held accountable for mastering the content *and* making equitable contributions.

Another way in which cooperative learning differs from other forms of group work is that activities are structured so that students must coordinate their efforts in order to complete the project. Students should perceive that they are linked with others in such a way that they cannot succeed unless their teammates do (and vice versa), and that their work benefits others and the work of others benefits them. This condition for cooperative learning is known as positive interdependence (Johnson, Johnson, and Holubec 1991). Positive interdependence requires structuring the activity so that students are given incentives to work together and help each other.

The importance of positive interdependence can be seen in the following comparison made by Johnson, Johnson, and Holubec (1991, 4:9–4:10).

When positive interdependence has been carefully structured, you tend to observe students:

1. putting their heads together over their work.
2. talking about the work.
3. drilling each other on the material being learned.
4. sharing answers and materials.
5. encouraging each other to learn.

FIGURE 4–1 Cooperative learning groups vs. traditional learning groups

COOPERATIVE LEARNING GROUPS	TRADITIONAL LEARNING GROUPS
individual accountability	no individual accountability
heterogeneous members	homogeneous members
shared leadership	one appointed leader
responsible for each other	responsible only for self
process-oriented	product-oriented
social skills taught	social skills assumed
teacher plays active role	teacher plays no role
group processing occurs	no group processing
no free rides	slackers let others do work

When positive interdependence has not been structured, you tend to observe students:

1. leaving their groups impulsively.
2. talking about topics other than the work.
3. doing their own work while ignoring other students.
4. not sharing answers or materials.
5. not checking to see if others have learned the material.

Figure 4–1 summarizes the differences between cooperative learning groups and traditional learning groups.

Ensuring Individual Accountability and Positive Interdependence

Many of the structures for ensuring individual accountability overlap with those for ensuring positive interdependence. Therefore, examples for ensuring the two conditions for cooperative learning will be presented here as one consolidated list:

1. Identify a mastery level (e.g., 90 percent) that all group members must achieve before any of the group members' grades will be recorded.
2. Require all group members to improve their scores from the previous one (unless it was 100 percent) before any of the group members' grades will be recorded.
3. Add or average the scores of all group members to determine an overall group score.
4. Each group member must produce a separate product. Then, randomly select one to represent the group's grade.

5. The group members must reach consensus and produce a single group product. All group members must sign it and be prepared to explain or defend its contents if called upon to do so.

6. Each group member receives the same reward for successfully completing an assignment. Either everyone gets the bonus or no one gets it. For example, if all group members score 90 percent on a test, everyone gets a five-point bonus. If not all group members score 90 percent, no one gets the bonus.

7. Provide resources (e.g., books, pencils, answer sheets, reference materials, and so on) that are fewer in number than group members. As a result, students must share and depend on one another to complete the task.

8. "Jigsaw" a set of instructional materials (e.g., article, vocabulary list, poem, chapter, problems, questions, instructions) by dividing it into equal parts. Give each student one part. That student will then be responsible for completing his or her part and teaching it to the rest of the group.

9. Assign each group member a different part of a single writing assignment.

10. Assign each group member a different role in completing the task (e.g., reader, writer/recorder, materials leader, checker, conceptualizer, presenter, questioner, paraphraser, reviewer, and so forth).

Importance and Benefits of Cooperative Learning

According to Johnson, Johnson, and Holubec (1991), cooperative learning has a long tradition in U.S. education. For example, it was used extensively in one-room school houses. However, competitive and individualistic learning has dominated U.S. schools for the last fifty years, probably because they served well the factory-model paradigm of education.

In competitive learning environments, students are required to compete with each other for goals that only a few can realistically attain. The students who succeed, in essence, do so at the expense of those who do not. In competitive educational models, the cards are generally stacked in favor of the more capable students, since evaluation is done by comparing students to one another. The stronger students are always the winners because they always perform better than the less capable students. This philosophy is not consistent with the synergistic philosophy associated with Total Quality teaching and the new paradigm of educaton. Although some competitive learning activities can be used appropriately in the new paradigm (for example, norm-referenced testing in which students' abilities are assessed in relation to those of their peers), the dominant learning structures should be cooperative (Johnson, Johnson, and Holubec 1991).

In individualistic learning environments, students work alone to attain learning goals unrelated to those of the other students. Students each have their own sets of learning materials and work at their own pace, without interacting with the other students. Students are evaluated according to their own individual efforts and attainment of goals. Of course, some individualistic learning activities are appropriate in the new paradigm. For example, students can be evaluated on a criterion-referenced basis by comparing their performance with a predetermined mastery level, or they can measure their success in terms of progress toward a goal. Such forms of assessment are consistent with the Total Quality principle of continuous improvement, which characterizes the new paradigm. However, although some individualistic learning activities are appropriate, the dominant learning structure should be cooperative (Johnson, Johnson, and Holubec 1991). You recall from Chapter 1 the importance of synergy for enhancing productivity and success in our highly competitive global economy. The emphasis Total Quality principles place on synergy points to the need to accentuate cooperative rather than individualistic learning situations.

In cooperative learning situations, students work together toward shared goals. The individual group members seek outcomes that are not only beneficial to themselves but also to their fellow group members. Applying the principle of synergy, students work together to maximize their own and each other's learning. They perceive that they can reach their goals only if their groupmates also reach their goals. Cooperative learning structures are a dominant guiding force in the new paradigm. However, both competitive and individualistic structures also should be included as appropriate to help students learn how to compete for fun and to pursue personal learning interests independently (Johnson, Johnson, and Holubec 1991). The role of cooperative learning can be seen in Figure 4–2, which summarizes some of the major differences between the old and the new paradigms.

Extensive classroom research supports the many benefits of cooperative learning (Johnson and Johnson 1989). Some of those benefits, as identified by Johnson, Johnson, and Holubec (1991), include the following:

1. Achievement is higher when learning activities are structured cooperatively rather than competitively or individualistically.
2. Cooperative learning experiences promote more frequent higher-level reasoning, deeper-level understanding, and greater competencies in critical thinking.
3. Cooperative learning fosters more positive attitudes toward the subject matter under study, school, and learning in general.
4. Cooperative learning promotes more on-task and less disruptive behavior.

FIGURE 4–2 The role of cooperative learning in the old vs. new paradigm of education

OLD PARADIGM	NEW PARADIGM
knowledge transferred from teacher to students	knowledge jointly constructed
students are passive vessels	students are active learners
teacher is a fountain of knowledge	teacher is a guide, model, resource, consultant, and facilitator
competition and individual achievement are emphasized	cooperation and synergy are emphasized
only the teacher teaches	students teach each other
quiet, isolated learning environment	"organized chaos"
teachers mostly responsible for learning	students take more responsibility for learning

5. Motivation to achieve and intrinsic motivation to learn are enhanced by cooperative learning.
6. Cooperative learning encourages students to listen empathically (i.e., understanding, but not necessarily agreeing), thereby resulting in a greater ability to view situations from others' perspectives.
7. Cooperative learning improves students' abilities in working and solving problems collaboratively.
8. Students gain greater social support through cooperative learning.
9. Cooperative learning generates appreciation of peers with different learning styles, interests, backgrounds, ethnicities, genders, abilities, social classes, and disabilities.
10. Cooperative learning improves self-esteem based on self-acceptance.
11. Cooperative learning results in greater psychological health, adjustment, and well-being.
12. Cooperative learning leads to improved social skills and interpersonal relationships.

Another benefit of cooperative learning involves the opportunities it affords students to teach each other. It is common knowledge that we learn something best when we teach it to someone else: students gain in two ways when they help teach their group mates. First, verbalizing a concept by saying it aloud or writing it provides an excellent means of allowing students to assess their own learning. If they cannot adequately verbalize the information, they may not understand it quite as well as they thought they did. Second, verbalizing the concepts can make it easier to internalize and retain the information.

Opportunities for students to teach each other are also beneficial because students sometimes understand something better when it is explained by a peer rather than a teacher. After observing students in cooperative learning situations over a period of time, you would probably conclude that the following benefits could be added to the list: Students become more responsible, independent, and self-motivated learners. Students learn to value synergy (everyone putting their best talents together to make a better product). Students strengthen their independent reading, writing, research, and study skills. Students develop an awareness of and appreciation for their own and others' strengths. As you can see, the benefits of cooperative learning are extensive enough to warrant the time and hard work it takes to structure it properly.

Team Building and Social Skills Development

One of the key elements of synergy for successful cooperative learning is to value differences. If each member of a group brings the same resources (e.g., talents, knowledge, and experiences) to a project, the benefits of working together are minimal. However, if each group member has something different to contribute to the project, the resulting product will likely have more breadth, depth, and substance.

One of the most difficult team-building and social skills to develop is the ability to recognize and appreciate differences. Human nature seems to involve a tendency to be fearful and skeptical of people who are different from ourselves. These feelings are exacerbated by another human tendency, which is to prejudge or judge too soon. However, students *can* overcome their fears, skepticism, and prejudices through their own concerted efforts in regular opportunities for cooperation, along with guidance and encouragement from teachers.

In your experiences with cooperative learning groups (at all levels, including elementary school, middle school, high school, and college), you have probably encountered situations similar to the following example. After students are assigned to groups, some of the group members become uncomfortable immediately and are resentful about not being able to work with their friends. Discomfort and resentment are not surprising; since getting to know people is hard work, it is much easier to work with someone you already know.

Rarely in the real world of careers and community service, however, are we given the luxury of being assigned to work on a project with friends or acquaintances we know well. A crucial first step in team building and social skills development is to get to know the other team members and identify their strengths and the different resources they bring to the project. Getting to know group members may be an arduous and uncomfortable task, particularly if you are working with people who are reluctant to get acquainted.

Another common situation you may have encountered in cooperative learning projects (with students of all ages) involves prejudging classmates on the basis of inadequate information. For example, a student did not do her or his homework, and therefore came to class unprepared. On the basis of that incident, her or his groupmates might be prone to label this person a slacker and respond by ignoring the person and leaving the individual out of the group discussion. However, if group members instead show kindness and concern by probing to find out why the student did not do the homework, they might discover a legitimate reason why he or she came to class unprepared. A respectful and mature response would be to express concern and offer assistance to make sure the student does not fall behind, and to welcome her or him into the discussion, bringing her or him up to speed as necessary.

Another specific example of prejudging involves a group member's early performance on homework, quizzes, or tests. Poor performance does not necessarily indicate ignorance, laziness, or apathy. Instead of concluding that they are "stuck with a loser" for a groupmate, students might express compassion for her or his lack of success and offer assistance to help the individual master the content. Others might be surprised to find that someone who failed an early test for personal reasons or because of inadequate preparation can ace the next test with some coaching and encouragement.

When students show compassion for a group member with a problem, make sure they do not become enablers; that is, they should not cover up for a groupmate or do the work for her or him. If the problem persists, the entire group should talk about the unacceptability of the recurring problems. They can then brainstorm and discuss possible solutions, follow up to ensure that changes are made, and if necessary ask the teacher to mediate. Giving and receiving honest feedback are very important social skills that must be developed for successful cooperative learning.

Being patient and positive are other social skills that are key to the success of cooperative learning; students must earn their teammates' trust by responding positively to their mistakes and omissions. Since everyone makes mistakes, and mistakes are an important part of the learning experience, they should be turned into opportunities for learning. Within their groups, students can seek to establish a climate of trust and compassion, where it is okay to make an error or use poor judgment. Certainly problems that affect the group should not be ignored but addressed in a calm and understanding manner, discussing possible options for remedying the situation. Rather than exasperation or disgust, teach students to show kindness, understanding, and encouragement to groupmates. Getting angry and resentful only breaks down group trust and makes some people even more reluctant to open up and become part of the group. Again, these team-building and social skills can be difficult and arduous to develop, but they are crucial to students' success as members of the learning community. Living and working in a vacuum is simply not possible in today's world.

Social skills must be developed through direct instruction and carefully-planned activities. Teachers should give students numerous opportunities to develop awareness of their own and classmates' strengths in learning and literacy. Remind students continually to look for and appreciate different ways of learning in their classmates and groupmates. Give them time and guidance in getting to know each other. Students who are lacking in self-confidence, successful experiences, or motivation initially might seem to be ignorant, incapable, or apathetic. Encourage students to get to know each other well enough to discover the real reasons behind problem or difficult behavior. Actions and attitudes that at first glance might be interpreted as ignorance or apathy might turn out to be a matter of temporary personal problems or simply a lack of self-confidence.

Effective Cooperative Grouping

Several basic guidelines are important for effective cooperative grouping. Once again, variety is one of the keys to success. Cooperative groups should exist for diverse tasks and different lengths of time. Some cooperative groups should be formed to complete a task within a short time frame within a single class (for example, fifteen to forty-five minutes). Others should be structured to complete a task by working on it during class over a period of several days, while still others should be established to allow students to work together with the same people over a period of weeks. Students need long-term group experience to develop team-building skills.

Another important guideline for effective cooperative grouping involves the size of the group. The smaller the group the better: the optimal number is two or three, especially while students are still developing their cooperative learning skills (Johnson, Johnson, and Holubec 1991). However, for certain tasks, groups of five or six members can also be effective.

A third guideline for effective cooperative grouping involves the composition of the group—again, variety is important. Students should have some opportunities to work with others of similar abilities, interests, and needs: homogeneous grouping can be used occasionally. Generally speaking, however, cooperative grouping works best when the membership is heterogeneous. Mix high, medium, and low achievers, genders, cultural groups, and motivation levels for maximum effectiveness. Students generally should not be allowed to work with their friends, except under special circumstances when you can structure and monitor the group carefully (Johnson, Johnson, and Holubec 1991).

Another guideline for effective cooperative grouping involves room arrangement. Tables or desks should be arranged to allow the group members to face each other in close proximity (within one to two feet). Having students face each other and sit closely together are keys to successful cooperative grouping and should be required (Johnson, Johnson, and Holubec 1991).

A fifth principle for effective cooperative grouping is to help students develop social skills by giving them time and directions for processing the group's performance (Johnson, Johnson, and Holubec 1991). Students should be provided with checklists that identify effective social skills and team-building behaviors. They should then assess their own and each other's performances with respect to those behaviors, giving each other feedback in the form of praise and suggestions for improvement. Finally, members must identify specific changes they want to make to improve the group's effectiveness.

The remaining guideline for effective cooperative grouping involves planning and managing the groups. You need to plan group activities carefully and provide detailed instructions for them in writing. You should then inform the students of your expectations, both in terms of group behavior and task behavior. Next, you should monitor the groups closely, intervening appropriately to provide guidance, get the group on track, model task behaviors, give feedback, or make modifications in a group's composition or task.

Cooperative Learning and Group Composition for Gifted and Talented (GT) Students

The concept of "cooperative learning" is sometimes confused with the concept of "grouping." Consequently, some educators oppose the use of cooperative learning with GT students (see definition of GT students in section on curriculum compacting earlier in this chapter). They contend that when GT students work in groups, they should work only with others of similar exceptional ability, i.e., homogeneous groups. A common argument against heterogeneous grouping is that combining GT students with students of lesser abilities unfairly takes advantage of the GT students by expecting them to tutor their teammates and do most of the work. Another argument often made against heterogeneous grouping is that the students of lesser abilities "drag down" and "hold back" the gifted students.

Opponents of cooperative learning for GT students are actually expressing opposition to heterogeneous grouping. Heterogeneous grouping refers to the practice of assigning students of varying ability levels to cooperate. On the other hand, homogeneous grouping, sometimes known as ability grouping, refers to the practice of assigning students of similar ability levels to work together.

Cooperative learning refers to an instructional procedure, *not* to the composition of the group using it (Johnson and Johnson 1993). Cooperative learning often is implemented with homogeneous groups of students, including homogeneous groups of GT students. You recall from earlier in this chapter that cooperative learning is an instructional format that, among other things, establishes positive interdependence (i.e., incentives and appreciation for working as a team) and individual accountability (i.e., holding each group member responsible for contributing to the group product and mastering the content).

Therefore, cooperative learning can be used with homogeneous groups of GT students, as well as heterogeneous groups of students with mixed abilities, talents, and interests. When structured properly, cooperative learning distributes the workload equitably and holds *everyone* in the group accountable for learning. As a result, the structure provided by cooperative learning helps prevent the drawbacks often cited for GT students in heterogeneous grouping.

In response to opponents of heterogeneous grouping for GT students, Sapon-Shevin and Schniedewind (1993) make an excellent case for using cooperative learning with heterogeneous groups of students. Following is their summary of the benefits of cooperative learning for *all* students, including GT students:

- Teaches students to value differences
- Teaches students how to interact successfully with people from a variety of racial, ethnic, religious, and socioeconomic groups
- Teaches students how to interact successfully with people who have widely divergent skills
- Prepares students for a multicultural society in which they will live and work with people from a variety of backgrounds
- Gives students opportunities to learn to work with others they perceive as "uncooperative"
- Helps students develop social skills
- Helps students develop creative problem-solving strategies for working with others of varying abilities, interests, and levels of motivation

■ Offers opportunities for students to experience and value the personal satisfaction that comes from helping and supporting others in need

From their fifteen years of research, Johnson and Johnson (1992) also report conclusions about the benefits of using cooperative learning with GT, or what they refer to as "high ability" or "high achieving," students in heterogeneous groups:

■ Cooperative learning is a powerful motivating device for gifted students who are bored, disinterested, or unwilling to commit the effort necessary for living up to their potentials.

■ Mastery and retention of assigned content by high-ability students is higher in cooperative tasks than in competitive or individual learning activities.

■ Cooperative learning improves the critical thinking and higher-level reasoning of high-ability students.

■ High-ability students who work in heterogeneous cooperative learning groups use higher-level reasoning strategies more often than do those who work competitively or individually.

■ High-ability students benefit academically from working with low- and average-achieving peers, because the cognitive restructuring and practice that occurs when explaining material fosters greater understanding and retention of the material.

■ High-ability students' achievement is *not* likely to be higher when working only with intellectual peers, because there tend to be fewer teaching opportunities. (Studies have shown that learning for the purpose of teaching or explaining what one is learning, as opposed to learning it to pass a test, increases the level of cognitive understanding of the material.)

■ Although the *quantity* of learning for high-ability students working in heterogeneous learning groups may go down, their *quality* of learning is increased.

■ The positive effects of cooperative learning can be transferred to homogeneous groups of high-ability students by including students of different learning styles and strengths.

■ Cooperative learning leads to increased appreciation and acceptance of high-ability students by their low- and average-achieving classmates, because through cooperative learning, students have a stake in one another's success and benefit from one another's efforts and abilities.

■ Cooperative learning can reduce the stress, isolation, and loneliness GT students often experience by providing a supportive and caring network of friends.

Sapon-Shevin and Schniedewind (1993, 63) beautifully summarize the importance of cooperative learning to GT students: "Isn't a truly gifted person one who has multiple repertoires and can adapt, talk, and relate to a wide range of others?" Cooperative learning activities and projects, when structured properly, challenge students through their multilevel and multidisciplinary emphases. Cooperative learning activities and projects often call for the "gifts" of a variety of learners, encouraging appreciation for multiple forms of intelligence (Sapon-Shevin and Schniedewind 1993).

Some would argue, however, that many students, including many GT students, do not *like* to work as a team—they prefer instead to work independently. Therefore, they believe students not be *required* to participate in cooperative learning. Perhaps the best solution, not only for GT students but for all students who do not prefer to work cooperatively, is *variety*. Give them opportunities to work independently. At the same time, provide carefully structured and monitored cooperative learning activities. One likely reason many GT and other students have negative attitudes toward cooperative learning is that they associate it with negative experiences they have had with small-group work. Many of them have ended up doing all the work in poorly structured small-group activities. It is no wonder that they shy away from anything resembling "group work." Perhaps their attitudes would change if you could demonstrate to them how you will ensure that everyone contributes equitably and masters the content, as well as the potential rewards for working as a team.

To ensure a variety of cooperative learning experiences, GT students need opportunities to work with others of widely varying abilities. Following are a few examples of the different types of learners you might team with GT students for cooperative learning:

- Other GT students
- Students who have not been identified as GT, but who have exceptional knowledge or abilities in certain content areas or topics
- Students who have average or below-average abilities, but who have special interests in certain content areas or topics
- Students who have not been identified as GT, but who have special talents (e.g., social skills, communication skills, organization skills, artistic design, creative thinking, writing, and so on)

Ultimately, the decision to provide GT students opportunities to cooperate with a variety of learners is based on the values we hope to instill. If you agree that acceptance of diversity, helping others, and building community across differences are values we want to develop in our students, cooperative learning in heterogeneous settings is important for *all* students, including GT students (Sapon-Shevin and Schniedewind 1993).

To ensure the maximum benefits of cooperative learning for GT students, Johnson and Johnson (1993) identify the following elements that must be present:

1. The activity and student roles must be highly structured to include a high level of positive interdependence to promote each other's success.
2. The physical arrangement and task must be structured so that members interact face-to-face with clearly defined roles and procedures.
3. Students need to be taught directly the interpersonal, social, and small-group skills necessary to coordinate efforts successfully.
4. Students must be guided in a process of self-assessment in terms of how well they worked together and what they will do to improve the quality of their group efforts.

COOPERATIVE LEARNING STRATEGIES

Cooperative learning strategies are an excellent complement to content area literacy strategies. When used as part of literacy-based strategies, they can significantly enhance the effectiveness of content area learning. For example, a cooperative learning strategy could be used as part of a Directed Reading Activity by having students work together with specific roles and tasks related to meeting the purposes set for reading. Cooperative learning strategies can be used before, during, and after reading to bolster the efficacy of content area literacy strategies.

Cooperative Learning for English as a Second Language (ESL) Students

Small-group cooperative learning activities are especially important for ESL students, because they provide a low-stress, nonthreatening learning environment. At first, select a small number of students (three or four) to work frequently with each ESL student to allow her or him to develop comfortable and effective working relationships. When selecting learning partners, remember to give your ESL students opportunities to experience a variety of personalities and learning styles. The learning partners you select, however, should be at least average-achieving students who are patient, compassionate, and willing to help fellow students. As ESL students get accustomed to working with small groups of classmates, gradually increase the number of different learning partners until they have had the opportunity to work with most of the students in the class. Although the following cooperative learning strategies are especially recommended for use with ESL students, they are excellent strategies for meeting the needs of *all* learners.

Student Teams-Achievement Division (STAD)

One cooperative learning strategy recommended by Reyes and Molner (1991) for use with ESL students is called Student Teams-Achievement Division (Slavin 1983). This strategy is beneficial to ESL students primarily because they work with small groups of classmates to master content. Peer tutoring in cooperative learning situations can be more effective than whole-class lessons for ESL students, because they become more highly involved and motivated, get more practice learning the content, and have more one-on-one attention. Following are a set of procedures adapted from those recommended by Reyes and Molner (1991):

1. Form heterogeneous teams of students, with no more than four or five students per team. Make sure that team composition reflects varying abilities, ethnicity, English proficiency, and gender.
2. Introduce the topic and give a whole-class presentation on it. Provide students with information sheets and/or reading assignments that summarize and reinforce the lesson.
3. Students work in teams to study and learn the material. They use peer tutoring, drill, and oral quizzes to master the information. Give individual quizzes on the material.
4. Design a system in which individuals earn points for their teams in two scoring categories. First, compare individual scores with previous scores. For example, students earn points for their teams according to the degree of improvement shown. Second, points are earned by comparing individual scores with other individuals of similar ability. For example, of the average-achieving students, the individual with the highest quiz score earns a certain number of points for his or her team.
5. Recognize and reward team performance.

Jigsaw

Another cooperative learning strategy recommended by Reyes and Molner (1991) for use with ESL students is the Jigsaw. This strategy is based on the notion that we learn best what we teach, and that sometimes, students learn best by teaching each other. Following is a set of procedures for the Jigsaw strategy.

1. Establish heterogeneous base groups of no more than five students each. Conduct team-building activities to help the group members get acquainted, learn to communicate effectively, and develop strategies for collaboration.
2. Divide the information to be learned into the same number of segments as group members. Assign each group member one of the information segments. For example, in a lesson on the geography of

Texas, divide the information into five segments: (1) West Texas mountains, (2) North Texas plains, (3) Central Texas hill country, (4) East Texas pine forests, and (5) South Texas coastline and river valley.

3. Students temporarily leave their base groups and join "expert" groups. These expert groups are comprised of the students from the other groups assigned the same segments of information. For example, all the students assigned to (1) West Texas mountains work together, all the students assigned to (2) North Texas plains work together, and so on. Each student is provided resources and information for her or his assigned segment or topic.

4. In their expert groups, students work together to pool resources and identify the concepts and supporting details they will share with their base groups. They then develop a presentation designed to teach that content to their base groups. Experts should be encouraged to develop visual aids and models to use when presenting the information to their base groups. In these expert groups, classmates can provide extra assistance to the ESL students in preparing to teach the information.

5. Students return to their base groups and take turns giving the presentations they developed in their expert groups. Each expert becomes a teacher of her or his content. Students' incentive for listening to each other is the quiz they will each take individually over *all* the material.

Finding Out/Descubrimiento

The third cooperative learning strategy recommended for ESL students by Reyes and Molner (1991) is called Finding Out/Descubrimiento, which they report was originally an English/Spanish cooperative inquiry-based science program. Following is a set of procedures adapted from their description of that program. This strategy is especially useful for helping ESL students become familiar with technical terms and instructional language.

1. From a content area topic, identify weekly themes that will connect the week's activities to the topic.

2. Design learning centers with hands-on activities and assignments that promote higher-order thinking (e.g., analyzing, comparing, contrasting, hypothesizing, predicting, asking questions, drawing conclusions, and so forth). Develop activity cards that provide instructions in both (or more) languages.

3. Assign students to groups that are heterogeneous in terms of language proficiency. Assign each student a different role and task

(e.g., recorder, reader, facilitator, checker, materials leader, clean-up worker).

4. Students move in groups from one learning center to the next, working cooperatively to complete the activities. Assess students individually both in terms of their role assignment and content mastery.

More Cooperative Learning Strategies

The cooperative learning strategies described in the previous section as recommendations for ESL students, Student Team-Achievement Division (STAD) and Jigsaw (Slavin 1983) are also excellent strategies for meeting the needs of all students through cooperative grouping. Following are some additional cooperative learning strategies. All of these tactics could be used as part of content area literacy strategies.

Jigsaw II

Another excellent cooperative learning strategy is Jigsaw II (Slavin 1983). This strategy is used most appropriately with narrative materials, usually in social studies, literature, and sometimes science. Students working in heterogeneous teams are given a reading assignment along with an expert sheet that assigns different topics on which each group member will focus while reading. After reading, students from different teams having the same topics meet together in an expert group to discuss their topic for about thirty minutes. The experts then return to their original groups and take turns teaching their teammates about their topics. Finally, each student takes a quiz that covers *all* of the topics, and the quiz scores become team scores, as in STAD.

Teams-Games-Tournaments

Still another excellent cooperative learning strategy is called Teams-Games-Tournaments (TGT). For a detailed description of preparing, implementing, and scoring TGT, see Slavin (1983). In this activity, the teacher first introduces the content in a class presentation. The teams, composed of four or five students, are heterogeneously grouped. The goal of the team is to prepare its members to do well on the quiz games covering material presented in class by the teacher. To this end, the team works together to study worksheets and share notes. Typically, preparation takes the form of students quizzing each other to make sure they understand the content. Students also can work together to solve problems (e.g., math) or to correct any of their teammates' misconceptions.

The team concept is emphasized. Students are continually reminded that they are to do their best for their team, and that the team is to do its best for its members. This concept emphasizes peer support for academic performance, as well as the mutual concern and respect that are so important for intergroup relations, self-esteem, and acceptance of special needs learners.

Once team members are prepared, the games are played in the structure of a tournament. The games are composed of simple questions designed to test the knowledge gained from the class presentation and team preparation. Games are played in groups of team representatives. To play, students take turns picking number cards and answering the corresponding questions from the question list.

To equitably match team representatives, you first need to rank the students within each team, based on past performance or performance in team practice. Then, when you set up the tournament, the top students from each group compete with each other, the students ranking second compete with each other, and so on. Keep record of the results of the tournament to help you rank students for the next tournament.

Use some sort of recognition to reward winning teams after each tournament; you also want to recognize teams for improving their scores. Team scores can be calculated in a variety of ways. For example, you could simply add the total points earned by each team member or assign a certain number of team points to the top scorer in each group, second highest scorer, and so forth.

Think-Pair-Share

In this cooperative learning strategy, students are presented with a question to be answered or a problem to be solved. First, they are instructed to **think** about how they might answer the question or solve the problem. After about thirty to sixty seconds, students are instructed to **pair** up with another student to discuss their thoughts and come to consensus about possible answers or solutions. After one to two minutes, each pair is instructed to form a quad with another pair to **share** their ideas and reach agreement. Finally, each quad reports back to the whole class for a discussion of possible answers or solutions. The teacher leads the discussion and helps the class come to consensus.

Group Retellings

Wood (1992) describes a cooperative learning strategy she calls *Group Retellings*, which can be used either with heterogeneous or homogeneous groups, depending on your instructional objectives and the students' needs. In this strategy, students work in pairs or small groups: each group member is given a different passage, chapter, section, article, or other piece of material related to the topic of the lesson. Students are instructed to read silently for the purpose of preparing to retell the information in summary form to their group members. During the retellings, other students may add to the accounts with similar information from their reading or experiences.

Cybernetic Sessions

Another strategy Wood (1992) describes is called "cybernetic sessions" and was originally developed by Nancy Masztal (1986). In this strategy, specific questions designed to elicit a variety of responses are written on chart paper or poster board and placed on the walls around the classroom. Use the same number of questions as groups, so that each group will be assigned to one of the questions. Chairs are placed around each question for the group assigned to that question.

One of the group members is designated the recorder and writes the group's responses directly on the chart paper or poster board under the question. At the end of a predetermined amount of time (about three to five minutes), groups are directed to rotate to the next question, and the role of recorder is rotated to another group member. This process continues until each group has responded to all the questions and has rotated back to its original question. At their "home" question, the group clarifies and consolidates all the responses. Finally, one member from each group presents to the whole class the synthesized responses for their question.

Structured Academic Controversies

A cooperative learning strategy called Structured Academic Controversies is described by Johnson, Johnson, and Smith (1991). In preparing for this strategy, you must first select one or more relevant controversies or issues for which there are clearly two sides (e.g., pro and con). Then, assign students to groups of four and divide each group into two pairs. The groups and pairs may be homogeneous or heterogeneous, depending on the needs of the students and your instructional goals. Assign each group one of the controversies or issues you have selected.

Assign one pair in each group a different side (i.e., pro or con) of the controversy or issue. Each pair then works together to learn the information supporting their assigned position for the purpose of preparing a presentation and series of persuasive arguments. You can provide students all the information they need for their presentations or require them to do some library research as part of their preparation. Students should be instructed to share with the other pair in their group any information they find on the opposing position while doing research.

When the pairs are ready, they present their positions and persuasive arguments to each other in their small groups of four. At this point, students should be told to listen to each other, taking notes to help understand and learn the opposing positions. Once both positions have been presented, students discuss the issue by probing, evaluating, and challenging each other's positions. They should ask for supporting data and clarification, as well as defend their own positions. Finally, students discuss the strengths and weaknesses of each position. If necessary, pairs should be allowed, at this point, to meet privately to regroup, uncover more facts, address challenges, and prepare new arguments.

The teacher's role is to encourage logical reasoning and argumentation, point out fallacies, take sides in support of pairs in trouble, play devil's advocate, and stimulate discussion. Once the pairs have exhausted their arguments, thoroughly understand each other's positions, and analyzed both arguments, have them switch positions. Now they become advocates for the opposing arguments, presenting those positions as sincerely and convincingly as possible. They should also add any new facts, information, or perspectives not mentioned by the other pair.

Once both pairs have had a chance to argue and discuss both positions, they should come to a consensus. As a group, they write a report that presents their conclusion, along with supporting evidence and rationales. This final position can be a third alternative derived or synthesized from the two original positions. All group members must agree with the contents of the report, be able to explain its content, and be prepared to be evaluated on all the positions examined in the controversy.

Give each group a test on its controversy. If all members of the group reach a predetermined mastery level, each member earns five bonus points. Have the group members discuss how well they functioned as a group and how they might do a better job working together next time. You should highlight specific conflict-management skills students have mastered or still need to master.

INDIVIDUALIZING INSTRUCTION THROUGH COOPERATIVE GROUPING

Meeting the special needs of your students can, at times, seem overwhelming. How can you select materials and adapt instruction for all your special needs learners, while also planning and implementing your regular curriculum for the rest of the students? Writing a lesson plan for each student to meet her or his individual needs is obviously not a very efficient solution. One practical and effective way of individualizing your instruction is by grouping students in various ways for cooperative learning. For example, you can put students with similar needs and interests together to work on the same tasks using the same set of materials.

The key to successful grouping is variety. Some groups should be formed for one activity or one class period only. Some groups should be formed for a short-term project lasting between one and two weeks. Some groups should be formed for long-term projects lasting an entire six-week period or longer. Each student needs to have the opportunity to work with many different classmates for a wide range of tasks and learning objectives. On any given day, a student might be a part of several different groups working on different activities and projects.

Another important factor in successful grouping involves following the principles of cooperative learning. You need to structure group activities carefully to ensure that the work is equitably distributed, every student is held accountable for learning the content (individual accountability), students are given incentives to help each other (positive interdependence), and the groups remain small (three to five members). You also must monitor the groups closely and give them regular opportunities to reflect on how well they work together and discuss ways they could improve (group processing).

Students can be grouped together in a multitude of ways. Karen Wood (1992) provides an excellent summary of some of the best grouping techniques for content area classrooms. The techniques she summarizes are described briefly in Appendix F. You will see that the possible variations are almost endless—with so many options, you should have no trouble maintaining variety in your grouping techniques. You will also notice that the numerous possibilities for grouping provide excellent opportunities for individualizing your instruction to meet the special needs of all your students.

SUMMARY

The Directed Reading Activity (DRA) and the Directed Reading-Thinking Activity (DR-TA) provide general frameworks for planning content area lessons. These frameworks emphasize reading as a medium of instruction and literacy as a tool for learning. The DRA and DR-TA have great flexibility and are applicable in a wide variety of content areas. The components of the DRA—preparation, directed silent reading, and follow-up—are based on the assumption that comprehension can be increased by building background knowledge, setting specific purposes for reading, and discussing and extending understanding after reading. The DR-TA, which helps students learn to make predictions as purposes for reading, leads students through a cycle of making predictions, reading to verify predictions, evaluating comprehension with respect to the predictions, and making new predictions.

Setting purposes involves both the general reasons for reading, as well as the specific information that should be gleaned from the assignment. Specific purposes generally should be written down and can be presented in a variety of formats. It is important to communicate to students that focusing on specific purposes will help them concentrate so they are better able to discover other information not necessarily related to the purposes. Although they do so in different ways, all content area literacy strategies set purposes.

A variety of instructional frameworks and strategies should be used in content area teaching for a number of reasons. Probably the most important reason for emphasizing variety in planning instruction is that it helps generate and maintain interest in and enthusiasm for learning. Both students and teachers need diversity to enhance motivation. Variety in lesson planning is also important for meeting the different needs of the students. The demands of the reading materials also must be taken into account when planning instruction. In addition to considering individual differences in students and textual materials, teachers must also consider their own individual teaching styles, as well as constraints in time and space.

A thematic unit is a set of lesson plans all related to a selected topic. The length of the unit can vary from one week to as many as six weeks, depending on the grade level and specificity of the topic. Just as the Instructional Framework provides a structure for planning within the context of a single lesson, the thematic unit provides a structure for organizing instruction around a set of lessons using a variety of activities, reading materials, and strategies. The thematic unit allows more options for coordinating a variety of information sources, and the lessons and activities are connected to give the students a sense of continuity.

Thematic units are particularly important for content area literacy because they allow the teacher to integrate literacy instruction with content instruction. Specifically, they provide a structure that encourages the teacher to consider the demands of the materials and identify the literacy tools necessary for successful learning of the content. Thematic units also help the teacher select strategies and activities that are appropriate for developing those literacy skills and guiding students in meeting the demands of the content materials. The thematic unit is significant to content area instruction, because it can provide a welcome change for both students and teachers from continuous single-text instruction. In fact, one of the most important features of the thematic unit is the integration of a wide variety of materials.

Cooperative learning when used as part of or in conjunction with content area literacy strategies is an important tool for effectively meeting the special needs of all learners. Many teachers, and students as well, hear the term *cooperative learning* and conclude that it is just a fancy new term for the typical group work or small-group projects most of us have experienced—often with negative outcomes—at one time or another.

Cooperative learning is a completely different concept and was specifically designed to avoid the pitfalls of traditional learning groups. The concept of cooperative learning differs from these other forms of group work in many ways. One of the most important differences involves individual accountability, meaning that activities are structured so that each student is held accountable for mastering the content and doing his or her fair share of the work. Another important way in which cooperative learning differs from other forms of group work involves positive interdependence: activities are structured so that students perceive that they are linked with others in such a way that they cannot succeed unless their teammates do (and vice versa), and that their work benefits others and the others' work benefits them.

Extensive classroom research supports the many benefits of cooperative learning, including the following: Achievement is higher. More frequent higher-level reasoning, deeper-level understanding, and greater competencies in critical thinking are promoted. More positive attitudes are fostered toward the subject matter under study, learning in general, and school. More on-task and less disruptive behavior is promoted. Motivation to achieve and intrinsic motivation to learn are enhanced. Cooperative learning encourages students to view situations from alternate perspectives. It improves students' abilities in working and solving problems collaboratively. Students gain greater social support. Cooperative learning generates appreciation of peers with different learning styles, interests, backgrounds, ethnicities, genders, abilities, social classes, and disabilities. Cooperative learning improves self-esteem and psychological health, adjustment, and well-being. Cooperative learning leads to improved social skills and interpersonal relationships.

ENRICHMENT ACTIVITIES

1. Borrow a teacher's edition of a content area textbook. Then, evaluate one of the lessons according to the lesson plan guidelines and components discussed in Appendix C. Write a critical analysis of the lesson plan recommended by the teacher's edition.
2. Select a chapter section from a content area textbook and write a lesson plan for teaching it, following the format of the Instructional Framework.
3. Choose a topic for a thematic unit. Define the scope of the topic by listing the three to five major concepts that will be covered. Write a one-paragraph rationale for teaching that information. Develop a bibliography of children and adolescent literature related to the topic; at a minimum, your bibliography should include ten books, including both fiction and nonfiction.

4. Design a cooperative learning activity that ensures individual accountability and positive interdependence. Describe through specific examples how you will hold all group members accountable for mastering the content and doing their fair share of the work, and how you will provide them incentives to work together and help each other.

5. Observe two or more classrooms and write brief descriptions about the classroom management systems used. Compare them to the recommendations offered in Appendix E. Create a list of ways you would alter the systems you observed for use in your own classroom.

REFERENCES

Betts, E. A. (1946). *Foundations of reading instruction*. New York: American Book.

Brozo, W. G., and C. M. Tomlinson. (1986). Literature: The key to lively content courses. *The Reading Teacher* 40, 288–293.

Charles, C. M. (1992). *Building classroom discipline*, 4th ed. White Plains, NY: Longman.

Fader, D. (1976). *The new hooked on books*. New York: Berkley Publishing.

Herber, H. L. (1978). *Teaching reading in content areas*, 2d ed. Englewood Cliffs, NJ: Prentice Hall.

Johnson, D. W., and R. T. Johnson. (1989). *Cooperation and competition: Theory and research*. Edina, MN: Interaction Book Company.

———. (1992). What to say to advocates for the gifted. *Educational Leadership* 50, 44–47.

———. (1993). Gifted students illustrate what isn't cooperative learning. *Educational Leadership* 50, 60–61.

Johnson, D. W., R. T. Johnson, and E. Holubec. (1991). *Cooperation in the classroom*. Edina, MN: Interaction Book Company.

Johnson, D. W., R. T. Johnson, and K. A. Smith. (1991). *Active learning: Cooperation in the college classroom*. Edina, MN: Interaction Book Company.

Larson, C. O., and D. F. Dansereau. (1986). Cooperative learning in dyads. *Journal of Reading* 29, 516–520.

Manzo, A. V., and U. C. Manzo. (1990). *Content area reading: A heuristic approach*. Columbus, OH: Merrill.

Masztal, N. B. (1986). Cybernetic sessions: A high involvement teaching technique. *Reading Research and Instruction* 25, 131–138.

McKenna, M. C., and R. D. Robinson. (1993). *Teaching through text: A content literacy approach to content area reading*. White Plains, NY: Longman.

Peterson, P. L. (1978). Teacher planning, teacher behavior and student achievement. *American Educational Research Journal* 15, 417–432.

Reis, S. M., and J. S. Renzulli. (1992). Using curriculum compacting to challenge the above-average. *Educational Leadership* 50, 51–57.

Reyes, M., and L. A. Molner. (1991). Instructional strategies for second-language learners in the content areas. *Journal of Reading* 35, 96–103.

Sapon-Shevin, M., and N. Schniedewind. (1993). Why (even) gifted children need cooperative learning. *Educational Leadership* 50, 62–63.

Slavin, R. E. (1983). *Student team learning: A practical guide to cooperative learning*, 3d ed. Washington, DC: National Education Association.

Stauffer, R. G. (1969). *Directing reading maturity as a cognitive process.* New York: Harper and Row.

———. (1976). *Teaching reading as a thinking process.* New York: Harper and Row.

Tuttle, F. B., L. A. Becker, and J. A. Sousa. (1988). *Characteristics and identification of gifted and talented students*, 3d ed. Washington, DC: National Education Association.

Vacca, R. T., and J. L. Vacca. (1993). *Content area reading*, 4th ed. New York: HarperCollins.

Wood, K. D. (1992). Fostering cooperative learning in middle and secondary level classrooms. In *Reading in the content areas: Improving classroom instruction.* Edited by E. K. Dishner, T. W. Bean, J. E. Readence, and D. W. Moore. Dubuque, IA: Kendall/Hunt Publishing Company.

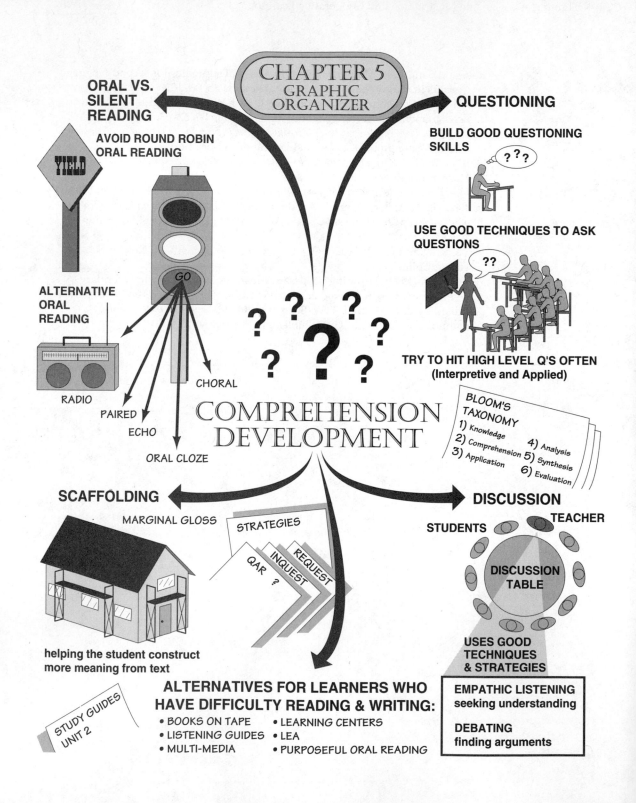

CHAPTER 5

Comprehension Development for Content Area Learning and Literacy

To demonstrate mastery of the content, the student will be able to do the following:

PART 1 OBJECTIVES

1. Identify the following strategy, describe its distinguishing features, and assess its significance to teaching content area literacy: ReQuest/InQuest.
2. Describe and assess the importance of effective teacher and student questioning techniques in content area comprehension and learning.
3. Distinguish discussion from recitation (turn-taking), addressing the appropriate uses of each.
4. Identify ways to avoid the overuse of recitation and describe effective discussion techniques.
5. Describe the phenomenon of gender bias in teacher-student classroom interactions and identify ways to promote gender equity.

PART 2 OBJECTIVES

1. Identify the following strategy, describe its distinguishing features, and assess its significance to teaching content area literacy: QAR.
2. Distinguish deductive and inductive approaches to teaching.
3. Explain the concept of "scaffolding reading comprehension."
4. Briefly describe three types of study guides designed to provide scaffolding.
5. Describe at least one type of scaffolding that is especially appropriate for ESL students.
6. Distinguish round-robin oral reading from purposeful oral reading.

PART 1 OBJECTIVES—continued

6. Distinguish empathic listening from debating skills, describing the role of each in the development of critical thinking.
7. Assess the role of thinking and comprehension taxonomies for effective teacher and student questioning.
8. Compare and contrast Bloom's taxonomy of thinking, Barrett's taxonomy of reading comprehension, and Herber's taxonomy of reading comprehension.
9. Define and provide a sample question (designed to check comprehension of Chapter 5, Part 1) for each of the three levels of comprehension in Herber's taxonomy: literal, interpretive, and applied.

PART 2 OBJECTIVES—continued

7. Summarize the disadvantages of round-robin oral reading by designing an argument against using it as an instructional strategy for content area classrooms.
8. Briefly describe the distinguishing features of three effective oral reading strategies.
9. Describe five alternate ways to teach content to learners who have difficulty reading and writing.

INTRODUCTION

The literacy-based study and instructional strategies you have learned in previous chapters are designed to develop students' comprehension of content area materials by helping them relate new information to what they already know about the topic. They help both students and teachers focus on the information by setting specific purposes for reading. Literacy-based strategies assist students to monitor and assess their comprehension during and after reading, guiding them in rereading when purposes have not been met. When teachers apply literacy-based strategies for content area instruction and teach students how to apply the literacy-based study strategies independently, they are developing and enhancing students' comprehension of the content.

Without becoming reading specialists or reading teachers, what else can content area teachers do to support their students' comprehension development? First, effective questioning techniques play a crucial role in the development of comprehension, especially at critical levels of thought. This chapter will distinguish questioning that *evaluates* comprehension from questioning that *develops* comprehension. It will then address ways teachers can use questioning techniques to enhance comprehension through active student involvement and critical thinking.

This chapter also will look at ways to increase students' metacognitive awareness by teaching them how to formulate good self-directed questions before, during, and after reading. Asking themselves questions is crucial to students actively engaging the text, making predictions, monitoring and assessing comprehension, fulfilling purposes for reading, and processing content at higher levels of thought. You will be introduced to two new instructional strategies, both of which are designed to help develop students' self-questioning abilities as part of metacognition.

The crucial difference between two types of classroom interactions that affect comprehension development—recitation (turn-taking) and discussion—will be addressed. Each of these types of verbalization has a unique role in content area instruction; discussion is essential for developing comprehension at critical levels of thought. You will learn some valuable discussion techniques that enhance content area learning while developing students' critical thinking abilities.

Additionally, this chapter introduces listening as both a discussion and comprehension skill. Two types of listening/comprehension skills crucial for the development of critical thinking are distinguished: empathic and debate. Empathic listening involves listening for the purpose of complete understanding through a process of sharing the speaker or author's experience. Debate listening involves listening for the purpose of responding to an author's message as it relates to a predetermined question, issue, or position. Both types of listening skills are important in comprehension development at the highest levels of thinking.

To develop comprehension at *all* levels of thought, teachers must understand the thinking processes involved at the various levels. This chapter will introduce you to several taxonomies of thinking and comprehension, and you will learn ways to use them in planning and implementing instruction. Using taxonomies can help the content area teacher develop students' comprehension at all levels, from literal to critical.

Guiding students' comprehension both with and without questions is another important tactic described in this chapter. Content area teachers can enhance comprehension by providing students with a variety of reading guides developed especially for specific reading assignments. Several types of reading guides will be presented for scaffolding or supporting students for successful text interaction. Reading guides allow the teacher to guide students through a difficult assignment without having to be present. They can be quite useful for providing support for homework assignments or allowing teachers the freedom to work with several groups in class at once.

Finally, this chapter will address the varying effects of oral and silent reading on comprehension development. Generally speaking, comprehension is better during silent reading; however, some oral reading strategies can also be effective for comprehension development. Round-robin oral reading (i.e., taking turns reading aloud with no purpose toward comprehension) is *not* one of them.

PART 1

STRATEGY: RECIPROCAL QUESTIONING (REQUEST)

One of the characteristics of good readers is that they ask themselves questions as they read. Self-questioning characterizes active and purposeful reading; it also indicates that the reader is metacognitively aware. The ReQuest Procedure was designed by Manzo (1969) for the following purposes: (1) to encourage students to formulate their own questions about the material; (2) to develop students' questioning behaviors; (3) to encourage students to adopt an inquiring attitude to reading; (4) to help students acquire reasonable purposes for reading; and (5) to improve students' independent reading comprehension skills. Following is an adaptation of Manzo's original strategy designed more specifically for use in content area instruction.

Preparing to Read

The passage is divided into segments by the teacher, depending on the age and abilities of the students, as well as the difficulty of the material. For example, for primary-grade (1–3) children, each section might consist of only one sentence. For intermediate-grade (4–6) children, each assignment might consist of a paragraph. For middle and high school students, the section might consist of a page or chapter section.

The teacher introduces the strategy by telling students that the purpose of the lesson is to help them understand what they read by asking themselves good questions. The teacher then tells the students that they will take turns asking and answering questions with the teacher. The teacher establishes the purpose for reading by telling students to formulate questions as they read. Students should be instructed to make up the kinds of *good* questions a teacher might ask for the purpose of finding out how well the students understood what they read.

Although the primary purpose of ReQuest is comprehension development, the questions students formulate can give the teacher feedback in terms of how well the content was understood by the students. The extent of understanding is often clear from the quality of the questions formulated. A question that could have been formulated from a subheading does not assure the teacher that the content was understood adequately. Of course, it does not necessarily mean that the content was not understood; it simply means that the question is inadequate for assessing comprehension. On the other hand, a question that could have been formulated only from a careful reading and thorough understanding of the content assures the teacher that the content has been adequately comprehended. Consequently, paying close attention to the questions your students formulate can give you important information for assessing the comprehension strengths and needs of your students.

The Value of "Stumping the Teacher"

This strategy can be highly motivating when presented to the students as an opportunity to "stump the teacher." For some teachers, the idea of not being able to answer a student's question might be uncomfortable or even intimidating. For this reason, teachers might avoid this strategy; however, being unable to answer a question provides an excellent opportunity to establish a classroom climate for risk-taking and a safe place to make mistakes.

When you model for students your willingness to be honest about not knowing an answer and guessing when you are unsure, you assure them that making mistakes is an important part of the learning process. You can show students ways to learn from their mistakes by referring to the passage and self-correcting. Through this process of guessing, making mistakes, and self-correcting, you are maximizing use of your role as master learner. Students can see that the characteristics of a master learner include the willingness to risk being wrong and knowledge of self-corrective strategies.

Another benefit of ReQuest is its emphasis on the changing role of the teacher from "fountain of knowledge" to "facilitator of knowledge." When you readily admit that you are not all-knowing and all-seeing, you are in an excellent position to demonstrate strategies for lifelong learning. One of the most important lifelong learning skills is knowing how to find answers to your questions; even more important than remembering specific pieces of information is knowing where to find them. ReQuest is not only a valuable strategy for teaching students how to formulate their own questions, it is also important in teaching them how to find answers to their questions.

Reading Silently and Formulating Questions

After the strategy and passage have been introduced, the teacher tells the students to read the first section (sentence, paragraph, page, or chapter section) for the purpose of formulating one or more questions that a teacher might ask students to find out how well they understood the material. Students should write down their questions to make it easier for the teacher to monitor their progress while they work. In addition, they should be asked to write down the number(s) of the page(s) where the answer or hints toward the answer can be found. Students also can be encouraged to write down questions about any part(s) of the passage they have difficulty understanding.

When students are first introduced to this strategy, no matter what their age or grade level, they may have some difficulty formulating questions. Until students develop confidence with this challenging task, allowing them to work with one or two other students to form questions can make the activity more enjoyable and productive. Also, while in the early learning stages of formulating questions, encourage students to focus predominantly on literal-level questions. Once they have mastered the art of formulating literal-level questions, begin modeling and instructing students in questioning at higher levels. Later in this chapter, you will learn the Question-Answer Relationships strategy, which is designed to teach students how to distinguish and formulate questions at different levels of thought.

As your students are reading and formulating questions, carefully monitor their progress. For students who might be having trouble initiating questions, model some good options by giving them two or three questions and having them choose one to write down. They then have a good written example to follow. When most students have at least one question written, stop them and begin the reciprocal questioning process.

The Reciprocal Questioning Process

Call on a student to read you a question. At first, until students develop some confidence with questioning, accept and praise every effort. Insist that all students show respect for one another by not judging negatively or laughing at each other's questions. Students will become reluctant to participate if their questions are met with displeased looks, disparaging comments, or snickering. If a question is so poor as to be virtually unanswerable, help the student change the wording slightly to make the question acceptable.

As you think about the question and try to recall the answer without looking back in the book, ask the class to do the same. Tell them that if you cannot answer the question, you will need their help; tell them to start looking for clues in the book. Before you respond to the question, model your thinking processes by thinking aloud. For example, you might say "Oh yes, I remember reading something about that. Let's see, I remember the book said this or that, and I believe the answer to your question is

_____." Ask the student if he or she agrees with your answer. If so, show the class the supportive information in the book; if not, ask the student to give you the page number(s), so that you can locate the answer. Again, model your thinking process as you refer to the appropriate page(s) and find the answer. Model healthy reactions to getting the answer wrong— do not berate yourself or make an issue of it. Instead, smile and say "Well, I was close," or "I just didn't remember that part very well, but I found the answer!"

After you answer or locate the answer to the student's question, it is your turn to pose a question. However, rather than addressing it only to the student who asked you a question, pose it to the entire class. Ask everyone to think of or locate the answer. When you pose a question to the entire class rather than to only one student, you significantly increase the utility of the question. It forces everyone to think and actively engage in the interchange; otherwise, everyone but the student who was called on can tune out and miss the opportunity to review the information and the process for rereading to locate the answer.

Continue by calling on another student to read a question. Repeat the process until the important points of the section have been addressed. Then go on to the next section, reminding students that their purpose for reading is to formulate and write down questions a teacher might ask. After reading, repeat the reciprocal questioning process. Once students develop skill and confidence with asking and answering their own questions, you might vary the ReQuest Procedure by having them pose their questions to fellow students instead of to the teacher.

Investigative Questioning (InQuest)

This procedure was developed by Shoop (1986) as a tool for self-questioning in a context that enhances critical thinking. As in ReQuest, students formulate their own questions, but instead of posing them to the teacher, they question each other in a role-playing activity that simulates an interview. Students are asked to read for the purpose of selecting a character (if the content area is literature or if historical fiction is being used in another content area) or person who is a focus of the assignment and write questions that might be asked in an interview. Students should be instructed to formulate only questions that can be answered or inferred by reading the passage.

At first, the teacher may want to model the procedure by assuming one of the roles in the role-playing situation. Later, the students should assume both roles in the "news conference" situation: investigative reporter and character or famous person being interviewed. Once students can successfully role-play by asking and answering questions based on the reading assignment, the project might be extended. For example, a good enrichment activity might be to have paired students research assigned characters or people and develop a skit using the information found in their research.

DEVELOPING COMPREHENSION THROUGH QUESTIONING

Teacher questioning plays a crucial role in comprehension development. The types of questions and the ways in which they are posed are critical to developing students' abilities to process information at various levels of thought. Since all content area teachers use questions, knowing how to use them effectively is an important way to develop content area literacy.

Assessing vs. Developing Comprehension

Teachers often plan to develop comprehension abilities by asking students questions after they read. However, too often these questions are convergent (i.e., having specific, predetermined answers) and do nothing more than tell you how well the students can read your mind. Obviously, these types of questions do little to develop students' comprehension and often do not even assess comprehension effectively.

If a student gets an answer right, the teacher might say "Good" or "Okay" and move on the next question. If the student does not guess the "right" answer, the teacher might say "No, can someone help her or him out?" or "Good guess, but that's not it." When questioning turns into a drill session with the teacher firing convergent questions and the students trying to guess which specific answer the teacher wants, the questions become more a test of the students' literal-level recall than a way to develop their comprehension and deeper critical thinking skills.

When drill dominates the questioning sessions, teachers rarely take the time to probe, examine, and model the thinking processes involved in answering the questions, nor do they discuss and explain the answers. When teachers expect students to know specific answers but do not model for them or guide them through the thinking processes for deriving those answers, the message being given to students is that it is more important to be able to recall and recite the information than to genuinely understand it. Furthermore, when question-and-answer sessions become drill sessions, teachers cannot tell if a student misses an answer because the student did not understand the question, had trouble constructing a response, or did not understand the material.

On the other hand, when teachers take the time to ask follow-up questions that allow students to extend, explain, or defend their answers, the questioning session becomes a tool for comprehension development. Not only do the students who are responding benefit from an in-depth interchange, but the others also benefit from hearing how the student arrived at that particular response. When students and teachers explain the thought processes they go through to arrive at an answer, they are modeling good comprehension for the listeners.

Good questioning techniques can be extremely effective in developing comprehension. Good questions and their appropriate use can not only help students understand content on a basic level but can also guide them in elaborative and critical thinking about that content. Effective questioning transforms students from information seekers to information users; they not only ask "What do I already know about this topic and what else do I need to learn?" but also "What is the significance of this information, how is it meaningful to me, and how can I apply it?" (Vacca and Vacca 1993). The difference between these questions reflects the difference between literal-level thinking and critical and analytical reasoning. Thus, questioning techniques can develop not only comprehension but comprehension at the highest levels.

If properly used, questions can be tools for comprehension development, but they can also become weapons against students. Students are put on the spot when they are caught daydreaming, thinking about something else for just an instant, or simply not reading the teacher's mind; when they are put in this position students often resort to wild guessing until someone gets the right answer. The time spent on such interchanges has little value, particularly in terms of comprehension development. Putting students on the spot can have detrimental effects by causing students to lose interest in the content and develop negative attitudes toward classroom interactions (Vacca and Vacca 1993).

Effective Teacher Questioning Techniques

A few simple techniques can make questions effective tools for comprehension development instead of weapons for destroying interests and attitudes. First, as described earlier in this chapter as part of the ReQuest Procedure, question the entire class. When you call on a student before posing the question, the rest of the class avoids responsibility. They essentially have been given permission to relax, tune out, and let someone else take care of the question. Techniques that ensure no one is excluded from the question are called ways of raising the level of concern. For example, tell the entire class to listen carefully to the question before posing it.

Second, after posing the question, allow plenty of think time or wait time. Typically, if a response is not made or offered within three seconds, the quietness becomes uncomfortable, and teachers tend to start calling on individuals. For many students, three seconds is not nearly enough time to formulate a response worthy of presenting to the class. After posing a question, you should wait at least five to seven seconds, or longer for an especially difficult question. While waiting, you might alleviate some of the discomfort of the extended period of silence by rephrasing the question several different ways. A change in wording often provides clarification, triggers recognition, or stimulates ideas. Eventually, both you and the students will become more comfortable with an extended wait time. During the think time, tell students to sit quietly until you give a signal. This strategy prevents eager volunteers from distracting others with waving arms and "call-on-me" noises.

Third, in addition to calling on eager volunteers, make it a point to call on others who do not volunteer. Students should know that paying attention pays off and that they could be called on at any time. Again, to raise the level of concern, they need to know that *not* volunteering will *not* let them off the hook. Even though you do not want to put students on the spot, they should know that they are expected to participate actively. If a student is caught off guard and is not paying attention, give him or her another chance to contribute as soon as possible. Many students are too shy or humble to volunteer, and the only opportunity they may have to participate is by teacher action.

Fourth, do not accept "I don't know" as an answer. When students use that response as an excuse, you are giving them the message that they do not have to pay attention, and you are willing to let them off the hook. Requiring students to respond in some legitimate way raises the level of concern. If a student does not know the answer, be kind and gentle. Establish a classroom atmosphere that is safe for students who pay attention but still do not know the answer, as well as for those who were not paying attention but want another chance. Follow up the question with some hints, choices, or even another question until the student gives a response. Then, give the student positive reinforcement through genuine praise. You also might allow the student some additional time to think by going on to another question and then coming back to him or her later. Just make sure you do not forget to return to the student for a response.

Fifth, when a student gives an incorrect response or a response that is different from one you had in mind, it is extremely important to *dignify* the response with a positive comment such as "Good thinking! Now think again about this part of the question." Respecting responses is crucial in the development of a safe and comfortable classroom environment with a risk-taking climate. Sometimes, it is difficult to think of something positive to say about an incorrect response, so plan ahead and keep in mind a few possibilities you might use. For example, you might say "You're thinking about _____. If the question had been _____, that would have been the answer." You could also say "No, but I know you know the answer. Would it be _____ or _____?"

Probing the student to make sure you understand the response is important because sometimes students interpret questions in different ways. When students give incorrect responses, it is important to follow up with hints or choices to lead them toward a correct or partially correct response. Giving students successful experiences with answering in class is important for building their confidence and encouraging further participation. Responding comprehensively to incorrect responses also provides you an excellent opportunity to reteach or clarify concepts.

Promoting Gender Equity

In 1972, in an effort to create gender-fair attitudes and practices in classrooms, Congress passed landmark legislation that banned sex discrimination in public schools. However, a recent report published by the American Association of University Women (AAUW) concluded that girls continue to receive an unequal education in U.S. schools. After examining over 1,000 recent studies about girls and education, researchers made a number of conclusions (Feder-Feitel 1993, 57). Among them were the following:

▌ Girls receive significantly less teacher attention than boys.
▌ Sexual harassment of girls by boys is increasing.
▌ The gender gap in math ability is small and declining, but girls are still not pursuing math-related careers in proportion to boys.
▌ Although African-American girls may try to get their teachers' attention more often than white girls, they are more likely to be ignored by teachers.
▌ Curricula commonly ignore or stereotype females.
▌ Most standardized tests are biased against girls.

Recent studies examined in the AAUW report found that, throughout elementary, middle, and high school, boys consistently receive more teacher attention than do girls. Some of the research concluded that one reason for this disparity is that boys tend to call out answers significantly more often than girls. When boys call out answers, the typical teacher response is to listen to their answers; however, when girls call out answers, the typical teacher response is to admonish them for answering without raising their hands. Studies also found that when boys do not volunteer, teachers are more likely to solicit their responses. Other studies reported by AAUW indicated that teachers are more likely to give boys specific feedback, both in terms of praise and constructive criticism (AAUW 1993).

Teachers involved in these studies probably would be surprised to discover that they favored boys over girls in classroom interactions. The bias is often so subtle that it is difficult to recognize, especially in oneself. In fact, gender bias is so deep-rooted from years of socialization that it is difficult for teachers to become aware of it in themselves, even if they are looking for it.

In a television report on gender bias in the classroom ("Failing and Fairness"), aired on NBC's *Dateline* on December 29, 1992, Jane Pauley interviewed a fourth-grade teacher who agreed to have her classroom videotaped. Confident that she was not guilty of gender bias, the teacher welcomed NBC's cameras into her classroom. She was astonished to discover that even though she was making a conscious effort toward gender equality, she still called on boys significantly more often than girls. From the videotapes, the teacher also discovered that the quality of her remarks and feedback was significantly better for boys than girls. For example, she was more likely to respond to a boy with a positive reinforcer such as "Good thinking," followed by probing, higher-level questions. For the girls, however, she was more likely to give a nonresponse such as "Okay" and then move on without following up.

In the television report, Jane Pauley also interviewed some of the children. The girls were all too aware that they were frequently ignored in favor of the boys. When asked why they thought that happened, they responded that it was because the boys were more aggressive in their attempts to get the teacher's attention. For example, they were more likely to stand up with their arms waving frantically in the air, calling out "Oh, oh, oh, I know, I know."

The videotape shown by Jane Pauley confirmed the girls' observations. The boys' histrionics designed to get the teacher's attention were indeed effective. She called on them much more often than she did the girls who were generally sitting calmly with their hands raised—sometimes directly in front of the teacher.

What can you do to avoid the insidious teacher behaviors associated with gender bias? First, you must be willing to examine yourself and allow your classroom to be videotaped. No one else need view the tapes but you, although it helps to have someone trained to point out behaviors that might be too subtle for you to notice. If you do not have access to a videocamera, you can ask a colleague, administrator, or teacher's aide to observe you.

When you are viewing your videotape or giving instructions to your observer, watch for these things:

▮ Make note of specific examples of your behavior toward boys and girls.
▮ Make note of specific examples of your follow-up responses to boys and girls.
▮ Tally the number of times you call on boys and girls.
▮ Tally the number of times you allow boys and girls to call out answers.

Feder-Feitel (1993, 58) recommends keeping a checklist as a reminder of your equal-opportunity behaviors. She includes these questions on her self-assessment:

- Do you call on girls as often as boys?
- Do you expect girls to solve difficult problems?
- Do you give girls specific feedback on problem-solving techniques?
- Are you afraid that girls may cry if you criticize them?
- Do you expect girls to do better in reading than in math?
- Do you compliment girls for their assertiveness? Or do you resent "pushy" girls?
- Do you encourage both males and females to try harder? Are males admonished for not trying hard enough while females are criticized for lack of ability?

Once you have developed an awareness of your classroom behaviors, select one type of behavior to work on at a time. For example, first set a goal to call on boys and girls equally. Then, develop a plan for changing your behavior. You could keep your own tally during classroom interactions or distribute different color tokens to boys and girls as you call on them, making sure to use the same number of each color. Give yourself at least six weeks to work on the change before doing a follow-up assessment by having yourself videotaped or observed again. You should be pleasantly surprised at how much you have reduced gender bias in your classroom.

When you are working on the problem of boys who call out, wave their arms in your face, or beg to be called on, simply remind the students of your expectations. Tell them that you expect everyone to prepare to be called on; they need not raise their hands to get called on, and if they do raise their hands, they should remain seated and quiet. Remind them not to call out answers. The trick is to be consistent with enforcing the rules: you must ignore or admonish all students who call out answers inappropriately. Also, avoid calling on students, girls or boys, who put on a "pick-me" performance. Look for and reinforce those who are meeting your expectations.

To promote gender equity in following up a student's response, make a personal commitment to answer *every* student's response with a higher-level question. Also, keep a list of positive words and phrases handy and make it a point to praise *every* student who responds appropriately, even if her or his answer is incorrect. Make sure "okay" and "all right" are not on your list, because these responses are too neutral to have the desired effect of a positive reinforcer.

The AAUW report (1993) also concluded that the following strategies are effective in promoting more gender-equitable learning environments: First, eliminate sexist language from your instruction and expand instruction beyond the use of a single text. Make sure you are fair in your treatment and expectations of girls and boys. Finally, emphasize a spirit of cooperation instead of competition by incorporating significantly more cooperative learning activities into class time.

DEVELOPING COMPREHENSION THROUGH CLASSROOM INTERACTION

In the previous section, you learned that questioning in the form of drill sessions in not an effective way to develop students' comprehension. However, drill sessions can serve a limited purpose. Knowing how and when to use them is just as important as knowing when *not* to use them. When you think about classroom interactions, you probably picture teacher-student interchanges. However, student-student interactions are equally important in comprehension development, particularly in terms of developing critical levels of thought.

The Role and Limited Value of Turn-Taking (Recitation)

Turn-taking, sometimes called recitation, involves teacher-student interaction. It generally begins with the teacher posing a convergent question (i.e., a question with a specific predetermined answer) and calling on someone to respond. After the student responds, the teacher either corrects or reinforces the response (Vacca and Vacca 1993). Then, the teacher poses another question and calls on another student to respond. The process continues until all the teacher's questions have been asked. The question-answer exchanges are brief, and the focus of the questions is usually on literal-level comprehension and recall. The turn-taking interaction is used in the drill sessions discussed in previous sections.

As Vacca and Vacca (1993) have pointed out, several rules are implicit in turn-taking interactions. First, teachers must speak in the form of questions and students must speak in the form of answers. Answers must be brief, giving just the information specified by the question, and directed toward the teacher. Once a student has been called on, another student is not allowed to participate in the interchange unless first recognized by the teacher to take a turn; students may not respond to another student's answer, because only the teacher is allowed to give feedback.

In fact, when used appropriately, one of the purposes of taking turns is to drill students on important information they need to understand and learn. Turn-taking can be a way to help students memorize basic content items that are requisite for future learning. When turn-taking is planned occasionally for this purpose, its use can be acceptable. Another acceptable use of turn-taking is in diagnosis. It is a way for the teacher to make a quick check at the end of a lesson, set of lessons, or part of a lesson to assess students' understanding and recall of basic content at the literal level. However, McKenna and Robinson (1993) argue that turn-taking questions designed for comprehension monitoring should be embedded into the context of broader, meaning-extended questioning. That way, the teacher can assess comprehension at the same time as he or she develops it.

A third acceptable use of turn-taking is to review before a test or alternate form of assessment. It can tell the students something about which pieces of content are important for understanding and retaining. It can also give them an opportunity to review and reinforce the concepts before being tested on them. When used appropriately and judiciously, turn-taking can have limited value in the content area classroom.

However, all too often teachers record on their lesson plans the verb "discuss" when, in reality, they do not allow the students to discuss the content at all. Instead, they lead a turn-taking session to test students' literal-level comprehension and recall, drill them on important (and sometimes unimportant) content, and review basic concepts. In fact, turn-taking questions stifle discussion by their very nature (Vacca and Vacca 1993).

The Role of Discussions

Real, honest-to-goodness **discussions** are "conversational interactions between teacher and students, as well as between students and other students" (Vacca and Vacca 1993, 81). The teacher's primary role is to get the discussion started and keep it focused. Discussions easily arise from divergent questions (i.e., questions with a variety of acceptable responses), but these questions are few and far between; those asked are carefully selected and used judiciously. Discussions are characterized by extended exchanges of ideas and active participation by the students (Vacca and Vacca 1993).

Discussions are vital for comprehension development because they present a variety of opportunities for improving, refining, and enriching comprehension (Alvermann, Dillon, and O'Brien 1990). They improve comprehension by allowing students to learn new concepts, clarify meanings, correct misunderstandings, and reinforce long-term retention. Discussions refine comprehension by encouraging students to compare their own interpretations with the interpretations of others, expand their vocabularies, and address apparent inconsistencies or contradictions. Finally, they enrich comprehension by giving students the opportunity to respond to and analyze what they read, share a variety of perspectives, explore issues, examine controversies, defend various positions, provide support for their own opinions, and listen to the viewpoints of others.

Discussions can seem risky, because the teacher essentially is turning over a significant amount of responsibility for classroom interaction to the students. However, if carefully planned and monitored, discussions are a terrific way to actively involve students in thinking about and applying the content. The active involvement generated by discussions not only develops comprehension at higher levels of thought but also generates enthusiasm for learning and excitement about practical applications of the content. Students are given the opportunity to ponder the relevance and value of the content in relation to their own lives, experiences, goals, and perspectives.

The advantages of discussion over turn-taking are obvious. Although turn-taking has its place, it does not provide the valuable opportunities for comprehension development afforded by discussions. The only way to avoid overuse of turn-taking is through careful planning and question selection. As a content area teacher, you must ask yourself the extent to which you expect your students to learn the information. Are literal-level understanding and simple recall sufficient, or do you expect students to be able to interpret, apply, and evaluate what they read? If the latter is your goal, design structured discussion sessions as part of your lesson plans. Discussions can be structured as follow-up activities after the assignment has been read and purposes have been met or as enrichment activities at the end of class. Your time would be spent wisely if you decided to devote an entire class period to discussing and processing important content.

Once you have determined your instructional objectives, look at the questions you choose or formulate. Do they probe for specific bits and pieces of information, or do they require students to integrate, compare, contrast, evaluate, and apply concepts? In the next section, you will learn some ways to structure different types of discussions for inclusion in lesson plans. Including discussions in your lesson plans is probably the best way to ensure that classroom interactions are not dominated by turn-taking.

Types of Discussions

Vacca and Vacca (1993) identify two types of discussions: guided and reflective. In a guided discussion, you have more teacher-student interchanges, i.e., the teacher interjects more questions to "guide" the discussion. For example, you might want to lead a guided discussion on the concept of Native American reservations in which your goal is to ensure that students understand the concept from an historical perspective. You might ask "What are Native American reservations?" Following student responses (you should get a variety of responses before continuing), you ask "When did the U.S. government create reservations and what were their purposes in doing so? You then continue, *leading* them toward the concept. As necessary, you interject corrections and information. Guided discussions are informational: they are primarily designed to develop and refine comprehension.

The teacher's role is that of guiding students in monitoring, assessing, and improving their comprehension. The key activity in the teacher's role is "guide," and caution should be taken to avoid dominating the interaction. If the teacher takes too great a role in a guided discussion, it becomes a turn-taking session. Guided discussions can improve comprehension by having students recall, interpret, and elaborate on the content.

Reflective discussions assume a solid understanding of the content and are designed primarily to enrich comprehension by engaging students in critical and creative thought about the content. Using the previous example about Native American reservations, a reflective discussion might start as follows: "Imagine that you are awakened one morning by an army of soldiers surrounding your house. They tell you and your family to pack what you can carry and leave immediately. Then they force you to leave your house, never to return. The soldiers make you walk for days, weeks, or even months and force you to live in a new place. How would you feel? Would you go? Why or why not? What would you do?" The discussion should be structured in a way that encourages students to engage in critical thinking activities such as examining controversial issues, defending various positions, analyzing values, and solving problems.

Once the teacher starts the discussion, his or her role shifts to that of participant. By participating, the teacher can model appropriate ways to contribute to a discussion, as well as a variety of ways to analyze the content. "Teachers can guide students to greater independence in learning by modeling different ways of responding and reacting to issues, commenting on others' points of view, and applying critical reading strategies to difficult concepts in the textbooks" (Alvermann, Dillon, and O'Brien 1990, 31).

Discussion types can also reflect the size of a group. Small-group discussions need to be structured carefully with a specific instructional focus, an appropriate number of participants (i.e., the least number needed for a successful discussion), and an appropriate mix of students (i.e., heterogeneous or homogeneous). With small groups, the teacher's role is primarily that of consultant. The teacher monitors the groups carefully, offering appropriate assistance, information, and guidance (Alvermann, Dillon, and O'Brien 1990).

Large-group discussions also need to be structured carefully. Their structure should be based on the teacher's knowledge of the students' diverse beliefs and value systems and the students' attitudes toward the discussion format. The ideal role of the teacher in large-group discussions is to remain completely neutral and silent. Until students become competent and confident with conducting discussions independently, the teacher may need to intervene occasionally to refocus or give direction to the discussion. However, as soon as possible, the teacher should turn the responsibility for the discussion over to the students. "When students direct questions or responses to the neutral teacher, they are redirected to other students in the group" (Alvermann, Dillon, and O'Brien 1990, 31). When students take complete responsibility for the discussion, the teacher does not participate, even to offer opinions, ask questions, or confirm responses.

Discussion Strategies and Techniques

Text-based discussions are important for putting students in control of their own learning and helping them avoid the feelings of isolation often experienced when interacting only with the text. Discussions must be planned before giving reading assignments, because the purposes given for reading will set the stage for the desired discussion format. For example, if a guided discussion is the instructional goal, the purposes for reading will focus more on understanding the conceptual information contained in the assignment. Conversely, if a reflective discussion is the instructional goal, the purposes for reading will focus more on evaluating and applying the content with relation to personal experiences, opinions, and values.

Alternatives to Teacher Questioning

One of the easiest and most effective ways to increase the number of discussions and the amount of participation is for the teacher to reduce or even eliminate teacher questioning. Dillon (1984) recommends the following seven alternatives to teacher questioning. First, start the discussion by making a declarative or factual statement on which students may elaborate or make a reflective statement (by reflecting on something a student says) to which students may respond. Describe your perception, which students may challenge, of a student's feelings or state of mind with respect to the content. Invite students to elaborate on a statement made by another student or encourage students to ask questions—especially of one another. Finally, maintain a deliberate silence (three or more seconds) to signal and encourage reflective thinking. In addition to reducing or eliminating teacher questioning, avoid reacting to every student response; otherwise, the teacher-student interaction will dominate over student-student interaction.

Listen-Read-Discuss

In Chapter 11, you will be introduced to a strategy called Listen-Read-Discuss, which was described by Manzo and Casale (1985). This strategy is designed to create a guided discussion following a short lecture (about fifteen minutes) and related reading assignment. After the lecture, the students read the material that formed the basis of the lecture. The purpose given for reading is to compare understanding of the lecture with the information presented in the reading assignment. The discussion that follows the reading should be guided with questions such as the following: What did you understand best from what you heard and read? What did you understand least from what you heard and read? What questions or thoughts did the topic raise in your mind?

Facilitating Successful Discussions

The success of discussions depends heavily on the classroom environment. First, desks or chairs should be arranged in a circle or semicircle to allow students to see and hear each other well. Students sitting in rows cannot interact adequately for a discussion. A physical arrangement that requires students to face each other is necessary for successful discussions.

Successful discussions also depend on the students' expertise and confidence with discussion etiquette, which should be explained and modeled by the teacher. A system of response should be established to keep more than one person from talking at a time. Students need to learn how to enter a discussion appropriately without interrupting and avoid dominating the discussion. Respectful listening skills are necessary—students must learn how to be polite listeners. They should demonstrate good listening skills by remaining silent while someone else is speaking, having good eye contact with the speaker, and maintaining appropriate facial expressions and body language. An important way to foster good listening habits is to avoid repeating students' questions and responses for all to hear. Students need to learn to speak audibly and listen carefully.

Help students develop good discussion skills by giving them regular and consistent opportunities to participate in meaningful discussions. Until they have confidence in a discussion setting, emphasize the use of small-group discussions. Ensure that discussions have a clear purpose related to the instructional objectives. The teacher is responsible for monitoring the discussions and intervening if necessary to keep them focused. The teacher should also monitor the discussion to make sure that it is not dominated by a few students. To ensure equitable participation, the teacher may need to impose flexible rules such as "Once you have contributed something to the discussion, you may not contribute again until everyone else has spoken." You may need to call on individuals who are too shy to participate voluntarily.

EMPATHIC LISTENING VS. DEBATING

Both empathic listening and debating are crucial for the development of critical thinking. Empathic listening, as defined by Covey (1990), refers not to agreeing with the speaker or author but to understanding completely the speaker or author's message. Generally, people listen for the purpose of responding; as a result, they project their own biases and perspectives onto what they are hearing. Empathic listening, on the other hand, requires objectivity and involves listening for the purpose of complete understanding through a process of sharing the speaker or author's experience. Again, the listener need not agree with the message but should be able to restate the message accurately as intended by the speaker. This type of listening is important for accurate comprehension at literal and interpretive levels of thought. Once the message has been accurately understood, appropriate and personalized responses can be formulated at the applicable level of thought. Empathic listening emphasizes the knowledge, comprehension, synthesis, and application levels of thinking.

Debate listening, on the other hand, involves listening for the purpose of responding to an author's message as it relates to a predetermined question, issue, or position. You are listening not for the purpose of sharing the speaker or author's experience; rather, your goal is to assess and critique that experience or position. This type of listening emphasizes analysis and evaluation to a greater degree than empathic listening.

Both types of listening skills are important in comprehension development at the highest levels of thinking. Figure 5–1 compares these two types of listening and outlines the scope of these comprehension skills.

FIGURE 5–1 An empathic listener vs. a successful debater

AN EMPATHIC LISTENER	A SUCCESSFUL DEBATER
listens with an intent to understand	listens with the intent to reply
is fair-mindedly critical	is close-mindedly critical
requires emotional and intellectual understanding	requires avoidance of opposing frames of reference
recognizes merit and truth in opposing arguments without necessarily agreeing with them	considers opposing points of view for the sole purpose of strengthening own position
reasons from various points of view	reasons from one point of view only
seeks first to understand the alternate or opposing points of view	seeks first to be understood
makes a good mediator	often makes a good attorney

TAXONOMIES OF THINKING AND COMPREHENSION

Taxonomies, i.e., classification systems, provide a practical way for guiding teachers to ask questions at all levels of thinking and comprehension. Since most teachers were themselves questioned primarily at the literal level throughout their school careers, they have a tendency to ask questions at the literal level. The fact that literal-level questions are the easiest and quickest to formulate coupled with the tendency toward focusing on the literal level can doom classroom interaction to turn-taking only. However, if teachers use taxonomies to formulate and assess questions during lesson planning, they can ensure that their classroom interactions move beyond turn-taking. Discussions require thinking at higher levels; students need much practice in answering questions and responding to material at critical levels of thought. A variety of taxonomies are available to help you develop a wide range of questions for lesson planning. A few of the more popular ones are presented in the next sections.

Bloom's Taxonomy of Thinking and Barrett's Taxonomy of Reading Comprehension

Bloom's (1956) taxonomy of thinking, well-known and quite popular among educators, categorizes the cognitive processes involved in learning. From Bloom's taxonomy, Barrett (1972) developed a simplified taxonomy specifically for reading comprehension. Figure 5–2 shows logical relationships between the two taxonomies, along with verbs to help you design objectives and activities that tap into each level.

As you can see from Figure 5–2, Barrett's literal level of comprehension corresponds with Bloom's knowledge and comprehension levels of thinking. Barrett's inferential level of comprehension corresponds with Bloom's application and analysis levels of thinking, and Barrett's evaluation level of comprehension corresponds with Bloom's synthesis and evaluation levels of thinking. Barrett's appreciation level of comprehension taps into the affective domain by focusing on the reader's value-laden personal and emotional responses to the reading. Therefore, Barrett's appreciation level of comprehension does not correspond with any of Bloom's cognitive levels.

All literal and some inferential questions are convergent, requiring a specific predetermined response. Other inferential questions and all evaluation and appreciation questions are divergent, having many possible answers and requiring students to think critically and defend their answers. All question types are important for assessing and developing comprehension, and using taxonomies as guides, teachers can ensure that a variety of questions guide their classroom interactions.

FIGURE 5–2 Verbs for lesson planning: Activities requiring different levels of thinking according to Bloom's Taxonomy and comprehension according to Barrett's Taxonomy

BLOOM	BARRETT	VERBS
knowledge	literal	cite, define, identify, know, label, list, match, name, pronounce, quote, recall, recite, recognize, remember, repeat, reproduce, state, tell, what?, when?, where?, who?
comprehension	literal	alter, change, convert, depict, describe, discover, explain, give examples, generalize, give main idea, illustrate, infer, interpret, manage, paraphrase, relate, rephrase, represent, restate, review, reword, substitute, summarize, transform, translate, vary
application	inferential	apply, classify, compute, demonstrate, direct, discover, employ, evidence, how many?, illustrate, manage, manifest, practice, prepare, predict, relate, report, show, solve, use, utilize, what is?, which?, write an example
analysis	inferential	ascertain, analyze, associate, categorize, classify, compare, conclude, contrast, designate, determine, diagnose, diagram, differentiate, discriminate, dissect, distinguish, divide, examine, find, infer, investigate, organize, outline, point out, reduce, separate, survey
synthesis	evaluation	combine, compile, compose, conceive, construct, create, design, develop, devise, expand, extend, generalize, how can we improve?, how can we solve?, imagine, integrate, invent, modify, originate, plan, pose, produce, project, propose, rearrange, revise, rewrite, synthesize, theorize, what if?, what would happen if?, write
evaluation	evaluation	appraise, assess, compare, contrast, conclude, criticize, critique, debate, decide, deduce, evaluate, judge, justify, recommend, select, verify, weigh
	appreciation	apply, analyze values, associate, express feelings, respond personally

Gray's, Herber's, Pearson and Johnson's, and Raphael's Taxonomies of Reading Comprehension

Gray's taxonomy of comprehension is possibly one of the easiest to understand and use. It contains three levels: reading the lines, reading between the lines, and reading beyond the lines. Reading the lines involves literal-level understanding of material explicitly (directly) stated in the text. Reading between the lines involves making inferences and drawing conclusions based on an interpretation of material implicitly (not directly) stated in the text. Reading beyond the lines involves schema-based understanding (based on prior knowledge) of the material in applying it to new or personal situations, including making value judgments and forming opinions.

Herber's taxonomy (1978) labeled Gray's three levels of comprehension: **literal** (reading the lines), **interpretive** (reading between the lines), and **applied** (reading beyond the lines). Herber and Nelson Herber (1993) describe the literal level as a process of acquiring basic information from text, i.e., determining what the author is saying. Literal comprehension is necessary but not sufficient for higher levels of comprehension.

Herber and Nelson Herber (1993) describe the interpretive level as the process of inferring ideas from information presented in text. In other words, interpretive comprehension refers to the process of determining what authors mean by what they say or discovering the implicit message. Interpretive comprehension requires the reader to analyze information acquired at the literal level.

The applied level of comprehension is described as the process of synthesizing ideas from multiple sources within text and making use of them (Herber and Nelson Herber 1993). Applied comprehension requires the reader to connect ideas within their schemata with ideas garnered from the text. The results of applied comprehension include generalizations based on notions from both sources.

Pearson and Johnson (1978) gave these three levels of comprehension still another set of labels, from which emerged Raphael's (1982) taxonomy. Pearson and Johnson (1978) refer to literal comprehension as **textually explicit,** because it requires the reader to identify explicitly stated information in text. They call interpretive comprehension **textually implicit,** because it requires the reader to identify information inferred from text. Applied comprehension is **scriptally implicit,** because it requires readers to relate ideas from background knowledge to ideas from text. Pearson and Johnson (1978) point out the importance of considering the answer to a given question in determining which level of comprehension it taps.

This relationship between the question and answer is important in assessing and developing comprehension.

Raphael (1982) developed a comprehension taxonomy based on the relationships between questions and answers. Her taxonomy identifies four types of questions in two categories: text-based questions and reader-based questions. Text-based questions include textually explicit, which she calls "right there" questions, and textually implicit questions, which she calls "think and search" questions. The answers to "right there" questions are generally easy to find in the text; in fact, often some of the words used in the question are found in the same sentence as the answer. The answers to "think and search" questions are not quite as easy to find. Usually, different parts of the answer are found in different parts of the text, and you have to put them together, make inferences, or draw conclusions.

Reader-based questions include scriptally implicit questions, which she calls "author and me" questions, and personal response questions, which she calls "on my own" questions. The answers to "author and me" questions are usually generalizations and applied examples derived from a combination of information in the text and your own background knowledge and experiences. The answers to "on my own" questions usually take some form of personal response to what was read; in fact, the answer cannot be found in the text. Some combination of personal experience, background knowledge, and value judgments is required for answering "on my own" questions.

Raphael chose these labels for the specific intent of teaching students how to distinguish question types independently. Raphael's strategy for teaching students the various levels of questions, **Question-Answer Relationships (QAR)** will be described in depth in Part 2 of this chapter. Figure 5–3 provides a chart that compares Gray's, Herber's, Pearson's and Johnson's, and Raphael's taxonomies of comprehension. Figure 5–4 presents this information in the format of a Graphic Organizer.

FIGURE 5–3 A comparison of comprehension taxonomies

GRAY	HERBER	PEARSON AND JOHNSON	RAPHAEL
read the lines	literal	textually explicit	right there
read between the lines	interpretive	textually implicit	think and search
read beyond the lines	applied	scriptally implicit	author and you
read beyond the lines	applied	scriptally implicit	on my own

FIGURE 5–4 Graphic Organizer illustrating a comparison of comprehension taxonomies

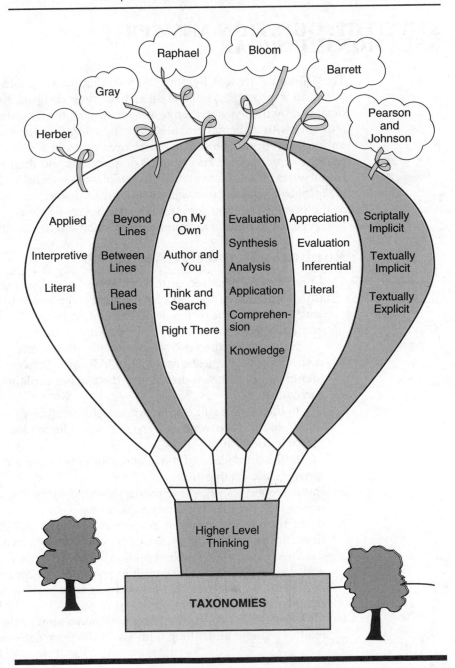

PART 2

STRATEGY: QUESTION-ANSWER RELATIONSHIPS (QAR)

The Question-Answer Relationships strategy was designed by Raphael (1982) to improve students' abilities to answer comprehension questions designed by the teacher, themselves, or classmates. The strategy provides students with systematic procedures for analyzing the task demands of various questions. Raphael's procedures provide a *deductive approach to teaching* students the various levels of questions and their relationships to the answers. *In a deductive approach, students are provided with an explanation of the concept followed by examples and supervised practice in applying it.* Refer to the previous section for a review of what distinguishes the four question types in Raphael's taxonomy of question-answer relationships.

Raphael's Deductive Approach

1. In Raphael's (1982) recommended procedures, the first lesson introduces students to the concept of different questions by having the teacher explain the difference between text-based ("in the book") and knowledge-based ("in my head") answers.

    Students are then provided examples in the form of passages to read, along with questions, whose QARs and answers have been identified; after the students read, the teacher explains the QAR for each question.

    In the second stage of the lesson, students are given passages, questions, and answers; as a group, the students identify the QAR for each question.

    In the third stage of the lesson, students identify the QAR and answer for each question.

2. In the second lesson, students are provided further review and supervised practice with longer passages.

3. In the third lesson, an even longer passage is divided into four sections. Six questions are presented for each section, two for each of the three categories. The first section is done together by the teacher and class as a review. The remaining sections are completed independently, with the students identifying the QARs and answering the questions.

4. In the fourth lesson, students are assigned a similar passage to be read as a single unit, along with six QARs from each category.

FIGURE 5–5 Question-Answer Relationships

IN THE BOOK (text-based)	IN MY HEAD (reader-based)
RIGHT THERE (literal)	AUTHOR AND ME (interpretive and applied)
THINK AND SEARCH (literal and interpretive)	ON MY OWN (applied)

Students are expected to read the passage, identify the QAR for each, and answer the questions.

5. Raphael then recommends weekly review sessions to reinforce students' competencies with QARs. Figure 5–5 summarizes a set of question types and labels recommended for use with QAR.

An Alternate Inductive Approach

Some teachers and students might prefer an *inductive approach to teaching* for introducing QARs. *In an inductive approach, students are led to discover the concepts for themselves, rather than having the concept defined for them.* Following is an adaptation of QAR designed specifically for content area instruction and literacy development using an inductive approach. If QARs are introduced using an inductive method, Raphael's recommendation of a period of intensive training followed by weekly review or maintenance activities still applies. Once students can successfully make question-answer relationships, you can reinforce their critical thinking by using the question-answer labels during daily turn-taking and discussion activities.

The following procedures can be accomplished in one lesson or can be extended over a period of several days, depending on both students' readiness for understanding and internalizing the concept of question-answer relationships, and the difficulty and length of the passage to be read. You may repeat any of the steps as many times as necessary to help students develop competence and confidence with the concepts. Students may work through these procedures individually, in pairs, in small groups, or as a whole class.

1. To introduce students to the strategy, prepare them for reading as you would in a Directed Reading Activity (DRA) by providing motivation, developing requisite background knowledge, introducing

vocabulary, and setting purposes for reading. Divide the passage into short sections and set purposes for reading the first section in the form of questions to be answered. Present the questions in writing in two labeled categories: *in the book* and *in my head*. Tell the students that the answers to these questions can be found either directly stated in the book, in the student's own knowledge of the subject, or through a combination of both. Have students read for the purposes of answering the questions and identifying the source of the information they used for answering them.

2. After reading, follow up on the purposes by checking responses to the questions. As each response is confirmed, help the students identify the information source they used for answering it. When they can point to the answer and read it from the book, identify the answer as an "in the book" answer. When they can locate hints from the book but also have to use what they already know, identify the answer as an "in my head" answer.

3. Set the purposes for reading the next section to reinforce the discoveries students made about questions and answers in the first section. Tell them to identify whether each question has an "in the book" or "in my head" answer in the process of answering the question. Again, follow up on the purposes by confirming and explaining the question-answer relationships. Then, have students create at least one question for each of the two categories. Once students are confident in distinguishing the two main categories of questions, introduce them to the two subcategories within each.

4. For the next section, set the purposes for reading with "in the book" questions only. Tell students that all of the questions are "in the book" questions, but that there are two different types of them. Have them read for the purpose of answering the questions and separating them into two categories of "in the book" questions. Emphasize the need to explain the difference between the two types of "in the book" questions. After reading, confirm the answers and lead students through a description of the two types of "in the book" questions. As each type is described, label it as either "right there" or "think and search."

5. Set the purpose for reading the next section as labeling the questions either "right there" or "think and search" while answering them. After reading, confirm and explain the relationship between the labels and answers. Then have students make up at least one question for each of the two "in the book" QARs.

6. Once students have mastered the concept of "right there" and "think and search" questions, introduce the two types of "in my head" questions. For the next section, set the purposes for reading

with "in my head" questions only. Tell students that all of the questions are "in my head" questions, but that there are two different types of them. Have students read for the purpose of answering the questions and separating them into two categories of "in my head" questions. Emphasize the need to explain the difference between the two types of "in my head" questions. After reading, confirm the answers and lead students through a description of the two types of "in my head" questions. As each type is described, label it either as "author and you" or "on my own."

7. Set the purpose for reading the next section as labeling the questions "author and you" or "on my own" while answering them. After reading, confirm and explain the relationship between the labels and answers. Then have students make up at least one question for each of the two "in my head" QARs.

8. Set the purpose for reading another section as labeling questions as either "right there," "think and search," "author and you," or "on my own." After reading, confirm and explain the relationship between the labels and answers. Then have students formulate at least one question for each of the four types of QARs. Continue providing practice by having students label and make up questions for each category on a regular and consistent basis—at least weekly—until the concept of question-answer relationships is internalized and students are confident with it.

SCAFFOLDING COMPREHENSION DEVELOPMENT WITH STUDY GUIDES

The Concept of Scaffolding in Literacy Instruction

In literacy instruction, the concept of scaffolding refers to the support teachers provide students for constructing knowledge from text. The concept is based on a metaphor of the scaffolding used by construction workers. Herber and Nelson Herber (1993, 138–139) describe the metaphor this way:

> Scaffolds allow workers to perform tasks they could not otherwise complete. Scaffolds provide a place to work, a position from which workers can accomplish what they are expected to do. Scaffolds also provide workers access to places they could not reach on their own. In these otherwise inaccessible places, they can complete tasks they could not otherwise perform.

The scaffolding provided students by teachers serves exactly the same function. It allows students access to material they might have difficulty understanding on their own and provides students the support necessary to enable them to comprehend and learn content effectively.

Study Guides as a Form of Scaffolding

Scaffolding can take many forms, one of which is study guides. Study guides are supplementary materials prepared by the author or teacher for students to read simultaneously with the text. The main purpose of study guides is to lead students toward key concepts and help them integrate and apply the concepts in a meaningful way. Study guides are especially useful for difficult material and supporting less competent readers. They allow the teacher to provide guidance without having to be present; therefore, study guides can free the teacher during class time to work with other students or provide support for students in completing assignments outside of class.

Many different types of study guides can provide scaffolding for comprehension development. Four of the most popular ones are described in the following sections. Study guides can be incorporated into other content area literacy strategies by using them to set purposes for reading and to guide the silent reading portion of the procedures. For example, in a Directed Reading Activity, after the selection has been introduced, students may be given a study guide that specifies the purposes for reading and guides them through the reading. Students can work on study guides independently, in pairs, or in small groups. In addition to Figures 5–6 through 5–10, Appendix G provides examples of different types of study guides.

Selective Reading Guide

Originally called the Selective Reading Guide-O-Rama, the Selective Reading Guide was designed by Cunningham and Shablak (1975) to lead students to main ideas and important supporting details, and to help them develop flexibility by identifying portions of the text that may be skimmed lightly. The concept of a Selective Reading Guide is supported by the notion that mature readers do not give equal attention to *everything* they read; they know how to "study read" and internalize the most salient parts and how to "skim read" for familiarity of the less important details.

McKenna and Robinson (1993) identify two common challenges of textbook reading assignments. First, readability tends to fluctuate significantly both among and within chapters. Second, the writing is often dense with information, not all of which is necessary to understanding the content (McKenna and Robinson 1993). A good Selective Reading Guide addresses these challenges by providing students a "model of purposeful and selective text reading" (Readence, Bean, and Baldwin 1992, 178).

In developing a Selective Reading Guide, first ask yourself these questions (Tierney, Readence, and Dishner 1990, 239–240):

1. What should students know when they finish this chapter?
    a. What are the major concepts that the students should understand?
    b. What supporting information or details should they remember on a long-term basis?
2. What should students be able *to do* when they finish the chapter? What background information is essential to perform the required tasks?

Use this information to develop statements and questions to guide students toward this information and away from information that might distract them from your identified goals.

After introducing the selection, give students the Selective Reading Guide to complete as they read the assignment. After reading, give them the opportunity to share and discuss their responses, findings, and reactions. Selective Reading Guides can be adapted for a wide variety of content areas, materials, difficulty levels, and student needs.

Figure 5–6 shows examples of the kinds of statements and questions that would be incorporated appropriately into a Selective Reading Guide.

FIGURE 5–6 Selective Reading Guide: Examples of appropriate statements and questions

p. 14, paragraphs 1–3. Read this section carefully. It explains some important background information. Make note of anything you do not understand in this section so we can discuss it in class.

p. 14, paragraphs 4–5. You may skip this part, since we will not be using this information at this point.

p. 15, paragraphs 1–4. Read the subheading and turn it into a question. Answer the question after you read this part. You may look back if you need to do so.

p. 15, paragraph 5. This paragraph gives a good example of the concept. If you already understand the concept thoroughly, you may skip or skim through this paragraph quickly. If you are still unsure about how to apply this concept, read the paragraph and see if you can think of another example similar to the one described.

p. 16, paragraph 4. This information is very interesting, and you may want to keep it in mind as resource information for future use. For now, you may skim this part quickly and go on. If you are interested in this topic, you may want to read it carefully just for fun.

Marginal Gloss

A Marginal Gloss (Singer and Donlan 1985) is a type of study guide that provides notes to the reader in the margins. These notes can be written by the author of the text or by the teacher. The notes are designed to walk the students through the material, pointing out especially important concepts, defining technical terms, providing examples, asking higher-level questions, and so on.

If marginal notes are not provided by the textbook author, the teacher can prepare a Marginal Gloss by placing a sheet of paper next to the textbook page and writing notes to the student so that the notes match up physically with the text to which they refer. This physical matching is a distinguishing feature of the Marginal Gloss and helps the students locate more easily the text being referred to in the marginal notes. A separate gloss should be provided for each textbook page, and the page number at the top of the gloss should match the textbook page number. Copies of the gloss are distributed to students who lay them next to each page and refer to them while reading. The Marginal Gloss can be a very effective way for teachers to provide indirect guidance to students for difficult material.

Figure 5–7 shows some examples of the kinds of notes to the student that might be appropriate for a Marginal Gloss.

Text Pattern Guide

The Text Pattern Guide, a variation of the Three-Level Guide (which is described in the next section), is designed to enhance reading effectiveness by helping students identify major patterns of text organization (e.g., chronological order, reasons, examples, cause-effect, compare-contrast,

---

FIGURE 5–7 Marginal Gloss: Examples of appropriate notes to students

p. 73   This section describes an important concept. Which of the following would be examples of that concept, as described in this section? You might need to read this section several times to be able to answer this question.

p. 75   Look at the words in boldface print. Can you pronounce them? If not, ask for assistance. Make sure you can explain these terms in your own words. You might start by looking them up in the glossary.

p. 77   As you read this section, think about how it relates to what we studied last week. If you are not sure, go back and read the summary from the last chapter.

p. 78   The most important thing to remember about this section is what it tells us about our upcoming field trip. After reading this section, decide which of the following will be most important in preparing for the field trip.

problem-solution, description, spatial order). The Text Pattern Guide also enhances metacognitive awareness by helping students understand how the identification of text patterns can improve their comprehension. Identifying text patterns can help readers attain higher levels of comprehension by showing them relationships among and between concepts (Herber and Nelson Herber 1993).

Following is an adaptation of the steps for designing and using Text Pattern Guides as recommended by Vacca and Vacca (1993). First, examine the reading selection and determine the primary pattern of organization in the text. Develop a Text Pattern Guide that requires students to manipulate the content using the selected pattern. For example, provide students with a list of causes and effects, which they must match. Second, while introducing the selection, explain the pattern to the students and guide them through examples of how to interpret the author's message in relation to the pattern. Third, give students the pattern guide to complete as they read the assignment. Next, have students compare responses in a small-group or whole-class discussion. Finally, provide assistance through explanation and examples if students had problems completing the guide appropriately; encourage the students to help each other as much as possible. Figures 5–8 and 5–9 provide examples of Text-Pattern Guides.

Three-Level Guide
Sometimes called Levels Guides, Three-Level Guides are based on Herber's (1978) taxonomy of comprehension, which as you recall from the discussion earlier in this chapter includes the literal, interpretive, and applied levels. A Three-Level Guide includes support for developing the reader's comprehension at all three levels. Teachers can also design Levels Guides that focus on only one or two of the comprehension levels, depending on the needs of the students and the demands of the text.

Keep in mind that as master learner, the Three-Level Guide you prepare in many ways reflects your own comprehension of the material. Since you are the most highly skilled reader and learner of content in the class, as well as the resident expert of the content being taught, the guide you design will serve as a model of how to comprehend text in your content area (Herber and Nelson Herber 1993). Your task in designing the guide is to support your students' comprehension development at each level.

In designing a Three-Level Guide, Herber and Nelson Herber (1993) recommend the following procedures. First, establish the organizing principle and examine the assignment to determine how it should be read. For the literal level, identify the significant information that supports the organizing principle and place this information in a set of declarative statements. Students are instructed to identify the statements

FIGURE 5-8 Text Pattern Guide developed for a reading selection on geography and history

Objective: The student will be able to identify causes and effects related to how geography has affected history and how people have influenced their environment throughout history.

Directions: In your reading selection on geography and history, find the causes that led to the effects listed. Write each cause in the space provided.

Section 1

1. Cause: _____
   Effect: They discourage the growth of dense population.

2. Cause: _____
   Effect: Nomads travel from place to place in search of food and water.

3. Cause: _____
   Effect: It is natural that the great centers of the world's population are found in the lowlands.

4. Cause: _____
   Effect: The people of England see a special meaning in the year 1066 A.D.

5. Cause: _____
   Effect: The seas and the oceans serve as broad highways and become friends of civilization.

6. Cause: _____
   Effect: It might be said that to know a country's rivers is to know its history.

Section 3

1. Cause: _____
   Effect: Improved their environment.

2. Cause: _____
   Effect: Weakened the political ties between Spanish and American colonies.

3. Cause: _____
   Effect: Stimulated development of the north-central U.S. and south-central Canada as the "bread-basket" of the world.

FIGURE 5–9 Text Pattern Guide developed for a math lesson

Directions: Our text presents much of its material in an "if-then" format. We learn that **if** a specific condition or CAUSE exists, **then** a corresponding specific outcome of EFFECT must be true.

Read pp. 78–81 in Chapter 2. Then read each statement in the "IF" column. Determine the "THEN" statement that best defines the outcome precipitated by the "IF" statement and write its letter in the blank. The "THEN" statements may be used more than once.

IF

_____ **1.** If a variable makes an open sentence a true statement,

_____ **2.** If a Mathematical Sentence contains the symbol >,

_____ **3.** If an equation contains variables,

_____ **4.** If every number in a set of numbers makes an Open Sentence true,

_____ **5.** If no number from a Replacement Set makes an Open Sentence true,

_____ **6.** If the symbol for a set is { },

_____ **7.** If a set of numbers is substituted for the variable in an open sentence,

THEN

a. then it is an Open Sentence.

b. then the set of numbers is a Solution Set for the sentence.

c. then it is a Solution of the Open Sentence.

d. then the Solution Set is the Empty Set.

e. then it is an Inequality.

f. then it is the Replacement Set.

---

that represent information found in the assignment and be ready to provide evidence for their decisions (Herber and Nelson Herber 1993). For examples of declarative statements at the literal level, see Figures 5–10 and 5–11.

For the interpretive level, identify the relationships that seem reasonable in light of the organizing principle; then create statements that reflect possible interpretations of the relationships, including inferences, deductions, and conclusions. Again, write out these possible relationships in the form of declarative statements, instruct students to identify the relationships that can be supported by information in the reading assignment, and be prepared to provide evidence (Herber and Nelson Herber 1993). For examples of declarative statements at the interpretive level, see Figures 5–10 and 5–11.

For the applied level, identify some universal ideas or generalizations that relate somehow to the organizing principle and can be illustrated by concepts from the text and students' own background knowledge and experiences. List these universal ideas or generalizations again as a set of

---

FIGURE 5-10 Three-Level Guide developed for a history lesson

"Mexico, the Community"

I. *Directions:* Check the statements that you believe say what the author says.

_____ **1.** More than 10 million people live in Mexico City.
_____ **2.** Spanish soldiers destroyed the capital city of the Aztecs in 1521.
_____ **3.** The President of Mexico works in the National Palace.
_____ **4.** September 16th is the day the Spanish won their independence from the Aztecs.
_____ **5.** The eagle and the snake are symbols of the Mexican flag.
_____ **6.** The battle of the Alamo was a famous fight during the Mexican-American War in 1836.

II. *Directions:* Check the statements that you believe say what the author said between the lines.

_____ **1.** Mexico City is the capital of a country to the south of the United States.
_____ **2.** Mexico is a democracy.
_____ **3.** The people in Mexico speak Spanish today because of the Spanish conquerors in 1521.
_____ **4.** Independence Day in Mexico is an important national holiday.
_____ **5.** The coat of arms on the Mexican flag symbolizes an Aztec legend.
_____ **6.** The battle of the Alamo was important because of the cottonwood trees that surround the mission.

III. *Directions:* Check those statements you agree with and be ready to support your choices with your own knowledge or beliefs.

_____ **1.** It would be easier to build a pyramid today than it would have been in 1500.
_____ **2.** Texans celebrate Cinco de Mayo because a lot of people with Mexican heritage live in Texas.
_____ **3.** Texas won its freedom from Mexico because there were men like those at the Alamo who were willing to die for their beliefs.
_____ **4.** National holidays celebrate important days in the history of a country.

---

declarative statements. Students identify the statements that can be supported with evidence from the text and their own knowledge and experiences and are ready to support their decisions (Herber and Nelson Herber 1993). For examples of declarative statements at the applied level, see Figures 5–10 and Figures 5–11.

FIGURE 5–11   Three-Level Guide developed for a math lesson

Bill and Ted's Math Adventure

Bill and Ted bought a new house in Austin. The house is at 2413 Smith Drive. The house has two stories. The house has a rectangular shaped pool. Sara the house contractor/designer said the area of the pool is 252 ft^2. Sara also said the perimeter of the pool is 64 ft. Bill and Ted were wondering what the length and width of the pool are. Bill and Ted knew that there were formulas from Algebra I class that could help them, but they were on an adventure that week and missed out. Can you help Bill and Ted find the length and width of the pool?

Directions:

I. Facts of the Problem

Read the word problem above. Check column A if it is a fact from the problem. Then check column B if it will help you solve the problem.

A   **B**

_____   _____   Bill and Ted own a new house

_____   _____   The pool has an area of 252 ft^2

_____   _____   Their Contractors/Designer's name is Sara

_____   _____   Bill and Ted live on Smith Drive

_____   _____   The pool has a perimeter of 64 ft

II. Math Ideas

Check the statements which contain math ideas in the problem. You might use part 1 for help.

_____   volume of rectangles   _____   subtraction properties

_____   multiplication properties   _____   distributive property

_____   perimeter of rectangles

III. Numbers

Below are possible ways of getting an answer for this problem. Check those that will help solve the problem.

_____ $A = lw$

_____ $252 - 64$

_____ $64 \div 4$

_____ $x(32 - x) = 252$

Anticipation Guide

Chapter 6 describes in detail the Anticipation Guide which, in addition to being a study guide, is a motivational strategy. The Anticipation Guide consists of a set of statements to which students respond. Before reading, students decide whether they agree or disagree with the statements. It is important that the statements go beyond the literal level. In other words, this should not be a True/False exercise. Rather, students should be required to use their background knowledge and interpretive or applied-level thinking to form an opinion. Therefore, the statements should reflect gray-area beliefs or opinions that could be argued from various perspectives.

The purpose for reading is to decide whether the author would agree or disagree with each statement. After reading, students respond to the statements as they think the author would respond. They must use specific passages and information from the text to support their decisions. After considering the author's perceived responses, students can choose whether to change their original responses. Finally, students engage in discussion and/or reflective writing about their own responses and how they compare with those of the author and their classmates. In addition to Figure 5–12, Chapter 6 provides examples of Anticipation Guides.

FIGURE 5–12 Anticipation Guide developed for an art appreciation lesson

The Importance of Art Outside the Classroom

Directions: Before reading, decide whether you agree or disagree with each statement below. In the left column, put an A if you agree and a D if you disagree. Then, read for the purpose of deciding whether the author would agree or disagree. Put those responses in the column on the right.

YOU   *AUTHOR*

_____ **1.** Art is a universal language.   **1.** _____
_____ **2.** Art is a means of communication.   **2.** _____
_____ **3.** Art is personal.   **3.** _____
_____ **4.** Video is a form of art.   **4.** _____
_____ **5.** Art is purely decorative.   **5.** _____
_____ **6.** We can learn about other cultures through their art.   **6.** _____
_____ **7.** Art is historical.   **7.** _____
_____ **8.** Painting and sculpture are the only pure forms of art.   **8.** _____

After reading, decide whether you would change any of your original responses. Do you disagree with any of the author's responses?

Scaffolding Instruction for ESL Students

Kang (1994) recommends the use of a variety of study guides and glosses with ESL students for three broad purposes. First, to provide linguistic or language support, the guides and glosses should explain key vocabulary, expand meanings, simplify concepts, make comparisons and contrasts, and provide additional context. The guides also can be used to direct students' attention to textual study aids including pictures, charts, graphs, diagrams, and other visual displays of information that can aid comprehension. In addition, guides can be used to help ESL students learn independent strategies for vocabulary development.

The second broad purpose for using study guides and glosses as recommended by Kang (1994) is to provide knowledge or content support. Specifically, you can use guides to direct the ESL students' attention to the most salient terms and information. Guides can also emphasize text organizational patterns (e.g., cause-effect, compare-contrast, chronological order, reasons, examples, description, simple listing, and so forth) and how to use those patterns for understanding and distinguishing relationships between important ideas and concepts. Three-Level Guides can be especially useful for helping ESL students with higher-level comprehension.

Kang's (1994) third broad purpose for using guides and glosses with ESL students during reading is to provide literacy or reading/writing skill support. For this purpose, process-oriented guides would be most appropriate; for example, process-oriented guides can be used to lead students to apply appropriate reading and study strategies. They could also be used to help students adjust their reading rate appropriately for the difficulty of the material and purpose for reading. Another example of how process-oriented guides can provide literacy support is by helping students develop appropriate strategies for monitoring their comprehension, making predictions, drawing conclusions, and solving problems.

A strategy recommended by Reyes and Molner (1991) is the Experience-Text-Relationship Method (ETR) (Au 1979). It is a scaffolding technique that builds on background knowledge, connecting it with content as the teacher guides students through a reading assignment one section at a time. Following are a set of steps adapted from Reyes and Molner's (1991) recommendations. Be sure to include your ESL students in every step and notice the similarities between this strategy, Semantic Maps (see Chapter 1), and the PReP (see Chapter 9).

1. Identify key concepts from the assignment and lead a discussion on what students already know about them.
2. Have students read a short segment of the material. Then, ask questions designed to assess comprehension. If necessary, clarify any misconceptions or misunderstandings about the content.

3. Lead another discussion designed to help students understand relationships and relevance between their prior knowledge and the
   reading. Allow students to discover for themselves, as much as possible, how the new content relates to what they already know.

ORAL VS. SILENT READING

"Round-robin" oral reading involves students taking turns reading a segment out loud while the rest of the group or class follows along silently
(Tierney, Readence, and Dishner 1990). Students take turns either by seat-
ing arrangement or teacher selection; either way, students are put on the
spot to read aloud without preparation. This type of oral reading is too
often used in the content area classroom by teachers who claim that reading the material aloud in class is the only way to make sure students are
exposed to the content in the textbook. Teachers who are frustrated when
students either cannot or will not read the book on their own resort to
spending class time having students take turns reading aloud from the
text. However, this practice of round-robin oral reading is not supported
by research. In fact, research suggests that this practice of oral reading is
not defensible if comprehension of the material is the instructional goal
(Allington 1984; Anderson, Mason, and Shirey 1984; Bruinsma 1981).

The Disadvantages of Round-Robin Oral Reading

Some teachers defend the use of round-robin oral reading as a way to
make sure that students are exposed to content presented by the text.
However, exposing students to the content does not guarantee that they
will learn or even understand it. Since comprehension is generally better
during silent reading, students who read orally or listen to others read
orally often have difficulty paying attention.

As you have already learned, content area literacy strategies are
designed specifically to help students attend to the text for maximum concentration and comprehension. If you compare round-robin oral reading
to these strategies, you will notice that it is in fact not a strategy at all;
rather, it is an activity that uses class time but has little instructional value.
In fact, not only is it ineffective in terms of helping students learn content,
it can actually be harmful for several reasons.

First, overemphasis on round-robin oral reading can give students the
misconception that reading is little more than a performance. They learn
to associate the concept of reading with the act of pronouncing words
aloud. These assumptions can lead to poor attitudes toward reading in
general and reading to learn in particular.

Students also learn to associate the concept of good reading with good oral reading skills. As a result, they begin to value pronunciation and fluency over comprehension, metacognitive awareness, and critical thinking. The concept of content area literacy can then be misinterpreted in the minds of the students as a hollow act of verbalization. Missing the point of content area literacy means missing out on crucial opportunities to develop independent reading and learning skills.

Listening to others read orally, especially poor readers, can be extremely tedious and boring. If students associate content area learning experiences with the empty and sometimes painful experience of round-robin oral reading, poor attitudes toward content area learning can result. Also, when students are distracted during oral reading, important information is missed.

Similarly, round-robin oral reading can be very stressful to the oral reader, especially if she or he is not a competent and confident oral reader. The embarrassment of giving a poor oral reading performance can contribute further to poor attitudes toward content area reading and learning. Worse yet, experiencing embarrassment in front of one's peers can lead to or complicate existing emotional or self-confidence problems.

Fifth, round-robin oral reading does not reinforce good silent reading habits, which are an essential part of content area literacy. The ultimate goal of content area literacy is the development of students who can set their own purposes for reading, read actively to achieve those purposes, monitor their own reading, and assess their reading with respect to their established purposes. These independent reading skills can only be developed with experiences that approximate real-life reading-to-learn situations.

Finally, round-robin oral reading is not purposeful; that is, its goal is proper pronunciation and good fluency rather than comprehension and learning. Therefore, it does not activate schemata, encourage metacognition, or emphasize content learning as goals. Valuable class time that could be devoted to further the goals of content area literacy is lost.

Evidence of many of these disadvantages can be seen in the following testimonials written by college students in a teacher education class:

> With regard to oral reading, I always hated it. I'm not that outgoing and reading in front of the class always stressed me out. I always felt like an idiot when reading aloud and was afraid my peers would make fun of me. In second grade, I remember having problems with the pronunciation of the "ch" and "sh" sounds. One day, our teacher had me read aloud and I had trouble with the "sh" sound (which is common for native Spanish speakers like myself). She tried to correct me, but I could not pronounce the sound she wanted. I was extremely embarrassed and even started to cry because my peers began to laugh at me. Ever since, I've always hated reading aloud.

I remember a history class I had my freshman year of high school in which we did a lot of oral reading. I am a good oral reader, but I hated this exercise because it was so boring. Many of the students in the class were poor readers so the process was often slow and tedious. I also do not have good comprehension when I read orally.

I don't remember any distinct experience reading orally in school. I remember feeling slightly queasy, and the numbing feeling of listening to people who couldn't read. I remember trying to stifle giggles, and feeling horrible about how mean I was.

One recent experience I had was in reading aloud in Spanish class. This has a slightly different emphasis, because some of what we are learning is how to pronounce correctly, so even word calling is a halfway acceptable attempt. But the funny thing to me is that even though I am an adult, am paying lots of money to be in the class, and come voluntarily to class, I still have that dread in my stomach, and still look ahead to my part and try to practice when the people ahead of me are reading. This is true even though the atmosphere is accepting and not competitive. During my turn, I am so focused on pronouncing words correctly, that I have very little idea about what is being said in the passage, unless it is very simple. We generally read short newspaper articles and are supposed to have a discussion afterward. I have learned to look at the selections at home, so that I can keep my brain from freezing with anxiety in class.

In my freshman year in high school, I was required to take American history. It was totally an oral reading experience. We would read straight from the book, round-robin style. I hated and dreaded this class. I am not a confident oral reader because I have some speech problems. I also prefer reading silently in order to understand the text. The only comfort I got was that I could predict which paragraph I would have to read. I would practice the paragraph silently instead of listening to the others. If I realized that there was a word or words I couldn't pronounce, I would make excuses not to read, like having a sore throat or having to use the bathroom. We did this every day. It was a very negative experience. I would get nervous and stressed. I can't even remember learning American history!

I remember oral reading to be a negative and positive experience for me. It was a positive experience because I liked to read and when I was chosen I felt important to the class and the teacher. It was in my English class that I experienced most of my oral reading, because we never read silently in that class. Not reading silently played a part in my negative experience in oral reading. After I read a portion of the text, I was told to explain out loud what I read. I never could explain the material. I was worried about pronouncing every word correctly, what other students were thinking when I was reading, and what the teacher was thinking. If I had the chance to read silently, I would have been able to understand and explain the text.

Often, when teachers shift away from round-robin oral reading and begin using content area literacy strategies, they encounter resistance from the students, which is not surprising. Many students have learned to associate round-robin oral reading with reading and learning, and feel uncomfortable about redefining the concepts. Also, students cling to round-robin oral reading because they are used to it, it is familiar and comfortable, and it requires less active involvement. The alternate content area literacy strategies require students to work much harder, since round-robin oral reading is actually not work at all. It is a rote activity that requires little thinking; many students will be resistant to strategies that require cognitive energy and effort. However, once they begin reaping the benefits of their hard work, they will become disenchanted with the old, familiar round-robin oral reading. The interest and enthusiasm generated by content area literacy strategies cannot be compared with the boredom and tedium too often associated with round-robin oral reading.

Round-Robin Oral Reading vs. Purposeful Oral Reading

Not all oral reading is bad. In the previous sections, a case was made against round-robin oral reading as a strategy for content area literacy; however, some oral reading practices are beneficial and even necessary in certain situations. For example, fluent and confident oral reading is a lifelong communication skill used to deliver information or entertain (Tierney, Readence, and Dishner 1990). Oral reading is a skill that is mastered through practice; therefore, providing students opportunities to improve their oral reading skills is a worthwhile investment of time. When used properly, oral reading is done for a specific purpose toward comprehension, communication, and/or entertainment.

To be used properly, the pitfalls of round-robin oral reading should be avoided. It is preferable to give students the opportunity to read the passage silently beforehand to reduce the stress of performing in front of their peers. Keep the emphasis on the content and not on pronunciation by introducing the passage appropriately and providing specific purposes for reading and listening. These purposes should be followed up after reading, just as with silent reading strategies. Finally, students should be put in pairs or small groups to read orally, thus minimizing the stress associated with reading in front of a large group.

Here are several examples of oral reading used appropriately in content area literacy instruction. Oral reading is used appropriately as part of a follow-up comprehension check and discussion of the content. For example, it is often beneficial to have students read orally evidence from the text that supports their positions or answers to questions. Teachers can diagnose word recognition problems by listening to students read orally in one-on-one settings. Students should be encouraged to share with the class their writing products by reading them orally. Finally, some students need the auditory reinforcement of hearing information while reading it; however, this reinforcement is effective only if the oral reading model is a good one.

In literature classes, oral reading is often a vital part of sharing creative works such as poetry and drama. However, when reading literary works aloud in class, it is crucial that students be given the opportunity to prepare by first reading silently. They should know in advance what they will be expected to read aloud and for what purpose. Also, before the oral reading begins, the teacher should set specific purposes for listening.

The difference between these acceptable forms of oral reading and round-robin oral reading is that these examples are purposeful; that is, they serve a specific purpose toward comprehension, learning, communication, and/or entertainment. The only purpose served by round-robin oral reading is to verbalize the material in class. When used appropriately, oral reading activities can enhance content area literacy and learning.

Effective Oral Reading Alternatives

In content area classrooms, the examples of purposeful oral reading activities presented in Appendix H should be incorporated as components of content area literacy strategies. For example, the oral reading activities may be used in place of the silent reading portions. Keep in mind that passages should always be appropriately introduced, necessary background knowledge generated, vocabulary introduced, purposes set, and comprehension increased through questioning and discussion.

LEARNERS WHO HAVE DIFFICULTY READING AND WRITING

Regardless of whether students have difficulty reading and writing because they have a learning difference such as dyslexia or because they are slow learners, they will probably have difficulty reading the text or other assigned materials at one time or another. Using the content area literacy strategies described in this textbook will certainly enhance comprehension and learning for all students, even learners who have difficulty reading and writing. However, students who have trouble reading and writing about assigned text materials may, at some point, need special adaptations to help them learn the content and improve their literacy skills. This section offers a wide selection of possible adaptations for poor readers and writers who need support beyond the basic content area literacy strategies.

In addition to cognitive support for content area learning and literacy, students who have difficulty reading and writing often need affective support as well to boost their self-confidence and motivation. As Coley and Hoffman (1990) point out, these at-risk learners are often caught in a cycle of failure, leading them to poor self-concepts. After repeated failures, they come to view themselves as incapable and helpless. They then develop coping behaviors for "learned helplessness," best described as a passive attitude toward learning. In a sense, they give up and rely on others to tell or show them what to do. To overcome this sense of helplessness, which often characterizes poor readers and writers, Coley and Hoffman (1990) suggest that direct access to metacognitive strategies will encourage such students to see themselves as capable learners and productive thinkers.

Coley and Hoffman (1990) recommend a three-facet model for helping students develop metacognitive awareness, view themselves more positively as learners, and strengthen their capabilities in asking and answering varied types of questions. First, double entry/response journals can be used to guide students in reflecting on their own comprehension and metacognition. Each page of the journal is divided into two parts. On the left two-thirds of the page, students take notes on their learning. Some examples of student entries include graphic organizers, key words and phrases from a reading assignment, and summary notes from cooperative learning projects. On the right one-third of the page, students record and reflect on the steps they followed in completing assignments. In this portion of the journal entry, students also reflect on and respond to the work represented by the left-hand entry.

Space is also provided in this right-hand portion of the journal entry for the teacher to respond and comment on the students' entries. Teacher comments provide a critical link in leading students to verbalize their stages of cognitive processing, including planning, monitoring, and evaluating. Additionally, teacher comments help students view themselves and their learning potentials more positively.

The second facet of Coley and Hoffman's (1990) model for overcoming the learned helplessness of poor readers and writers is self-evaluation. Each week students respond to three questions about themselves as learners. For the first question, "What kind of thinker were you this week?" students respond using a 5-point Likert scale, with 1 representing poor and 5 representing excellent. The remaining two questions, "What was the best thing you did this week?" and "What do you hope to do next week?" are answered in narrative form. Using self-evaluation is important for students to recognize and appreciate their progress. It also is important for reinforcing the notion that students are in control of their own learning.

The third facet of Coley and Hoffman's (1990) model for overcoming the learned helplessness of poor readers and writers is the use of picture symbols to identify different levels of questions. Through direct instruction, e.g., using the Question-Answer Relationships strategy, students are taught the various graphic symbols, type of thinking represented by each, and sample questions for each type of thinking. Then visual cues are posted in the classroom, and the teacher reminds the student to think about the different types of thinking required for asking and answering various questions. Having a visual frame of reference for distinguishing questions and levels of comprehension is important for helping students develop self-confidence and gain a sense of control over their own learning.

You recall from Chapter 4 that one of the steps in planning thematic units of content area instruction is selection of materials. You should select a wide variety of materials covering related topics and subtopics and make them available in your classroom library. Following the thematic unit system of planning instruction, have ready different reading materials and other media designed to teach the content. Having these materials available is important for providing suitable alternate materials to meet the special needs of your students, especially those who have difficulty reading and writing.

Alternatives for Teaching Content

You should not eliminate completely reading and writing tasks for your poor readers and writers. They need plenty of support and practice in developing content area literacy skills. However, to ensure adequate communication of content, you can supplement reading and writing activities by communicating the content in other ways.

Books on Tape/Listening Guides

One alternative to reading is communicating the content through taped recordings. At one time or another, all of your auditory learners would benefit from listening to instructional tapes. Therefore, it is a good idea to devote a permanent area in your room to a listening center or station. In this space, you should have tape players and headphones available both for individual listening and for small groups to listen to the same tape.

You can develop a classroom audiotape library of textbook chapters and other content reading materials you use for instruction. You may do the recording yourself or ask for assistance from parent volunteers, teachers' aides, older students, and good oral readers in your own class. Have your oral readers do a short test tape, so you can check it for quality before they do extensive recordings. If necessary, give them instructive feedback to ensure that they read slowly yet naturally, speak distinctly and with adequate volume, and use appropriate expression, intonation, and inflection.

For effective listening, most students need visual support. At the very least, they should follow along in the book as it is being read to them on tape. Either you, teachers' aides, or student partners need to monitor them closely to ensure they are following along in their books while they listen. The auditory and visual reinforcement provided by this activity can actually help improve the students' reading abilities while also communicating the content.

Another way to provide visual reinforcement and support for students listening to taped recordings is through the use of Listening Guides (Castallo 1976). Originally designed as a notetaking device for lectures, the Listening Guide can also be used for providing guidance to students listening to books on tape. The Listening Guide usually consists of a skeletal outline of the major concepts, presented in the same order and with the same relationships as communicated on the tape. The outline helps students focus on and record the most important information to be learned. As they listen to the tape, students complete the Listening Guide. They should also have a copy of the text available to aid them in spelling. See Figure 5–13 for an example of this type of Listening Guide.

Listening Guides can also consist of a set of comments and questions designed to provide specific types of guidance and focus. This type of Listening Guide is particularly valuable because it can help students go beyond the literal level of understanding required for completing an outline. In addition to helping students identify important information, the Listening Guide's comments and questions are designed to help students make inferences, recognize relationships, draw conclusions, make critical judgments, and assess the information in terms of personal experiences and values. See Figure 5–14 for an example of this type of Listening Guide.

Lectures and Notetaking

Although often overused, lectures can be an excellent way to communicate and reinforce content, especially for learners who have difficulty reading and writing. However, be careful to avoid the habit of giving lectures over the exact content covered in reading assignments. Your students, both good and poor readers, will learn quickly that if they pay attention in class, they do not really have to read the assignments. If you give a reading assignment, make sure that you hold the students accountable for at least some material that you do not cover in lectures. Otherwise, what is the point of giving reading assignments at all? For your students who are poor readers and writers, you will need to direct them to

FIGURE 5–13 Listening Guide developed for a social studies
lesson (outline)

I. Regions and cities of Texas
    A. Central Texas Hill Country
        1. Austin
        2.
    B.
        1. Houston
        2.
    C.
        1. Dallas
        2.
    D.
        1. El Paso
        2.
    E.
        1. Brownsville
        2.
II. History of Texas
    A. Spanish Missions in Texas
        1. The Alamo
        2.
    B. Flags Over Texas
        1. United States
        2.
        3.
        4.
        5.
        6.
    C. Famous Texans and their Accomplishments
        1. Stephen F. Austin
            a.
            b.
        2. Sam Houston
            a.
            b.
        3. Lyndon Baines Johnson
            a.
            b.
        4. Ann Richards
            a.
            b.

FIGURE 5–14 Listening Guide developed for a literature lesson (comments and questions)

Instructions:

Read these questions before you begin.

Think about them as you listen to the first chapter of "The Scarlet Letter."

Follow along in your book as you listen.

Stop the tape often to review the questions and take notes.

If you do not understand something, rewind the tape and listen to it again.

1. This story took place in the 1600's. Why might we be interested in this story, even though it took place so long ago?

2. The main character's name is Hester Prynne. She lived in a community of Puritans. How would you describe these people?

3. For the Puritans, committing a sin was the same as breaking the law. What does that tell you about their religious beliefs?

4. The scarlet letter stood for the sin committed by Hester. What is that word and what does it mean?

5. How did the Puritans punish women who committed the sin that Hester committed?

6. What color was the scarlet letter? Why do you think they chose that color?

7. Were men who committed the same sin as Hester punished? If so, were they punished in the same way?

8. Why was it easier to find out that women had committed that sin and harder to know that men had?

9. Based on what you have learned about the Puritans in the 1600's, how would you have felt about being part of their community? Why?

10. If you had lived in Hester's community, how would you feel about her punishment? What would you do about it, if anything?

the points in the reading assignments for which they are responsible. You can provide such guidance in the form of study guides.

Since many poor readers and writers have poor notetaking skills as well, they will probably need some support and instruction in notetaking if lectures are to be effective. Listening Guides provide an excellent structure for teaching notetaking skills (see Figures 5–13 and 5–14 for examples of a Listening Guide). In fact, they were originally designed by Castallo (1976) to help students listen for the key points made in lectures and record that information in an organized fashion.

Another way you can provide notetaking support for poor readers and writers is to identify some of the best notetakers in class and make copies of their notes. Distribute these copies to students having difficulty with notetaking but be careful not to allow students to become totally dependent on the notetaking skills of others. Rather, tell students that occasionally you will provide them with samples of good sets of notes. They should compare these samples with their own notes to make sure their notes are complete, accurate, and well organized. You should also collect and assess students' notes regularly, giving them feedback on how they could improve their notetaking skills.

Other Instructional Media

As you plan thematic units, check with your school and community librarians for catalogues of films, filmstrips, videotapes, audiotapes, video discs, computer multimedia software, and so on related to the topics of instruction. Develop annotated bibliographies of what is available and then update your bibliography each year. A tremendous amount of content is available for presentation through audio and visual media. Most of the media programs available today are quite good, although you should preview it before actually using it.

All too often, teachers use media presentations inappropriately. They assume that the media programs are self-contained units, needing no introduction or follow-up. You have probably seen teachers introduce films or videos by saying nothing more than "Now we're going to watch a video about _____." Then, afterwards they say nothing in review or response to the presentation; instead, they dismiss class or move on to another activity as if the end of the program constitutes the end of the lesson. However, presenting a media presentation without adequate preparation before, guidance during, and assessment afterward is just as ineffective as giving a reading assignment without introducing it, setting purposes, and following up to ensure purposes have been met.

To use media programs effectively in communicating content, you need to use them in the context of strategies for content area literacy. For example, just as with reading assignments, you should introduce vocabulary, develop background knowledge, activate schemata, set specific purposes for viewing/listening, follow up to assess learning, and reteach if necessary. *Never* present a media program without a proper introduction and without telling students what information they should be able to identify. Listening Guides can be quite useful for setting purposes for media viewing/listening, helping students identify key information, and assessing their understanding of the content.

Learning Centers

Learning centers are areas in the classroom set up for self-contained independent and small-group activities. They are self-contained in that they provide instructions, materials, and self-checking devices. Since they are designed for students to work independently of the teacher, instructions must be simple, clear, and complete; all necessary materials must be provided along with places for finished work; and self-checking devices must be self-explanatory and easy to use. Students may work alone, in pairs, or in small groups to complete learning center activities. They are responsible for starting the tasks, managing their time, and asking for assistance. They are allowed to talk and work with classmates and generally are rewarded with free time when they finish.

Learning centers are excellent for developing independent work habits, helping students become responsible for their own learning, and freeing the teacher to work with individuals or small groups of students. They are also excellent for communicating and reinforcing content in a variety of ways. For example, you could have any combination of the following types of centers: reading center, listening center, viewing center, writing center, computer center, and games center.

Using learning centers, you can make adaptations for learners with reading and writing problems in several ways. One way is to have special centers devoted to those students. In the special centers, you could provide instructions and answer keys on tape, reduce the quantity and difficulty of tasks, and emphasize key content from the reading assignments. Another adaptation is to have two or more sets of instructions at each center, each set reflecting a task at a different level of difficulty. Then, you can give students assignment sheets or cards telling them which task(s) to complete at each center. You can vary the number of tasks you assign to each student at each center and also let students select the tasks they wish to complete. Still another adaptation is to assign heterogeneous partners so that at least one of the partners can be responsible for the reading and writing done by the pair.

More Alternatives: Partnership Strategies and Activities

Students with reading and writing difficulties can benefit from working with more able partners in a variety of ways. First, partners can serve as models for helping students develop their abilities in metacognition, word recognition (see Chapter 8), concept development (see Chapter 8), application of reading and study strategies, higher-level comprehension, questioning, notetaking, outlining, summary writing, annotating, and so forth. Partners can serve as effective peer tutors for teaching and reinforcing content and guides who walk students through difficult tasks, assignments, and activities by giving step-by-step instructions, monitoring progress, and giving immediate feedback. Finally, partners can read difficult materials to other students, discuss the content with them, and serve as the recorder in completing the written portion of the task.

Oral Reading Strategies

You remember from earlier in this chapter that some oral reading strategies can be effectively used in content area learning. Three of these activities are especially useful for having student partners provide support for

In Radio Reading, a purposeful oral reading activity, the reader plays the role of a radio announcer reading a script. (See Appendix H for more information about Radio Reading and other effective alternatives to Round-Robin oral reading.)

learners who have difficulty reading and writing. These effective oral reading strategies are Radio Reading, Paired Reading, and Echo Reading. See Appendix H for more detailed descriptions of these strategies.

Language Experience Approach

Chapter 1 provides a detailed description of the Language Experience Approach, which can be an effective strategy for adapting instruction for students who have difficulty reading and writing. In this strategy, students generate reading materials related to the content using their own language. Consequently, partners can monitor and evaluate each other's learning. By using their own language, students can also make the content their own by relating it to prior knowledge. The steps include presentation of content, discussion of content, dictation to summarize content, and reading the summaries.

The first step, presentation of content, can take many forms. For example, it can be a reading assignment (read aloud by the able reader in the partnership), video, guest speaker, individual or group student presentation, computer hypertext program, slide presentation, lecture, discussion, or field trip. Once the content is presented, it should be discussed by the whole class in a teacher-led discussion with questions that require students to think at all levels. In this step, students should do most of the talking. The teacher's role is to keep the discussion focused, as well as to help students assess and complete any apparent gaps in their understanding and learning of the content.

Once students have had time to discuss the content thoroughly, and the teacher is satisfied that the level of learning is adequate, the students work with partners to compose their own summaries of the information. The dictation should be done by the student who is a poor reader and writer, with her or his partner serving as recorder. The student who is dictating the summary should be allowed to consult with her or his partner to formulate the sentences orally before they are recorded.

Once the dictated summaries are complete and accurate, students should be given opportunities to reread them silently or orally with their partners. The recorded summaries should then be copied so that each partner has her or his own to keep. These summaries, written in the students' own language, provide important study aids, especially for poor readers and writers.

Guided Listening Procedure

This strategy follows the same steps as the Guided Reading Procedure (see Chapter 2), except that instead of "reading to remember everything," students are instructed to "listen to remember everything" (Readence, Bean, and Baldwin 1992). When using this strategy as an adaptation for students who have difficulty reading, the able reader in the partnership reads a passage to the poor reader. After reading, the listener recalls aloud anything and everything he or she can remember from the passage. The reader, at this point, becomes the recorder, writing down everything the listener recalls.

Once the listener has stated everything he or she can remember, the reader rereads the passage. While the passage is being reread, the listener looks at the dictated statement to see if he or she can think of anything that was excluded or remembered incorrectly. The listener can stop the reader at any point to ask her or him to make corrections in the notes recalled or to reread parts if necessary. After rereading, the reader checks the notes for accuracy and completeness, making additions and corrections as necessary. The reader and listener then work together to organize the notes in some fashion. Once the pair has decided how they want to organize the information, the listener does the rewriting with the reader checking for accuracy and making suggestions as necessary.

SUMMARY

When teachers apply literacy-based strategies for content area instruction and teach students how to apply literacy-based study strategies independently, they are developing and enhancing students' comprehension of the content. Without becoming reading specialists or reading teachers, what else can content area teachers do to support their students' comprehension development? First, effective questioning techniques play a crucial role in the development of comprehension, especially at critical levels of thought. Both teachers and students can use questioning effectively to enhance comprehension at all levels.

Students must ask themselves good questions for the purposes of actively engaging the text, making predictions, monitoring and assessing comprehension, fulfilling purposes for reading, and processing content at higher levels of thought. Two content area literacy strategies, the ReQuest Procedure and Question-Answer Relationships, are designed to improve students' self-questioning abilities.

Two types of classroom interactions affect comprehension development: recitation (turn-taking) and discussion. Each of these interaction types has a unique role in content area instruction. Discussion is essential for developing comprehension at critical levels of thought. Some discussion techniques enhance content area learning while also developing students' critical thinking abilities.

Two types of listening/comprehension skills are important both for discussion and critical thinking. Empathic listening involves listening for the purpose of complete understanding through a process of sharing the author's experience. Debate listening involves listening for the purpose of responding to an author's message as it relates to a predetermined question, issue, or position. Both types of listening skills are important in comprehension development at the highest levels of thinking.

For teachers to develop their students' comprehension at all levels of thought, they must understand the cognitive processes involved at the various levels. Several taxonomies of thinking and comprehension can be useful in becoming familiar with those processes. These taxonomies can also serve in planning and implementing instruction to develop students' comprehension at all levels from literal to critical.

Content area teachers can enhance comprehension by "scaffolding instruction," i.e., supporting students for successful text interaction. They can provide this instructional support in the form of study guides developed especially for specific reading assignments; study guides can provide support for homework assignments or allow teachers the freedom to work with several groups in class at once.

Generally speaking, comprehension is better during silent reading. However, some oral reading strategies can also be effective for comprehension development—round-robin oral reading is *not* one of them. Therefore, in content area instruction, only purposeful oral reading should be used, and it should be used judiciously.

ENRICHMENT ACTIVITIES

1. Borrow a teacher's edition of a content area textbook. Select a chapter and examine the recommended teacher questions. Write a critical analysis of the questions. In your analysis, address whether the questions are designed primarily to evaluate or develop comprehension and provide support for your judgment. Also, include a summary of the extent to which the levels tap into each of the three levels of comprehension in Herber's taxonomy.

2. Select a chapter section from a content area textbook and write a set of questions designed to develop comprehension at all levels of thought.

3. Visit a school in your community and observe a content area lesson. Record the teacher's questions for the entire lesson. A tape recorder or video camera would be preferable if permission is obtained. Label each question as literal, interpretive, or applied. Write a brief summary of your findings. Is the teacher emphasizing one level over the others or ignoring one or more of the levels? How would you assess the effectiveness of the teacher's questioning techniques? What conclusions can you draw about the overall efficacy of the questions in terms of promoting content area learning?

4. Visit a school in your community and observe a content area lesson in which the teacher incorporates oral reading. Write a critical assessment of what you observed, addressing the following questions. Was round-robin oral reading used? If so, what effects on the students did you observe? If not, what distinguished it from round-robin oral reading? Was the oral reading used effectively? Why or why not?

5. Form a group with three of your classmates. Make plans to meet outside of class for an hour. When you meet, form two pairs. Have one pair discuss the following controversial statement for fifteen minutes: *Abortion should remain legal.* While one pair is discussing the statement, the other pair should be observing and taking notes on whether each participant is engaging in empathic or debate listening. After fifteen minutes, stop and have the observers share their observations with the discussants. Then the whole group can talk about ways that empathic listening could have been used or increased in the discussion. Have the discussants apply the suggestions for empathic listening by having another discussion of the same statement for another fifteen minutes. Then, switch roles and repeat.

REFERENCES

Allington, R. L. (1984). Oral reading. In *Handbook of reading research.* Edited by P. D. Pearson, R. Barr, M. L. Kamil, and P. Mosenthal. New York: Longman.

Alvermann, D. E., D. R. Dillon, and D. G. O'Brien. (1990). *Using discussion to promote reading comprehension.* Newark, DE: International Reading Association.

American Association of University Women (1993). *The AAUW report: How schools shortchange girls.* Washington DC: AAUW Educational Foundation and National Education Association.

Anderson, R. C., J. Mason, and L. Shirey. (1984). The reading group: An experimental investigation of a labyrinth. *Reading Research Quarterly* 20:6–39.

Au, K. (1979). Using the experience-test-relationship method with minority children. *The Reading Teacher* 32:677–679.

Barrett, T. C. (1972). Taxonomy of reading comprehension. In *Reading 360 Monograph.* Lexington, MA: Ginn.

Bloom, B. C. (1956). *Taxonomy of educational objectives: Cognitive domain.* New York: David McKay.

Bruinsma, R. (1981). A critique of "round-robin" oral reading in the elementary classroom. *Reading-Canada-Lecture* 1:78–81.

Castallo, R. (1976). Listening-Guide—A first step toward notetaking and listening skills. *Journal of Reading* 19:289–290.

Coley, J. D., and D. M. Hoffman. (1990). Overcoming learned helplessness in at-risk readers. *Journal of Reading* 33:497–502.

Covey, S. R. (1990). *The seven habits of highly effective people.* New York: Fireside.

Cunningham, D., and S. L. Shablak. (1975). Selective reading guide-o-rama: The content teacher's best friend. *Journal of Reading* 18:380–382.

Dillon, J. T. (1984). Research on questioning and discussion. *Educational Leadership* 42:50–56.

Ericson, B., M. Hubler, T. W. Bean, C. C. Smith, and J. V. McKenzie. (1987). Increasing critical reading in junior high classrooms. *Journal of Reading* 30:430–439.

"Failing and Fairness," *Dateline*, NBC. December 29, 1992, show #130.

Feder-Feitel, L. (1993). How to avoid gender bias. *Creative Classroom* 56–62.

Frandsen, B. (1993). *Diversified teaching: An anthology of strategies.* Austin, TX: St. Edward's University.

Heckelman, R. G. (1969). A neurological-impress method of remedial-reading instruction. *Academic Therapy* 4:277–282.

Herber, H. L. (1978). *Teaching reading in content areas,* 2d ed. Englewood Cliffs, NJ: Prentice Hall.

Herber, H. L., and J. Nelson Herber. (1993). *Teaching in content areas with reading, writing, and reasoning.* Needham Heights, MA: Allyn & Bacon.

Kang, Hee-Won. (1994). Helping second language readers learn from content area text through collaboration and support. *Journal of Reading* 37:646–652.

Manzo, A. V. (1969). The ReQuest procedure. *Journal of Reading* 2:123–126.

Manzo, A. V., and U. P. Casale. (1985). Listen-read-discuss: A content heuristic. *Journal of Reading* 28:732–734.

McKenna, M., and R. Robinson. (1993). *Teaching and learning through text.* White Plains, NY: Longman.

Pearson, P. D., and D. D. Johnson. (1978). *Teaching reading comprehension.* New York: Holt, Rinehart and Winston.

Raphael, T. E. (1982). Question-answering strategies for children. *The Reading Teacher* 36:186–190.

Readence, J. E., T. W. Bean, and R. S. Baldwin. (1992). *Content area reading: An integrated approach,* 4th ed. Dubuque, IA: Kendall/Hunt Publishing Company.

Reyes, M., and L. A. Molner. (1991). Instructional strategies for second-language learners in the content areas. *Journal of Reading* 35:96–103.

Richardson, J. S., and R. F. Morgan. (1994). *Reading to learn in the content areas,* 2d ed. Belmont, CA: Wadsworth.

Searfoss, L. W. (1975). Radio reading. *The Reading Teacher* 29:295–296.

Shoop, M. (1986). Inquest: A listening and reading comprehension strategy. *The Reading Teacher* 39:670–675.

Singer, H., and D. Donlan. (1985). *Reading and learning from text.* Hillsdale, NJ: Erlbaum.

Tierney, R. J., J. E. Readence, and E. K. Dishner. (1990). *Reading strategies and practices: A compendium,* 3d ed. Needham Heights, MA: Allyn & Bacon.

Vacca, R. T., and J. L. Vacca. (1993). *Content area reading,* 4th ed. New York: HarperCollins.

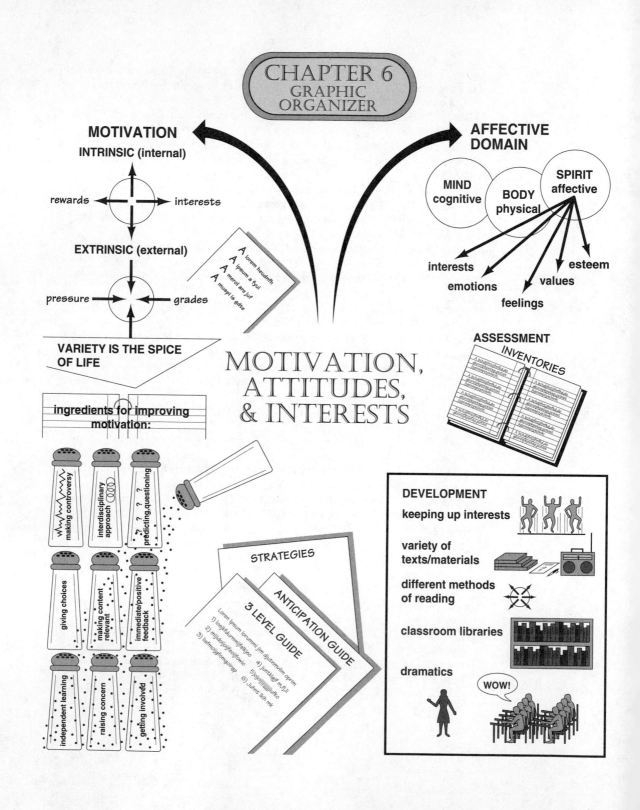

CHAPTER 6
GRAPHIC
ORGANIZER

MOTIVATION

INTRINSIC (internal)

rewards ← → interests

EXTRINSIC (external)

pressure → ← grades

A lorem heudnth,
A ipsum a fyil
A merol are juf
A muspl is gdte

VARIETY IS THE SPICE
OF LIFE

ingredients for improving
motivation:

making controversy

interdisciplinary approach

predicting, questioning

giving choices

making content relevant

immediate/positive feedback

independent learning

raising concern

getting involved

MOTIVATION,
ATTITUDES,
& INTERESTS

AFFECTIVE
DOMAIN

MIND
cognitive

BODY
physical

SPIRIT
affective

interests

emotions

feelings

values

esteem

ASSESSMENT
INVENTORIES

STRATEGIES

ANTICIPATION GUIDE

3 LEVEL GUIDE

Lorem Ipsum lorummj jim diurtmvilm oprm
1) loejkfdummjifekijeo   4) Jumtkgif m.fj.li
2) mjjdoljoijfedjfowio   5) jogeljjjjjjiiJiuRo
3) liefmoijgfomgorigp   6) Juhnt kih mk

DEVELOPMENT

keeping up interests

variety of
texts/materials

different methods
of reading

classroom libraries

dramatics

WOW!

Motivation, Attitudes, and Interests

To demonstrate mastery of the content, the student will be able to do the following:

PART 1 OBJECTIVES

1. Explain the key to motivation in content area learning and why it is a simple concept, but not necessarily easy to accomplish.
2. Identify the following strategy, describe its distinguishing features, and assess its significance to teaching content area literacy: Anticipation Guide.
3. Identify and briefly describe two ways to assess attitudes and two ways to assess interests in content area instruction.
4. Discuss the importance of assessing students' attitudes and personal interests in the content area classroom.

PART 2 OBJECTIVES

1. Identify the following strategy, describe its distinguishing features, and assess its significance to teaching content area literacy: Cooperative Reading Teams.
2. Generalize the effect students' attitudes toward literacy and learning can have on their motivation.
3. Briefly explain the factors that influence students' attitudes toward literacy and learning, including teacher attitudes.
4. Justify content area teachers' investments of time and energy to improve their students' attitudes toward literacy.
5. Distinguish intrinsic from extrinsic motivation, briefly examining the role of each for improving students' attitudes toward learning.

6. Create a set of planning guidelines designed to intrigue students at the beginning and hold their attention throughout each lesson.
7. Compose a descriptive list of five additional motivational techniques (i.e., not addressed in the preceding objective) that you perceive as most valuable to you.

INTRODUCTION

Can students learn if they are not motivated to do so? Perhaps, but the learning process can be much more effective and enjoyable, both for students and teachers, if everyone is a willing participant. This chapter is written with several assumptions in mind. First, student motivation is important to the success of content area learning through literacy. Second, students are not necessarily self-motivated and do not automatically perceive the value of content area learning and literacy. However, teachers can motivate students and help them perceive the value of learning by making instruction interesting, challenging, enjoyable, meaningful, and relevant. Finally, teachers can achieve these goals simply through a careful selection of materials, strategies, and activities based on informal assessment of students' attitudes and interests.

The topic of motivating students is so important that an entire chapter is being devoted to it in this textbook. However, motivation is also addressed throughout the rest of the book as a critical component of the overall concept of content area literacy. In content area learning, students have the opportunity to experience the importance and practical value of literacy skills. Motivation helps define content area literacy because, as discussed in Chapters 1 and 2, content area learning involves real-life reading-to-learn experiences. As a result, students are empowered to satisfy natural curiosities and appetites for knowledge. This empowerment is a motivator that transforms reading to learn into reading for fun, fostering positive attitudes toward reading and writing.

Motivation is crucial to every aspect of content area literacy. For example, notice how literacy-based strategies are designed to motivate students by actively involving them in the learning process and giving them more control over their own learning. Although students are often motivated through active involvement in and control over the learning process, sometimes they need more. In other words, applying sound literacy-based strategies for content area learning is important but may not be sufficient for ensuring motivation. Sometimes students need help establishing personal goals for learning and identifying possible approaches and tools for reaching their goals.

You recall from Chapters 1 and 2 that literacy provides tools for learning, and literacy skills develop as the need arises to use them. Students perceive needs for learning in many ways. For example, they may have natural curiosities and innate urges to fill them, personal interests that they find rewarding to develop, certain goals for achievement and a desire to enjoy the satisfaction of reaching them, or desires for the external rewards (e.g., money, praise, status) associated with being educated. Perhaps students want to feel better about themselves through self-improvement, find personal satisfaction in the process of acquiring knowledge, get fulfillment from being knowledgeable about the world around them, or perhaps they simply want to do everything possible to find the best that life has to offer. All of these perceived needs are examples of motivation.

The key to motivation is simple but not necessarily easy to accomplish. The key is this: *The content area teacher must demonstrate to students how instruction is relevant to their personal interests, experiences, and perceived needs for learning.* Indeed, the notion is a simple one and seems quite obvious; however, communicating the relevance of instruction is not necessarily an easy task. Students often have difficulty perceiving how the content topics and instructional activities are related to their own lives and personal needs for learning. As a result, content area teachers simply cannot take for granted that students appreciate the value of each lesson. Rather, for each lesson, teachers must consciously and deliberately demonstrate to students how the topic and activity is relevant to their individual learning needs. Demonstrating the relevance of each lesson is possibly the most important part of the lesson but can also be the most challenging and frustrating. This chapter will show you ways to make this task easier.

When students have poor attitudes toward literacy or school in general, they generally have little motivation to learn. Teaching can be a painful and ineffective endeavor if you are trying to force information on unwilling learners. On the other hand, students with favorable attitudes toward literacy and learning are more likely to have higher motivation to learn. Improving students' attitudes is an important and worthwhile aspect of content area teaching, especially if you want it to be a successful and enjoyable experience. Content area teachers can facilitate students' positive attitudes toward learning and literacy. This chapter will show you ways you can learn more about your students' attitudes, as well as ways to help them develop more positive attitudes toward learning and literacy.

Information about students' personal interests is necessary for planning instruction, selecting materials that are motivating, and effectively communicating the relevance and value of lessons. When content area teachers can relate a topic to something of personal interest to the students, the relevance and value of learning about that topic becomes much more obvious. This chapter will show you ways to discover your students' personal interests, as well as ways to use that information for planning lessons, selecting materials, and making instruction meaningful.

PART 1

STRATEGY: ANTICIPATION GUIDE

Herber (1978, 178, 180, 181) recommended a set of procedures based on the use of predictions as a motivator and an aid to comprehension. He identified the following instructional principles in support of having students make predictions:

1. Students' interest is aroused when you treat the curriculum in a way that lets them discover that much of their prior knowledge and experience is relevant to each new topic.
2. Motivation for staying with the lesson seems assured when the students' prior knowledge and experience becomes the basic "stuff" of the lesson, creating a student-centered lesson in which each has invested intellectually and emotionally.
3. Students' comprehension will increase when you show them how to relate information and ideas in the resource materials to their own knowledge and experience.

Herber (1978) suggested that a lesson begin by having students work in small groups to brainstorm lists of words related to the topic of the lesson; students then share and discuss the lists as a whole class. This activity is designed to activate students' background knowledge on the topic. Students are then given a set of opinion-type statements and asked to decide whether they would agree or disagree with each one. Finally, they are asked to predict whether the author would agree or disagree with each one. Their purpose for reading is to check the accuracy of their predictions (Herber 1978).

The Anticipation Guide consists of a set of procedures similar to those recommended by Herber and was developed by Readence, Bean, and Baldwin (1992) as a motivational prereading strategy. It is designed to activate students' prior knowledge and stimulate interest in the reading assignment's topic. Anticipation Guides can also be used to introduce nonprint media such as lectures, videos, and field trips. They lend themselves to a variety of content areas including science, art, physical education, and history (Readence, Bean, and Baldwin 1992). Anticipation Guides are used best in pairs, small groups, or cooperative learning situations so that students can discuss more easily their opinions and perceptions. Their versatility and motivational effect make Anticipation Guides a valuable strategy for content area learning and literacy.

Developing Motivation and Activating Schemata

The Anticipation Guide consists of five to ten interpretive- or applied-level statements related to the topic of the passage being introduced. Before reading the assignment, students are asked to respond to each statement by writing either *agree* or *disagree* next to it. They should be instructed to decide whether they agree or disagree on the basis of their prior knowledge and experiences, even if they have little previous knowledge about the topic. Students must provide support for their opinions by identifying the information or experiences that led them to those opinions. Readence, Bean, and Baldwin (1992) recommend that students record their justifications in writing to serve as reference points for discussion. You can easily see the motivational value of this strategy, since most students have opinions they are eager to share and discuss. You can also see how this strategy activates schemata, since students have to decide whether they agree or disagree using what they already know or have experienced about the topic; schemata are further activated when students record and discuss their justifications for the positions they have taken.

Composing the Statements

The Anticipation Guide should *not* consist of literal-level true/false statements; it is *not* a true/false exercise. Statements of the "Ho-hum-who-cares?" variety defeat the purpose of the strategy. Rather, the relevance to the students' own lives and experiences should be obvious. Statements designed to challenge commonly held beliefs and misconceptions about the topic are most effective; they should be somewhat controversial, involving something about which students are likely to have an opinion. One of the distinguishing features of the Anticipation Guide is that it allows students to examine misconceptions about the topic. When giving instructions, make it clear to the students that the Anticipation Guide is *not* a true/false test; rather, it is an activity designed to get them thinking actively and forming opinions about the reading assignment (Readence, Bean, and Baldwin 1992).

Duffelmeyer (1994) cautions against the following common pitfalls in composing statements for Anticipation Guides. First, avoid statements that require more background knowledge than students are likely to have. Literal-level facts stated as true/false statements are one example of a statement type requiring more knowledge than students are likely to have before reading. Second, avoid statements based on supporting details rather than on the major concepts; literal-level facts of little significance to the big picture are an example of statements that focus on subordinate information rather than on major ideas. Third, avoid using statements that are considered common knowledge, i.e., that most students would already know without having to read the passage. An exception, of course, would be statements that reflect commonly held misconceptions; these are the types of statements the Anticipation Guide is designed to address.

If you avoid these pitfalls you should end up with an effective set of statements that, according to Duffelmeyer (1994), have the following characteristics. First, they convey a sense of the major ideas students can expect to encounter in the reading. They also activate and build upon students' prior experiences and are general rather than specific. Finally, they challenge students' beliefs (see Figures 6–1 and 6–2).

Anticipating the Content by Discussing Responses to the Statements

After students have responded in writing to each statement by agreeing or disagreeing with it, lead a brief discussion to allow students to share and defend their opinions. This discussion is important for at least two reasons. First, it gives students the opportunity to hear varying and alternative perspectives and points of view. Second, it gives the teacher the opportunity to assess students' background knowledge and misconceptions regarding the topic (Readence, Bean, and Baldwin 1992). This information can then serve as a starting point for postreading discussions, making it easier for the teacher to evaluate students' comprehension of the passage.

Setting Purposes for Reading

Once opinions about the Anticipation Guide statements have been discussed, students should read for the purpose of deciding whether the author might agree or disagree with each statement. While reading, they should write down what they think the author's opinion might be regarding each statement and prepare to defend their decisions. Students should keep in mind their own and classmates' opinions, as well as ways in which the passage relates to the group discussion (Tierney, Readence, and Dishner 1990).

FIGURE 6–1 Anticipation Guide for a social studies lesson on World War II

Directions: Before reading, decide whether you agree or disagree with each statement. In the column labeled "YOU," put an **A** if you agree and a **D** if you disagree. Then, read for the purpose of deciding whether the author would agree or disagree with each statement. Put those responses in the column labeled "AUTHOR."

		You	Author
1.	World War II was a necessary war.		
2.	One should fight for what he/she thinks is right.		
3.	One should use any type of force necessary to end war.		
4.	The atomic bombs that were dropped on Hiroshima and Nagasaki were necessary.		
5.	All men and women who died fighting for their country should be heroes.		
6.	It was wrong for us to use the atomic bomb in World War II.		
7.	Hitler's final solution was wrong.		
8.	The Holocaust is an example of genocide.		
9.	The U.S. should have tried to stop the genocide in Germany.		
10.	The German officers who carried out this genocide should be punished.		

After reading, decide whether you would change any of your initial responses. Do you disagree with any of the author's responses?

Reactions after Reading

After reading, have students respond again to each statement in light of the information gleaned from the reading. These reactions then serve as a springboard for a postreading discussion. Students should explain why they did or did not change their original positions. Make it clear to the students that they do not necessarily have to agree with the author as long as they can reasonably support their own positions (Tierney, Readence, and Dishner 1990).

AFFECTIVE ASSESSMENT

The **cognitive domain** of learning refers to the learner's thought processes involved in understanding and learning content. Therefore, cognitive assessment involves evaluation of the content learned, in terms of both quantity and quality. Chapter 9 provides a detailed look at cognitive assessment in the content area classroom.

The **affective domain** of learning, on the other hand, refers to the learner's emotions and attitudes relevant to the content and learning processes. Therefore, affective assessment involves evaluation of the learner's feelings about and attitudes toward the content and learning processes. Since the affective domain can have a significant impact on the cognitive domain, affective assessment is crucial to understanding and meeting students' needs.

As discussed in the introduction to this chapter, students with positive attitudes toward literacy and learning are more likely to be self-motivated. Improving students' attitudes is an important and worthwhile endeavor of the content area teacher; teaching students with good attitudes is much more enjoyable and effective than teaching students who are anguished or disinterested. Content area teachers can indeed improve their students' attitudes toward learning and literacy, and the results are well worth the small amount of time and effort involved.

Also discussed in the introduction was the importance of teachers' knowledge about their students' personal interests; this information is necessary for the teacher to plan instruction that is meaningful to the students. When content area teachers relate a topic of study to something of personal interest to students, the relevance and value of learning about that topic are much more obvious. Teachers need information about their students' personal interests in order to plan activities and select materials that students are likely to find interesting and enjoyable.

Before teachers can decide how to improve attitudes and relate learning to students' personal interests, they must first gather some information about their students. Collecting information about students' attitudes and interests is vital for two reasons. First, when teachers take the time and trouble to gather personal information about their students and use it for planning activities and selecting materials, it communicates to students a caring attitude and commitment to their needs. Students are more likely to meet a teacher halfway in the learning process when they see evidence that the teacher genuinely cares and is making a real effort to make learning meaningful. However, gathering information is not sufficient, in and of itself, for motivation. Any motivation generated by the process of collecting information will be lost if not acted upon. Second, teachers need the information to make instructional decisions that are more likely to make learning interesting, enjoyable, rewarding, and valuable to their particular students.

Assessing the affective characteristics and needs of students is an important part of the application of Total Quality principles to education. In particular, the principles of continuous improvement and ongoing self-evaluation rely heavily on the feedback provided by the assessment of attitudes and interests. Teachers need that feedback on a regular basis to evaluate the effectiveness of instructional decisions and make improvements based on what worked and what did not. In addition, it is important to include students in the decision-making process by assessing their needs and interests and then using that information to plan instruction and select materials. In the process of giving feedback, students are empowered to make choices about topics of study, instructional activities, and reading materials.

Assessing Attitudes

When considering attitudes, we need to distinguish attitudes about literacy skills from attitudes about the content area. Some students can have negative feelings about reading and writing, for example, but enjoy learning about the content area. In particular, students who have experienced repeated failure with reading and writing probably do not enjoy those activities. However, they may find the subject matter interesting and be eager participants in class discussions or enthusiastic listeners to lectures on the topic.

Other students might have positive attitudes about reading and writing but have prejudices or misconceptions about a content area. For example, some students might have math anxiety, others might experience science phobia, and still others might believe that there is no inherent value in learning about "dead people" in history class. To complicate matters further, some students might express a negative attitude about a content area or reading assignment when in fact they are actually having difficulty understanding the material. Therefore, it is equally important for content area teachers to develop an awareness of their students' attitudes toward both literacy and the content areas. It is also important to observe students carefully to identify reading and writing problems being masked by poor attitudes toward the content area.

Informal Observation

Generally speaking, students' attitudes are fairly easy to identify through informal observation (both in and out of the classroom), class discussions, and private conversations (e.g., in one-on-one conferences). Teachers can keep track of informal observations of students' attitudes and attitude changes through anecdotal records and/or checklists of characteristics. This information can be quite useful in selecting materials, planning instruction, and forming cooperative learning groups.

Often, it is all too obvious which students harbor negative attitudes: their classroom behaviors serve as a continual reminder that they do not like to read, write, listen, think, or learn. Negative attitudes about literacy are often manifested when students repeatedly refuse to read or write, complain vociferously when asked to do so, whine about how hard the work is or how tired they are, or ask "Why do we have to do this?" By contrast, it also can be obvious which students have positive attitudes toward literacy. These students can be seen frequenting the library, carrying books and other reading materials besides textbooks, talking with classmates about books or articles they have read, writing in journals, solving puzzles, and asking higher-level questions.

Informal observations, discussions, and conferences can also reveal students with negative attitudes toward the content area or topic of study. For example, if they have fears or misconceptions about the content area, they frequently repeat such sentiments as "I can't do math!" or "Science is too hard!" or "Who cares about what happened a long time ago?" In the same respect, students with positive attitudes toward the content area can also be identified. They often complete assignments with enthusiasm, eagerly participate in class discussions, voluntarily bring in outside materials relevant to the topic, and talk about related information or experiences from television, outside reading, or other classes.

Attitude Surveys

Information garnered through observations, discussions, and individual conferences can be supplemented with informal attitude surveys. Generally, these surveys consist of a series of statements to which students respond, indicating the extent to which they agree or disagree with each statement. The statements might focus on such areas as attitudes toward reading and writing in general, reading and writing to learn, reading and writing for fun, and self-concept and self-confidence involving reading and writing abilities.

Constructing a survey. One popular survey of reading attitudes is the BJP Middle/Secondary Reading Attitude Survey (Baldwin, Johnson, and Peer 1980). For elementary students, the length of the survey could be shortened and the statements simplified. Thomas Estes (1971) developed such a survey; in fact, it is versatile enough to be used with students in grades 3–12. Figure 6–3 provides some examples of the kinds of statements that might be included on a reading attitude survey. Generally, students select their responses from a Likert scale, similar to the one shown in Figure 6–3 at the top of the survey.

The same type of survey could be developed for attitudes toward other literacy skills including writing, listening, and critical thinking.

FIGURE 6–2 Anticipation Guide for a math lesson

Problem Solving Strategy: Account for All Possibilities

Directions: Before reading, consider each statement below. Decide whether you agree or disagree and write your responses in the blanks on the left side. Then, read your assignment for the purpose of deciding whether the author would agree or disagree with each statement. Record those responses on the right side.

YOU   **AUTHOR**

_____ **1.** Drawing a diagram is always the best strategy to use when solving a problem. _____

_____ **2.** It is not always possible to write a mathematical equation for a word problem. _____

_____ **3.** It is always possible to identify every solution for an equation. _____

_____ **4.** A systematic approach is always the best method to use when solving an equation. _____

_____ **5.** It is always best to use computers when solving an equation with an infinite number of solutions. _____

_____ **6.** There will always be a finite number of ways for solving a problem. _____

After reading, decide whether you would change any of your initial responses. Do you disagree with any of the author's responses?

FIGURE 6–3 Reading attitude survey: Examples of appropriate items

---

    strongly agree   **agree**   **disagree**   **strongly disagree**

1. Reading is something I like to do for fun.

2. I like going to the library.

3. Reading is boring.

4. Bookstores are fun.

5. I like to read during summer vacation.

6. I don't like to read.

7. Reading is not cool.

8. I love getting new books.

9. Reading is more fun than watching television.

10. Free reading time at school is a waste.

Additionally, surveys could be created to assess attitudes toward particular content areas and even specific topics within those content areas. As with the reading attitude surveys, content area attitude surveys could include statements related to the students' self-concepts and confidence with respect to their abilities in a particular content area. The surveys could also address common misconceptions and prejudices related to the content area or topics of study.

Communicating purpose and maintaining anonymity. Some teachers require students to put their names on the attitude surveys, so they can identify and counsel individually those with poor attitudes. However, for several reasons, some reading specialists argue that students should complete the surveys anonymously (Readence, Bean, and Baldwin 1992). First, students with poor attitudes might be reluctant to share that information honestly with the teacher—and justifiably so. Teachers, as human beings, easily could feel some degree of prejudice against students with bad attitudes. Students who need to be counseled can be identified easily through observation. The primary purpose of the surveys should be to assess overall group attitudes; more importantly, surveys should be used to measure the effectiveness of selected materials, strategies, and activities in terms of improving overall group attitudes.

When administering attitude surveys, it is important to explain your intentions to the students; otherwise, they might become very confused and suspicious about why you are collecting information on their personal opinions regarding school. One of the most effective ways to communicate your intentions is to precede the survey with an informal class discussion about attitudes toward school in general or your content area in particular. Let your students know that your goal is to make learning as interesting and enjoyable as possible and to accomplish that you will be relying on regular input from them. Assure them that the feedback will be anonymous, since you want them to respond honestly. Explain exactly how you plan to use the group results to make decisions about topics, activities, and materials. Such a preliminary discussion will set the tone for an interactive, participatory class, as well as become a precedent for regular class discussions (similar to town meetings) to get student feedback about the progress of the class. Hopefully, such discussions will lead to a climate of trust, making anonymous surveys unnecessary.

Making effective use of results.   Although teacher use of attitude surveys for instructional decision making communicates to students the teacher's sense of caring and commitment, the simple process of completing the survey is probably not enough to improve students' attitudes. The process itself can be beneficial to students by helping them develop an awareness of personal attitudes toward literacy and learning; awareness is often a prerequisite to personal change. Beyond developing an awareness, however, the act of completing a survey does little toward influencing the attitudes reflected by it.

Once the teacher has a good idea of the group's overall attitudes, the information should be considered for instructional decision making related to materials, strategies, activities, topics of study, and sequencing of instruction. Therefore, the group results of the survey should be kept readily available for frequent referral by the teacher. If the survey results are filed, forgotten, and not used to influence instructional decisions, there is little hope that attitudes will improve on their own. Instructional decisions should be evaluated by readministering the attitude survey as a reassessment later in the semester or year.

Assessing Interests

The importance of assessing the interests of students is emphasized by Readence, Bean, and Baldwin (1992, 60):

> All students can learn to enjoy reading if teachers are capable of helping them find sufficiently interesting materials and are willing to give them the time to read.

Later in this chapter we will discuss the notion of giving students time to read for enjoyment in class. Before committing class time for free reading of materials related to the topic of study, however, teachers must first find materials their students are willing to read. The task of locating such materials is not always an easy one. Content area teachers who know something about the kinds of topics their students are likely to find interesting have an advantage over teachers who try to predict what their students will like. Since individual patterns of reading interests cannot be predicted on the basis of sex, age, or ethnic origin, teachers who attempt to do so can end up engaging in the worst kind of stereotyping (Readence, Bean, and Baldwin 1992). In the long run, the most efficient process for selecting materials begins with collecting information on students' individual interests.

The process of selecting reading materials to serve as alternatives or supplements to content area textbooks will be discussed in detail in Chapter 7. Before such materials can be selected and classroom libraries established, however, content area teachers must assess the personal interests of their students. Information gathered on students' interests can be used throughout the school year to update and restock classroom libraries as the topics of study change.

Informal Observation

As with attitudes, student interests can be investigated through informal observations, class discussions, and student/teacher conferences. Students frequently give clues as to the kinds of topics that spark their interest. For example, teachers can gather valuable information just by paying attention to informal conversations students have with teachers and other students, contributions students make to in-class discussions, and dialogues between students during cooperative learning activities. As with attitudes, student interests can be summarized and recorded by the teacher in the form of anecdotal notes or checklists of topics. This information can be especially useful to the teacher in matching partners and planning cooperative learning projects.

Interest Inventories

Since students cannot always be overheard talking about topics of interest, particularly those that relate to the content area or unit of study, teachers often need to supplement informal observations with another form of assessment. A variety of interest inventories can be used for this purpose, all of which have the following potential benefits. First, they stimulate students' thinking about the many possible subtopics related to major topics of study, hopefully piquing new interests. Second, they give students the opportunity to participate in the decision-making process by giving them some choice in the materials and topics of study. Third, they offer the teacher ideas about general interests that might somehow be made relevant to the topic or unit of study.

As with attitude surveys, make your intentions clear before administering an interest inventory. Assure students that it is not a test and will not be scored. Explain that it will help you make decisions about which topics to study, how long to spend on each, and which materials might be interesting and enjoyable. McKenna and Robinson (1993) recommend reading the inventory aloud to the students as they complete it. Not only does this practice allow you to elaborate or explain some of the topics and perhaps provide some examples, but it also helps ensure that the poor readers in the class understand the questions.

General inventories.   The first of the two basic types of interest inventory is a general interest inventory, which gives students the opportunity to share with the teacher their general interests. These interests are manifested in everyday activities such as hobbies, television viewing, sports and leisure activities, pleasure reading, and extracurricular activities. The format of the inventory usually consists of a list of possible areas of interest from which students choose; in addition, space is provided for students to add other topics not on the list.

General interest inventories could also include a section asking students to identify the kinds of things that motivate them. Knowing the types of incentives and rewards that might be effective motivators and positive reinforcers for your students will be important. One possibility is to provide a list of incentives and rewards and have students rank them in order of preference. Figure 6–4 is a partial list of both internal and external motivators you might include.

Content-specific inventories.   The second type of interest inventory is the content interest inventory, which focuses more specifically on topics and subtopics related to the content area or unit of study. In generating a list of topics and subtopics, McKenna and Robinson (1993) emphasize the importance of including aspects of the subject matter that will likely have the greatest appeal to students. Often, the most appealing aspects are those that are unusual, strange (McKenna 1986), or potentially controversial. Also, look for the aspects that might be related somehow to current events or the students' own lives and experiences.

FIGURE 6–4 Examples of internal and external motivators

Internal Rewards

____ learning something because you are curious about it
____ being an expert on something that interests you
____ learning something so you'll know more about it than your friends know
____ learning something new just for fun
____ knowing more about the world around you
____ finding out more about something you've seen on television
____ feeling good about being smart
____ feeling good about your abilities
____ being intelligent and educated
____ feeling confident in yourself
____ liking yourself more

External Rewards

____ getting good grades and making the honor roll
____ money or tokens to be spent on something fun
____ praise from the teacher, your parents, the principal, or other teachers
____ popcorn, candy, gum, and soda
____ free time, hall pass, or other privileges
____ free time to read or write whatever you want
____ books, toys, stickers, colored markers, and other fun things
____ stars, happy faces, and teacher comments written on your work
____ progress charts
____ time to play computer games

The format of the content interest inventory is basically the same as that of the general interest inventory: provide a list of possible topics or subtopics from which students choose. In addition, space is provided for students to add other topics not on the list. The content interest inventory can include general topics such as ecology, war, crime, animals, space travel, computers, money, architecture, fashion, and sports medicine. You could also break one or more general topics into a variety of subtopics. For example, within ecology you might include air pollution, pesticides, oil spills, endangered species, economic development, and rain forests. For a math unit, you could include a variety of careers in math and computer technology, along with practical applications of mathematical concepts (e.g., automotive maintenance, cooking, shopping, building design and construction, fashion design and sewing, and so forth).

Systems of response. One way students could respond is simply by checking or circling topics of interest to them. However, this method of response makes it difficult to synthesize results into any kind of meaningful data; basically you end up with a long list of topics, which is actually where you started. If the students' responses tend to cluster around the same topics, this method might prove useful. However, if the students respond with widely-varying choices, then the system's lack of discrimination between favorite topics and topics of mild interest would make it impractical.

Readence, Bean, and Baldwin (1992) suggest having students prioritize or give weight to stronger interests by using a rating system something like a traditional grading system. Have the students "grade" each topic by assigning it A, B, C, D, or F, with A showing enthusiasm, B showing interest, C showing indifference, D showing distaste, and F showing aversion. From these results, you can rank the topics for the class, from most interesting to least interesting topics.

Another system of response suggested by Readence, Bean, and Baldwin (1992) is to have students rank their top three subtopics under each general topic, identifying them with 1, 2, or 3. With this system, the subtopics could be ranked in separate groups, rather than having all the subtopics competing with each other. If instruction focuses on only one group of subtopics at a time, it might be more useful to have the results separated according to the unit of study.

PART 2

STRATEGY: COOPERATIVE READING TEAMS

Chapter 4 discussed in detail the concept of cooperative learning, which can be an effective tool for improving students' attitudes toward literacy and learning. Madden (1988) recommends the use of cooperative learning specifically for improving the attitudes of poor readers. He bases his recommendation on Glasser's (1986) "control theory," which attributes students' motivation to a sense of control over the ability to get their basic needs met. Basic needs can include such things as food, shelter, clothing, love, pleasure, and power. According to Glasser, students can gain a sense of power and importance by achieving academically: through academic activities and achievement, students can discover the power they have in controlling their own destinies. Therefore, motivation can be enhanced with cooperative learning activities, which offer opportunities for students to feel their self-worth, value, and power in an academic setting. Cooperative learning allows students to get immediate feedback from their peers and teachers in terms of their value to the group. Through the group dynamics in cooperative learning activities, students can develop a positive sense of self as a necessary or wanted component for overall group and individual success.

The "cooperative reading teams" suggested by Madden (1988) for content area instruction consist of heterogeneous groups of students who share a common interest in a particular topic. A research project is carefully structured by the teacher to focus on specific purposes and questions. The task of researching the topic is divided among the group members, and research activities are assigned to students based on their abilities to complete them. After completing their individual tasks, group members share their findings with each other. Then, as a group, they analyze and synthesize the information in response to the specific investigative questions originally posed. Finally, each group prepares to share its information with the rest of the class. Some of the possible formats include oral and written reports, construction of research books or booklets, bulletin board displays, exhibits, dramatizations, filmstrips with audiotapes, and videotapes (Madden 1988).

According to Madden (1988), the use of cooperative reading teams can improve attitudes because it provides all students, particularly poor readers, with positive learning and social experiences. Positive experiences result from students making contributions toward a common goal on a high-interest task. Students enjoy the opportunity to share common interests and make important contributions to a group of students with a variety of abilities and talents.

AFFECTIVE DEVELOPMENT

Attitudes and interests are key elements of motivation. Once you have assessed your students' attitudes and interests, you are ready to use that information to make instructional decisions designed to help motivate them. Your instructional decisions should address both attitudes and interests, since one tends to influence the other. For example, as students develop more varied and intense personal interests in learning, their attitudes toward learning and literacy are likely to improve as well.

Keep in mind that both attitudes and interests can be significantly affected by students' experiential backgrounds. For example, attitudes toward learning and literacy will likely need strengthening for students who come from homes where little value is placed on books and schooling. Unfortunately, many students have not had the opportunity to see family members (or other significant adults or peers) reading or writing for pleasure or personal growth. Such students are obviously at a disadvantage in terms of appreciating the value of learning and literacy. Therefore, when you address attitudes and interests in your instructional decisions, consider ways to strengthen and bridge possible gaps in students' background experiences with literacy and learning.

Attitudes and interests also can be influenced significantly by students' self-concepts. For example, students who view themselves as slow learners or poor readers will probably have negative attitudes toward learning and reading; it is not surprising that they view unfavorably tasks about which they have little self-confidence. Often, self-concepts are the result of prior experiences. Therefore, students who have had little success with certain content areas or literacy skills probably have negative attitudes toward them; again, it is not surprising that they would dislike something with which they have experienced repeated failure. Consequently, when making instructional decisions, it is important to include ways to help students understand and appreciate their individual ways of learning, potentials for learning, and abilities in literacy skills. Giving students every opportunity to experience success on a regular basis is crucial for helping them develop the self-confidence they need for positive attitudes and strong interests.

Teacher Attitudes

Some of the most important considerations to make in planning content area instruction include your own attitudes toward literacy, as well as your own personal interest in and enthusiasm for the subject matter. It is virtually impossible for teachers to improve their students' attitudes toward reading unless they themselves have favorable attitudes toward reading, which they communicate through their actions and words. For example, teachers lose credibility when they tell their students that reading is a pleasurable and rewarding leisure activity but are never seen reading during a break or talking about books they have read. Such mixed messages can sabotage your efforts to improve students' attitudes.

The effect of teacher attitudes was demonstrated in a study reported by Rieck (1977, 647), in which three hundred students from the classes of fourteen content area teachers responded to the following questionnaire with the following results:

1. Do you like to read?
   (52% yes, 38% no, 10% no response)
2. Do you read your assignments in this class?
   (15% yes, 81% no, 4% no response)

3. Do your tests mainly cover lecture and discussion, or reading assignments?
(98% lecture and discussion)
4. Are you required to discuss your reading assignments?
(23% yes, 73% no, 4% no response)
5. Does your teacher give you a purpose for reading or are you only given the number of pages to be read?
(95% pages, 5% purpose)
6. Does your teacher bring in outside material for you to read and recommend books of interest for you to read?
(5% yes, 95% no)
7. Does your teacher like to read?
(20% yes, 33% no, 47% don't know)

If you study these results, you will see the significant effect the teachers' actions had on the students' perceptions and attitudes. Although the teachers were giving reading assignments, the facts that they rarely set purposes for reading or held students accountable for the assignments gave a different message to the students. As Rieck (1977) points out, the real message might be: "You really don't have to read the assignments because I'm not going to test you on them, and we probably won't even discuss them in class. You should read the assigned pages, but there is no real reason to do so. Reading isn't as important as listening to the lectures."

The fact that the teachers gave their students little indication about their own personal reading attitudes and preferences and rarely brought in or recommended interesting books related to the topic of study also sent students a distinct message. That message, Rieck (1977) suggests, might have been: "Reading really isn't important, outside reading is of little value in my class, and my students have no way of knowing whether I like to read or what my reading preferences are."

An important implication of these results is that teachers' own attitudes about content area literacy and literacy-based strategies, as communicated through their classroom behaviors, have a significant influence on their students' attitudes. If teachers are going to effect improvements in their students' attitudes and perceptions, they must first convince the students of their own beliefs in the importance of literacy for learning, and the value of the content. As master learners, teachers of content have the responsibility to model for students their own desires for and satisfaction gained from acquiring knowledge. The teachers' attitudes about learning and literacy, as well as their enthusiasm for the content, is contagious. Unfortunately, even their negative attitudes and lack of enthusiasm are visible and contagious. If you want your students to have positive attitudes and enthusiasm, you must be a believer yourself and remember that your actions speak louder than your words.

Your classroom climate is the sum of your attitudes not only toward learning and literacy but also toward your job, your subject, and your students. Your classroom should be a pleasant, comfortable, and secure place for the students; they should look forward to being there and enjoy the time they spend with you. It is important that you maintain and convey a calm, relaxed manner. At the same time, be generous with smiles and positive comments. Show your students the sincere concern you have for them as individuals and especially as learners. Listen and respond to their needs, problems, ideas, and suggestions; celebrate their successes; be their advocate and supporter; show them your respect and trust. Most of all, create a positive learning environment through praise, encouragement, and a good sense of humor.

Improving Student Attitudes toward Literacy

Why would teachers of content want to invest time and energy improving their students' attitudes toward literacy? After all, isn't it the job of elementary teachers, reading specialists, and English teachers to develop students' abilities and attitudes involving literacy? First, you recall from Chapter 1 that often, in classrooms where teachers do not use literacy as a learning tool, students and teachers alike begin to associate textbooks with boredom and drudgery. Teachers complain that students either cannot or will not read their assignments; in turn, many students complain that the text is boring and that the same old assignments are nothing but busy work. When teachers of content can improve students' attitudes about the text and other instructional materials, feelings of boredom and drudgery dissipate, and students are motivated to read their assignments.

Second, when students have positive attitudes and appreciate the value of literacy in the classroom, they are more likely to be motivated participants in the learning process. The joys of teaching students who are enthusiastic about learning seem obvious, especially compared with the agony of dragging unwilling learners through the motions. In other words, when students have good attitudes about reading and writing to learn, they are more likely to be pleasant and successful members of the learning community in the content classroom.

Third, students with favorable attitudes toward reading and writing tend to become better at those skills than students with negative attitudes toward them. One likely reason they have better skills is that students with positive attitudes toward literacy, particularly reading and writing, tend to engage in those activities more often. The more they read and write, the better readers and writers they become. "Practice makes perfect" certainly applies in the development of literacy skills. The bottom line for teachers of content is that their jobs become easier and more pleasurable when students' attitudes and skills in literacy improve. Students with strong literacy abilities are more likely to be independent, responsible, and self-directed learners. Having students with these qualities makes teaching a completely different experience; instead of spoon feeding, force feeding, and hand holding, you spend more time leading, guiding, facilitating, and consulting. The teacher's job becomes more exciting and rewarding as the teacher and students become partners in learning.

Fourth, when positive attitudes toward literacy lead to improved abilities in reading, writing, and critical thinking, students become more successful learners of content. Think about how much and how often learning in the content classroom is accomplished through reading and writing. Students with poor literacy skills are at a distinct learning disadvantage in every content classroom—even math. Since improved learning outcomes are the ultimate goal of the content teacher, they provide documentation of the teacher's instructional effectiveness.

General Recommendations
From their review of research producing recommendations for improving student attitudes, Richardson and Morgan (1994, 36) summarized a set of recommendations specifically for helping teachers improve students' attitudes towards reading:

1. Actively listen to student comments and discussions.
2. Make reading fun and rewarding.
3. Encourage students to read on their own.
4. Make reading assignments shorter for poor readers.
5. Have frequent group and sharing experiences.
6. Speak well of reading and share the books he or she is reading.

They also recommend using sound instructional frameworks that include a Preparation phase, Assistance phase, and Reflection phase. Their recommended framework, PAR, represents the before, during, and after segments of other basic instructional strategies in content area literacy such as the Directed Reading Activity (DRA). Using strategies such as the PAR and DRA is important to ensure that the reading task is clear. Specific purposes for reading should be established so that students know exactly what is expected of them. Students should be guided in preparing themselves for reading by relating their background knowledge to the reading assignment. After reading, students should follow up to ensure the purposes have been met and think critically about the content.

Using a Variety of Reading Materials as Text Supplements and Alternatives
One of the most important ways to help students improve their attitudes toward literacy is to provide them with a wide variety of reading

experiences. As discussed earlier in this chapter, many students come to school with few or no experiences with books or other reading materials. Therefore, their first experiences with books and literacy involve a great deal of instruction with textbooks. You would probably agree that textbooks are generally not the most exciting and pleasurable reading materials available. As a result, students whose primary experiences with reading have involved textbook instruction begin to associate the specific act of textbook reading with the general concept of "reading." Not surprisingly, such students often develop negative attitudes toward reading and literacy in general.

Teachers of content play a crucial role in helping students avoid or overcome misconceptions about the purposes, utility, and versatility of reading. It is important that students be made aware of the wide range of materials available for different needs including learning and pleasure. Chapter 7 discusses in detail how to use a variety of reading materials including children's and young adult fiction and nonfiction as supplements or alternatives to textbooks.

Providing Opportunities for a Variety of Reading Experiences

In addition to making readily available a wide variety of interesting, relevant, and appealing reading materials, it is important to provide students opportunities to explore, read, and share those materials. You must somehow incorporate them into your daily lesson plans, using them to either supplement the text with enrichment activities or replace the text for literacy-based strategies. It is also important to provide students regular opportunities (daily or every other day) to read content-related nontextbook materials such as books and magazine articles simply for fun. Chapter 7 describes various strategies and activities you can use to ensure that your students have opportunities for a wide range of reading experiences beyond the textbook.

Improving Student Attitudes toward Learning

Following are some of the perceived needs for learning that can affect students' attitudes toward learning:

- satisfying natural curiosities
- developing personal interests into expertise
- acquiring knowledge for its own sake
- being knowledgeable about the world around us
- reaching personal goals for achievement
- enhancing self-concept through self-improvement
- taking advantage of everything that life has to offer
- building self-confidence

When students develop and identify their own needs for learning, they can more readily perceive the value of learning; as a result, attitudes toward learning are enhanced. Teachers can help students develop and identify personal needs for learning in a variety of ways. For example, they can share with students through modeling and discussion their own personal needs for learning. Through class discussions, teachers can introduce students to the various reasons people have for wanting to become educated. In small groups, students can share with each other things that motivate them to become more knowledgeable. As part of the introduction to each lesson, students can discuss with the class their own purposes for learning (i.e., what they want to learn and why). Journal writing can give students the opportunity to explore and personalize various needs for learning. The time spent in helping students perceive their own needs for learning is a wise investment that should save time in the long run. Students who have good attitudes toward learning because they perceive its value in getting their needs met will likely be more willing and successful members of your content learning community.

Intrinsic vs. Extrinsic Motivation

The perceived needs for learning identified in the previous section are examples of intrinsic motivation. They originate internally or within the student. Extrinsic motivation, on the other hand, originates externally or outside of the student. Examples of extrinsic motivation include the following:

- good grades, progress charts, and honor rolls
- money
- praise, respect, and status
- food and beverages
- free time, parties, and other special privileges
- pleasurable reading books
- toys and other material possessions
- parent, teacher, and employer approval
- acceptance by friends and family
- good jobs
- field trips and guest speakers

Some students are more motivated by extrinsic rewards than others. For students who are extrinsically motivated, such rewards can be quite useful. For example, for students who do not perceive a need for learning, extrinsic rewards can provide an incentive to get involved in the learning process. Hopefully, through active involvement, the students will recognize and appreciate the intrinsic rewards of participating in the learning process.

Knowledge about what motivates your students is crucial for creating a system of positive reinforcement and classroom management that incorporates both intrinsic and extrinsic motivators. Use information gleaned from interest inventories to help you determine which types of rewards are likely to be effective for each student. However, some combination of intrinsic and extrinsic rewards is important to give students the opportunity to experience both types of motivation.

From interest inventory results, you should have a fairly clear idea of which students might benefit from extrinsic rewards. Use this information to set up a flexible classroom management system that allows students to make choices from a variety of rewards. For extrinsic rewards to provide effective positive reinforcement, they need to be given as soon as possible after they have been earned. However, use your extrinsic reward system sparingly, preferably only when needed. Overuse of external rewards can sometimes undermine the development of intrinsic motivation.

Ultimately, your goal should be to help students develop intrinsic motivation by helping them perceive their own needs for learning. Your instructional planning should emphasize the development of intrinsic motivation. During the sometimes lengthy and challenging process of developing students' intrinsic motivation, however, extrinsic rewards can be quite effective as temporary motivators.

General Recommendations

From a review of research, Richardson and Morgan (1994) summarize a set of recommendations for teachers to improve student attitudes in general. Many of these suggestions seem like common sense but easily can be overlooked in the lesson planning process. Therefore, consider these suggestions as part of the development of every lesson plan. Look for ways to incorporate them daily through your selection of reading materials, strategies, activities, classroom interactions, and nonprint media.

For example, the recommendation to "trust students and exude warmth" at first glance would not seem appropriate to include in a lesson plan. However, if you think about it as part of your instructional decision-making process, you might develop a specific way to demonstrate to students that you trust and have a warm, caring attitude towards them. One way to show your trust is to give students a set of choices for a homework or in-class assignment; let them know that you trust them to select the options best suited for them and complete the assignments to the best of their abilities.

One way you could exude warmth is to have individual conferences with students who do not complete their assignments or do not complete them satisfactorily. The purpose of the conference would be for you to listen as the student explains the circumstances or reasons that interfered with completion of the assignment. You could then decide whether to give the student another chance, and if so, what adjustments might need to be made. The fact that you are willing to listen and make considerations based on individual circumstances rather than automatically doling out punishments or zeros shows a great deal of warmth and compassion on your part. You can see how important it would be to plan ahead, though, for something like individual conferences. If this idea is going to be realistic, you would need to plan it into the next day's activities.

Following are the recommendations summarized by Richardson and Morgan (1994, 36):

1. Accept students as they are.
2. Assume students want to learn.
3. Expect considerable achievement.
4. Praise whenever appropriate.
5. Be critical in a constructive manner.
6. Be honest with students.
7. Accentuate the positive—that is, build on strengths.
8. Talk *with* students, not *at* students.
9. Have a sense of humor.
10. Learn some interesting characteristics of each student.
11. Trust students and exude warmth.
12. Be enthusiastic.
13. Call students by first name or preferred name.

All of these recommendations are important in the development of a positive and supportive classroom climate, which is essential to foster positive attitudes toward learning. In addition to the previous recommendations, it is also important to communicate to students that you believe in them and their abilities, and you will not give up on them. Perhaps most crucial is that teachers must value and demonstrate the value they place on inquiry, problem solving, and reasoning. This value can be demonstrated by being open-minded and encouraging students to participate in open-ended discussions (Richardson and Morgan 1994).

Setting Goals

As discussed in Chapter 3, teachers can help their students set goals, both long and short term. Whole-class discussions, small-group discussions, or individual conferences with students can be used to give students the opportunity to express their own hopes for the future, as well as to ponder alternatives expressed by their classmates. Students who have a solid vision of what they want out of their education and what they want out of life are in a better position to appreciate the value and relevance of learning. As a result, they are more likely to have positive attitudes toward learning and be interested in the topics of study.

Teachers can help by including in the curriculum some career awareness activities and materials. It is extremely important for students to know about a variety of career options related to the various content areas. Relating content area instruction to career choices can make learning more meaningful to students. When students explore career opportunities as part of content area learning, they are able to see the application and practical value of the topics they study.

Choices, Rewards, and Consequences

In the process of improving students' attitudes toward learning, teachers should emphasize to their students that learning is optional—no one can force them to learn. In other words, the choice is theirs. When students realize that they have the power to control their own learning, they may be in a better frame of mind to develop positive attitudes. Whatever their attitudes, however, teachers should emphasize to students that the choices they make have a direct effect on their lives.

Teachers should also make students aware of the rewards available to them if they choose to learn, as well as the possible consequences if they choose not to learn. Rewards and consequences are not always obvious to students. Short-term rewards and consequences are often so inconsistent that students are confused about what they can expect; long-term rewards and consequences are often so far in the future that students can easily ignore them. Teachers need to communicate short-term rewards and consequences clearly and follow through with them consistently by using a system of positive reinforcement and classroom management. They also need to make the long-term rewards and consequences more visible through regular class discussions, student conferences, and reading materials about how their choices of today can expand or limit their options in the future.

In a previous section of this chapter, the distinction was made between intrinsic and extrinsic motivation. Short-term rewards usually involve extrinsic motivation; these rewards are more tangible and provide more immediate reinforcement. Long-term rewards, on the other hand, usually involve intrinsic motivation. These rewards are more abstract and difficult to appreciate but ultimately result in students who are self-motivated. When students have a clear understanding of their choices, as well as the resulting rewards and consequences, they are generally in a better position to develop positive attitudes toward learning.

Setting Priorities through Values Exploration and Clarification

To foster positive attitudes toward learning, students also need to be reminded regularly that the choices they make are affected by their values and the priorities inherent in those values. They should be given opportunities to explore, discuss, and write about their own values. Figure 6–5

FIGURE 6–5 Examples of values

A value is a principle or characteristic that is intrinsically valuable or desirable. What others can you add to this list?

ambition	honesty
beauty	individuality
charity	inner peace
cleanliness	justice
comfort	loyalty
common good	obedience
compassion	open-mindedness
competence	peace
consistence	pleasure
courage	pride
courtesy	privacy
creativity	prosperity
duty	quality of life
economic efficiency	recognition
enjoyment	safety
equality	security
excitement	self-discipline
fairness	self-esteem
forgiveness	social harmony
freedom	social responsibility
friendship	spirituality
happiness	tradition
health	wisdom

---

provides a list of values that could be used to generate exploration activities, e.g., requiring students to rank order a given set of values or identify the values held by opposing parties in a controversy or ethical dilemma. Such opportunities can also be provided appropriately in applied-level questioning and discussions. Value-laden questions should be posed regularly to students to allow them to make decisions about the values that will guide their choices and actions. When students have a clear understanding of their values and the priorities they represent, they are more able to appreciate the importance of learning.

Value-laden questions should also require students to demonstrate how their choices and actions are consistent with their expressed values. Additionally, students need opportunities to examine the priorities implied by their chosen values. Through these explorations, students can uncover inconsistencies between priorities, choices, actions, and their expressed values. Identification of inconsistencies should be followed by opportunities for students to make their own decisions about whether they want to make their values, priorities, choices, and actions consistent. If so, they need to decide what they want to change to achieve consistency. Students who make choices based on their values are in a better position to develop positive attitudes toward learning.

Applied-Level Questioning and Discussion

These difficult issues can be interwoven into instructional discussions on a wide variety of topics in many different content areas. Emphasizing the applied level in instruction is therefore an important tool in motivating students. When students are constantly stuck with literal-level assignments and questioning, they easily become bored and disinterested. When the focus shifts to more challenging and relevant application of the content, they become more motivated to learn. Emphasis on applied-level questioning and discussion gives the teacher many opportunities to make the topic relevant to the students' own lives and experiences. Applied-level instruction also allows for more focus on controversial issues related to the topic. Again, students are much more motivated by and interested in controversy than in rote learning.

Capitalizing on Students' Personal Interests

Positive attitudes are only one side of the motivation coin; personal interest in the content is the other side. Obviously, students are going to be more motivated to learn about a topic if they have a personal interest in it. Personal interests are influenced by the students' curiosities, background experiences, personal situations, and perceived needs for learning. Student interests should have a major influence on instructional planning. By focusing on topics of interest, relevance, appeal, and meaning, you can draw students into your learning community.

Of course, it would be impossible to select your entire curriculum around the interests of your students. However, if students are interested in a significant portion of what you teach, they have reason to feel confident in your instructional decisions. In other words, they will trust that your selection of topics, even those in which they have no particular interest, are important and worthwhile.

Also, interest can be stimulated even if students initially perceive no real connection with the topic. For example, if you are familiar enough with your students, you will be able to connect seemingly obscure topics to previous experiences, current events, relevant controversial issues, and their perceived needs for learning. In fact, as discussed in Chapter 4, it is important to begin each lesson with an introduction that relates the topic to the students' own background knowledge and experiences.

Grabbing Attention at the Beginning of Every Lesson

The introduction to every lesson should somehow grab students' attention by zeroing in on their personal interests and experiences. Begin with questions that will involve them actively and immediately. For example, in a social studies lesson you might ask "Has anyone ever visited a foreign country, or do you know someone who has? Tell us about it. What was it like? How did you feel? What did you enjoy most? How was it difficult?" In a math lesson, you might ask "Has anyone ever bought something yourself with your own money? Did you get change back? Are you sure you got the right amount of change? How do you know?"

You must follow up these questions with opportunities for at least several students to respond. If you ask the questions and move on without calling on anyone, you are sending them this message: "These questions are not really important, but they are on my lesson plan so I asked them." Only by giving students a chance to share their personal experiences and background knowledge can you capture their attention by capitalizing on their personal interests. Students are always interested in things they personally have done, seen, or heard about. Take advantage of this "hook" by somehow relating the content to something they have likely experienced, even vicariously. Sometimes, it takes a real stretch to relate the topic to their background of experiences.

For topics that require a stretch for students to appreciate, you have to build a bridge to help them see the value and relevance to their lives. For example, if you are teaching a science lesson about protozoa, students will probably have some difficulty appreciating the importance of one-celled microscopic organisms to their daily lives. However, if you show them pictures of microorganisms that live in various water supplies, you can show them some of the effects of pollution. They might be interested to know that having those strange-looking creatures in the water they drink is a partial indication that the water is safe for drinking. Conversely, the absence of protozoa from a water supply is an indication that the water is seriously polluted.

Selecting Interesting and Varied Reading Materials

The idea of giving students time to read in the content classroom was discussed earlier in this chapter. Providing regular opportunities for students to read a wide variety of materials related to the topic of study is important for cultivating positive attitudes toward literacy and learning. Even more important is the need to allow students to select materials that interest them. Therefore, teachers of content must make available materials that are likely to appeal to their students. The assessment of interests, discussed earlier in this chapter, is important in helping teachers select interesting and appealing materials to have available. Chapter 7 shows you ways to select appropriate materials and incorporate them into your lessons.

Generating Student Interest in Content

From a review of research on interest-promoting techniques, Mathison (1989) identifies five general techniques to stimulate readers' interest in text. First is the use of analogies. Analogies are an important way to develop interest by connecting new information to prior knowledge; they make the "strange familiar and the familiar strange" (Mathison 1989, 171). Through analogies, students can activate the schema necessary to appreciate the relevance of the new material; they provide the "cognitive hooks" for grasping new information (Ausubel 1968). They allow students to begin with familiar territory from which a bridge can be built to reach new shores. Analogies develop interest by helping students look at prior knowledge and experiences in new and different ways. For example, a sixth-grade science lesson on keeping the heart healthy can incorporate the analogy of the "heart" of a city, along with its major roads or "arteries" in and out of the city (Mathison 1989).

The second technique is relating personal anecdotes. Since students are often curious about their teachers' personal lives, you can capitalize on this natural curiosity. You can develop students' interests by sharing your own experiences to help them appreciate the importance and relevance of a topic or text passage. As with analogies, personal anecdotes provide students a personal context in which to place new information. For example, in a fourth-grade geography lesson on climate and temperature of deserts, the teacher could begin with a personal anecdote about visiting or camping in a desert.

Mathison also recommends disrupting students' expectations. Students have a natural inclination, as we all do, to retain what is familiar and comfortable. As a result, they have certain expectations and make logical predictions consistent with their own knowledge and experiences. The surprise and confusion resulting from the disruption of expectations is one way in which students' interests can be developed. Teachers of content should constantly look for challenging ideas to develop students' interests by pushing them beyond their comfort zones. For example, in the lesson about the desert previously described, students' expectations about what type of clothing to pack for a camping trip could be disrupted: they would probably be surprised to find that clothing you would wear during the day would be insufficient for nighttime temperatures.

The fourth technique for developing interest is to challenge students to resolve a paradox. When students are presented with information that contradicts their own knowledge and beliefs, an uncomfortable state of cognitive dissonance is created. This discomfort creates in students a desire to explain the "mystery" and resolve the apparent contradiction. As a result, students' interests in reading the information necessary to resolve the paradox are developed. For example, in an eleventh-grade history lesson on the U.S. homefront during WWII, after reviewing Hitler's persecution of the Jews in Europe, the teacher could introduce the fact that a similar thing actually happened to another group of people here in the United States during the war.

Mathison's fifth technique is to introduce novel and conflicting information or situations. The value of novelty in getting students' attention has long been realized by teachers; however, keeping the students' attention once you have it can be a real challenge. Continued interest can be ensured by focusing students' attention on conflicting ideas within the new information presented; students are more likely to be interested in reading the text to help them analyze and resolve these conflicts. For example, in a ninth-grade American citizenship lesson on equal rights and opportunities, the teacher could present a controversial situation involving charges of discrimination, from at least two different points of view; one perspective could be that of the person *charging* discrimination and the other that of the person *being charged* with discrimination. Students could then be asked to argue from both points of view to explore the conflicting perspectives and search for a resolution.

In addition to these five techniques of developing interest, Mathison (1992) makes the following general recommendations for planning. First, connect and stay connected to your students. For example, you could keep your students' interest and attention focused on task by connecting the information to their current knowledge and then sustain the connection by introducing a "new twist" or problem to be solved. Second, design the introductory activity to develop interest in a relatively short period (five to twenty minutes). Third, keep the activity focused by providing students with questions that can only be answered by reading their assignment. Other ways to keep the activity focused include directing attention to students' personal and prior knowledge and directing discussion toward key concepts. Finally, integrate language arts and content-specific information by engaging students in reading, writing, listening, and speaking about the topic.

MOTIVATIONAL IDEAS AND TECHNIQUES

Of course, *all* of the ideas presented thus far for assessing and improving attitudes, as well as for generating and capitalizing on interests, are designed to enhance motivation. This section will describe ten additional suggestions for motivating students in the content classroom. Many of these ideas and techniques overlap with recommendations previously made in this chapter; however, they are so important that they bear repeating. All of these suggestions should be taken into consideration when making and carrying out instructional plans.

Motivating ESL Students

Reyes and Molner (1991) recommend motivating ESL students by connecting their writing assignments with community resources in culturally relevant and authentic forms of expression. For example, students could conduct home and community interviews and surveys on current and relevant topics and issues (e.g., immigration, the value of education, the benefits of being bilingual, single-member voting districts, neighborhood crime, gang violence, environmental concerns, and so on). Then, teachers provide guidance and modeling to help students write papers summarizing the results of their field work.

Field-work activities are important for integrating the interests and needs of the ESL students into the curriculum for the whole class. Because of the importance of culturally-relevant schema to reading comprehension (Pritchard 1990), making school/community connections can be a valuable tool for enhancing content learning. Community issues also provide a fertile ground for motivating students to write, whether to communicate concerns, summarize findings, or write letters to the editor and government representatives. When ESL students can share community concerns with their classmates, they have moved from the periphery to become an integral part of the classroom community.

Emphasizing Variety and Novelty

Continually remind yourself that variety is, indeed, the spice of life—especially in the classroom. Some students need more variety than others, so be prepared to provide options. However, even students who are comfortable with routine and reluctant to make changes can eventually get tired of the same old thing. Using a variety of strategies and activities can be an easy and effective way to motivate your students. Of course, you need to give students ample opportunity to master a strategy, especially when it is first introduced; however, as soon as most of the students get the hang of it and feel comfortable with it, try something new. You can then return to familiar strategies periodically to make sure your students maintain their confidence once it is developed.

Always be on the lookout for ways to bring a novel approach or outlook to both content and activities. For example, present content from varying perspectives by giving students different contexts for learning. An excellent way to present content from various perspectives and points of view is through role playing. Give individual students or small groups of students different situations from which to consider the same set of information to answer an applied-level question. Then have them share and defend their responses.

The desired effect of novelty can also be attained through something as simple as rearranging the room occasionally or wearing a costume to class. Think of ways to shake up your students' expectations; surprise them. Change your classroom routine or plans at the last minute, especially if the students seem particularly listless or disinterested. Wake them up by putting on a hat and singing a song or playing an instrument (even a kazoo will get their attention!).

Of course, the ideas described in the previous paragraph are designed to do nothing more than get the students' attention. Once you have their attention, the hard part is to hold it throughout the lesson. This task is never easy, but the following ideas can be quite effective for motivating students once you get their attention.

Making Content Relevant and Meaningful through Controversy

The idea of making the lesson relevant and meaningful to the students' own lives cannot be overemphasized. Whenever you can somehow demonstrate the connection between the topic of the lesson and things that matter to the students, motivation takes care of itself. One of the most effective ways to make this connection between the content and the students is through controversy.

Students love controversy. If they "take the bait," controversy can "hook" them solidly into the lesson. Look for ways content can be related to some controversial issue, preferably one that affects students directly. Present the controversial issue right away, in the introduction to your lesson and give students the opportunity to respond to it. Actively involve them immediately. Ask for their opinions. Ask them to share prior knowledge or experiences that led them to their opinions. Allow other students to present opposing viewpoints.

Then, once you have their attention, explain carefully how today's topic relates to the controversial issue you have been discussing. Even if the topic and controversy are only remotely related, you have opened the students' minds to the possibility that this topic is something in which they have an interest. Throughout the lesson, refer continually to the controversy, demonstrating for them the connection of the topic to the issue under discussion.

Teaching with an Interdisciplinary Focus

Another effective way to make learning meaningful and relevant is to help students see the connections between disciplines that exist in the real world. Schools built around the nineteenth-century factory model tend to separate the curriculum into discreet parts, like automobile parts riding on an assembly-line conveyer belt. Originally, the idea behind this system of education seems to have been that by the end of the school day, each student would have moved through the entire assembly line and accumulated each part of the curriculum.

Today this factory model of education is outdated, as students can readily see. The assembly line model presents a distorted view of content that clearly does not parallel real life. In day-to-day living, we face challenges, solve problems, make decisions, and answer questions using a combination of approaches from a variety of disciplines. Rarely do we face a situation or dilemma that requires us to apply *only* the principles we learned in social studies, or *only* the principles we learned in biology, or *only* the principles we learned in math. Instead, we must integrate the application of principles from two or more disciplines. For example, when deciding how to vote on a proposed city ordinance to allow commercial development near a local water supply, we need to consider at least the following things: environmental impact statistics, effects on the real estate market, population changes in surrounding neighborhoods, traffic flows, endangered species, and disruption of community activities.

When school curricula can demonstrate to students how principles and information from a variety of disciplines can be combined to address real-life issues, students can more readily see the value and relevance of the content. Whenever possible, look for connections with other disciplines. Probably the best way to ensure an interdisciplinary focus is to team with faculty members from other disciplines and work together to plan instructional units. If students are working on the same or similar real-life issues and problems in more than one class, they have a better chance of recognizing and appreciating content applications.

Many teachers have already discovered the benefits of interdisciplinary planning. For example, a program called International, Multicultural, and Global Education (IMAGE) was developed by a "vertical team" of schools (Travis Heights Elementary School, Fulmore Middle School, Travis High School, and St. Edward's University) in Austin, Texas. The three K–12 schools were selected by the National Education Association's National Center for Innovation to be one of six schools in the nation to make up the Mastery in Learning Consortium.

The project concentrates on a thematic, interdisciplinary approach to the curriculum, as well as team teaching and other innovative practices. For example, at the high school, teachers in biology, English, mathematics, and world geography worked together to plan instructional units based on a common theme. If the theme were a current issue like the North American Free Trade Agreement (NAFTA), teachers and students might work together in teams to do research, draw conclusions, identify implications, ask questions, and report on their findings.

Biology topics might be addressed in terms of the environmental impact of the agreement on each country. English topics might include relevant fictional and nonfictional literature designed to give the students a better understanding of differences and similarities between the three countries. Other English topics could be addressed in terms of the research, writing, and oral presentations of findings. Topics in mathematics might be addressed in terms of the agreement's impact on national budgets, trade deficits and surpluses, business profits and losses, stock markets, and world trade figures. Topics in world geography might be addressed in terms of cultural comparisons between the three countries, impacts of geographical differences on the needs of the people and their ways of life, and the environmental resources available to each country.

Even as the topics within each subject are investigated, several disciplines can emerge at once. For example, the environmental impact of NAFTA also involves the application of concepts in biology and world geography. Also, comparative figures of environmental impact studies involve the application of mathematical concepts, and English literature can be used to give insights on how each country relies on its environmental resources. Not only is interdisciplinary planning easy to accomplish, it is actually difficult to avoid!

Even if you do not find it possible to coordinate planning with other teachers, you can still look for ways to connect your content to other disciplines. For example, students could do journal writing in math class, making notes about what they learned, did not understand, or found interesting, confusing, or frustrating. Students in English classes could incorporate statistics into writing projects to support their positions or conclusions. Another example of teaching with an interdisciplinary focus involves students in middle or high school science classes who manufacture their own paint using principles from biology, chemistry, and mathematics; they then use the paint to create their own paintings as an art project. Still another example of interdisciplinary teaching would be a unit on the history of sugar plantations and slavery that includes as a subtopic the evolutionary and metabolic effect of sugar on humans. Through the use of examples, issues to be addressed, problems to be solved, and projects to be researched, you can demonstrate to your students the importance of the content to a larger, real-life context. When you make instructional decisions using the format of a thematic unit, you can integrate more easily the principles of a variety of disciplines.

Helping Students Make Predictions and Ask Themselves Questions

Herber (1978) emphasized the importance of predictions in the motivation of students for two reasons. Not only is student interest aroused when they discover that much of their background knowledge and experience is relevant to the topic, but their interest is also held when their background knowledge and experience becomes the heart of the lesson.

When students make predictions, they are not only activating their prior knowledge but also actively engaging themselves with the content. Predictions involve a personal response to the topic; therefore, students have a vested interest in checking the accuracy of their predictions. Students who automatically make predictions as they read are motivated through active involvement with the text.

You can teach students how to make logical predictions and develop the habit of making predictions while reading. Use the Directed Reading-Thinking Activity (Chapter 4) and frequently ask students to make and share predictions before and during a reading assignment. Always follow through by having students assess the logic of their predictions and provide support for their analysis.

Another important way in which students actively engage with the text is through self-questioning. As with predictions, students who automatically ask themselves questions as part of the comprehension process are motivated through active involvement with the text. When students are seeking answers to their own questions, as opposed to those provided by the teacher or text, their knowledge quest becomes that of satisfying personal curiosities rather than completing an assignment. The motivational value of fulfilling curiosities over "doing homework" is obvious.

You can teach students how to ask themselves good questions while reading and help them develop the habit of doing so. Using the Reciprocal Questioning Procedure and the Question-Answer Relationships Strategy (Chapter 5) teaches students the value of asking their own questions and asking questions at higher levels of thinking. Another good strategy for helping students learn how to ask themselves questions as purposes for reading is the KWL (Chapter 1). Also, by using study strategies like SQ3R (Chapter 3), students can be taught first how to frame questions from subheadings, then how to formulate their own questions based on their own interests and curiosities.

Empowering Students by Giving Them Choices

One of the most effective ways to motivate students is to give them more control over their learning. You can empower them by showing them you trust them enough to select the option most appropriate for them. When students can make their own choices, they become more active participants in the learning process. They enjoy making their own decisions occasionally instead of constantly following orders.

Some students will probably feel somewhat uncomfortable making their own choices. For these students, you can restrict their choices more carefully, but you should still give them opportunities to become more comfortable making their own decisions. Eventually, you will be able to expand their choices, giving them more decision-making power.

Choices can be given in a variety of ways. However, teachers always should maintain ultimate control by providing a predetermined set of acceptable options from which students may choose. Students can be allowed to choose which questions they will answer or problems they will

Cooperative Reading Teams can be motivating because they allow students to gain a sense of control over their own learning, feel like a valued part of the team, and develop self-confidence in an academic setting.

solve and the order in which they complete a given set of tasks. They can be allowed to choose, within reason, where they will sit and with whom they will work. They can be allowed to choose topics or subtopics they will investigate and the materials they will use to complete an assignment. They can be allowed to choose a format for presenting the completed assignment (e.g., oral summary, written report, role playing, graphic, or bulletin board exhibit). They can also be allowed to choose how they will demonstrate to the teacher that they have mastered the content.

Giving Students Successful and Enjoyable Learning Experiences

Success is probably the best motivator of all. We naturally tend to want to do something we have done well and to avoid those things we have not done well. One of the keys to success in the content area classroom is to apply the literacy-based instructional and study strategies described throughout this book. These strategies are designed to provide students the support and guidance they need for successful use of reading and writing as tools for learning. If you model content area literacy strategies for your students while also requiring them to apply the strategies consistently, they should enjoy success in content area learning.

Another key to success in content area learning is to individualize your instruction. Making instructional decisions on an individual basis maximizes each student's chances for success. You can individualize your instruction by giving students choices and assignments that vary the content, activities, and time limits according to their needs.

Cooperative learning is another practical way to individualize for successful and enjoyable learning experiences. One of the reasons cooperative learning is so motivating is that it discourages competition between students. Students who might have difficulty finding success on their own often find it through the support, guidance, and encouragement of group members. Make sure your groups are composed of students with varied abilities and background experiences, so they can benefit from synergy, each making unique contributions according to their resources.

Although you should prepare students for success, you also want to be careful not to assume that something is too difficult for them. Avoid labeling students and making assumptions about what they can and cannot do. Give them opportunities to choose for themselves the level or amount of work they feel comfortable doing.

Students need to be challenged constantly to stay motivated. However, a fine line exists between challenging students and frustrating them. Although students will generally rise to your level of expectations, your expectations should be within reason. Be flexible enough to make adjustments if you discover that an assignment is too easy or too difficult for a student.

Learning experiences will be enjoyable if you have established a classroom climate that makes it okay to make mistakes. Take advantage of every mistake you make, both in the classroom and out, to teach this concept. Many teachers are terrified about making a mistake in front of their students. However, making mistakes in front of your students is one of the best ways to motivate them to take risks and dive into the learning process with gusto. Talk to them about your mistakes, what you learn from them, how they happen, and how you might prevent them from happening again. The most important lesson you can teach your students is how to achieve success as a direct result of learning from mistakes.

Giving Immediate and Positive Feedback

An important way to help students stay motivated in the classroom is to keep them constantly aware of their progress. They need to know how they are doing, how far they have come, and how far they need to go to meet your expectations. Give them feedback while they are working and as soon as possible after they complete each assignment. Make your feedback very specific. Give them examples of what you liked about their work and specific suggestions and examples for making improvements or corrections.

Make your feedback as positive as possible. You should always make the effort (and sometimes it is a major one!) to find something good to say about every assignment. Then, frame your criticisms constructively by telling the students exactly how to make the desired changes. Be careful with your written comments. A comment written in a lighthearted, humorous spirit can be interpreted by the student as snide and sarcastic. Your feedback should be framed in such a way that will make students feel they have achieved at least some measure of success. Your feedback should also motivate and inspire students to correct their work and avoid the same mistakes next time.

Providing Opportunities for Independent Learning

As you get to know your students, you will be able to provide them with more and more opportunities for independent learning. These opportunities allow them to put into practice the literacy-based strategies that provide them the tools for independent learning. When teachers put their trust in students to make choices about what and how they will learn, students are motivated to prove themselves by putting forth their best efforts. Although teachers should provide guidance and monitor independent work, for the most part, the students are responsible for making decisions about materials, procedures, and formats for presenting their products. Such independence is, of course, the ultimate goal of content area literacy: teachers need to give students ample opportunities to practice independent application of the literacy tools for lifelong learning of content.

Raising the Level of Concern

When teachers raise the level of concern in their classrooms, they communicate to students their expectations that all the students will participate in and contribute to the lesson. When they lower the level of concern in their classrooms, teachers communicate to students a lack of caring about whether the students participate. This communication can be either verbal, nonverbal, or both.

For example, when teachers give an assignment and then retire to their desks to complete paperwork, they have lowered the level of concern through a nonverbal message. The message sent to the students is this: "I have given you this assignment because I am the teacher, and that is what I am supposed to do, but I am really more concerned with the paperwork on my desk than I am about whether you complete the assignment. As long as you seem to be working and are not bothering me, I am not really concerned about whether you complete the assignment."

When the level of concern is low, you can see how students' motivation is likely to be low as well. If you are serious about motivating your students, you must somehow raise the level of concern in your classroom. For example, instead of removing your physical presence from the students as they are working, you need to maintain a strong physical presence by walking around and carefully monitoring each student's progress.

Your monitoring needs to be perceived by the students as serious. If you are walking around and looking at their work, but not really checking to make sure they are successfully reading and completing the assignment, you have failed to raise the level of concern. Many students have become deserving of Academy Awards for acting as if they are reading or working on an assignment. If you are serious about raising the level of concern, you need to call their bluff by asking them questions about what they are reading or how they are otherwise completing the assignment.

Other ways to raise the level of concern include the following. You should give positive reinforcement to those students who are doing a good job and extrinsic rewards to those who complete the assignment satisfactorily. Give students feedback in the form of guidance and suggestions as they work. Have individual conferences with students who are not participating to get to the root of the problem. For example, perhaps they are feeling emotionally distracted that day; perhaps they do not understand the assignment; perhaps they are unable to read the assignment or solve the problems. Whatever the reason, you need to make adjustments to provide appropriate support for the student.

Getting Students Actively Involved

Another way to raise the level of concern in your classroom is to encourage and even require active involvement from all your students. Too often, teachers rely on the same students to respond over and over again. Make sure you call on individuals who do not volunteer; if students you call on do not know the answer, avoid putting them on the spot. You could give them hints or choices, or tell them to think about it and call on them again later. To encourage reluctant students to volunteer, you might say something such as "I want to hear from someone who has not yet shared something today." Perhaps you can give everyone a chance to respond before calling on the same person twice.

Another idea to aid reluctant participants is called "Turn to your neighbor." After posing a question or problem to the entire class, ask the students to turn to their neighbors to discuss possible responses. Then have them raise their hands when they have a response about which they feel confident. Instead of taking volunteers, you could also begin calling

Students attitudes toward reading can be enhanced by providing a wide variety of reading materials along with opportunities for a wide range of reading experiences.

on individuals after they have had at least thirty seconds to consult with their neighbors.

Another way to get more active involvement is to use yes/no response cards ("yes" on one side, "no" on the other; or green on one side for "yes," red on the other for "no") or thumbs up/thumbs down signals. You ask a yes/no question or give a true/false or agree/disagree statement and have all students respond. Then call on several individuals to explain their responses.

Writing is an excellent way to get all students actively involved. Each student must jot down a response and expect to explain it when called on by the teacher. A cooperative learning activity called **Think-Pair-Share** also involves writing and is another good way to get more students actively participating. In this strategy, a question or problem is posed and each student is given about thirty seconds to *think* about it individually and jot down a response. Then, each student forms a *pair* with another student to compare and discuss responses for about a minute. Each pair then forms a "quad" with another pair to *share* and discuss their responses for one to two minutes. Finally, the teacher calls on individuals to share with the whole class some of the responses from each group.

SUMMARY

This chapter was based on the assumption that the learning process is much more effective and enjoyable, both for students and teachers, if everyone is a willing participant. Therefore, motivation is a key component of every aspect of content area literacy. Applying sound literacy-based strategies for content area learning is important but may not be sufficient for ensuring motivation. Sometimes students need help establishing personal goals for learning and identifying possible approaches and tools for reaching their goals.

Students perceive "needs" for learning in many ways: natural curiosities, personal interests they find rewarding to develop, satisfaction in the process of acquiring knowledge, fulfillment from being knowledgeable about the world around them, the satisfaction of reaching their goals for achievement, desires for external rewards (e.g., money, praise, status), and desires to feel better about themselves. All of these perceived needs are examples of intrinsic rewards. Some students can be motivated on a short-term basis with extrinsic rewards (like grades and privileges), but intrinsic motivation is ultimately more effective and enduring.

The key to intrinsic motivation is simple but not necessarily easy to accomplish: The content area teacher must demonstrate to students how instruction is relevant to their personal interests, experiences, and perceived needs for learning. Students often have great difficulty perceiving how the content topics and instructional activities are related to their own lives and personal needs for learning. As a result, content area teachers cannot take for granted that students appreciate the value of each lesson. Demonstrating the relevance of each lesson is possibly the most important part of the lesson but can also be the most challenging and frustrating. This task can be made easier in a variety of ways.

First, it is important to relate the topic to background knowledge and experiences the students are likely to have. Teaching with an interdisciplinary focus is another way to make the value and relevance of the content more obvious. Since students make predictions and formulate questions using their own prior knowledge and experiential background, helping them learn to make predictions and ask themselves questions is another effective way to make the content more personally meaningful. Activating students' background knowledge is crucial to helping them appreciate the value and relevance of the content. The Anticipation Guide is an excellent way to activate background knowledge and help students relate it to the content.

Knowledge about students' personal interests is vital to the process of making learning relevant and valuable. When content area teachers can relate a topic to something of personal interest to the students, the relevance and value of learning about that topic becomes much more obvious. Two ways you can find out about your students' personal interests are through informal observations and interest inventories. This information is important for planning ways to capture students' attention at the beginning and hold it throughout each lesson. Information about student interests is also important for selecting a variety of appealing reading materials.

When students have poor attitudes toward literacy or school in general, they generally have little motivation to learn. Therefore, improving students' attitudes is an important and worthwhile aspect of content area teaching, especially if you want it to be a successful and enjoyable experience. Content area teachers can facilitate students' positive attitudes toward learning and literacy.

Before you can help your students develop positive attitudes, you need to get an idea of the kinds of attitudes they already possess. Two ways to assess attitudes are through informal observation and through the use of anonymous attitude surveys. You can help your students develop more positive attitudes toward learning and literacy by providing rich and varied opportunities for reading, as well as a wide range of high-interest materials.

Probably the most important way to have a positive influence on students' attitudes toward literacy and learning is for the teacher to model an enjoyment of reading and enthusiasm for learning. If you expect your students to be motivated to learn the content, you must show enthusiasm for the subject matter yourself. You must also be careful to avoid sending students mixed messages of the "Do as I say, not as I do" variety. Your actions always speak louder than your words when modeling attitudes toward literacy and learning.

ENRICHMENT ACTIVITIES

1. Develop an attitude survey and general interest inventory appropriate for primary (K–2), intermediate (3–5), middle school (6–8), or high school (9–12) students. Develop a content-specific interest inventory. Administer all three instruments to a class of students and compile the results into a format useful for instructional planning.
2. Observe a class in a neighborhood school, watching for messages the teacher is sending to the students about the importance of the content and the literacy skills being used as learning tools. Also notice the teacher's level of concern in the class. Take notes during your observation, keeping in mind that the teacher might want to read what you wrote; later summarize your findings in a one-page essay.
3. Survey ten teachers each from an elementary, middle, and high school about whether they read aloud to their students. Make the survey brief, asking questions similar to the ones that follow. Summarize your findings.
   - Do you read to your students?
   - If so, how often?
   - Why do you read to them?
   - Do they enjoy it?
   - How do you choose the reading material?
   - What books or other materials do you enjoy reading aloud?
4. Make separate lists of intrinsic and extrinsic rewards that would be appropriate motivators and reinforcers for your classroom.

REFERENCES

Ausubel, D. (1968). *Educational psychology: A cognitive view.* New York: Holt, Rinehart and Winston.

Baldwin, R. S., D. Johnson, and G. Peer. (1980). *Bookmatch.* Tulsa, OK: Educational Development Corporation.

Duffelmeyer, F. A. (1994). Effective anticipation guide statements for learning from expository prose. *Journal of Reading* 37:452–457.

Glasser, W. (1986). *Control theory in the classroom.* New York: Harper & Row.

Herber, H. L. (1978). *Teaching reading in the content areas.* Englewood Cliffs, NJ: Prentice Hall.

Madden, L. (1988). Improve reading attitudes of poor readers through cooperative reading teams. *The Reading Teacher* 42:194–199.

Mathison, C. (1989). Activating student interest in content area reading. *Journal of Reading* 33:170–176.

———. (1992). Stimulating and sustaining student interest in content area reading. In *Reading in the content areas: Improving classroom instruction.* Edited by E. K. Dishner, T. W. Bean, J. E. Readence, and D. W. Moore. Dubuque, IA: Kendall/Hunt Publishing Company.

McKenna, M. (1986). Reading interests of remedial secondary school students. *Journal of Reading* 29:346–351.

McKenna, M., and R. Robinson. (1993). *Teaching and learning through text.* White Plains, NY: Longman.

Pritchard, R. (1990). The effects of cultural schemata on reading processing strategies. *Reading Research Quarterly* 25:273–295.

Readence, J. E., T. W. Bean, and R. S. Baldwin. (1981, 1985, 1989, 1992). *Content area reading: An integrated approach.* Dubuque, IA: Kendall/Hunt Publishing Company.

Reyes, M., and L. A. Molner. (1991). Instructional strategies for second-language learners in the content areas. *Journal of Reading* 35:96–103.

Richardson, J. S., and R. F. Morgan. (1994). *Reading to learn in the content areas.* Belmont, CA: Wadsworth.

Rieck, B. J. (1977). How content teachers telegraph messages against reading. *Journal of Reading* 20:646–648.

Tierney, R. J., J. E. Readence, and E. K. Dishner (1990). *Reading strategies and practices: A compendium,* 3d ed. Needham Heights, MA: Allyn & Bacon.

BEING VERSATILE

Magazines

TIME

NEWS

Variety

Newspapers

NEW YORK TIMES

COVER UP

USING BOOKS

class library

AVAILABILITY

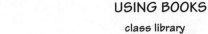

TRADE BOOKS

GUIDE TO BOOKS !

CHECK OUT CARD

TEACHING WITH BOOKS

UNIT 3

books

USING CHILDREN'S & YOUNG ADULT LITERATURE
AS ALTERNATIVE AND COLLATERAL MATERIALS TO THE TEXTBOOK

Multicultural Literature

Gender Bias (AVOID IT!)

Readability

STRATEGIES:
READ-ALOUDS

SUSTAINED SILENT READING

FOLLOW UP ACTIVITIES

BOOK REPORTS ? / **ENRICHMENT**

provide alternatives

ILLUSTRATED LITERATURE

FRY'S GRAPH

TEACHER TIME SAVER*
Consult literature guides for available & appropriate fiction & non-fiction

LITERATURE GUIDES

Children's and Young Adult Literature: Periodicals and Other Alternatives and Collateral Materials for Textbooks

To demonstrate mastery of the content, the student will be able to do the following:

PART 1 OBJECTIVES

1. Summarize the role and value of children's and young adult literature as alternate or collateral materials in the content classroom.
2. Identify the following strategy, describe its distinguishing features, and assess its significance to teaching content area literacy: Sustained Silent Reading (SSR).
3. Summarize the value to students of incorporating multicultural literature and explain how multicultural literature can help students appreciate and value differences among people while also strengthening their own cultural identities.

PART 2 OBJECTIVES

1. Identify the following strategy, describe its distinguishing features, and assess its significance to teaching content area literacy: Read-alouds.
2. Prepare a set of practical guidelines for selecting trade books appropriate for instructional objectives.
3. Choose a theme for a thematic unit in the content area of your choice, describe at least three ways you could incorporate literature into the unit, and list at least five appropriate book titles.
4. Give five examples of alternatives to traditional book reports.

PART 1 OBJECTIVES—continued

4. Describe a five-phase model for incorporating multicultural literature.
5. Distinguish "gender bias" from "sexual harassment" in the classroom and create a plan for promoting gender equity through literature in your own classroom.
6. Create a checklist composed of criteria for evaluating and selecting content area reading materials, including those for the gifted and talented.
7. Distinguish the general concept of readability from the limited concept measured by readability formulas.
8. Distinguish the appropriate uses of readability formulas from potential misuses.
9. Create an argument that justifies the classroom space and teacher time necessary for maintaining a classroom library and compose a list of guidelines for establishing and maintaining a classroom library.
10. Devise a practical and realistic plan for helping students develop confidence with library skills and become voluntary "regulars" at school and community libraries.

PART 2 OBJECTIVES—continued

5. Compare and contrast the value of picture books for elementary children with the value of picture books for middle and high school students and identify three examples of picture books appropriate for middle and high school students, along with three examples of ways picture books can be used with older students.
6. Distinguish fiction from nonfiction books and identify types of each appropriate for content area instruction.
7. Summarize the benefits of incorporating periodicals into content area instruction and describe five ideas for teaching content using magazines or newspapers.

INTRODUCTION

Textbooks can be a valuable resource in the content classroom. They provide teachers with a scope and sequence of topics and sometimes literacy skills taught at each grade level. In addition, most textbook teachers' editions suggest teaching strategies, comprehension questions, enrichment activities, and bibliographies. Used properly, they can serve as a valuable guide for teachers in lesson planning.

Proper use involves judicious selection of appropriate topics, strategies, questions, problems, activities, and collateral materials for instructional units and individual lesson plans designed by the teacher to meet the individual needs of students. You recall from Chapter 4 that instructional units allow the teacher rather than the textbook to be the instructional decision maker. After all, the textbook cannot possibly know the needs and interests of your students as well as you do. Textbooks provide a starting point for planning, along with a menu of topics and ideas. However, teachers should use them to serve instructional plans based on the needs and interests of the students.

In addition to serving as a resource for teachers in lesson planning, textbooks serve another valuable purpose in the content classroom: they often serve as reference books that provide general information on a wide range of topics within each content area. Students can use them as they would encyclopedias or other reference books; for example, students can look up definitions of technical vocabulary, identify important general concepts, get clarification on areas of confusion, verify predictions or hearsay about a topic, and investigate topics of particular interest to them. Textbooks can be good starting points for research projects because they often provide general overviews of topics, along with suggested bibliographies of related books and other materials.

Improper use of textbooks usually involves teachers automatically following the suggestions in the teachers' manuals, assuming that those procedures will be effective for their students. In these situations, teachers are usually determined to cover the material without due consideration of students' interests and mastery of content. Unfortunately, the result of this attitude is often the use of round-robin oral reading. (Chapter 5 defines round-robin oral reading, discusses its disadvantages, and offers effective alternatives.)

Although textbooks play a valuable role in content area learning and literacy development, alone they do not serve all the needs of students. Some teachers mistakenly assume that their instructional responsibilities are fulfilled by having students read the textbook aloud in class and answer questions related to the content. However, simply reading aloud the material to be learned in class is not sufficient for effective teaching. Students' mastery of content and their development of content area literacy must also be considered. You recall from Chapters 1 and 2 that when you help students apply content area literacy skills as tools for learning, you are developing lifelong, independent learners.

For content teachers to help their students become such learners, a variety of materials must be offered as textbook alternatives or collateral reading. The term *collateral reading* connotes that the nontextbook materials are equal partners with the text and should be used as resources parallel to the text. As you learned in earlier chapters, different types of materials are read using different strategies, for differing purposes, and with varying rates. Students need opportunities to experience a variety of materials in their development of content area literacy.

Varied materials are also important for content mastery. Textbooks generally have to cover such an extensive range of topics that they cannot go into depth about each one. Usually their purpose is to introduce a topic, provide an overview of it, and perhaps offer a cursory summation of relevant details and background knowledge. Alternate or collateral materials that provide more in-depth descriptions, explanations, examples, and applications are important for students to master content at critical levels of thinking.

As discussed in Chapter 6, another important reason to provide alternate or collateral materials to the text is motivation. Students who are motivated to read content area materials are more likely to master the content and develop their literacy skills. When students have positive attitudes toward the books they are reading in the content area classroom, they tend to put forth more energy and spend more time reading to learn.

By definition, textbooks were not designed to be motivating. Their purpose is cognitive—not affective—development. To emphasize the nonmotivational nature of textbooks, Baldwin and Leavell (1992) ask the rhetorical question "When was the last time you read a textbook just for kicks?" Unfortunately, many students find textbooks boring and if not boring, difficult. Textbooks tend to present large amounts of information and technical vocabulary in an impersonal, nonemotional way, often using advanced-level, sophisticated language. As a result, it is not surprising that many students tend to consider textbook reading drudgery. Even the finest textbooks available might be perceived by students as boring, irrelevant, or difficult (Baldwin and Leavell 1992).

Also, textbooks generally avoid controversial issues or information, because in most states they must be reviewed and approved for classroom use. Since publishers are in the business of selling textbooks, they wisely hesitate to include issues or information that might be construed as inappropriate by parents, legislators, school administrators, or the general public. As a result, textbooks tend to be bland in nature, and the coverage of topics is often scant. Typically, they present one-sided points of view rather than a comprehensive exploration of different ideas.

Students should be encouraged not only to question information provided in their textbooks but also to be on the lookout for information that might be omitted. Textbooks can be used to introduce topics and generate curiosity about such items as details, causes, explanations, applications, and the like. However, students then should be guided in searching for additional information in alternate or collateral materials. When students generate their own curiosities, questions, and interests in a topic, their motivation to read and learn is significantly enhanced.

Although textbooks serve an important educational purpose, they are not the best means of promoting independent learning, developing lifetime reading habits, and encouraging positive attitudes toward the content and learning. For these purposes, the textbook needs to be augmented or replaced with trade books (i.e., library books), paperback books, and periodicals. Trade books include a wide variety of children's and young adult fictional and nonfictional literature. Along with periodicals, they offer a variety and depth of information that simply cannot be provided by textbooks alone. These advantages not only motivate students but also provide valuable background knowledge that can enhance comprehension of textbooks (Baldwin and Leavell 1992).

This chapter will show you ways to make readily available to your students a variety of interesting and appealing books and periodicals. It will also show you ways to incorporate these materials into your lesson plans as collateral or replacement materials for the text. Various uses of fiction and nonfiction books to enhance content area learning and literacy will be addressed. Also, you will learn how to use alternate and collateral books and periodicals to develop lifelong readers and learners.

This chapter will address ways you can avoid gender bias and stereotyping in the selection and use of trade books. You will learn how to select and incorporate books with a multicultural or multiethnic focus and select appropriate materials using various readability criteria and readability formulas. A checklist for helping you select appropriate materials will be presented. In addition, you will learn ways to help students select their own books appropriate for their purposes and abilities. Finally, you will be introduced to two important strategies for helping students appreciate the books you and they have selected: Sustained Silent Reading and Read-alouds.

PART 1

STRATEGY: SUSTAINED SILENT READING

A useful strategy for providing students with regular opportunities to read nontextbook materials for enjoyment is Sustained Silent Reading (McCracken 1971). There are four distinguishing features of this strategy:

- Students select their own materials to read.
- Their primary purpose for reading is enjoyment.
- They are *not* held accountable for what they read.
- Everyone (including the teacher) reads silently without interruption for a predetermined amount of time (at least 5 minutes).

Setting aside a few minutes at the beginning of the class or lesson for sustained silent reading is an excellent way to help students settle down and focus on the topic of study. It also starts the class on a positive note, reminding students that reading content-related materials is personally rewarding and fulfilling. This time commitment is another way to send to students the message that you think reading is a valuable activity, and that textbook alternatives can be interesting and enjoyable sources of information and literature.

In addition, SSR is an important strategy for enrichment in content area instruction. It allows students to read a variety of interesting and enjoyable materials related to the topics of study. Students therefore have opportunities to investigate a topic further, study particular aspects of a topic more fully, and become familiar with a wide range of subtopics. Since they have input in selecting their reading materials, SSR is also a motivating activity. It gives students the opportunity to take control over the range and depth of study they pursue on a particular topic.

Preparation and Rules

Tierney, Readence, and Dishner (1990) suggest that the key to the success of SSR is adequate preparation. The idea should be discussed with students several days before beginning implementation. To ensure that all students understand the rules of SSR, present guidelines a day or two in advance to allow discussion of the importance of the rules. Then, review the rules just before the first SSR session.

The following rules should be followed strictly for about a month before you initiate variations (McCracken 1971, 521–522).

1. Each student must read silently.
2. The teacher reads and permits no interruption.
3. Each student selects a single book (or magazine or newspaper).
4. A timer is used.
5. There are absolutely no reports or records of any kind.

Emphasize to students that they will be allowed to choose whatever they want to read from the materials provided by the teacher in the classroom library. They should be encouraged to bring their own materials from home as long as they are appropriate for the topic of study. Make clear any parameters that you feel would define "appropriate" materials. Although students are encouraged to bring their own materials, the teacher should have suitable materials available in the classroom for students who forget or choose not to bring their own. Make sure you have a variety large enough to suit varied interests and reading levels. Change or add materials often to ensure a variety of new material.

Timing the Sessions

When determining the amount of time for the first SSR session, keep in mind that it should be long enough for the majority of students in the class to sustain their reading easily without tiring or losing their attention. Obviously this period will vary depending on age groups, but generally for primary-grade students (K–2), three to five minutes is probably enough; for intermediate-grade students (3–5), about five to ten minutes; and for middle and high school students, ten to fifteen minutes is probably about right (Tierney, Readence, and Dishner 1990).

The period should be gradually increased, depending on the interest and ability levels of the students, as well as the amount of time available during the instructional period. Primary-grade students should eventually be able to sustain their reading for fifteen to twenty minutes. Intermediate-grade students should eventually be expected to sustain their silent reading for twenty to thirty minutes. Middle and high school students should be able to work up to thirty or more minutes.

Of course, you may not be able to devote thirty minutes of class time daily to SSR. However, in the content area classroom, that time becomes a wise instructional investment, since students select materials related to the topic of study. Even if you do not set aside extended periods of time for SSR on a daily basis, you could do so once, twice, or three times a week.

Do not use the classroom clock for timing. Keep the time with a kitchen timer, alarm clock, or some other device that signals the end of the silent reading session. Place the timer where students cannot read the time. The idea is to prevent "clock watching" as an interruption to the sustained reading session. Using a timer also prevents interruptions from students asking the teacher if time is up.

Be consistent about stopping as soon as the alarm sounds and moving on to another activity. Much class time can be lost waiting for individuals to reach different stopping points in their books. However, if you wish, you could establish a system that provides one or more additional minutes at the end of each session to allow students to reach more comfortable stopping points. However, those who finish early should make a concerted effort to remain quiet until everyone has finished or the time is up.

The Teacher's Role

The role of the teacher is crucial to the success of SSR. You must set an example of good silent reading (McCracken 1971). Given the significant number of minutes students are quietly engaged in reading, it is tempting to take advantage of that time in a "productive" manner. You will likely hear the call of the attendance records, papers to be graded, lesson plans, or any of the numerous daily administrative chores trying to get your attention. However, if you do other work while expecting your students to read, you send the message that reading is important for them but not for you (Tierney, Readence, and Dishner 1990). In other words, you create an unrealistic expectation by asking students to do as you say but not as you do. Students will notice the discrepancy between your words and actions and will be less likely to take the SSR session seriously. As a result, they may start using that time to discreetly write notes to their friends or work on homework instead of reading.

Neither should the teacher walk around the room and monitor the students as is appropriate for other content area literacy strategies such as the Directed Reading Activity. The teacher walking around the room during SSR serves both as a distraction and potential interruption. The importance of the teacher as model cannot be overstated. You must follow the same rules and instructions as the students, including choosing your own materials for pleasure, using whatever constraints (like limiting materials to a given set of topics), if any, put on the students. Then, together, you and your students should sit and read silently.

Dealing with Interruptions

Despite your best efforts to minimize distractions during the SSR session, occasional interruptions are likely to occur, especially during the first few times you implement the strategy. To lessen the probability of interruptions, let your colleagues and administrators know what you are doing and when. Make special requests asking them to refrain from interrupting your class during those times. A "do not disturb" sign could also be posted on the door during SSR sessions to minimize the risk of distractions.

When an interruption does occur, whether from outside the class or from one of your students, do not turn it into a big issue. If the interruption causes you and a large number of your students to look up, stop the session for that day. Again, do not reprimand anyone for the interruption, simply say "I'm sorry, but that signals the end of our SSR session for today. Please put your reading materials away and get ready for the next activity." After the SSR procedure is solidly established, minor and unintentional interruptions may be handled discreetly without ending the reading session.

Following Up

Although sharing what was read should not be required, it certainly can be encouraged. After about a week, or whenever the SSR habit is firmly established, encourage sharing by first setting an example. McCracken (1971, 524) suggests the following ways to encourage sharing through your example:

1. Summarize in one sentence the main idea of a book.
2. Read a paragraph from [your] book and relate it to current happenings, national political events, or something in school.
3. Use the dictionary to check a word, comment about its unusual usage, or remark that it is a word [you] cannot recall ever seeing before.
4. Have the pupils question [you] about [your] book and develop models of questioning so that students learn how to go beyond simple recall.
5. Describe how some episodes in the book have suggested ideas or given [you] possible insight into how to teach or work with students.
6. Begin to keep a response journal of interesting words, ideas, epithets, and so on.
7. List the books [you] read or the pages read daily.

To involve students in following your examples, Tierney, Readence, and Dishner (1990) make the following suggestions. At the end of a session, make a brief comment about something you read and encourage volunteers to do the same. Ask students if they read something that might be of interest to the class or relevant to the current topic of study. You might also have students keep a log of the books and number of pages they read, or an optional journal in which they jot down anything they especially liked, questioned, found interesting, or thought memorable. At all times, however, students should be reminded that the primary emphasis of SSR is enjoyment and not reporting or recording what they read.

APPRECIATING DIVERSITY THROUGH MULTICULTURAL LITERATURE

Books that provide insights into cultural and ethnic similarities and differences should be an essential component of any school and classroom library. Norton (1990) does an excellent job of summarizing the importance of studying multicultural literature. First, students are given the opportunity to understand and appreciate a diverse literary heritage; for example, students learn to identify with people, from both past and present, who created the stories. They also discover a wealth of folktales, fables, myths, and legends that clarify values and beliefs. In addition, they are introduced to the threads that weave the past with the present and the themes and values that continue to be important to people today.

Studying multicultural literature also awards students tremendous personal gains (Norton 1990, 28):

1. They gain understandings about diverse beliefs and value systems.
2. Students gain aesthetic appreciation and respect of the artistic contributions and literary techniques of people from a variety of cultural backgrounds.
3. Students expand their understandings of geography and natural history.
4. They increase understanding of historical and sociological change.
5. They become sensitive to the needs of others, realizing that people have similarities as well as differences.

In studying similarities and differences among people, it is important to help students develop an appreciation for rather than fear of differences. You recall from Chapters 1 and 4 that one of the key elements of synergy for successful cooperative learning is to value differences. If each member of a group brings the same resources (e.g., talents, knowledge, and experiences) to a project, the benefits of working together are minimal. However, if each group member has something different to contribute to the project, the product will likely have more breadth, depth, and substance.

One of the most difficult team-building skills to develop is the ability to recognize and appreciate differences. Human nature seems to be fearful and skeptical of people who are different from ourselves. Fear and skepticism are exacerbated by another human tendency, which is to prejudge or judge too soon. However, students can overcome their fears, skepticism, and prejudices through concerted efforts to learn about other cultures. They also need to be encouraged and given opportunities to get to know their classmates better.

Teachers should give students numerous opportunities to develop awareness of their own and classmates' different strengths in learning and literacy. Remind students continually to look for and appreciate different ways of learning in their classmates and groupmates. Encourage students to be supportive of each other in resolving conflicts and understanding differences.

One of the most important ways students can learn about themselves and each other is through exposure to a variety of multicultural or multiethnic literature. Multicultural awareness is crucial for understanding and valuing differences in learning and communication. Many misunderstandings can occur as a result of not knowing about differences in verbal and nonverbal communication, some of which are cultural in nature.

For example, many students mistakenly assume that students who do not volunteer in class are not as smart as those who do. However, in some cultures, students learn from an early age that speaking out in class is not appropriate; for example, some cultures consider it an insult to the teacher, and others consider it boastful and pretentious.

Students should be given ample opportunities to read and talk about various cultures in small-group settings. Multicultural literature allows students to appreciate and celebrate diversity by exposing them to the varied talents of people from different cultures. Such literature also helps students break down myths and stereotypes and appreciate the rich texture of America's cultural tapestry. By reading about a diversity of cultures, students can gain a deeper understanding of and appreciation for cultures other than their own. Finally, learning about other cultures is one of the best ways to increase understanding of one's own culture.

In addition to helping students appreciate their classmates from different cultures, culturally diverse literature can also do much to enhance the self-concepts of students from various cultures. Multicultural literature serves to validate students' cultural identities by projecting positive images of them and their cultures. Also, when such personal validation emerges from the classroom, students' positive identification with school is also enhanced (Alvermann and Phelps 1994).

Culturally relevant literature can also serve as an important tool in developing literacy. Books that validate culturally diverse characters and personalities help students form a more intimate link between their own experiences and the text, thus enhancing comprehension. Motivation is enhanced by the personal appeal of reading about culturally-familiar subjects.

Norton (1990) describes an excellent five-phase model for studying multicultural literature:

1. The first phase focuses on a broad awareness of one cultural group by studying some of its folktales, fables, myths, and legends.
2. The second phase narrows the focus to one or two tribal or cultural areas, again by studying some of their folktales, fables, myths, and legends.
3. The third phase moves to autobiographies, biographies, and informational literature that focuses on the cultural group being studied. Students evaluate this nonfictional literature using knowledge gained from studying the cultural group's literature in the first two phases.
4. The fourth phase continues with historical fiction centering on the cultural group under study.
5. The fifth phase concludes the model with contemporary realistic fiction, poetry, and biography, again using books that represent the same cultural group.

As students move through each phase, they develop understandings that build upon each other. For example, in the first two phases, students identify traditional values and beliefs of the culture as represented in its folktales, fables, myths, and legends. Then they use this information in later phases as they search for values and beliefs in historical fiction, biographies, contemporary poetry, and realistic fiction. Also, they use knowledge gleaned from analyzing the nonfictional literature and biographies to evaluate the quality and authenticity of historical fiction.

Through the process of moving through this five-phase model, students look for common threads in the literature. They compare works written by authors who are members of the culture under study with works by authors outside the culture. Authors within the culture, who are writing from personal experience, often have different perspectives than authors who are writing about a culture other than their own. These cross-cultural comparisons allow students to identify similarities and value differences both within and between cultures (Norton 1990).

Two excellent sources for African-American and Hispanic literature are the August, 1984 (Growing Up Black) and June, 1985 (Growing Up Hispanic) issues of *Booklist*. Other excellent sources for multicultural literature are listed in Appendix K.

PROMOTING GENDER EQUITY THROUGH LITERATURE

Chapter 5 outlined some of the conclusions of the report on the state of gender equity in the classroom sponsored by the American Association of University Women (AAUW). One of those conclusions was that curricula commonly ignore or stereotype females. To make sure you are an "equal-opportunity teacher," Feder-Feitel (1993, 58) recommends that you ask yourself the following questions (among others):

- Do you read more stories that have male rather than female protagonists?
- How often do you include female contributions in your studies of math, science, and social studies?

Following are some examples of books recommended by Cline and McBride (1983) to promote gender equality in the classroom:

- *New Women in Social Sciences* by Kathleen Bowman
- *Women Who Shaped History* by Henrietta Buckmaster
- *Women of Courage* by Dorothy Nathan
- *Demeter's Daughters: The Women Who Founded America* by Selma R. Williams

Feder-Feitel (1993) also suggests several activities to help promote gender equity in your classroom. One activity is designed to help students focus on the qualities that comprise heroism, and to point out that both men and women can be heroes/heroines. Following the discussion and writing activity Feder-Feitel recommends for establishing possible traits of a hero/heroine, students could examine a variety of books on both men and women who might be considered heroes or heroines. The students could then compare the qualities described in the books to the criteria established through discussion to conclude whether they would consider each person a hero/heroine.

Another activity recommended by Feder-Feitel (1993) involves increasing student recognition of sexism in written materials. Choose three textbooks or trade books and have the class examine them to see if the authors' language is unfair to females. For example, does the author use the word "men" to mean "people"? Is a doctor, fire fighter, president of a corporation, or other authority figure always described as "he"? Are the historical figures included predominantly men?

Alvermann and Commeyras (1994) recommend a similar approach to classroom analysis and discussion of gender inequalities in text. First, pose a broad question to guide the analysis such as "How are women positioned in this textbook?" Then have students survey the index to locate all references to women and selectively read each page containing such a reference. Finally, students take notes on the pages they read using a three-column approach.

In the first column, students copy excerpts from passages containing references to women. In the second column, they comment on the content the authors chose to include in their treatment of the subject. Students comment on the author's choice of language in presenting the content in the third column.

The culminating step involves student discussion of the patterns they observed across their readings. Discussions should begin in pairs or small groups before involving the whole class or larger groups. Guide students in considering their observations from a variety of perspectives. These discussions should lead to additional insights about the apparent gender inequalities they observed.

A third activity recommended by Feder-Feitel (1993) to promote gender equality in the classroom involves students scanning newspapers and magazines for stories about women in the news. Guide students in examining differences in attitudes toward sex roles in different publications, especially between tabloids and conventional periodicals. Have the students create a bulletin board or scrapbook with their clippings. They could also do some follow-up reading and research on the women in the articles.

Teachers need to make a conscious effort to select and include books that promote the following recommendations included in the AAUW report (1993, 85–86):

▌ Teachers must help girls develop positive views of themselves and their futures, as well as an understanding of the obstacles women must overcome in a society where their options and opportunities are still limited by gender stereotypes and assumptions.

▌ School curricula should deal directly with issues of power, gender politics, and violence against women. Better-informed girls are better equipped to make decisions about their futures. Girls and young women who have a strong sense of themselves are better able to confront violence and abuse in their lives.

▌ Curricula for young children must not perpetuate gender stereotypes and should reflect sensitivity to different learning styles.

SELECTING ALTERNATIVES FOR GIFTED AND TALENTED STUDENTS

If your GT students are not challenged by the assigned text or other instructional materials, you should have available some suitable alternatives. To locate appropriate materials, you first need to know the approximate reading levels of your GT students. Following are some suggestions for determining approximate reading levels.

1. Examine students' cumulative folders for standardized test results and other diagnostic information that might be available.

2. Administer a content area reading inventory (CARI) (see Chapter 9). This test serves as a screening device to identify students for whom the text is too easy (as well as those who may have difficulty reading the text).

3. Administer an informal reading inventory (IRI) (see Chapter 9). This test is given individually to students identified by the CARI as potentially bored and unchallenged by the assigned reading materials. The IRI is given individually to determine the highest level at which the student can successfully read with instructional support (i.e., the instructional reading level) and the highest level at which the student can successfully read materials independently without instructional support (i.e., the independent reading level).

4. Administer a series of cloze tests (see Chapter 9). Once you have some idea of the student's instructional and independent reading levels (from standardized test, CARI, or IRI results), select what you

believe will be appropriate alternate (more challenging) materials. Then, verify your selections with cloze tests. Each cloze test is developed from the actual reading materials you select. The test is designed to give you a yes or no answer to the questions "Can this student read this material successfully with instructional support?" and "Can this student read this material successfully without instructional support (independently)?" On the basis of the answers to these questions, you may have to select and try different materials until you find those suitable.

Once you know the approximate instructional and independent reading levels of the GT students you suspect might be bored with and unchallenged by the assigned text, you can begin locating appropriate materials. After selecting what you believe will be appropriate materials, check their suitability with cloze tests (see Chapter 9). Following are some suggestions for locating materials:

1. Meet with your school administrator in charge of textbooks (often an assistant principal) to discover what supplementary or alternate textbooks are available.
2. Ask your local parent-teacher association, school librarian, or school administrator in charge of curriculum funds to help obtain more challenging books and periodicals on various content area topics for the school library or your classroom library collection.
3. Collaborate with your school and community librarians to develop a bibliography of trade books on the topics covered by the textbook. Categorize the trade books by grade level, either from information provided by the publishers or from your own readability assessment. Ask your local parent-teacher association, school librarian, or school administrator in charge of curriculum funds to help obtain higher-level books from this bibliography for the school library or your classroom library collection.

READABILITY

Readability is a characteristic of the reading materials themselves. It is a rather complex concept that involves a number of criteria. Basically, the criteria are designed to determine how "readable" a given piece of reading material is for a particular student or group of similar students. When you talk about *readability*, you are assessing how difficult or interesting a set of reading materials will be for certain students. Materials that are highly readable for certain students are said to have a high readability level with respect to those students; materials that are not very readable for a given group of students are said to have a low readability level for those particular students.

It is not appropriate to talk about the readability levels of your students. Chapter 9 shows you ways to assess the *reading levels* of your students, but *readability levels* refer to materials, not students. You must have some information regarding the reading levels of your students to assess the readability of materials, but the concept of readability characterizes the reading materials themselves.

Knowing what makes a textbook, trade book, or periodical readable for your students is crucial. You are responsible for making available a variety of materials appropriate for their interests, levels of background knowledge, reading abilities, and study skills. Consider that literally hundreds of thousands of trade books and periodicals are available for children and young adults, and you will probably have at least several different textbooks available. You might also find yourself on a textbook committee composed of teachers and administrators whose duty it is to select textbooks that will be purchased by the school according to a state-adopted list. Another possible committee assignment is to a library committee, which assists the librarian in setting priorities for book purchases.

How will you know which textbooks you should select? Which trade books and periodicals should be ordered for the library? How will you select materials for your classroom library? Readability criteria provide you the tools for the often arduous task of selecting materials appropriate for your students' needs and wants. This task can be made much easier, as well as more enjoyable and rewarding, if you know what to look for in the process of identifying appropriate materials.

No doubt you have heard educators discuss readability and readability levels. When someone talks to or asks you about the readability or readability level of a book, you need to ask for clarification. Are they referring to the broad concept of readability involving a wide range of criteria including organization, style, content, print, and study aids? Are they referring to the limited definition provided by readability formulas? Too often, teachers talk about readability only in terms of the linguistic factors assessed using readability formulas.

A readability formula focuses on linguistic complexity, which is only one of many readability criteria. Linguistic complexity usually is measured in terms of sentence and word length. Readability formulas are based on the theory that the longer the sentences and words in a passage, the more difficult it is to read. The validity of this theory will not be discussed here; regardless of whether readability formulas are valid indicators of text difficulty, they remain in widespread use today.

You can be sure that as a professional educator you will at some point be asked by administrators, parents, colleagues, and sometimes even the students themselves about the readability or readability levels of certain materials. You may be asked to determine the readability of a given set of materials or explain or interpret readability levels identified by computer software or published in the materials themselves. Whether you believe in the validity of readability formulas or not, you will be expected to know what they are, how to use them, and how to interpret the results properly, avoiding the pitfalls of misinterpreting the readability levels identified by readability formulas.

Readability is a concept that involves two distinct sets of criteria, both of which are required for matching the characteristics of the materials with those of the reader. You must first know your students before you can select readable materials for them. What might be difficult or boring to one student might be easy or interesting to another. Therefore, before looking for and selecting appropriate materials, you first must have some basic information about your students including their interests, motivation levels, levels of background knowledge, and reading abilities. Chapter 6 shows you ways to assess the interests and motivation levels of your students. Chapter 9 provides ways to assess the background knowledge and abilities of your students.

Another set of criteria refers to the characteristics of the reading materials themselves. The next section of this chapter will help you develop a comprehensive set of criteria for assessing readability. In the process of assessing a given set of materials, you must consider its characteristics with respect to the characteristics of your students. Readable materials are those whose characteristics match the needs, interests, and abilities of your students. Chapter 9 describes the Cloze Test, which really is not a test at all but rather an informal procedure for deciding whether the materials you have selected match the characteristics of your students.

Criteria for Assessing and Selecting Materials

Ask yourself the following questions: What characteristics make a book readable to me? What characteristics distinguish books I enjoy and look forward to reading from those I avoid and find tedious or boring? Why do I enjoy or at least not mind reading some textbooks, while I despise reading others? If you sit down and brainstorm, you might find some of your responses in the list of characteristics presented in Figure 7–1. This list was compiled from responses to the previous questions posed to several different classes of college students in teacher education. See if you can add any others.

This list provides a sample set of characteristics involved in readability. Criteria for assessing readability can be developed from characteristics like these. Before deciding whether to develop your own set of criteria,

---

FIGURE 7–1 Characteristics assessed by readability criteria

CHARACTERISTICS OF THE MATERIALS	CHARACTERISTICS OF THE READER
length of chapters	interest in the topic
chapter questions	expertise in the area
size and style of print	perceived value of the content
author's style	prior knowledge of the topic
use of simple, everyday language	confidence with study skills
difficulty level of vocabulary	attitude toward subject
density of difficult concepts	efficiency of study skills
length and complexity of sentences	reading abilities
length of chapter sections	level of motivation
number of headings and subheadings	
chapter introductions and summaries	
bibliographies and reading lists	
cover, photographs, and illustrations	
charts, graphs, and diagrams	
amount of technical jargon	
the table of contents and index	
glossary and appendix	
use of bold-faced print and italics	
sequence and organization	
demonstration of applications	
use of relevant and concrete examples	
absence of ethnic, gender, and cultural bias	
interesting presentation	
attention-getting devices	
descriptive headings and subheadings	
size of margins	
author's use of humor	
author's integrity and tone	

---

you might want to review the readability checklist developed by Irwin and Davis (1980) to assess textbooks according to criteria developed from characteristics of the book itself. They separate the criteria in their checklist into two broad categories: understandability and learnability. The understandability category includes assumptions made by the text concerning background knowledge, the quantity of new concepts presented, the quality of their presentation, clarity of writing, and the extent to which new concepts are linked to prior knowledge.

The learnability category is divided into three subcategories: organization, reinforcement, and motivation. Organization includes the way the chapters are laid out (e.g., clear organizational pattern) and the reading aids provided (e.g., introductions, summaries, index, and glossary). Reinforcement includes quality of questions provided, opportunities for application and practice, and graphic aids (e.g., charts, graphs, diagrams, and illustrations). Motivation includes stimulating introductory activities, chapter headings and subheadings, writing style, the extent to which the value and relevance of the content is conveyed, and the extent to which it provides positive models for both sexes and all racial, ethnic, and socioeconomic groups.

Irwin and Davis' (1980) checklist provides an excellent example of a set of criteria that can be developed from text characteristics identified as important to readability. In developing your own checklist, you would essentially frame a question designed to assess each characteristic. You might also want to develop a set of criteria designed to assess reader characteristics.

Characteristics of the reader might include interest in the topic, prior knowledge, motivation, attitude, reading ability, and confidence with study skills (see Figure 7–1). You could develop a checklist of criteria that frame questions designed to assess these characteristics. Here are several examples of questions designed by Tonjes and Zintz (1992, 67).

1. Is the topic of particular interest to you?
2. Do you have the necessary background experiences or prerequisites in the subject matter?
3. Are your reading skills adequate for the task at hand?

Some older students might be able to answer these questions themselves. For younger students and other older students, however, you could answer questions with data you gather from informal assessments. Informal assessment procedures for interests, attitudes, and motivation are described in Chapter 6. Informal assessment procedures for reading and study skill abilities are described in Chapter 9.

Many excellent checklists are available for assessing readability and matching readers with text. A wide range of possibilities exists for developing a practical system to assess textbook readability. You should examine some of these possibilities before deciding whether or how to develop a checklist specially tailored to your own priorities, teaching levels, content areas, and instructional objectives.

Many of the criteria included in textbook assessment checklists might also be included in a checklist designed to assess trade books and periodicals. For example, the cover, illustrations, writing style, length of chapters, and print size should also be considered in selecting appropriate trade books and periodicals. Later in this chapter, a set of questions developed from Cullinan's criteria for selecting nonfictional books (cited in Moss 1991) is presented. These questions provide a good start for a checklist to assess the readability of trade books and periodicals. Such a checklist should also include criteria appropriate for fiction (e.g., plot, character development, setting, true to form) and periodicals (e.g., relevance of articles, quality of stories, effective presentation, appropriate illustrations).

Formulas for Assessing Linguistic Difficulty

As previously mentioned, the validity of readability formulas will not be discussed in this text, nor will the validity of the premises on which they are based. Since readability formulas remain in widespread use today, it is important to understand what they are, what they can tell you, and perhaps more importantly, what they cannot tell you. Applying a readability formula to a sample passage or set of passages yields a grade-level score that serves only as an approximate indication of difficulty. This grade-level score does not necessarily mean that a student with the same reading achievement level can successfully read the passage(s). Readability formulas provide an *estimate* of text difficulty only: they do not provide a precise measure of difficulty, nor are they intended for that purpose.

Readability formulas do not yield an exact level of difficulty because they are designed to measure only one of the many criteria that indicate text difficulty. The criterion measured by readability formulas involves linguistic complexity, generally defined in terms of sentence and word length. Readability formulas are based on the following premises:

- The longer a sentence is, the more difficult it is to read.
- The longer a word is, the more difficult it is to read.
- The more long words and long sentences there are in a passage, the more difficult it is to read.

Uses and Misuses of Readability Formulas

One way the estimated difficulty level offered by readability formulas can be useful is in making at-a-glance comparisons between materials. For example, if you have selected a set of books on a particular topic from the library, you can use a readability formula to help you compare the approximate difficulty levels of the books. You can then use this information to help you match the more difficult books to the better readers in the class. It is also useful to apply readability formulas in making quick-look comparisons between available textbooks.

A second way readability formulas can be useful is in making comparisons within materials. For example, you can identify particularly difficult chapters within the same book or passages within the same chapter.

You may then wish to provide extra preparation or guidance for your students when they read the more difficult parts.

A third way in which an estimated difficulty level can be helpful is in selecting materials for your students. When used in conjunction with a readability checklist, the estimated level of difficulty provided by readability formulas offers additional information to help you select appropriate materials. For example, when selecting materials from a library or bookstore, you could consider the readability level, along with the other criteria on your checklist, to help you narrow the possibilities. When ordering books, the estimated readability levels provided by publishers can guide you to make difficult decisions about books you have not actually seen.

Unfortunately, readability formulas often are misused in schools today. These misuses are generally the result of a mistaken assumption that readability levels obtained from formulas signify absolute measures of difficulty. Nelson (1978) cautions against the faulty assumption that matching the readability score of materials to the reading achievement scores of students will lead to comprehension. For example, assume you are a sixth-grade teacher selecting materials for your classroom library. In the process, you apply a readability formula to a book in order to assess its linguistic difficulty. The book yields a grade-level score of 6. How would you interpret that result? First, you cannot assume that students who can read other sixth-grade materials (e.g., textbooks, basal readers, test passages, and so on) will be able to read that book successfully. Second, you cannot assume that students who are unable to read other sixth-grade materials will not be able to read that book successfully. In other words, a book yielding a sixth-grade readability level from a formula does not necessarily mean that it is readable for a student with a sixth-grade reading achievement level. So many factors are involved in the concept of readability that a formula based on word and sentence length only cannot possibly provide an absolute measure of difficulty.

Be especially careful to avoid misuses of readability data that involve inappropriate assumptions or invalid conclusions about students' abilities. For example, if a sixth-grade student has trouble reading a book estimated to have a sixth-grade readability level, you cannot conclude that the student has reading problems. He or she might be able to read other materials that have a sixth-grade readability level. Likewise, you cannot assume that a sixth-grade student who can read a book estimated to have a seventh-grade readability level has special talents in reading, he or she may have difficulty reading other books with a seventh-grade reading level. If you use readability formulas as a tool for quick-look comparisons and general estimates of difficulty only, you should be able to safely avoid their common misuses.

Another problem often related to readability is publishers' labeling of books with specific readability levels. The problem results when there are a range of readability levels in a single book. For example, readability levels ranging from fourth to tenth grade might be found in a book labeled by the publisher as sixth grade level.

The Fry Readability Graph

Many different readability formulas are in widespread use. These include the SMOG (McLaughlin 1969), the Raygor Readability Estimate (Raygor 1977), the Rix (Anderson 1983), and the Fry Readability Graph (Fry 1977). Possibly the most popular and widely known of these is the Fry Graph. It was developed as a quick and easy-to-use readability formula, based on two variables. The first is sentence length and is measured in terms of the number of sentences in a one hundred-word passage. (The fewer sentences in the passage, the greater the sentence length.) The second is word length, and is measured in terms of the number of syllables in a one hundred-word passage. (The more syllables in the passage, the greater the word length.) According to Fry (1977), the graph estimates readability within one grade level.

Many software packages are available to apply the Fry or other readability formulas for passages typed into the computer. If you do not have access to a computer or appropriate software, the Fry Graph is easy to apply yourself. With a little practice, you can use it quickly and accurately. Always double check your accuracy, of course—especially if you are using the information to make instructional decisions, such as selecting materials, matching materials to students, or planning guidance for students—based on the estimated difficulty of the materials.

Counting syllables can be a tedious process, in which it is easy to lose count. The process is made easier and less prone to error if you use the following technique. Since each word obviously has at least one syllable, and you are using a one hundred-word passage, one hundred of the syllables have been automatically counted for you. Adding them to your count significantly increases the number of marks you have to count, thereby complicating the counting process and making it easier to make a mistake. So, if a word has only one syllable, make no mark at all. If a word has more than one syllable, make no mark for the first syllable; begin making marks for the second and successive syllables. When you have finished making marks, for each additional syllable in the words, count the marks. Then, add one hundred to the number of marks you made to determine the total number of syllables in the one hundred-word passage.

If you are using a photocopy of the passage or a personal copy of the book, you can make the marks directly above each syllable being counted. If you do not wish to mark in the book, you can make the marks on a separate sheet of paper. When making the marks, it helps to read the passage aloud and slowly, emphasizing each syllable while pronouncing the words.

Figure 7–2 presents the Fry Graph, and Figure 7–3 provides the instructions for applying it. Fry recommends selecting three different one hundred-word passages, especially for an entire book or lengthy chapter, one from the beginning, one from the middle, and one from the end. Data from the three passages are then averaged to obtain an overall estimate of readability.

FIGURE 7–2 Fry's Graph for Estimating Readability—Extended

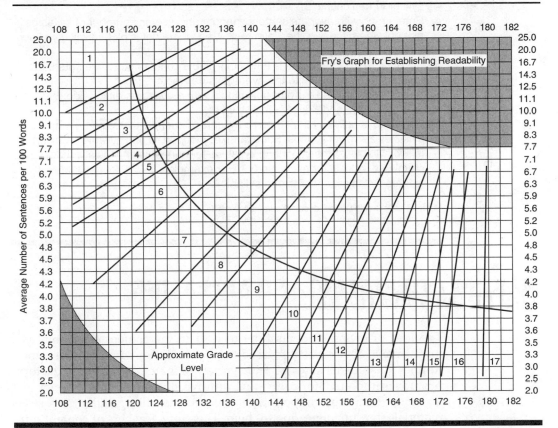

FIGURE 7–3 Expanded directions for Fry's readability graph

Expanded Directions for Fry's Readability Graph

1. Randomly select (3) sample passages and count out exactly 100 words each, beginning with the beginning of a sentence. DO count proper nouns, initializations, and numerals.

2. Count the number of sentences in the hundred words, estimating length of the fraction of the last sentence to the nearest one-tenth.

3. Count the total number of syllables in the 100-word passage. If you don't have a hand calculator available, an easy way is to simply put a mark above every syllable over one in each word, then when you get to the end of the passage, count the number of marks and add 100. Small calculators can also be used as counters by pushing numeral 1, then push the + sign for each word or syllable when counting.

4. Enter graph with *average* sentence length and *average* number of syllables: plot dot where the two lines intersect. Area where dot is plotted will give you the approximate grade level.

5. If a great deal of variability is found in syllable count or sentence count, putting more samples into the average is desirable.

6. A word is defined as a group of symbols with a space on either side: thus, *Joe, IRA, 1945* and *&* are each one word.

7. A syllable is defined as a phonetic syllable. Generally there are as many syllables as vowel sounds. For example, *stopped*, is one syllable and *wanted* is two syllables. When counting syllables for numerals and initializations, count one syllable for each symbol. For example, *1945* is four syllables. *IRA* is three syllables, and *&* is one syllable.

Note: This "extended graph" does not outmode or render the earlier (1958) version inoperative or inaccurate: It is an extension. (REPRODUCTION PERMITTED—NO COPYRIGHT)

MAKING INTERESTING AND APPEALING MATERIALS AVAILABLE

The idea of giving students time to read in the content classroom as a motivational device was discussed in Chapter 6. Providing regular opportunities for students to read a wide variety of materials related to the topic of study is important for cultivating positive attitudes toward literacy and learning. Even more important is the need to allow students to select materials that are interesting to them. Therefore, teachers of content must make available materials that are likely to appeal to their students.

Maintaining a Classroom Library

To offer students a wide range of reading materials that appeal to a variety of interests, a classroom library is essential. Many teachers' first reaction to this idea is "But my classroom is too small to squeeze in an area for a library." Keep in mind that all you need for a classroom library is a shelf where you keep a selection of books and other reading materials for use in classroom instruction. Some teachers have transformed coat closets into library centers by adding shelves. Many teachers find that they can provide a small reading area next to their classroom library shelf to encourage students to "read for fun" if they finish their work early. Allowing students to read for pleasure on the floor, on pillows, in rocking chairs, under tables, or any place but their desks, reinforces the notion that reading is an enjoyable free-time activity.

The assessment of interests, discussed in Chapter 6, is important in helping teachers select interesting and appealing materials to have available. The results of interest inventories, supplemented by teacher observations, can be summarized into a list of topics or subtopics related to a current or upcoming unit of study. This list should then be examined with the assistance of the school librarian, who can help you make a list of appropriate books. Books that have earned Caldecott or Newbery awards for outstanding literature are always excellent choices, especially when starting your classroom library. Ideally, a significant number of the books (thirty to forty) should be borrowed from a larger library for your classroom library. You should restock your library regularly, approximately every two weeks.

These books can be used for in-class assignments, enrichment activities, and free reading. If students wish to borrow any of the books, you must decide whether your other students will need them in class. If so, tell students they may borrow the books at the end of the unit; if not, allow them to check them out while their interest is piqued. Unless you are willing to take responsibility for books checked out by students, it is probably a good idea to have the students check out the books directly from the library.

In addition to books, keep your room library stocked with a wide variety of current magazines and newspapers. One of the best ways to stir interest in a topic of study is to relate it to current events. Students get especially excited when they find articles on their own that relate the "real world" to current topics of study. Although periodicals are not recommended for use with Sustained Silent Reading, they can be used for research, in-class collaborative assignments, and enrichment activities. (See the section on incorporating periodicals in this chapter.)

Encourage your students to bring their own books and periodicals related to their personal interests and current topics of study for the classroom library. Many students get excited about finding books and other reading materials to share with their classmates. Students who enjoy looking for books at the school or public library can have a positive influence on their classmates, who might just be inclined to take up the habits of their peers. This phenomenon is a positive example of peer pressure at work.

When teachers of content stock their classroom libraries with a wide variety of books, magazines, and other materials, they are teaching their students that textbooks are not the only places to find relevant and interesting information and stories related to the topics of study. They are making it easier for students to find materials of personal interest and providing more opportunities for students to read self-selected materials for personal satisfaction. When students have pleasurable and self-fulfilling reading experiences, their attitudes toward literacy are more likely to be positive.

Frequenting School and Community Libraries

Another important opportunity for varied reading experiences involves the school and community libraries. Many students do not feel comfortable in a library. They do not know how to locate books on particular subjects, by particular authors, or of particular genres. Once they have found the appropriate library section they do not know how to select a book they might enjoy reading. Teachers of content have an obligation to help their students become confident and comfortable in a library by providing regular and varied library experiences. They also need to provide guidance to students in locating materials for research or enrichment projects (a process for research is described in Chapter 10). Teachers must also teach students how to choose books of personal interest. Show students how to read the first page or two of several books until they find one that is appealing and not too difficult for independent reading.

Only after extensive visits to libraries on a regular basis with specific tasks to accomplish and guidance toward successful completion will students begin to feel comfortable. Eventually they should be confident and motivated enough to frequent libraries on their own. If enough students who are considered leaders by their classmates are seen hanging out in libraries, it might even become a "cool" thing to do. This phenomenon can only happen, though, if enough teachers are committed to spending quality time with their classes in their school and community libraries on a regular basis. As with attitudes toward learning, the teachers' attitudes and the value they place on libraries as sources of learning and enjoyment will be conveyed to their students.

One way to get students into libraries after school hours is to set up scavenger hunts. Students then go to public libraries to find the required information or books. A system of points and prizes can be set up as incentives.

Learning Centers

Learning centers (see Chapter 11) provide another excellent opportunity to make a variety of interesting and appealing reading materials available to students. Books and other materials from your classroom library can be used for the learning center activities. Each center could offer one or more activities allowing students to read and write about the books and other materials. Students can be given choices, both in terms of the reading matter and accompanying writing activities.

Learning center activities allow for the integration of content areas and literacy skills. For example, students could choose from among fiction and nonfiction books provided on a particular topic. They could then choose from among activities inviting them to investigate and reflect on the topic from a combination of two or more perspectives (e.g., social studies, mathematics, environmental studies, history, psychology, sociology, business, economics, life science, earth science, space science, and so on).

PART 2

STRATEGY: READ-ALOUDS

Reading aloud to your students is one of the best ways to share with them a variety of content-related literature. When you read aloud to your students, you are sending them very important messages. First, you are letting them know how important and enjoyable reading is to you. Second, you are demonstrating to them that adults who are experts in their fields actively pursue and enjoy reading relevant materials. Third, you are creating interest by showing them the wide range of reading materials available on content-related topics (Alvermann and Phelps 1994).

Reading aloud to students *of all ages* is an important way to enrich the reading experiences of students. Traditionally, reading aloud to students has been a staple of the elementary classroom. Most children love to be read to, from very early ages. However, most teachers who have read aloud to their middle and high school students would agree with Martha Rapp Ruddell (1993, 364) when she says "no one ever gets too old to enjoy being read to." To prove her point, she even reads to her university students at the beginning of every class period excerpts from materials including favorite books, newspaper columns, magazine articles, poetry books, children's books, and young adult literature.

You could start a class by reading a current events article related to the topic of study. Students also love cartoons and comic strips: starting a class with humor can be a very effective attention-getter.

Even high school students enjoy having picture books read to them. For example, a university intern who read Dr. Seuss's *The Butter Battle Book* to a class of inner city high school students was amazed by their positive response. The students, in an honors social studies class, had been studying the Cold War. The intern brought the Dr. Seuss book and set the following purposes for listening. She told them to listen for specific examples of how the "Butter Battle" was similar to the Cold War between the United States and the Soviet Union. She also told them to listen for elements of satire in the story. As she read the story to them, she held up the book so they could see the pictures. This class of thirty-five high school juniors was completely mesmerized by having the children's book read aloud to them. This example demonstrates that students of all ages can indeed enjoy having children's and young adult literature read aloud to them.

As the previous example demonstrates, many opportunities arise in the course of teaching content to read aloud both fictional and nonfictional literature to your students. This chapter provides information on how to select appropriate literature for all content areas—even math. An excellent way to introduce students to the books in your classroom library is to read an excerpt from the beginning or just before a particularly interesting or exciting part; encourage students to find out what happens or what comes next by reading the book for themselves.

One of the reasons students of all ages enjoy being read to is that it is an important and possibly the only way for many students to experience classic children's and young adult literature. Many students come to school with little or no experience with books; unfortunately, that means many of them never had books read to them as preschoolers. Therefore, being read to at school is an important way students can build experiential background. Also, many middle and high school students, even if they were read to as young children, might have missed some of the classic children's literature books and new classics are coming out all the time. Finally, the classics can be enjoyed over and over again, even into and throughout adulthood.

Earlier a case was made for reading picture books to middle and high school students, as well as elementary students. These books provide excellent read-aloud material, as do other fiction books and short stories. In addition, nonfiction books, as well as magazine and newspaper articles, are excellent sources of read-aloud material. Read-aloud materials, carefully chosen to emphasize topics under study and their relevance to current events, can enhance the value of direct instruction by adding pizzazz, generating enthusiasm, and modeling the value of literacy.

In Read-alouds, the teacher generally reads aloud to the students. The concept of teacher as model is very important to the success of the strategy. When you read aloud to your students, you are actively promoting reading for enjoyment and learning. When you take the time to select and read materials you enjoy to your students, your enthusiasm for the materials and the content can be contagious.

Occasionally you might allow student volunteers to read something aloud to the class as long as certain rules are followed. First, make sure the student volunteer is a confident, competent, fluent, and expressive oral reader. Second, make sure the student practices reading the material in advance and has some enthusiasm about the material to communicate through the Read-aloud experience. Finally, establish a clear purpose for listening before the student begins reading and follow up on the purpose after reading.

In content area teaching, you can use Read-alouds for many different purposes. For example, you might use Read-alouds to introduce a unit or lesson, provide support for principles and theories, give examples of concepts, demonstrate practical applications of knowledge, examine implications of information, analyze controversies, or simply share with your students an enjoyment of literature. Many valuable teaching moments can occur during Read-alouds: you may wish to read aloud to your students every day. If you are serious about generating positive attitudes toward books and reading, you should read aloud to your students at least once a week.

The length of each Read-aloud is determined by you according to the time available, length of the passage you wish to share, students' interests and attention spans, and your purpose in reading. For example, if you are introducing a lesson, providing support, or giving examples, you may only want to read a brief passage, article, or book for about five minutes. If you are introducing a unit, examining implications, or analyzing controversies, you may wish to read a little longer (ten to fifteen minutes). If you are demonstrating practical applications or simply sharing related literature for enjoyment, an even longer Read-aloud session (twenty to thirty minutes) might be appropriate.

An excellent source of tips on reading aloud, ideas for teaching, and lists of appropriate books is Trelease's *The New Read-Aloud Handbook*. Following are some Read-aloud guidelines recommended by Trelease (1989, 80–84):

1. Begin with picture books before moving on to stories and novels.
2. Vary the length and subject matter of your read-aloud sessions.

3. Once you start a book or story, make sure you finish it unless the students clearly have a negative reaction to it. After giving it a fair chance (some books start slower than others), give up and choose something else.

4. Occasionally challenge your students by reading something above their intellectual levels, but never read something above their emotional levels.

5. Select materials you are enthusiastic about and enjoy reading yourself.

6. Preread the material and make thoughtful decisions about whether to read the whole piece. If you decide on selected excerpts or passages, choose them carefully to serve your purposes. Identify stopping points for higher-level questions and discussion.

7. Avoid long descriptive passages unless you are fairly certain your students' imaginations and attention spans can handle them. Do not hesitate to shorten or eliminate them.

8. Choose suspenseful spots as stopping points to pique the students' interest in the next read-aloud session.

9. Practice reading the material beforehand. Read *slowly* and with expression and eye contact. Change your tone of voice appropriately for dialogue.

10. Allow students a few minutes to settle down and get in the mood by reviewing or asking questions about what happened last. Set a casual, friendly tone for each read-aloud session. Avoid authoritarian admonishments such as, "Now settle down and be quiet!"

11. Both you and your audience should be comfortable. Sit or stand where the students can easily see the pictures and hear you. Make sure your head is above the heads of your listeners to allow your voice to carry all the way to the back of the group. Do not sit or stand in front of bright windows: they strain the eyes of your audience.

12. Encourage your students to ask questions and generate discussion during read-aloud sessions. Be patient in allowing students to share their curiosities, thoughts, hopes, fears, and discoveries without quizzing them about the story.

13. Make sure you do not impose your own opinions, points of view, and interpretations on your students.

14. Bring authors to life by sharing something interesting about them from *About the Author*, which should be available at your library, or by reading information from the book jacket.

15. Reluctant readers and extremely active children often have a difficult time sitting still and listening. You can help them remain attentive by providing them paper and pencil or crayons to keep their hands busy.

Reading aloud to your students is an excellent way to improve their attitudes toward books and literacy. At the same time, it is a way to complement textual content with examples, historical perspectives, practical applications, value-laden controversies, and other valuable support tools. For some teachers, reading aloud effectively and confidently takes some practice. However, your efforts will likely be rewarded by an overwhelmingly positive response from your students.

INCORPORATING LITERATURE

Children and young adults who frequent libraries and bookstores are already aware of the almost overwhelming number of exciting new and classic trade books (commonly called library books) available today. Literally dozens of interesting, enjoyable, attractive, and up-to-date books can be found on just about any subject you can name. Students who have not had the privilege of spending time in bookstores and well-stocked libraries are missing out on a valuable dimension of life. The millions of high-quality books available allow students to explore a wider range of interests, satisfy their curiosities, and choose personally rewarding entertainment.

Students who choose the expansive entertainment options open to them through books are empowered to enjoy and pursue a wider range of interests and curiosities. You recall from Chapter 6 that in influencing students' attitudes toward books and reading, your actions speak louder than your words. So, you must set a good example by talking to students about the books you read. You also have to prove to them that they are capable of finding books they will enjoy reading. Undoing misconceptions about books and negative attitudes toward reading will probably not be easy. However, you can make a difference by providing a wide variety of interesting and attractive reading materials in your classroom, along with daily opportunities to enjoy them. If you can help your students discover that entertaining books exist and that they can learn how to find these exciting books, you will have given them a lifelong gift of stimulating entertainment.

Brozo and Tomlinson (1986) suggest that trade books be used in tandem with textbooks to make the content more interesting, comprehensible, and memorable. Since textbooks provide limited coverage of topics, they cannot be expected to develop important concepts adequately. Therefore, trade books are recommended to develop salient concepts, as well as to promote students' interest in and involvement with the content, both of which should enhance learning.

Many students are under the misconception that textbooks are only for learning and trade books are only for fun. While consensus on the best use of trade books in content area instruction may never be reached, it is important to avoid this false dichotomy (Alvermann and Phelps 1994). Incorporating trade books into content area teaching is important not only for enhancing learning, but also to teach students the value of trade books for learning about topics of interest and satisfying curiosities. If students are to become independent, lifelong readers, they must appreciate the value of trade books for learning and personal fulfillment. Thematic units and research projects are two examples of organizing instruction to integrate textbooks and trade books.

Selecting Books to Match Objectives

In order to incorporate trade books into content teaching, you must first identify the salient concepts of the lesson or unit. The textbook can be a useful resource in helping you identify the major concepts students should be expected to master. Remember, you must make the final decisions about your instructional objectives. In making your decisions, Brozo and Tomlinson (1986, 289) suggest asking yourself questions such as the following:

1. What are the driving human forces behind the events?
2. What phenomena described in the textbook have affected ordinary people (including me and my students) or may do so in the future?
3. What universal patterns of behavior related to this reading should be explained?

Of course, you must also consider any literacy and content objectives outlined by the school district or administration. However, you will probably find that most if not all specified objectives will be addressed in terms of the literal-level information needed to answer the above questions. In other words, using a literature-based approach, your instruction is more likely to take students above and beyond the identified competencies than to shortchange them. An approach that incorporates literature used as alternatives or collateral materials to the text requires students to understand the facts by manipulating, evaluating, and applying them. Not only do they learn the content, they also develop advanced skills in literacy including higher-order thinking.

Guzzetti, Kowalinski, and McGowan (1992) confirmed the possibility of addressing a school district's predetermined instructional objectives. They planned and implemented a sixth-grade social studies unit on China using a literature-based approach. They found that 70 percent of the district's objectives for reading and 68 percent for social studies could be addressed by the forty-two trade books they selected for the unit. Any objectives not addressed by the trade books you select could be taught using either the textbook or nontextual media including computers, videos, or lectures.

After you have identified the salient concepts to be taught, select appropriate trade books to help teach the concepts (Brozo and Tomlinson 1986). Ask your school librarian to help you with this step; you might also need to use public libraries as an additional resource. Many guides to children's and young adult literature are now available to help you identify appropriate books. Be proactive about ensuring that some of these resources are available to teachers in your school's curriculum library. In addition to the list provided in Appendix I, several journals devote regular columns or issues to reviewing and recommending trade books for various subjects. For example, the October issue of *The Reading Teacher* publishes a book list of "Children's Choices." Also, the April/May issue of *Social Education* publishes a list of "Notable Children's Trade Books in the Field of Social Studies," compiled through a joint effort of the Children's Book Council and the National Council for the Social Studies. In addition, an annotated bibliography of "Outstanding Science Trade Books for Children" is published annually through the combined efforts of the Children's Book Council and the National Science Teachers Association.

Organizing Instruction

Zarillo's research on literature-based programs (cited in Moss 1991) identified the following as three effective methods to organize teaching. Using the first method, the teacher chooses a book to be read by all the students in a class, and the students choose their own ways to respond to the book and share it with the class. Another method to organize teaching involves the use of a variety of books, all related to a central theme. In this thematic unit approach, the teacher reads some of the books aloud to the whole class, and other books are read by small groups, assigned according to interests and abilities. The third method uses individualized instruction. Each student selects a book to read according to her or his personal interests. In this type of instruction, students read their books silently on their own and at their own pace. They confer with the teacher periodically, participate in activities designed to enhance literacy skills, and choose some way to share their books with the rest of the class.

Thematic Units

As described in Chapter 4, thematic units provide a structure that allows the teacher to integrate a variety of materials around a central theme. The thematic unit is an excellent approach for incorporating literature and other textbook alternatives and corollaries into content area instruction.

Thematic units allow students to explore, investigate, query, examine, reflect, analyze, and criticize in a real-world approach to study and learning. They identify and focus on the concepts and facts as they relate to the theme, question, or issues under investigation.

Brozo and Tomlinson (1986) suggest that teachers be prepared to use trade books interchangeably with textbooks throughout any lesson or unit, and they recommend the following instructional combinations. One approach is to use one or more trade books to introduce a unit or lesson. Present an appropriate book or books for building schemata and interest in the topic before reading the text. You might read aloud selections that highlight concepts and information that will be emphasized in the text. You might also have students read independently or in small groups after you have identified the key parts for which they should look while reading.

Another approach is using trade books to elaborate on concepts, extend content, and provide relevant examples during and after reading the text. After reading a section of text for specified purposes designed to tie the content to the trade books, students work in small groups to search related trade books for additional and supporting information. Students might also read specific portions of trade books for the purpose of explaining the significance of each book or selection in relation to the content. The importance of giving students opportunities to share their favorite passages and discuss the content of the trade books in light of the concepts presented in the textbook cannot be over emphasized. Appendix I provides examples of children's and adolescent literature appropriate for various content areas and topics.

Social Studies

The following example of a sixth-grade literature-based social studies unit on China, designed and implemented by Guzzetti, Kowalinski, and McGowan (1992, 116) illustrates an approach that emphasizes the students' own interests, prior knowledge, and curiosities. Their study of the efficacy of this approach showed significant gains in students' concept acquisition.

> We designed and continually refined our instructional program by capitalizing on students' interests and curiosity about China. We engaged students in cooperative and purposeful activity that would answer their personal queries while providing the strategies necessary for students to find the answers they sought.

They began the unit by assessing the students' prior knowledge in the following fashion. First they asked the students to brainstorm everything they knew about China as they recorded their responses on an overhead transparency. Recording was done in the form of a Semantic Map that clustered ideas and diagrammed their relationships. They repeated this activity throughout the unit to assess students' progress in learning.

They began each lesson with a ten to fifteen-minute read-aloud program designed to activate students' prior knowledge and clarify any misconceptions. Following the read-aloud introduction, students were questioned and encouraged to come up with questions of their own. From the students' questions emerged cooperative groups based on interests, each group focusing on a different aspect of the theme. For example, a cooperative group might have been formed to design and construct a salt-dough map of the Yangtze River. These students might be particularly interested in reading *Young Fu of the Upper Yangtze* by E. Lewis in order to visualize the river and make connections with their map.

Another strategy they employed involved a "Think Sheet," which consisted of a sheet of paper with a central question at the top and three labeled columns: *My questions, My ideas,* and *Text ideas.* In the first column, students generated their own questions related to the central question. In the second column, they listed their ideas about those questions and in the third column, they recorded answers obtained from the trade books. As they observed students seeking answers, the researchers found that the trade books offered students more opportunities to answer their own questions than a single text would have done. Students came up with such questions as "What does a communist believe?" "Is the military in China as powerful as ours?" "What exactly is a socialist country?" "Which is more powerful in China, the communist organization or the socialist?"

In fact, the students became so enthusiastic about the knowledge they gained from completing their Think Sheets, they created their own question-and-answer books on various topics. The students then exchanged books to answer each other's questions. They used paper markers to mark pages in the trade books containing information that conflicted with their impressions or that they wanted to investigate further.

Trade books were also used to "foster students' sense of world citizenship and develop their abilities to function as global citizens" (Guzzetti, Kowalinski, and McGowan 1992, 117). For example, the 1990 Caldecott-winning Chinese folktale *Lon Po Po* by E. Young was read aloud and compared with the American folktale "Little Red Riding Hood." Students therefore had the opportunity to develop an appreciation for the similarities and differences between the two cultures.

Two activities were used by Guzzetti, Kowalinski, and McGowan (1992) to help students become personally involved with the literature. They felt that personal responses would facilitate attainment of cognitive and affective goals. When students completed reading books of their choice, they were given the option of responding in one of two ways.

First, students could construct a paradigm that related the author's ideas and thoughts to the reader's interests and experiences. Creating paradigms involved students developing visual displays on posterboard to demonstrate the relationships between their hobbies and interests and the events in a story. For example, one student used his interest in fishing to interpret the Newbery honor book *Dragonwings* by L. Yep. "This is the story of an 8-year-old boy who sailed from China to live with his father in San Francisco" (Guzzetti, Kowalinski, and McGowan 1992, 119).

Second, students could design a character chart involving a visual representation of individual characters in the story along with a caption. The visual representation was a display of images using the students' own illustrations or photographs from magazines or newspapers. The caption provided a justification for the particular images selected for a specific character, along with an explanation of how the images relate to the character's attitudes, beliefs, personality traits, and actions. The images students create should be based on their individual reflections and visualizations.

An excellent reference for developing thematic social studies units specifically on the topic of war is Phyllis K. Kennemer's (1993) *Using Literature to Teach Middle Grades About War.* She presents sample literature units on the Revolutionary War, Civil War, World War I, World War II, Vietnam War, and the Gulf War. Her sample units include a selected chronology, recommended picture books, factual books, biographies, and fiction books, sample lesson plans, and suggested questions and activities. Another excellent source for literature related to various social studies themes is *Literature-Based Social Studies: Children's Books and Activities to Enrich the K–5 Curriculum* by Mildred Knight Laughlin and Patricia Payne Kardaleff (1991). Appendix I provides examples of literature appropriate for use in a variety of thematic social studies units.

Math and Science

Although math and science might seem unlikely content areas for incorporating trade books into instruction, keep in mind that literacy instruction is crucial in every content area. Even in math, reading and writing play key roles in learning. For example, students must be able to interpret symbols, learn new vocabulary, read instructions, read word problems, demonstrate applied-level thinking, formulate questions, record procedures, identify salient information, and write out the steps followed in problem solving. The importance of literacy in science is more obvious; good reading and writing skills are essential for the collection, analysis, and manipulation of data, as well as for drawing conclusions, answering questions, and testing hypotheses.

The role of literature in math and science instruction may not be as obvious as it is in social studies. Math and science teachers are often skeptical that trade books can be of any real value in the teaching of math. However, once they start using them, teachers quickly discover that trade books can be extremely valuable in the math curriculum for students at all levels. Thematic units make it especially easy to integrate relevant literature into math and science instruction. An excellent annotated bibliography of literature related to various math concepts is *The Wonderful World of Mathematics: A Critically Annotated List of Children's Books in Mathematics* edited by Diane Thiessen and Margaret Matthias (1992).

Literature is valuable to the math and science curricula for several reasons. First, interesting and enjoyable books involving math and science concepts can help dispel anxiety and phobia related to those subjects. Appendix I provides examples of literature that are excellent motivational books.

Second, books can help inspire students to consider careers in math and science, especially girls and other groups who have traditionally not pursued math and science careers. Career awareness is perhaps one of the most important areas of math and science exploration. Books can enlighten students about all the bright futures possible through competence in math and science. For older students, trade books serve the valuable role of developing interest in math and science topics, as well as confidence in their own abilities in math and science. Appendix I provides examples of such books.

Third, books can make abstract mathematical and scientific concepts more concrete and meaningful to students. Appendix I provides examples of books appropriate for this purpose. Trade books are especially useful for developing a solid foundation of number concepts, the basis of all mathematical learning, especially for younger children. *What is One?* by Nancy Watson and *Numerals, New Dresses for Old Numbers* by Irving Adler are two examples of such books. Number concepts develop slowly over several years and can be reinforced with a variety of children's literature trade books. Following are examples of math concepts that could be reinforced for elementary school students using trade books (Radebaugh 1981):

1. Illustrations in children's literature can help students distinguish geometric shapes and identify them in familiar objects.
2. The concept of relative size can also be reinforced.
3. Sequencing in stories helps students understand the concept of ordinal numbers as they retell stories according to what happened first, what happened second, what happened third, and so forth.
4. The concept of one-to-one correspondence between numbers and objects being counted is easily reinforced with many different types of trade books. (*Anno's Counting Book* and *Anno's Counting House* by Mitsumasa Anno are good examples of such books.)

5. Addition can be reinforced by having students add rather than count objects, characters, or animals in counting books.
6. The historical foundation of our Hindu-Arabic number system can be explored with a number of trade books.
7. Subtraction and the concept of *zero* can be reinforced with a variety of nursery rhymes.
8. General number concepts can be reinforced with a variety of fairy tales.

Fourth, books can help students appreciate the practical applications of math and science in day-to-day living. Although many trade books do not deal directly with math and science concepts, they do allow students to explore and reinforce those concepts. Trade books can also be used to reinforce math and science concepts with older students. Middle school and high school students need to see practical applications of mathematical concepts in everyday life. Both fiction and nonfiction books provide many opportunities for students to see math and science in action. For example, concepts such as probability can be explored in puzzle and activity books; also, many concepts about money, environmental issues, animals, space exploration, and physics are addressed in a wide variety of trade books. Appendix I provides examples of such books.

In addition, students can learn about famous mathematicians and scientists and the contributions they made to life as we know it. Appendix I provides some examples of such biographies.

Computer science is another area of instruction that can be enhanced with literature. For example, "An unusual book, *Magic Squares*, by Paul Calter is a fantasy novel based on computer characters, problems, and math terms. Computer problems are cleverly inserted into the narrative" (Cline and McBride 1983, 189). Other examples of books appropriate for use in computer science teaching are provided in Appendix I.

Technological advances in science can be explored using a variety of science fiction literature. Examples of science fiction books appropriate for classroom instruction are provided in Appendix I.

Art and Music

Literature and literacy-based strategies can even be used in art and music. Keep in mind the importance of students practicing literacy as a learning and communication tool in every area of their lives. Literacy skills are tremendously important for learning in *every* content area including art and music. For example, both require students to interpret symbols, read instructions, develop a body of background knowledge, master technical vocabulary, express themselves, and make interpretations. The use of literature not only fosters the development of literacy skills, it can also significantly enhance learning and creativity in art and music.

An excellent source of ideas for incorporating literature into thematic units in art and music is *Literature-Based Art and Music: Children's Books and Activities to Enrich the K–5 Curriculum* by Mildred Knight Laughlin and Terri Parker Street (1992). They suggest that literature can be used to teach such artistic themes as color and value, shape and space, media and methods, and style. Laughlin and Street (1992) suggest literature as a valuable tool for learning about well-known artists, from the old masters to contemporary artists. They suggest the use of literature to teach musical themes such as timbre, pitch and dynamics, tempo and rhythm, form and style, folk songs, the mechanics of music, and composers and musicians. A few examples of the books they recommend for thematic units in art and music are provided in Appendix I.

Health and Physical Education

The importance of literacy-based instruction in the content area of health is obvious. As with social studies and science, for example, reading and writing play major roles as learning tools in health. The value of literature parallels that of instruction in other content areas. A large number of trade books, both fiction and nonfiction, are available to introduce, explore, and reinforce concepts related to health and wellness. Two excellent sources for annotated bibliographies of books appropriate for instruction in health are *Adventuring with Books: A Booklist for Pre-K–Grade 6* by Jett-Simpson (1989) and *Books for You: A Booklist for Senior High Students* by Carter and Abrahamson (1988). Appendix I provides a list of examples, including books they recommend.

The importance of literature and literacy-based instruction in physical education is perhaps not so obvious. From your own experiences with traditional physical education, you may have difficulty imagining how reading and writing could possibly be used to improve instruction. You might also have difficulty seeing how literature might be used in a physical education class. However, reading, writing, and literature can all be quite effective as instructional tools in physical education. Ask any coach or serious sports player about the importance of reading and writing for mastering the game. They appreciate the importance of play books, studying, and self-reflection.

Students who are given the opportunity to *read* and *write* the rules, strategies, and techniques for various sports and games *before* hearing and discussing them are at an obvious advantage over those who merely listen passively. They can internalize the information by writing it in journals or summarizing it in Graphic Organizers they create. Journals can also be used to help students explore, examine, and reflect on their attitudes toward various sports and physical activities. Writing can be an effective tool for helping them face their fears, improve their self-concepts, and develop confidence in physical performance.

Literature also can be used to guide students in physical education classes through a process of self-reflection. Great benefits can be reaped by having students read about characters (both fictional and real) who have faced similar challenges or have similar goals. Literature can also be used to help students identify and ponder sports figures who are their role models and heroes. Books related to sports and recreation can introduce students to a wide range of hobbies and physical activities available for lifelong wellness. Literature can help students develop background knowledge in a wide range of physical education themes. Carter and Abrahamson's (1988) book list is an excellent source of annotations of books related to sports and recreation. Appendix I provides a few examples of the literature they recommend.

Interdisciplinary Themes

This chapter has demonstrated the value of literature to instruction in all content areas. One of the greatest advantages of using literature for content area instruction is the versatility it affords in focusing on several content areas related to a single theme. Interdisciplinary themes are crucial to the new paradigm of education: deemphasizing or preferably eliminating altogether the disjointed focus of separate content areas that played such a major role in the factory model of education is important. Instead, it is time to emphasize the interdisciplinary nature of learning in the real world. Every issue, controversy, interest we investigate and contemplate involves many different content areas. Separating content instruction is a contrived and unnatural way to view and understand the world.

Teachers should work together to plan and implement instruction in various content areas using interdisciplinary thematic units. Every event, problem, question, situation, and issue can be studied from a variety of perspectives. For example, a unit on the Vietnam War can address history by examining the chronology of events. Social studies could be addressed by examining social issues related to the war, and math could be studied by examining the economic impact of the war. Science could be studied by examining the environmental and ecological impacts, and health issues could be addressed by examining the effects of drugs and chemical herbicides on the war veterans. Art, music, and recreation could be studied by comparing the cultures of the countries involved in the war.

Current events also lend themselves nicely to interdisciplinary instruction. For example, the January 1995 earthquake in Kobe, Japan could be used as an interdisciplinary theme. History could be studied by tracing the development of the city itself and art by examining the architecture of buildings. Social studies could be addressed by comparing the response of the Japanese society to the disaster with the response of American society to the recent earthquakes in California. Math could be used to identify the economic impact of the disaster on both Japan's and the world economies. Science could be studied by examining the environmental impact of the disaster both to the Japanese and the rest of the world.

Students should be encouraged to help select and develop interdisciplinary themes for instruction. Their personal interests and curiosities can lead to some fascinating thematic units. You can provide them some ideas and choices to get them started, but when students choose their own courses of study, the ownership they feel is a tremendous motivator. They often become inspired to investigate issues and controversies close to their own lives. Such topics are meaningful and relevant; that consequently, students generate their own interest and excitement in learning.

Sometimes a single book can inspire an interdisciplinary theme. For example, *Journey to Topaz* by Yoshiko Uchida tells the story of a Japanese-American family forced into a detention camp during World War II. This book could be used as a springboard for instruction in a variety of content areas. History could be addressed by examining the chronological events of the detention of Japanese-Americans in the context of World War II. By examining and comparing various historical and current examples of racial discrimination, social studies ideas can be represented. Science could be addressed by studying the living conditions at the detention camps and examining possible causes of the poor physical condition of the detainees. Health could be studied by examining the types of illness and disease most prevalent in the camps. Examining mortality rates of the people who were detained, by sex and age uses math concepts. Also, the financial holdings of the detainees could be investigated to determine the economic impact on the families.

For younger children, a book such as *Wagon Wheels* by Barbara Brenner could be used as the basis for an interdisciplinary thematic unit. This historical fiction book is based on the true story of an African-American pioneer family moving to Kansas in response to an offer of free land. History could be studied by looking at the whole westward pioneer movement. Social studies could be addressed by comparing life as a pioneer with life as we know it today, in terms of things like clothing, food, housing, technology, comfort, work, school, and entertainment. Geography could be studied by tracing some of the most popular pioneer trails and examining the terrain along the way. Incorporate math by having students calculate the amounts of provisions the family might have needed for such a trip, the distance they would have traveled, and the time it would have taken them to reach their destination. Science could be studied by comparing the plant and animal life in the eastern regions the pioneers were leaving and the western regions they wanted to call home.

Enrichment Activities

Enrichment activities are important for allowing the students to interpret and personalize new knowledge, as well as to help the teacher assess learning and identify misconceptions. These activities should be considered an essential part of the lesson and designed to synthesize text and trade book learning (Brozo and Tomlinson 1986).

Since follow-up activities are an important part of the lesson, they should not be considered an "add-on" or something for students to do only if they finish early. However, you may certainly allow students to begin the enrichment activity as soon as they finish the previous portion of the lesson. In fact, your enrichment activities should be enjoyable enough to serve as an incentive for students to finish their other work as quickly as possible.

You may want to allow individual group members to begin working on the enrichment activity once they have finished their other work. The remaining group members should join in as soon as they have finished. If the activity requires full-group participation, allow those who finish their other work early to choose a book or magazine related to the topic to read until most of their group members are ready to begin the enrichment activity. Never make individual students sit idly while others finish; however, make sure that you do not "keep them busy" by giving them extra work. Their reward for being efficient should be free reading for pleasure, or a fun, interesting, and challenging enrichment activity. Make sure you design your follow-up activities to enrich learning by challenging students at interpretive and applied levels of thinking.

Many of the sample enrichment activities described in the next sections can be very time consuming. The benefits gained from applying higher-level thinking, oral and written communication skills, and applying newly acquired concepts, ideas, and information, however, make it worthwhile (Brozo and Tomlinson 1986). Lengthy enrichment activities need not be done every day; rather, you can choose appropriate points during or after a unit to do some follow-up activities that allow students to synthesize what they are learning.

Reading

If you do not have enough trade books on the lesson's topic for each student to have one, divide the class into groups according to the number of books you have. Give each group one book along with specific instructions. For example, assign a reader in each group; give that student the book, and have him or her read either a selection you have marked, the book jacket, foreword, preface, table of contents, and so forth. For younger or less able readers, provide picture books and have students describe the book cover and one or more of the illustrations in the book.

Tell the listeners that their purpose for listening is to decide how the book relates to today's lesson. After the passage is read aloud or pictures described, the group should discuss the book's relationship to the topic and come to some consensus about it. Hold each group member accountable by telling them that you will be calling on one of them at random to describe the book and explain its relevance to today's topic.

Another possibility would be to have each group select a passage to read or picture to describe to the rest of the class. The passage or picture the group selects should demonstrate how the book relates to today's lesson. Again, each group member should be prepared to explain to the class why they chose that passage or picture as an example of how the book relates to the topic of study.

You might also have each group discuss whether members would want to read this book on their own for fun and why or why not. Tell them to be prepared to share with the rest of the class their decisions and the reasons behind them. Students should also be prepared to provide examples from the book in support of their decisions.

Another topic for the group's discussion could be the author's purpose in writing the book. Students should be prepared to surmise the author's intent, supporting their position with answers to questions such as: Who is the intended audience? What is the author's perspective or point of view in addressing this topic? What is the author's background or expertise on this topic? What is the author's overall message or position? What is the author's tone? How would you describe the author's style?

Another possibility is to give each group an applied-level question to answer after the selected passage has been read aloud or picture has been described. Again, the group should be prepared to share its question and answer with the rest of the class. Members should also use examples from the passage or illustrations in support of their responses.

Still another possibility would be to have the students do a "quickie" research assignment. Give each group a topic along with page numbers from the book to use as a resource. Then, assign a role to each group member. For example, each group could have a reader or researcher, notetaker, checker or editor, and presenter. Students should prepare a one-minute summary of the information they located on the research topic. Make it clear that group members must paraphrase and summarize the information and will not be allowed to read information aloud from the book itself when presenting research.

Writing

Chapter 10 addresses numerous ways to incorporate writing activities. Here are a few examples of using writing in enrichment activities, as described by Brozo and Tomlinson (1986). First, you might have students do some simple writing activities, including describing places or events mentioned in the text and detailed by trade books or having students assume the persona of fictional characters and write letters to historical figures. Both of these activities allow students to use factual knowledge in a personal way.

Second, they recommend more involved writing activities such as developing a dialogue between historical figures and fictional characters. Students might develop their own informational picture storybooks, modeling the plot after a trade book and incorporating facts from both the trade book and textbook. They also recommend whole-class writing activities, including writing a newspaper or newsletter centered around a theme (e.g., ecology). Finally, the class might develop fact sheets about famous historical figures.

Drama

Brozo and Tomlinson (1986) recommend the following use of drama for enrichment activities. Drama provides nonthreatening opportunities to try out different roles, ideas, and perspectives. It also motivates students to become actively involved with the content.

For example, students might do extemporaneous reenactments of scenes or events mentioned in the textbook or described in trade books. They might develop original scenes pertaining to the concepts, using the text and trade books as models. The scenes could be either impromptu or scripted. Students in the audience might then take the role of film critic.

Students might also do informal, on-the-spot interviews of characters or historical figures encountered in textbooks or trade books. Conducting interviews allows students to play with and apply factual information and concepts as they formulate questions and answers. Students could even do some actual interviewing, in which they interview local people who have some knowledge of the era, area, or concept under study.

Another possible drama activity would be to have students put on radio plays. Students select a scene or invent a likely scene from an historical event and then write a script with dialogue and action. They could then tape record it with sound effects and "broadcast" it later. Students could broadcast it either for the class or an invited audience from other classes.

Book Report Alternatives

Many of us still cringe at the idea of a "book report." Experience tells us that writing, presenting, and listening to book reports can be extremely boring and tedious. Not surprisingly, students who have had negative experiences with book reports tend to have misconceptions and negative attitudes toward them. Often their conceptions of book reports involve reading a book they do not particularly want to read and for no particular reason.

If the idea is to encourage students to read on their own for pleasure, allow them to select books they want to read. Students should also set their own purposes for reading each book and be given freedom of choice in deciding how to share their reading experience with the rest of the class. Sometimes, responses to books are so personal that they may wish to keep their reactions private. Journal writing provides a safe, nonthreatening mode of response for students who choose not to share their thoughts and feelings with the rest of the class.

Sanacore (1990) emphasizes the importance of avoiding conditions that might dissuade students from reading, such as book reports. To avoid the drudgery often associated with book reports, he recommends two alternatives originally described by Criscuolo (1977). The first is called *computerized dating.* In his activity, students attempt to "date" a book. They complete a "dating application," which includes their name, age, hobbies, favorite television programs, titles of books they have enjoyed, and types of books they like. The completed applications are posted on a bulletin board, and classmates recommend books to each other in a process of matchmaking friends and books.

A second alternative to book reports is "Book a trip." In this activity, students select books of personal interest related to places where they would like to travel. After reading the books, they make oral presentations using photographs, pictures from magazines, postcards, slides, and so on. (Many of these materials can be obtained from travel agencies free of charge.)

Another option would be to give students a set of interesting questions from which to choose. In addition, allow them to add other questions of their own. They can then construct a presentation by mixing and matching responses to the questions they choose. Some examples of possible questions are listed below (Peck 1978, 1, 7). As you can see, these questions require higher level understanding than do "typical" book report questions such as "Who are the characters, what is the setting, and what happens in the plot?"

1. What would this story be like if the main character were of the opposite sex?
2. Why is this story set where it is (not *what* is the setting)?
3. If you were to film this story, what characters would you eliminate if you couldn't use them all?
4. Would you film this story in black and white or in color? Why?
5. How is the main character different from you?

6. Would this story make a good television series? Why or why not?
7. What's one thing in this story that's happened to you?
8. Reread the first paragraph of Chapter 1. What's in it that makes you read on?
9. If you had to design a new cover for this book, what would it look like?
10. What does the title tell you about the book? Does it tell the truth?

A good source for interesting book report alternatives is *Explorations in the Teaching of English* (Mitchell 1989). This book includes a section called "Responding to Literature," which lists eighteen excellent ideas for book reports. Another source for inspiring book report ideas is *Ideas for Teaching English in the Junior High and Middle School* (Carter and Rashkis 1980). It includes a section called "Thirty-four alternatives to book reports." It also describes an activity called a "Book Pass," which gives students the opportunity to explore a variety of books in a short period of time. The teacher brings in a large variety of books, each one marked with a numbered card. Students begin by making four columns on a sheet of paper: book number, book title, author's last name, and number of lines read. Pass out one book to each student. When you say "start," students record the book number, title, and author before they begin reading. Call "time" after about one to two minutes, at which point students record the number of lines they read and pass their book on to the next person. This activity gives students practice in the art of book selection. By the end of the Book Pass, they should be able to identify at least one book they would like to read.

Here are a few more ideas for book report alternatives described by Cline and Hartman (1990) as ideas for linking novels with writing:

1. Ghost Chapter. Students write an additional chapter for the book.
2. Letter Writing. As a form of journal writing, students and teachers write back and forth about the books students are reading.
3. One Word, One Line. Each student chooses one word, phrase, or sentence that best represents one scene, one chapter, or the entire book. Students then write justifications for their selections and meet in groups to decide whose selection best represents their group.
4. "I Wonder." Students write down several "I wonder" statements, which pose questions about why a character acts in a particular manner, how a character would change if the storyline were a bit different, or how a change in the setting might affect the plot. (These statements can become the basis for Ghost Chapters.)
5. Moving Characters. As students put a character from one novel into the situation from another novel, they consider how the character's strengths and personality could improve a situation or how his or her weaknesses might change an event.

6. Rewriting. Students select an episode from their books and rewrite it from a different point of view.

Picture Books for All Ages

Picture books were once reserved for "story time" or "free reading" time for children. However, in recent years the value of picture books in content area learning and literacy has been discovered. For example, Smardo (1982) recommends using children's picture books to clarify science concepts. An important stage of the cognitive development of young children is the distinction between what is possible in the real world and what is fantasy or make-believe. Picture books can introduce science lessons by raising questions about what is realistic and what is fictitious.

One example described by Smardo (1982) involves a story of a tadpole changing into a frog. This phenomenon might seem quite implausible to young children, when of course, the transformation of tadpole to frog is a scientific fact. Another example involves a story that makes reference to the moon being made of cheese. Just as easily as the tadpole story might seem implausible, the moon-is-made-of-cheese theory might seem quite possible to a young mind. "Each of these situations deals either with an aspect of the natural world which seems so strange that children assume it is fictitious, or with a fanciful episode which seems so believable that children assume it is true" (Smardo 1982, 267). The stories offer rich and varied opportunities for discovery in science. They can be used to raise questions that can guide instruction and make it more meaningful to the students.

Although picture books have traditionally been reserved only for younger children, Neal and Moore (1991) make an excellent case for using them with older students in content area teaching. They offer the following five points as a rationale for using picture books with students of all ages. First, themes of picture books have universal value and appeal to students of all ages. Topics span a wide range of interests including such varied topics as love, self-fulfillment, humor, nostalgia, and endangered species. Also, a variety of literary genre are available to suit many tastes including biographies, historical fiction, tall tales, fantasies, science fiction, and mysteries.

Second, students may have somehow missed exposure to some picture book classics when they were younger. Many of the classics may have been published since they were young children.

Third, many of the issues addressed in picture books demand a maturity level not possessed by younger children. Although younger children can certainly enjoy such books on a surface level, they are often appreciated on a deeper level by older children, adolescents, and adults.

Fourth, the short format offered by picture books makes it easy to incorporate them into content area lessons. Since the content is presented in a concise and illustrative manner, students can quickly grasp the concepts without frustration.

Fifth, students have been conditioned by our visually-oriented society to rely on pictures as comprehension aids. Therefore, picture books are attractive and stimulating to most students.

Selecting Appropriate Books

A wide variety of high-quality picture books are available today. Neal and Moore (1991, 292) categorize them into five forms:

1. *Wordless picture books:* a story is told entirely through pictures.
2. *Near-wordless picture books:* illustrations and a few words tell the story.
3. *Standard picture books:* illustrations are the primary means of communication, with text occupying 1 to 25 percent of a page.
4. *Picture storybooks:* pictures and text are equally important in telling the story; text is narrative.
5. *Informational picture books:* subject-oriented books with easy-to-read text and many illustrations, written in either expository or narrative style.

You should carefully select picture books appropriate for your instructional purpose. Keep in mind, especially for older students, that appropriate picture books generally do not feature young children as characters, nor do they focus on the day-to-day concerns and activities of young children. Rather, you should select books that illustrate a concept, introduce an issue, serve as a model for student writing, or provide a resource for independent reading or group projects. Ultimately, *you* must enjoy the book. Perceiving your enthusiasm, your students will usually respond favorably (Neal and Moore 1991).

One example of a picture book appropriate for use with older students, even high school juniors and seniors, is Dr. Seuss's *The Butter Battle Book.* This book provides a satirical and enlightening view of the Cold War and ensuing arms race. It would make an excellent introduction to a unit on the Cold War; it would also provide an excellent stimulus for a follow-up discussion after the Cold War has been studied. Another example of a picture book enjoyed by older students is Dr. Seuss's *Yertle the Turtle,* which provides an insightful perspective into societies ruled by dictators. This book would enrich any unit on World War II, Hitler, or Nazi Germany.

Still another example of a picture book attractive to older students is Jon Scieszka's *The True Story of the Three Little Pigs.* In this book, students read a favorite fairy tale from a different perspective: that of the wolf. From the wolf's perspective, the story is entirely different from the way the pigs told it. This book gives students an excellent example of the literary element of perspective or point of view and its importance in critical evaluation of content.

More Ideas for Teaching

Picture books can be used to add pizzazz to lessons in most any content area including math, science, foreign languages, health, physical education, English, social studies, and art.

In English/language arts/reading classes, picture books can be used to help students develop writing ability and fluency. Many stories have simple patterns that can serve as excellent models for students' writing and publishing efforts. Picture books also provide a rich resource for vocabulary development.

Story structure (e.g., flashback, linear, retraceable, parallel, and circular) and genre (e.g., tall tale, mystery, realistic fiction, legend, satire, folktale, historical fiction, allegory, ballad, fable, and fantasy) can both be taught using picture books as examples. Picture books can also be used to facilitate the study of literary conventions (e.g., allusion, symbolism, parody, foreshadowing, metaphor, and mood). Neal and Moore (1991) recommend a book called *Using Picture Storybooks to Teach Literary Devices* (Hall 1990) as a source for selecting appropriate picture books for instruction.

In social studies content instruction, picture books provide an excellent introduction to such varied concepts as culture, prejudice, the work ethic, class structure, fame, community, and family. They can also be used to explore a variety of values such as privacy, freedom, individuality, common good, equality, fairness, wisdom, courage, social harmony, charity, peace, and health. Also, picture books allow students to examine interesting aspects of famous historical figures not addressed by textbooks often. Additionally, not-so-famous but nonetheless important historical figures not generally mentioned in textbooks can be studied. Other important topics that can be introduced or taught effectively using picture books include war, the global community, changing demographics, patriotism, and peace-making.

Neal and Moore (1991) make several excellent teaching suggestions. One idea is to help students compare the accounts of historical events portrayed in picture books with the descriptions provided by a textbook. Students can take clues from the dialogue often provided by picture books and role play historical events, taking the identities of famous historical figures. Sharing and discussing a picture book before composing predictions about what happened after the depicted events may be very valuable for students. Finally, they can study current issues such as homelessness in newspapers and compare the coverage with story details in related picture books.

In art classes, picture books offer a rich resource for teaching students about various artistic elements (e.g., style, medium, and technique). Picture books themselves serve as an art form to be studied, particularly in terms of their history, outstanding artists, and the special art of illustration. Students can also study picture books to gain important insights into the relationship between art and written text. After studying one or more picture books that provide good examples of the art of illustration, students can create their illustrations according to their own interpretations. They could also work cooperatively with creative writing classes to produce their own picture books.

Fiction Books

The two basic types of fiction best suited for content area instruction are realistic fiction and historical fiction. Realistic fiction portrays characters who are believable as real-life people and events that are believable as real-life occurrences. Often they depict characters struggling with realistic personal problems involving such topics as AIDS, sexual abuse and harassment, divorce, death and dying, drunken driving, puberty and adolescence, sexuality, mental illness, physical handicaps, drug and alcohol abuse, and peer pressure. Students can get tremendous benefits from bibliotherapy, which involves reading about real problems of real people to help them deal with their own problems. Realistic fiction also deals with broader social concerns including crime, environmental protection, war, poverty, homelessness, child abuse, human rights, and racism.

Historical fiction recreates past events in a narrative fashion, allowing readers to vicariously experience events of the past. Usually the characters portray actual historical figures; sometimes fictional characters are created to make it easier for modern-day readers to relate to events of long ago. Through historical fiction, students can gain deeper insights into people who played important roles in shaping history. They can also find greater appreciation for what happened in the past and how those events influenced current events, as well as their potential for shaping future events.

Vacca and Vacca (1993, 301–305) make a strong case for using other types of fiction in content area teaching by demonstrating appropriate uses of fantasy, folk literature, myths, poetry, drama, and cartoons as follows.

- using fantasy books about the aftermath of a nuclear holocaust to teach students about the realities of that potential terror
- using folktales about monsters to teach students about prejudice and strength of character

▪ using myths from different countries to help students develop multicultural awareness and appreciation

▪ using poetry for giving students opportunities to ponder universal human experiences and "unanswerable" questions

▪ using drama to portray life in other countries to offer students glimpses of differing cultural norms for human behavior

▪ using cartoons to personify animals to give students greater insights into the human condition, even tragedy such as the Nazi Holocaust. They recommend that teachers not rule out any fictional genre. In addition to those mentioned, important teaching tools may be found in animal realism, mysteries, sports stories, adventure stories, and romance books (Vacca and Vacca 1993)

Nonfiction Books

The term nonfiction generally refers to information books and biographies. One type of information book is the nonfiction narrative, which provides an interesting narrative account (including dialogue) of actual events. Nonfiction narrative books are based on the recollections, recordings, and written accounts of actual participants. Another type of information book is the "how-to" book, which describes how to do something such as play a game, cook, solve a problem, conduct an experiment, create a piece of art, or fix a car. How-to books are especially useful in science, math, vocational arts, and fine arts.

The use of nonfiction books as alternative or collateral materials is becoming increasingly popular because nonfiction trade books compensate for many of the weaknesses of content area textbooks. Teachers are discovering that the use of nonfiction books with textbooks can enrich content area learning (Moss 1991).

Nonfiction trade books have numerous advantages over textbooks; Moss (1991) elaborates on five of them. First, the use of nonfiction books allows teachers to individualize instruction, because they can choose books for individuals or small groups according to reading levels and interests.

Second, nonfiction trade books have interesting content and are generally more visually appealing. Since they present factual information in an interesting and detailed fashion, students are often attracted to them over other types of trade books, as well as textbooks. Nonfiction trade books also have exciting cover designs, attractive graphics, and effective illustrations.

Third, nonfiction trade books can go into greater detail than textbooks and are allowed greater freedom of expression since they do not have to undergo the scrutiny and approval required for textbooks. Because they provide such in-depth information on a wide range of topics, they allow students to discover and explore how knowledge in various disciplines is organized, applied, and related. This foundation of knowledge develops essential schemata, thereby providing an important context for understanding and learning.

Fourth, nonfiction trade books generally present information arranged in a more logical and coherent fashion than do textbooks. Since textbooks provide skimpy coverage over a multitude of topics, students often have difficulty discerning and prioritizing main ideas, supporting details, important facts, and more importantly, the implications and significance of all that information. However, nonfiction books present information concisely and organize facts in a way that makes it easier for the reader to analyze and synthesize them in a meaningful context.

Fifth, nonfiction trade books provide more up-to-date information and are more readily accessible than textbooks. As a result, students can more easily relate them to current events and their own day-to-day experiences. Since they are generally easier to obtain, teachers have more flexibility in planning, and students have access to a wider variety of resources.

Moss (1991) recommends using Bernice Cullinan's three criteria for selecting children's nonfiction trade books (cited in Moss 1991). You can use these criteria for stocking your classroom library, and even more importantly, you can teach them to your students to encourage them to be critical readers. Since students should be allowed to select their own books anyway, it is important that you provide them a wide variety from which to choose. Once they learn the qualities of good nonfiction literature, they can apply the criteria themselves in selecting books.

The first criterion involves the integrity of authors, which refers to whether and to what extent they are honest with the readers. The following questions should help you judge the integrity of authors:

- To what extent do they reveal their point of view and communicate to the reader their motivation for writing?
- To what extent do they encourage a questioning attitude in the reader?
- To what extent do they reveal their sources?
- How clearly do they distinguish and label facts, opinions, and theories?
- Do they present different viewpoints objectively?
- Do they support generalizations with facts?

The second criterion involves the tone of the book, which is partially determined by the extent of the author's presence. The reader should be able to hear the writer's voice clearly enough to perceive the person behind the information. The following questions should help you judge the tone of the book:

- Does the author have a distinctive and effective communication style?
- Does the author use an informal, yet informative tone of "voice"?
- Does the author seem to be communicating with the reader or just transmitting facts?

The third criterion involves the content of the book. The content should be both comprehensible and appealing. The following questions should help you judge the content of the book:

- How well is the material organized?
- To what extent are the ideas presented in a logical and coherent fashion?
- What kinds of reading aids are provided (e.g., index, bibliographies, appendices, reference notes, graphics, and glossaries)?
- Is the content presented in well-designed layouts with effective illustrations?

In selecting nonfiction books, an important thing to remember is the value of variety. Take advantage of the opportunity to expose students to a wide variety of perspectives. Provide enough variety so that students can make their own choices to suit their personal interests and tastes. In addition to making available books that are relevant to the instructional content, include in your classroom library some nonfiction trade books that allow students to explore and examine critical issues of personal concern. For example, nonfiction books address a wide range of practical issues and social problems, including career choices, educational opportunities, prison life, sexually transmitted diseases, cigarette smoking, domestic violence, violence against women, and sexual abuse.

Nonfiction trade books for children and young adults are widely available today. Many of them have teacher's guides with suggested activities for instruction and enrichment. Moss (1991) makes several excellent suggestions for helping teachers build a classroom library. First, communicate your needs to your school and community librarians; often they are willing to purchase additional copies for classroom use. Take advantage of the low-cost treasures frequently found at garage sales, used-book stores, and book sales sponsored by schools and community organizations. Get your students involved in book clubs like those offered by Scholastic and Trumpet. These clubs offer opportunities for teachers to get free or low-cost books. Talk to your school administrators about submitting grant proposals to foundations, corporations, parent-teacher organizations, or local businesses. Finally, talk to your school administrators in charge of textbook purchasing. More and more schools are being allowed the freedom to purchase trade books in addition to or instead of textbooks. Sometimes textbook purchases can be deferred, allowing teachers to build a diversified classroom library.

INCORPORATING PERIODICALS

According to Olson, Gee, and Forester (1992, 112), magazines are popular as supplementary reading materials because "they are visually attractive; provide contemporary articles of high interest; contain *short* articles that can be read in one sitting; and they often contain challenging and amusing games and puzzles." For these reasons, their appeal is obvious, and reading magazines in the content classroom for recreation is both appropriate and desirable. However, magazines also make excellent collateral materials for learning content.

Children's periodicals engage students in reading a variety of genres for a variety of purposes. Often overlooked as a resource for content area instruction, periodicals are extremely valuable alternative and collateral materials for the text. Seminoff (1986) identifies six benefits of using periodicals:

1. The material is current and relevant to students' interests.
2. Periodicals offer a wide range of readability, both in terms of interest and difficulty.
3. Periodicals include both fiction and nonfiction, thereby encouraging students to be strategic readers, i.e., those who use a variety of reading strategies appropriate for the demands of the materials and task.
4. The quality and quantity of the illustrations and photographs that often accompany the articles provide another source of content for improving comprehension.
5. The relatively low cost of periodicals makes them readily accessible.
6. Periodicals present content in a way that is more concise and manageable than textbooks.

As Moore and Moore (1983) point out, magazine articles do not assume that the teacher will be present to explain concepts or eliminate confusion, as do textbooks. Rather, articles are largely self-contained and self-explanatory. Periodical authors usually select a few major concepts to explore in detail in the context of the readers' prior knowledge.

Criscuolo and Gallagher (1989) recommend the use of newspapers as an especially good instructional tool for troubled adolescents in middle and high school. The reasons they offer in support of this recommendation indicate that newspapers might be an effective way to develop interest for all students.

1. Newspapers offer a "freshness" of content; they focus on what is happening around students right now.
2. They provide relevance of content; most topics covered in newspaper articles affect students personally in one way or another.
3. Newspapers are disposable (and can be recycled!); students can cut them up, manipulate and rearrange material, and throw them away. As a result, students can personalize the materials by choosing what they want to use and discarding the rest.
4. Since newspapers do not look like textbooks, they do not provoke the negative attitudes often associated with textbooks.
5. Because newspapers are not labeled according to reading or grade level as are most textbooks, students lacking in academic success and self-confidence are not stigmatized; they use the same materials as the honor students.
6. Newspapers are generally associated with free-time activities, increasing students' interest in reading them.
7. Most major U.S. newspapers are written between a fourth- and sixth-grade reading level, making them useful for students in a wide range of age and ability levels.
8. Using newspapers for instruction develops and reinforces an important tool for lifelong learning.

Selecting and Obtaining Periodicals

One of the finest sources available for teachers in selecting magazines is a publication titled *Magazines for Children* (Stoll 1990). This booklet provides an exhaustive annotated list of children's magazines along with a subject index and age/grade index. Another excellent source to aid teachers in selecting magazines is a booklet titled *Easy Reading: Book Series and Periodicals for Less Able Readers, 2d ed.* (Ryder, Graves, and Graves 1989). Figure 7–4 offers are a few examples of the children's magazines recommended by Seminoff (1986), listed by general category.

Moore and Moore (1983) suggest a number of ways to obtain magazines and newspapers easily and inexpensively. For example, you can ask for donations from students, parents, librarians, magazine dealers, and local newspapers. Also, since subscriptions are usually quite reasonable, parent-teacher organizations often are willing to help with funds.

Multiple subscriptions are not necessary, but they do make it easier for more students to enjoy them. Single issues are still a valuable resource and can be used for a number of activities. For example, they can serve as a model for students to produce their own classroom magazines (Moore and Moore 1983).

FIGURE 7–4 Examples of children's periodicals

SCIENCE
Odyssey
Scienceland
3-2-1 Contact
Ranger Rick's Nature Magazine
National Geographic's World
Your Big Backyard

HEALTH
Children's Digest
Child Life
Children's Playmate
Humpty Dumpty
Jack and Jill
Turtle

SOCIAL SCIENCE
Cobblestone
Penny Power
Faces

LITERATURE
Classical Calliope
Cricket

GENERAL INTEREST
Electric Company
Highlights
Sesame Street

Ideas for Teaching

From their study of 290 teachers who indicated that they used magazines in their classrooms to teach content, Olson, Gee, and Forester (1992, 113, 114) summarize the following suggestions for incorporating magazines into content classes:

1. Collect a wide range of magazines related to specialized content areas and allow students to choose them for Sustained Silent Reading and recreational reading when they have free time after finishing their work.
2. Have groups of students read different articles on the same topic. After each group has written a summary, have the groups share and compare summaries. They should focus on similarities and differences in the authors' perspectives and points of view, as well as purposes in writing the articles.
3. Distribute an article to the entire class and conduct a Directed Reading Activity.
4. Have students read two articles with opposing viewpoints and compare the authors' credentials, treatment of the subject, sources and accuracy, and purposes for writing the articles. Help students distinguish fact from opinion, prejudice from reason, and propaganda from information.
5. Help students apply reading strategies to activate prior knowledge, make predictions, and relate the content to their own experiences.

Sustained Silent Reading is a useful strategy for giving students regular opportunities to read non-textbook materials for enjoyment.

6. Guide the students in analyzing the writer's craft by examining and analyzing an article's organization, effectiveness of opening and closing paragraphs, paragraph development, and the author's use of language and examples.
7. Update textbook information with current magazines.
8. Have students compare and contrast television, newspaper, and magazine coverage of the same topic.
9. Encourage students to respond to an article they particularly enjoyed or disagreed with by writing a letter to the editor or author.
10. Help students summarize key points of an article by having them create and discuss outlines, graphic organizers, or annotations.
11. Provide magazines as resources for students to use in report writing. Have students follow these steps. First, students should make a column for each magazine on a sheet of paper. Second, as they read, have them summarize important information in the appropriate column (using columns helps reinforce the importance of giving credit to the appropriate source).

Seminoff (1986) suggests that even younger children can enjoy periodicals by reading articles, looking at the pictures, and listening to selections read aloud by the teacher. She also suggests that simply reading a selection aloud to the class and then leaving the magazine in a readily accessible place is a sufficient "hook" for students of all ages. Following are several examples of incorporating periodicals as offered by Seminoff (1986, 892):

▌ In a literature unit, have students compare several versions of the same folktale.
▌ In a social studies unit, have students draw on information from magazines to develop their own travel brochures for specific places or historical points of interest.
▌ In a math unit, have students compare the cost of a variety of publication subscriptions from around the world.

An idea described by Moore and Moore (1983) is designed to encourage self-questioning by students. They suggest placing library card pockets in magazines and having students write questions on cards. Students enjoy trying to answer their classmates' questions, as well as trying to stump their friends with their own questions. You could then compile a bank of the students' questions for use in educational games.

Criscuolo and Gallagher (1989) described a number of ways they incorporate newspapers into instruction:

1. They used articles about controversial and relevant issues to stimulate class discussions. Students then wrote paragraphs stating and defending their positions. For example, they read articles related to crime and criminal activity; following discussion, they created their own plans for reducing crime.
2. They used political campaign advertisements to help students distinguish information that is directly stated from implied information. Students examined the candidates' biographical sketches, identifying facts and implications.
3. They developed a newspaper scavenger hunt to teach students how to locate information in a newspaper and how to read for details. Clues were provided, and students were challenged to locate information in the appropriate sections of the newspaper.
4. They used "Dear Abby" columns to help students examine and discuss real-life problems and dilemmas.
5. They used newspapers to teach students how to uncover practical information for themselves. For example, they worked on exercises designed to help them locate potential jobs, housing, and used cars.
6. They used newspapers to help students identify, characterize, compare, and contrast their heroes and heroines.

SUMMARY

Using children's and young adult literature and periodicals as alternative and collateral materials to the textbook is possibly the most effective way to make content area literacy and learning fun and interesting. Although the textbook serves its own purpose, alone it is not sufficient for providing students the wide range of reading experiences demanded by content area literacy. A wide variety of interesting, attractive, and enjoyable literature is crucial to instruction in content area literacy. Students need experiences with varied materials to learn how to read, write, and think critically in the unique language of each content area. They also need wide-ranging literary experiences to understand and appreciate the value of literacy as a tool for learning the content.

Trade books, magazines, and newspapers are a valuable source for developing multicultural concepts to promote awareness, understanding, tolerance, and appreciation. Through literature students can vicariously travel around the world and meet people from many different cultures. These "travels" enrich their background knowledge and stimulate curiosities about the world around them. Through periodicals students can experience current events around the world. They can "be there now" to learn firsthand about commonalities and differences between their own communities and those around the globe. Learning about the rest of the world is crucial to understanding themselves and their own cultures.

Through books and periodicals students can venture from familiar surroundings to face the reality of a world community. This reality requires that they become aware of how everything they do affects other people all over the world. Up-to-date books and other publications give students the opportunity to put the content they are learning into a larger context, one that makes the content meaningful, practical, and valuable to their own lives.

Careful selection of materials is important to avoid perpetuating gender bias and to promote gender equity among your students. Consider first the characteristic abilities, needs, interests, and attitudes of your students. Then, select materials that best match those student characteristics. To help you examine and select materials, consider their "readability" with respect to the characteristics of your students. Develop a checklist of criteria that you and your students believe make a book or periodical "readable."

Attractive and current books, magazines, and newspapers can be extremely motivational to students, especially if they associate textbooks with boredom and drudgery. Students tend to be more interested in learning from real-life materials, and are therefore more motivated to develop the literacy skills needed to master them. As a result, when students are able to expand their reading experiences with a variety of materials related to content area learning, they are more likely to improve their attitudes toward literacy and learning. Providing interesting and enjoyable materials is an effective way to motivate your students to want to read and learn.

At the same time, providing varied materials of high quality is an effective way to help students master the content. Trade books and periodicals provide up-to-date information often presented in compelling, attractive, and meaningful ways. Many students find such materials easier and more enjoyable to read and study. Also, through literature and periodicals, students can more easily see the practical value of the content and its relevance to their own lives.

Furthermore, selecting and incorporating a variety of trade books and periodicals can be an inspiring and rejuvenating experience for teachers, who are often just as bored with the textbook as are their students. The investment of time and money for establishing a classroom library is a wise one; both teachers and students will benefit from the increased enjoyment of and enthusiasm for learning inspired by good books and articles. Developing the habit of constantly looking for interesting and relevant books and articles can be very motivating and rewarding for both teachers and students alike.

ENRICHMENT ACTIVITIES

1. Develop a comprehensive checklist of readability criteria, including application of a readability formula, for textbooks. Then, evaluate two textbooks using your checklist. From your evaluation, decide whether you would select each textbook. Write a letter to your school principal explaining and defending your decisions.

2. Develop a comprehensive checklist of readability criteria, including application of a readability formula, for trade books. Then, evaluate two trade books (one fiction and one nonfiction) using your checklist. From your evaluation, decide whether you would select each trade book. Write a letter to your school principal explaining and defending your decisions.

3. Observe a class in a neighborhood school, watching for evidence of gender bias or gender equity. Prepare a set of questions to guide your observations, beginning with the following suggestions. When responding to your questions, include specific examples of what you observed.

- Does the teacher call on boys more than girls or girls more than boys? Does the teacher probe boys for more information, but not girls, or vice versa?
- Does the teacher use gender-biased language (e.g., "he" when referring to both genders, "policemen" when referring to police officers)?
- Does the teacher use examples that stereotype roles for men and women (e.g., a woman cooking dinner, a man working on a car)?
- Does the teacher promote gender equity through the reading materials available in the classroom (e.g., a variety of materials that are not gender biased and do not portray stereotypical sex roles)?
- Does the teacher promote gender equity through class discussions and direct instruction (e.g., addressing sexual harassment, identifying appropriate vs. offensive behavior, promoting nontraditional career opportunities for both boys and girls)?

4. Identify a topic or theme that could be studied from an interdisciplinary perspective. Then, prepare an annotated bibliography of at least thirty books related to that topic or theme that would be appropriate for your classroom library.

5. Visit five classrooms that have classroom libraries. Describe what you saw. Did you have a hard time finding classrooms with libraries? On your way out of the school, stop by the school library and ask how many teachers regularly check out books for their classroom libraries; ask the librarian whether teachers are encouraged to do so. Summarize your results.

6. Select a topic for a thematic unit in the content area of your choice (e.g., the Civil War for a social studies unit). Identify a set of five to ten important concepts you want to highlight (e.g., justice, courage, slavery, economics, death and loss, racial equality, patriotism, and fear). Develop an annotated bibliography of books, articles, and other materials you might use in teaching these concepts. In your annotations, include examples of ways you could use the materials for instruction or enrichment.

7. Survey ten teachers each from an elementary, middle, and high school about whether they read aloud to their students. Make the survey brief, asking questions similar to the ones that follow. Summarize your findings.
- Do you read to your students?
- If so, how often?
- Why do you read to them?
- Do they enjoy it?
- How do you choose the reading material?
- What books or other materials do you enjoy reading aloud?

REFERENCES

Alvermann, D. E., and M. Commeyras. (1994). Inviting multiple perspectives: Creating opportunities for student talk about gender inequalities in texts. *Journal of Reading* 37:566–571.

Alvermann, D. E., and S. E. Phelps. (1994). *Content reading and literacy: Succeeding in today's diverse classrooms.* Needham Heights, MA: Allyn & Bacon.

American Association of University Women. (1993). *The AAUW report: How schools shortchange girls.* Washington, DC: AAUW Educational Foundation and the National Education Association.

Anderson, J. (1983). Lix and rix: Variations on a little-known readability index. *Journal of Reading* 26:490–496.

Baldwin, R. S., and A. G. Leavell. (1992). When was the last time you read a textbook just for kicks? In *Reading in the content areas: Improving classroom instruction,* 3d ed. Edited by E. K. Dishner, T. W. Bean, J. E. Readence, and D. W. Moore. Dubuque, IA: Kendall/Hunt Publishing Company.

Brozo, W. G., and C. M. Tomlinson. (1986). Literature: The key to lively content courses. *The Reading Teacher* 40:288–293.

Carter, B. C., and R. F. Abrahamson. (1988). *Books for you: A booklist for senior high students,* 5th ed. Phoenix: Oryx Press.

———. (1990). *From delight to wisdom: Nonfiction for young adults.* Phoenix: Oryx Press.

Carter, C., and Z. Rathkis. (Eds.). (1980). Ideas for teaching English in the junior high and middle school. Urbana, IL: National Council of Teachers of English.

Christensen, J. (Ed.). (1983). *Your reading: A booklist for junior high students.* Urbana, IL: National Council of Teachers of English.

Cline, R. K. J., and K. J. Hartman. (1990). Practical ideas for linking novels with students' writing. *The ALAN Review* 17:38–41.

Cline, R. K. J., and W. McBride. (1983). *A guide to literature for young adults: Background, selection, and use.* Glenview, IL: Scott, Foresman and Company.

Criscuolo, N. P. (1977). Book reports: Twelve creative alternatives. *The Reading Teacher* 30:893–895.

Criscuolo, N. P., and S. A. Gallagher. (1989). Using the newspaper with disruptive students. *Journal of Reading* 32:440–443.

Estes, T. H. (1971). A scale to measure attitudes toward reading. *Journal of Reading* 15:135–138.

Feder-Feitel, L. (1993). How to avoid gender bias. *Creative Classroom* 7:56–62.

Fry, E. (1977). Fry's readability graph: Clarifications, validity, and extension to level 17. *Journal of Reading* 21:242–252.

Guzzetti, B. J., B. J. Kowalinski, and T. McGowan. (1992). Using a literature-based approach to teaching social studies. *Journal of Reading* 36:114–122.

Hall, S. (1990). *Using picture storybooks to teach literary devices.* Phoenix: Oryx Press.

Irwin, J. W., and C. A. Davis. (1980). Assessing readability: The checklist approach. *Journal of Reading* 24:124–130.

Jett-Simpson, M. (Ed.). (1989). *Adventuring with books: A booklist for pre-K–grade 6,* 9th ed. Urbana, IL: National Council of Teachers of English.

Laughlin, M. K., and P. P. Kardeleff. (1991). *Literature-based social studies: Children's books and activities to enrich the K–5 curriculum.* Phoenix: Oryx Press.

Laughlin, M. K., and T. P. Street. (1992). *Literature-based art and music.* Phoenix: Oryx Press.

McCracken, R. A. (1971). Initiating sustained silent reading. *Journal of Reading* 14:521–524, 582–583.

McKenna, M. C., and R. D. Robinson. (1993). *Teaching through text: A content literacy approach to content area reading.* White Plains, NY: Longman.

McLaughlin, G. H. (1969). SMOG grading—A new readability formula. *Journal of Reading* 12:639–645.

Mitchell, D. (1989). *Explorations in the teaching of English.* New York: Harper & Row Publishers.

Moore, D. W., and S. A. Moore. (1983). The clip sheet: Periodically reading. *The Reading Teacher* 36:456–458.

Moore, D. W., S. A. Moore, P. M. Cunningham, and J. W. Cunningham. (1994). *Developing readers and writers in the content areas K–12,* 2d ed. White Plains, NY: Longman.

Moss, B. (1991). Children's nonfiction trade books: A complement to content area texts. *The Reading Teacher* 45:26–31.

Neal, J. C., and K. Moore. (1991). *The very hungry caterpillar* meets *Beowulf* in secondary classrooms. *Journal of Reading* 35:290–296.

Nelson, J. (1978). Readability: Some cautions for the content area teacher. *Journal of Reading* 21:620–625.

Norton, D. E. (1990). Teaching multicultural literature in the reading curriculum. *The Reading Teacher* 44:28–40.

Olson, M. W., T. C. Gee, and N. Forester. (1992). Magazines in the classroom: Beyond recreational reading. In *Reading in the content areas: Improving classroom instruction,* 3d ed. Edited by E. K. Dishner, T. W. Bean, J. E. Readence, and D. W. Moore. Dubuque, IA: Kendall/Hunt Publishing Company.

Peck, R. (1978). Ten questions to ask about a novel. *The ALAN Review* 5:1, 7.

Radebaugh, M. R. (1981). Using children's literature to teach mathematics. *The Reading Teacher* 34:902–906.

Raygor, A. L. (1977). The Raygor readability estimate: A quick and easy way to determine difficulty. In *Reading: Theory, research, and practice: Twenty-sixth yearbook of the National Reading Conference.* Edited by P. D. Pearson. Clemson, SC: National Reading Conference.

Richardson, J. S., and R. F. Morgan. (1994). *Reading to learn in the content areas,* 2d ed. Belmont, CA: Wadsworth.

Ruddell, M. R. (1993). *Teaching content reading and writing.* Needham Heights, MA: Allyn & Bacon.

Ryder, R. J., B. B. Graves, and M. F. Graves. (1989). *Easy reading: Book series and periodicals for less able readers,* 2d ed. Newark, DE: International Reading Association.

Sanacore, J. (1990). Creating the lifetime reading habit in social studies. *Journal of Reading* 33:414–418.

Seminoff, N. W. (1986). Children's periodicals throughout the world: An overlooked educational resource. *The Reading Teacher* 39:889–895.

Smardo, F. A. (1982). Using children's literature to clarify science concepts in early childhood programs. *The Reading Teacher* 36:267–273.

Stoll, D. R. (Ed.). (1990). *Magazines for children.* Glassboro, NJ: Educational Press Association of America; Newark, DE: International Reading Association.

———. (Ed.). (1994). Magazines for kids and teens. Glassboro, NJ: Educational Press Association of America; Newark, DE: International Reading Association.

Thiessen, D., and M. Matthias. (Eds.). (1993). *The wonderful world of mathematics: A critically annotated list of children's books in mathematics.* Reston, VA: National Council of Teachers of Mathematics.

Tierney, R. J., J. E. Readence, and E. K. Dishner. (1990). *Reading strategies and practices: A compendium,* 3d ed. Needham Heights, MA: Allyn & Bacon.

Tonjes, M. J., and M. V. Zintz. (1992). *Teaching reading thinking study skills in content classrooms,* 3d ed. Dubuque, IA: Wm. C. Brown.

Trelease, J. (1989). *The new read-aloud handbook.* New York: Penguin Books.

Vacca, R. T., and J. L. Vacca. (1993). *Content area reading,* 4th ed. New York: HarperCollins.

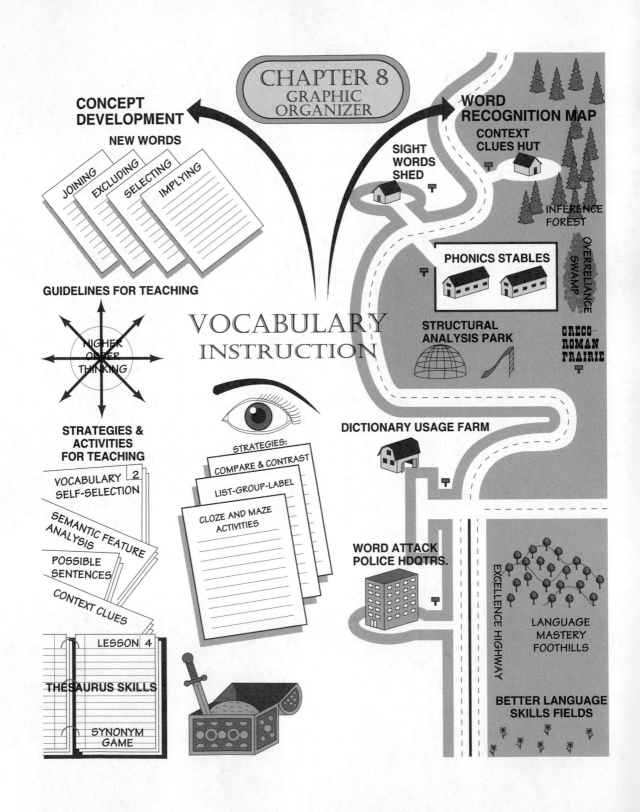

CHAPTER 8
GRAPHIC
ORGANIZER

VOCABULARY
INSTRUCTION

CONCEPT DEVELOPMENT

NEW WORDS

JOINING

EXCLUDING

SELECTING

IMPLYING

GUIDELINES FOR TEACHING

HIGHER ORDER THINKING

STRATEGIES & ACTIVITIES FOR TEACHING

VOCABULARY SELF-SELECTION 2

SEMANTIC FEATURE ANALYSIS

POSSIBLE SENTENCES

CONTEXT CLUES

LESSON 4

THESAURUS SKILLS

SYNONYM GAME

STRATEGIES:

COMPARE & CONTRAST

LIST-GROUP-LABEL

CLOZE AND MAZE ACTIVITIES

WORD RECOGNITION MAP

CONTEXT CLUES HUT

SIGHT WORDS SHED

INFERENCE FOREST

PHONICS STABLES

OVERRELIANCE SWAMP

STRUCTURAL ANALYSIS PARK

GRECO-ROMAN PRAIRIE

DICTIONARY USAGE FARM

WORD ATTACK POLICE HDQTRS.

EXCELLENCE HIGHWAY

LANGUAGE MASTERY FOOTHILLS

BETTER LANGUAGE SKILLS FIELDS

Vocabulary Instruction

To demonstrate mastery of the content, the student will be able to do the following:

PART 1 OBJECTIVES

1. Identify the following strategy, describe its distinguishing features, and assess its significance to teaching content area literacy: Compare/Contrast.
2. Distinguish word recognition from concept development in terms of vocabulary instruction.
3. Identify and define each of the five word recognition skills.
4. Summarize the most important principles for teaching each of the five word recognition skills.
5. Suggest ways to coach students in applying each of the five word recognition skills.

PART 2 OBJECTIVES

1. Identify the following strategy, describe its distinguishing features, and assess its significance to teaching content area literacy: List-Group-Label.
2. Describe the keys to effective concept development.
3. Define and assess joining, excluding, selecting, and implying as techniques for introducing and reinforcing concepts.
4. Compile a list of ten guidelines for teaching vocabulary concept development the student considers most important for her or his content area(s) and grade level(s).
5. Evaluate the following strategies in terms of how they follow recommended guidelines for teaching vocabulary concept development:

PART 2 OBJECTIVES—continued

- Knowledge Rating
- Vocabulary Self-Collection Strategy
- Semantic Feature Analysis
- Possible Sentences
- Contextual Redefinition
- Preview in Context

6. Describe at least one concept development activity that is especially appropriate for ESL students.
7. Distinguish instruction in context clues and dictionary usage for word recognition versus concept development.

INTRODUCTION

Imagine yourself as a teacher in the following classroom scenario: After introducing and setting purposes for a reading assignment (for example, as part of a Directed Reading Activity), you instruct your students to begin reading silently. While they are reading, you walk quietly around the room monitoring their reading. The purpose of your monitoring is to ensure they are handling the material successfully. To address this purpose, you are providing guidance, coaching, and encouragement; answering questions; and asking questions. As you walk around, stopping briefly at individual desks, some students begin raising their hands to ask you for assistance. One student after another begins asking you, "What's this word?"

What would you do or say to these students? Think about it for a minute and jot down some possible reactions or responses. See if any of your responses resemble the following possibilities, that are commonly suggested by teacher education students:

- Pronounce the words for them.
- Explain the meanings of the words.
- Pronounce the words and explain their meanings.
- Ask whether they are referring to what the word means or how it is pronounced.
- Ask them to "sound out" the words.
- Tell them to "look up" the words.
- Tell them to try to figure out the words on their own.
- Ask them to think of words they know that would make sense in those particular sentences and paragraphs.
- Stop and teach the words to the whole class.

The primary purpose of this chapter is to teach you what to do and say to the many students who ask for assistance with words while reading. As you can see from the many possible responses, *vocabulary instruction* involves two important components: *decoding* and *meaning*. Instruction can focus on decoding as separate from meaning, or it can focus on both components at the same time.

The first component of vocabulary instruction, decoding, focuses on word pronunciation and is commonly referred to as word recognition. It is also known as word attack or word identification. Word recognition involves decoding the written symbols into spoken or signed language. Graves, Slater, and White (1989) identify three content area word-learning tasks that involve decoding: (a) learning to read known words, (b) learning new words representing known concepts, and (c) learning new words representing new concepts. The first two emphasize the decoding of words that represent concepts already familiar to the students, while the third word-learning task requires the student to learn the new concepts or meanings of the words once they have decoded them.

Readers must be able to decode (i.e., pronounce) a word before (perhaps only a fraction of a second before) deciding whether they understand its meaning in the given context. Students *at all levels* need instruction and coaching in decoding, which is, as mentioned above, commonly known as word recognition, word attack, or word identification. Although word recognition skills are taught as part of the learning-to-read process in elementary school, students must continue to develop their decoding skills as the content vocabulary becomes increasingly challenging. In fact, the more advanced word recognition skills cannot be taught meaningfully until students begin reading content area materials in middle and high school.

Through simple activities and coaching techniques, you can help students of all ages develop word recognition skills that work for them. This chapter will show you ways to develop your students' abilities to decode words on their own. In addition to helping the reader decode unfamiliar symbols into familiar pronunciations, word recognition skills have another purpose. They also offer the reader ways to remember words so that they can be recognized the next time they are encountered. Therefore, time invested in developing word recognition skills should yield a significant reduction in the number of students needing your assistance in decoding words. More importantly, their improved decoding abilities should enhance their learning of content.

The second component of vocabulary instruction focuses on word meanings and is commonly referred to as concept development. *Concept development* involves word meanings in various contexts. For content area literacy, students need to master the technical language and jargon of each content area. Graves, Slater, and White (1989) identify three content area word-learning tasks that involve word meanings.

The first, *learning new meanings for known words,* requires students to learn new meanings for words they can already pronounce and understand in a particular context. For these familiar words, students must learn new word meanings that are specific to a particular content area or context. Just because a student recognizes and can pronounce a word does not necessarily mean he or she will understand its meaning—or understand its meaning in the particular context in which it is used. For example, in decoding the word *lugubrious,* one could recognize it because he or she has heard it pronounced and read it in context. However, even though a person is able to pronounce it, he or she still may not know what it means. If the word has not been encountered or applied frequently enough for one to have internalized its definition, an individual may not be able to recall its meaning. If the same person decodes the word *point,* he or she recognizes it: not only has the person heard it before, he or she probably knows what it means. However, if the word *point* is encountered in a geometry lesson for the first time, one may not understand its meaning in that particular context.

The other two content area word learning tasks identified by Graves, Slater, and White (1989) are *clarifying and enriching the meanings of known words* and *moving words into students' productive vocabularies.* Both tasks require students to become actively engaged with the words. For example, they must read and listen to them modeled frequently and in various contexts. They must also "play" with the words by exploring, analyzing, comparing, and contrasting them extensively, in both oral and written language. Finally, students must use the words frequently in meeting their expressive communication needs in content area literacy.

This chapter will provide you with some basic guidelines for effective concept development, as well as some activities for helping students master and internalize word meanings. All the strategies and activities in this chapter can be used as part of other content area literacy strategies. In previous chapters, you have learned the importance of preparing students for a reading assignment. Almost all strategies for content area literacy include a preparation phase before reading. One of the critical aspects of the preparation phase is the introduction of vocabulary. In this chapter you will learn effective and efficient ways to introduce key vocabulary that students will encounter in their reading assignments.

Word recognition and concept development activities can also be used during reading to help students decode new words and learn their meanings in context. Strategies and activities for vocabulary instruction can be incorporated into the postreading phase of most content area literacy strategies and lesson formats: they can be used as part of the comprehension development and assessment phase after reading. Finally, vocabulary strategies and activities can be incorporated into enrichment activities designed to strengthen students' word recognition skills and help them internalize important concepts.

PART 1

COMPARE-CONTRAST: A WORD RECOGNITION STRATEGY

Cunningham (1975, 1976) reported improved word recognition skills of primary grade children with a Compare/Contrast strategy for decoding unfamiliar monosyllabic words. She also found that these students showed a significantly greater ability to decode polysyllabic words. The Compare/Contrast strategy teaches students to look at an unfamiliar word and compare parts of that word to words they already know. The resulting pronunciation is then checked for meaning in the sentence. Following a study of fourth- and fifth-grade students, Cunningham (1979, 778) concluded that "training in a compare/contrast strategy can result in a significant increase in the ability to decode unfamiliar words."

Cunningham (1978) also recommended using the Compare/Contrast strategy with middle and high school students as well, particularly for remedial readers. She based her recommendation on the principle of building on strengths and starting with what a student already knows. She noted that most middle and high school remedial readers know a large number of simple, monosyllabic words and have knowledge of initial consonant, blend, and digraph sounds. This knowledge provides a foundation for applying the Compare/Contrast strategy and developing phonemic awareness with students who have difficulty decoding.

The Pretest

Students for whom this strategy is appropriate can be identified easily and quickly with the following simple word pronunciation activity. This activity should be done individually with the student and teacher and can be used with students of all ages.

1. Prepare a set of flashcards for the list of words presented in Figure 8–1. On one side of each card, print the two-syllable word. On the back of the card, print the two commonly occurring one-syllable words that could be used in the Compare/Contrast decoding strategy.
2. Ask each student to pronounce the words on the fronts of the cards. Place any word the student misses in a separate pile.

FIGURE 8–1 Compare/Contrast Strategy: Flashcards
(Cunningham 1975–1976)

FRONT	BACK		FRONT	BACK	
garnish	car	fish	bladder	had	her
pigment	big	went	chowder	how	her
slander	ran	her	fungus	run	us
decoy	he	boy	splatter	cat	her
pewter	few	her	varnish	car	fish
harpoon	car	soon	whimper	him	her

3. After the student pronounces all twelve words, turn over the pile of words missed.
4. If the student can pronounce the familiar words on the backs of the words missed, he or she will probably benefit from learning to apply the Compare/Contrast strategy for decoding.

The Lessons

This series of lessons is designed to lead students through a step-by-step procedure for decoding polysyllabic words and developing phonemic awareness using monosyllabic words they already know. At first, students will use a set of cards, each of which has a familiar monosyllabic word, to match physically the known words to the appropriate parts of the unknown words. Later, this "word store" need not be used; simply ask students to think of words they know that are similar to the parts of unknown words.

Step 1

Have students develop their own sets of word store cards by writing each of the five words listed in Figure 8–2 on index cards. Tell students that you are going to show them a two-syllable word. Their job is to find the two cards from their word stores that match the parts of the word you are showing. You can have students either write down the words they select or simply place their selected cards side by side. After most of the students have made their selections, ask a volunteer to share his or her selections with the rest of the class. After the words have been appropriately matched, ask a student to pronounce the two matching words and the two-syllable word. Have students practice matching and pronouncing words as quickly as possible. Figure 8–2 suggests some examples of words recommended for practice.

FIGURE 8–2   Compare/Contrast Strategy: Step One
(Cunningham 1975–1976)

WORD STORE CARDS	WORDS FOR MATCHING WITH WORD STORE CARDS			
he	banter	cancer	tangent	serpent
went	defer	German	repent	banner
her	regent	garment	charter	canter
can	garter	percent	ferment	merger
car	barber	panther	meter	Herman

FIGURE 8–3   Compare/Contrast Strategy: Step Two
(Cunningham 1975–1976)

WORD STORE CARDS		WORDS FOR MATCHING WITH WORD STORE CARDS		
he	in	bitter	center	bandit
went	at	bitten	remit	blister
her	then	batter	jerkin	ginger
can	it	winter	latter	fitter
car	is	cretin	render	vermin
		batten	hermit	scatter
			margin	Berlin
			charter	

Step 2

Have students add five more cards to their word stores as in Figure 8–3. Using all ten cards in their word stores, guide students in matching the appropriate cards to the words listed in Figure 8–3.

Step 3

Have students make cards to add five more words to their word stores as in Figure 8–4. Using all fifteen word cards, help them identify matches for the words listed in Figure 8–4.

Step 4

After a great deal of practice using the fifteen-word set of cards, have students practice decoding words without the cards. Begin by giving each student some blank index cards. Then, show them a two-syllable word with a line drawn between the syllables. Have them think of and write two matching words from their memorized word stores. When most

---

FIGURE 8–4   Compare/Contrast Strategy: Step Three
(Cunningham 1975–1976)

WORD STORE CARDS			WORDS FOR MATCHING WITH WORD STORE CARDS		
he	in	let	market	banish	disband
went	at	fish	clannish	catfish	shetland
her	then	sun	trigger	decent	punish
can	it	big	hunger	secret	misspent
car	is	and			

---

students have written their selections for matching words, have them share and discuss their selections.

Continue this process with more words until students have had extensive practice applying the strategy without using their word-store cards. Then, begin presenting two-syllable words without the line drawn between the syllables. These words are more effectively presented in the context of sentences, giving students practice in applying the Compare/Contrast strategy in a more realistic reading situation. Presenting the words in sentences also allows students to check their pronunciations to see if they have identified words that make sense.

Many words can be used for practice in this step. You should look for opportunities to select key words from their content area reading assignments. Cunningham (1978, 611) suggests starting with the list in Figure 8–5.

Step 5

Once students become proficient at applying the Compare/Contrast strategy with two-syllable words, guide them in applying the strategy to decode three-syllable words. Again, put the words into the context of sentences and make sure students check their pronunciations against the meaning of the sentence. Cunningham (1978, 611, 612) suggests starting with the list in Figure 8–6.

WORD RECOGNITION SKILLS

Five different word recognition skills can be used to decode words:

1. context clues
2. sight words
3. phonics
4. structural analysis
5. dictionary usage

FIGURE 8–5   Compare/Contrast Strategy: Step Four (Cunningham 1975–1976)

basket	moment	pungent	betray	viscus	rattan
fender	recent	boyhood	German	repeat	butler
refer	butter	gusset	relay	binder	handsome
bunker	hinder	restore	cutlet	invade	russet
igloo	retreat	delight	jasmine	Roman	defame
veto	depend	luster	whisper	delay	mango
defeat	mannish	withstand	zero	deter	matter
ferment	member	gender	fritter	musket	devout
destroy	orphan	splinter	magnet	trawler	retreat
convoy	display	decide	devour	frozen	mister
bereft	pinto	harpoon	defend	Peter	rebound
profound	litter	robot	resound	focus	scarlet
sandwich	order	rely	simmer	repay	dement
shimmer	reply	sponsor	Shinto	wither	rampage
prevent	tender	splinter	payment	border	simper
permit	sincere	powder	corner	slender	potter
sober	platter	massive	sordid	plaster	statement
shampoo	splendid	selfish	varnish	gutter	splutter
engage	dismiss	sewer	cluster	snobbish	present
hammer	pinball	Spanish	remind	zenith	refuse
depart	demand	blender	grocer	wiggler	cinder

FIGURE 8–6   Compare/Contrast Strategy: Step Five (Cunningham 1975–1976)

engagement	attentive	betterment	unimpressive	wonderful
expensive	employment	inactive	apartment	chimpanzee
amendment	abdomen	powerful	diplomat	entertainment
indignant	enrichment	manpower	enjoyment	sarcastic
encampment	romantic	enlistment	independent	important
surrender	consider	insincere	contestant	underline
unrepentant	fisherman	unimportant	entertain	unresistant
turpentine	informant	passenger	unobservant	disorder

These skills can be used alone but are generally more effective when used in combination with one another. Because individual students have unique perceptual strengths and weaknesses, some will have more success with a particular word recognition skill than others. For example, students who are strong visual learners will probably have an easier time learning sight words than students who have poor visual memory. Also, students who are strong auditory learners may have an easier time applying phonics than students who have poor auditory discrimination.

You need not become a reading specialist to coach your students in word recognition and help them develop skills that work for them. However, teachers at *all* levels need to be prepared to help their students with decoding skills. Even in high school, content area teachers may be faced with a significant number of students who are lacking even the most basic decoding skills—and the good readers in high school are ready to continue developing advanced decoding skills. A few simple exercises and coaching techniques can go a long way in developing independent readers who can decode most words on their own. You will see that some of the instruction for word recognition also strengthens concept development, and vice versa.

Context Clues

Context clues refer to the use of surrounding word, sentence, and paragraph meaning to decode words or determine their meanings. Instruction in context clues combines both components of vocabulary instruction, decoding and concept development. It emphasizes the use of context in decoding words *and* determining their meanings. This section will address the use of context clues for word recognition only. The use of context clues for concept development will be discussed in Part 2.

Of the word recognition skills, context clues may be the most important for two reasons. First, context emphasizes decoding for the purpose of finding meaning. Second, it should be used in conjunction with all the others; if a decoded word does not make sense in context, it probably has not been decoded correctly.

When you teach students to use context as a word recognition skill, you are reminding them to attend to meaning rather than word calling. You are emphasizing the important concept that word pronunciation without meaning is not reading. The importance of helping your students use word recognition skills as tools for understanding the content cannot be overstated.

You can easily recognize students who have been "overcoached" in word recognition skills, particularly phonics. These students labor over the letter sounds and pronunciation of word after word, often suggesting words that may look similar but make no sense in the context of the sentences. In extreme cases of overemphasis on decoding words in isolation, students may even produce a nonsense word, i.e., a word that does not exist at all, but that they have concluded is the pronunciation for that particular sequence of letters.

You can help correct the tendency to overanalyze and decode isolated words in two ways. First, you can give students exercises that will help them learn to use context clues as a word recognition skill. Second, you can coach them in applying context clues as a *first* step in decoding, and then again later *in conjunction* with other skills. When you coach them in these ways, you are reminding students that their goal is to decipher the message of the sentences, not the pronunciation of words.

Cloze Activities

The term *cloze* is a shortened form of the word *closure.* The concept of closure involves the inclination and ability to fill in missing pieces of information based on what is known. We use closure every day for all sorts of activities. For example, in conversation with someone, if he or she pauses to think of a word or choose just the right word, many of us try to help by guessing or offering possible words intended by the speaker.

Cloze activities are basically fill-in-the-blank activities. They are not to be confused with a cloze test or inventory, an informal measure designed to tell you whether students can adequately comprehend materials you have selected for them. In the cloze inventory, which is described in detail in Chapter 9, students must fill in the blanks using the exact words as the original author.

Cloze activities, rather than serving to assess comprehension, are designed to teach students how to use context clues for decoding words and uncovering word meanings. In cloze activities, students are presented with one or more sentences containing one or more missing words in each sentence. They must then use surrounding word, sentence, and paragraph meaning to think of words that would make sense in the blanks. Sample items for a cloze activity are presented in Figure 8–7.

The missing words must be carefully selected and placed. If you are introducing the idea of context clues or want to emphasize the concept as a word recognition tool, use sentences that provide enough clues to the missing word(s). You can choose sentences from the content area materials being used in class for instruction; if you do so, you may need to rewrite some of the sentences to make sure that ample clues are provided.

FIGURE 8–7 Sample items for a cloze activity

Notice that in these examples no phonetic clues are provided, and significant context clues are provided.

1. Austin is the _____ of Texas.

2. The _____ sign is used to subtract numbers.

3. The sun is at the _____ of our solar system.

4. George Washington was the first _____ of the United States.

5. The _____ is the state flower of Texas.

6. People around the world speak different _____ .

7. _____ is the study of life.

8. Today scientists learn about dinosaurs from _____ .

9. Lava flows from an active _____ .

10. Charles Lindburgh flew across the _____ ocean.

You should accept any word the student provides as long as it makes sense and is used appropriately in the sentence. The point of the exercise is to develop students' abilities to apply closure for understanding a message, not to develop her or his ability to read your or the author's mind. Cloze activities teach students how to narrow the possibilities for decoding unknown words.

Provide cloze activities on a regular basis until students automatically attend to the meaning surrounding unknown words. Once students have mastered the concept of closure, you can begin emphasizing the use of context clues in conjunction with other word recognition skills. For example, you can introduce *modified cloze* activities, which provide one or more letters for the missing words. These activities give students practice in concentrating on phonetic clues along with context clues. An example of a modified cloze activity would be to provide the initial or final consonant, consonant blend (e.g., *bl, pr, sn, str*), or consonant digraph (e.g., *sh, ch, th, wh*).

FIGURE 8–8 Sample items for a modified cloze activity

Notice that in these examples phonetic clues are provided, and that without the phonetic clues, at least two words could fit in each sentence.

1. M_____ is a mathematical operation.

2. One of the North American countries is C_____ .

3. The United States fought against G_____ in World War II.

4. M_____y is a planet in our solar system.

5. A pr_____ is a single-celled organism.

6. A fraction stated in a different form is a p_____ .

7. As of 1995, Ch_____ is still a communist country.

8. Because rainforests are part of our e_____m, their destruction has harmful effects for all of us.

9. During World War II, Hitler killed 7,000,000 Jews as part of his plan to carry out g_____ of the Jewish people.

10. A square has four equal a_____ .

With modified cloze activities, students have additional clues with which to narrow the possibilities of acceptable words. When you begin providing these additional clues, make sure you frame the sentences so that without the phonetic clues, at least two different words could fit. Students then must rely on a combination of the context and phonetic clues to make their choices. See the sample items in Figure 8–8.

Maze Activities

The maze activity, a variation of the cloze activity, was originally described by Guthrie, Burnham, Caplan, and Seifert (1974) as a technique for assessing and monitoring comprehension. However, it also can be used as a type of cloze activity for developing context clues. The maze differs from the cloze in that it provides choices for students in filling in the blanks. The choices you provide can require students to use different skills, and their responses can give you some diagnostic information about how they decode in context. Therefore, you can obtain valuable information about how your students are processing information by carefully selecting the options provided in maze activities.

For example, on some of the items in a maze activity, you could provide three choices that look similar but have very different meanings. See the examples in Figure 8–9. If a student consistently misses these types of items, chances are that he or she is not attending closely to meaning, does not understand content, or does not understand key terms.

Another example of how you might control the choices in a maze activity is to provide three choices that look similar but represent different parts of speech. Students who consistently miss these types of items may have some gaps in their knowledge of grammatical structures (see the examples in Figure 8–10.) If you are not an English teacher, you may be inclined to ignore these particular weaknesses. However, investing a few minutes to point out and remind students about grammatical structures can make a significant difference in terms of learning quality of the content and the development of content area literacy.

FIGURE 8–9 Sample items for a maze activity: Similar appearance, different meanings

---

Notice that in these examples the choices look similar, but have different meanings.

1. Monkeys and humans are both
    primates.
    privates.
    prelates.

2. The Renaissance was the age of
    enlightenment.
    endangerment.
    encroachment.

3. Did Columbus really
    uncover
    recover
    discover
    America?

4. The values on both sides of an equation are
    equivocal.
    equal.
    equable.

5. Our solar system has nine
    planets.
    plants.
    planes.

FIGURE 8–10 Sample items for a maze activity: Similar appearance,
different parts of speech

Notice that in these examples the choices look similar but are different parts of
speech.

                                                  species.
1. Bald eagles are an endangered special.
                                                  specify.

                                                              reacting.
2. For every action, there is an equal and opposite reaction.
                                                              reactive.

    Magical
3. Magnify is the melted rock beneath volcanoes.
    Magma

        fabricate
4. A fabulous is a story that teaches a lesson.
        fable

                        supper
5. Prices are determined by supply and demand.
                        supple

Coaching Context Clues

Whenever a student asks for assistance with a word, make sure that he or
she has thoroughly considered all available context clues for decoding. To
coach students in consistently applying context clues as a word recognition skill, your first response to their requests for assistance should resemble the following:

- What word can you think of that would make sense there?
- Read the rest of the sentence and think of a word that would make
  sense there.
- Read the sentence from the beginning and see if you can think of a
  word that would make sense there.
- Remember the fill-in-the-blank exercises we have been doing? Pretend that word is a blank. What word might fit there?
- Read the paragraph from the beginning, looking for clues as to
  what the word might be.
- Keep reading the rest of the paragraph and the following paragraph for clues as to what the word might be.

Structural Analysis

Structural analysis is a sophisticated term for a simple concept. Analyzing the structure of a word refers to breaking it into its component parts of syllables, prefixes, and suffixes. Many students feel overwhelmed at the prospect of decoding multisyllabic words. As whole units, large words can seem rather intimidating; however, you can show students how to tackle these giants by dissecting them.

Affixes and Inflected Endings

The first step in dividing a word is to look for "add ons" including affixes and inflected endings. Separating these added features from the root word can be very effective in helping students decode. Often they know the root word but do not immediately recognize it with the various attachments.

The two types of affixes are prefixes and suffixes. A prefix is added to the beginning of a word to change its meaning; a suffix is added to the end of a word to change its meaning or part of speech. Every content area has commonly used prefixes and suffixes. Make a list of these affixes and teach them to your students. Recognizing commonly used prefixes and suffixes is a valuable word recognition tool. Appendix J provides lists of commonly used prefixes and suffixes. Unlike suffixes, inflected endings do not significantly change the meanings of words: rather, they produce variations of the words. The most common inflected endings are *-s*, *-ed*, and *-ing*.

Compounds and Contractions

Compound words are comprised of two words joined together. When students can identify smaller words as part of larger words, decoding is made easier. Contractions are shortened forms of two words put together; letters are omitted, and their omission is indicated by an apostrophe. Students should be aware that apostrophes indicate contractions. Distinguishing the two conjoined words sometimes helps make decoding contractions easier.

Syllabication

Although there are many exceptions to the syllabication rules in English, knowing the rules can be helpful for decoding. In terms of structural analysis, being able to divide words into syllables can be an effective way to break an unmanageable word into manageable units. Syllabication principles can also help determine pronunciation; for example, in an open syllable, which ends with a vowel, the vowel is usually pronounced as a long vowel (e.g., ta•ble). In a closed syllable, which ends with a consonant, the vowel is usually pronounced as a short vowel (cab•in). If application of these principles does not produce recognition, the word may be an exception. In that case, students should try another pronunciation for the vowel.

Following are some common syllabication principles and rules that might be helpful to your students in applying structural analysis as a word recognition skill.

1. Each syllable contains one vowel sound.
2. Prefixes and suffixes usually form separate syllables (e.g., pre•view, age•less).
3. Compound words are divided between the two component words, as well as between the syllables of each word (e.g., room•mate, un•der•state•ment).
4. Consonant blends and digraphs are not separated to divide syllables (e.g., ap•ply, e•ther).
5. When a vowel (V) is followed by two consonants (C) and another vowel, the syllables are usually divided between the two consonants (VC•CV, e.g., yel•low).
6. When a vowel is followed by one consonant and another vowel, the syllables are usually divided between the first vowel and the consonant (V•CV, e.g., ra•cer). (Caution: There are numerous exceptions to this rule.)
7. When a word ends in a consonant followed by *le*, those three letters constitute the final syllable of the word (e.g., ca•ble).

Coaching Structural Analysis

When students ask for assistance with an unknown word, coach them in ways similar to the following:

- Cover the suffix. Do you recognize the root word?
- Cover the prefix. Do you recognize the root word?
- How would you break this word into syllables?
- Can you think of another word that looks like and perhaps rhymes with this one?
- Do you see a familiar phonogram (word family) in this word?
- Do you recognize any smaller words within this word?
- What two words make up this compound word?
- What two words are represented by this contraction?

Sight Words

Sight words are of two types. The first category of sight words includes words that cannot be "sounded out" because they do not follow phonetic rules. Sight words of this type must therefore be memorized from the way they look.

Once sight words, which cannot be sounded out, are committed to memory and can be recognized on sight, they have become sight words of the second type. The second category of sight words includes all those words a reader has memorized from repeated use and, therefore, recognizes on sight. For proficient adult readers, almost all words have become sight words.

The first type of sight words are most relevant to word recognition instruction. As a teacher, you must constantly look for words that may present confusion by not following sound-to-symbol rules for pronunciation. Unfortunately, English has a significant number of such words. Many students tend to overuse phonics and get frustrated when phonetic rules work for some words but not others. When phonics will not help, which probably is most of the time, your students need to be equipped with other decoding tools including a significant store of sight words.

When teaching sight words as a word recognition skill, emphasis is placed on memorizing each word by studying it visually as a whole unit. Refrain from breaking the word into parts for decoding. Instead, point out the overall configuration of each word and teach students how to notice the general shape of a word. Once students have memorized a sight word by its visual configuration, teach them how to spell it by focusing on the individual letters and their sequencing.

Visual Configurations

An excellent exercise for helping students be aware of the overall shapes of words is the visual configuration activity. In this activity, students are given a list of sight words printed on the left side of the page. Provided on the right side of the page are a set of boxes that, if placed over the words, would fit around the words according to their overall shapes. Provide one box for each word but jumble the order of the boxes so students have to match each word with the box that represents its overall visual configuration. When matching the words, have students write each word inside the appropriate box. Each box should be the same length as the word it matches. It should have tall spaces for the tall letters (*b, d, f, h, i, k, l, t*) and spaces below the line for letters that fall beyond the baseline (*g, j, p, q, y*). See the sample items in Figure 8–11.

You can include any number of words, depending on the amount of practice you want for the students. At first, you will need to show students some examples and assist them until they understand the activity. Also, begin with shorter words of simple configurations. Once students have mastered the concept, progress to longer words with more complicated configurations. Figure 8–11 provides sample items from beginning

---

FIGURE 8-11 Sample items for a visual configuration activity

The boxes are not jumbled in this presentation of sample items. For an actual visual configuration activity, present the boxes in jumbled order. Have students match them by writing the appropriate word in each box.

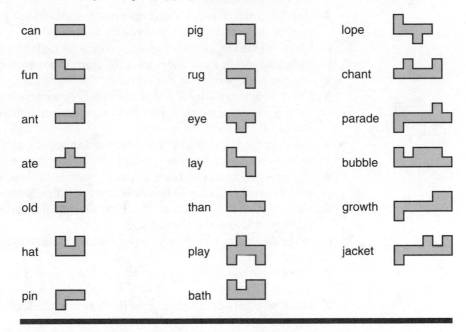

---

to more advanced word configuration exercises. Once students have mastered the concept of overall visual configuration of words, they are ready to receive direct instruction in memorizing sight words.

Teaching Sight Words

To select words to teach as sight words, keep an ongoing list of key words in various content areas that cannot be sounded out. Also, encourage or require your students to keep their own lists of words that they discover and cannot pronounce. From these lists, identify a small number, no more than five to eight at a time, to teach as sight words.

Teach sight words using the following guidelines.

1. Always introduce sight words in meaningful contexts, making sure that students understand their meanings.
    ▌ The only way students can memorize sight words is through repeated encounters in meaningful contexts.

■ When introducing a sight word, present it in the context of a sentence designed to give clues to the word's meaning.

■ Highlight the word by underlining it or putting it in bold-faced print.

■ Read the sentence to the students, pronounce the word, and explain its meaning.

■ Ask students questions and encourage them to ask questions to ensure they understand the word's meaning.

2. Provide practice in identifying sight words in isolation while also paraphrasing their meanings or using them in meaningful sentences.

■ Put the sight words on flashcards.

■ On the back of each card, put a picture, synonym, simple definition, or meaningful sentence that communicates the meaning of the word.

■ Give students practice in recognizing the words, talking about their meanings, and using them in meaningful contexts.

■ For words that have identical visual configurations, emphasize the differences that will help students distinguish them.

■ Have students play games in which they drill each other on the sight words and their meanings.

3. Once students can recognize a word on sight, teach them how to spell the word.

■ Pronounce the word to the students, then spell it while pointing to each letter.

■ Have students practice writing the word while looking at the model.

■ As they write, have students say each letter out loud.

■ Have students practice writing the word without looking at the model.

■ Students should check themselves immediately and rewrite the word if necessary to correct it.

■ Play games with each word. For example, cut the word into letters and have students put it back together again. You could also write the word incorrectly and have students correct it orally and in writing.

■ Have students practice spelling the words in different ways. For example, use paper and pencil, cutout letters, magnetic letters, painting, finger painting, sand writing, foam writing, and tracing (both with pencil and finger).

4. Have students practice using the words in their own expressive and receptive vocabularies.

■ Have students use the words to dictate or write their own sentences, paragraphs, stories, or summaries (expressive).

▌ Have students practice reading the words by reading what they have dictated or written (receptive).

5. Have students practice reading the words in a variety of contexts.

▌ Have students read sentences, paragraphs, or passages from content area materials that use the same or similar meaning for each word.

▌ Students can locate their sight words in the content area materials they are reading.

▌ Have students compare the meanings of the located words in context with the meanings they learned.

▌ Ask comprehension questions to assess students' understandings of the words in various contexts.

▌ Ask higher-level questions that require students to apply the sight words in their responses.

Coaching Sight Words

When students ask for assistance with sight words, coach them in ways similar to the following:

▌ "This is one of our sight words. It means _____. Do you remember it?"

▌ "This is a sight word. Look at its overall shape. Do you recognize it?"

▌ "This is a word that cannot be sounded out. Add it to your sight word list to learn later. The word is _____."

▌ "This is a new word. I will add it to our sight word list to learn later. The word is _____."

▌ "This is a sight word that you have to remember by the way it looks. The word is _____. Notice how long it is; notice the tall letters; notice the letters that go below the line."

▌ "This is a sight word that you will have to remember by its overall shape. Draw a box to fit around it."

Phonics

Phonics involves the application of sound-to-symbol relationships for decoding. Certainly, knowledge of letter sounds can be an important tool for decoding, especially for students who have strong auditory discrimination and auditory memory. Jeanne Chall, in her book *Learning to Read: The Great Debate* (1967), concluded from an extensive review of classroom research on beginning readers that systematic phonics instruction, when used as part of a program that emphasizes reading for meaning, has a significant positive effect on early reading achievement. In the revised version of her book, Chall (1983) reiterated this conclusion by reporting updated research evidence supporting early and systematic phonics instruction.

However, Chall (1967) cautioned against misinterpreting this evidence. Her fear, which ultimately proved to be well-founded, was that educators would overemphasize phonics instruction at the expense of reading-for-meaning practice. Indeed, it seems the research conclusions supporting phonics instruction as presented by Chall and others (Bond and Dykstra 1967; Dykstra 1968; Spache and Spache 1973; Becker and Gersten 1982) have been misinterpreted significantly. Many educators began implementing programs that emphasized phonics exercises presented in isolation from meaningful text and deemphasized instruction in reading for meaning. This misuse of phonics instruction occurred not only for beginning readers but also for upper elementary and even middle and high school readers. The results of this tragic misinterpretion were staggering for many students whose reading achievement suffered from a lack of well-rounded instruction in decoding and comprehension.

As a content area teacher, you may encounter students whose reading abilities have suffered from an overemphasis on phonics. For such students, who tend to overuse it as a word recognition skill, you should probably deemphasize phonics. For example, you may observe students relying heavily on the"sounding-it-out" technique. Many of them have heard this prompt from teachers so often, they automatically tell themselves to sound it out as soon as they encounter an unknown word. Therefore, it might be wise to remove the phrase "sound it out" completely from your instructional vocabulary for these students.

Instead, encourage the use of phonics as a supplemental word recognition skill. Applying phonics can be much more valuable when used in conjunction with other skills, especially when text meaning is emphasized. For example, encourage students to use initial letter sounds as clues to narrow the possibilities of words that would fit into the context. Also, show students how to differentiate rhyming words, a structural analysis skill, by their initial consonants, consonant blends, and consonant digraphs.

You can certainly instruct and correct students for the purpose of increasing their knowledge of letter sounds. However, be sure to emphasize the use of letter sounds as a tool to be used in support of and in conjunction with other word recognition skills to unlock meaning. When used properly, phonics can be an extremely valuable decoding skill. However, when overused, especially with students who have poor phonemic awareness, auditory discrimination, and auditory memory, the results can be disastrous.

The overuse of phonics is especially ineffective in the English language. Because a significant number of words and word parts simply do not follow the rules of phonics, letter sounds alone are not very effective for decoding words. Most of the phonics rules have so many exceptions that applying them can be quite confusing. On the other hand, in languages such as Spanish phonetic rules can be relied on for decoding almost without exception. Therefore, when teaching in Spanish, emphasizing knowledge and application of phonics is time well spent. The extent that the language of instruction follows phonetic rules certainly should be a factor in determining the degree of emphasis on phonics. Considering its limited utility in English, an overemphasis on phonics used alone as a word recognition skill would not seem prudent.

Sharyl's Story: Overreliance on Phonics

Sharyl's story could easily be the subject of an entire book. However, her story will be simplified here to emphasize a particular point about the possible danger of overreliance on phonics. Sharyl's situation was complicated by significant learning disabilities with which she has learned to cope. However, reading and writing have always been and continue to be difficult and time consuming tasks for her. Regardless, she has learned to compensate for her learning disabilities and is a remarkable success story.

About twelve years ago, Sharyl was a fifth grader who was virtually a nonreader and nonwriter. She was referred for testing by a diagnostician. The informal reading inventory results indicated that she could handle reading instruction at only the primer level, which is the level just below the first-grade level. Since she could not spell even first-grade–level sight words, her writing was extremely poor as well.

On the other hand, Sharyl's potential for learning, as measured by an intelligence test, was at least average. In other words, she had the intellectual capability to read, but for some reason had not been successful in learning. Her intelligence was not surprising: anyone could tell just from talking with her that she was a bright child. The listening comprehension test indicated that Sharyl could easily understand fifth-grade–level materials that were read to her. Obviously, lack of intelligence and verbal ability were not significant factors in her reading disability.

The diagnostician noted from interviewing her that Sharyl was *very* eager to learn and *extremely* motivated to learn how to read. She loved books and learning and wanted desperately to be able to read and learn for herself. Not surprisingly, she was also quite embarrassed by her inability to read, because most of her fifth-grade classmates seemed able to do so with ease. In spite of her tremendous motivation to learn, however, Sharyl faced many obstacles.

The auditory perception tests indicated that auditory perception was a severe weakness for Sharyl. She had extremely poor auditory discrimination, meaning that most letter sounds, especially vowel sounds, generally sounded the same to her. She also had poor auditory memory, suggesting that she had a hard time remembering the sound(s) associated with each letter.

In the oral reading segment of the informal reading inventory, her decoding efforts and errors were analyzed. Astonishingly, virtually the only word recognition tool she employed was phonics. The experience seemed to be an agonizing one for her as she struggled and labored over "sounding out" each letter of each word. She seemed to have no focus on meaning at all, but was bent on getting the words pronounced correctly. Not surprisingly, the experience was a painful one for both Sharyl and the diagnostician.

Sharyl's inability to apply phonics as a decoding skill was not surprising in light of her poor auditory perception skills. What was surprising, however, was that she seemed to have no other tools available for decoding words—not even sight words. A learning modalities test indicated that visual memory was a strength for Sharyl, and that she was able to learn sight words rather easily. However, her store of sight words was virtually nonexistent, as if no one had provided her significant direct instruction with sight words. After examining Sharyl's test results, the diagnostician reviewed her school records and talked with her mother, school principal, and teachers.

All sources confirmed the observations that Sharyl was a bright and verbal child who was highly motivated. Her parents, teachers, and principal were all concerned about Sharyl because their efforts at remediation had failed. The school sources provided revealing information about the basal reading program employed by the school to teach students how to read.

The reading program used by the entire school at that time was heavily phonics based. Starting in first grade, efforts had been made to teach Sharyl to read with a phonetic approach. Because of her severe auditory weaknesses, Sharyl failed to do so. Consequently, she was placed in a remedial reading program designed to teach her phonics, which the classroom teacher had been unable to do.

Each school day for the next three years, Sharyl worked on phonics. At times she would seem to catch on and begin making some progress. Then, she would inexplicably forget everything as if she were just beginning the program. Her teachers were infinitely patient, developing and implementing a wide variety of multisensory activities and techniques designed to help her learn phonics. Ultimately, however, all efforts failed, and Sharyl and her supporters grew more and more frustrated.

By the fourth grade, her classroom teachers began to lose hope that Sharyl would ever learn how to read. As a result, they developed ways to help her learn the science, social studies, math, and English content without requiring her to read. Since she could easily understand what she heard and remember meaningful content, she was able to keep up with her classmates in every area except reading and writing.

Immediately following the revelations from the test results and information about her previous instructional programs, Sharyl's tutor began to teach her context clues and sight words. They worked on cloze and maze activities with primer-level materials, as well as with stories she dictated using the Language Experience Approach. Sharyl understood almost immediately and was an expert at guessing appropriate words to go in the blanks. They quickly moved to cloze and maze activities with more difficult materials.

At the same time, they began developing a store of sight words for Sharyl. An index card was made for each new word she learned; because she was learning about ten new words per week, her stack of cards began to grow thicker and thicker. With an emphasis on their meanings and use in sentences she composed, Sharyl was not only able to learn sight words quickly but also remembered them on a long-term basis.

Phonics was completely deemphasized, and her tutor would not allow her to sound out anything. Eventually Sharyl learned to rely on the context of the sentence immediately, rather than sounding out unknown words. After she mastered the application of context clues and developed a solid store of sight words, Sharyl's tutor began teaching her some structural analysis skills and dictionary usage as supplemental word recognition skills.

Because of her intense desire to learn and her motivation to read, Sharyl's progress was almost amazing. The tutor started working with her in the fall semester of her fifth-grade year. By the end of the school year, Sharyl was reading third-grade materials. As a result of her success, she began reading voraciously. She read library books, magazines, and textbooks. She even *enjoyed* reading textbooks. Sharyl was excited about being able to read them and fascinated with the content she was able to absorb independently. Because Sharyl read such a wide variety of materials so frequently, she continually progressed.

Her tutor continued working with Sharyl twice a week for the next five years. By the time she was in the eighth grade, she was reading materials at her grade level. By the time Sharyl was a sophomore in high school, she was not only a satisfactory reader and writer, she also had excellent study habits, was extremely well organized, managed her time better than most adults, was driven to succeed, loved to read for fun, and placed her education as a priority above everything else in her life. After she graduated from high school, she got her associate's degree from a junior college and eventually became a licensed vocational nurse.

The absence of phonics from her tutoring program certainly does not attribute to Sharyl's tremendous success. As previously mentioned, her internal motivation for learning and self-improvement was exceptional. She also had support from home: her mother passed on to Sharyl her own love of books, reading, and learning, as well as the drive to become educated, independent, self-sufficient, and self-satisfied.

However, the deemphasis of phonics, along with a strong emphasis on other word recognition skills, gave her the opportunity to benefit from her own strengths. The point of this story is to avoid overemphasis of any one word recognition skill and to be aware of students who overrely on phonics. For many students, phonics is a strong and valuable decoding tool—but not for all students.

For younger children having trouble with phonics, if you have reason to believe they can be successful with phonics, some remediation is probably beneficial. If they still are not proficient after serious attempts to remediate, give them alternate and supplemental word recognition tools. The bottom line is this: If phonics is not working for students, give them some decoding skills that *do* work for them.

Phonemic Awareness and Sound Blending

Phonemes are speech sounds that are blended together to form syllables and words. For students to be successful at learning letter-sound correspondences for decoding, they must first become aware of phonemes. Unfortunately, phonemic awareness can be difficult to acquire.

Marilyn Jager Adams (1990) makes a strong case for helping students develop phonemic awareness, beginning with their awareness of spoken words, then syllables, and finally, the two parts of syllables or monosyllabic words. The first part, called an *onset*, consists of the consonant sound or sounds that precede(s) the vowel. The second part, called the *rime*, consists of the vowel and any consonant sounds that follow it. Adams provides examples of words separated into onsets and rimes similar to those presented in Figure 8–12.

Adams (1990) makes the following instructional recommendations for helping students develop awareness of onsets and rimes. First, begin with a rime without an onset such as *an*. As the students are looking at the word, explain to them that the *a* says /a/, and the *n* says /n/. Next, lead the students in pronouncing these separate sounds before blending them together.

Second, add a consonant such as *t* to the beginning of the syllable. Again, explain that the *t* says /t/, and that, as they learned before, the *an* says /an/. Next, guide the students in blending the onset (*t*) with the rime (*an*) to produce /tan/. Repeat this process with single-consonant onsets until they have been "comfortably mastered" (Adams 1990, 324). Only then should instruction move on to sounding and blending onsets with consonant clusters (e.g., *br, sc, scr, thr*).

FIGURE 8–12 Sound blending with onsets and rimes (Adams 1990)

WORD	ONSET	RIME
in	—	in
ash	—	ash
pet	p	et
buy	b	uy
coin	c	oin
sky	sk	y
plan	pl	an
blank	bl	ank
sprout	spr	out
scrap	scr	ap
scrounge	scr	ounge

Recognizing common rimes is an important part of applying structural analysis as a word recognition skill. It is also important in the development of phonemic awareness, which is so essential to success in phonics instruction (Adams 1990). Recognizing rimes is also key to the success of the Compare/Contrast strategy, which was described earlier in this chapter. The appendix section provides a list of commonly used rimes, along with examples of words made from blending them with onsets.

Phonetic Terms

If you have students for whom phonics is a valuable word recognition tool, you might want to be familiar with some of the more commonly used phonetic terms:

Consonant: Any letter other than *a, e, i, o,* or *u* (including *w* and *y* in the initial position of a word or syllable).

Consonant blend: Two or more adjacent consonants that represent a merger of their individual sounds (e.g., *bl, gr, cr, pl, sw, tr, sm, spl, str, scr*).

Consonant digraph: Two adjacent consonants that represent a single, totally different sound (e.g., *th, ch, wh, sh, ph, ng*).

Vowel: *a, e, i, o,* or *u* (and *y* and *w* in the final position of a word or syllable, and *y* in the middle position of a word or syllable).

Long vowel: A vowel sound that has the same pronunciation as the name of the vowel itself.

Short vowel: A vowel sound that has a different pronunciation than the name of the vowel itself.

Vowel digraph: Two adjacent vowels that represent a single sound (e.g., *ea, oa, ie, ee, ai, oo*)

Diphthong: Two adjacent vowels that represent a blending of their individual sounds (e.g., *ou, ow, oi, oy, aw, oo*).

Schwa: The sound of short *u.*

Coaching Phonics

When students ask for assistance with an unknown word, coach them in ways similar to the following. Notice that you are pointing out to them key phonetic clues without having them sound out the entire word.

- With what letter sound does the word start?
- What word that starts with that letter would make sense there?
- What vowel sound does that syllable have?
- With what consonant does it end?
- What rhyming word can you think of that would make sense there?
- What sound do those letters make together?
- What word that starts with that sound makes sense in that sentence?
- This word starts with the same sound as _____.

Dictionary Usage

Dictionaries and glossaries are valuable word recognition tools, especially with content area materials. However, they should be used as a last resort, after all the other word recognition skills have been applied. When students develop the ability to apply the other word recognition skills immediately and effectively, little fluency is lost. Stopping to look up words takes time and doing so excessively causes constant interruptions that can adversely affect comprehension.

When a student has applied all the other word recognition skills and is still unable to decode a word, the ability to use the dictionary or glossary quickly and successfully is a valuable skill. However, simply providing dictionaries and glossaries is not enough. You *cannot* assume that students know how to look up words, nor can you assume that once they have located words they will know how to interpret the pronunciation symbols.

Students must be taught how to use dictionaries and glossaries through direct instruction, modeling, and supervised practice. Many skills are important for using the dictionary effectively. Those necessary for word recognition will be addressed here. Students must be able to locate words efficiently and determine pronunciations through proper interpretation of the symbols.

Locating Words

As students, how many times have we ourselves heard the familiar directive, "Well, look it up"? Even adults and accomplished dictionary users
still avoid looking up words as much as possible and instead read to look
for context clues. Many times readers decide that the unknown word
simply does not affect overall comprehension enough to force dictionary
usage. Even for an expert, using a dictionary can be a tedious and time-
consuming process; however when the reader lacks confidence in his or
her understanding of a main idea, an unknown word might hold the key
to understanding.

Alphabetical order.   As teachers, we cannot assume that our students
know the alphabet well enough to make snap decisions about whether a
given letter comes before or after another. Students need practice working with the alphabet in groups of about four to six letters at a time.
Working with smaller groups of letters makes it easier to develop skill at
alphabetizing.

Games are an excellent way to help students become skilled at alphabetizing. You could give each student a set of construction paper letters
and time them as they put them in alphabetical order. The student who
puts them in order accurately in the shortest time is the winner. You could
also have teams of students work together to put magnetic letters in order
on a chalkboard.

Once students are skilled at alphabetizing letters, they need to be
taught how to alphabetize words. Make sure they understand how to
alphabetize words beginning with the same letter, same two letters, same
three letters, and so on. Provide much guided practice in alphabetizing
words so that students can make snap judgments about whether a word
goes before or after another word. Deciding the order of words is important for learning to use guide words effectively.

Guide words.   The ability to use guide words is essential for locating
words efficiently, not only in the dictionary but also in the phone book and
other similarly indexed reference books. Guide words, the two words at
the top of each page in a dictionary or glossary, indicate the first and last
word on the page. Students must be able to decide quickly whether a given
word would be alphabetized between the two guide words. If so, they
know the word will be located on that page; if the word does not fall alphabetically between the guide words, they need to know where to look next.

As with alphabetizing, students need direct instruction in the use of
guide words followed by much guided practice. If students cannot use
guide words effectively, the process of looking up words will not only be
tedious and time consuming but probably quite frustrating as well. Drill
students, requiring them to think quickly in deciding whether a word

would fall between two given guide words. With practice, they should be able to decide at a glance whether the word would be found on that page.

Once students know how to and are skilled at using guide words, remind them to look at the guide words *first*, before looking down the page. Many students and even many adults who know perfectly well how to use guide words still manage to avoid them. Locating words without the assistance of guide words is certainly possible; people do it all the time. The difference between those who use them and those who do not is the amount of time it takes to locate a word. The process is simply easier and more efficient when you use the guide words, which is important for getting students into the habit of looking up words when appropriate.

Variants and derivatives.   If a student is looking for a word that is a variant or derivative of another word, it might be hard to find. If the word is not listed alphabetically, it is probably listed as part of the root word entry. Therefore, it is very important to teach students to check for and look up the root word, if the word they are trying to locate is not listed alphabetically. Once the variant or derivative is located, students must be taught how to combine the pronunciation of the root word with the additional or altered components. This skill is obviously an advanced one, and students will need much assistance, modeling, and practice in mastering it.

Pronouncing Words

As a word recognition tool, the dictionary is only useful if students can interpret the pronunciation provided for each word. If a student can successfully locate a word but is unable to decipher its pronunciation, he or she is no closer to recognizing the word. Learning to interpret pronunciation guides is no small task, but its importance cannot be overstated. If you want your students to be able to look up words they do not recognize and therefore cannot pronounce, you must also teach them how to decode the phonetic spellings.

Pronunciation key.   The pronunciation key is the guide provided by the dictionary for interpreting phonetic spellings (diacritical markings). Some phonetic symbols are universal, but some will change from dictionary to dictionary. Therefore, to interpret the symbols accurately, students should consult the pronunciation key. Eventually, after looking up words regularly from the same dictionary, they will memorize the sound-to-symbol relationships.

The first step in learning how to use a pronunciation key is locating it. In some dictionaries it is located in the front of the book, in others it is located in the back of the book, and in still others it is located on each page. Once students can readily locate the pronunciation key, teach them how to interpret it.

Pronunciation keys provide sample words that demonstrate sounds represented by the diacritical markings. Students need to be able to combine the individual sounds represented by the symbols into words. Therefore, a basic knowledge of phonics (letter sounds and putting them together to form words) is necessary. Students who have difficulty isolating individual letter sounds or synthesizing them into words will also have difficulty interpreting pronunciation keys and phonetic spellings. To help students master the pronunciation key, they will need regular and consistent modeling and guided practice.

Accent marks.   Teaching your students the concept of accented syllables is crucial for proper pronunciation. Accent marks identify the syllable that receives the stress in pronunciation of the word. Some dictionaries provide only one accent mark for each word. Others will provide a primary accent mark to indicate the syllable that receives the major stress and a secondary accent mark to indicate the syllable that receives minor stress.

Coaching Dictionary Usage

When students ask for assistance with an unknown word, coach them in ways similar to the following:

- Have you tried to figure out a word that would make sense in that context?
- Have you thought about words that would make sense there and have those initial letter sounds?
- Have you tried comparing the word with other words you already know and that look similar?
- Let's look it up together.
- Let's check to see if it's listed in the glossary.
- Let's use the pronunciation guide in the back of the dictionary.
- Look at these guide words. Would it be on this page?

PART 2

STRATEGY: LIST-GROUP-LABEL

This strategy developed by Readence, Bean, and Baldwin (1992) is similar to the Graphic Organizer and Semantic Map (both of which are detailed in Chapter 1) in that it is a classification technique emphasizing word relationships. List-Group-Label was originally designed by Taba (1967) as a technique for teaching vocabulary in elementary social studies. However, as with Semantic Mapping, it can be used with all ages and content areas

FIGURE 8–13 Example of List-Group-Label used in a science lesson

TOPIC: WEATHER

List of words brainstormed by the class:

rain	hot	cold	freezing	hail
windy	tornado	hurricane	warm	cool
thunderhead	drizzle	misty	foggy	stormy
snow	thunder	lightning	dust	cloudy
sleet	cumulous	nimbus	cirrus	cumulo-nimbus

Groups of words formed and labeled by the class:

precipitation	*storms*	*conditions*	*temperatures*	*clouds*
rain	thunder	misty	hot	cumulous
snow	hurricane	cloudy	cold	cirrus
drizzle	tornado	foggy	freezing	nimbus
hail	dust	stormy	tropical	thunderhead
sleet	lightning	windy	cool	cumulo-nimbus

to help students learn word meanings. Figure 8–13 provides an example of the list, groups, and labels that might be produced in this strategy.

List

In preparing for the lesson, select a topic or subtopic that represents a major concept from the content under study. Write the stimulus topic at the top of the chalkboard, overhead transparency, computer LCD panel, or chart paper so that it can be seen easily by all the students. Students then brainstorm about the topic by calling out any word, phrase, or expression related to the topic that comes to mind. Record their responses so the entire class can see.

Group

Instruct students to break the list of words brainstormed by the class into smaller groups. These groups should consist of words that somehow correspond. Explain to the students that they should be prepared to label each of their groupings by identifying what the words in each have in common.

Label

Have students share with the class some of their word groupings while you record them for all to see. As students explain what the words in each group have in common, help them identify appropriate descriptive labels. The class then discusses each group of words and its label. Discussion serves to activate and develop background knowledge on the concepts by helping students explore various word meanings and their relationships. Readence, Bean, and Baldwin (1992) suggest that the teacher lead the discussion by commenting on the classifications and rationales, asking for clarification, and suggesting alternate ways to categorize the words.

Modifications

Tierney, Readence, and Dishner (1995) offer a few modifications for students who are younger or poorer readers and writers. The teacher could:

- model the process by constructing the first category and explaining how all the words fit together.
- provide the initial list of words to be grouped and labeled, making sure that the word categories are fairly simple and obvious.
- provide the groupings and have students label them.
- provide the labels and have students categorize the words accordingly.

CONCEPT DEVELOPMENT

Concept development refers to teaching and learning word meanings. The processes of word recognition and concept development are so closely related and intertwined, it would be difficult to separate them completely. However, instruction can certainly emphasize one process at a time. Students' overall vocabulary mastery can be enhanced by providing instruction both in word recognition and concept development.

Often the processes of word recognition and concept development occur simultaneously. For example, when you apply context clues, both processes of word recognition and concept development are at work. From surrounding word meaning, it is possible to gain enough clues to recognize a word and understand its meaning at the same time. However, it is also possible to recognize a word based on context because you have seen it or heard it used before without fully comprehending its meaning. At that point, you have recognized and pronounced the word but still need to learn its meaning in that particular context.

The importance of concept development to word recognition can be seen in the emphasis on using context clues to enhance the effectiveness of other word recognition skills. Concept development is also part of attention to word meanings for teaching and learning sight words. The meaning of a word certainly serves as an effective device for recalling the pronunciation of that particular set of symbols.

Concept development involves learning word meanings on several different levels. For example, it includes the ability to understand the meanings of both unfamiliar and familiar words. Concept development also involves the ability to internalize meanings for future use as part of one's own expressive vocabulary and later recognition.

An important key to concept development is the utility of the vocabulary. Words perceived as useful to students, in terms of their own communication needs, tend to be more easily learned and recalled. On the other hand, words that students do not perceive as useful are more difficult to learn and recall. Technical vocabulary, especially, is difficult for students to appreciate in terms of utility. Therefore, the more you can demonstrate to students the personal value of recognition and use of technical vocabulary, the more success they are likely to have with concept development.

Another key to concept development is the opportunity to practice recognizing and using new words in meaningful ways. Effectively internalizing new vocabulary involves two essential ingredients. The first is repeated encounters with new words. The more you see the words in context, the more they are reinforced for you. The second involves integrating new words into your expressive vocabulary. Using new words in speaking or writing makes them part of your working vocabulary.

Introducing and Reinforcing New Vocabulary

Think back for a minute to the vocabulary activities you can recall from your elementary, middle, and high school experiences. See if your recollections are similar to these: Do you remember being given a list of isolated words at the beginning of the week to prepare for a vocabulary test, usually administered on Friday? Early in the week, were you given daily activities that included looking up the words in a dictionary or glossary and copying the definitions? Later in the week, did the daily activities focus on memorizing the definitions, and did they usually include writing the words in sentences of your own composition?

If you recall these or similar activities, you probably remember doing them the same way week after week. During the process of looking up and copying definitions, do you recall ever being frustrated when more than one meaning was listed for a word (which was probably most of the time)? Having to copy and memorize multiple definitions may have made this already tedious task even more burdensome.

During the process of composing and writing sentences, do you recall being frustrated with unfamiliar words? If you had no recollection of seeing or hearing a word used before, did the task of using it appropriately in a sentence seem almost overwhelming? Even for familiar words, thinking of an isolated sentence to stand alone in demonstration of a word's meaning was probably extremely difficult and tiresome.

However, in spite of your frustrations, did the drudgery seem to pay off on Fridays? Were you somehow able to remember the word meanings well enough to ace the test? If so, the format of the test probably involved some type of recognition of the word meanings. Did the task require matching words with their meanings? Were sentences provided in which you filled in the blanks with appropriate words from the list provided? Whatever the format, the test probably required memorization of word meanings for short-term recall.

For the purpose of short-term recall of memorized word meanings, copying definitions and composing sentences were probably at least somewhat effective. However, even if you managed to perform well on those weekly vocabulary tests, did the majority of the vocabulary you learned in that manner actually stay with you beyond each test? For six-week tests, for example, did you have to go back and memorize the words all over again? Worse yet, even after memorizing them twice, did you still not include most of the words in your personal vocabulary?

If you answered yes to most of these questions, like many students, you may have graduated from high school with a relatively poor vocabulary. Not only was your vocabulary limited, you probably had few or no effective skills for learning new words for long-term recall. Consequently, improving your vocabulary in college probably presented quite a challenge.

Effective ways to build your personal vocabulary do exist. One way in which you could build your personal vocabulary effectively involves the manner in which you are introduced to new words. In terms of life-long learning, you will be introducing words to yourself; the manner in which you handle the new words you encounter can significantly influence the effectiveness of your vocabulary development.

Another way to build your vocabulary involves reinforcing new vocabulary. In other words, what do you *do* with a new word once you have uncovered its meaning? For example, do you substitute a familiar synonym into the context, then continue reading and forget about it? Do you jot the word down in the margin as part of a key phrase related to the content? Do you make an effort to use new words when speaking? While writing, do you check the thesaurus for new words you have previously encountered but rarely, if ever, use?

Four concept development activities designed to introduce and reinforce vocabulary will be described in this section. These activities—joining, excluding, selecting, and implying—are based on cognitive operations involved in concept learning (Henry 1974). Each of these activities represents a way to help students incorporate new vocabulary for personal use by modeling the kinds of mental activities required for independent, lifelong vocabulary development.

As you read about the activities, think about how they are similar. What is it that makes them effective for concept development? What distinguishes them from activities involving copying and memorizing definitions? How might they be used both to introduce and reinforce new vocabulary? How might they be incorporated into some of the strategies for content area literacy and learning?

Also, keep in mind the appropriate uses of these activities. They are *not* designed to be used as worksheets in isolation from other content area learning and literacy activities. Rather, they should be part of whole-group and cooperative learning activities led and supervised by the teacher. Concept development activities, when used properly, give students many meaningful and valuable vocabulary-enhancing opportunities to

▌ talk about the words and use them in the context of everyday language.
▌ listen to a variety of perspectives and ideas about the words.
▌ develop background knowledge about the words and their relationships.
▌ understand the words in the context of the content under study.
▌ internalize the words as part of the language of the content area.
▌ assimilate the words into personal expressive vocabularies.

Joining

Joining, as a concept development activity, involves grouping together words according to categories. This categorizing activity can be used to introduce words by first providing students a set of grouped, familiar words labeled by category. Present the new words in the context of sentences, introducing each word individually, by reading its sentence aloud. Then briefly explain and allow discussion of its meaning.

After introducing and discussing the first word, model for students the process of joining. Explain why the words are grouped the way they are and how they relate to the categories. Then tell them which group the new word should join and explain why.

Continue with the remaining words. After each word is introduced and discussed, ask students to compare the new word to the grouped words provided and decide which group it should "join." Students can

---

FIGURE 8–14 Concept development activity for a geography lesson:
Introducing vocabulary using *joining*

---

1. The <u>rainforests</u> are being cut down for wood and farmland.

2. <u>Crafts</u> can be both useful and artistic.

3. The <u>monsoons</u> provide water needed for growing rice.

4. Fresh water <u>springs</u> are important in areas with little rain.

5. In Bali, <u>celebrations</u> are held almost every day.

6. Frozen <u>tundra</u> makes up much of Siberia.

Which of the following groups of words, labeled by category, should each of the underlined words above join?

land formations	*bodies of water*	*climate*	*culture*
islands	rivers	temperate	religion
mountains	creeks	tropical	clothing
deserts	streams	arctic	traditions
plains	lakes	humid	customs
valleys	oceans	arid	entertainment

---

place each word into more than one category as long as they can justify their decisions. See Figure 8–14 for an example of how a joining activity could be used to introduce new words for concept development.

Joining can also provide reinforcement of words once they have been introduced. Through the processes of comparing and contrasting them with other words, students come to fully understand the words' meanings. Also, one of the important ways we learn new concepts is by comparing and contrasting them with concepts we already know. Actively engaging new words in a mental activity that integrates them with familiar vocabulary facilitates the process of internalization.

Figure 8–15 provides an example of a joining activity that could be used to reinforce new vocabulary for concept development. Students could complete such activities independently, in pairs, or in small groups. Discussing and sharing thinking processes to complete the activities makes them even more effective.

FIGURE 8–15 Concept development activity for a geography lesson: Reinforcing vocabulary using *joining*

Place each of the words listed below under the appropriate category. Some of the words might fit into more than one category. Make sure you can explain why you placed each word in the category you chose.

land formations	*bodies of water*	*climate*	*culture*
islands	arid	valleys	oceans
rivers	customs	tropical	clothing
arctic	streams	deserts	traditions
plains	lakes	humid	creeks
temperate	entertainment	mountains	waterfalls
crafts	rainforests	springs	monsoons
mild	religion	celebrations	tundra

Excluding

As a concept development activity, excluding involves identifying a word or words that do not belong with the others in a group. Key to understanding and learning a new concept is the clear understanding of what that concept is *not*. To fully understand a word's meaning, students must be able to distinguish it from others that are similar but clearly not the same. The act of excluding helps students distinguish similar words, especially those with fine distinctions.

When using excluding as a way to introduce new vocabulary, first present the new words in the context of sentences. Introduce each word, one at a time, by reading its sentence aloud. Then, briefly explain and allow discussion of its meaning.

After you have introduced and discussed the first word, model for students the process of excluding. Present a list of at least three or four other words that could be categorized together. Explain to the students why these words fit together in the same category. Then explain why the new word would *not* fit with the others. Continue with the remaining words. After introducing and discussing each word, ask students to explain *why* each word does not fit with the others. See Figure 8–16 for an example of how an excluding activity could be used to introduce new words for concept development.

Excluding can also provide reinforcement of words once they have been introduced. For students to decide whether certain words fit together with other words requires that they have a clear understanding of the word meanings. The process also requires that they understand fine distinctions between words with similar meanings. When students work

---

FIGURE 8–16 Concept development activity for a geometry lesson: Introducing vocabulary using *excluding*

---

1. A <u>point</u> is a position with no dimensions.

2. A <u>rhombus</u> is a parallelogram with equal sides.

3. A unit of measure for angles is a <u>degree</u>.

4. A <u>right triangle</u> has three sides and three angles, one of which is a right angle.

Why would each of the italicized words below *not* fit with the other words listed below it?

point	*rhombus*	*degree*	*right triangle*
line	cone	arc	parallelogram
angle	cylinder	radius	square
line segment	cube	diameter	rectangle
ray	sphere	chord	quadrilateral

---

through the excluding process, they mentally manipulate the terms and meanings in a way that helps them internalize the concepts. Figure 8–17 provides an example of how excluding could be used to help students reinforce terms and the concepts they represent.

Several variations of excluding can be used as effective concept development activities. First, as shown in Figure 8–17, students select the word in a list that does not belong with the others and then identify the organizing concept of the remaining words. Second, as shown in Figure 8–18, the words in each list could be organized in more than one way; the task is the same as the one in Figure 8–17, but more than one correct response is possible. Third, as shown in Figure 8–19, students select the word that does not belong because that word actually represents the category under which the others fall.

Selecting

As a concept development activity, the process of selecting involves identifying appropriate synonyms. One of the key ways we internalize words and make them our own is by associating them with familiar words that have similar or opposite meanings. Once students associate new words with appropriate and familiar synonyms, they can begin to make finer distinctions between synonyms. In other words, they can begin to distinguish synonyms in terms of context and usage.

FIGURE 8–17 Concept development activity for a history lesson: Reinforcing vocabulary using *excluding* (Examples of correct responses are underlined.)

Mark through the word or phrase in each group below that does not fit with the others. Then write in the blank the organizing concept (word or phrase) that describes the remaining words.

genocide
Holocaust
blitzkrieg
ethnic cleansing
extermination
blitzkrieg/killing off a race of people

Jews
gypsies
non-Aryans
German Aryans
Slavs
German Aryans/people killed in Nazi
  extermination camps in WW II

Cold War
detente
containment
domino theory
arms race
detente/U.S. military build-up to
  prevent spread of communism

colonialism
imperialism
colonization
paternalism
democratization
democratization/policies describing and
  rationalizing stronger countries taking
  over weaker ones

When using selecting as a way to introduce new vocabulary, first present the new words in the context of sentences, reading each sentence aloud. Then, briefly explain and allow discussion of each word's meaning. After you have introduced and discussed the first word, model for students the process of selecting. Under each sentence, present four to six words that should be familiar to the students.

At first, make sure that only one of these words is a synonym for the meaning of the underlined word in that particular sentence. Explain to the students why each word under the sentence either would or would not be a synonym for the underlined word. Continue with the remaining sentences. After introducing and discussing each word, ask students to help you decide whether each word below the sentence would or would not be a synonym. Figure 8–20 provides an example of how a selecting activity might be used for introducing words and concepts by helping students identify their synonyms.

Once students develop some competence with identifying one synonym from a list, begin including more than one synonym in the list and

---

FIGURE 8–18   Concept development activity for a life science lesson: Reinforcing vocabulary using *excluding* (Examples of correct responses are underlined.)

Mark through a word or phrase in each group below that does not fit with the others. Then write in the blank the organizing concept (word or phrase) that describes the remaining words. Keep in mind that more than one correct response is possible for each group of words.

bacteria
bacillus
blue-green bacteria
saprophytes
parasites
1. bacteria/types of bacteria
2. bacillus/types of Monera

diffusion
permeable membrane
active transport
respiration
osmosis
1. diffusion/cells move from more crowded to less crowded cell areas
2. active transport/cells move from less crowded to more crowded areas

root hairs
root cap
xylem
phloem
photosynthesis
1. photosynthesis/food transportation system in plants
2. root cap/food making and transporting in plants

acquired immune deficiency syndrome
acquired immunity malfunction
human immunodeficiency virus
infectious disease
nucleic acid
1. nucleic acid/AIDS
2. infectious disease/AIDS virus

---

have students identify all the synonyms. Make sure that all the synonyms listed are appropriate for the meaning of the underlined word as it is used in that particular sentence.

Once students become confident with the selecting process, you can help them begin to make distinctions between synonyms. One way of making distinctions between synonyms involves the multiple meanings of words. Because a word can have several different meanings, students must not only be able to identify synonyms but those appropriate for a given context. Begin by including at least two synonyms in the list of words below each sentence, only one of which is appropriate for the context of the sentence. The context of the sentence should clearly indicate which of the synonyms is appropriate for that particular sentence. Make sure you explain that more than one word in the list might be a synonym for the underlined word. See Figure 8–21 for an example of a selecting

---

FIGURE 8–19 Concept development activity for an earth science lesson: Reinforcing vocabulary using *excluding* (Examples of correct responses are underlined.)

In each group of words that follows, identify the word that describes the organizing concept (category) for the other words in the group.

protostars	quartz
stars	feldspar
white dwarfs	micas
supernovas	talc
pulsars	silicates
stars	*silicates*
conglomerate	mantle
sandstone	silicon
breccia	oxygen
clastic	iron
shale	magnesium
clastic	*mantle*

---

activity with more than one synonym, only one of which is appropriate for the context provided.

Selecting can also be used to provide reinforcement of words once they have been introduced. Students must have a clear understanding of the word meanings before they can select acceptable and appropriate synonyms. The selecting process also requires that they understand fine distinctions between words with similar meanings, particularly in terms of appropriate usage. When students work through the selecting process, they are internalizing the concepts by mentally comparing and contrasting them with familiar terms and concepts. When students can decide which synonyms would be most appropriate for certain contexts, they have mastered the concept on a level required for ownership of the words; in other words, they are ready to use the words in their own oral and written language. Figure 8–22 provides an example of how selecting could be used to help students reinforce terms and the concepts they represent.

Implying

As a concept development activity, the process of implying involves making analogies. The ability to make analogies is a valuable critical thinking skill requiring clear understanding of the concepts involved. Because it can be difficult to master, students should be introduced to the concept

---

FIGURE 8-20 Concept development activity for a mathematics lesson: Introducing vocabulary using *selecting* (identifying synonyms)

---

1. A comparison of one number to another is called a(n) <u>ratio</u>.

integer	function
rational number	equation
fraction	whole number

(The only synonym is <u>fraction</u>.)

2. In a scale drawing, the dimensions of the objects are reduced by the same <u>scale</u>.

amount	ratio
size	equation
measurements	length

(The only synonym is <u>ratio</u>.)

3. A number in <u>decimal</u> form is a type of ratio.

rational	final
reduced	equivalent
percentage	extended

(The only synonym is <u>percentage</u>.)

---

early (even in primary grades). Making analogies is a skill that can only be mastered with practice; repeated use of the format is necessary for students to become comfortable and confident with the language and processes involved. Making analogies helps students understand and internalize concepts by identifying the relationships between words. Implying is the most advanced concept development process because it includes all three of the others (joining, excluding, and selecting).

When using implying as a way to introduce new vocabulary, present a sample set of analogies containing the new words. Present them in proper analogy format:

_____ : _____ : : _____ : _____

(Read as "_____ is to _____ , as _____ is to _____ .")

Each analogy contains only one new word, which should be underlined. Each new word should be surrounded in the analogy by familiar words

---

FIGURE 8–21 Concept development activity for a mathematics lesson: Introducing vocabulary using *selecting* (distinguishing synonyms in terms of context)

---

1. A price <u>discount</u> is calculated by subtracting a percentage of the regular price.

increase	disregard
reduction	amount
inflation	total

(The synonyms are <u>reduction</u> and <u>disregard</u>, but only <u>reduction</u> is appropriate in this context.)

2. When finding a percentage of a number, it is helpful to <u>estimate</u> the answer first.

guess	choose
determine	understand
record	assess

(The synonyms are <u>guess</u> and <u>assess</u>, but only <u>guess</u> is appropriate in this context.)

3. A <u>commission</u> is a fee based on a percentage of sales.

delegate	value
salary	committee
cost	price

(The synonyms are <u>salary</u>, <u>delegate</u>, and <u>committee</u>, but only <u>salary</u> is appropriate in this context.)

---

that help students understand the new concept by comparing it with familiar ones. Introduce each new word individually by explaining and allowing discussion of its meaning; then briefly review the meanings of the familiar words. After you have introduced and discussed the first word, model for students the process of implying. First, describe the relationship between the first pair of words in the analogy. Then, explain how the second pair of words exhibits the same relationship. Continue with the remaining analogies. After introducing and discussing the words in each analogy, ask students to help you determine and explain the relationship between the first pair of words. Then ask them to do the same with the second pair of words.

FIGURE 8–22 Concept development activity in a world geography lesson: Reinforcing vocabulary using *selecting*

Mark the words following each sentence that are acceptable synonyms for the underlined word. Identify only those synonyms appropriate for the context of the sentence provided. Be prepared to defend your choices.

1. Earthquakes occur along <u>faults</u> in the earth's surface.

weaknesses   flaws

illnesses   errors

problems   sins

(The acceptable synonyms are <u>weaknesses</u> and <u>flaws</u>.)

2. The earth's surface is made of <u>plates,</u> which move gradually.

saucers   segments

sections   sheets

dishes   panes

(The acceptable synonyms are <u>sections</u> and <u>segments</u>.)

3. Changes in the earth's <u>crust</u> happen slowly from forces deep in the center.

dough   exterior

hardening   cake

surface   wall

(The acceptable synonyms are <u>surface</u> and <u>exterior</u>.)

Once you have guided students through the implying process with sample analogies, provide new analogies using the same set of new words being introduced. In the new analogies, provide a blank in place of the last word of each, followed by three or four word choices. Use the first analogy to model for students the implying process involved in filling in the blanks. Continue with the remaining analogies by having students decide the appropriate word for completing the analogy. Figure 8–23 provides an example of how an implying activity might be used for introducing words and concepts by helping students analyze analogies.

Implying can also be used to provide reinforcement of words once they have been introduced. Students must have a clear understanding of the word meanings before they can analyze and complete analogies. The

---

FIGURE 8–23 Concept development activity in a health lesson: Reinforcing vocabulary using *implying* (The correct responses are underlined.)

How are the first two words in the following analogies related to each other?

Which of the four options would give the second pair of words the same relationship as the first pair?

1. gene : hemophilia : : virus : _____ .
   (cancer, <u>AIDS</u>, strep throat, diabetes)

2. filth : disease : : sanitation : _____ .
   (sickness, bacteria, <u>health</u>, virus)

3. liquor : alcoholism : : cocaine : _____ .
   (<u>addiction</u>, drug, inhalants, marijuana)

4. nicotine : cigarettes : : alcohol : _____ .
   (tobacco, caffeine, coffee, <u>beer</u>)

5. water : pipe : : blood : _____ .
   (heart, <u>vein</u>, flow, river)

6. nose : olfactory : : skin : _____ .
   (smell, visual, auditory, <u>tactile</u>)

---

implying process also requires that they understand fine distinctions between concepts and their relationships. When students work through the implying process, they internalize the concepts by analyzing the relationships of new words with familiar terms and concepts. When students can complete analogies, they have mastered the new words on a level required for ownership. In other words, they are ready to use the words in their own oral and written language.

Once students have mastered the art of completing analogies by filling in blanks placed at the end, you can begin moving the blanks. Students need practice with the varied thinking processes required for completing blanks in different positions. Figure 8–24 provides an example of how implying could be used to help students reinforce terms and the concepts they represent.

FIGURE 8-24 Concept development activity in an English literature lesson: Reinforcing vocabulary using *implying*

Complete the analogies that follow with one of the four choices provided.

1. fourteen : sonnet : : haiku : _____ .
(<u>three</u>, five, eight, ten)

2. onomatopoeia : sound : : _____ : comparison.
(poem, <u>metaphor</u>, allusion, idiom)

3. biography : _____ : : novel : fiction.
(literature, short story, <u>nonfiction</u>, realism)

4. *Macbeth* : drama : : *The Odyssey* : _____ .
(novel, poem, fable, <u>epic</u>)

5. _____ : Nash : : sonnets : Browning.
(haiku, <u>limericks</u>, proverbs, cliches)

6. climax : plot : : _____ : characterization.
(<u>antagonist</u>, setting, theme, conclusion)

Guidelines for Teaching

Before reading further, stop for a few minutes and think about the following purpose for reading, which was established for the previous section:

> How are the four concept development activities, *joining, excluding, selecting,* and *implying,* all alike? What is it that makes them effective for concept development? What distinguishes them from activities involving copying and memorizing definitions?

Making a list of the things that joining, excluding, selecting, and implying activities have in common will give you a good start on guidelines for effectively teaching concepts. Your list would probably include the following guidelines, all of which are based on reviews of research related to vocabulary instruction. Can you think of others?

According to Beck and McKeown (1991):

▌ Design instruction with the goal of enhancing students' abilities to engage vocabulary in complex language situations *not* with the goal of helping students match words to definitions.

■ Incorporate a variety of techniques into instruction including both those that emphasize context and those that emphasize definitions.
■ Repeatedly expose students to new words in a variety of contexts.

According to Vaughn, Crawley, and Mountain (1979):

■ Teach vocabulary directly, not incidentally.
■ Categorize words.
■ Use strategies to promote mental imagery.

According to Nelson-Herber (1986):

■ Involve students in the learning process instead of having them memorize definitions.

According to Blachowicz (1985, 1986):

■ Activate any previous knowledge of the words being introduced.
■ Guide students in making predictions about word meanings, word relationships, and connections among the words, topic, content and structure of the passage.
■ Have students begin reading, even if they do not yet fully understand the word meanings or concepts; remind them to read for the purpose of checking their predictions and finding clues to the word meanings.
■ After reading, guide students through the process of considering their predictions in light of new information, and if necessary, revising and clarifying their notions about the word meanings.
■ Help students internalize the words by giving them opportunities to use them in meaningful reading and writing situations.
■ Use categories to introduce vocabulary in related sets in order to build a schema for learning the new words.
■ Involve students in the learning process rather than just telling them the definitions.
■ Teach vocabulary that will be most useful for serving your students' communication needs.
■ Provide many opportunities for students to use new vocabulary.
■ Make vocabulary development ongoing.
■ Provide opportunities for follow-up.
■ Introduce your students to books on word study.
■ Teach students how to learn word meanings independently.
■ Teach students how to apply usage of the dictionary, thesaurus, and context.

According to Carr and Wixson (1986):

■ Help students relate new concepts to their background knowledge and experiences.

- Require students to manipulate the concepts represented by new words in the combined context of background knowledge and text presentation.
- Provide for active student involvement in learning new words.
- Help students build strategies for developing vocabulary independently.

According to Readence, Bean, and Baldwin (1992):

- Be an enthusiastic model of vocabulary development by using the dictionary and thesaurus in class, using the words you expect your students to learn, and sharing interesting new words you encounter and learn.
- Make vocabulary meaningful by defining it in multiple contexts, drawing it from immediately relevant experiences, and defining it in terms of and with examples from the students' prior knowledge.
- Reinforce vocabulary by providing opportunities to use new words in reading, writing, speaking, and listening activities in meaningful ways.

According to Ruddell (1992):

- Help students develop associations with other words.
- Incorporate activities that encourage higher-order thinking.
- Design activities that lead students to many different resources.
- Use activities that acknowledge and capitalize on the social nature of learning.

Strategies

This section describes some of the more popular concept development strategies and activities. All of these strategies and activities follow the guidelines suggested by research that were presented in the previous section. As you read the descriptions, refer to the list of guidelines for teaching. See if you can identify how each strategy or activity fits one or more of the guidelines.

Knowledge Rating

Blachowicz (1986) recommends Knowledge Rating as a way of helping students ponder what they already know about a topic and related key words. First, have students individually complete Knowledge Rating forms. See Figures 8–25 and 8–26 for examples. Then, lead a discussion of the words to help you and the students assess their background knowledge of the words. Once unknown words have been identified, follow up the discussion by helping students make connections between the unknown words and any related knowledge already possessed. At this

---

FIGURE 8–25 Vocabulary Strategy: Knowledge Rating format for a math lesson (Sample A)

How much do you know about these words?

Mark "**X**" in the column that indicates your understanding.

	Can define	**Have seen/heard**	**?**
radical sign	_____	_____	_____
index	_____	_____	_____
roots	_____	_____	_____
radicand	_____	_____	_____
expression	_____	_____	_____
principle Nth root	_____	_____	_____
quotient	_____	_____	_____
product	_____	_____	_____
simplest radical form	_____	_____	_____

---

point, guide students in making predictions about word meanings in the context of the passage to be read. Students then read for the purpose of looking for clues to make connections between the words and what they already know, their predictions about the words, and the meaning of the passage.

Vocabulary Self-Collection Strategy

The Vocabulary Self-Collection Strategy (VSS) (Haggard 1982) emphasizes vocabulary concept development as an integral part of content area learning. It also emphasizes vocabulary acquisition in developing the language of an academic discipline. The strategy is designed to help the class generate its own list of vocabulary to be learned and help students use their own interests, experiences, and world knowledge to enhance vocabulary development.

FIGURE 8–26 Vocabulary Strategy: Knowledge Rating format for a math lesson (Sample B)

How much do you know about these words?

Mark "**X**" in the column that indicates your understanding.

	Can define	Have seen/heard	?
empty set	_____	_____	_____
equation	_____	_____	_____
inequality	_____	_____	_____
open sentence	_____	_____	_____
replacement set	_____	_____	_____
solution	_____	_____	_____
solution set	_____	_____	_____
factor	_____	_____	_____
sum	_____	_____	_____
product	_____	_____	_____
multiplicative inverse	_____	_____	_____

Following are a set of steps that Ruddell (1992) recommends for implementing the strategy:

1. Following discussion of a reading assignment or any learning stimulus, ask each student to nominate one word for the class list. Tell students to choose words they would like to learn more about and that are important to the topic.
2. Put students into nominating teams of two to five people to respond to the following questions about their words:
   a. Where did you find the word? (Record the sentence if found in text or the context if recalled from discussion.)

    b. What do you think the word means in this context?

    c. Why do you think the class should learn it?

3. Give groups about three to five minutes to accomplish this task. Keep the time limited to help keep students focused. You can then extend the time if it is really needed. Monitor the groups closely, providing guidance as needed.

4. Have a spokesperson from each group present the nominated words, one at a time, telling where each was found, what the group believes it means, and why it was chosen.

5. As each word is presented, write it for all to see and lead a discussion to define it, first from context, then, if needed, from references available in the classroom. The discussion should include contributions from other class members so that definitions are extended and personalized.

6. After all the groups have presented their words, nominate a word yourself to be added to the list, using the same format for presenting and discussing the word. You should have several words prepared in advance for presentation, from which you select one.

7. Modify the list by eliminating duplicates, words most students feel they already know, and any that are not appropriate for whatever reason. Mark the eliminated words but do not erase them.

8. The final class list should contain no more than five to six words. These words are then redefined and written along with their definitions in the students' vocabulary journals or study maps.

9. Words not chosen for the class list may be recorded by individual students who wish to include them on their personal vocabulary lists.

10. Once the list is determined from the initial introductions and discussions of words, follow-up activities should be designed for reinforcement. Students must be provided with planned opportunities that follow the guidelines for effective vocabulary instruction, especially the following. Activities should:

    ▋ allow students to use new words in meaningful ways.

    ▋ allow students opportunities to associate new words and concepts with their own background knowledge and experiences.

    ▋ encourage higher-order thinking.

    ▋ lead students to many different resources.

    ▋ acknowledge and capitalize on the social nature of learning.

    ▋ help students develop associations between words (e.g., with Semantic Mapping [see Chapter 1] or Semantic Feature Analysis).

Semantic Feature Analysis

Semantic Feature Analysis (SFA) (Johnson and Pearson 1984) is designed to help students improve their vocabulary through categorizing, comparing, and contrasting related words. Figure 8–27 provides an example of a blank matrix and Figure 8–28 provides an example of a completed feature matrix developed from an SFA. Following are six steps adapted from those recommended by Tierney, Readence, and Dishner (1995) for implementing the strategy:

FIGURE 8–27   Semantic Feature Analysis grid for an art history lesson

Directions: Students will list all the periods of art history by brainstorming.
Students will decide what time-periods they fall under.
Students will decide what art-forms apply to the different periods of art.
(Hint: There could be more than one application.)

Periods of Art History	Pre–1900	1900–1950	1950–Present	Architecture	Sculpture	Painting

FIGURE 8–28 Semantic Feature Analysis matrix completed in a life science lesson

CATEGORY: ARTHROPODS

	exoskeleton	jointed legs	vertebrae	wings	body sections
lobster	+	10	–	–	2
spider	+	8	–	–	2
grasshopper	+	6	–	+	3
centipede	+	many	–	–	many
butterfly	+	6	–	+	3
millipede	+	many	–	–	many
crawfish	+	10	–	–	2
mite	+	8	–	–	2
ant	+	6	–	+	3
tick	+	8	–	–	2
bee	+	6	–	+	3
crab	+	10	–	–	2
moth	+	6	–	+	3

1. Select a category that is concrete and familiar to the students. (You can begin to use more abstract and less familiar categories once students become accustomed to the strategy.). Begin a feature matrix labeled with the category at the top.
2. Develop a list of words related to the category. As students become more familiar and confident with the strategy, they can supply the word themselves. Continue the feature matrix by listing the related words vertically down the left side of the page, board, transparency, and so on.
3. Develop a set of features or characteristics to be compared and contrasted. Again, as students develop confidence with the strategy, they can create their own set of features, and you can increase the number of features explored. Continue the feature matrix by listing the features horizontally across the top.
4. Guide the students in completing the feature matrix by helping them decide whether each word possesses each of the identified features. At first, use a + or – to indicate "yes" or "no." Eventually,

you can begin using more sophisticated systems of response such as a Likert scale, which indicates frequency (e.g., 1 = never, 2 = some, 3 = always) or degrees (e.g., 1 = a little, 2 = some, 3 = a lot).

5. Expand the matrix by generating new words to be added and new features to be analyzed. At first, you will need to provide the new words and features; eventually, the students should be expected to provide them.

6. Complete the matrix by analyzing and recording the results for the newly added words and features. Help students explore the matrix by examining and discussing how all the words are related yet clearly unique. Again, students should eventually be expected to explore and discuss the matrix with little help from you.

Possible Sentences

Possible Sentences (PS) (Moore and Moore 1992) is designed to help students learn new vocabulary by making predictions about sentences found in the reading assignment. The strategy aims to prepare students for reading by focusing their attention on key vocabulary. Students are then guided in using context clues to infer word meanings while checking their predictions. Following are the four recommended steps for this strategy:

1. Select and list key words defined adequately by their context. Each word is presented to the class and pronounced several times.

2. Ask students individually to select two words from the list and compose one sentence using both words. As each student dictates, record the sentence for all to see, underlining the key words. (Write the sentences exactly as dictated, even if the information is not accurate.) Continue by calling on another student to select two words, compose, and dictate a sentence. Continue recording sentences until a predetermined period has elapsed, a specified number of sentences has been created, or students can produce no more. Students may choose words that someone else previously used, but eventually, each word on the list should be presented in a sentence.

3. Have students read the passage for the purpose of checking the accuracy of their classmates' "possible" sentences.

4. Using the reading assignment as a reference, evaluate the sentences generated before reading using questions such as the following:
   ∎ Which ones are accurate?
   ∎ Which ones need further elaboration?
   ∎ Which ones cannot be validated because the passage did not provide enough information?

Guide students in making necessary changes to their sentences to make them accurate. Remove sentences that cannot be validated. After evaluating and modifying the original sentences, ask students to dictate new ones. As they are being recorded, students may challenge each other's sentences as inaccurate, incomplete, or unknowable. Have students respond to challenges by quickly referring to the text. Students should copy the final, acceptable statements into their notebooks or vocabulary journals.

Concept Development for ESL Students

Schifini (1994, 70) notes that vocabulary development for second-language learners is most effective when used to label experiences or concepts related to direct experiences. He specifically recommends avoiding dictionary, glossary, and memorization activities in favor of concrete learning experiences with as many hands-on activities as possible. For example, vocabulary development should include such activities as simulations, role-play situations, dramatizations, games, demonstrations, experiments, field trips, and discovery learning (Schifini 1994, 70). These kinds of activities are especially useful because they provide a meaningful social context for constructing meaning and relating concepts with words.

Schifini (1994) also recommends the use of *Semantic Mapping* (see Chapter 1) and Semantic Feature Analysis (see previous section) for vocabulary development. In addition, he recommends Gipe's (1979) strategy for interacting with vocabulary in context. In this interactive vocabulary-learning method, you present a new word in a simple written sentence, which include phrases that define the concept. You can then give students immediate practice in using the word. Following is an example of the interactive vocabulary-learning method used to introduce the word *extinct* in a science lesson:

Scientists have not yet determined why dinosaurs became *extinct*.

Specific types of animals that no longer exist are said to be *extinct*.

What animals can you think of that have become *extinct*?

List as many possible reasons as you can to explain why animals might become *extinct*.

Context Clues for Concept Development

The use of context clues as a word recognition skill was discussed in Part 1 of this chapter. Now, the use of context clues for concept development will be examined. The utility of context clues for determining word meanings depends on the richness of the context. If enough clues are provided, you can usually figure out an unknown word without resorting to a dictionary. However, if the context does not provide enough clues, finding the meaning of an unfamiliar word can be extremely difficult, if not impossible, without outside help.

Context clues generally are of three types: *definition, description,* and *contrast* (Readence, Bean, and Baldwin 1992). See Figure 8–29 for an example of each. Definition generally provides the strongest context clues. Since the definition of the word is directly stated, the reader does not have to infer its meaning. Unless the definition of the word is poorly stated, the reader should have little or no difficulty figuring out its meaning. Sometimes, definitions will offer synonyms for the word.

Description does not provide as many context clues as definitions. Depending on the sentence, however, descriptions can still offer readers ample clues for finding the meanings of unknown words. Since descriptions only allude to meanings rather than directly stating them the available clues are only useful if the reader is skilled at making inferences. Sometimes, descriptions will compare the word to similar concepts.

The third type of context clues, contrast, also provides implied meanings. Clues are implied by offering the reader antonyms (words of opposite meaning) or by describing what the concept is *not*. As with descriptions, the reader must infer meanings based on the clues provided.

FIGURE 8–29   Examples of three types of context clues

TYPE	EXAMPLES
definition	**1.** The Ancient Egyptians built pyramids as burial rooms, called **tombs,** for their kings.
	2. The study of light and vision is referred to as **optics.**
	3. An **acid** is a compound that forms hydrogen atoms when dissolved in water.
description	**1.** Biologists classify animals **phylogenetically** by tracing their ancestral characteristics.
	2. People sometimes build **aqueducts** to carry water to cities and irrigate dry farmland.
contrast	**1.** As opposed to **organic** matter, inorganic matter does not contain carbon.
	2. While a square is **symmetrical,** a rectangle does not necessarily have equal sides.

Even if context clues are implied and vague, a skilled reader and critical thinker can put the available hints together effectively. With practice, a reader can make greater use of available context clues. Because context clues are only as effective as the reader's ability to recognize and infer them, activities that give students practice using context clues can be quite valuable.

Cloze Activities

As discussed in Part 1 of this chapter, cloze activities are fill-in-the-blank exercises. In addition to helping students learn to use context for decoding, cloze activities can also give students practice in using context for concept development. At first, the sentences you use for cloze activities should offer many clues, preferably in the form of directly stated definitions. You also should initially provide students with choices for filling in the blanks (maze activities). The choices should be familiar words so that emphasis at this point is on the process of using context clues rather than on the terms themselves. You should also model for students your thinking processes in identifying and piecing together context clues to make educated guesses about the meanings of unknown words.

Once students begin to develop confidence with the process of identifying and combining context clues, you can make the clues less obvious. At first, you will need to provide choices for these more advanced exercises (maze activities). For technical terms or especially difficult words, you might also need to provide the meanings along with the choices. That way, emphasis is on the process of matching meanings with context rather than on the terms themselves.

Again, you should model your thinking so that students can see how to make inferences to identify clues. Also, allow students to work in pairs or triads to model for each other their thought processes in making inferences and piecing together clues. Eventually, students should be able to work on the activities independently, but they first need good models and opportunities to apply what they observe. Ultimately, students need to practice recognizing and applying all three types of context clues: definition, description, and contrast. They also need practice with varying amounts of clues at various levels of concreteness. Students especially need practice making inferences about clues not directly stated.

Contextual Redefinition

Contextual Redefinition (Cunningham, Cunningham, and Arthur 1981) is designed to help students learn to use context for making educated guesses about word meanings. It is also designed to introduce vocabulary with meaningful associations derived from context. Following are the five steps for implementing Contextual Redefinition:

1. Examine the reading assignment and select unfamiliar words that are important for understanding the major ideas and that might give students trouble. These are the words you will introduce to students in preparation for the reading assignment.
2. Provide context either by copying the sentences that use the words or composing sentences yourself. Make sure the sentences offer ample and varied context clues.
3. Present the words in isolation for all to see. After pronouncing each word, ask students to guess the meaning based on their past knowledge and experiences. Students should provide rationales for their definitions so that the class can briefly discuss possible meanings before coming to consensus. Record the consensual meanings for the class.
4. Present the words in the context of sentences. After reading each sentence aloud, ask students to consider the context clues before making educated guesses about the word meanings. Students should be asked to explain their guesses so that other students get a model of the thinking processes involved in using context clues and making inferences. Record the new meanings.
5. Ask students to check the new meanings with dictionaries or glossaries. After a student reads aloud a dictionary definition, lead a class discussion comparing it to the students' educated guesses. Point out the difference in quality of predictions when the words were presented in isolation as opposed to when they were presented in context. Students should conclude that context clues provide much useful information for guessing the meanings of unfamiliar words.

Preview in Context

Preview in Context is designed to use informal discovery for introducing new words (Readence, Bean, and Baldwin 1992). It also helps students use their prior knowledge along with context clues to learn new vocabulary. Following are the four steps recommended for its implementation:

1. From the reading assignment, select a few words that are vital to understanding the major ideas. Choose words with which students are likely to be unfamiliar and that are likely to be troublesome.
2. In preparation for reading the assignment, direct students to each word in context. Read aloud the word and its surrounding context as the students follow along silently. Then have the students reread the material silently.
3. Through questioning and discussion, the teacher guides students in using their prior knowledge along with context clues to make educated guesses about word meanings.

4. Once students understand a word's meaning in the given context, expand its meaning by briefly offering and discussing synonyms, antonyms, and alternate contexts.

Dictionary and Thesaurus Skills

As discussed in Part 1 of this chapter, you cannot assume your students know how to use reference materials independently. Students need to learn at an early age the value of using the dictionary and thesaurus effectively and efficiently. If possible, each student should have her or his own dictionary and thesaurus to keep at her or his desk to encourage their regular and frequent use.

You need to diagnose each student's ability to use a dictionary and thesaurus. Here are some skills you want to assess:

- alphabetizing speed and accuracy
- using guide words
- recognizing and interpreting information about etymologies (word origins)
- identifying parts of speech
- narrowing and selecting from multiple meanings the best one for a given context
- identifying synonyms and antonyms

Diagnosis can be done informally simply by observing students as they use the reference books. A written diagnosis can be done by giving students a brief set of questions to answer while looking up words. For example, you might ask "What are the guide words for the page on which _____ is found?"

Making definitions meaningful. Many times students successfully locate a word in the dictionary only to be frustrated because they do not understand the definitions provided. Some words are more easily understood by comparing them with familiar synonyms or antonyms. Consequently, each student should be provided with a thesaurus and the skills to use it.

Other times, students successfully locate a word in the dictionary and become frustrated because they cannot guess which of the multiple meanings listed matches the context of the word. For this reason, students need practice matching dictionary definitions to words in context. They also need experience identifying a word's part of speech as it is used in context and then locating in the dictionary or thesaurus the word used as the same part of speech.

Etymology. Each content area has a core set of commonly used prefixes, suffixes, and root words, many of which are derived from Greek and

Latin. Students need to learn the meanings of these word parts and how to use them in understanding the meanings of the words containing them. Since students will likely encounter them repeatedly, the time invested in teaching the meanings of affixes and roots common to the language of the content area is well spent. Appendix J presents a list of commonly used prefixes and suffixes, as well as affixes and roots derived from Greek and Latin.

The "Synonym Game." The Synonym Game is designed to give students practice in using the thesaurus and commonly used content area terminology. The game can be played with teams or individuals. It can also be played as the Antonym Game. Here are the rules:

1. The first player or team representative draws a card on which you have written a sentence using a key word from the topic currently under study. The word should be underlined. That player first reads aloud the underlined word and then the sentence that provides context for the sentence.
2. Her or his opponent or opposing team representative then looks up the word in a thesaurus and identifies another word that he or she believes could be appropriately substituted for the underlined word.
3. The player who reads the sentence must then decide whether the word choice is acceptable.
4. As the teacher, you serve as judge by giving your verdict. If the player with the thesaurus made an appropriate word choice, he or she gets a point. If the player who read the sentence evaluated correctly the word choice, then he or she also gets a point.
5. Play continues until a predetermined amount of time has elapsed or number of points has been reached.

SUMMARY

In the content area classroom, vocabulary instruction should be of two types. The first is word recognition, which refers to decoding skills. The second is concept development, which refers to internalizing word meanings. Both types of vocabulary instruction are important for students of all ages. In order for students to understand unknown words and internalize new concepts on their own, they need a variety of skills in word recognition and concept development.

Unfortunately, many middle and high school students have not yet mastered a set of word recognition skills that allow them to decode words independently. As a content area teacher, you can coach students to show them how to apply each of the five word recognition skills: context clues, sight words, phonics, structural analysis, and dictionary usage. You can also help them decide which of these skills works best for them.

Concept development activities must emphasize the usefulness of the words, make the words meaningful to students, and provide opportunities for students to manipulate and use the words in communication. Activities that require joining, excluding, selecting, and implying are effective for introducing and reinforcing new words. These activities go beyond copying and memorizing definitions: they require students to become actively engaged with the meanings, relate them to prior knowledge, and compare and contrast them with words they already know. These activities result in greater long-term retention of concepts.

These and other concept development strategies and activities should be incorporated into the more comprehensive content area literacy strategies such as the Directed Reading Activity (DRA) or Directed Reading-Thinking Activity. For example, Possible Sentences or Preview in Context could be used as part of the preparation step of the DRA. The Vocabulary Self-Collection Strategy or Semantic Feature Analysis could comprise the follow-up step of the DRA. Vocabulary instruction should be an ongoing and integral part of your content area literacy instructional program.

ENRICHMENT ACTIVITIES

1. Develop a set of flashcards for the Compare/Contrast strategy. Include the instructions on another set of cards. Your finished product should allow you to meet with a student, administer the pretest, and then implement the strategy.
2. Develop a set of cloze and maze activities designed to develop students' abilities to use context as a word recognition tool in a content area of your choice. Develop another set of cloze and maze activities designed to develop students' abilities to use context for concept development in the content area of your choice.
3. Select twenty key sight words for the content area of your choice. Make a set of flashcards with the word on one side of each card and the meaning, synonym, or picture of the word on the other side. Then make visual configuration exercises for the words.
4. Select twenty key words (not necessarily sight words) for the content area of your choice. Design a set of joining, excluding, selecting, and implying activities for the twenty words (five words for each of the four activities).
5. Make a list of key Greek and Latin (or other) roots, prefixes, and suffixes for the content area of your choice. For each root, prefix, and suffix, identify its meaning and provide an example of a word containing it.

REFERENCES

Adams, M. J. (1990). *Beginning to read: Thinking and learning about print.* Cambridge, MA: The MIT Press.

Beck, I., and M. McKeown. (1991). Conditions of vocabulary acquisition. In *Handbook of reading research: Volume II.* Edited by R. Barr, M. L. Kamil, P. B. Mosenthal, and P. D. Pearson. White Plains, NY: Longman.

Blachowicz, C. L. Z. (1985). Vocabulary development and reading: From research to instruction. *The Reading Teacher* 38:876–881.

———. (1986). Making connections: Alternatives to vocabulary notebook. *Journal of Reading* 29:643–649.

Bond, G. L., and R. Dykstra. (1967). The Cooperative Research Program in first grade reading. *Reading Research Quarterly* 2:5–142.

Carr, E., and K. Wixson. (1986). Guidelines for evaluating vocabulary instruction. *Journal of Reading* 29:588–595.

Chall, J. S. (1967). *Learning to read: The great debate.* New York: McGraw-Hill.

———. *Learning to read: The great debate* (revised). New York: McGraw-Hill.

Cunningham, P. M. (1975–1976). Investigating a synthesized theory of mediated word identification. *Reading Research Quarterly* 11:127–143.

———. (1978). Decoding polysyllabic words: An alternative strategy. *Journal of Reading* 21:608–614.

———. (1979). A compare/contrast theory of mediated word identification. *The Reading Teacher* 37:774–778.

Cunningham, J. W., P. M. Cunningham, and S. V. Arthur. (1981). *Middle and secondary school reading.* New York: Longman.

Dykstra, R. (1968). The effectiveness of code- and meaning-emphasis beginning reading programs. *The Reading Teacher* 22:17–23.

Gipe, J. P. (1979). Investigating techniques for teaching word meanings. *Reading Research Quarterly* 14:624–644.

Graves, M. F., W. H. Slater, and T. G. White. (1989). Teaching content area vocabulary. In *Content area reading and learning.* Edited by D. Lapp, J. Flood, and N. Farnan. Englewood Cliffs, NJ: Prentice Hall.

Guthrie, J. T., N. A. Burnham, R. I. Caplan, and M. Seifert. (1974). The maze technique to assess, monitor reading comprehension. *The Reading Teacher* 28:161–168.

Haggard, M. R. (1982). The vocabulary self-collection strategy: An active approach to word learning. *Journal of Reading* 26:203–207.

Henry, G. (1974). *Teaching reading as concept development: Emphasis on affective thinking.* Newark, DE: International Reading Association.

Johnson, D. D., and P. D. Pearson. (1984). *Teaching reading vocabulary.* New York: Holt, Rinehart and Winston.

Moore, D. M., and S. A. Moore. (1992). Possible sentences: An update. In *Reading in the content areas: Improving classroom instruction,* 3d ed. Edited by E. K. Dishner, T. W. Bean, J. E. Readence, and D. W. Moore. Dubuque, IA: Kendall/Hunt Publishing Company.

Nelson-Herber, J. (1986). Expanding and refining vocabulary in content areas. *Journal of Reading* 29:626–633.

Readence, J. E., T. W. Bean, and R. S. Baldwin. (1992). *Content area reading: An integrated approach*, 4th ed. Dubuque, IA: Kendall/Hunt Publishing Company.

Ruddell, M. R. (1992). Integrated content and long-term vocabulary learning with the vocabulary self-collection strategy. In *Reading in the content areas: Improving classroom instruction*, 3d ed. Edited by K. Dishner, T. W. Bean, J. E. Readence, and D. W. Moore. Dubuque, IA: Kendall/Hunt Publishing Company.

Schifini, A. (1994). Language, literacy, and content instruction: Strategies for teachers. In *Kids come in all languages: Reading instruction for ESL students*. Edited by K. Spangenberg-Urbschat and R. Pritchard. Newark, DE: International Reading Association.

Spache, G. D., and E. B. Spache. (1973). *Reading in the elementary school*, 3d ed. Boston: Allyn & Bacon.

Taba, H. (1967). *Teacher's handbook for elementary social studies.* Reading, MA: Addison-Wesley.

Tierney, R. J., J. E. Readence, and E. K. Dishner. (1995). *Reading strategies and practices: A compendium*, 4th ed. Needham Heights, MA: Allyn & Bacon.

Vaughan, S., S. Crawley, and L. Mountain. (1979). A multiple-modality approach to word study: Vocabulary scavenger hunts. *The Reading Teacher* 26:180–186.

**CONTENT
MASTERY
TESTS**

TEST QUESTIONS:
1) TRUE/FALSE
2) MATCHING
3) MULTIPLE CHOICE
4) SHORT ANSWER
5) ESSAY

good tests utilize a well balanced approach, and are valid and reliable

VALIDITY
Does the test measure what it is supposed to?

RELIABILITY
Is the test consistent?

A bchdjifntijfmfkd,do gkoroipkpstsp,potist jiyposspoys;isok;
A bchdjifntijfmfkd,do gkoroipkpstsp,potist jiyposspoys;isok;
A bchdjifntijfmfkd,do gkoroipkpstsp,potist jiyposspoys;isok;
A bchdjifntijfmfkd,do gkoroipkpstsp,potist

COVINGTON M.S.

**ASSESSMENT
TECHNIQUES**

**COOPERATIVE
GROUP TESTING**

CONSENSUS AND
COLLABORATION

JAMAL

TERESA

ANNE

NEW STRATEGIES!

**FORMAL
(STANDARDIZED)
TESTS**

CRITERION
REFERENCED

NORM
REFERENCED

SCORES

raw

scaled

percentile

stanine

age
equivalent

grade
equivalent

**AUTHENTIC
ASSESSMENT**

TEACHER OBSERVATION

INTERVIEWS/CONFERENCES

STUDENT SELF-EVALUATIONS

PORTFOLIOS

BEST
WORK

NARRATIVE
REPORT CARDS

SEMANTIC FEATURE
ANALYSIS (SFA)

PRE READING PLAN
(Prep)

How did I do?
1) Lorem ipsum is a Greeting
2) Type Face to be Used
3) When you want to
4) Indicate Type

**INFORMAL TESTS
(diagnostic)**

IRI

CLOZE

CARI

Learners with Special Needs

To demonstrate mastery of the content, the student will be able to do the following:

PART 1 OBJECTIVES

1. Identify the following strategy, describe its distinguishing features, and assess its significance to teaching content area literacy: PreReading Plan (PreP).
2. Define and assess the importance of validity and reliability as desirable test characteristics.
3. Distinguish norm-referenced from criterion-referenced tests.
4. Interpret the following standardized test scores: raw scores, scaled scores, percentile scores, grade equivalent scores, age equivalent scores, and stanine scores.
5. Distinguish formal (standardized) from informal tests.

PART 2 OBJECTIVES

1. Identify the following strategy, describe its distinguishing features, and assess its significance to teaching content area literacy: Semantic Feature Analysis (SFA).
2. Assess the importance of criterion-referenced mastery tests in the content area classroom, both as assessment and instructional tools.
3. Summarize the five guidelines for test construction you believe will be most valuable to you in developing valid and reliable content area mastery tests.
4. Define cooperative group testing and design a system for using it in the content area(s) and grade(s) level of your choice.

PART 1 OBJECTIVES—continued

6. Provide examples and assess the value of diagnostic tests in the content area classroom.
7. Identify and define the four reading levels in terms of their use in the process of selecting appropriate content area materials.
8. Distinguish the cloze inventory and content area reading inventory in terms of the purposes they serve, their distinguishing features, advantages, and disadvantages as informal assessment techniques in the content area classroom.

PART 2 OBJECTIVES—continued

5. Define the concept of authentic assessment, summarize its distinguishing characteristics, and assess its significance in the content area classroom.
6. Define the concept of portfolios, identify five different types of student work samples, and design your own system of portfolio assessment, including a reporting system you could use as a supplement or alternative to report cards.

INTRODUCTION

In this chapter, assessment will focus on the collection of information about students. Evaluation, on the other hand, will focus on the analysis of that data once they are collected. The process of evaluation is crucial to instructional planning. Evaluation involves making decisions about the best ways to meet the identified learning needs of students. Key to the evaluation process are the selection and development of appropriate assessment instruments, as well as the accurate interpretation of the assessment results.

As a content area classroom teacher, you must be able to interpret formal (standardized) achievement tests properly. You will need to interpret test scores to determine starting points for selecting appropriate materials, as well as for making cooperative grouping assignments. You will also be expected to interpret and explain test scores to parents who often harbor misconceptions about the meanings of some standardized test scores. In this chapter, you will learn to distinguish norm-referenced from criterion-referenced tests. You will also learn how to correctly interpret both types of test scores.

You should be prepared to evaluate standardized test data by noting any discrepancies between your students' test scores and their performances in class. For example, if they demonstrate mastery in class but not on standardized tests, you need to examine and perhaps develop your role as "test facilitator." In this role, you guide students through the process of mastering the types of tasks required of students on standardized tests.

In addition to formal assessment, you will need to be familiar with a variety of informal tests as well. For example, know when and how to use the end-of-chapter and end-of-book tests provided by textbook publishers to assess your students' levels of content mastery. You will also need to design appropriate tests, quizzes, and other means of assessment to match your instructional objectives. This chapter will show you how to use commercially available content mastery tests (i.e., end-of-chapter and end-of-book tests), as well as how to design your own.

One of the most effective ways to use content mastery tests as both teaching and assessment tools is through the use of cooperative group testing. You will learn some ways to design and implement tests that require students to collaborate in small groups. You will also discover ways to score cooperative group tests so that you can assess individual students' content mastery both before and after group collaboration.

This chapter also presents effective alternatives to traditional tests for assessing and documenting mastery of content and literacy skills. You will learn ways to assess authentically students' mastery of content. Through authentic assessment, you can help your students develop portfolios of work that demonstrate progress in literacy skills and content mastery. Authentic assessment portfolios also allow students to demonstrate their abilities to apply content in practical ways and understandings at higher levels of thought. Finally, authentic assessment provides crucial data for the teacher in evaluating teaching effectiveness and planning appropriate instruction.

Two strategies that have been introduced briefly in previous chapters will be developed further in this chapter. The PreReading Plan (PreP) was introduced in Chapter 2 as a means of assessing and activating background knowledge. Semantic Feature Analysis (SFA) was introduced in Chapter 8 as a concept development strategy and an important strategy for English as a second language (ESL) learners. Both of these strategies can be valuable means of assessing background and vocabulary knowledge.

PART 1

STRATEGY: PREREADING PLAN (PREP)

The PreReading Plan (PreP) was developed by Langer (1981) as an easy-to-use set of procedures for assessment and instruction related to students' background knowledge. Through group discussion, both teachers and students can assess students' prior knowledge of text-related information.

You can determine how much information students have on a particular topic and observe and make judgments about the language students use to express their background knowledge. Finally, you can evaluate this information and make decisions about whether students need to develop background information and vocabulary before being able to comprehend the text.

As its name implies, the PreP takes place in preparation of a reading assignment. Your role is that of observer, questioner, and recorder—not critic. In other words, you guide students in their own discovery and processing of what they already know about a concept. In the process, you gain valuable information about your students' levels of background knowledge. At the same time, students benefit by listening to each other's ideas and interpretations.

The following procedures are adapted from the PreP as described by Langer (1981):

1. *Initial associations with the concept.* Select one or more key concepts to present for discussion one at a time. Present the first concept and have students brainstorm ideas they associate with that concept. For example, ask something such as "What comes to mind when you see or hear the term *pollution?*" Record students' responses, even those that are incomplete or inaccurate. The discussion during this phase gives students the opportunity to recognize associations between their prior knowledge and key concepts of the text. For example, ask questions such as "Have you ever seen and smelled *smog?* What did it look like? How did it smell? Is it dangerous to breathe smog? Why or why not? Is it more dangerous than smoking cigarettes? Why or why not?"

2. *Reflections on initial associations.* Lead a discussion to allow students to reflect on and explain their initial associations. Ask such questions as "What made you think of that?" or "Where did you learn that?" The discussion during this phase helps students expand their awareness of prior knowledge by examining relationships and networks of information. For example, ask questions such as "How do you know all this about *air pollution*? How did you know it was dangerous? Why do some places have problems with smog while others don't? Should we be worried about air pollution? Why or why not? What should we do about it? How did you come up with that solution?" This discussion also affords students the opportunity to become aware of their changing ideas as they listen to each other's ideas and explanations. As they participate in the discussion, they have opportunities to consider and then accept, reject, revise, or integrate ideas. For example, ask such questions as "How do cars

cause air pollution? What else causes air pollution? How can we stop polluting our air? Is that solution practical? Is it worth the money it will cost? Why or why not?"

3. *Reformulation of knowledge.* Guide students in making elaborations, additions, deletions, or changes, if any, following the discussion. Ask questions such as "Since our discussion about air pollution, have you thought of anything new you would like to add?" or "Based on our discussion about smog, is there anything you want to take out or change?" This discussion gives students the opportunity to verbalize any elaborations and changes in their ideas.

4. *Assessing levels of prior knowledge.* Following the discussion, you need to decide whether each student has "much," "some," or "little" prior knowledge regarding the topic. The responses of students with much prior knowledge usually involve superordinate concepts, definitions, analogies, or the linking of one concept with another. The responses of students with some prior knowledge include examples, attributes, or defining characteristics. The responses of students with little prior knowledge usually take the form of low-level associations involving morphemes (e.g., prefixes, suffixes, and root words), words that sound similar to the term(s) representing the concept, or personal experiences that are not directly relevant.

5. *Evaluating prior knowledge.* Once you have assessed your students' prior knowledge, evaluate this information and formulate a plan for instruction. Students with little prior knowledge will need opportunities to develop some background knowledge before being expected to master new content. Students with some prior knowledge will need minimal background instruction, and students with much prior knowledge should be ready to meet the challenge of mastering new content. In many cases, students with some or much prior knowledge can help the students with little prior knowledge develop key background concepts.

VALIDITY AND RELIABILITY

Validity and reliability are test characteristics that influence the quality of the test. A test must be *both* valid and reliable to be an effective means of assessment. Therefore, whether you are choosing a commercially available test or developing your own test, you need to consider the extent to which the test is valid and reliable. In the process of developing your own tests, you need to check for validity and reliability and revise the test as necessary to ensure these qualities.

Validity, probably the most important characteristic of a test, refers to the test's ability to measure what it is intended to measure. In other words, does the test actually measure what it says it measures or is supposed to measure? To be useful and beneficial, a test must assess the literacy skills and content mastery you are intending to assess.

Reliability, which refers to consistency, is a prerequisite for validity. For example, if your bathroom scale shows your weight at 130 pounds one minute and 140 pounds the next minute, it is not very reliable (Baumann 1988). In the same way, a test must produce consistent results from the same students—or even from similar students with similar knowledge and skills—to be considered reliable.

Although reliability is a necessary prerequisite for validity, it does not guarantee validity. For example, if your bathroom scale consistently shows your weight at 130 pounds from one minute to the next, it is consistent; however, if your actual weight is 140 pounds, the scale is not a valid indicator of your weight. Although it is consistent, it is still not valid (Baumann 1988). Similarly, a test that produces consistent results is reliable but not necessarily valid.

FORMAL (STANDARDIZED) TESTS

Formal tests, also known as standardized tests, are commercially published assessment instruments developed according to systematic procedures. The publishers determine the content of the test by examining appropriate curricula and instructional materials and conferring with experts in the content or skills areas to be assessed. The test items are prepared by professional writers according to specific criteria. The test is then piloted with a large population of students across the country. From the information gathered by piloting the test, a final version is prepared.

Formal tests are standardized in that they are administered and scored according to a uniform or standard set of conditions, rules, and procedures. Each formal test has specific instructions for administration that are developed as part of the piloting process (e.g., time limits, methods of response, directions to students, and so on). For valid results, those specific instructions must be followed. In addition, each formal test has its own set of specific scoring procedures that must be followed. Both the administration and scoring of formal tests are standardized.

There are two types of formal tests: norm referenced and criterion referenced. Both tests are standardized in terms of administration and scoring but serve different purposes. Being familiar with both types will allow you to interpret the tests and use the information appropriately. Formal tests can be quite useful for helping you identify starting points for instructional materials, content, and grouping. The most important reason for you to be confident about interpreting standardized test results may be an increased ability to explain to parents, and sometimes students, what the scores mean in terms of educational placement and programs. Parents and teachers who misinterpret standardized test scores often misuse the information, resulting in inappropriate instructional decisions for the students involved.

At the secondary level, guidance counselors and other resource personnel should be available to help you interpret standardized test results. However, you have a responsibility to evaluate your students' test results so that you are better able to note any discrepancies between their classroom and standardized test performances. If your students demonstrate mastery of knowledge and competencies in class but not on standardized tests, you may need to explore and develop your role as "test facilitator." That is, you can help prepare your students for taking tests by guiding them through the types of tasks required on standardized tests.

Although standardized tests have been criticized as culturally prejudiced, gender biased, and possibly unreflective of actual learning, they remain today the most cost-effective, valid, and reliable means of measuring student learning outcomes on a large scale. As a result, students' performances on standardized tests have serious implications. For example, test performance determines whether students should be passed from one grade to the next, whether they should graduate from high school, whether they should be admitted to college, and whether they should be admitted to graduate school.

Standardized test scores also have serious implications for teachers and schools. The current trend toward outcome-based education often leads to an overemphasis on standardized test scores. The concept of outcome-based education is well-founded in principle, but the realistic effect may prove devastating. The idea behind outcome-based education is that teaching effectiveness is measured in terms of student-learning outcomes. This concept can be beneficial because it allows individual teachers and schools the freedom to make appropriate instructional decisions as long as student learning can be documented. An unfortunate consequence of outcome-based education, however, is the sole use of standardized tests to measure student learning. Until more authentic forms of assessment (see Part 2 of this chapter) become cost effective, this emphasis on standardized test scores is likely to continue.

Standardized tests as the sole indicator of student learning allows funding and accreditation to be tied directly to test scores. As a result, many teachers and administrators take the short-sighted approach. They begin "teaching to the test" by implementing curricula designed primarily to prepare students for standardized test performance. When test performance becomes the sole educational objective, generally the result is short-term rote learning of disjointed and seemingly irrelevant information.

Unfortunately, this phenomenon of teaching to the test seems to be an increasing trend. Many teachers design their lessons to help students recognize and memorize fixed bodies of knowledge and discrete skills covered on a standardized test. However, these teachers quickly discover that the result of such instruction is boredom and apathy. Students quickly lose interest in learning if the sole purpose is to perform well on a test. Even if students appreciate the significant role standardized test scores can play in their lives, they have difficulty being motivated and enthusiastic about the kinds of passive learning and low-level thinking so often involved in test preparation. The most tragic result of this type of instruction is students who drop out of school. With high school dropout rates in most parts of the country soaring to 30 percent, one has to wonder if improved achievement test scores are worth the price to be paid. If test scores are good, but students have little interest in education or the value of learning, long-term educational benefits have been sacrificed for superficial short-term gains.

The good news is that content area teachers can help their students maximize their performance on standardized tests without teaching to the test. For example, you can make sure your students are familiar and confident with the various formats of standardized test items. Also, if students' knowledge and skills are to be validly assessed, they must have good test-taking skills. You can help your students develop skill and confidence at taking standardized tests by giving them practice and review exercises using a variety of test formats. After discussing each format, give students test-taking tips for different types of questions, and then give them opportunities to practice. (See Chapter 3 for suggestions and ideas on teaching test-taking skills as a study skill.) When standardized tests are a fact of life, the most effective and valuable curriculum for long-term educational gains may be characterized by meaningful and relevant content area instruction and literacy development that incorporates test-taking skills and practice.

Norm-Referenced Tests

Norm-referenced tests are formal tests from which scores are used to compare the performance of a student with that of similar students in the *norming population*. The norming population usually consists of a wide cross-section of students from across the country who were administered the test for the purpose of developing "norms." Norms are statistics such as percentile ranks that indicate relative performance (i.e., how well a student performed in comparison with her or his peers who took the test).

Norm-referenced tests can be used to compare the performance of individual students with one another, individual students with groups of students, or groups of students with one another.

Some commonly known norm-referenced tests include the Iowa Tests of Basic Skills (ITBS), the Comprehensive Tests of Basic Skills (CTBS), the Metropolitan Achievement Tests (MAT), the Pre-Scholastic Aptitude Test (PSAT), the Scholastic Aptitude Test (SAT), the Academic Competencies Test (ACT), the Graduate Record Exam (GRE), the Law School Admissions Test (LSAT), and the General Medical Aptitude Test (GMAT). Norm-referenced tests can produce several types of scores: Make sure you know how to interpret and evaluate these scores appropriately. If instructional decisions are based on misinterpretation of standardized test scores, by both teachers and parents, students can experience serious problems.

Raw Scores

One type of score is the *raw score*, which is simply the number of correct responses. Some raw scores make an adjustment for guessing. Others can include the time taken to complete the test or the number missed. However, most raw scores are stated as the number of items correct.

Scaled Scores

A second type of score is the *scaled score*, which presents the results of a subtest in terms of a continuous scale with equal intervals. This type of score allows you to make comparisons across grade levels. For example, you could compare the score made on a reading subtest by a fifth grader with the scores on the same subtest made by students at other grade levels. Keep in mind, however, that when using scaled scores, you can only make comparisons between grade levels, *not* between subtests. For example, you could not compare a fifth grader's reading subtest score with math subtest scores at any grade level.

Percentile Scores

The third type of score, one of the most commonly used norm-referenced scores, is the *percentile score*, sometimes known as a *percentile rank*. Be careful not to confuse percentile scores with *percentage scores*, which indicate the percent of responses that are correct. Percentile scores show how well a student performed relative to other students within the same grade level of the norming population. Specifically, the percentile score ranks a student's performance by comparing it with the scores earned by the students in the norming group at that grade level. For example, a percentile score of 70 indicates that the student performed as well as or better than 70 percent of the students at that grade level in the norming population.

Grade Equivalency Scores

The fourth and probably the most widely misunderstood, misinterpreted, and misused norm-referenced score is the *grade equivalency score*. The only information a grade equivalency score gives you is how well the student performed compared to other students at different grade levels. Grade equivalency scores represent the average performance, or score, for students at a particular grade level. A grade equivalency score consists of one or two digits followed by a decimal point and another single digit (e.g., 2.9 or 10.1). The digit(s) before the decimal point represent the grade level. The digit following the decimal point represents the month in the traditional nine-month school year (0 through 9).

Every educator must be able to interpret grade equivalency scores appropriately for curricular planning and instructional decision making. Also, every teacher should be able to explain clearly and simply to parents and older students the correct interpretation and implications of grade equivalency scores, avoiding the two following misinterpretations of them.

One frequently encountered misinterpretation is the confusion of grade equivalency scores with the notion of instructional reading level. For example, if a fourth-grade student scored a 6.0 on a reading achievement test, a commonly made mistake is to assume that the student should receive instruction using sixth-grade materials. Too often, you will hear parents or teachers interpreting such a score by saying "This fourth grader is reading at the sixth-grade level. " Although it may very well be the case that this fourth grader is capable of reading sixth-grade–level materials, that conclusion cannot be drawn from a grade equivalency score. A test designed specifically to identify instructional reading levels, such as an informal reading inventory, would have to be administered to determine what grade-level materials the student is capable of reading. Instead, the grade equivalency score indicates that this particular fourth grader performed as well on this particular test as did students who were beginning sixth grade. The correct interpretation is that this fourth grader's reading achievement, as measured by this particular test, is indeed above average.

A second frequently encountered misinterpretation of grade equivalency scores is their use as standards of performance rather than comparison. For example, many school administrators or faculty will set the admirable goal that they want all or almost all of their students reading (or performing in some other area) at or above grade level. There is certainly nothing wrong with such a goal. The problem is the use of grade equivalency scores to measure achievement of the goal, that is, how many students are reading at or above grade level. First, as mentioned previously, the use of grade equivalency scores to identify reading levels is inappropriate. Second, grade equivalency scores are based on the average performance of the norming population, which is determined by the mean (average) or median (middle-ranked) score. Therefore, approximately half of the students in the norming group were above grade level, and the other half were below grade level. Since grade equivalency scores represent average performances, it is not statistically possible to have more than about half of your students earning grade equivalency scores that are at or above grade level.

Age Equivalency Scores

Not surprisingly, age equivalency scores are similar to grade equivalency scores. The difference is that instead of comparing a student's performance to that of students at other grade levels, age equivalency scores compare a student's performance to that of students at other ages. The interpretation of these scores is basically the same as that for grade equivalency scores. Be careful to avoid the same pitfalls of misinterpretation.

Stanine Scores

Stanine scores are a type of *standard score*, which is a score converted on a scale. The relationship between raw scores and converted scores is the same throughout the scale because standard scores are evenly spaced across the scale, unlike percentiles, which have more scores toward the middle and fewer scores at either end. Stanines consist of single-digit scores, ranging from 1 to 9. Stanines from 1 to 3 represent below-average performances, 4 to 6 represent average performances, and from 7 to 9 represent above-average performances. As you can see, stanines are fairly easy to interpret and can be compared across tests and subtests.

Criterion-Referenced Tests

A *criterion-referenced test* is different from a norm-referenced test in that it does not compare a student's performance to that of others. Instead, criterion-referenced tests measure a student's performance relative to her or his previous performance or relative to a predetermined set of mastery criteria. Mastery is determined by comparing a student's score with the established standard or "cut-off score," which indicates mastery for that particular test or subtest.

Criterion-referenced tests are useful as pretests to determine which students have already mastered the skills or content and which students need instruction. Criterion-referenced tests are also useful as posttests to determine which students have successfully mastered the skills or content and which students need reteaching. Considering these uses, you can see why criterion-referenced tests are sometimes called objective-referenced tests or mastery tests. Some commonly known criterion-referenced tests include the Stanford Diagnostic Reading Test (SDRT), Texas Academic Skills Program (TASP), the Test of Academic Achievement in School (TAAS), and the Examination for Teacher Certification (ExCet).

Many criterion-referenced tests can be used to assess subskill knowledge and competence. Once evaluated, this information can be useful for grouping students according to specific skill needs. In addition, some of these tests including the Fountain Valley Test and the McGraw Hill Test offer a reference guide for teachers. This guide identifies the texts and page numbers appropriate for reteaching specific subskills.

INFORMAL DIAGNOSTIC TESTS

Following is a comprehensive definition of informal tests according to Baumann (1988, 7):

> *Informal tests* are assessment instruments that are usually diagnostic and criterion-referenced. They are not usually standardized. Such instruments may be either teacher-made or commercially available. They may be administered to either a group or an individual. The essence of informal tests as opposed to standardized tests, however, is that they are intended to provide specific (often diagnostic) information about an individual pupil's performance so that concrete, instructional decisions can be made about the learning program for the individual.

Several types of diagnostic tests can be helpful to you as a content area teacher. Most of them are designed to help you assess your students' literacy skills including reading, writing, critical thinking, vocabulary, and study skills. Some are commercially available and should be an important part of every school's curriculum library. Some are teacher made to fit your particular curriculum and instruction. Although they can be time consuming to create, diagnostic tests can be easily filed and reused. The valuable information you can gain from informal tests makes instructional planning and decision making much easier. Therefore, the time investment is a wise one.

Informal Reading Inventories (IRIs)

The IRI is administered individually with the teacher or some other qualified person. This test can give you substantial information about a student's reading levels and strengths and weaknesses in terms of reading skills such as word recognition, concept development, and various levels of comprehension. For example, as a content area teacher, IRI data can be evaluated for deciding how best to help students who have trouble reading the materials or seem bored and unchallenged by the curriculum. Therefore, you should be ready when the need for diagnosis arises by keeping at least one informal reading inventory (IRI) that you know how to use in your classroom. Ask your school's diagnostician or reading specialist to show you how to use it. You will need a few dress rehearsals with students before actually using it for diagnosis.

Reading Levels

The IRI identifies four different reading levels for the student (see Figure 9–1). Understanding these levels is crucial to the process of evaluating IRI and other informal test results. Knowing your students' reading levels and listening comprehension potentials can help you select materials that are challenging but not frustrating.

The *independent level* is the highest level at which a student can be expected to read without assistance. Students who read extensively for pleasure or have special reading talents generally have independent reading levels at or above their grade levels. These students generally can be expected to read grade-level materials with little or no assistance and may even become bored or unchallenged by grade-level materials. Knowing your students' independent reading levels is important for selecting books and other materials for enrichment and independent work. For example, if you have a sixth grader with an independent reading level of fourth grade, you will need to provide some fourth-grade–level materials for independent reading and research. Using Betts' (1946) criteria (see Figure 9–1), a student's independent level is the level at which word recognition is almost 100 percent (at least 99 percent) accurate, and comprehension is at least 90 percent accurate.

The *instructional level* is the highest level at which a student can be expected to read with guidance from the teacher or study guides. Students who are average readers generally have an instructional level at grade level and can therefore be expected to read grade-level materials with adequate preparation for reading including developing of background

FIGURE 9–1 Criteria for estimating reading levels in an informal reading inventory

WORD RECOGNITION ACCURACY	COMPREHENSION ACCURACY	READING LEVEL
99–100%	at least 90%	independent
95–98%	at least 75%	instructional
below 95%	below 75%	frustration
not applicable	highest level with at least 75%	listening

knowledge and vocabulary, setting specific purposes for reading, monitoring by the teacher during reading, and following up or evaluating through discussion after reading. Strategies for content area literacy instruction provide the guidance needed at students' instructional reading levels. Knowing your students' instructional reading levels is important because you may need to provide books and other alternate materials for instruction. For example, if you have an eighth grader with an instructional reading level of sixth grade, you may need to provide sixth-grade–level materials for instruction. Likewise, if you have an eighth grader with an instructional reading level of tenth grade, you may need to provide some tenth-grade–level materials for instruction. Using Betts's (1946) criteria (see Figure 9–1), a student's instructional level is the level at which word recognition is between 95 and 98 percent accurate, and comprehension is at least 75 percent accurate. Baumann (1988) suggests that in some cases (depending on the content, materials, student, and so forth), an instructional level can be indicated by word recognition accuracy that is at least 91 percent and comprehension accuracy that is at least 50 percent.

The *frustration level* is the level at which a student cannot be expected to read successfully, even with extensive guidance from the teacher. Students are generally frustrated because they do not have the background knowledge, vocabulary, word recognition skills, or reading experience necessary to read at that level. These students need alternate materials or adapted instruction (see Chapters 2, 3, 5, and 11). It is important to know your students' frustration reading levels for the same reason you need to know their independent and instructional levels: you may need to provide alternate materials. For example, a seventh grader with a frustration reading level of seventh grade may need lower-level materials for instruction. At the same time, a seventh grader with a frustration level of tenth grade may need to be provided with more challenging materials. Using Betts's (1946) criteria (see Figure 9–1), a frustration level is clearly indicated by word recognition accuracy of 90 percent or less, and comprehension accuracy of 50 percent or less. Baumann (1988) suggests that, in some cases (depending on the content, materials, student, and so forth), a frustration level can be indicated by word recognition accuracy that is 94 percent or less, and comprehension accuracy that is 74 percent or less.

The *listening level* or *capacity level* is the highest level at which a student can comprehend satisfactorily materials read orally to her or him (i.e., at least 75 percent comprehension). The listening level indicates the student's potential for successful reading. In other words, if a student can comprehend the content read orally to her or him, he or she should have the requisite language development and background knowledge for learning to read at that level. Therefore, the listening level for an average reader should match her or his instructional level. A student with reading problems may have a listening level higher than her/his instructional level. With special instruction (e.g., in decoding skills) and appropriate materials (e.g., instructional level), that student should be able to learn to read successfully at her or his listening level.

Commercially Published IRIs

Informal reading inventories (IRIs) can be either teacher made or commercially published. Because the quality of the commercially available informal reading inventories is excellent and the process for developing IRIs can be extremely complicated and time consuming, content area teachers are encouraged to use commercially made IRIs. Any or all of the ones recommended in this section or Appendix L would make valuable additions to your school or classroom curriculum library.

Because it must be administered in a one-on-one situation, the IRI can be very time consuming. Therefore, you will need to plan occasional times when you can work individually with students and identify places where you can work privately. You could also train a teacher's aide to administer IRIs or ask the school's diagnostician or reading specialist to do it for you. Appendix L provides a list of some commercially available IRIs.

Group IRIs

Some group IRIs are also available such as the *Group Assessment in Reading* (Warncke and Shipman 1984) and the *Johnston Informal Reading Inventory* (Johnston 1982). The advantage of group IRIs is obvious: they are less time consuming because you can give them to more than one student at a time. However, if it seems too good to be true, it probably is. Although group IRIs can be useful for estimating reading levels for groups of students, they are not as valid or informative in terms of evaluating and diagnosing strengths and weaknesses as individually administered IRIs.

One major disadvantage of group IRIs is the lack of a word-identification measure. To obtain such a measure, have each student read aloud a one hundred-word passage for a quick count of word recognition errors. Although having students read aloud short passages to check word recognition accuracy actually takes little of the teacher's time; you can also train a teacher's aide or parent volunteer to take the oral reading sample. Another alternative is to have students read the passage into a tape recorder (Baumann 1988).

Convert the errors to a percentage of words correctly identified (e.g., five errors in a one hundred-word passage indicates a 95 percent word recognition accuracy). As mentioned in the section on reading levels, an independent level is usually indicated by almost 100 percent accuracy. An instructional level is indicated by at least 95 percent, although sometimes it can be as low as 91 percent. A frustration level is shown by 90 percent or less, although sometimes it can be as high as 94 percent.

Cloze Inventories

The *cloze inventory,* also known as a cloze test, is similar to the cloze activity, which was introduced and discussed in Chapter 8 as an activity for helping students develop the use of context clues as a word recognition skill. As an assessment tool, the cloze inventory is a screening device used for helping teachers determine whether selected materials are appropriate for their students' needs and abilities. The cloze inventory is based on the concept of closure or filling in unknown information based on what is known. The spelling of *cloze* is derived from the pronunciation of the word *closure.*

A cloze inventory consists of a passage with words deleted at regular intervals. Students are given the passage, without reading it in advance, and asked to fill in as many blanks as possible. The idea behind the cloze inventory is that students who can satisfactorily read the passage should be able to fill in at least half the blanks.

The major advantage of the cloze inventory is that it is very easy to develop, administer, and score. The disadvantage is that it provides rather limited information for evaluation. Basically, the cloze inventory answers only two yes/no questions: *Are these particular materials appropriate for instruction for this student? If not, are they too easy or too hard?* If the answer to the first question is "no," you can then use the answer to the second question to select different materials. Administer another cloze inventory to check the suitability of the newly selected materials. If the answer to the first question is "yes," it needs to be verified by following up with another assessment inventory, such as a content area reading inventory (CARI) (see next section), which gives you more detailed information for the evaluation of each student's abilities to read the materials.

Developing Cloze Inventories

A cloze inventory is relatively quick and easy to develop. Preferably, the passage you choose should be retyped using double spacing and uniform blanks (ten to fifteen typed spaces) for each deleted word. Following are recommended procedures for developing a cloze inventory:

1. Select a passage of about two hundred to four hundred words in continuous text (i.e., do not leave out or rearrange text); a shorter passage can be used with primary-grade materials. The passage should be one not previously read by students and representative of the difficulty level of most of the text. The passage should be selected from the beginning of a chapter or chapter section so that

understanding it is not significantly dependent on previous material. If possible, the passage should be long enough to allow at least fifty blanks (according to the instructions that follow).

2. Leave intact the first sentence for primary grades and the first few sentences (about twenty-five words) for intermediate and upper grades. Also, leave the last sentence of the passage intact. These complete sentences are important in providing students with sufficient information for closure.

3. Beginning with the first sentence after the "lead-in" sentence(s), delete every fifth, seventh, or tenth word depending on the grade level, length, content difficulty, concept density, and linguistic complexity of the passage. Be consistent; for example, if you choose to delete every fifth word, then use that pattern throughout the passage.

4. Develop a brief set of written instructions to precede the test. The instructions should communicate the following:

   ▌ Because this activity is not a test or assignment, you will not be graded on it.

   ▌ This activity is called an *inventory*, and the purpose of it is to help me, the teacher, decide if this book is too hard, too easy, or just right for you.

   ▌ Although you will not receive a grade, this inventory is very important, so you should do your best in completing it.

   ▌ You should fill in each blank with only one word.

   ▌ If you do not know what word should go in the blank, take a guess. Even if you are not sure, you should not leave any blank.

   ▌ Do not worry about spelling. As long as I can figure out what the word is supposed to be, it does not have to be spelled correctly.

   ▌ You should have plenty of time to finish this inventory. However, since you will not receive a grade, do not worry if you have not finished when time is up.

   ▌ Before filling in any blanks, read the whole thing to yourself. Think carefully about the words around the blanks. Use those words to help you figure out what words should go in the blanks.

   ▌ After reading through the whole test, go back and read it again. While reading it the second time, begin filling in the blanks. You may read it as many times as you wish.

   ▌ Deciding what words should go in the blanks can be very difficult. Do not worry if you cannot figure out many of them. You are only expected to guess about half of them correctly.

Administering and Scoring Cloze Inventories

Before administering a cloze inventory, prepare your students by giving them some practice with the format. Do a sample inventory with them, showing them how you use the words provided to decide which words go in the blanks. After guiding them through a sample inventory, have them complete one or more samples independently for additional practice. Reiterate that students will not be graded on this activity, and that it is very important that they do their very best in completing it.

After ensuring your students are familiar with the format of the cloze inventory, administer and score it using the following procedures:

1. After guiding students through a short sample of a cloze inventory, pass out the tests and read the instructions orally while students follow along silently.
2. Give students adequate time to finish the inventory. One way is to allow about 45 minutes to an hour (to those who need that much time). Another way is to observe students carefully while they are completing the inventory and stop them only when almost all students have finished.
3. Encourage those who finish early to read back over their inventories for careless mistakes and any items they may have left blank. Have a quiet activity planned for those who finish early; for example, make sure students have leisure-reading books at their desks.
4. Do not allow students to score the inventories themselves. Even though a low score (e.g., 50 percent) can represent an acceptable performance on a cloze inventory, such a score can be very discouraging and degrading. Students are not accustomed to such low scores being acceptable.
5. You can score the cloze inventory in one of two ways. The first way—accepting the exact word only—is recommended because it is much quicker and easier, while being equally valid. The second way, accepting synonyms, is extremely difficult, time consuming, and subjective, with few advantages to make it worthwhile. In addition to the process being very tedious, subjective judgments about which synonyms are acceptable can vary. Therefore, the results can also be highly inconsistent. Perhaps surprisingly, research comparing both techniques of scoring cloze inventories has found virtually no difference between the two in terms of reading level placements (McKenna 1976). Based on cloze test research, most reading specialists use and recommend the exact-word scoring method. The synonym method is more appropriately used for cloze activities designed for instruction and vocabulary development.
6. Count the number correct and compute a percentage by dividing it by the total number of blanks. Use the ranges provided in Figure 9–2 to find the answers to the questions the cloze inventory is designed to answer: *Are these particular materials appropriate for instruction for this student? If not, are they too easy or too hard?*

FIGURE 9–2   Criteria for estimating reading levels with a cloze inventory

PERCENTAGE CORRECT	ESTIMATED READING LEVEL
61–100	independent
40–60	instructional
0–39	frustration

7. If a student scores in the independent or instructional range, the materials are probably appropriate, and you are ready to follow up with a content area reading inventory (CARI) as described in the next section. For students in the instructional range, you need to use the information you obtain from the CARI to provide enough preparation, guidance, and follow-up for reading assignments.

8. For students who score in the independent range, the possibility exists that they will be bored and unchallenged by the materials. Thus, you should obtain materials that are more challenging and repeat the cloze inventory. When you find appropriate materials, keep them in case you need to use them as enrichment or alternate materials. (See the section on gifted and talented students in Chapter 11 for enrichment ideas and suggestions for selecting and using alternate materials.)

9. For students who score in the frustration range, you need to obtain easier materials and try the cloze inventory again. When you find suitable materials, follow up with a CARI. With the information you obtain from the CARI, you may need to design instruction for these students to provide a great deal of structure, support, guidance, and monitoring. (See Chapters 3, 5, and 11 for ideas on finding or developing alternate materials and adapting instruction for students who have difficulty reading the material.)

Content Area Reading Inventories (CARIs)

Once you have identified appropriate materials using a cloze inventory, follow up with a *content area reading inventory* (CARI), also known as a *group reading inventory, content reading inventory,* or *content informal reading inventory.* The purpose of the CARI is to gather specific information about each student's strengths and weaknesses with respect to reading and studying the identified materials—information not afforded by the cloze test. Although the CARI is more time consuming than the cloze test to develop, administer, and score, the CARI tells you much more about students' abilities and needs than the cloze test. For example, it can help you assess content mastery, background knowledge, vocabulary, and study skills. The CARI is designed to help content area teachers assess the variety of factors necessary to determine whether students are capable of reading and learning the content using specifically identified materials.

Some commercially published CARIs are available such as *Content Inventories: English, social studies, science* (McWilliams and Rakes 1979). However, making your own CARIs is recommended so that you can use the actual materials you have selected for instruction. The inventory then becomes a more valid predictor of each student's ability to read, study, and learn the content using those particular materials. Although creating CARIs can be time consuming, you can file and reuse them. Also, since the diagnostic information you get from them is directly related to the students' abilities to learn from your specific instructional materials, planning becomes easier and more efficient.

Developing Your Own CARIs

Following is a set of procedures recommended to help you develop your own CARIs. These procedures are designed for developing a CARI for a content area textbook, but they can be modified easily for use with nonfiction, reference materials, or other content area instructional materials. Keep in mind that the CARI should have two main parts. One part should assess the student's literacy skills, and the other content mastery.

Part 1: Literacy skills. Part 1 of your CARI should assess the students' abilities to do the following. First, you should see how well they can use components of the textbook as study aids (e.g., table of contents, glossary, pictures, charts, and graphs). Second, evaluate how well students can use library and classroom reference materials (e.g., encyclopedias, the card catalogue, *The Reader's Guide to Periodical Literature,* and dictionaries). Third, determine to what extent students can apply study skills (e.g., SQ3R, previewing, setting purposes, formulating questions, monitoring comprehension, outlining, and adapting rate). To assess the aforementioned abilities, develop Part 1 of a CARI by following these steps:

1. Decide which of the following textbook study aids students need to use to read and learn the material. Although you may use the following list to guide you in making your selections, you need not use all of them, and you need not limit your CARI to these features. You may think of others you want to include instead of or as well as these.

   ____table of contents   ____glossary
   ____index   ____appendices
   ____bibliographies   ____preface
   ____chapter introductions   ____chapter summaries

        ____chapter questions   ____chapter outlines
        ____chapter objectives   ____graphic organizers
        ____headings and subheadings   ____charts, tables, and graphs
        ____maps and keys   ____flow charts and diagrams
        ____photographs and captions   ____illustrations and captions

2. Next decide which of the following classroom and library reference materials students must be able to use to read and learn the material. You may think of others you want to include instead of or in addition to these.

        ____encyclopedias   ____content-specific reference books
        ____*The Reader's Guide*   ____dictionary
        ____card catalogue   ____thesaurus

3. Decide which of the following study skills or strategies students need to be able to use to read and learn the material. Again, you may think of others you want to include instead of or in addition to these.

        ____SQ3R   ____previewing
        ____setting purposes   ____formulating questions
        ____monitoring comprehension ____outlining
        ____adapting rate   ____developing graphic organizers

4. Depending on the number of textbook study aids, reference materials, and study skills you identified as important, write between ten and twenty items designed to assess students' knowledge of and abilities to use them. You can develop these items in the form of objective questions (e.g., matching, multiple choice, or fill-in-the-blank) or subjective questions (e.g., open-ended short answer or essay). These items will comprise Part 1 of your CARI. Following are some examples:

▮ Match the textbook part in the left-hand column with its description in the right-hand column:

    table of contents   list of recommended readings
    glossary   introduction to the book
    preface   list of topics and page numbers
    index   alphabetical list of terms and definitions
    bibliography   alphabetical list of terms and page numbers

▮ Select the best choice to answer each of the following questions:

When should you read the chapter questions?

    a. before reading the chapter
    b. while reading the chapter
    c. after reading the chapter
    d. before, while, and after reading the chapter

How should you use the chapter objectives?

    a. as purposes for reading
    b. to monitor your understanding while reading

    c. to find out how much you learned after reading

    d. all of the above

Where would be the best place to begin looking for articles on a particular topic?

    a. encyclopedias

    b. the card catalogue

    c. *The Reader's Guide to Periodical Literature*

    d. a dictionary

Where would you look to find out what books a library has on a particular topic?

    a. *The Reader's Guide to Periodical Literature*

    b. the card catalogue

    c. the appendix

    d. an encyclopedia

■ Fill in the blank in each of the following sentences with the most appropriate word from the list that follows. You may use each word no more than once:

    appendices   appendix

    headings   subheadings

    When you want to see an example of or more information about the topic, look in the _____ in the back of the book.

    The main topics of a chapter can be previewed before reading by looking at the _____ in boldfaced print.

    The list of _____ in the table of contents tells you what additional information can be found at the back of the book.

    Important details related to the main topics of a chapter can be identified by looking at the _____ .

■ Use your textbook to answer the following questions:

    On what page does Chapter 3 begin and what is the title of Chapter 5? _____

    What is the meaning of the term _____ ?

    What information is summarized on the chart on page 47?

    _____

    Describe in your own words the process shown in the flow chart on page 62. _____

    On what pages is the concept _____ explained?

    According to the table on page 29, what are the meanings of the following symbols? _____

    Look at the map on page 70. What distance is represented by each centimeter? _____

On the map on page 14, what is represented by the color brown? _____

Read the caption of the photograph on page 84 and describe in your own words how this picture is related to the information described on page 83. _____

Formulate a question from each subheading on pages 23–25.
_____

▮ Answer the following questions about how you would read and study a textbook assignment:

Identify and briefly describe each of the five steps in the SQ3R study strategy. _____

What should you think about in deciding how to adapt your reading rate appropriately? _____

What should you do if you come across a word you cannot pronounce? _____

What should you do if you come across a word you can pronounce, but whose meaning you do not understand?
_____

What does "setting purposes for reading" mean? _____

Why and how should you set purposes before reading? _____

How can you check yourself to make sure you are understanding what you are reading? _____

Should you ever go back and reread parts of or all of an assignment? If so, when? _____

Distinguish an outline from a graphic organizer. In reviewing a chapter, would you prefer to outline it or develop a graphic organizer for it? Why? _____

Part 2: Content mastery.   While Part 1 assesses literacy skills, Part 2 of the CARI should assess knowledge of content. First, it should assess quantity and quality of students' background knowledge. Second, it should assess students' understandings of key vocabulary and their mastery of the content, including key concepts. To develop Part 2 of your CARI, follow these steps:

1. Select a textbook chapter or chapter section from the beginning of the book (i.e., within the first three chapters) that students could be expected to read in about ten to forty minutes. The passage length will depend on the grade level, difficulty of the material, and length of the class period. A good guideline is to "study" read, i.e., read slowly, the material for about half the time of a regular class period. Then, select about half the amount you were able to read in that amount of time. Primary-level (i.e., grades 1–2) children might be

expected to read for about ten to fifteen minutes. Intermediate (3–5) and middle school (6–8) students might be expected to read for about twenty to thirty minutes, and high school students thirty to forty minutes. In addition to age, you should also consider the abilities of your students and the concept density (i.e., the number of difficult concepts) in determining the length of the passage.

2. Using the textbook passage you selected, identify or summarize the background knowledge including specialized vocabulary that students need to have in order to read and learn the material. The textbook teachers' guide can be quite helpful in providing or helping you determine requisite background knowledge.

3. Again using the textbook passage you selected, identify the key vocabulary students need to learn rapidly, either with assistance from you or on their own, using textbook study aids and external reference materials. In other words, these are vocabulary words students need not have mastered before instruction, but they should be capable of learning them with some teacher assistance. Again, the textbook teachers' guide can be helpful in identifying key vocabulary.

4. Identify from the selected textbook passage the key concepts that represent the content students will be expected to master. As with vocabulary, students do not need to demonstrate prior mastery but do need to be able to master the concepts from reading the text with guidance from the teacher and support from external references. Once again, check the textbook teachers' guide for assistance in identifying the key concepts students will be expected to learn.

5. Depending on the amount of requisite knowledge and the number of vocabulary and concepts students will be expected to master, develop between ten and twenty items. Some of the items should be designed to assess background knowledge, and others understandings of key vocabulary gained from reading the passages. The remaining items should assess comprehension at all levels of thought, including literal-level recall of facts, interpretive-level inferences, and applied-level judgments. The items can be either objective (i.e., multiple choice, matching, true/false, fill-in-the-blank, and so on) or subjective (i.e., open-ended short answer or essay).

Administering and Scoring CARIs

Plan to administer the CARI in one or two class periods. For elementary students especially, administer Parts 1 and 2 on different days. Although middle and high school students should be able to complete both parts in one class period, you may want to administer the parts on different days so that those who need more time will have it.

Develop written directions to precede Part 1 of the CARI. Make sure that you read orally and discuss the directions with the students immediately before they begin completing Part 1. Your directions should include the following:

- Because this activity is not a test or assignment, you will not be graded on it.
- This activity is called an *inventory*, and the purpose of it is to help me, the teacher, plan lessons that will help you learn better.
- Although you will not receive a grade, this inventory is very important, so you should do your best in completing it.
- You should answer every question, even if you have to guess.
- You should have plenty of time to finish this inventory. However, since you will not receive a grade, do not worry if you have not finished when time is up.
- Part 1 of this inventory is designed to help me find out how much you know about the parts of your textbook, various library reference books, and different kinds of study skills.
- You will need to use your textbook to answer the questions about its parts.

Develop a set of written directions to precede Part 2 of the CARI. Again, you should read orally and discuss these directions with your students immediately before they begin Part 2. Your directions should include the following:

- Part 2 of this inventory is designed to help me find out how well you can read and study this textbook. I will use this information to plan lessons that will help you learn better and have fun learning.
- In this part of the inventory, you will read several pages and then answer some questions about it.
- If you are interested in assessing comprehension more than recall, tell students that they will be allowed to look back in the passage to answer the questions. If you allow them to look back, be sure that you print the questions on separate paper to make it easier for them to refer to the passage. (These responses should be evaluated rather stringently.)
- If you are more interested in assessing recall, tell students that they will not be allowed to look back in the passage to answer the questions. (These responses may be evaluated more leniently.)
- If you want to know your students' rates of reading the passage, have them all begin at the same time. Then, tell them to write down the time when they finish reading. For younger students who cannot tell time, keep the elapsed time written on the board and tell them to copy it down when they finish.

Prepare students for reading the passage for Part 2 in the following ways:

- Provide any background knowledge necessary for understanding its content.
- Introduce the passage by briefly stating its content.
- Somehow relate the passage to the students' personal lives and experiences.
- Set a purpose for reading by telling students that they will be expected to answer "right there" questions about important vocabulary, facts, and main ideas. Tell them also that they will need to answer some "think and search" and "in my head" questions.

You should score the CARI in two parts. First, develop a class checklist for mastery of literacy skills. Down the left-hand side of the page, list the students' names. Across the top of the page, label columns for the literacy skills and content mastery you are assessing (e.g., parts of a textbook, library reference materials, study skills, vocabulary, and comprehension). You may divide these skills into subskills; for example, the parts of a textbook could be listed as four (or more) columns, e.g., table of contents, index, graphic aids, and glossary. Another option is to divide "comprehension" into subskills, e.g., literal, interpretive, and applied. Make a grid by drawing lines for rows and columns. Then, place symbols (e.g., check, plus, minus, and so forth) in the appropriate boxes of the grid to indicate each student's skill mastery or need for instruction. See Figure 9–3 for a sample of a checklist of skill mastery for a class. Use this master list for grouping students, selecting materials, and planning instruction according to the specific needs of your students.

Second, score Part 2 of the CARI by identifying mastery criteria for vocabulary knowledge and comprehension or recall. If students are allowed to refer to the passage to answer the questions, set your criteria toward the higher end of the range. If students are not allowed to refer to the passage, set the criteria at the lower end of the range. If they are allowed to refer to the passage for some but not all of the questions, set the criteria toward the middle of the range. See Figure 9–4 for recommended criteria ranges.

The scores and information about students' strengths and weaknesses obtained from a CARI will be helpful in the evaluation process involved in selecting materials, planning instruction, and grouping students. This information is especially useful at the beginning of the year or semester or whenever you have new students. Remember, however, that this information is designed to provide you with starting points only. You will need to observe and monitor the progress of your students carefully to make sure that the materials are challenging without being frustrating. Make adjustments after your initial decisions using CARI results.

FIGURE 9–3 Sample content area reading inventory checklist of skill mastery for a class

STUDENTS: Anson, Julie; Barrett, Ken; Cheng, Nina; Davis, Brent; Eagle, Tom; Flores, Rosa; Gates, Terry; Hill, Denise; Ingall, Laura; Jones, David; King, Donell; Lopez, Juan; McFar, Lisa

PARTS OF A TEXTBOOK
- table of contents
- index
- graphic aids
- glossary
- chapter introductions
- chapter summaries
- headings and subheadings

LIBRARY REFERENCE MATERIALS
- encyclopedias
- The Reader's Guide
- card catalogue
- dictionary and thesaurus
- content-specific references

STUDY SKILLS
- SQ3R (or variation)
- setting purposes
- monitoring
- adapting rate
- previewing
- formulating questions
- outlining
- developing graphic organizers

VOCABULARY
- context clues
- prefixes
- suffixes
- root words

LITERAL COMPREHENSION
INTERPRETIVE COMPREHENSION
APPLIED COMPREHENSION

FIGURE 9–3 Sample content area reading inventory checklist of skill mastery for a class—continued

STUDENTS

Column headers (skill categories):

PARTS OF A TEXTBOOK
- table of contents
- index
- graphic aids
- glossary
- chapter introductions
- chapter summaries
- headings and subheadings

LIBRARY REFERENCE MATERIALS
- encyclopedias
- The Reader's Guide
- card catalogue
- dictionary thesaurus
- content-specific references

STUDY SKILLS
- SQ3R (or variation)
- setting purposes
- monitoring
- adapting rate
- previewing
- formulating questions
- outlining
- developing graphic organizers

VOCABULARY
- context clues
- prefixes
- suffixes
- root words

LITERAL COMPREHENSION
INTERPRETIVE COMPREHENSION
APPLIED COMPREHENSION

Students (rows):
- Nguyen, Lan
- Oster, Randy
- Prince, Karen
- Quinten, Sara
- Ramos, Hector
- Samson, Mark
- Torres, Luci
- Umber, Casey
- Vinson, Jill
- Weston, Amy
- Xavier, Mary
- Ybarra, Jose
- Zader, Jan

FIGURE 9–4 Criteria for estimating reading levels with a content area reading inventory

PERCENTAGE CORRECT	ESTIMATED READING LEVEL
85–100	independent
65–84	instructional
0–64	frustration

Students who score in the independent range might be bored and unchallenged by the materials; consider making materials available that are more challenging for them. (See the section on gifted and talented students in Chapter 11 for enrichment ideas and suggestions for selecting and using alternate materials.) Students who score in the instructional range should find the materials challenging and with adequate instruction should be able to master them without experiencing frustration. For these students, you will need to provide sufficient preparation, guidance, and follow-up for reading assignments. Students who score in the frustration range will probably not be able to handle these materials even with support and guidance; you should consider adapting the materials or finding suitable alternatives, as well as providing a great deal of structure, support, guidance, and monitoring. (See Chapters 2, 3, 5, and 11 for ideas on finding or developing alternate materials and adapting instruction for students who have difficulty reading the material.)

PART 2

STRATEGY: SEMANTIC FEATURE ANALYSIS (SFA)

The Semantic Feature Analysis (SFA) (Johnson and Pearson 1984) was introduced in Chapter 8 as a strategy designed to help students improve their vocabulary through categorizing, comparing, and contrasting related words. Although originally designed as a concept development strategy, SFA can also be used for assessment purposes. For example, it can be used as a prereading activity to assess students' prior understandings of vocabulary and key concepts. It can also be used as a postreading activity to measure the extent to which students have mastered key vocabulary and concepts.

Figure 9–5 provides an example of a completed feature matrix developed from an SFA. Procedures for implementing the strategy should provide a significant amount of teacher guidance at first. Begin by choosing categories that are concrete and familiar to the students (e.g., plants, dinosaurs, geometric shapes, insects, sports). Gradually use more abstract and less familiar categories (e.g., communities, countries, heroes/heroines, cultures, diseases). Prepare the matrix by listing words in the category down the left margin of the page and features across the top.

At first, guide students through the process of completing the matrix by modeling and thinking aloud as you decide whether each word possesses each of the identified features. At first, use a + or – to indicate "yes" or "no." Eventually, you can begin using more sophisticated systems of response such as a Likert scale that indicates frequency (e.g., 1 = never, 2 = some, 3 = always) or degree (e.g., 1 = a little, 2 = some, 3 = a lot) (Tierney, Readence, and Dishner 1995). Help students examine and discuss how all the words in the matrix are related yet clearly unique.

Once students become familiar with the process, they should complete the matrix on their own, in pairs, or in small groups. Then they can begin to participate in the process of developing the matrix itself. Until they develop confidence with the process, help them limit the number of words and features in the matrix. Eventually, students can expand the

---

FIGURE 9–5   Semantic Feature Analysis matrix completed for a geography lesson

---

CATEGORY: SOUTH AMERICAN COUNTRIES

	mountains	rain forests	coastline	desert	Spanish-speaking
Argentina	+	–	+	–	+
Bolivia	+	+	–	+	+
Brazil	+	+	+	–	–
Chile	+	–	+	+	+
Colombia	+	+	+	–	+
Ecuador	+	+	+	+	+
French Guiana	+	+	+	–	–
Guyana	+	+	+	–	–
Paraguay	–	–	–	–	+
Peru	+	+	+	+	+
Surinam	+	+	+	–	–
Uruguay	–	–	+	–	+
Venezuela	+	+	+	–	+

matrix by generating new words to be added and new features to be analyzed. Again, over time students should analyze and discuss the matrix with little help from you. The completed matrices can then be evaluated by the teacher to make instructional planning decisions.

CONTENT MASTERY TESTS (CRITERION-REFERENCED)

Content mastery tests are usually criterion-referenced tests because they are designed to determine whether students have achieved acceptable levels of mastery and are ready to move on to more advanced content. This type of testing also provides important feedback to teachers to help them evaluate and, if necessary, modify or redesign instruction (Taylor 1987). You can use both commercially made and teacher-made criterion-referenced tests to assess your students' content mastery.

Commercially Made

Commonly used commercially made content mastery tests include end-of-book and end-of-chapter tests that accompany the textbook. Also, many teachers' guides provide test banks of possible items for assessing your students' content mastery. You will need to examine the commercially made tests and test items available to you and decide whether they validly assess your particular curriculum and instruction. Even if they accompany the textbook or other instructional materials you use, they may not evaluate the content you have emphasized during instruction. Further, they may not evaluate understanding at the levels you expect of your students. Although commercially made tests can be very convenient, analyze them thoroughly before deciding whether they suit your assessment needs. You might also consider using parts of them along with items you design to develop a test that provides a valid reflection of your students' learning.

Teacher-Made

Teacher-made tests are probably the most commonly used type of content mastery test. If constructed properly, they can provide valid indicators of your students' levels of content mastery. However, test construction is something of an art, which takes a great deal of time, preparation, practice, consulting, and rewriting. You need to begin now to think about how you can fairly and accurately assess your students' learning.

Tests are important for several reasons. First, they provide crucial feedback to the students to let them know how they are doing, how they need to adjust study habits and strategies, and what they need to improve. Second, tests provide important feedback to the teacher, which allows him or her to modify instruction and materials as necessary to meet the needs of the students. Third, if grades are required in your school, tests help you assign them as reflections of learning.

Fourth, and perhaps most importantly, your tests communicate to your students what content is important in your discipline. The content over which you test provides students with information that guides them in their methods of study. Therefore, your tests should reflect the content you emphasize in your lessons and assignments. If you emphasize understanding of general concepts and their relationships, for example, then knowledge of general concepts and their relationships should be necessary for passing the test. If you instead test literal recall of minor details, you are at best sending mixed messages to your students. At worst, you are telling them that although you emphasized key concepts in class, what is really important in your discipline is the knowledge of minor details required for passing the test.

Furthermore, your tests communicate to your students the types of thinking and other literacy skills that are important in your discipline. The way you test content communicates to your students the types of activities in which they should engage for study and learning. For example, if you emphasize analysis, synthesis, and application of concepts in your lessons, then analysis, synthesis, and application of concepts should be required for passing your test. If you require nothing more than memorization of information about concepts for passing the test, again, you are sending mixed messages to your students. Essentially you are telling them that in your discipline, the kinds of thinking that are really important are memorizing and paraphrasing rather than analysis, synthesis, and application (Taylor 1987).

In other words, testing is more than assessment; it is also an important instructional tool. Therefore, your tests should be constructed with your lessons in mind, and your lessons should be constructed with your tests in mind. In order for your tests to match your instructional emphases, you must have clearly stated daily objectives that are communicated to the students (Taylor 1987). These objectives should include verbs that indicate activities or tasks requiring whatever levels of thinking you want to emphasize (see Chapter 5 for a list of verbs that correspond to each level of Bloom's taxonomy of thinking). Your tests should require performance of similar activities and tasks.

Different kinds of questions are appropriate for different content and levels of thinking. Therefore, when constructing your tests, make careful decisions about the types of questions you use and whether they require similar types of thinking. The information in Appendix K is designed to help you select question types that match your instructional objectives.

COOPERATIVE GROUP TESTING

Many teachers attempt to use their tests as teaching tools by reviewing the graded tests with the class as a whole. However, while spending time going over a test might be well spent in terms of clarifying test items and the responses you expected, it actually does little to enhance students' learning of the content. From the teacher's perspective, reviewing the test means learning more about the content by discussing why each answer was right or wrong. From the students' perspective, however, going over the test usually means arguing for more points. The test is over, and unless they are going to be given another test over the same material, they wonder why they should learn the information now. From personal experience, you probably know that when going over a test, most students are more interested in the grade they earned and any points they might be able to argue than in learning how they might have done better.

Although certainly some learning of content might be enhanced by going over tests, the time spent on such endeavors might be more effectively spent on cooperative group tests. If you want your tests to be teaching tools as well as assessment tools, you might consider the use of cooperative group quizzes and tests. The format of such tests can take many forms. Following are several basic formats, which can be modified according to time constraints, student needs, difficulty of content, and the purpose of the test. You will be able to adapt these formats in creating your own versions of cooperative group tests.

In order to assess individual student learning *before* collaboration with classmates, you can give the test twice. The first time students take it, they take it on their own as they would any traditional test. This first administration of the test assesses individuals' content mastery. The second time they take it, students collaborate in their assigned groups. This second administration of the test enhances students' learning of the content. Consequently, the test becomes both a teaching and assessment tool. Students' grades can be a combination of the two performances so that they are motivated to perform well on their own and not rely too heavily on their groups.

Because the test is given twice, you can either shorten the test so that you can give it twice in the same class period, or you can administer it in two consecutive class periods. Students are going to be allowed to collaborate the second time, so it will not matter if they know the questions from taking it the first time. In fact, the more time they spend looking up answers in preparation for taking it the second time, the more of a teaching tool the test becomes.

When students collaborate in their groups, the focus is on discussing the content and not on how many points they earned. This collaboration is an excellent teaching tool, because students' understandings of content are deepened by listening to each other's ideas, perspectives, recollections, and analyses. Internalization of content is also facilitated by verbalizing and examining it through discussion. Also, students often understand difficult concepts better from their classmates' explanations and interpretations than from those of the teacher or textbook.

You can have students take the "double" test in a variety of ways. For example, you could have them take the test on their own, all using the same color of ink. Then, you could have them use another color of ink when they retake the test in their groups. This method reduces paper consumption and copy costs because students only need one copy of the test. Paper consumption can be further reduced by using separate answer sheets. When taking the test the second time, students only need to rewrite their responses if they are going to change an answer. Any answers left in the original color ink will be scored the same for both tests.

When students collaborate in their groups, they do not have to come to consensus on an answer. After discussing a question, each student is free to make her or his decision about which answer to record. Allowing the freedom to choose their own answers requires students to take responsibility for their own choices while also having the benefit of feedback from their groups. You can encourage students to help each other by offering bonus points if every member of the group reaches a predetermined mastery level (e.g., 80 percent).

However, requiring students to come to consensus has advantages. For example, when the group's consensus reflects a portion of each individual's grade, students are more motivated to contribute to the group discussion. They are also more likely to articulate clearly and convincingly answers they strongly believe are correct. If the group chooses an incorrect answer in spite of the objections of a minority of its members, rather than blaming the majority, the minority members need to work on their ability to communicate their positions and provide persuasive evidence supporting them.

If you require group consensus for the second administration of the test, provide each group with one answer sheet. Each member of the group puts her or his name at the top, and the group chooses a recorder. Following discussion of each question, the group can vote to decide which answer will be recorded. Before recording it, those in the minority have one more chance to argue for their preferred answer; if they cannot convince their group members to change their minds, the minority must accept the group's decision as their own. Because requiring group consensus and allowing individual decision making both have their advantages, you might want to consider using a combination of cooperative group formats.

AUTHENTIC ASSESSMENT

Although including some traditional assessment (e.g., multiple choice, analogies, matching, true/false, and so on) is a good idea in terms of helping your students develop test-taking skills and confidence, you should also include more authentic forms of assessment in your classroom. Authentic assessment refers to the process of collecting representative samples of students' work, along with recorded observations of their classroom behaviors. These work samples and descriptions of observed behaviors serve to document students' literacy skills, knowledge of content, and abilities to apply that knowledge in meaningful ways. The value of authentic assessment lies in the notion that it is more likely than traditional tests to reflect students' true abilities (Ruddell 1993).

Another valuable aspect of authentic assessment is that it may be the most effective way to combine teaching and assessment. Authentic assessment is designed to monitor and evaluate student progress in ways that approximate real-life applications of knowledge and literacy more than traditional tests. Furthermore, authentic assessment is designed to teach students to evaluate their own progress; this emphasis on self-evaluation is a key component of Total Quality and is likely to be a key element of twenty-first century schools.

Characteristics

According to Ruddell (1993), authentic assessment is characterized by the following:

1. *Authentic assessment should be planned and systematic, occurring frequently and regularly.* In addition to sampling the products of instruction, assessment sampling should also occur during instruction.
2. *Authentic assessment should include information from a variety of sources.* These sources should include daily work (both homework and in-class activities), teacher observations of both guided and independent activities, conferences and interviews with students, students' self-evaluations, and conferences with other teachers (who may have had opportunities to observe the students).
3. *Authentic assessment should occur while students are engaged in literacy tasks including both reading and writing.* Writing samples should document students' progression through the writing process, from first draft through finished product. You will want to keep systematic records that describe and evaluate students' expressive communication during discussion and writing activities. Students should summarize and reflect on their own learning using such journal

techniques as learning logs, which document students' learning from the beginning to the end of a particular unit of study.

4. *Authentic assessment should rely heavily on teacher observation as a source of information about how well and in what ways students are able to verbalize content knowledge.* Teachers must be trained and skilled in techniques of analyzing student behaviors observed during the course of regular classroom activities. You must develop record-keeping procedures that are systematic, efficient, informative, and unobtrusive. Finally, developing confidence in your own judgments, especially if they conflict with test results, is extremely important.

Teacher Observation

Because observation is a key tool for gathering information about students' literacy skills and content knowledge, you need to engage in both formal and informal observations. Formal observations occur whenever you are looking for something in particular. For example, you might observe students who are reading to determine whether and to what extent they preview the selection and set purposes for reading. You might also observe students during a discussion to determine how well they understand and can apply a certain concept. Informal observations occur whenever you are *not* looking for anything in particular but are attuned to the possibility of noticing student behaviors that might tell you something about their strengths and weaknesses in terms of literacy skills and content knowledge.

Your record-keeping system is critical to the effectiveness of your observation techniques. A series of checklists is probably most efficient for structured observation. These checklists should reflect your instructional objectives, i.e., the information you expect students to learn and the literacy skills you expect them to master in documenting their learning. Ideally, your checklists should include space for describing examples of how students demonstrated knowledge of content or mastery of skills. Computer spreadsheets can provide especially efficient checklist systems. Documenting formal observations can also be done using any of the following methods recommended for informal observations.

For informal observations, choose a method that is accessible and easy to use. For example, you could keep a daily observation journal in which you make notes about what individual students do and say. Your journal can be set up so that each page represents observations made on a particular day or for a particular student. Later, you can evaluate your journal entries and transcribe them into individual student folders. Another good system for informal observations is an index card file, in which you designate a card for each student. During class, you can pull students' cards as necessary to record your observations and evaluations. Computer databases also make efficient record-keeping systems for informal observations.

Although anecdotal records based on teacher observations are crucial to authentic assessment, they must be focused somehow on instructional objectives. Your observation records must demonstrate a clear purpose related to assessment of how well and in what ways students are able to demonstrate achievement of your objectives. Unfocused and seemingly irrelevant teacher comments can be easily misinterpreted by parents and administrators. To ensure that your recorded comments are focused on and relevant to assessment of your curricular goals, you should probably begin with a formal observation system. Once you become skilled and confident with observation techniques for authentic assessment, you can expand your database using informal yet focused observation systems.

Interviews and Conferences

Interviews and conferences with students can be formally structured to allow you to assess your students' abilities to articulate the content they have learned and the literacy skills they have mastered. Such formal interviews and conferences can take the place of or supplement traditional tests. They can be brief (three to five minutes) or lengthy (twenty to thirty minutes), depending on the extent of content and literacy skills you are assessing. Interview assessment can be recorded in the form of checklists supplemented with conference notes and/or audiotapes.

Interviews and conferences need not be formal or lengthy to be effective. Any time you talk with a student, either in class or outside of class, your are conducting an informal interview. In class, you can conduct on-the-spot interviews and conferences with students to verify understandings of concepts and applications of skills. You can also use such informal interviews and conferences to find out why students might be having difficulty with a particular assignment or task. This information can be important in documenting the learning process for particular students. Whenever students ask for assistance, take advantage of the opportunity to conduct an informal interview. All you have to do is listen for information you can use to document students' understandings, misunderstandings, abilities, and skill needs. As soon as you have identified a piece of vital information, jot it down in your observation journal or otherwise record it in whatever observation system you choose.

Both formal and informal interviews and conferences can be conducted in the form of questionnaires. Students can complete questionnaires independently or you can record their responses in a one-on-one setting. In addition to being useful for authentic assessment, information garnered from questionnaires can also be useful for diagnosing student needs and grouping for instruction.

Student Self-Evaluations

Having students reflect on their own learning and evaluate themselves is one of the most important and valuable aspects of authentic assessment. Students who can conduct honest and accurate self-assessments are more likely to take responsibility for their own learning, effectively develop skills and processes for content learning and study, learn from their mistakes, and develop successful lifelong learning habits. Until students can effectively conduct self-evaluations on their own, you will have to provide them with specific daily tasks designed to develop their abilities to reflect on their own learning. For example, daily processing of group work and written journal entries can help students become comfortable, confident, and accurate in evaluating themselves.

Journal writing needs to be well structured and should be planned using a process similar to the following suggested by Ruddell (1993):

1. Identify specific goals for the journal-writing task in terms of how it will be used to reflect your instructional objectives.
2. Decide on, communicate to your students, and consistently use specific journal-writing procedures and policies. Address such questions as these:
   - Will journal writing influence grades, and if so, how?
   - How often and when will journal writing occur (e.g., daily at the beginning of class, weekly at the end of class, and so on)?
   - Will journal entries consist of free-writing summaries and reflections of learning, or will they contain responses to specific questions (i.e., writing prompts)?
   - Will time limits be set for journal writing, and if so, what will they be?
3. Make logistical decisions about starting and maintaining journals. Address such questions as these:
   - Will students bring their own journals or will they be provided?
   - Will a particular type of notebook be used or will students be allowed to choose their own?
   - Where will the journals be kept?
   - Will students be allowed to take them home?
4. Decide on and communicate to your students the behaviors they can expect from you. Address such questions as these:
   - What will you do while your students are writing?
   - Will you model journal writing by writing while they write and sharing your entries with them?

■ Will your responses to students' writing provide corrective feedback, be evaluative, critical, encouraging, positive, and so on?

■ Will you read and respond to all students' journal entries, or will you rotate and respond to only some students' entries each time?

■ How will you respond to students' journal entries, and how soon can they expect you to respond?

The learning log (see Chapter 10) is a particular type of journal used both as a tool for learning and as a way to document learning. It usually consists of journal entries that are responses to writing prompts. A prompt is a question or unfinished statement designed to guide students in reflecting on a particular topic, skill, or piece of the learning process. Learning logs are designed to document a student's progression of learning from the beginning of a unit of study (preassessment) to the end of the unit (postassessment). They provide an authentic view of the students' learning processes and assessment of their learning products.

Portfolios

Portfolios comprise the heart of authentic assessment. They are collections of work samples that document each student's literacy skills and content learning. The work samples should represent a wide range of presentation formats, and students should be given a wide variety of choices for documenting their learning and skill mastery. They should be encouraged to experiment with many different formats before deciding which types will be emphasized in their portfolios.

A common misconception about portfolios is that they should include only a student's best work. Achievement is more clearly documented when finished products are accompanied by first drafts and other early learning products. Therefore, for the samples of a student's best work to be meaningful, they should be accompanied by examples of previous work completed as part of the learning process. In addition to documenting what the student can do, the purpose of the portfolio is to demonstrate how much the student has learned and how her or his literacy skills have improved. Consequently, work samples that demonstrate progress made by the student should be selected for inclusion in the portfolio. Students should be allowed to revise or correct work so that their work samples can document improvement.

You will need to guide students in selecting items for inclusion in the portfolio. The amount of guidance you provide will depend on the age of the students and the experience they have had with portfolio development. Primary-age students will need a great deal of guidance; in fact, for the most part, you should select for them the work they will include in their portfolios. However, even for these young children, explain why you chose the particular items you did. You should also provide them some choices by identifying appropriate items and allowing them to make selections from those. As early as possible, teach students about the portfolio concept and involve them in the development of their own portfolios.

Show older students who have not had much experience developing portfolios a variety of portfolio models. Also, provide them with lists and checklists of appropriate items they should select for inclusion in their portfolios. When you provide written feedback on their work, note for them which items would be especially appropriate for their portfolios. Make sure you help them understand that their portfolios should include early work that may not be their best work so that the work samples can show how much they have improved. Set aside at least a few minutes each week to help students select work to place in their portfolios.

Types of Student Work Samples

Following are some examples of the kinds of work appropriate to include in a portfolio (Ruddell 1993; Vacca and Vacca 1993). What others can you add?

- writing samples that show work over time (e.g., brainstorming notes, outlines, first drafts, revisions, and final products for essays, research papers, paragraph writing, summary writing, and so on)
- reading logs that document books, articles, and other materials read (e.g., annotated bibliographies and written responses to materials read)
- reading-response logs completed to document understanding and learning from assigned readings (e.g., summaries, notes, impressions, critiques, reflections, and evaluations)
- vocabulary journals or logs that demonstrate words the student has selected for concept development (e.g., word lists including definitions, synonyms, or sentences using the words and written concept development activities completed)
- projects completed as part of documentation of content mastery and communication skills (e.g., videotapes, audiotapes, photographs, graphic organizers, models, drawings, plays, and songs)
- group projects including detailed written descriptions of the individual student's contributions to the final product and the group's work leading up to the finished product (e.g., papers, models, presentations, and self-evaluations)
- daily journals of students' perceptions, thoughts, ideas, and reflections concerning the learning activities, assignments, materials, learning process, and so forth
- daily learning logs that document students' learning and reflections concerning the content (e.g., questions, notes, essays, creative writing, summaries, annotations, and analyses of data, issues, and arguments)

- study questions formulated by the student and other products generated by applying various reading and studying strategies (e.g., predictions, diagrams, summaries, annotations, outlines, preview notes, notes taken during readings and lectures, purposes set for reading, metacognitive "think aloud" sheets completed by the student, and so forth)
- checklists, questionnaires, inventories, interview notes, conference notes, and observation notes completed by the teacher and student
- letters exchanged with teachers, other students, parents, school administrators, community leaders, classroom visitors, pen pals, and so forth
- writing and artwork related to topics of study
- self-evaluations and peer evaluations
- homework assignments, in-class assignments, tests, and quizzes

Portfolio Assessment

Consider the following questions recommended by Ruddell (1993, 223) for establishing the criteria and procedures you will use for assessing your students' portfolios:

1. *What will be the criteria for assessment?* What am I looking for? What do I want students to demonstrate? How will I make sure students know what needs to go into their portfolios? What kind of mix do I want between daily work, individual work, group work, tests, first draft and polished writing, and outside work?
2. *Whose responsibility is it to do what?* How directive should I be regarding portfolio contents? How much leeway should I give students to determine what they each want in their portfolio? Should I rule certain things out? Should I require certain things?
3. *What will the guidelines be?* How will students be able to judge the quality of their own work? By what standards will I judge the quality of their work?
4. *How shall materials be collected?* Where will the portfolios be housed? How shall materials be presented? What categories of work and what self-evaluations should be included? How many items should be presented for each category of work?
5. *What will the working procedures be?* When and how often will portfolios be evaluated? How will I report evaluation to students? What is my commitment for returning portfolios to students?

Alternatives to Report Cards

Traditional report cards that provide a number or letter grade for academic performance and another for classroom behavior provide parents and students with little information about the students' abilities and achievements. Traditional report cards are especially inappropriate for reporting authentic assessment. Many schools, especially those that emphasize authentic assessment, are supplementing or replacing report cards with other types of reporting systems. Providing constructive feedback to students is extremely important to the learning process. At the same time, parental concern and involvement can positively influence students' motivation and academic achievement. Therefore, you might consider supplementing traditional report cards, even if your school does not emphasize authentic assessment or does not have an alternate reporting system in place.

One way to supplement or replace traditional report cards is with parent conferences. Many schools alternate parent conferences with report cards, resulting in at least one parent conference each semester or quarter. This system of alternating conferences with report cards makes it easier for the teacher to schedule, prepare for, and implement conferences. You might want to consider inviting older students to the parent conferences. Although it is certainly an option, having a parent conference for every student at the end of every reporting period can be extremely time consuming, especially for middle and high school teachers.

What do you do if the parents either cannot attend (e.g., because of work schedules) or refuse to attend a conference? Requiring parents to attend is very difficult; all you can do is offer the opportunity and encourage them to take advantage of it. Parents who work during the day might appreciate conferences scheduled during evening hours. Parents who feel intimidated by teachers and schools might be willing to accept a telephone conference or even a home visit. Once parents see that you are genuinely interested in helping their children, they are usually eager to meet with you, work with you, and support you in whatever ways they can.

Another way to supplement or replace report cards is through the use of checklists. Fairly detailed checklists can communicate to students and parents the content and literacy skills they are expected to master in your class. This specific information lets the students and their parents know exactly where they stand in terms of what they have achieved and what they still need to master. Detailed information about students' strengths and weaknesses is important for helping the students and their parents make necessary adjustments to improve study habits and enrich students' learning experiences outside of class.

Both report cards and checklists can be supplemented with brief narratives that summarize each student's strengths, achievements, attitudes, special needs, and classroom behaviors. The narratives should include specific examples of particularly impressive achievements and any critical needs students may have for improving learning, literacy skills, or behavior. Narratives are especially useful when parent conferences are not possible. The length of the narrative can vary anywhere from a paragraph to a page. Factors affecting the length include the extent of the students' accomplishments and needs, the number of narratives to be written by each teacher, and the number of teachers involved with each student.

SUMMARY

Assessment techniques in the content area classroom serve a variety of purposes. For example, evaluating scores on formal (standardized) tests can be useful in determining instructional starting points for content, materials, and grouping. Formal tests can be either norm referenced or criterion referenced. Norm-referenced tests compare a student's performance with that of other similar students in the norming population. Criterion-referenced tests compare a student's performance with predetermined criteria designed to indicate mastery of skills or knowledge.

Standardized test scores are reported in a variety of ways, and as a content area teacher, you must be able to interpret and evaluate them appropriately. Some of the more common forms of reporting standardized test results include raw scores, scaled scores, percentile scores, grade equivalency scores, age equivalency scores, and stanine scores. In addition to interpreting and evaluating test scores for instructional decision making, materials selection, and grouping, you will also be expected to interpret standardized test results and their implications to parents and students. Especially important, and most often misunderstood, are grade equivalency scores. Make sure you are able to translate these types of scores appropriately for instructional decision making and can interpret grade equivalency scores and their implications for parents and students.

Informal tests are not standardized and can be either commercially published (e.g., end-of-chapter and end-of-book tests) or teacher made. In the content area classroom, several types of informal teacher-made tests and inventories are crucial for diagnostic and content mastery assessment. The informal reading inventory (IRI) is administered on an individual basis and is designed to help teachers diagnose a student's reading level, along with reading skill strengths and weaknesses. The IRI can help you identify students' independent, instructional, frustration, and listening (or capacity) reading levels.

The cloze inventory is another diagnostic tool designed to help teachers decide whether materials selected for instruction will be appropriate for the reading abilities of the students. The content area reading inventory is a diagnostic instrument that provides teachers with detailed and specific information about students' strengths and weaknesses in their reading and study abilities with selected materials.

Students' prior knowledge can be assessed informally using content area reading and vocabulary strategies. For example, the PreReading Plan is a discussion technique that helps teachers assess students' background knowledge prior to a unit of study, at the beginning of a lesson, or before giving a reading assignment. Another example is the Semantic Feature Analysis, a vocabulary strategy that can be used to help you determine how well students understand requisite concepts. This strategy can also be used for teachers' assessment of how much students may already know about the key concepts that will be introduced in a reading assignment or new study unit.

Informal criterion-referenced content mastery tests developed by teachers are important for assessing students' achievement of the content area curricular objectives. In addition to being assessment tools, content mastery tests are important instructional tools as well. For example, the test you develop communicates to students the types of content, thinking, and literacy skills important to learning in that content area. Also, content mastery tests provide valuable feedback to the students in terms of how they are doing and how their learning can be improved. Of course, these tests also provide valuable feedback to you so that adjustments for improved instruction can be made.

Cooperative group testing is one way to ensure the use of content mastery tests as instructional and assessment devices. You can design systems in which students first take a test on their own and then again in a cooperative learning group. In their groups, students discuss the test items in ways that enhance their learning of the content.

As with all tests, teacher-made tests must be developed in such a way to ensure validity and reliability. Validity is a test characteristic indicating that the test assesses what it purports to measure. Reliability is a test characteristic referring to consistency of results. To ensure validity and reliability, you must carefully develop tests that match your instructional objectives and incorporate appropriate items for assessing those objectives.

Authentic assessment is a concept that refers to the evaluation of student learning using actual literacy tasks that require application of knowledge in realistic ways. Actual student work samples are selected collaboratively by teachers and students and compiled along with other documentation of students' learning and achievement in a portfolio. Other documentation comes from a variety of sources including observations by the teacher, interviews and conferences with students, and student self-evaluations. Teaching students to evaluate themselves accurately and automatically can be one of the most valuable aspects of authentic assessment.

Because assessment and evaluation are vital to instructional planning in the content area classroom, you need to be familiar with a wide variety of assessment techniques. Regular and consistent assessment is necessary to ensure continuous improvement and reflective teaching and learning. You must be engaged in an ongoing process of diagnosing and evaluating student needs, planning instruction and selecting materials according to those needs, evaluating instruction and materials, and making necessary adjustments. A variety of assessment techniques is crucial for implementing each step of the evaluation and decision-making process.

ENRICHMENT ACTIVITIES

1. Select a content area textbook at the grade level of your choice and develop a cloze inventory for it. Include written instructions and administration and scoring procedures. Administer it to at least one student at that grade level and summarize your findings.

2. Select a content area textbook at the grade level of your choice and develop a content area reading inventory for it. Include written instructions and administration and scoring procedures. Administer it to at least one student at that grade level and summarize your findings.

3. Design a cooperative group testing system. Construct a short content mastery quiz or test for identified instructional objectives. Administer the test to one or more groups of students using your cooperative group testing system. Develop a chart that summarizes the students' individual and group scores. Reflect on and evaluate your system. How could you improve it?

4. Write a letter to the parents of the following child, interpreting and explaining the standardized test scores provided.
   Student: George Darwin   Grade: 6
   Reading grade equivalency score: 8.5
   Reading percentile ranking: 90th percentile
   Math grade equivalency score: 5.5
   Math percentile ranking: 45th percentile

5. Design an authentic assessment system you could use in your classroom. Identify the grade level, and if middle or high school level, the content area. Address each of the following questions:
   ▪ How will you assess students' abilities to read, write, and think in the language of the content area?
   ▪ How will you assess students' mastery of content?
   ▪ How will students demonstrate progress and achievement?
   ▪ What types of student work samples would be required in each student's portfolio?

▌ What criteria will you use for assessing student portfolios?

▌ What type of record-keeping systems would you use for making formal and informal observations?

▌ How will students evaluate themselves?

▌ Will you use journal writing or learning logs, and if so, how?

▌ How will you record and report the results of formal and informal interviews and conferences with students?

▌ What type of reporting system will you use as a supplement or alternative to traditional report cards?

REFERENCES

Baumann, James F. (1988). *Reading assessment: An instructional decision-making perspective.* Columbus, OH: Merrill.

Betts, E. A. (1946). *Foundation of reading instruction.* New York: American Book Co.

Johnson, D. D., and P. D. Pearson. (1984). *Teaching reading vocabulary,* 2d ed. New York: Holt, Rinehart and Winston.

Johnston, M. C. (1982). *Johnston informal reading inventory.* Tucson, AZ: Educational Publications.

Langer, J. A. (1981). From theory to practice: A prereading plan. *Journal of Reading* 25:152–156.

McKenna, M. (1976). Synonymic vs. verbatim scoring of the cloze procedure. *Journal of Reading* 20:141–143.

McWilliams, L., and T. A. Rakes. (1979). *Content inventories: English, social studies, science.* Dubuque, IA: Kendall/Hunt Publishing Company.

Readence, J. E., T. W. Bean, and R. S. Baldwin. (1992). *Content area reading: An integrated approach,* 4th ed. Dubuque, IA: Kendall/Hunt Publishing Company.

Ruddell, M. R. (1993). *Teaching content reading and writing.* Needham Heights, MA: Allyn & Bacon.

Taylor, W. (1987). *Test construction manual.* Oakton, IL: Oakton Community College.

Tierney, R. J., J. E. Readence, and E. K. Dishner. (1995). *Reading strategies and practices: A compendium,* 4th ed. Needham Heights, MA: Allyn & Bacon.

Vacca, R. T., and J. L. Vacca. (1993). *Content area reading,* 4th ed. New York: HarperCollins.

Warncke, E. W., and D. A. Shipman. (1984). *Group assessment in reading.* Englewood Cliffs, NJ: Prentice Hall.

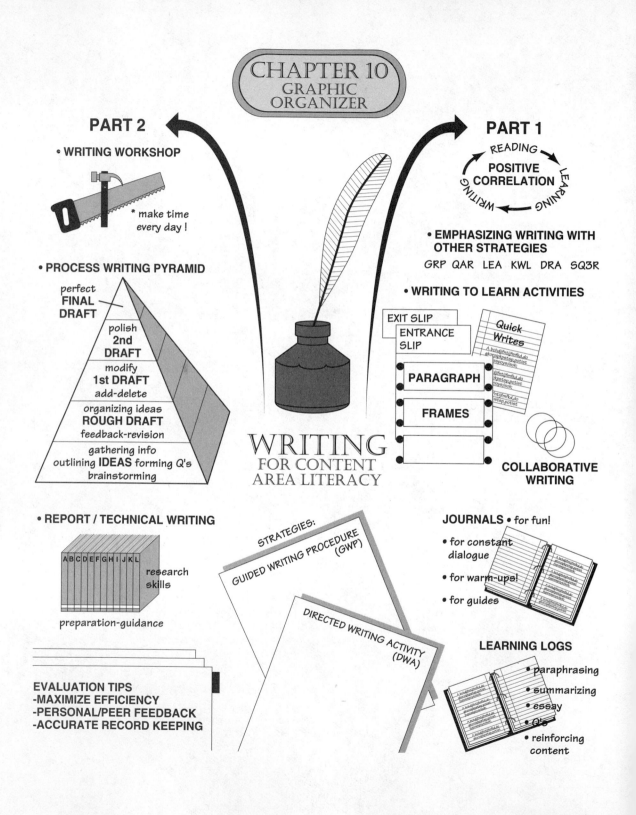

CHAPTER 10
GRAPHIC ORGANIZER

PART 2

• WRITING WORKSHOP

* make time every day !

• PROCESS WRITING PYRAMID

perfect
FINAL DRAFT

polish
2nd DRAFT

modify
1st DRAFT
add-delete

organizing ideas
ROUGH DRAFT
feedback-revision

gathering info
outlining **IDEAS** forming Q's
brainstorming

PART 1

READING
POSITIVE CORRELATION
LEARNING
WRITING

• EMPHASIZING WRITING WITH OTHER STRATEGIES

GRP QAR LEA KWL DRA SQ3R

• WRITING TO LEARN ACTIVITIES

EXIT SLIP
ENTRANCE SLIP

Quick Writes
A lschdjlfntjlfmfkd.do akomplpkpetsepopotiet aepoyodsock

jljlfntjlfmfkd.do lkpetsepopotiet poyodsock

ntljlfmfkd.do iotpot potiet

PARAGRAPH

FRAMES

COLLABORATIVE WRITING

WRITING
FOR CONTENT
AREA LITERACY

• REPORT / TECHNICAL WRITING

ABCDEFGHIJKL

research skills

preparation-guidance

EVALUATION TIPS
-MAXIMIZE EFFICIENCY
-PERSONAL/PEER FEEDBACK
-ACCURATE RECORD KEEPING

STRATEGIES:
GUIDED WRITING PROCEDURE (GWP)

DIRECTED WRITING ACTIVITY (DWA)

JOURNALS • for fun!

• for constant dialogue

• for warm-ups!

• for guides

LEARNING LOGS

• paraphrasing
• summarizing
• essay
• Q's
• reinforcing content

Writing for Content Area Literacy

To demonstrate mastery of the content, the student will be able to do the following:

PART 1 OBJECTIVES

1. Identify the following strategy, describe its distinguishing features, and assess its significance to teaching content area literacy: Guided Writing Procedure (GWP).
2. Identify and characterize relationships between reading, writing, and learning.
3. Assess the value of writing activities for helping students learn.
4. Identify and briefly describe at least three examples of writing-to-learn activities that would be appropriate for the grade level or content area of your choice.
5. Describe at least one writing-to-learn activity that is especially appropriate for ESL students.

PART 2 OBJECTIVES

1. Identify the following strategy, describe its distinguishing features, and assess its significance to teaching content area literacy: Directed Writing Activity (DWA).
2. Define the concept of writing workshop and assess its significance as an instructional tool for content area learning and literacy.
3. Define, including the steps involved, the process approach to writing and assess its significance to content learning and literacy development.
4. Describe at least three examples of prewriting activities designed to provide guided practice in planning, organizing, and outlining.

INTRODUCTION

You have undoubtedly noticed that writing is an integral component of the content area literacy strategies and activities described in this textbook. Because writing is so crucial to the development of content area literacy, and because it is often overlooked or deemphasized as a tool for content area learning, an entire chapter of this text is devoted to it. Just as students need to develop their reading and thinking skills with a variety of reading experiences in all content areas, they also need to develop their writing skills with extensive and varied writing experiences. As Shanahan (1988) points out, although the research clearly indicates a close relationship between reading and writing skills, it also suggests that reading and writing do not overlap to the extent that instruction in one will sufficiently replace instruction in both. In other words, it is important to teach both reading and writing daily in as many content areas as possible.

Even primary-grade students and students with poor writing abilities should be expected to write daily in a variety of content areas. Providing students frequent opportunities to write for a variety of purposes is the only way they can be expected to improve their writing skills. Writing assignments should be tailored to meet students' needs and abilities. They should be challenging but not frustrating. Also, you can tailor your evaluation system to provide instructional feedback and fair assessment according to students' individual needs and abilities.

Writing is a valuable tool for learning in a number of ways. For example, writing helps students reflect on and determine how much they already know about a topic. It encourages students to assess how well they understand new information and allows them to integrate new information with prior knowledge. Through writing, students can understand information at deeper levels. Writing can make knowledge meaningful and more easily retained. In short, writing is a valuable literacy tool for enhancing content area learning.

Too often, writing is overlooked or avoided as a literacy tool for content area learning. Many teachers assume that incorporating writing activities and assignments automatically means that they will have overwhelming stacks of papers to grade. Others are unaware of ways they can use writing as a learning tool in their particular content areas. For example, math and science teachers sometimes assume that writing is not an important literacy skill students need for developing knowledge in their content areas.

One purpose of this chapter is to present a variety of ways in which writing activities and assignments can be used to enhance content area learning and literacy *without* resulting in significantly more papers to grade. Emphasizing the role writing plays in the implementation of content area literacy strategies is another goal. Still another purpose is to provide you with ideas for using writing on a daily basis to help students learn more at higher levels of understanding and evaluate their own learning. Finally, daily writing provides you, the teacher, with ongoing diagnostic feedback about how well your students are learning.

You will be introduced to two new content area literacy strategies that emphasize writing to support and enhance students' abilities to read, think, and study. The first strategy is the Guided Writing Procedure, and the second is the Directed Writing Activity. Both are variations of content area literacy strategies and are designed not only to improve students' writing skills but also to guide them in using writing as a tool for learning.

PART 1

STRATEGY: GUIDED WRITING PROCEDURE

The Guided Writing Procedure (GWP), designed by Smith and Bean (1980), is a strategy that uses the writing process to facilitate students' learning from text. In addition to increasing learning of content, the GWP is also designed to activate and assess background knowledge and evaluate and improve students' writing abilities (Tierney, Readence, and Dishner 1990). The GWP is recommended by Reyes and Molner (1991) as an effective strategy for use with ESL students.

The procedures of the GWP—designed to be implemented over a period of at least several days—involve two major components. The first component of the GWP includes informal diagnosis of students' background knowledge and writing abilities, the second, instruction in content and writing.

The following steps of the first component, diagnosing background knowledge and writing skills, have been adapted from Smith and Bean's (1980) original description:

1. Present in writing the topic under study. Ask students to brainstorm everything they can think of in relation to that topic. Record the information verbatim for all to see.
2. Have students vote to distinguish major ideas from supporting details. Guide the students in designing an outline that presents the information in clusters.
3. Using the outline as a guide, students write one or two brief paragraphs as their "first draft." Collect the drafts and, after setting a purpose, assign the students to read.
4. Using a short checklist for each student, quickly examine the drafts, analyzing them for content (e.g., completeness and accuracy), organization (e.g., topic sentences and supporting information), style (e.g., clarity, syntax, and word choice), and mechanics (e.g., spelling, grammar, and punctuation). The checklists should indicate for each student whether he or she has mastered each criterion or still needs improvement.

The following steps of the second component, teaching content and writing skills, have also been adapted from Smith and Bean's (1980) original description:

1. Display a sample draft for all to see. To avoid singling out students, develop a sample draft that is a composite of various parts of several different drafts. The sample draft should demonstrate good aspects of writing, as well as problem areas needing revision.
2. Using the checklist along with information gained from the reading assignment, guide students in editing and revising the sample draft.
3. Return the students' first drafts. Have them use the checklists you completed and information recalled from the reading assignment to edit and revise their first drafts.
4. Collect the second drafts and give students a quiz on the reading assignment, a vocabulary concept development activity, or an activity designed to reinforce the content.

5. As soon as possible, examine the second drafts, comparing them to the checklist results from the first drafts. Schedule individual conferences with students who did not show improvement on the second drafts or who still exhibit serious writing problems or content misunderstandings.

Konopak, Martin, and Martin (1987, 113) conducted an investigation of the effectiveness of a modified version of the GWP. From their research, they concluded that writing can benefit learning in the content area classroom because "students who compose their thoughts on paper become actively involved with new facts and ideas and better understand the relationships among them." The following are a set of procedures adapted from their modified version of the GWP, which deletes the diagnostic checklist and instead emphasizes fluency and coherence of ideas.

1. Activate background knowledge with individual, pair, or small-group brainstorming, discussion, or notetaking.
2. Students share their experiences and knowledge through whole-class brainstorming or discussion.
3. Students clarify their ideas by writing their understanding of the discussion in paragraph form. This written expression will be assessed for content and clarity only, not for style and mechanics.
4. Prepare students for reading the assignment by introducing vocabulary and setting a purpose for reading.
5. Students read the assignment after they have been instructed to relate any new information to what they already know about the topic.
6. After reading, students rewrite their paragraphs, integrating any new information learned from the reading assignment.
7. Conduct a whole-class discussion of the content contained in students' individual writings. Lead the discussion by modeling good questions and responses related to key concepts from the reading assignment.
8. In small groups, students read their paragraphs aloud and discuss their understandings of the content. Discussions should be guided by questions developed by the group or provided by you. Circulate among the groups, serving as a facilitator.
9. Students rewrite their paragraphs using new or corrected information gained from the small-group discussions. These rewritten versions can then serve as class notes on the topic.
10. Evaluate learning with short essay questions or similar writing assignments.

RELATIONSHIPS BETWEEN READING, WRITING, AND LEARNING

Reading, like listening, is a *receptive* language skill, and writing, like speaking, is an *expressive* language skill. Both receptive and expressive skills are necessary and important for effective communication. Because learning processes rely heavily on communication skills including understanding information conveyed by others (reading and listening) and articulating information to others (writing and speaking), both reading and writing skills influence students' abilities to learn.

As written language skills, reading and writing are correlated: although there are exceptions, good readers tend to be good writers and poor readers tend to be poor writers. Also, the act of reading is similar to the act of writing in that both processes involve the construction of meaning. Both readers and writers construct meaning by interpreting information in terms of their prior knowledge and experiences.

Readers and writers engage in similar thought processes. For example, readers survey or preview a passage, and writers organize or outline their thoughts. Readers make and check their predictions, and writers develop a first draft, then seek feedback and suggestions. Readers elaborate on or modify their predictions, and writers make revisions; readers monitor their comprehension to make necessary adjustments, and writers edit their work. Finally, readers evaluate their learning, and writers assess the effectiveness of their final drafts.

Because of the relationship between reading and writing, instruction in one may enhance ability in the other. More importantly, instruction in both reading and writing can positively influence achievement and instructional efficiency (Shanahan 1988). Research by Tierney, Soter, O'Flahavan, and McGinley (1989) suggests reading and writing in combination are more likely to facilitate critical thinking. Therefore, as important learning and literacy tools, both reading and writing should be emphasized in the content area classroom. Students should be provided with daily and varied experiences to read about content information and then process it with writing activities at all levels of thinking.

As mentioned in the introduction to this chapter, writing is an integral part of literacy-based strategies for content area teaching and learning. You can control the extent to which you emphasize writing over oral communication, or vice versa. Many of the procedures that call for oral questions or responses from students can be modified easily to emphasize written questions or responses. Appendix L provides examples of ways to modify content area literacy strategies to incorporate or emphasize writing. As you read the examples, see whether you can think of other modifications for increasing the emphasis on writing when applying content area instructional strategies.

WRITING-TO-LEARN ACTIVITIES

Writing-to-learn activities can be used before, during, or after lessons for a variety of purposes designed to enhance learning. For example, writing activities can be used before reading or at the beginning of a lesson to activate students' background knowledge. During reading or in the middle of a lecture, writing activities can help students monitor their understanding and process new information. Writing activities used after reading or at the end of a lesson allow students to evaluate their learning, reflect on new information at higher levels of thought, and integrate that new information with prior knowledge.

Quick Writes

Quick Writes can be done on paper or index cards or in journals. As described by Ruddell (1993), Quick Writes are short (three to five minutes), open-ended writing assignments, usually given during or at the end of a lesson. Students write about what they learned or did not learn, liked or did not like, did or did not understand about the lesson, what kinds of activities they would like to do more often, what they would like to see changed, and any other impressions of the lesson, its content, and their own learning processes. Quick Writes may be anonymous if you are looking for general feedback about the effectiveness of a lesson, but students should put their names on them if you seek diagnostic information for individual students.

Quick Writes can be especially useful in the middle of a lesson if you suspect that the students are having trouble (Ruddell 1993). You can get valuable feedback on how well students are understanding, whether they are ready to move on, and if not, what needs to be reviewed or retaught. Even if students are not struggling with the lesson, Quick Writes assigned in the middle of a lesson will help students think about, reflect on, and process what they are learning.

Quick Writes can also be used at the beginning of a class or lesson to give students a chance to settle down and focus on the topic. Students respond to questions related to reflections on the homework, the previous day's lesson, prior knowledge about the topic, concerns and problems related to recent or upcoming lessons or assignments, and so on. Quick Writes can also help refocus students as different parts of the lesson begin, for example, to help them shift gears from a whole-class discussion to an independent reading activity.

Entrance and Exit Slips

Entrance slips are pieces of paper or index cards students turn in as they enter the classroom or begin a new lesson. The entrance slip assignment is given at the end of the previous day's lesson. Students answer a specific question about the lesson, reading assignment, homework, previous or upcoming topic, study strategy, and the like. Then, at the beginning of class after the entrance slips have been collected, start the lesson by reading aloud a few of the students' responses, maintaining their anonymity. Then lead a brief discussion designed to review previous material, focus on a new topic, or develop metacognitive awareness.

Exit slips are turned in at the end of a class as students are leaving or after a lesson before progressing to the next activity. Students are assigned to summarize information, respond to certain content, ask questions about the lesson, and give feedback about instructional activities and strategies. After collecting exit slips, you may simply read them for diagnostic feedback and return them the next day or read a few aloud and discuss them at the beginning of the next class or lesson.

Collaborative Writing

Richardson and Morgan (1994) describe two examples of writing-to-learn activities that involve collaboration of a small group of students. In the first example, each student in the group reads an article and reacts to it independently. Then the group members share their individual reactions. Working as a group, students produce a common first draft that incorporates the individual reactions. Next, each student revises the draft and brings suggestions back to the group. Finally, the group collaborates to evaluate, edit, and rewrite the draft into final form. One final draft is submitted by each group to the teacher for evaluation.

The second example involves the use of collaborative writing in math classes. Students work together in small groups to compose meaningful word problems that require application of particular operations. Such collaboration helps students develop confidence with the tasks involved in the writing process (e.g., prewriting, drafting, revising, evaluating, and editing). Another benefit to the use of collaboration in writing-to-learn activities is a significant reduction in the number of papers that must be graded.

RAFT Assignments

Role, audience, format, and topic (RAFT) are key ingredients for developing writing assignments (Santa, Havens, and Harrison 1989). *Role* refers to the role or perspective of the writer, while *audience* refers to the reader(s). *Format* relates to the form the final writing product will take, and *topic* concerns the specific subject guiding the development and organization of the writing. Because RAFT assignments are specific and well focused, they can be much more enjoyable for both writers and readers (Santa, Havens, and Harrison 1989).

The role of the writer in a RAFT assignment is important for introducing and reinforcing the concept of perspective and point of view. The concept of the author's perspective and point of view is not only a critical writing skill but also crucial for reading and interpreting what others have written. Roles specified in RAFT assignments can give students opportunities to consider situations or issues from more than one perspective or point of view. Students especially need opportunities to write from perspectives that differ from their own. In addition to people, roles can reflect the perspectives of animals, plants, or even inanimate objects. For example, a description of the destruction of rain forests could be written from the point of view of an animal or indigenous person living there, a tree in the forest, or even fossils lying beneath the earth.

The audience is another important concept to consider in writing-to-learn activities. For example, if the audience is the teacher, the need for clarity and specificity is not as great as if the audience had little or no prior knowledge of the topic. Thus, when you specify an audience other than the teacher, students are charged with the responsibility of providing clear explanations, descriptions, and examples of concepts. As with roles, the audience can be people, animals, plants, or inanimate objects.

Students also must be given opportunities to produce in a variety of writing formats; they need to learn how to identify appropriate formats according to their purposes for writing. Additionally, students should learn how to set a tone of writing appropriate for the identified format (Santa, Havens, and Harrison 1989), or more realistically, how to identify a format that is appropriate for the tone of writing to be used. Examples of writing formats include poems, expository essays, memoranda, letters, telegrams, editorials, dialogues, narratives, and persuasive essays.

The topic of the RAFT assignment should be clearly specified so that students know the purpose of their writing. To guide your students in the organization and development of their writing for the identified format, avoid using the word *write* in the assignment; instead, use a verb that specifies the type of writing appropriate for the identified format (e.g., *describe, explain, compare, contrast, persuade, convince, or demonstrate*) (Santa, Havens, and Harrison 1989).

Santa, Havens, and Harrison (1989) offer an example to demonstrate the creative possibilities of a RAFT assignment within a science class. The role of the writer could be that of a blood cell serving as a "tour guide" for other blood cells; the audience could then be other blood cells in the circulatory system. The assignment could take the form of a travelogue, with a description of what happens to blood cells as they travel through the circulatory system.

Writing Guides

Writing Guides, as described by Alvermann and Phelps (1994), are similar to Study Guides (see Chapter 5) in that they are a type of scaffolding. In other words, they allow you, the teacher, to provide support for students in constructing meaning. Writing Guides help students understand what and how to write by leading students through the steps necessary for completing the writing task.

Each Writing Guide describes for students a clear purpose, voice, perspective, and tone for the writing assignment. They offer students hints that provide guidance about what should and should not be included in the writing product. Students can be given choices to help guide them through the writing process. For example, Writing Guides can offer two or more organizational structures (e.g., chronological order, compare/ contrast, cause/effect) appropriate for the identified product from which students choose one.

The importance of revising and editing are emphasized by Writing Guides by including instructions for those steps in the process. For example, guidelines for reviewing another student's paper or a list of criteria for evaluating and editing papers can be included.

Paragraph Frames

Paragraph Frames were designed by Cudd and Roberts (1989) to help students write about what they are learning in the content area classroom. Paragraph Frames "can be used to review and reinforce specific content and to familiarize students with the different ways in which authors organize material in order to inform" (Cudd and Roberts 1989, 392). They employ a cloze format by providing sentence starters that include specific signal words or phrases designed to guide the students in organizing and developing a paragraph. Each paragraph is framed according to a particular organizational pattern (e.g., sequential, enumeration, reaction, and comparison/contrast).

Instruction with Paragraph Frames begins with a sample paragraph and follows several steps. First, select an organizational pattern and introduce students to it by presenting a sample paragraph that clearly follows that particular pattern. When first introducing the concept of organizational patterns, begin with sequential ordering. This type of organizational pattern is probably the easiest for students to recognize and use in their own writing. Make sure the sample paragraph contains signal words and phrases appropriate for the organizational pattern (e.g., *first, next, then, finally*).

Second, copy the sentences onto sentence strips or transparency strips large enough for the class to see. With the whole class, review the topic and discuss the logical sequence of events. Third, students should arrange the sentence strips in correct order and read the completed paragraph together with the class. Finally, scramble the sentences again and have each student reorder them and copy the completed paragraph independently.

After students have practiced sequential paragraph organization, they can gradually begin filling in their own supporting information within the context of the framed paragraph. Paragraph Frames can also be adapted for math lessons. For example, an Algebra Frame can be used to reinforce the procedures involved in solving different types of problems. Figures 10–1 through 10–4 present examples of sentence starters adapted from those offered by Cudd and Roberts (1989).

Activities for ESL Students

Graves (1994) stresses the importance of ensuring ESL students do not feel alienated and confused. To help them feel secure in the classroom and

---

FIGURE 10–1   Sequentially-Organized Paragraph Frames

Butterflies and moths go through major changes before becoming adults.

First, _____.
Next, _____.
Then, _____.
Finally, _____.

The process of starting an ant farm is easy.

To begin, _____.
Next, _____.
To continue, _____.
Last, _____.

To solve this math problem, you follow these steps.

First, you _____.
Next, you _____.
Then, you _____.
Finally, you _____.
To check your work, you _____.

FIGURE 10–2 Enumeration Paragraph Frames

Bees are very important insects.

First, _____.
Second, _____.
Third, _____.
Finally, _____.

As you can see, bees have important jobs.

FIGURE 10–3 Reaction Paragraph Frames

My favorite character in this story is _____.

This character _____.
I like her/him because _____.

Yesterday, our class walked to the creek behind our school. I learned some important things about this creek.

I learned _____.
I also learned _____.
Another important thing is _____.
In addition, I learned that _____.
One thing about the creek I would like to learn more about is _____

_____

Before I read this article, I thought that bats were harmful.

After reading, I found out that bats _____.

Besides this, I learned some other new things about bats.

First, I learned _____.
Second, I learned _____.
Finally, I learned _____.

practice their English through writing, he makes the following recommendations. First, carefully choose student mentors to sit next to the ESL students. These mentors should be able and willing to help interpret as much as possible, provide assistance without doing the work for them, and offer encouragement appropriately.

FIGURE 10–4 Comparison/Contrast Paragraph Frames

The geography and natural resources of the United States and Mexico are alike in some interesting ways.

First, _____.
Second, _____.
Finally, _____.

Humans differ from apes in several ways.

First, humans _____, while apes _____.
Second, humans _____, while apes _____.
I think the biggest difference between humans and apes is _____
_____.

Second, the use of "pictionaries" helps ESL students develop a vocabulary of nouns. Pictionaries can be made from the illustrations of other students. The key items in the illustrations are labeled, and the labeled illustrations are photocopied and collated into personal pictionaries for ESL students.

A third recommendation for helping ESL students write in English is to allow and encourage them to write in their first language. Even if they are not fluent writers in their first language, they can benefit from first-language writing practice. Students who have extensive experience writing in their first language often have an easier time learning to write in English.

Graves (1994) also suggests helping ESL students write letters. They can write to relatives and friends, both in this country and others. ESL students can also write to you and their classmates; they can write the letters in English and their native languages. Responding to their letters by writing back is an especially good way for teachers and classmates to help ESL students feel welcome and appreciated by their learning communities.

A final recommendation is to take photographs of ESL students involved in various classroom and school activities. The students can then arrange the photographs in an album and write captions for them. Again, this activity not only provides opportunities for writing practice but also reinforces a sense of belonging to the school and classroom communities.

For ESL students, Schifini (1994) recommends using writing activities as prereading activities. For example, Quick Writes (i.e., brainstorming on paper), journal writing, and responding to writing prompts can be used to prepare students for a reading assignment. Kang (1994) recommends using writing activities as postreading activities to reinforce and extend learning, as well as to offer experience recognizing and using organizational patterns (e.g., cause/effect, compare/contrast, chronological order, reasons, examples, description, simple listing, and so on).

Writing Guides used as postreading activities encourage additional cognitive and affective involvement with the text. They can also extend ideas in the text by connecting them with ideas for compositions. Guides and other writing activities are important for emphasizing to students the connections between the communication processes of reading and writing (Kang 1994).

Activities for Writers with Poor Handwriting, Spelling, Grammar, and Punctuation

Graves (1994) emphasizes the importance of focusing primarily on the content and working on one type of problem at a time. He suggests categorizing writing problems into three major areas: handwriting, spelling, and conventions (i.e., grammar and punctuation). He also recommends allowing the student to decide which area he or she wants to study first.

Instructional technology is an especially important tool for students with writing problems. Graves (1994) suggests that writing on a computer or typewriter can help students with poor handwriting improve their spelling. He also believes that producing work with computers or typewriters is important in adding prestige to the students' work. It follows that prestigious writing products may serve to increase the confidence and self-esteem of writers who have had little prior success.

When helping writers with grammar problems, Graves (1994, 45) recommends that teachers "treat conventions as tools, not rules." In such an approach, rather than teaching the conventional rules of comma placement, commas are emphasized as tools for helping to "slow down" the writing. Another example is to emphasize the functional use of quotation marks in identifying dialogue, rather than the conventional rules for placement of quotation marks in making writing "correct."

Conferences are especially important for coaching students with writing problems. Graves (1994) suggests that conferences be structured so that the writer takes the lead in identifying areas needing improvement. Instead of pointing out errors, ask questions that lead the writer to discover and identify potential problems. Make sure you help the student focus on only one problem during each conference. For example, if the writer has chosen spelling as a goal for improvement, then focus the conference on helping her or him identify and correct words the student believes are or may be misspelled.

JOURNALS

Journals can take many forms, have many uses, and serve a variety of purposes. Basically, journals are written records of students' and teachers' personal observations and questions about content, practical applications, higher-level interpretations, learning processes, instructional activities, and study strategies. Journals are designed for self-reflection and correspondence between students and teachers: they offer a means for students and teachers to think about what and how they are learning, the effectiveness of instruction, applications of study skills, and so on. Journals also allow students to communicate personal thoughts to the teacher who can then respond with guidance, support, encouragement, individual attention, and adjustments for more effective instruction. For the teacher, journals provide an excellent way to record observations and evaluations of daily events. This information provides valuable feedback for lesson planning.

As a teacher, you need to make sure that students understand the nature of journals. That is, since journals are designed to serve as a means of communication, students need to understand that you will be reading their entries at least occasionally and sometimes on a daily basis. Although a great deal of journal writing involves self-reflection, students need to be aware that their reflections will probably be shared with you. The nature of students' written messages will be influenced by the knowledge that their audience is you, the teacher. Let them know that you care and are concerned about them and that you will use the information from their journals to help make learning more enjoyable and successful for them.

Remind students that they may share with you anything that might be on their minds, even if not directly related to the content of the class. Let them know that you are their listener and that you want to hear what they have to say. However, if students write something of an extremely personal nature that they specifically ask you not to read, you should honor their wishes. To prevent overuse of such a request, you should expect these students to write an additional entry that they *will* allow you to read.

At the same time, assure students that no one but you will have access to their journals. Each student needs to feel confident that her or his journal entries will remain private. Continually reassure your students that no one but you will read their journal entries. Their journals will be private property to which only you will have access. They will not be shared with other students, teachers, parents, or administrators. Unless students trust you with their personal thoughts, feelings, and observations, their entries are not likely to be honest reflections. When journal entries do little more than tell you what students think you want to hear, the time spent on writing them is not well spent.

To avoid this potential problem, avoid setting topics. Instead, encourage students to tell you whatever is on their minds. At first, begin with short periods of writing (about five minutes), allowing no distractions. If students have questions, they should be instructed to write them down. If they need help with spelling, they should underline the words they want you to correct. Students can write about anything on their minds that might influence learning including things they like to do, problems they are having, help they need, school work they enjoy or find difficult, and significant events in their lives. If students complain that they cannot think of anything to write, tell them to describe the events of the day until they think of something they want to tell you (Strackbein and Tillman, 1987).

You might also begin by having students draw a picture and then describe it in a journal entry. Other ways to help students get started and build confidence in journal writing include having them write in response to class discussions, personal and social activities, sentence starters, or questions. For primary-grade children, encourage use of "invented spelling" (i.e., spelling the words however they think the words might be spelled) if they are not confident enough to write fluently. You might need to have these students read their entries to you if their spelling inventions are indecipherable (Bode 1989).

Dialogue Journals

A dialogue journal is an ongoing written conversation between a student and teacher, with the partners exchanging messages daily or weekly. The student makes the first entry, and you respond by addressing questions and comments made by the student. The student takes the active role in directing the conversation. Your role is to expand and modify content not to direct or correct. Occasionally, you may need to take a more active role to avoid or resolve communication breakdowns (Dolly 1990). Some underachieving readers may not have made the connection that writing is conversation in print. For such students, spend a little time at the beginning of the process reading your entries aloud at the same time the student reads them silently.

Dialogue journals are designed primarily to allow students and teachers to do self-reflections and communicate those reflections with each other on a regular basis. As a means of self-reflection, journals allow students and teachers to take the time to ponder past events, decide what they have learned from their experiences, set goals for making changes, relate their life experiences to classroom learning experiences, and so forth. As a means of communication, dialogue journals allow students to share with teachers their personal thoughts about anything related to their learning of the content, their relationships with other students, or their experiences at home and in the community. Dialogue journal writing empowers students to think critically about their learning environments and personal lives and to express that critical thought to their teachers (Bode 1989).

Through dialogue journal entries, you can make vital connections with your students not afforded by other types of assignments and activities. Because you do not correct mistakes in the students' entries, emphasis is placed on meaningful communication rather than direct literacy instruction (Bode 1989). As a result, you can get to know your students on a more personal level, and the more you know about individuals, the easier it is to teach them. When students share their personal thoughts and feelings with you, a sense of mutual respect, trust, and understanding is fostered.

Dialogue journals can serve as valuable learning tools in several ways. They can help students and teachers concentrate on the topic and task at hand and help students evaluate and modify their learning and study strategies. Dialogue journals can give you valuable insights about your students' metacognitive awareness, diagnostic feedback about their literacy skills, and general information about attitudes, interests, and motivation. Finally, dialogue journals can provide teachers with ongoing feedback about the effectiveness of instruction. The feedback offered by dialogue journals is vital to the process of continuous improvement and adjustment according to students' individual needs.

Getting Focused at the Beginning of Class

Although students should be encouraged to keep their journals available for jotting down things they want to recall, reflect, and share with the teacher, a certain time should be set aside each day for students to elaborate on those jottings. You might consider setting aside a few minutes at the beginning of each day or class for journal writing. One of the greatest challenges faced by teachers is getting their students—and sometimes even themselves—focused on the subject and task at the beginning of class. Much instructional time can be wasted in efforts to get students' attention and begin the lesson. Understandably, both students and teachers can have trouble shifting to new topics. For example, they may still be thinking about previous classes, personal problems, something that happened between classes, homework, personal and professional relationships, incomplete work, responsibilities, and so forth. Considering the number of potential distractions, preparing everyone to work can be quite a challenge.

The ability to put unfinished business aside for full concentration is a valuable skill that must be nurtured and practiced on a lifelong basis. Writing in dialogue journals for a few minutes at the beginning of each class is an excellent way to teach students how to focus on the present topic and activity. Students should be allowed to clear their minds by writing down anything that might be troubling them or otherwise occupying their minds, whether related to the class or not. Since writing can be an effective way to relax and concentrate by purging the mind of distracting thoughts and feelings, the few minutes invested in journal writing at the beginning of class makes normally wasted time productive.

If you begin each class with a few minutes of journal writing, model the process and its importance for your students by writing along with them. You should have the same or a similar type of notebook for your journal and be prepared to share some of your entries with your students. Because they will be sharing their personal thoughts with you, you need to be willing to do the same. Sharing your personal thoughts also serves to model for students the many kinds of entries appropriate for dialogue journals.

Literacy Skill Development

Because dialogue journals allow for the functional use of language (Bode 1989), they provide excellent opportunities for literacy skill development. For example, student entries can reflect language functions such as giving opinions, reporting facts, responding to questions, making predictions, giving directives, making apologies, expressing gratitude, conducting evaluations, making suggestions, asking informative questions, and articulating complaints. Providing opportunities and encouraging students to complain is an especially important language function of dialogue journals. In most traditional classrooms, students are discouraged from voicing complaints. As a result of this "culture of silence," many students learn and internalize passive roles in the classroom (Bode 1989).

When students are allowed to voice their complaints, and teachers respond by making appropriate adjustments, students become partners in the learning process. Students assume more of the responsibility for the effectiveness of instruction. If a student has a complaint and does not share it with the teacher, the student is suggesting that the complaint is not serious or realistic. If, on the other hand, the student's complaint reflects a legitimate concern, he or she must learn how to express it constructively.

Asking questions is another important language function developed through dialogue journals (Bode 1989). Students have the opportunity to practice formulating meaningful questions at all levels of thought; the ability to ask good questions is an important literacy skill in all content areas. Also, when students are encouraged and rewarded for asking challenging questions, they are empowered with greater responsibility for their own learning. Through questioning in dialogue journals, students also develop questioning attitudes and begin to view the world around them with a critical and inquisitive eye. By developing confidence with formulating and posing questions, students can become more active and effective participants in their classrooms and communities.

Through the medium of dialogue journal writing, teachers can integrate and emphasize both reading and writing as literacy skills and tools for learning. For example, students must read the teachers' entries made in response to their own entries; because the teachers' entries serve as models for good spelling, punctuation, grammar, and syntax, the students are exposed to an indirect editing process (Bode 1989). Also, since dialogue journals require both expressive and receptive literacy skills, they provide a meaningful context for literacy development in the content area classroom.

Metacognitive Reflections

Dialogue journal writing can be an excellent way to encourage students to think about their own thought processes, learning strategies, and study habits. You can guide their thoughts in this direction with general questions designed to make them stop and think about how they came to a particular conclusion, completed a particular homework assignment, read a particular passage, studied for a particular test, or collaborated on a particular project. At first, students will probably need a great deal of guidance. Making a conscious effort to articulate thought processes that are often automatic and taken for granted can be quite difficult. With guided practice, however, metacognitive awareness can be developed to the point that students automatically reflect on their own thinking and learning, even without your guidance.

Thinking about and recording the steps students follow in answering questions, solving problems, learning new vocabulary, studying difficult concepts, reading difficult material, and making adjustments when an approach is not working is a valuable process. Through this approach, students can evaluate their learning and study strategies to determine what works and what does not work well for them. Using this information, they can effect positive changes. Students, by developing their metacognitive awareness, can have more control over the outcomes of their learning, take more responsibility for their own learning, and build a repertoire of effective learning and study strategies. In addition to developing students' autonomy in managing their academic activities, dialogue journal writing can help them become more autonomous in managing their interpersonal affairs (Bode 1989).

Diagnostic Feedback

By analyzing students' self-reflections, dialogue journals can offer you valuable insights about your students' metacognitive awareness, literacy skills, attitudes, interests, and motivation. First, you can use this information to plan content area lessons that effectively incorporate literacy-based strategies and build literacy skills. Second, using this information can make the content more meaningful to your students' personal lives. Further, it can make the content more practical in terms of meeting students' perceived needs and achieving their personal goals. The insights can also make the content more relevant to students' real-life experiences, and students' self-reflections can be used to help you select interesting and motivating materials. Finally, use this information to plan learning activities that match students' likes and interests. In short, dialogue journal writing can personalize education by helping you meet each student at her or his point of need (Bode 1989).

Independent Projects

Students need at least occasional experiences with self-directed learning projects. Independent projects involve some instruction and guidance from the teacher, but the students are primarily responsible for their own work. Such projects help students develop competence and confidence with independent work, as well as a sense of responsibility for and control over their own learning. Additionally, students are able to apply and practice lifelong literacy, study, and research skills for various content areas. Gifted students in particular can benefit from independent projects designed to challenge and inspire them to pursue personal learning interests.

In addition to students working alone, independent projects can also involve students working in partnerships or small groups. Whether working alone, in partnerships, or in small groups, students need regular teacher contact and feedback. Although independent projects do not involve a great deal of teacher supervision, at least some contact with the teacher is important. Dialogue journals allow students to maintain that contact while working independently by providing an excellent system for students and teachers to communicate regularly about work the students are assigned to complete independently.

When students work on independent projects, especially those of a long-term nature, they need to keep careful records of their activities, progress, problems, questions, and achievements. Using dialogue journals, students can document their independent work and ask questions about content or procedures. You, in turn, can answer students' questions and give them feedback, guidance, direction, encouragement, and positive reinforcement. Students working in partnerships and small groups are able to share concerns and questions with you about their working relationships with other students. With this information, you can make adjustments in the groups, instructions, responsibilities, and so on to ensure positive interdependence (incentives to work as a team) and individual accountability (every student doing her or his fair share).

Student Input for Continuous Improvement of Instruction

Finally, dialogue journals provide an excellent way for students to give you regular feedback about the effectiveness of instruction. They can use the opportunity to share privately any problems or concerns they might have about instructional materials, strategies, and activities. At first, students may be reluctant to be candid with you about whether they enjoyed a lesson or found it valuable. You may have to ask some leading questions until they are comfortable evaluating classroom activities and assignments. Also, they will probably be skeptical about how candid you really want them to be; therefore, you will have to prove to them that you can handle the truth and that you genuinely want to know their opinions.

Model for and guide students in ways to give feedback constructively. Show them how to couch a complaint in positive terms by suggesting specific alternatives. General negativisms such as "boring," "too much homework," and "tests too hard" are not very useful forms of feedback. Instead, show them how to tell you *specifically* what topics, materials, or activities are boring, what they would like to see changed, and what particular topics, materials, or activities they would like to see instead.

Student complaints can provide a valuable perspective that you simply cannot get from evaluating a lesson yourself. Feedback from students empowers you to make adjustments accordingly by supplementing, changing, repeating, or continuing your original course of instruction. Of course, you will need to learn how to look for trends and commonalities amidst the feedback you receive. You do not want to make drastic changes to satisfy the demands of one or two disgruntled students. However, if you notice a significant number of students repeating the same kinds of complaints made legitimate by specific suggestions for improvement, you may want to consider some minor or even major adjustments.

Learning Logs

A learning log is a type of journal that emphasizes writing as a tool for learning and a means for keeping written records of content learned. Martin (1992) identifies three major purposes of this type of journal. One goal is to give students opportunities to practice and reinforce course concepts. Journal writing is an excellent tool for helping students master and internalize course content.

A second purpose is to provide students and teachers with documentation of students' learning. This documentation is another piece of vital feedback for you, the teacher, in terms of meeting students' individual needs. Learning logs can help you identify students who have mastered the content and are ready to take on more responsibility, work on independent activities, and progress to new and more advanced content. At the same time, learning logs can help you identify students who have not mastered the content and need reteaching, reinforcement, and special attention.

A third purpose of this type of journal is to give students the opportunity to practice articulating course concepts before being tested or otherwise held accountable for learning them. Journal writing is an excellent way for students to develop the habit of reflecting on and assessing their own learning. Regular opportunities to express in writing the concepts they have learned allows students to decide for themselves which concepts they believe they have mastered and which ones they need to review and study.

Learning log entries can take a variety of forms and can be used at any time before, during, or after a lesson or unit. For example, students can paraphrase and summarize lectures and reading assignments. In preparation for a test or other assessment activity, they can respond to higher-level essay questions related to the content. Students can brainstorm and make predictions before a lesson or unit to activate and assess background knowledge. Learning logs used throughout a lesson or unit during stopping points give students a chance to digest and reflect on newly acquired concepts. At the end of a lesson or unit, students can summarize, review, and evaluate their learning before moving on to new concepts.

Paraphrasing

Paraphrasing can be used for learning log entries in a variety of ways. For example, students can paraphrase reading assignments either while they are reading or after they have finished reading to demonstrate their understanding of the text. They may paraphrase reading assignments in their learning logs in preparation for tests or other assessment activities. Students can also paraphrase their lecture notes or notes taken while reading to check their own understanding and recall of key points. Paraphrasing a wide range of materials in their learning logs both for internalizing information and documenting learning of content can prove very helpful.

Paraphrasing involves rewriting text into one's own words, an activity that can improve comprehension, interest, concentration, and recall (Shugarman and Hurst 1986). Comprehension is improved because paraphrasing helps students construct meaning in a process of assimilating text information with prior knowledge and interpreting the meaning into their own language. Metacognition is also enhanced by paraphrasing because the required rereading, manipulation, and rewording of the text helps students focus their attention on what they do and do not understand.

Paraphrasing can improve the quality and quantity of students' receptive and expressive vocabulary abilities, as well as their spelling abilities (Cunningham and Cunningham 1976). Vocabularies are improved because of the emphasis on substituting appropriate synonyms for key words in the paraphrasing process. Also, putting new concepts into their own words helps students internalize and retain them.

Shugarman and Hurst (1986) identify three types of paraphrases. The first, *simple rephrasing*, involves paraphrasing short passages, paragraphs, or topic sentences. The second, *summarizing*, includes highlighting major points in longer passages or series of paragraphs. For both simple rephrasing and summarizing, students develop a parallel form of the original meaning of the text. The third type, *elaborating*, involves a purposeful integration of the text's meaning with the students' previous experiences, prior knowledge, and creative thought. Elaboration is a more advanced and involved process in which students construct new forms to represent the original meaning of the text. For example, a text passage could be elaborated in the form of a chart, cartoon, picture, map, or dialogue.

During the process of paraphrase writing, interact with your students to clarify and compare personal understandings with each other and the original text. To guide this process, first model the process and guide students through it orally before asking them to paraphrase in writing. The process of paraphrase writing should be reinforced with a variety of individual, paired, small-group, and whole-class activities that involve paraphrasing and discussion. These activities help students explore content beyond facts and vocabulary. They also provide opportunities for students to enhance their interpersonal communication skills, social skills, and creativity (Shugarman and Hurst 1986).

There are a variety of activities designed to teach and reinforce the process of paraphrasing (Shugarman and Hurst 1986). One example is an activity that should be carried out in the early stages of the development of the paraphrasing process. Give students a short passage and two sample paraphrases of it. One of the samples should be well constructed and the other poorly constructed. Discuss with students the strengths and weaknesses of each sample. Then, guide them through the process of determining meaning and interpreting it to paraphrase appropriately.

A second example involves providing students with a short passage and a well-constructed paraphrase of it. Emphasize to students how the different, simpler, and more concise wording of the paraphrase represents the same meaning. Then, ask students to paraphrase a short passage by answering the questions you have prepared to guide them through the process. Eventually, offer students longer passages to paraphrase and either decrease or eliminate the guide questions (Shugarman and Hurst 1986). The paraphrases students develop from guide questions—and then later on their own—can be recorded in their learning logs to help document their improvement and achievement in the skill of paraphrasing.

A third example of a paraphrasing activity pairs able readers with less-able readers. Ask the less-able reader to teach her or his partner how to develop a paraphrase of a given passage. Assign the able reader the tasks of reading the passage and checking the meaning of the paraphrase against the original meaning of the passage. If necessary, the able reader can assist her or his partner in the development of the paraphrase (Shugarman and Hurst 1986). Both partners can then record the paraphrase in their learning logs for later use in preparing for tests or otherwise reviewing previously learned content.

A fourth example suggests dividing the class into two teams and one panel of "experts." Each team is assigned to read and develop a paraphrase for a passage. The panel must decide which paraphrase is best and articulate why (Shugarman and Hurst 1986). After listening to the panel's decision and supporting arguments, the rest of the class members can then decide for themselves which paraphrase is best before recording it in their learning logs. In addition to the paraphrase, students should also write their reason(s) for choosing it.

Shugarman and Hurst's (1986) fifth example involves playing a popular song while students read the lyrics provided on a handout. Students then work in pairs, in small groups, or as a whole class to paraphrase the song or parts of it. Students can bring their own songs for the class to paraphrase. They may also record the paraphrases of their songs in their learning logs along with an explanation of how that song's lyrics are related to the content or topic of study.

A sixth example of a paraphrasing activity has students read and paraphrase advertisements, newspaper articles, letters to the editor, and so on. Guide them in distinguishing important from trivial information and help them identify persuasion techniques and marketing devices (Shugarman and Hurst 1986). Again, students can record their paraphrases in their learning logs along with brief explanations of the significance of the content in relation to the topic of study.

A seventh example involves students bringing passages from newspapers, magazines, trade books, and reference materials. Have them write paraphrases of their passages and share them with partners, small groups, or the whole class. After sharing paraphrases, students compare and discuss the meanings of the paraphrases with those of the original passages. Following the discussion, allow students to make changes, corrections, or additions to their paraphrases. They can then record their paraphrases in their learning logs.

A final example of a paraphrasing activity is sustained student summary writing (SSSW), which was developed by Cunningham and Cunningham (1976) to give students practice in putting concepts into their own words. After reading a passage, students are given about five minutes to write in their own words the most important information they recall. After writing, students share their summaries with the class, as you record the major ideas for all to see. Finally, the class uses these ideas to dictate a group summary recorded by you, the teacher.

Another use of SSSW involves summarizing information learned in class through reading, lecture, or other instructional activities. Toward the end of a class, students spend about five minutes writing summaries of the information they recall. Again, after writing, the students share their summaries with the class as you record the major ideas, and the class uses these ideas to dictate a class summary. These summaries—which can be copied and distributed to students for review and study—are especially helpful to students who are poor note takers.

Responding to Essay Questions

Using essay question responses as learning log entries is an excellent way to document students' learning of content and their ability to think critically about that content. Also, having students respond to essay questions in their learning logs is an excellent way to help them process information at higher levels of thinking. For example, Langer (1986) found that when writing essays, her students integrated information and engaged in more complex thought. They seemed to ponder the text after reading it, and in so doing reconceptualized the content in ways that integrated ideas and focused on more general issues or topics. Langer (1986) discovered essay questions helped her students focus on manipulating and reorganizing information. By contrast, when completing short answer study questions or taking notes from assigned text, they seemed to focus more on literal interpretations of the content.

Additionally, because learning logs are not graded, they provide a nonthreatening atmosphere for students to practice outlining and composing responses to the various types of essay questions typically found on tests. Students need practice in responding to the various terms used in essay questions (e.g., *compare, contrast, evaluate, defend, analyze, examine, critique, create, design, synthesize, distinguish, demonstrate, apply*, and so forth). If the only opportunity students have to respond to essay questions is on tests, they cannot possibly develop the competence and confidence necessary for outlining and composing responses. Therefore, without adequate practice, students' essay responses on tests may not validly reflect the quantity and quality of their knowledge. Before having students respond to essay questions in their learning logs, provide some modeling and direct instruction for outlining and composing responses for different essay question directives. Make sure you carefully define each term, provide an example of an appropriate response, and then give students time to practice responding to each type of essay question. An excellent way to prepare students for answering essay questions is a study strategy described in Chapter 3 called Predict, Organize, Rehearse, Practice, Evaluate (PORPE) (Simpson 1986).

Brainstorming and Predicting (Before Lesson or Unit)

At the beginning of a lesson or unit, students can write in their learning logs for a variety of purposes. For example, they can activate their background knowledge by brainstorming everything they already know about a particular topic. Then, following a whole-class discussion of what students brainstormed in their learning logs, they can add to their entries any other information they might have recalled or discovered. You can then use these learning log entries to assess students' prior knowledge and, if necessary, develop prerequisite concepts before introducing new concepts.

Students may also record any general questions they have or any specific questions they hope will be answered about the topic. They can record predictions about the lesson or what they will learn about the topic. Later, students can refer to their learning logs to compare what they learned with what they already knew about the topic and what they predicted about the lesson.

Processing and Reflecting (During Lesson or Unit)

At any point during a lesson or unit, you can stop and have students write about the content in their learning logs. Paraphrasing and précis (pronounced "pray-see") writing are excellent activities for processing and reflecting on the content during a lesson or unit. Précis writing involves summarizing the essence of the original text, including its emphasis and point of view, into abstract form that is less than one-third the length of the original text (D'Angelo 1983). Giving students opportunities to process the content helps them internalize it and understand it at higher levels of thought. Any of the writing-to-learn activities described earlier in this chapter could be used as learning log entries in the middle of a lesson or unit. For example, Quick Writes, collaborative writing, RAFT assignments, Writing Guides, and Paragraph Frames can all be used as opportunities for students to process the content in their learning logs.

Learning log entries throughout a lesson or unit are also important for students and teachers to reflect on how much and how well the students are learning. Specifically, these reflections help teachers identify gaps in learning, as well as any points of confusion. These gaps can then be filled and points of confusion clarified before moving on to new and more advanced concepts and information. When students have the opportunity to reflect on what they have learned, they are able to judge whether they understood the content as well as they thought they did. Then, if they discover missing pieces of information or misunderstandings about the content, they can ask you, the teacher, or other students for assistance and clarification.

Summarizing and Refocusing (After Lesson or Unit)

Summarizing requires that the main ideas and major supporting details be identified and restated concisely. As a form of summarizing, précis writing can provide an excellent learning log activity following a reading assignment, lesson, or unit. The process of précis writing involves reading a passage and then expressing one's understanding of the passage by selecting, rejecting, and paraphrasing ideas to compose a concise abstract of the passage. This activity can improve students' report and research writing, prepare them for tests, increase students' attention in class, and improve their vocabularies (D'Angelo 1983). Also, précis writing can improve students' comprehension, because paraphrasing and elaborating on text using their own words requires greater cognitive effort and deeper processing than merely copying text verbatim (as reported by D'Angelo 1983).

A prerequisite skill for précis writing is the ability to locate important ideas in a passage. If students have not mastered this ability, they need guidance and practice in identifying main ideas before they can be expected to master the process of précis writing. You cannot assume that your students already know that main ideas are often stated in a topic sentence that is supported by the other sentences in the paragraph.

Neither can you assume students know that topic sentences can be located anywhere in a paragraph, and that some paragraphs have implied main ideas not stated in topic sentences at all. Provide students with sample paragraphs containing topic sentences located at the beginning, middle, and end, as well as paragraphs with implied main ideas. Following direct instruction, students need practice identifying and formulating topic sentences for all types of paragraphs.

Students should also be able to explain why each sentence in a paragraph is or is not a topic sentence. After rejecting a sentence as a topic sentence, students must be able to identify it as either too general (i.e., it refers to more information than is addressed by the paragraph) or too specific (i.e., it refers to only part of the information addressed by the paragraph). Finally, after recognizing a paragraph with an implied main idea, students need to be able to formulate an appropriate topic sentence that expresses the main idea.

D'Angelo (1983) recommends using paragraphs taken directly from content area materials for practice. Students need guided and independent practice using these materials for distinguishing topic sentences from supporting details. They also need experience identifying topic sentences at the beginning, middle, and end of paragraphs and formulating topic sentences for paragraphs with implied main ideas.

Once students have demonstrated mastery summarizing paragraphs by identifying main ideas, they are ready to begin the process of précis writing. The first step in précis writing is identifying main ideas and restating them using fewer, simpler, and more familiar words (i.e., paraphrasing). In this process, students should supply synonyms for the key words in topic sentences, for which students need competence with use of a thesaurus and dictionary. If they have not mastered use of these reference materials, they need direct instruction and guided practice (see Chapter 8).

Before expecting students to paraphrase topic sentences in writing, you must provide substantial oral practice. As a group, students need sufficient opportunities to supply synonyms for key words in the text and then discuss and defend their choices. Such oral activities help students develop rephrasing skills, and "the actual writing of paraphrased ideas then becomes an extension of what students do orally" (D'Angelo 1983, 537).

Following oral lessons and written practice exercises in selecting topic sentences from different positions within paragraphs and identifying key words and replacing them with appropriate synonyms, students are ready for the actual writing of the précis itself. Once students have developed confidence with the requisite skills, the process of précis writing actually involves less time than the skill development. Keep in mind, however, that the process of précis writing is difficult, and students must practice and master the skills involved (D'Angelo 1983).

Until students become proficient with précis writing, you will need to provide them with guidance and coaching. Remind them continually to apply the skills they have practiced. In particular, "students must remember three key things to help them write an accurate and concise précis: Identify topic sentences, rephrase in your own words, and as you write, keep the order of the text" (D'Angelo 1983, 538).

Keeping the order of the passage is an important part of the learning process for précis writing. However, once students become proficient with précis writing, keeping the order of the text is not necessary. In fact, changing the sequence of ideas or information often clarifies a passage and the points it emphasizes, especially in précis form (D'Angelo 1983).

Another valuable strategy for teaching students how to summarize is Generating Interaction between Schema and Text (GIST) (Cunningham

1982). In this strategy, students begin by reading the first sentence of a paragraph and formulating a statement of fifteen words or less to summarize it. Next, they read the second sentence and rewrite their summary statement to summarize both sentences. This process continues until students have read the entire paragraph and summarized it in a single sentence of fifteen words or less.

Once students have developed competence and confidence summarizing paragraphs using the GIST strategy, they can begin summarizing passages. The process is the same. After reading the first paragraph, students summarize it in a sentence of twenty words or less. Then, after reading the second paragraph, students summarize both paragraphs by revising their sentence. The process continues until they have read all the paragraphs and summarized them in a sentence of 20 words or less.

Summarizing, in any form, is a valuable technique for helping students in transition between activities, lessons, or unit topics. It can be used to assist students in getting closure on one topic and refocusing on the content objectives. In fact, some form of summarizing should be used to conclude every lesson in order to "bring it all together" for the students. Sometimes the various learning activities in a lesson can seem like isolated events to students who need to see how it all relates to the objectives and expectations stated at the beginning of the lesson. Summarizing can also provide the regular review that is so important for long-term retention of information.

Diagnostic Feedback

Learning logs are an important source of diagnostic feedback in terms of how well students have learned the content. You should read them regularly throughout, as well as at the end of a study unit. Then, instruction can be modified or repeated as necessary according to how well students demonstrate their understanding of the content in their learning logs. The diagnostic information provided by learning logs can also be valuable for planning future lessons and units.

Although learning logs can provide a vital source of information about how much and how well students are learning, they may not always offer sufficient feedback by themselves. Some students, e.g., primary-grade children and students who are poor writers, may know more about the content than is evidenced by what they have written in their learning logs. At the same time, other students may not understand the content as well as their learning log entries might lead you to believe: they may have copied information from other students, lecture notes, or the textbook without understanding it on more than a superficial level. Therefore, you may need to supplement the information provided by learning logs with information obtained through other means including teacher conferences, observations, quizzes, tests, homework assignments, and in-class activities. During conferences, students should refer to their learning logs to guide them in responding to your questions and requests for clarification.

Diagnostic information gleaned from journal entries and conferences can be recorded in various ways. You can keep a checklist for groups and classes of students. Anecdotal information can be recorded on cards, in notebooks, or in files for individual students. As you read and comment on each journal entry, note important insights and perceptions about that student's progress. These notes provide useful information about students' strengths and problem areas needing attention (Martin 1992). All of this information will be valuable to you in the authentic assessment of students, as well as in future instructional planning. (For more information on authentic assessment, see Chapter 9).

Reading Response and Character Journals

Simpson (1986) described her use and success with reading response journals in literature classes. Each day, after reading aloud from a piece of literature, she and her students wrote in their journals for three to five minutes. To prepare students for writing the first time, she and the class brainstormed a list of appropriate journal responses, e.g., predictions, comments on characters and character development, insights into evolving themes, and appreciation for or critique of the author's technique. Until students became comfortable and confident with writing their responses, she suggested topics from which they could choose.

After writing in the journals, Simpson (1986) and her students voluntarily shared and discussed issues from their writing. At first, she shared comments from her own journal to demonstrate her interest, commitment, and involvement in the project. She also wanted to model for the students responses that went beyond summarizing to reflect critical thinking. Later, she shared her responses only when she wanted to emphasize something in particular or guide the direction of the discussion.

Simpson (1986) reported several benefits of reading response journals. First, the communal sharing of the literature and literacy processes emphasizes to students that you are their partner in learning and their equal in enjoyment, praise, and criticism of the literature. Second, the students and you, the teacher, experience an appreciation of the unique and varied contributions made by each individual. Third, instruction in literary devices is accomplished by guiding the students in their own discovery and applications of the devices. For example, students discovered and wrote about character motivation and development, foreshadowing, flashback, setting description, effective use of dialogue, interjection of humor, anticipation of audience questions, and alternate techniques available to authors. Fourth, Simpson (1986) concluded that the development of critical thinking is enhanced by the discussions. Students move from summarizing events and actions to giving opinions supported by reason and evidence. They also learn that there are no right or wrong answers; as long as a comment is logical and well supported, it is acceptable. Fifth, students have daily nonthreatening opportunities for writing that emphasize thoughts, perceptions, and insights rather than mechanics and spelling. Finally, students develop active listening skills during the discussions by sharing and defending their own comments and responding to others' comments.

Since Simpson (1986) read her students' journals once a week, she had the opportunity to respond to those students who were reluctant to share their entries in class. She was able to positively reinforce students whose entries showed deep, critical, and insightful thought. At the same time, she was able to model and provide direction for students having difficulty moving beyond the level of superficial summarizing.

A variation of reading response journals, *character journals,* was described by Jossart (1988). At times, she asked her students to respond to something they read or that was read to them by having them select a character and write a journal entry from the perspective of that character. The students' goal was to provide enough hints in their journal entries to allow a reader or listener to identify the character. Jossart (1988) reported that students learned quickly that at least several different characters could easily write the same entry. Their challenge became to add one or two details that would give away the perspective of one particular character.

After writing, Jossart (1988) had her students share their journal entries and guess each other's characters. She reported that the ensuing discussion led to active listening for the purpose of challenging and defending entries. Not only did this journal activity serve as a writing opportunity for her students, Jossart (1988) concluded that it also provided lessons in such literary devices as point of view, characterization, and mood, and comprehension skills including making inferences and identifying supporting details.

Giving Students Feedback and Assessing Their Journal Entries

Many teachers avoid using journals in their classrooms for fear of overwhelming themselves with grading and written feedback. However, systems of feedback, assessment, and diagnosis can be established to minimize the amount of time and effort required by the teacher. By establishing an efficient system, you can save yourself time and energy while also providing students sufficient feedback for their writing. The task of responding to and grading student journals need not be burdensome. The benefits of journal writing including diagnosis of student needs and the enhancement of content learning and literacy skills far outweigh the time spent on evaluating and providing feedback.

Grading and Written Comments

Grades send powerful messages to students about what is important. Students often learn quickly what they have to do to earn good grades. Because students eventually understand the criteria associated with high grades and then focus their energies accordingly, teachers need to carefully consider and consciously identify the criteria they use for evaluation. The criteria for grading journals might include certain numbers of pages, entries, or responses to specific journal assignments (Martin 1992). Teachers should communicate these criteria to their students and remind them on a regular basis what criteria will be used for evaluation. Much learning time is wasted by making students guess the criteria on their own through a process of trial and error.

One of the most common systems for grading journals is the all-or-none approach of giving credit or no credit. If students meet the required criteria, they earn a grade that indicates full credit. If they do not meet the criteria, they earn no credit (Martin 1992). You might consider allowing students to redo their entries, add to their entries, or complete additional journal assignments to earn partial credit. Giving these students full credit would not be fair to the students who earned full credit the first time and might serve as a disincentive for students to do their best on the first attempt. However, giving them a chance to earn partial credit offers students an incentive to improve their performance.

A modified version of the credit/no credit system is a system of symbols (e.g., checks, pluses, and minuses) or points that indicate various levels of success in meeting the criteria. This type of system allows you to make more distinctions between quality levels of performance. Another modified version of the credit/no credit system works well within numerical point-averaging grading systems. In this system, a specific number of points is assigned to either the journal as a whole or to specific journal assignments. "These point totals should not be so large that students feel anxiety over losing points for insignificant aspects of their responses; rather, they should allow the students to feel pride in easily accumulating points for contributing to their journal" (Martin 1992, 316).

Keep in mind that points should never be taken off in journal writing for mechanical errors, i.e., spelling, grammar, and punctuation. One of the many benefits of journal writing is the freedom from worry afforded students by the knowledge that teachers will not be attacking their spelling, grammar, and punctuation with red ink. However, if students receive no feedback at all, they may get the impression that journal writing is not important work, and that if it is not graded, it has little worth.

According to Martin (1992, 314), "the most important aspect of evaluating student journals is the manner in which the teacher responds to students' entries." Students should expect feedback and grading that focuses on the content of the writing rather than the mechanics of the written expression. They should also expect that your comments will be as positive and constructive as possible. Such feedback motivates students to improve and gives them the confidence to keep practicing.

Your responses help guide students toward desired objectives in future journal work. Therefore, responses must be genuine and more specific than such nondescript responses as *good* or *interesting*. Instead, share your own personal perspectives and insights that help open communication channels between you and each student (Martin 1992).

Minimizing Time Spent on Evaluating and Responding to Journals

The idea that journals and other writing assignments overburden content area teachers with excessive grading is a misconception that has minimized or even prevented the use of writing as a learning tool in the content area classroom. Although you will probably have to make some changes in your classroom procedures and grading schedules, you can effectively include journal and other writing assignments without giving yourself extra work.

One way to minimize the time of grading journals is to create a manageable schedule for collecting and reading journals. For example, instead of having all your students' journals due at the same time, stagger them by assigning different due dates to different groups. That way, you have fewer journals to read at one time. However, you also need to build some flexibility into the system, so that students' individual needs are met. Some students may legitimately need more time to complete their journal assignments, while others may need to get feedback from you more often than others (Martin 1994).

A second way you can minimize the burden of grading journals is to make sure you collect and respond to them regularly and frequently—at least once a week. Such a schedule prevents you from being overwhelmed with large numbers of entries to read for each journal. "For journals to be most effective, both students and the teacher need to keep up with them" (Martin 1994, 315).

Another way to reduce time spent on assessing journals is to teach students how to evaluate themselves and their peers. Keep in mind, however, that students cannot be required to let peers read their papers. The Privacy of Information Act protects students who wish to keep the contents of their papers confidential. Therefore, you may suggest peer review as an option but emphasize their option of confidentiality by making it clear that peer review must be done on a voluntary basis only.

In training students for peer review, you will need to show them some examples of journal entries at various levels of quality. Model for them some appropriate responses for giving positive and constructive feedback. Remind students to avoid worrying about spelling and other mechanics for this task and focus instead on the message being communicated.

Student Self-Evaluations

Although self-evaluations should not replace feedback given by the teacher, they can significantly reduce your work load. Also, self-evaluation is a valuable skill that is especially vital to the process of good writing. Students learn to read their own writing for the purposes of editing and revising. They will need some direct instruction and supervised practice before they are ready to evaluate their own writing.

First, present a list of criteria for evaluation, along with samples of good journal entries. Discuss with students the specific criteria and how each is either demonstrated by or missing from the sample entry. Second, provide sample journal entries that have some common problems and mistakes; again using a checklist of criteria, demonstrate how each is either demonstrated or not present. In addition to identifying the problems and mistakes, explain how they can be remedied as well. Provide students with some guided practice in evaluating and revising a variety of writing samples according to a given checklist of criteria.

When students are ready to evaluate their own entries, provide them with checklists of criteria. Because the mechanical aspects of writing should not be evaluated in journal writing, include only criteria related to communication of the content. For example, you could provide a list of key vocabulary or concepts students should address in their entries. You might also identify as criteria the various aspects of good written expression such as organization, topic sentences, supporting details, introductions, summaries, transitions, sequencing, paraphrasing, and quoting. Once students have evaluated their own journal entries using the criteria checklists, offer them incentives to revise. For example, you might offer credit as an in-class activity or homework assignment.

Peer Reviews and Teacher Conferences

As with self-evaluations, peer reviews should not replace feedback from the teacher but can significantly reduce the teacher's workload. Students will need some instruction, modeling, and guided practice for reviewing work and offering feedback. When you use peer reviews, make sure you inform students, before they write their entries, that their classmates will be reading them and giving feedback on the clarity and content of the message. Tell them to avoid including anything in their journal entries that might be embarrassing to themselves or others.

Peer reviews can be more meaningful than feedback from the teacher. Often students can more easily understand the difficulties their peers are experiencing, as well as the explanations they offer. (Martin 1992) Following peer-review sessions, hold class discussions so that you can evaluate students' understandings of the content and address problem areas. Such discussions also allow you to assess the quality and appropriateness of the feedback students give to each other.

Before employing peer reviews, spend some time teaching students how to give positive and constructive feedback to one another. Using sample entries and checklists of criteria, model for students how to frame suggestions in the form of questions, i.e., "Would it sound better if you said it this way?" or "What are you trying to say in this sentence?" Once students have had ample opportunities to practice giving feedback in whole-class, small-group, and partnership activities, they are ready to participate in the peer review process.

First, assign partners carefully, so that each student is capable of suggesting improvements to the other. Shift emphasis from mechanics to the message and have each writer read her or his entry aloud to her or his partner. The partner responds by first saying something positive about the entry and then asking questions for clarification and making suggestions for improvement. After the writer rereads the entry, the partner asks more questions and makes more positive comments about the quality of the written message. Finally, partners switch roles and repeat the process.

You may want to schedule occasional teacher/student conferences with individuals, partners, or small groups. During these conferences, allow students to ask questions, discuss content, or otherwise address their journal entries. At the same time, you can answer students' questions, make clarifications, reteach content, follow up on comments, and ask them questions about their journal entries. Some students need occasional personal contact for encouragement and reinforcement. Also, if you want to give a student extensive feedback, you can supplement your written comments with oral statements and explanations. Doing so can save you time and can also provide more effective feedback, because you reinforce the information both orally and in writing.

Teacher Self-Reflections, Observations, and Record-Keeping

As mentioned earlier in this chapter, you need to write in your own journal every time your students write in theirs. In so doing, you not only model the process but also send your students the message that this activity is important and worthwhile for *everyone,* including the teacher. When writing in your own journal, you may respond to the same assignment as your students, especially if you want to share examples of entries appropriate for the assigned task. In addition to or instead of responding to the students' assigned task, you can record reflections about your teaching and observations about your students. These reflections and observations will be helpful to you in developing lesson plans and selecting materials. Besides writing in your journal simultaneously with your students, you can also record your reflections and observations in your journal throughout the day and after school.

If you keep your journal nearby while grading papers, you can record the perceptions and insights you gain about students' learning and literacy needs. While reading, evaluating, and commenting on your students' journal entries, make note of which ideas seem to be clearly understood by most and which ideas still seem to be confusing to some. A practical system for recording this information is to keep in your journal a checklist of ideas and concepts you expect your students to master. You may also keep anecdotal progress records on individual students, groups of students, and whole classes of students (Martin 1992).

Using your journal for record keeping is a handy way to keep all the diagnostic information you gather in one place. In addition to recording diagnostic feedback and planning concerns, you can also assess your own teaching effectiveness and progress (Martin 1992). For example, make note of what worked, what did not work, and what changes you want to make. Making regular and routine journal entries is an excellent way to get into the habit of daily self-reflection and continuous self-improvement.

PART 2

STRATEGY: DIRECTED WRITING ACTIVITY (DWA)

The Directed Writing Activity (DWA) was developed by Blake and Spennato (1980) as a strategy for developing writing skills and using the writing process to enhance content area learning. Like the Directed Reading Activity, it provides a basic framework for teaching a content area lesson. Instead of emphasizing reading as a tool for learning, however, the DWA emphasizes writing. This strategy can be used at almost any grade level and in any content area. It is an instructional framework that allows for considerable flexibility in terms of the types of writing assignments you choose. Following are a set of procedures modified from Blake and

Spennato's (1980) original description. Students can work individually, in pairs, or in small groups to follow these steps:

1. Prepare students for writing by helping them select an appropriate topic, that is neither too broad nor too narrow. You may provide possible topics from which they can choose, guide them in choosing their own topics, or provide a specific topic for them. Then, help students develop lists of possible sources of information they will need to complete the assignment.

2. Help students formulate questions that should be answered in the writing assignment. You may provide students with a list of questions, provide choices from which they select a specified number, or help them formulate their own questions. Then, help students decide which possible sources would be most helpful in answering each question.

3. Guide and consult with students as they gather and organize the information necessary for answering the questions. Help them delete irrelevant or extraneous information and fill in any gaps to ensure complete and accurate information. Then, students write a first draft using the information they have collected and organized.

4. Each student reads her or his first draft to you, a partner, or a small group of classmates for feedback and suggestions. Ask listeners to respond first by complimenting some aspect of the writing. They should then offer suggestions in the form of questions (e.g., "What exactly do you mean in that sentence?" or "Would it be better to say it this way?"). Students take notes to record the suggestions offered.

5. After revising their first drafts according to the suggestions offered by you or their classmates, students either turn in their second drafts or exchange them with a partner. Next, either you or the student partners edit the second drafts by identifying mechanical problems that need to be corrected (e.g., spelling, capitalization, grammar, punctuation, and so on). The editor should also provide a written compliment of some aspect of the content, along with written comments that identify any content that is unclear or otherwise problematic.

6. Students write and turn in their final drafts. They should receive feedback as soon as possible—you can provide written feedback, oral feedback in individual conferences, or some combination of both.

WRITING WORKSHOP

Writing workshop refers, very simply, to a time set aside each day for writing (Atwell 1989; Calkins 1986; Graves 1983). As a concept, writing

Writing activities can be used before, during, or after reading to enhance content area learning.

workshop emerged from the work of the National Writing Project. Although originally developed as an activity for English classes, writing workshop can be used for content area literacy in any classroom. Its application in content area classrooms is summarized by Ruddell (1993, 175–176):

> The essential notion of writing workshop is that in every classroom there is a time set aside, daily if possible, when everyone in the room is immersed in writing. This time is established and maintained consistently, so that students can depend on its daily (or alternating day, or three-times-a-week) occurrence. The purpose of the workshop is to give students frequent, regularly scheduled opportunities to write about the subject matter of that class and their relationship to it.

One of the purposes of writing workshop is to turn students into writers in one or more content areas. To accomplish this goal, regular and frequent opportunities for personal involvement with writing are essential. When students are invited to choose their own subject, form, voice, and audience, they begin to take ownership and responsibility for their writing. This transformation changes writing from an assigned task to a personally relevant project. When students are in the routine of writing at certain times on certain days, they begin to expect, look forward to, and mentally prepare for it. They begin thinking ahead about information and ideas, as well as various ways of saying what they want to say. The writing workshop provides a way for writing to become a deeply personal experience.

Using the writing workshop in content area classrooms provides a way for not only writing but also the content to become deeply personal. During this time, students reflect on the content as it relates to their own lives and experiences. Through this regular and frequent reflection, students can make the content their own. The writing process allows them to integrate the content with their background knowledge, while it heightens students' awareness of when and how concepts and ideas are revealed in their daily lives.

Ruddell (1993) recommends setting aside ten to fifteen minutes daily at the beginning or end of class for the writing workshop. Both of these times are typically filled with routine tasks that waste instructional time: implementing the writing workshop can make a significant amount of wasted class time productive. Ruddell (1993) suggests a hard and fast rule for the writing workshop: Whether at the beginning or end of class, students are to be in their seats writing at a designated time.

Crucial to the success of the writing workshop in the content area classroom is the role of the teacher. Instead of *instructing* you *guide* by designing writing prompts and ideas rather than assigning topics and tasks. Instead of lecturing, consult with writers and conduct mini-lessons (Calkins 1989). Rather than working on something else while the students write, consult with individual writers to offer feedback and give direction. Finally, use conferences to enhance students' understanding of the content and develop their abilities in becoming independent and competent writers and learners in the content area (Ruddell 1993).

Seven Principles for Writing Workshop

Atwell (1989) offers seven principles to guide development and implementation of the writing workshop:

1. Writers need regular blocks of time to think, write, confer, read, change their minds, and write some more.
2. Writers need their own topics, so they can use writing as a way to think about and give shape to their own ideas and concerns.
3. Writers need helpful response during the composing process from their peers and the teacher, who models the kinds of restatements and questions that help writers reflect on the content of their writing.
4. Writers learn mechanics in context from teachers who address errors as they occur within individual pieces of writing.
5. Students need to know adults who write, so teachers need to write, share their writing with students, and demonstrate what experienced writers do in the process of composing.
6. Because writers need to read, they must have access to a wide variety of texts, prose, poetry, fiction, and nonfiction.

7. Writing teachers must take responsibility for their knowledge and teaching by seeking out professional resources, becoming writers and researchers, and observing and learning from their own and their students' writing.

Mini-Lessons

A mini-lesson is a brief meeting (generally five to ten minutes) of the whole class to begin writing workshop. Lead a discussion of issues that might have surfaced in previous workshops or in students' writing. Atwell (1989) suggests that the discussion topic might have something to do with the mechanics of writing, the editing process, techniques of organization and style, or literary modes and genres. Until students are veterans of writing workshop, mini-lessons might focus on procedural issues including classroom procedures for using the daily writing folders or journals, resources and materials available to the writers, self-editing steps, where to put writing that is ready for teacher editing, and what to do in conferences. For example, in a mini-lesson on conferences, you might discuss effective and helpful ways of responding and then model conferencing techniques in role-play situations. Mini-lessons provide excellent opportunities for you to share with the whole class hints about writing that you learn from working with individual students. In fact, the point of the mini-lesson is to share personal knowledge of writing (Atwell 1989).

Conferring and Editing

Atwell (1989) describes how, after the mini-lesson, she begins the writing process by modeling appropriate behavior for her middle school students. If possible, she sits down at an empty student desk and starts writing. She does not look up to see who is writing and who is not. She is busy writing, and her posture indicates that she means business and that she expects everyone else to join her in becoming a writer. And they do! After about ten minutes, she looks up from her own writing, and sees that all her students are writing. At this point, she puts aside her own writing and begins to move among her students, quietly conferring with them one at a time. If a student is not still writing at this point, she moves to her or him first to conduct a brief conference on her or his topic.

Atwell (1989) reports that her students know she will respond to their writing in person during the writing process rather than giving written comments at the end of the process. She describes the importance of conferring and conferences to writing workshop: "The purpose of writing workshop is to help kids develop their abilities as writers, not to assign sink-or-swim tests of writing ability, denying help along the way" (Atwell 1989, 47). Therefore, she never writes comments on students' writing. The only marks she makes are for straight editing of the final draft to correct or indicate errors students missed when they did their own editing.

According to Atwell (1989), teachers who wait to give comments on a final draft make three unreasonable assumptions. First, they assume that students actually read the comments. Second, they assume that students will recall the comments as they are working on the next writing assignment. Third, they assume that students will be able to transfer that advice to a completely different situation.

When teachers spend time in class conferring with students about their writing, they significantly reduce their grading time. Another way to decrease grading time with writing workshop is to allow flexible due dates. Atwell (1989), who allows students to write and finish their papers at their own paces, reports that she never has more than five or six papers to edit at one time.

Atwell (1989) recommends conferring with students by carrying your chair from desk to desk, so that you can interact with the student at her or his workspace. She suggests this strategy rather than creating a specific conference area at a table or desk and having students take turns coming to you. When you move from desk to desk, you have greater control over how much time you spend with each student. By controlling time spent with each student, you should be able to confer, at least briefly, with each student every day.

During a conference, if a student hands you her or his paper and asks you to read it, Atwell (1989) suggests handing it back and telling the student that you do not read drafts. Rather, you listen to what the student has to say about the draft, especially what he or she thinks about it. That way, you can give guidance and direction without accepting responsibility for the writing. As much as possible, you should ensure that the writer takes responsibility for what happens in the conference. You can do this by beginning each conference with an open-ended question or directive such as "Tell me about your paper" or "How is it coming?" Eventually, students will learn that they must take the lead in the conference and will be ready to start the dialogue without a prompt from you. The purpose of the conferences is not to force writers to revise; rather, it is to confer with them about the content of the paper. Speak with students in terms of what is working, what is not working, and what, if anything, they might change or add (Atwell 1989).

Atwell (1989) suggests that when you finish editing a paper, you prepare for the editing conference by making two kinds of notes. First, note the skills the writer has used correctly. Second, note the skills the student still needs to master. These notes will be valuable to you as you plan future mini-lessons and hold parent conferences. The skills you should focus on while editing include syntax, usage, spelling, punctuation, format, and style. You can add others as appropriate for each content area.

Group Share

The group share is a mini-lesson held at the end of class (usually seven or eight minutes) instead of at the beginning. Group share serves two important general purposes for writing workshop: It brings closure to the workshop and it allows students to discover what the other writers are doing.

Atwell (1989) suggests using this time to model ways of listening and responding to writers. She also provides this time for the whole class to "confer about conferring," i.e., about the kinds of responses that help and do not help writers. As a result, students learn how to give positive and constructive feedback. Additionally, Atwell (1989) uses the group share time to follow up on mini-lessons.

The writers can use the group share time for a variety of purposes. For example, they can experiment with new ideas, share a successful technique, try out alternatives to something that did not work, and get feedback from a wide range of perspectives. Generally, only a couple of students will have time to share during one session. The students who share can be either volunteers or writers you invite to speak because there is something in particular you want them to share with the class. You might also ask writers to share when you want them to get reactions other than the teacher's (Atwell 1989).

THE PROCESS APPROACH TO WRITING

Manion (1988) uses writing workshops to teach students the various steps involved in the production of a written composition. This application of writing workshop involves the process approach to writing. Process writing is an approach that emphasizes the way writing is accomplished rather than the final product. By using the process approach to writing, teachers can emphasize writing to learn and the quality of the ideas students present. When students are involved with the content through process writing, the content becomes personalized, and hopefully, internalized (Sensenbaugh 1989).

To implement a process approach, Manion (1988) set aside two days a week for writing workshop. She began each of these classes with a mini-lesson over such things as class procedures, topic choices, revision and editing strategies, techniques for good writing, and samples of good writing.

After writing their first drafts, students reflect on their own writing. Writers then participate in peer conferences to share their work with partners who listen carefully and raise questions that might lead to revision of the content. These conferences are important because they help writers learn to ask high-quality substantive questions of themselves during self-reflection. Also, through conferences, writers learn to analyze their own work and begin to develop audience awareness. An additional benefit of peer conferences is the support system that evolves through collaboration (Manion 1988).

Following peer conferences, you, the teacher, hold a conference with each student, in which you raise questions that might help polish the piece, particularly in terms of balance, form, and style. After completion of the peer and teacher conferences, writers must decide what they will do next: they need to decide what revisions, if any, will be made and whether anything needs to be added to the paper (Manion 1988).

After revisions are made, and writers are satisfied with their second or third draft, they begin editing their papers. Following a checklist developed for the particular purpose of the writing, students reread their drafts and correct mechanical errors. Afterward, the students review their papers with partners who make suggestions about various mechanical corrections that might be considered. Finally, the writer confers with you, the teacher, as you praise what has been done well and make suggestions to improve punctuation, language usage, syntax, and clarity. The edited papers are then rewritten into polished final form and submitted for evaluation (Manion 1988).

The application of writing workshop described by Manion (1988) for teaching the process approach to writing is characterized by three features included in writing lessons. Good writing lessons model the process for students and provide guided practice. They also offer feedback that helps students see how they succeeded and how they might improve their writing in the future (Cunningham and Cunningham 1987).

In every content area, students must become competent in all phases of the writing process. They must first learn how to prepare for writing and outline or otherwise plan their paper. Students should then receive objective feedback from others and make revisions based on that feedback. Next, they must edit their papers to correct mechanical errors. Finally, students rewrite their papers into final finished products. All of these steps of process writing can be taught in any content area using the writing workshop format.

Process writing can be used to produce written expression in a variety of genres. In most content areas, it is used for writing expository essays on some particular facet of the content. In English literature, process writing can be effective in writing narrative essays (i.e., stories), as well. No matter what the genre, purpose for writing, or required elements of the written expression, the steps in the process remain basically the same.

Prewriting Strategies

The first step in the writing process is preparation. Activities designed to prepare students for writing should help them develop background knowledge, select and narrow appropriate topics, consider the audience, decide on techniques to be used, brainstorm ideas, do research, and organize thoughts. Students need time and direction in class as they complete prewriting activities. Some of these activities can be completed as a whole class; others should be completed in small groups, in partnerships, or by individual writers.

Before they begin writing, students need guidance first in widening their perspectives of the topics. This process might require that they narrow their topics to manageable units. Next, they need assistance in identifying the subtopics and their relationships to the main topic. One way to help students get an overall view of their topics and identify appropriate subtopics is the card strategy lesson, which is described in the next section. Finally, students must develop a plan for organizing the topics in an appropriate sequence. Although the plan may change throughout the writing process, it is still important in guiding them. Devices for helping students organize their thoughts and subtopics include the cognitive map and web, the feature matrix, and of course, the traditional outline.

Card Strategy Lesson

Kucer (1986) describes the card strategy lesson as a way to help writers focus on their topics in the prewriting phase of the writing process. Through this lesson, you can guide students in the process of constructing a framework of meaning that consists of a sequence of subtopics. Following are the steps recommended by Kucer (1986):

1. Give each writer three or four index cards; ask them to brainstorm possible writing topics, each on a separate card. A topic related to the current unit of study may be specified, or students may choose their own topics. If you assign a topic, make sure it is general enough to allow students to generate sufficient subtopics. Students should be encouraged to share ideas with one another in generating potential topics. From the list of topics they generated, each writer selects one. You may want to file all the unused topics as a source of ideas for future use.

2. Each writer considers the major ideas related to his or her topic. Students who have sufficient background knowledge of the topic can brainstorm to generate major ideas related to it. As they generate major ideas, they record them on index cards—one to a card—as words, phrases, clauses, or sentences. During this process, students are encouraged to review related class readings and notes for relevant ideas. Through this process, they will be making conceptual connections among the related information from which the major ideas are generated. In other words, they will be looking for the big picture in their class readings and lecture notes, as well as in their

writing. Students should then share their ideas in small groups and help each other generate more ideas.

3. Students who do not have sufficient background knowledge of the topic will need to research the subject before generating major ideas. Introduce students to various reference sources and note-taking strategies: students should be required to read and take notes on their topics from at least three articles or other sources. After building prior knowledge, have students review their notes and generate major ideas as previously described.

4. Each writer selects the major ideas he or she wants to use. The unused cards are set aside but kept available in case they are needed. Students should be allowed to make changes in their cards any time they wish by adding, rejecting, or modifying them.

5. After selecting the major ideas, each writer organizes her or his cards in a meaningful order. Have students place the cards, below the topic card, in the order they choose. After deciding on the order of her or his cards, each writer shuffles the cards and exchanges them with a partner. The partner then arranges them in a meaningful sequence and explains the rationale behind that particular sequence. Next, the writer places the cards back in their original sequence, explaining the rationale to her or his partner. Following discussion of the two sequencing options, the writer decides on a final arrangement.

6. Using their cards as a guide, students write their first draft.

To introduce this strategy, particularly with younger children and poor writers, precede these steps with a whole-class Language Experience Approach (see Chapter 1). Using this approach, the entire class contributes major ideas to the same topic. Begin by asking students to brainstorm possible topics and then record them for all to see. The class chooses one of the topics and brainstorms major ideas related to it. Once again, record the ideas so that the class can decide which ideas should be included and in what order they should be presented. Finally, individual students dictate the text for each major idea as you record the information.

A Cognitive Mapping Strategy

Peresich, Meadows, and Sinatra (1990) describe a cognitive mapping strategy for use in content area classrooms. This strategy allows teachers to show students, through discussion and mapping, how a content theme or topic is organized. Students then use the strategy independently to gather and organize information in preparation for writing. Following is a set of procedures adapted from those described by Peresich, Meadows, and Sinatra (1990):

1. First, you read about and conceptualize the unit or topic by connecting major and minor ideas according to the text structure. You then

construct a cognitive map to show the hierarchical arrangement of the ideas. Subtopics are placed in geometric shapes and connected with lines to show their relationships to the main topic and to each other.

2. After students read the relevant material, you, the teacher, present them with a blank version of the cognitive map, i.e., the shapes and lines only, without the words. Then guide the class in filling in the map in one of two ways. One way is to elicit from students the topic or central thesis and record it. As students offer main ideas, discuss them, and explain why they are either accepted and recorded or rejected. Once all the main ideas have been identified and listed, students offer subordinate ideas, which are also discussed and either recorded or rejected.

3. A second way to complete the map is one section at a time. In this technique, you and your students work through one main idea at a time, considering subordinate ideas and information related to each subordinate idea. Both of these techniques require students to refer to the reading for locating, pondering, and evaluating information, eventually completing the map as conceptualized by you.

4. Next, provide students with guided practice in conceptualizing their own cognitive maps. After reading an assigned passage, students work individually, in pairs, or in small groups to develop a cognitive map of the content. Students then present their maps to the whole class, and you lead a discussion of the various conceptual configurations. Students can offer suggestions and possible changes for the maps.

5. Another activity designed to provide guided practice in cognitive mapping is called a synthesis drill. In this activity, distribute copies of a blank map and a list of subordinate ideas and detailed facts randomly ordered. Students then work to arrange the facts and subordinate ideas in logical clusters. Next, they generate subheadings and designate a title or thesis for their completed cognitive maps.

6. Finally, distribute a blank map that students complete on their own while reading. When the map is completed, each student uses it as a guide to write an essay reflecting the ideas on the map.

A Web Outlining Strategy

Another instructional device useful in preparing students for writing is the web, which is an easy outlining technique to use for those texts with numerous subtopics within a single topic. The web is a practical alternative to traditional outlines because it uses a simpler, more visual format without all the complicated lettering and numbering (Cunningham and Cunningham 1987). Web outlining is taught first by having you, the teacher, model the process.

As the lesson begins, introduce the topic of the reading by placing it at the top or center to begin the web. After enclosing the topic with a geometric shape (e.g., circle, square, rectangle, triangle, or oval), ask the class what they already know about this topic. As students contribute information for the web, record it for all to see. As the information is recorded on the class web, individual students record on their own webs only those contributions they believe are valid (Cunningham and Cunningham 1987).

When the web of students' background knowledge of the topic is completed, students read the assignment for two purposes. The first goal is to look for information from the web and check its accuracy. The second purpose is to search for new information that should be added to the web. As they read, they can make additions and changes to their own webs. After reading, students discuss the content of the class web in relation to information gleaned from the reading. During the discussion, they refer to the reading passage to clarify issues and resolve disagreements about the material on the web, after which you make changes to the class web according to information contributed by the students (Gahn 1989; Cunningham and Cunningham 1987).

When the web is complete, lead the class in a writing activity. Again, begin by modeling the process of writing a paragraph, e.g., composing a topic sentence and developing the paragraph with supporting ideas. "Think aloud" while demonstrating the process of writing a paragraph related to one of the major ideas from the web. Then students work individually, in pairs, and in small groups to write another paragraph related to a different major idea from the web. When the paragraphs are completed, volunteers share their own or their groups' paragraphs with the whole class by reading them aloud (Cunningham and Cunningham 1987). After each paragraph is read, lead an analysis of its content and structure.

A Feature Matrix Outlining Strategy

The feature matrix, a device for helping writers gather, compare, and contrast information for several items within a category, can be used as a prewriting strategy. (See the examples of Semantic Feature Analysis in Chapters 8 and 9.) To prepare the matrix, read the text to identify a major category and a number of items (five to ten) within that category. Next, identify relevant features that describe some, all, or none of the items for use in comparing and contrasting them (Cunningham and Cunningham 1987). Prepare the matrix by putting the major category at the top as the title, listing the items vertically down the left-hand side, and listing the features horizontally across the top. Then, draw vertical and horizontal lines to form boxes in completing the matrix form. The matrix itself is completed by filling in the boxes with some type of symbol that indicates whether each item possesses each of the features.

To use the matrix, first present it to the students in its skeletal form, i.e., with none of the boxes completed. Display the matrix for all to see and provide students with copies of it or have them copy it themselves on their own paper. Then lead the class in filling in the feature matrices based on what they already know about the category and specific items. Students use symbols (e.g., plus signs) in the boxes when they believe that the item possesses a feature, and other symbols (e.g., minus signs) when they believe the item does not possess the feature (Cunningham and Cunningham 1987). Encourage students to use pencils or erasable ink, so that they can make changes, if necessary, after reading the assignment.

When students have completed their feature matrices based on their background knowledge, they read the related assignment for the purpose of confirming or changing the symbols they placed in the boxes. Once students have finished reading, confirming, and changing symbols in their individual matrices, ask them for contributions in completing the class matrix (Cunningham and Cunningham 1987). When consensus is reached following discussion, referrals to the text, and rereading parts of the text, put the appropriate symbol in each box. Consensus should be reached only when sufficient supporting evidence is presented.

For the writing portion of the lesson, which might occur one or two days later, lead the class in contributing sentences for a paragraph about one of the items on the feature matrix. Students then work individually, in pairs, or in small groups to create another paragraph about an item on the matrix. When their paragraphs are completed, volunteers share some of the paragraphs with the class by reading them aloud. As the paragraphs are read, in addition to positive reinforcement, offer suggestions by encouraging students to add information not contained in the matrix and to use complex sentences. As students gain skill in writing paragraphs, they can combine paragraphs into short compositions (Cunningham and Cunningham 1987).

Traditional Outlines

The traditional outline is certainly a staple for many writers, especially those who are analytic learners (see Chapter 1). Since analytic learners tend to be linear thinkers who are detail oriented, they often feel more comfortable with the format of traditional outlines than with more visually oriented outlines (e.g., graphic organizers such as maps and webs). Even if students prefer to use graphic organizers, they can still benefit from instruction in developing traditional outlines. So much information in texts is presented through traditional outline format that some experience with it is important for students. Although many writers prefer to write without the guidance of an outline, for students who are learning the process of writing, outlines can be a valuable tool in the planning process.

Outlining for ESL Students

Schifini (1994) recommends teaching students how to use outlining to restructure text information by synthesizing, categorizing, and highlighting relationships. Some students will benefit from using traditional outlines to reinforce learning and organize writing. Other students might have difficulty working with the linear format of traditional outlines. Therefore, Schifini also suggests using diagram formats including the array and radial (see Figures 10–5 and 10–6), which can be used to distinguish and emphasize coordinate, subordinate, and superordinate ideas. Also, the nonlinear, more visually oriented outline format of Graphic Organizers (see Chapter 1) might be more appropriate for some ESL learners.

Graphic Organizers that represent information gleaned from *wh* and *how* questions (i.e., *who, what, when, where, why,* and *how*) can also be beneficial to ESL learners (Schifini 1994). Another outline format that emphasizes *wh* and *how* information is the Herringbone Technique, in which you guide students in completing the Herringbone form (see Figure 10–7). On

---

FIGURE 10–5 Sample diagram format for notetaking: The array

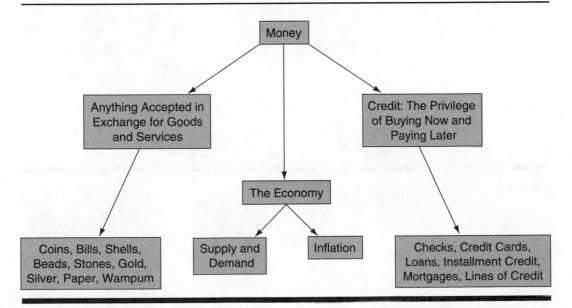

FIGURE 10-6   Sample diagram format for notetaking: The radial

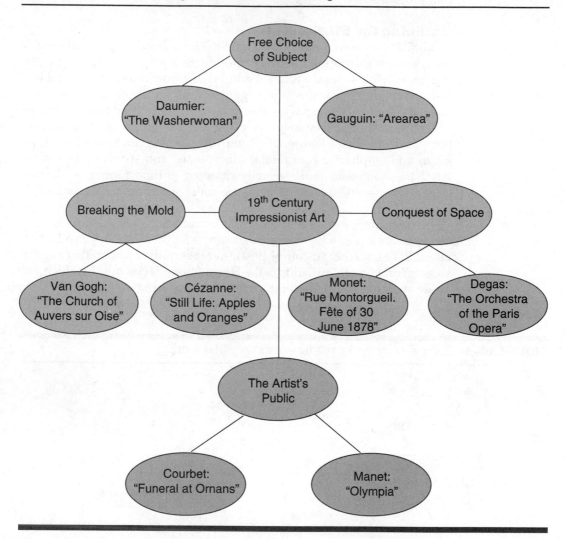

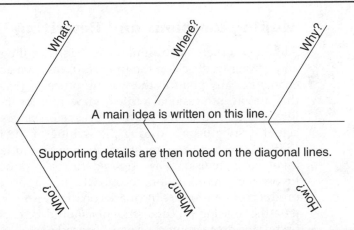

FIGURE 10–7 Sample diagram format for the Herringbone Technique for outlining

the long, horizontal line, the main idea of the selection is written; on the diagonal lines above and below the main idea line are written the six *wh* and *how* questions. Answers to each question are summarized next to each diagonal line.

Writing and Getting Feedback on the First Draft

First, encourage students to get their ideas down on paper or computer without worrying about spelling, punctuation, grammar, handwriting, and so on. Encourage them to double space the writing of their first draft, making it easier for revisions and insertions later. Provide opportunities for students to talk with you and their classmates for feedback while writing their drafts. Close supervision is important to prevent students from wasting writing time if they get on the wrong track. Through careful observation, you can provide valuable guidance and instruction when it is most needed and most effective, i.e., *during* the writing process.

Students need direct instruction in peer editing. Model and supervise the process until they can effectively and appropriately provide constructive feedback. The writer can either read the draft to a peer editor, or the peer editor can read the draft silently. After listening to or reading the draft, the editor first tells the writer something he or she liked about it. Then, the editor demonstrates understanding of the message by restating it in her or his own words. After restating the message, if the editor has misunderstood the message, he or she offers suggestions for rephrasing.

Suggestions should be posed in the form of questions, for example, "Would it sound better to say it this way?" or "What's another word you could use here?"

Making Revisions and Rewriting Drafts

Although writers often think of revisions as the next step after writing and getting feedback on the first draft, revision actually "means making changes at any point in the writing process" (Fitzgerald 1988, 124). For this reason, professional writers view revision as the heart of writing. Revision is a recursive process, because changes can occur before the actual writing begins, during the writing of the first draft, or after the draft is finished. You must emphasize to student writers the *process* involved in revisions, as opposed to the product. The act of revising involves the reprocessing, reconceptualizing, or rethinking of ideas; the products of revision are the marks on the paper (Fitzgerald 1988). To facilitate the revising process, students should be encouraged to write their first drafts on computers or word processors.

Fitzgerald (1988) specifies three guidelines she believes are important to any teacher interested in helping her or his student writers learn how to revise. First, revising activities should occur within the context of a broader writing program designed to teach knowledge about the content to be communicated, the characteristics of good writing, and the steps in the writing process. Second, revising activities should emphasize the concept of revision as a problem-solving process that creates, recreates, and conveys meaning. Third, revision should be seen as an integral part of the writing process for many types of writing including creative, expository essay, research report, and letter writing.

Fitzgerald (1988) also recommends three approaches to teaching the revising process. The first approach is called *naturalistic classroom support*, which refers to providing opportunities for student writers to experiment. In this approach, writers are also encouraged to treat failure as a chance to try again. Numerous opportunities to write and revise, along with peer and teacher conferences, are examples of naturalistic support for revision.

The second approach is called *direct instruction in the problem-solving process of revision*. Following are procedures for this approach adapted from those recommended by Fitzgerald (1988):

1. In this approach, you first give an introduction and overview of the process, then model the process by "thinking aloud" while revising a sample passage displayed for all to see. While modeling, point out key aspects of the revising process such as identifying discrepancies between intended and actual meaning, identifying problem areas, deciding how to fix them, and then effecting the changes.

2. After modeling, and on another day, the students have guided practice, in which they work in pairs to complete a task that leads them through the revision of a sample passage. Following completion of the task, lead a discussion of the revisions students elected to make, eliciting from them their reasons for making those particular changes.

3. Finally, on still another day, the students engage in independent practice of the revision process. They first revise a section of material supplied by you. Then, the students write and revise their own compositions.

Fitzgerald's (1988) third approach is called *procedural facilitation of revision*. Following are procedures for this problem-solving approach to revision, adapted from those described by Fitzgerald (1988):

1. Students review a passage they have written.

2. Then, they choose from lists of evaluative statements to identify problems needing attention. These evaluative statements include such comments as "This part is confusing," "This part is good," "The reader might not understand what I mean here," "This sentence (or paragraph) doesn't really fit here," "This word doesn't sound right," or "This is an interesting beginning."

3. Next, students choose from lists of diagnostic statements that indicate what, if anything, should be changed. These diagnostic statements include such comments as, "I need to rewrite this sentence," "I need to use a different word here," "I need to change the order of these sentences (paragraphs)," "I need to write a better conclusion," "I need to delete this part," or "I need to explain this part better."

4. Finally, with teacher supervision, the students make the changes they have identified.

A variation of this last approach is to have students analyze their own papers according to a checklist of criteria. Roe, Stoodt, and Burns (1991) suggest that you, the teacher, or you and the students cooperatively develop a checklist of criteria, presented in the form of questions, that students can use to critique their own papers. Following are a few examples suggested by Roe, Stoodt, and Burns (1991) that might be appropriate for such a checklist:

- Does the introduction capture the reader's interest and state your thesis?
- Is the information presented in a logical sequence?
- Does the ending reiterate the thesis and summarize your conclusions?
- Do all your sentences represent clear and complete thoughts?

- Is the vocabulary you chose appropriate for the meaning you intended?
- Did you use correct spelling, punctuation, and grammar?
- Did you stay focused on the topic and leave out irrelevant information?

Editing and Writing the Final Draft

Editing is a process similar to revising in that the writer looks for problems, decides how to fix them, and then makes the changes. However, editing usually involves less substantive changes because the revising and rewriting process has already taken place. Although editing includes a focus on the message or content of the composition, more emphasis is placed on finding and fixing mechanical problems. At this stage in the writing process, most writers should have refined their piece to the point that they can now look primarily for spelling, punctuation, and grammatical errors. Many excellent "spell check" programs are available for students who write their papers on computers or word processors.

Some student writers make the mistake of assuming that these kinds of errors are not important, so they either spend little time editing or skip it altogether. Of course, anyone who has tried to read compositions full of typos, misspellings, poor syntax and usage, and incorrect or insufficient punctuation can tell you that mechanical errors are extremely detrimental to the overall effectiveness of the written expression. No matter how good the content of the message, excessive mechanical errors can ruin the effectiveness of the communication. In other words, too many careless mechanical errors can ruin a composition just as much as content errors such as poor organization, confusing sentences, vague references, lack of focus, and poor word choice.

Students need to learn two things about editing. First, they must learn that they should never ask someone else to edit their papers until they have done so themselves. By paying careful attention, the writer can catch many of her or his own careless errors, thereby saving valuable time and effort for the next editor, e.g., friend, classmate, teacher, or parent. Thus, the first step in the editing process is for the writer to read the composition carefully herself or himself, looking for mechanical errors, and of course, always looking for ways to improve the presentation of the content.

The second thing students need to learn about editing is that they should always have objective readers edit their papers after they have done so themselves. Because the writer has a clear picture in mind of what he or she intended to say, he or she can easily miss mechanical errors. In other words, the writer can overlook an error because he or she is visualizing in mind what is supposed to be there, rather than what actually exists. Therefore, the second step in the editing process is to find an objective reader to edit the paper, looking for mechanical errors primarily, but also making note of any problems with the content such as lack of clarity.

Following is a set of procedures adapted from those recommended for the second stage of editing by Harp (1988) for one-on-one editing, i.e., *editing partners:*

1. Students exchange papers and read their partners' papers silently.
2. On the back of each paper, each editor writes something he or she liked about the paper, suggestions for changes, and a list of misspelled words, spelled correctly.
3. The editor makes punctuation corrections directly in the text, and flags each one with a ✓ in the margin.
4. After reading the paper aloud to the writer, the editor reads and discusses the positive comments and suggestions with the writer. If the partners cannot agree on what changes, if any, need to be made, they ask a third student. Then, if agreement still cannot be reached, they ask you, the teacher.

An alternative to editing partners is *editing committees,* which consist of three to five students charged with a single editing task, e.g., to read a draft and check for complete sentences, proper punctuation, or even a specific type of punctuation (Harp 1988). Following is a set of procedures adapted from those recommended for the second stage of editing by Harp (1988) for editing committees:

1. Select a writing skill you wish to highlight and teach a lesson on that skill either to the whole class or to a group of students needing such instruction.
2. Next, analyze students' writing products to identify students who correctly use the skill.
3. Then select three to five of these students to serve on the editing committee.
4. During editing time, these students sit together with a sign identifying their area of expertise, e.g., comma committee. More than one editing committee can be available for assistance.
5. Writers submit their drafts to the appropriate editing committee only after they have done partnership editing or have worked with an editing group.

An *editing group* is ideally composed of six students who work together all year. The stability of the group is important for developing a sense of trust and connectedness. The editing group members' task is to edit for both content and mechanics. You will need to prepare the members for this task (see approaches for teaching the revising process earlier in this chapter) and monitor their work closely. Following is a set of procedures for editing groups adapted from those recommended by Harp (1988):

1. Each member reads her or his composition to the others in the editing group.
2. Each group editor then responds by telling the writer at least one thing he or she liked about the composition and one suggestion for improvement.
3. The writer records the group editors' comments on the back of the composition or at appropriate places within the composition and asks the editing group if anyone has any additional comments or suggestions.
4. After everyone in the group has read and gotten feedback on their papers, the group members pair off and exchange papers to edit carefully for mechanics.

Before participating in editing partnerships, editing committees, or editing groups, students will need some direct instruction and supervised practice with the editing process. Harp (1988) recommends keeping the following points in mind as you prepare students for the editing process:

1. Explain each editing process step-by-step, making your expectations very clear and specific. Then, display the steps on a chart where they can be seen easily by the students.
2. Create checklists of editing criteria for students to use as they work through the process.
3. Model the editing process with student work samples. Also, model for students—and reinforce frequently—appropriate and helpful comments they should use in giving feedback to writers.
4. Require students to use the feedback they receive to revise their papers.
5. Monitor the students carefully as they work through the editing process.

REPORT AND TECHNICAL WRITING

Students need to become proficient in the process approach to writing using familiar topics before they attempt to implement the writing process for report and technical writing on less familiar topics. Because the focus of report and technical writing is on content, sometimes involving new and complex concepts, the writing process itself should be automatic for the students. Unless students are competent and confident with the techniques involved in process writing, their struggle with the writing process will likely interfere with their understanding and reporting of the content.

Research Reports

The first step in writing research reports is choosing a topic. You can either assign students topics, let them choose their own topics from sets of acceptable topics, or guide students in the selection and development of their own topics. If students choose their own topics, they may need consultation and guidance for narrowing their topics to manageable units. Once they have selected their topics, the next step involves planning and gathering information. After students have made notes on all the information they already know and have about a topic, they are ready to do the research.

Before beginning the actual research, students need to be introduced to and provided guided practice with a variety of reference materials and other sources of information for research reports. In addition to the traditional reference and information resources found in most libraries, a number of excellent resources are also available through increasingly advanced instructional technology. For example, encyclopedias that offer information in writing, as well as through audio and video presentations, are available on CD-ROM at reasonable prices (see Chapter 12).

Moore, Moore, Cunningham, and Cunningham (1994) identify two types of reference materials: compendiums and special-interest publications. Compendiums include such commonly used reference materials as encyclopedias, dictionaries, atlases, and yearbooks. What these types of reference materials have in common is that they "usually have extremely dense text summarizing a great deal of information in very little space" (Moore, Moore, Cunningham, and Cunningham 1994, 31). Students are often overwhelmed and intimidated by this type of presentation of information. Also, students who do not have satisfactory strategies for gleaning information from such reference sources often resort to copying text verbatim from the book. Therefore, they need to learn how to locate information by skimming, select only relevant information, take careful notes, paraphrase properly, keep quotations to a minimum, and document their sources appropriately. Students are never too young to learn about the concept of plagiarism, the seriousness of this infraction, and how to avoid it. Unless students have had some direct instruction and guided practice with using compendiums, you can probably expect to see a great deal of word-for-word copying.

Special-interest publications include brochures, pamphlets, fliers, promotional literature, trade union publications, professional organization publications, government agency publications, maps, application forms, menus, food labels, legal documents, and telephone books (Moore, Moore, Cunningham, and Cunningham 1994). Again, students need to become familiar with as many of these types of publications as possible. They need direct instruction and guided practice in how to tap these sources for information. As with compendiums, students must learn how to paraphrase properly, quote sparingly, and document their sources appropriately.

A third source of information for research reports with which students need to become familiar is periodicals, which include, primarily, magazines, newspapers, journals, and newsletters. Students must have experience with the major periodicals that serve as reference sources for various content areas. They also need to learn how to use the *Reader's Guide to Periodical Literature* to locate articles from a variety of sources on a particular topic. Once they have located appropriate articles, students need guidance and practice in skimming to locate the most relevant information, taking notes, paraphrasing and quoting, and citing the sources appropriately.

A fourth source of information for research reports is nonfiction trade books, i.e., library books. If not already proficient with the process, students need instruction and practice in using the library's card catalogue and locating books on the shelves. They need opportunities to become familiar with the formats of both traditional card catalogues, i.e., drawers filled with index cards, and computerized card catalogues (see Chapter 12). Once students have located appropriate books, they need to learn how to skim through them for the purpose of either locating key information or rejecting them as sources. Then, once they have located relevant information, they need to know how to take notes, paraphrase accurately, quote sparingly, and cite their sources appropriately.

Collaborative Research Reports

After students have received direct instruction in requisite research skills, i.e., locating sources, taking notes, paraphrasing, quoting, citing sources, outlining, and so on, an excellent way to give them guided practice in putting all these skills together is through the use of collaborative research reports (Davey 1987). Students can work in pairs or small groups as the teacher guides them through the process of research and writing. At the beginning of each step, students need direct instruction, or if direct instruction has already been provided, at least a review of the procedures involved. Then, if they immediately apply the procedures in a meaningful, interesting, and relevant research project, students should develop competence and confidence with research and report writing.

The following procedures are adapted from those recommended by Davey (1987) for collaborative research projects designed to provide guided practice in research and report writing skills:

1. The first step, *topic selection*, begins with you, the teacher, providing a broad topic related to the content objectives. Then, either you, the students, or you and the students together can generate a list of appropriate subtopics. Make sure that the subtopics are narrow enough to allow thorough coverage within a reasonable length of time and space and that they are broad enough to provide sufficient and varied sources of information. Although the students should be allowed some input in selecting their research topics and partners or teammates, you should make the final decisions about groups and topics. In making grouping decisions, the reading and writing skill levels of the students are not as important as their common interests and abilities to work cooperatively.

2. The next step, *planning*, begins once the research teams have been formed. Students meet to produce their research plan. Some form of guided instruction should be used to keep students focused and on track. They will first need to brainstorm what they already know about the topic and what questions they want their report to address. Students should record each research question at the top of an index card and then group the cards into categories. Next, they should identify a variety of appropriate sources for researching their topics. The team proposes a schedule for completing each step of the research and writing process. Finally, they agree on a division of labor for researching the topic, e.g., everyone researching the same topic using different sources or each person researching a different aspect of the topic.

3. The third step, *researching the topic*, begins as the group members work individually or in pairs to locate information, take careful notes, and keep records of their citations. Students should keep a research notebook with one of their research questions at the top of each page. For each question, students locate relevant information and take notes by paraphrasing. They can either record their citations with their notes or on separate index cards using numbers to match notes with citations.

4. After the team members have completed their research, they are ready to begin *organizing*. Again, some other form of guided instruction should be used to help them evaluate and categorize their information. After each team member or pair of team members presents their notes, the group helps decide whether to delete or add information and how to organize the information into an overall outline for the paper. The students' notes in their research notebooks should

be coded so that they know where each piece fits into the outline. The final product of this stage should be an outline, in whatever form the group chooses, to guide the writing process.

5. For the fifth step, *writing,* students divide the task and begin working alone or in pairs to write the first draft according to their outline, one section at a time, in paragraph form. They should be encouraged to put their ideas on paper, focusing on presenting the content clearly without worrying, at this point, about spelling and mechanics. When the first drafts are finished, team members should exchange and compare their drafts for the purpose of checking thoroughness, clarity, and organization of content. Careful notes are taken on what should be revised and how the revisions should be made.

6. The final step, *revising and editing,* begins as students write their second drafts incorporating the changes agreed upon by the group. At this point, more emphasis is placed on sentence structure, transitions, and overall organization. Finally, after the revisions are complete, students share the task of proofreading and editing for spelling, punctuation, grammar, and other mechanical errors. The final version of the paper should be carefully read and understood by all members of the group. Each team member should be aware of the possibility that he or she will be called upon to present her or his team's report to the rest of the class. Consequently, everyone on the team must be thoroughly familiar with and in agreement with the final form and content of the report.

Collaborative Research Reports provide students with guided practice in research and report writing skills.

To ensure that the collaborative research project is instructional in terms of both content and research skills for *all* students involved, you need to provide specific group instructions, in writing, for each step of the process. These instructions must clearly specify a division of labor to ensure individual accountability (i.e., each person doing her or his share *and* learning the content) and positive interdependence (incentives to help each other and work as a team). Students who are not accustomed to working in cooperative learning groups will probably attempt to plan the project in such a way that each person works independently on a particular section, and the sections are put together to form the report.

To avoid the possibility of group members working in isolation, guide the students in dividing the labor in a way that allows them to help and monitor each other throughout the process, so that all members of the group participate in and are familiar with all sections of the final report. For example, if each member of the team researches a different aspect of the topic, they must all come together to share, evaluate, and agree upon the information to be included on each subtopic. Another way to communicate the importance and requirement of working as a team is to grade each team member in two ways. First, assign part of each grade according to the quality of the overall team product. Second, assign another part of the grade according to each student's individual contributions to and cooperation with the group.

Finally, both you and the students need to monitor and evaluate the groups' and individual members' progress and contributions at each step in the process. Students and teachers must provide ongoing feedback to both groups and individuals in terms of how well they are cooperating as a group and contributing equally. Monitoring and assessment checklists can be used to document this ongoing feedback.

Lab Reports

A staple of the science curriculum, lab reports are used at all levels to document laboratory experiences. The first step in teaching students how to write effective lab reports is to make sure that they understand the scientific method, which dictates the steps involved in experiments. Along with direct instruction, provide students with written guidelines for conducting an experiment.

Model the experimental process for students as you guide them through several whole-class experiments. Begin by identifying a problem or question to be investigated. Then, lead students in a discussion of prior knowledge and experiences. Following the discussion, help them generate educated guesses or hypotheses about possible solutions or answers. Next, brainstorm ways to test the hypotheses, including procedures and materials, before selecting an experiment for the task (Santa, Havens, and Harrison 1989).

Once students have completed the experiment, have them consider the original problem or question to determine whether their investigation resulted in a solution or answer. If not, have them explain why and suggest alternate ways to examine the problem or question. Work through as many of these whole-class experiments as necessary to develop students' competence and confidence with problem-solving methods.

At this point students are ready to learn how to document their investigations in laboratory reports. Begin by modeling as you develop reports together. After conducting an experiment, verbalize each part of the report as you discuss it with the class and record it for all to see. After modeling several reports, gradually give students more and more responsibility in contributing.

Eventually, turn the entire process over to the students, who work alone, in pairs, or in small groups. You can support students in the transition by providing lab report forms that guide them in preparing the report. The forms divide the report into appropriate sections, e.g., observations, problem, hypothesis, procedures, materials, data, analysis, and conclusion. The forms also provide blanks, questions, or prompts to guide students in thinking through and documenting the process. Once they become competent and confident in completing the lab report forms, you can begin to allow them more flexibility and encourage them to be creative in writing their reports.

EVALUATING STUDENTS' WRITING

As discussed earlier in this chapter, many content area teachers are under the misconception that evaluating students' writing involves lengthy and tedious reading and editing of content and mechanical problems. As a result, many teachers avoid writing assignments and activities because they fear having to spend hours and hours grading papers. However, the process of evaluating student writing need not be lengthy or tedious. Following are some valuable tips for effective and efficient grading of students' writing.

First of all, keep in mind that not *all* student writing needs to be or even should be evaluated. A great deal of student writing is valuable to the learning process even if it is not graded. For example, class notes and journal writing are valuable learning activities even if they are not graded. Also, outlines and first drafts of papers and reports are important parts of the writing process that need not be graded (Gahn 1989). Many writing activities, including the ones previously mentioned, can be monitored and checked for completion without the thorough analysis required for grading.

Second, as discussed in the section on journals, much student writing can be evaluated by students themselves. In fact, students need to learn how to assess and improve their own work and also how to give positive and constructive feedback to their peers. You can guide students in the development of effective assessment strategies by providing them with checklists of criteria for various types of writing assignments (Gahn 1989).

Another effective tool for helping students evaluate their own and others' writing is the *rubric* (Pearce 1984). A rubric helps assign a grade or level of quality to a piece of writing. It provides a list of traits that should be evident in the writing, as well as the characteristics that distinguish papers of various grades (e.g., *A, B, C, D,* and *F*) or levels of quality. Having students apply rubrics can be quite useful for helping them learn to assess their own and others' writing. Rubrics can also be valuable to teachers by significantly reducing their grading time. Figure 10–8 presents a sample grading rubric developed for a college-level teacher education course.

A third way to save time grading students' writing is through the use of holistic scoring. Before using this method, you need to prepare both students and their parents, since it is somewhat different from traditional grading of student writing. Instead of looking for and marking every error in mechanics and content, read the piece for an overall impression of the writing. Emphasis is placed on the message itself and the effectiveness of its communication. As a result, rather than seeing a paper covered in red ink, the student will see a summary of your impressions of the organization of the paper, development of the topic, coherence of the writing, and clarity of communication. Mechanical errors are noted if they are so excessive that they interfere with understanding the content. Certainly, mechanical errors are not ignored, but they are corrected after the content has been refined. Instead of students being overwhelmed with the prospect of having to revise almost every word and comma, they are given a manageable number of changes to focus on during the revision process. Holistic scoring, then, not only makes the evaluation process less stressful for the students, it also results in less grading time for the teacher.

FIGURE 10–8   Sample grading rubric

A = exceptional (95 points: Quality, *not* quantity, goes above and beyond
           expectations)
- Demonstrates mastery of at least 90 percent of the content objectives
- Presentation of work is worthy of a professional portfolio
- Information is almost totally paraphrased using the student's own words
- Student personalizes the material by interjecting examples of and reflections
  about how the content might or might not be applicable, useful, valuable, or
  practical to her or his future teaching experience

B = excellent (85 points: Superior quality, *not* quantity, in meeting expectations)
- Demonstrates mastery of at least 80 percent of the content objectives
- Presentation of work is worthy of a professional portfolio
- Information is mostly paraphrased using the student's own words

C = acceptable (75 points: Satisfactory quality and quantity in meeting
           expectations)
- Demonstrates mastery of at least 70 percent of the content objectives
- With some revision, presentation of work would be worthy of a professional
  portfolio
- About half the information is paraphrased and half is summarized using
  wording from the text

D = unacceptable quality (65 points: Does not meet expectations)
- Demonstrates mastery of less than 70 percent of the content objectives
- Needs substantial revision to be worthy of a professional portfolio
- Information is mostly summarized using wording from the text

F = no credit (0 points: Effort not worthy of credit)
- Demonstrates mastery of less than 70 percent of the content objectives
- Needs to be completely rewritten to be worthy of a professional portfolio
- Information inaccurately summarizes wording of the text

SUMMARY

Because writing is a literacy skill, and as such is closely related to reading
and learning, it has been addressed throughout this book. In fact, writing
is an integral part of most content area literacy strategies.

Writing is crucial to content area literacy, yet many content area teachers avoid writing activities and assignments; this entire chapter focuses

on writing as an instructional device. One of the most widespread misconceptions about writing in the content areas is that it results in excessive paperwork and grading for the teacher. This misconception is negated by the numerous examples of writing activities designed to enhance learning and literacy development without requiring much, if any, teacher evaluation.

Teacher grading time can be reduced in a number of ways. First, holistic scoring can replace traditional "points-taken-off-for-every-single-error" systems, which require lengthy and tedious marking of the papers. In holistic scoring, you read the whole paper without marking errors, then evaluate it on the basis of the overall impression it made. Rubrics can be useful to this process, because they identify the specific traits that should be evident in a paper at various levels of quality. Another way to reduce grading time is to grade only final products of students' writing and do quick "completion" checks during the different phases of the process. Finally, grading time can be decreased by teaching students how to evaluate their own and their peers' writing.

The value of writing as a learning tool cannot be overstated. When students write, they think critically about the content and process it in meaningful ways. Writing helps students internalize content as they integrate the information into their schemata. Writing also provides a context for applying information to real-life situations and experiences. Students need to write about the content in a variety of formats to retain the information on a long-term basis.

Because writing is a valuable lifelong learning skill, students need to develop a variety of skills necessary for completing various writing tasks. The only way for students to become confident and skilled writers is to engage in numerous and varied opportunities to write. As with reading, good writing can only be the result of a great deal of practice. We are cheating our students if we do not give them regular and frequent opportunities to write in content area classes throughout the school day.

Journal writing provides students with daily or frequent opportunities to write about the content and their learning processes. Model the importance and process of journal writing by writing in your own journal simultaneously with the students. Journals can serve as a valuable record-keeping device for you if you record observations of students, as well as reflections on various instructional techniques and activities.

Dialogue journals allow students to communicate regularly with you, the teacher. This contact helps you meet the individual needs of students, who can use the format of the dialogue journal to ask questions and discuss confusing issues they hesitate to mention in class. Dialogue journals also help the students take more responsibility for their own learning. Since dialogue journals encourage students to process their learning experiences, students have increased opportunities to develop metacognitive awareness.

Like dialogue journals, learning logs help you assess how much and how well your students are learning. Because learning logs provide a means for documenting students' learning in authentic ways, you can gain valuable insights about which students are ready to move on and which students need some review and reteaching. Learning logs can be used to assess and activate background knowledge by having students brainstorm and make predictions about topics. They can also help students process and reflect on content by paraphrasing and summarizing information. Finally, learning logs can give students practice in responding to essay questions requiring higher-level thinking and processing.

Writing workshop is a time set aside regularly and frequently (preferably daily) for students and teachers to write about the content in one form or another. During this time, students are given a great deal of choice and freedom in terms of their topics, form of writing, style of writing, and audience. By allowing and encouraging them to choose their own topics and forums, writing workshop gives students the opportunity to take ownership of the content. Students can use this time to make practical applications of the content, reflect critically on it, and relate it to personal experiences and knowledge. During writing workshop, your role is leader, guide, and consultant: move from desk to desk providing meaningful instruction in the context of what students need and want to know in order to communicate a message of their own creation.

The process approach to writing is a lifelong skill that students can master only through direct instruction, guided practice, and independent applications of the various steps. You will need to model procedures, provide guidance in the form of writing guides, and monitor closely the students' collaborative and independent efforts. Evaluation and feedback should be an ongoing process, with students regularly evaluating themselves and each other before final evaluation by you.

First, they need to learn how to *plan* by selecting and narrowing a topic, deciding what questions will be addressed, brainstorming what they already know, and gathering additional information. Second, they need to learn how to *organize* by categorizing, prioritizing, and sequencing the information into some type of outline. Outlines can take the linear format of the traditional outline or the visually oriented format of graphic organizers such as cognitive maps and webs. Third, students must learn how to write a first draft with an emphasis on putting their ideas on paper without worrying so much about the mechanics. Fourth, they read their drafts with a critical eye for ways to improve the presentation of content.

They also seek feedback from their peers and teacher, who frame suggestions in the form of questions to ensure that the feedback given is both positive and constructive. Fifth, students consider all feedback and make decisions about what changes to make. Then the first draft is rewritten to incorporate the planned revisions. Because the revision process is recursive, the draft may be rewritten at various and repeated points in the writing process. Sixth, the revised draft is self-edited with a critical eye for mechanics and any other changes that might improve the presentation of content. After self-editing, the writer finds an objective reader, either a peer or the teacher, to edit it again for mechanical errors. Finally, the mechanical errors are corrected in the writing of the final draft.

The two strategies introduced in this chapter emphasize writing as a learning tool. The Guided Writing Procedure (GWP) is a variation of the Guided Reading Procedure. The Directed Writing Activity (DWA) offers a basic instructional format for writing, just as the Directed Reading Activity offers a basic instructional format for a content area reading lesson. Both the GWP and DWA can be used in all content areas and at all grade levels. Their flexible formats encourage teacher modification according to instructional objectives and the needs of the students.

REFERENCES

Alvermann, D. E., and S. F. Phelps. (1994). *Content reading and literacy: Succeeding in today's diverse classrooms.* Needham Heights, MA: Allyn & Bacon.

Atwell, N. (1989). Writing workshop. *American Educator* 13:14–50.

Blake, H., and N. A. Spennato. (1980). The directed writing activity: A process with structure. *Language Arts* 57:317–318.

Bode, B. A. (1989). Dialogue journal writing. *The Reading Teacher* 42:568–571.

Calkins, L. M. (1986). *The art of teaching writing.* Portsmouth, NH: Heinemann.

Cudd, E. T., and L. Roberts. (1989). Using writing to enhance content area learning in the primary grades. *The Reading Teacher* 42:392–404.

Cunningham, J. W. (1982). Generating interactions between schemata and text. In *New inquiries in reading research and instruction.* Edited by J. A. Niles and L. A. Harris. Thirty-first Yearbook of the National Reading Conference. Washington, DC: National Reading Conference.

Cunningham, P. M., and J. W. Cunningham. (1976). SSSW, better content-writing. *Clearinghouse* 49:237–238.

———. (1987). Content area reading-writing lessons. *The Reading Teacher* 40:506–512.

D'Angelo, K. (1983). Précis writing: Promoting vocabulary development and comprehension. *Journal of Reading* 26:534–539.

Davey, B. (1987). Team for success: Guided practice in study skills through cooperative research reports. *Journal of Reading* 30:701–705.

Dolly, M. R. (1990). Integrating ESL reading and writing through authentic discourse. *Journal of Reading* 33:360–365.

Fitzgerald, J. (1988). Helping young writers to revise: A brief review for teachers. *The Reading Teacher* 42:124–129.

Gahn, S. M. (1989). A practical guide for teaching writing in the content areas. *Journal of Reading* 32:525–531.

Graves, D. H. (1983). *Writing: Teachers and children at work.* Portsmouth, NH: Heinemann.

———. (1994). Be a better writing teacher. *Instructor* 104:43–45

Harp, B. (1988). When the principal asks, "Why aren't you using peer editing?" *The Reading Teacher* 41:828–830.

Jossart, S. A. (1988). Character journals aid comprehension. *The Reading Teacher* 42:180.

Kang, Hee-Won. (1994). Helping second language readers learn from content area text through collaboration and support. *Journal of Reading* 37:646–652.

Konopak, B. C., M. A. Martin, and S. H. Martin. (1987). Reading and writing: Aids to learning in the content areas. *Journal of Reading* 31:109–115.

Kucer, S. B. (1986). Helping writers get the "big picture." *Journal of Reading* 30:18–24.

Langer, J. A. (1986). Learning through writing: Study skills in the content areas. *Journal of Reading* 29:400–406.

Manion, B. B. (1988). Writing workshop in junior high school: It's worth the time. *Journal of Reading* 32:154–157.

Martin, S. H. (1992). Using journals to promote learning across the curriculum. In *Reading in the content areas: Improving classroom instruction.* Edited by E. K. Dishner, T. W. Bean, J. E. Readence, and D. W. Moore. Dubuque, IA: Kendall/Hunt Publishing Company.

Moore, C. W., S. A. Moore, P. M. Cunningham, and J. W. Cunningham. (1994). *Developing readers and writers in the content areas K–12,* 2d ed. White Plains, NY: Longman.

Pearce, D. L. (1984). Writing in content area classrooms. *Reading World* 23:234–241.

Peresich, M. L., J. D. Meadows, and R. Sinatra. (1990). Content area cognitive mapping for reading and writing proficiency. *Journal of Reading* 33:424–432.

Reyes, M., and L. A. Molner. (1991). Instructional strategies for second-language learners in the content areas. *Journal of Reading* 35:96–103.

Richardson, J. S., and R. F. Morgan. (1994). *Reading to learn in the content areas,* 2d ed. Belmont, CA: Wadsworth.

Roe, B. D., B. D. Stoodt, and P. C. Burns. (1991). *Secondary school reading instruction: The content areas.* Boston: Houghton Mifflin Company.

Ruddell, M. R. (1993). *Teaching content reading and writing.* Needham Heights, MA: Allyn & Bacon.

Santa, C., L. Havens, and S. Harrison. (1989). Teaching secondary science through reading, writing, studying, and problem-solving. In *Content area reading and learning: Instructional strategies.* Edited by D. Lapp, J. Flood, and N. Farnan. Englewood Cliffs, NJ: Prentice Hall.

Schifini, A. (1994). Language, literacy, and content instruction: Strategies for teachers. In *Kids come in all languages: Reading instruction for ESL students*. Edited by K. Spangenberg-Urbschat and R. Pritchard. Newark, DE: International Reading Association.

Sensenbaugh, R. (1989). Writing across the curriculum: Evolving reform. *Journal of Reading* 32:462–465.

Shanahan, T. (1988). The reading-writing relationship: Seven instructional principles. *The Reading Teacher* 41:636–647.

Shugarman, S. L., and J. B. Hurst. (1986). Purposeful paraphrasing: Promoting a nontrivial pursuit for meaning. *Journal of Reading* 29:396–399.

Simpson, M. K. (1986). A teacher's gift: Oral reading and the reading response journal. *Journal of Reading* 30:45–50.

Simpson, M. L. (1986). PORPE: A writing strategy for studying and learning in the content areas. *Journal of Reading* 29:407–414.

Smith, C., and T. W. Bean. (1980). The guided writing procedure: Integrating content reading and writing improvement. *Reading World* 19:290–298.

Strackbein, D., and M. Tillman. (1987). The joy of journals—with reservations. *Journal of Reading* 31:28–31.

Tierney, R. J., J. E. Readence, and E. K. Dishner. (1990). *Reading strategies and practices: A compendium,* 3d ed. Needham Heights, MA: Allyn & Bacon.

Tierney, R. J., A. Soter, J. F. O'Flahavan, and W. McGinley. (1989). The effects of reading and writing upon thinking critically. *Reading Research Quarterly* 24:134–173.

CHAPTER 11
GRAPHIC
ORGANIZER

ESL
students for whom
English is a second
language
main challenges:
comprehension,
confidence
strategies: build schema,
develop vocabulary,
provide support,
emphasize writing,
use cooperative learning

LEARNING
DIFFERENCES
(e.g., dyslexia)
main challenges: diagnosis,
comprehension
strategies: utilize multi-media
approaches, make adaptations
for reading and writing
deficiencies, find alternative
ways of learning,
use cooperative learning

G/T
gifted and talented
main challenges: keep interested,
work to full potential
strategies: offer enrichment activities,
encourage exploration,
use cooperative learning

MORE ABOUT
LEARNERS WITH
**SPECIAL
NEEDS**

ATTENTION DEFICIT/
HYPERACTIVE DISORDER
main challenges: attention,
behavior
strategies: keep classroom
uncluttered, foster calm
atmosphere, provide
individual copies of information
from chalkboards and overheads,
develop daily routines, use
consistent signals for attention,
provide taped recordings of
instructions

STRATEGIES:
LISTEN, READ, DISCUSS
LEARNING CENTERS

More about Learners with Special Needs

To demonstrate mastery of the content, the student will be able to do the following:

PART 1 OBJECTIVES

1. Identify the following strategy, describe its distinguishing features, and assess its significance to teaching content area literacy: Listen-Read-Discuss (LRD).
2. Design a plan for observing and identifying students who may be gifted and talented.
3. Describe the special needs of the gifted and talented (GT) learner in terms of program design and instructional adaptations.
4. Design a plan for creating a nonthreatening classroom climate that serves the special needs of ESL students by emphasizing self-esteem, mutual respect, trust, acceptance, empathy, inclusion, integration, collaboration, and the value of bilingualism.

PART 2 OBJECTIVES

1. Identify the following strategy, describe its distinguishing features, and assess its significance to teaching content area literacy: Learning Centers.
2. Devise a plan for identifying students who might need special instruction because of dyslexia or a related learning difference.
3. Summarize five adaptations for content area instruction appropriate for students with dyslexia or a related learning difference.

PART 1 OBJECTIVES—continued

5. Devise a plan for regular and consistent collaboration with resource personnel in meeting the special needs of ESL students in the content area classroom.
6. Propose five guidelines appropriate for enhancing instruction for ESL students in a specific content area or grade level.

INTRODUCTION

A significant program in widespread use across the country has emerged with the new paradigm of education. This program, called "Inclusion," mainstreams to the regular classroom learners who were previously served in special education classrooms. The concept of Inclusion implies cooperative planning and instruction among regular and special education teachers. However, because special education teachers cannot always be present, the classroom teacher must be prepared to serve a wide variety of special-needs learners.

As a content area teacher, you want to maximize learning for *all* of your students including those with special needs. Learners bring to school a great diversity of needs. What comes to mind when you think about the special needs of students? What kinds of special needs do you expect to encounter in the classroom? Think about it for a minute. You can probably think of many challenges students might bring to your classroom. Do any of the following come to mind? What others can you think of?

- visual impairment
- hearing impairment
- mobility impairment
- emotional disturbance
- attention deficit–hyperactive disorder
- giftedness
- mental retardation
- remedial needs (slow learning)
- learning differences (disabilities)
- limited English proficiency

Of course, you will not be expected to become a special education expert in all or even some of these areas. Your school should have specially trained faculty and staff to consult with you about how best to serve the needs of students with special challenges. You should find out and become knowledgeable about the services available to your special-needs students. Stay in regular and frequent contact with special education personnel to make sure your special-needs students are getting the best possible education.

For obvious reasons, most special-needs learners are now "mainstreamed" into regular classrooms as much as possible. *All* students benefit from educational and social interaction with students of differing backgrounds, needs, abilities, and talents. Inclusion programs parallel the reality of our integrated society. Students will be better prepared for the real world if they learn to value differences and appreciate the contributions of a variety of learners.

Because students with a variety of needs may be mainstreamed into your classroom, you need to know how to tailor instruction to facilitate their learning. All of the strategies and activities described in this text are designed to meet the needs of a wide variety of learners. Strategies and activities for content area literacy can be adapted easily to meet most special needs. This chapter will show you some additional ways to make adjustments according to the special needs of some of your students.

The primary focus of this text is on content area literacy; consequently, only the challenges most likely to influence content area learning and literacy development will be addressed. These challenges include students who are gifted and talented, students with limited English proficiency (ESL), students who are slow learners (e.g., remedial readers or writers), students with learning differences/disabilities (e.g., dyslexia), and students with attention deficit–hyperactive disorder.

Most of the special-needs students you encounter will probably have one or more of these particular challenges. This chapter will provide you some practical suggestions to facilitate content area learning and literacy development for your students. You will also learn how to facilitate learning by identifying your students' learning preferences (e.g., auditory, visual, kinesthetic, tactile, combination) and then designing instruction to maximize the benefits of those learning strengths.

Of course, it is certainly not practical to design a separate lesson plan for each student. This chapter will also show you how you can use grouping to individualize instruction in meeting a wide range of needs. Finally, you will learn from this chapter how to make special adaptations of general classroom procedures. You will find that you can make small, simple changes that can significantly enhance learning for some of your special-needs students. For example, the ways you give instructions, structure assignments, arrange your classroom, make handouts, and use the chalkboard can be easily modified for maximum effectiveness.

Two new strategies will be introduced in this chapter, both of which offer excellent ways to provide support for students with special learning needs and varying learning preferences. For example, Listen-Read-Discuss emphasizes auditory learning through a preparatory lecture and follow-up discussion. Therefore, it is an excellent strategy for remedial readers, auditory learners, and students with dyslexia. It can also be adapted nicely to emphasize critical thinking and meaningful applications for gifted students.

PART 1

STRATEGY: LISTEN-READ-DISCUSS

Listen-Read-Discuss is a variation of the Directed Reading Activity (see Chapter 4). It was designed by Manzo and Casale (1985) to prepare students for reading assignments with a brief lecture before reading and reinforce learning with a student-centered discussion following reading. Hence, the LRD consists of three basic steps: presentation, reading, and discussion.

Procedures

1. **Presentation.** Give a brief lecture (about fifteen minutes) concerning the contents of the reading assignment. The lecture can either summarize the key points of the assignment or focus on one or two of the most important concepts. The goal of this mini-lecture is a clear presentation of ideas to build students' confidence for reading.
2. **Reading.** Students then read the assignment covered by the lecture. Instruct students to take a few notes while reading. Model the note-taking process for them and monitor the quality of their notes frequently. Show them examples of different note-taking systems (see Chapter 3) and types of notes such as summarizing key points and jotting down key words and concepts. Students should also make note of any concepts that were hard to understand, did not seem consistent with the lecture, or about which they have questions. Tell them they will be using these notes for discussion following the reading.
3. **Discussion.** The first part of the discussion should be focused on *reducing uncertainties*, that is, answering questions to clear up any confusion or misunderstandings. Your goal for this part of the discussion should be to make sure that students targeted and understood the key points. The second part of the discussion should move on to *raising uncertainties*, that is, asking higher-level questions to guide students in thinking critically about the information. At this point, model comprehension, self-monitoring, and critical thinking by sharing your own thoughts and questions about the material.

Special Adaptations

The LRD lends itself nicely for adaptations according to the needs of students. For example, you can vary the difficulty of the questions or change the order of the steps. You might have the discussion first to allow students to activate background knowledge, make predictions, and share personal thoughts and opinions. Doing so allows students to experience a free flow of ideas, uninfluenced by the teacher. Finally, for some students, having the discussion first is more motivating (Manzo and Casale 1985).

Another adaptation involves changing the purposes of the lecture and the reading assignment. For example, you could use the lecture to present facts and then the reading to raise critical issues and questions about the information. The lecture raises critical issues and questions for students to think about as they read the facts (Manzo and Casale 1985). Then, the discussion could focus on the facts as they relate to the issues.

For students who have difficulty reading the text, you could supply them with the key points in the lecture. Then set very specific purposes for reading, guiding them to focus on those key points. The follow-up discussion allows them to hear other key points raised by their classmates. They would then have a better chance of gleaning more important concepts from the reading assignment.

For gifted and talented students, including some advanced-level material related to the assignment in the lecture should prove beneficial. You could then give them different purposes for reading. For example, instead of zeroing in on the facts, you could pose some higher-level questions challenging students to apply the facts in meaningful ways. You could also give them specific roles in the discussion. For example, ask students to formulate and pose questions to you and their classmates. You could also ask them to elaborate on some of the facts, emphasizing practical applications of the information.

GIFTED AND TALENTED LEARNERS

Gifted and talented (GT) learners are those who exhibit above-average potential for achievement in most or all subjects. The key word in this definition is *potential*, because some GT learners may not be achieving their potential in all areas. They may exhibit particular strengths in one or more content areas, but even in their weaker areas, they are capable of above-average achievement. As a classroom teacher, you are in an excellent position to identify through observation which students may be gifted and talented.

Keep in mind when observing your students that giftedness does not necessarily manifest itself in positive ways. Many teachers typically think of the following positive characteristics as indicators of possible giftedness: rapid skill mastery, exceptional academic achievement, long-term retention of information, curiosity, self-confidence, independent thinking and learning, complex problem solving, abstract thinking, risk taking, strong motivation, superior language skills, and higher-level thinking. Indeed, these characteristics are among those that identify gifted students. However, along with these characteristics, gifted students are just as likely to exhibit some of the following negative characteristics: bored, disruptive, rebellious, argumentative, perfectionism, highly critical, daydreamer, unfinished work, overextended involvement, boastful, interrupts, and gets off task easily (Tarver and Curry 1992).

Identifying gifted students from disadvantaged backgrounds (i.e., those deprived of the economic and educational benefits enjoyed by those in the cultural mainstream) can be especially difficult because of their socioeconomic and cultural differences. Because most IQ tests have been standardized with middle- and upper-class populations, they do not take into account the economic and cultural realities of disadvantaged communities. Therefore, multiple criteria including those identified through observation should be used for identifying the gifted. Also, teachers should be trained to recognize the needs and characteristics of their disadvantaged or culturally different students, so they are better able to identify those who are gifted (Tuttle 1983).

Keep in mind that the instruction you design for your GT students could also be appropriate for other students who show particularly strong abilities and potential in one or more content areas. *Any* student who masters the curriculum quickly and easily needs special attention to prevent boredom, poor study skills, and disenchantment with school in general (Reis and Renzulli 1992). In designing and adapting instruction for your GT students and other strong achievers, probably the most important tenet to keep in mind is to design *different* assignments, not *more* assignments for them. Too often, teachers mistakenly assume that if students can complete the assigned work in less time than the rest of the class, they should be given more work to keep them busy until everyone else is finished. However, students quickly understand that the faster they do their work, the more they have to do. Rewarding efficient work with more work generally leads to reduced rather than increased production. *Any* student, but especially a gifted one, learns quickly that slower work means less work. When students begin intentionally performing tasks slowly, or not at all, the result can be boredom, disinterest, and apathy, quickly followed by behavior problems.

Rather than completing a greater quantity of the same work, instructional goals for GT students should encourage and challenge them to reach their various potentials. Strategies and activities should help them build on their strengths, stimulate their interests, fulfill their curiosities, examine critical issues, develop social skills, synergize (i.e., work with others of differing talents for enriched learning), and apply knowledge in meaningful ways. Ultimately, as a teacher, you are responsible for helping your GT students find a comfortable, rewarding, and valuable role in your learning community. To this end, you need to design a variety of supplemental or alternate activities appropriate for their abilities, interests, and motivation.

Although activities for GT students should be challenging, be careful to avoid frustrating them. If the specially designed activities and materials seem overwhelming or extremely difficult to the GT students, their attitudes can be just as negative as when they are faced with a greater quantity of less challenging work. Rather, the activities and materials should be interesting and fun, as well as challenging.

Resources

The National Education Association has published some helpful source books on teaching GT students in content area classrooms. These books, presented in Appendix L, are excellent resources for helping you identify GT students and offering sample activities in helping you design and adapt instruction for GT students at all levels and in a variety of content areas. They would be a valuable addition to your school or classroom curriculum library.

Activities

Because interdisciplinary activities are recommended for gifted students, goals in the various content areas should be combined and addressed through thematic units as much as possible. Through these activities, problem-solving skills should be emphasized: GT students need to learn the following problem-solving process (Wright 1983):

1. Examine all possibilities for solving the problem.
2. Develop ideas into a plan of action.
3. Communicate and implement the plan effectively.
4. Follow up implementation of the plan with an objective evaluation.

The elements of a language arts program recommended by West (1980) are summarized by the acronym **SPLICE-P**, and characterize any good interdisciplinary program:

> ▌ The *subject* matter should be *significant* and, often, *student selected*.
> ▌ To be challenging, the subject matter needs a *purpose* and *plan*.
> ▌ The program must provide training in *leadership*.

▌ Many activities should be, at least in part, *independent* and *interdisciplinary*.

▌ Activities should emphasize *creation* and *creativity*.

▌ Through creative and cooperative group efforts, activities should generate *energy* and *extension* (i.e., synergy).

▌ The *products* of cooperative creation should be varied and include *performances* (e.g., plays, pantomimes, poetry readings), *publications* (e.g., newspapers, magazines, books, reports, anthologies), and *productions* (e.g., models, drawings, paintings, catalogs, inventions, machines).

English and Language Arts

Activities in English and language arts should be designed around some of the following instructional goals (Wright 1983):

▌ developing reading and writing fluency and flexibility

▌ nurturing creativity and originality

▌ developing the ability to elaborate, synthesize, and evaluate

▌ interpreting the author's mood, tone, style, perspective, and purpose

▌ drawing conclusions about relationships among plot, characterization, setting, and theme

▌ evaluating the effectiveness of the author's technique

Mathematics

Activities in mathematics should involve as much real-world application as possible. They should also be designed around some of the following instructional goals (Wright 1983):

▌ drawing conclusions from data

▌ making predictions

▌ designing word problems

▌ comparing and contrasting mathematical concepts

▌ applying problem-solving techniques to mathematical concepts

▌ recognizing interrelationships among various mathematical operations

▌ applying mathematics to situations in other content areas

Science

A balanced program in science for GT students should incorporate opportunities to learn about, appreciate, and value the world of nature. Also, the program should provide opportunities to develop a powerful and sophisticated awareness of natural processes, limitations, and possibilities. The ultimate goal of such a program might be to motivate students to spend time in an active pursuit of scientific understandings. To this end, exercises in perception, awareness, observation, and creativity are essential. Also essential is an examination of the relationship between science and values and of the concept of synergy, which is the interconnectedness of circumstance, innovation, progress, and understanding (Romey and Hibert 1988). Activities in science should be designed around some of the following instructional goals (Wright 1983):

▌ making predictions
▌ drawing conclusions from data
▌ formulating and verifying hypotheses
▌ matching principles and applications
▌ designing and conducting experiments
▌ distinguishing between scientific evidence and personal opinion
▌ understanding how society influences science and technology
▌ understanding how science and technology influence society

Social Studies

Because few GT students thrive on the lecture approach, activities in social studies need to engage them in an active study of people and society. They should be involved in the examination of values, relationships, and skills, as well as the sharing and testing of ideas. Independent study, small-group seminars, field trips, internships, and simulations should also be offered to GT students in social studies. Program options should include opportunities for direct communication and work with practicing social scientists (Plowman 1980). Activities in social studies should be designed around some of the following instructional goals (Wright 1983):

▌ comparing and contrasting things, ideas, events, and situations
▌ identifying unifying concepts
▌ recognizing the interrelationships among social, political, cultural, physical, and economic factors
▌ making reasonable predictions based on generalizations
▌ comparing and contrasting different cultures
▌ drawing conclusions and making inferences from evidence
▌ analyzing alternate solutions to problems
▌ identifying the implications and consequences of alternate solutions
▌ developing critical understandings and methods of evaluating current issues

LEARNERS FOR WHOM ENGLISH IS A SECOND LANGUAGE (ESL)

Classroom teachers must plan content area instruction for increasing numbers of students, who because it is not their native language, have limited proficiency with English. How can you teach content to students who cannot speak English, especially if you cannot speak their native language(s)? What will you do with students in your classroom who do not understand what is happening well enough to follow directions, let alone master the content? This situation can be frustrating for both teachers and students. You need to know some basic guidelines and strategies for effectively including ESL students in content area lessons. If you are prepared to make minor modifications in classroom procedures and lesson plans, you will feel more comfortable and confident about welcoming ESL students into your classroom. In turn, your ESL students will feel more comfortable and confident about participating in the learning process and becoming a member of your classroom learning community.

When teachers do not know how to include students with language differences into lessons, both teachers and ESL students can become isolated. Teachers may unwittingly ignore ESL students, sometimes even physically separating them to the back or periphery of the class. Also, the ESL students themselves may tend toward isolation or segregation with other ESL students. Not surprisingly, they often feel embarrassed and awkward in classroom situations. As a result, they seek isolation or segregation to avoid the possibility of having to participate in a lesson.

However, isolation and segregation are obviously detrimental to their learning and language development. Therefore, the recommendations in this section will emphasize inclusion and integration of ESL students into both small-group and whole-class activities. Small-group cooperative learning activities are especially important for ESL students because they provide a low-stress, nonthreatening learning environment. If possible, pair your ESL students with appropriate study partners to assist with translations and explanations. Once ESL students begin developing confidence and improving their language skills with a partner, they will be ready to work with other students in small groups and eventually with larger groups and the whole class.

For inclusion and integration to be effective, you must make every effort to establish a comfortable climate of security, trust, and mutual respect. The key to developing such a classroom climate for ESL students is to express admiration and respect for their language differences. Rather than viewing their ESL status as a *deficiency*, recognize it as valuable opportunity to become bilingual. Let them and the other students know that you value bilingualism and that the ESL students have an excellent opportunity to become bilingual or even multilingual. Remind them that once they become proficient with English, their bilingualism will be a valuable skill for succeeding in our increasingly global society and economy.

At the same time, encourage the other students to learn from your ESL students words and phrases from their native languages. Use your

ESL students as a valuable resource for your classroom community. Let them know that they are a welcome and valued addition to your classroom. The self-esteem they develop as a result will be crucial to building positive attitudes toward learning and motivation to learn English. Further enhance their self-esteem by showing empathy for their language barrier. Share with them and encourage other students to share personal frustrations you may have experienced visiting other countries where you could not speak the language.

One of the best ways to build security and win ESL students' respect and trust is to ask them occasionally to teach *you* how to say certain key words in their native language(s), making a concerted effort to learn them. In your attempts to speak their language(s), show them that it is okay to make mistakes. If you can laugh at and make light of your own mistakes, without giving up, you are modeling for ESL students the natural process of language learning. Encourage the other students to try various word pronunciations with you, so that the ESL students feel more comfortable attempting difficult English pronunciations.

To establish a climate of security, it is important to respond positively from the beginning to every word offered by an ESL student. You must prove to all your students but especially your ESL students that it is okay to take risks and make mistakes. Your early responses will set the tone for the rest of the school year. Let students know how pleased you are that they are willing to *try* and that their willingness to participate is more important to you than their accuracy.

Resources

Although it would certainly be a good idea, it may not be practical or even necessary for you to become an expert in teaching English as a second language. Your school or school district should have an ESL specialist on staff. You would be wise to consult with an ESL expert, as well as a reading specialist, as soon as you know that you will be teaching one or more ESL students. The ESL and reading teachers can show you ways to modify instruction for enhancing content learning while also improving the students' language and literacy skills. After initial consultations, you should plan regular collaboration with the ESL and reading teachers to review successes and failures, plan new strategies, and share instructional materials.

Kang (1994) strongly encourages collaboration between content area, ESL, and reading teachers because content area teachers alone typically do not have the time, expertise, or motivation to modify materials and instruction for ESL students. As a content area teacher, you will need support in such tasks as analyzing reading assignments to identify key vocabulary, organizational patterns, critical concepts, and necessary reading and study skills. Then, once text material has been analyzed, you will need help in adapting instruction to meet the particular needs of your ESL students and developing support materials. All of these responsibilities can be very time consuming and difficult, so you will appreciate the support of your colleagues in various areas of expertise.

Three forms of collaboration are recommended by Kang (1994). The first involves the curriculum, so that all teachers are building on, supporting, and reinforcing the instruction of the others. This type of collaboration is important for ensuring efficient use of instructional time.

The second form involves sharing time and expertise in planning instruction and developing materials. In this type of collaboration, the ESL and reading teachers help the content area teacher select or adapt materials and instruction. The goal is to make the content easier to learn and more conducive to language and literacy development.

The third form of collaboration involves sharing knowledge and expertise through consultation and training. In this type of collaboration, for example, content area teachers can get advice from ESL and reading teachers regarding specific problems or students. Reading teachers can learn from ESL teachers how to develop literacy skills for second-language learners and from content area teachers the specific demands of materials in their fields. Finally, ESL teachers can get advice from reading teachers on how to develop specific literacy skills.

Guidelines

Here are a few basic guidelines to keep in mind for meeting the special needs of your ESL students:

- Speak to them slowly and distinctly, making sure they can see your face and hear your voice. Ensure their fellow students do the same.
- Simplify the language of instruction for them, at first using as few words as possible for directives (e.g., *read, read this, listen, repeat, listen and repeat, write, copy this, answer this question,* and so on).
- If possible, provide them with an English translation dictionary or hand-held computer.
- Use much repetition, keeping communication brief at first (words and phrases).
- Have students repeat key words and phrases from the content and the language of instruction you typically use.
- Assign them student partners to help explain content and directions. Allow them to work as partners with a variety of students in the class. Their partners do not need to be able to speak their native language(s), but it helps if they do. Make it a privilege to work with ESL students as a study partner.

■ Give them many opportunities to practice English through small-group discussions, problem-solving activities, and review sessions.

■ Rewrite textual material by condensing it and using simpler language.

■ Use a wide variety of media to support your instruction (e.g., pictures, videotapes, audiotapes, charts, graphs, diagrams, computers, slides, and so on).

PART 2

STRATEGY: LEARNING CENTERS

Learning Centers provide opportunities for individualized and self-directed learning. Students can work independently, with a partner, or with a small group at each center. A variety of types of instructional technologies can be used to support special-needs learners in Learning Centers (see Chapter 12). For example, students can work through a computer program or develop their own. They can watch and listen to a multimedia presentation, video, slide/tape presentation, or video laserdisc. They can work through an interactive video program or practice word processing for writing assignments. The possibilities are almost endless.

Each Learning Center should be set up in a specific location within the classroom. Each classroom can have several Learning Centers, allowing students to rotate between them. The specific location of each Learning Center should be clearly marked, so that students know exactly where to go—or where not to go, if those working at a particular Learning Center are not to be disturbed. Bulletin boards make excellent locations for Learning Centers. Such instructional bulletin boards maximize the efficiency and effectiveness of learning space in the classroom.

At each Learning Center, a set of simple instructions should be posted, so that students know what to do when they get there. The instructions should be easy to read and understand and should be illustrated with samples. They should not require additional explanations or examples from the teacher. One of the ideas behind Learning Centers is to give students practice in following directions independently. For primary-age children, you might consider putting the directions on tape, so they can listen to them as they read them. This technique can actually help them learn to read the written instructions.

Each Learning Center should also be self-checking; that is, answer keys or sample answers should be available for students to check themselves. With experience, students will quickly learn that there is no value in cheating because the work is not graded; instead, the process and completion of the work is emphasized. Making the Learning Center self-checking is important for two reasons. First, it enhances the opportunity for self-directed and independent learning. Second, it teaches students how to evaluate themselves and correct their work in order to learn from their mistakes. Each Learning Center needs to provide a place for students to put their completed and self-evaluated work.

Finally, some means for having students evaluate each Learning Center should be provided. For example, instruct students to complete an assessment form you make available at the center. You might also ask them to make entries in an assessment journal kept at each center. You need students' feedback to supplement the information you gather from examining their completed work. Specifically, you need to find out how easy the instructions were to follow, how interesting the information was, how enjoyable the activities were, and how the students think you could make it better. Using this information, you might make adjustments to improve the effectiveness of your centers.

Much of the effectiveness of Learning Centers depends on the development of responsible, self-directed behavior. You and your students should compose and discuss a set of basic rules for appropriate Learning Center behavior. You need to enforce those rules, reminding students regularly of their responsibilities and then noticing and praising them when they behave appropriately. When students finish early by working through Learning Centers effectively and efficiently, they should be rewarded with some quiet free time with their friends or free reading time in the classroom library.

Students should be encouraged to offer each other assistance and answer questions, but they also need to be taught how to help their classmates without actually doing the work for them. Peer tutoring is a valuable skill that can be developed at Learning Centers. Knowing how to be an effective peer tutor is a skill that can benefit the tutor as much as the "tutee."

Students will also need practice following different types of directions. You should use simple directions repeatedly until students become proficient with them. You can then begin to mix and match simple directions to formulate more complex ones. Eventually, students should become familiar with all the types of directions you give, then spend more time on the learning activities than on deciding exactly what you expect them to do.

Students should be discouraged from asking you questions because they can easily become dependent on your help. When you give directions to students orally and demonstrate for them what they are supposed to do, you are robbing them of the opportunity to develop independent skills in following written instructions. However, although one of the Learning Center rules should be that students do not ask you questions, you can certainly monitor their progress. By circulating from center to center, you can usually identify students who are having problems or are off task. A simple suggestion or gentle reminder is generally all that is needed to get them back on track.

Learning Centers provide a flexible and versatile instructional approach. They can free you to work with individuals or small groups of students and also allow you to individualize instruction by designing activities to meet specific student needs. Student learning can be reinforced with Learning Center activities and Learning Centers can also be used to reteach concepts not yet mastered by students. Additionally, they can offer challenging enrichment activities for gifted students.

Because Learning Centers serve a variety of instructional functions and are designed to meet a variety of student needs, you need to change them regularly and frequently. Make sure that your Learning Centers reinforce and supplement your instruction appropriately. Start and maintain a file of Learning Center activities so that you can offer a wide variety of learning experiences. Also, talk to your schools' instructional media and technology specialist about equipment available or accessible for your Learning Centers.

LEARNERS WITH DYSLEXIA AND RELATED LEARNING DIFFERENCES

The term *dyslexia* is often used inappropriately to refer only to reading and writing problems that involve "mirror" reading or writing, i.e., reading or writing letters or words backwards or transposing the order of letters or words. However, this characteristic is only one of many possible indications of dyslexia and related disorders.

A more accurate definition of dyslexia is more inclusive. Dyslexia refers to any congenital disorder generally manifested by difficulty in reading, writing, and/or spelling in spite of normal conditions in classroom instruction, intellectual potential, and sociocultural opportunity. The term is used to characterize a discrepancy between potential and achievement. Related disorders include *dysphasia* (a disorder of mental processing manifested by problems with receptive and expressive language) and *dysgraphia* (a handwriting disorder), as well as problems with spelling and organizational ability (Frandsen 1993).

If you have reason to suspect that any of your students might have some form of dyslexia or a related disorder, you should refer her or him to your school's diagnostician for formal assessment. The student may qualify for special assistance. Also, this student may have significant learning differences that require special instructional techniques and materials. Following assessment, you should consult and collaborate with the diagnostician, resource teacher, or special education specialist to determine how best to meet that learner's special needs. These experts are essential resources for helping you efficiently adapt materials and modify instruction to ensure maximum learning for that student.

Students of all backgrounds and ability levels can have some form of dyslexia or related disorders. These learning differences are not limited to students of any particular background or ability level. Gifted students can be just as likely to exhibit learning differences as mildly retarded students. Remember, the distinguishing characteristic of a learning difference such as dyslexia is that the student is not living up to her or his potential for learning, whatever that potential might be. Identifying students who are not achieving acceptable mastery of content or literacy skills is the easy part. The hard part is deciding whether those students are slow learners (i.e., performing to the best of their ability; living up to their potential) or dyslexic.

One way you can informally screen underachievers for possible learning differences is to administer an informal reading inventory (IRI) (Frandsen 1993). The IRI (see Chapter 9) is a test given individually to students for the purpose of determining the reading level appropriate for instruction. It is further used as a diagnostic instrument to identify specific word recognition and comprehension problems that are interfering with reading achievement.

The IRI can also be used to determine reading potential. Students should be able to read successfully any material they can comprehend through listening. Therefore, the highest level at which a student can comprehend a passage read to her or him orally is that student's *listening level* (see Chapter 9). Slow learners generally have listening levels commensurate with their reading levels. Dyslexic learners, on the other hand, generally have listening levels significantly higher (two or more years) than their reading levels. If a student is unable to comprehend adequately at her or his listening level by reading it to herself or himself, then the student might have a discrepancy between potential and performance. Students you identify using an IRI for screening should be referred to the diagnostician for further evaluation.

Adaptations for Content Area Instruction

Consult with the diagnostician, resource teacher, special education teacher, and/or reading specialist about ways you can effectively modify instruction for students with learning differences. It is especially important to observe the students to determine their strongest learning modalities (visual, auditory, tactile, kinesthetic, or a combination). The physical environment can also be very important in terms of being conducive to learning. Consider conditions such as the following (Carbo, Dunn, and Dunn 1986; Frandsen 1993):

1. Does the student learn better in bright or dim light?
2. Does the student learn better while hungry or after eating? What kinds of nutrition create the best opportunities for learning?
3. Does sugar, food coloring, or caffeine affect the student?
4. Does the student learn better in a warm or cool environment?
5. Does the student prefer to sit at a desk, table, couch, or on the floor?
6. Does the student prefer frequent or infrequent feedback from the teacher?
7. Does the student learn best working alone, with a partner, or in a small group?
8. Does the student learn better during particular times of the day? If so, when?
9. Is the student distracted by background noise either inside or outside the classroom?
10. Does soft background music help the student learn?
11. Is the student distracted by too much visual stimulation (e.g., attractively decorated bulletin boards)?
12. Is the student motivated more by internal or external rewards? What types of each?

A tremendous resource for making instructional adaptations are media and technology. Instructional media and technology offer powerful supplements to textual materials when introducing and reinforcing content. The vast array of reasonably priced videos, multimedia software, CD-ROMs, computers, and so forth available today are an invaluable asset to the content area classroom. Both literacy development and content learning can be enhanced by incorporating instructional media and technology (see Chapter 12).

Also, the effectiveness of textual materials can be enhanced when supplemented with a variety of textbooks, trade books, and periodicals that cover an array of reading levels. These books could be incorporated using the structure of thematic units on meaningful and relevant topics. Using a variety of textual materials on topics of interest is crucial for meeting the varied needs of students (see Chapter 7).

Following is a list of possible adaptations to enhance content learning for different students (Frandsen 1993). If you use any of these adaptations for your students with learning differences, it is very important to communicate the situation honestly with the rest of the class. Explain that everyone learns in different ways and has different talents. Tell them that some of the students in the class learn better with different types of materials, assignments, lessons, and classroom procedures. Further explain that, for every student in the class, you will be selecting materials, planning lessons, and developing assignments that you hope will improve learning. As a result, some students will have different materials, assignments, and instructions than others. Within reason, you might even want to offer some of the same adaptations to any of the other students who feel they would benefit from them. Observe their performances after the adaptations have been made; if their learning has improved, there is no reason to stop making adaptations for them as well as the students with learning differences.

1. Use Graphic Organizers and Semantic Maps.
    ▌ Keep them simple, focusing on the most important concepts.
    ▌ Use geometric shapes and colors to represent different ideas and their relationships.
2. Incorporate a variety of instructional media.
    ▌ After showing overhead transparencies, allow students to study and copy from them at their desks.
    ▌ Whenever possible, provide students with their own desk copies of anything they have to copy from the front of the room, because they often have difficulty visually tracking written information.
    ▌ When using an overhead projector, cover all items except the one being discussed.
    ▌ When using an overhead projector, go over each idea orally while students are looking at the transparency or copying down information.
3. Use special procedures when incorporating filmstrips, movies, or videos.
    ▌ Stop after approximately five to ten minutes (depending on the age of the students and length of presentation) and have all the students write down everything they can recall to this point.
    ▌ After writing, put students in heterogeneous pairs to compare notes, make additions, changes, and so forth.
    ▌ Before resuming, remind all students to refocus on the purposes you set for listening.
    ▌ Stop periodically and repeat the three procedures.
    ▌ At the end help students, together as a class, organize their notes.
    ▌ Give students copies of the final version of the organized notes with the main points highlighted.

4. Use problem-solving groups and discovery learning.
    ▌ Plan a variety of cooperative learning activities with heterogeneous groups of no more than two or three students.
    ▌ Provide opportunities for real-life applications.
    ▌ Use small-group discussions to reinforce and extend learning.
    ▌ Emphasize higher-order thinking skills and experiential learning.
    ▌ Use as many manipulatives and concrete examples as possible.
    ▌ Use multisensory approaches that involve various combinations of reading, writing, listening, speaking, touching objects, manipulating pictures, sitting, standing, moving around the room, role playing, and so on.
    ▌ Use hands-on approaches (e.g., constructing a chart, working on a group project, or creating a model).

5. Ask parents, parent-teacher associations, and administration for personal copies of textbooks for students.
    ▌ Show students how to highlight and take marginal notes.
    ▌ Teach students how to annotate, illustrate, and develop study maps for the most important parts of their assignments.
    ▌ For test preparation, highlight portions of the chapters.
    ▌ The physical acts of highlighting, mapping, and annotating while studying should maximize learning for students who have strong tactile and kinesthetic learning modalities.

6. Teach students research skills for independent learning.
    ▌ Introduce students to a variety of informational sources including libraries, bookstores, videotape and audiotape libraries and catalogues, content experts on campus and in the community, and so forth.
    ▌ Give cooperative learning assignments to heterogeneous pairs or small groups to plan, implement, and report research findings.

7. Plan special activities to help students prepare for tests.
    ▌ Provide students with copies of class notes from students who are especially good note takers.
    ▌ Highlight the class notes before giving them to students.
    ▌ Assign study partners to students.
    ▌ Give students specific instructions for reviewing.
    ▌ Help students make flashcards and show them different ways to use them for drill and review (e.g., having someone else check accuracy; physically moving the cards around to group them by various categories, sequence, and so on).
    ▌ Provide study guide questions in a format similar to the test.
    ▌ Help students determine the most important information to study.

8. Provide special adaptations for testing.
  ▌ Leave space between test questions.
  ▌ Allow students to take tests orally (either at a separate time or in the resource room) or read answers into a tape recorder.
  ▌ Allow students to complete tests on computers or typewriters.
  ▌ Allow students with learning differences more time to complete tests.
  ▌ Color code important instructional terms (e.g., *list, describe,* or *compare*).
  ▌ Reword questions into simpler language.
  ▌ Calculate the percentage correct in terms of the number of items *attempted*.
  ▌ Consider using alternate, more authentic forms of assessment (see Chapter 9).
  ▌ On standardized tests, enlarge the computerized answer sheets and transfer the answers at a later time.
  ▌ Encourage students who have difficulty sequencing and organizing answers to use a piece of scratch paper to brainstorm and plan answers.

9. Use tape recorders as much as possible.
  ▌ Record oral instructions as you give them and allow students to listen to the tape as many times as necessary while carrying out the instructions.
  ▌ Record class discussions and allow students to study them at home or in class.
  ▌ Prepare tapes of key vocabulary presented in meaningful sentences, followed by synonyms or discussions of their meanings.
  ▌ Have students who are good oral readers, parent volunteers, or teachers' aides record text material for students to listen to while following along in their books.

10. For content mastery, provide extensive opportunities for repetition.
  ▌ Fast learners can generally master information after only about fifteen to fifty repetitions.
  ▌ Average learners require anywhere from fifty to five hundred repetitions for mastery.
  ▌ Students with learning differences may need up to fifteen hundred repetitions for mastery.
  ▌ The key to mastery is to keep repetitions short and focused.
  ▌ Use short, daily reviews for mastery.

Adaptations for General Classroom Procedures

Following are some adaptations for general classroom procedures (Frandsen 1993). They are designed to maximize learning for students with learning differences such as dyslexia and related disorders:

1. Provide clear and simple instructions both orally and in writing.
   - Provide written copies of instructions in bold, easy-to-read print with color-coded key words (e.g., *match, underline, choose, fill in the blanks,* or *write*).
   - Prepare students for oral instructions by announcing that you are about to give them instructions, giving them time to turn their attention to you, and speaking differently (e.g., changing tone, volume, or pitch).
   - Stand close to and touch either the student or her or his desk while telling her or him to look at you and listen to you.
   - Ask students to repeat the instructions orally.
   - Give step-by-step instructions, only one or two at a time.
   - Show models and examples of finished products while giving directions.
2. Use chalkboards and bulletin boards appropriately.
   - Keep chalkboards uncluttered.
   - Erase from left-to-right to reinforce left-to-right processing for students who tend to confuse directionality.
   - Use colored chalk to emphasize main points.
   - Post a daily schedule on the chalkboard or on a chart on the bulletin board.
   - Refer to the schedule with each change of subject, checking off subjects or activities as they are completed.
   - Keep bulletin boards simple.
   - Use bulletin boards to reinforce important concepts.
   - Use bulletin boards to celebrate students' successes in literacy development and content learning.
3. Follow an established routine for beginning assignments.
   - Set a timer or use a clock to pinpoint the starting time.
   - Divide each assignment into small increments using small, frequent rewards.
   - Notice and respond frequently to the work and progress of students.
   - Use a blank page to cover all but one part of an assignment and set a time goal for completing that part. At the end of the time, if students have completed the work satisfactorily, reward them appropriately.
   - Make sure the amount of time allowed for the assignment is appropriate for the length and difficulty of the assignment.
4. Frequently offer a variety of choices.
   - Allow students to choose a certain number of questions to answer or problems to solve.
   - Allow students to choose a certain number of questions or problems that they do *not* have to answer or solve.

■ Allow students the option of completing their work at the regularly scheduled time or at a later time predesignated for free time, catching up on unfinished work, or making up missed work.

5. Make sure the difficulty, quantity, and time limits of assignments are appropriate.
   ■ Reduce the quantity or extend the allotted time as necessary for improving the quality of work.
   ■ Be flexible with due dates and time.
   ■ As long as content mastery is demonstrated, academic standards are not lowered by reducing quantity or allowing more time.
   ■ When the quality of work improves, resist the temptation to increase the quantity.
   ■ Communicate with parents to determine how much time students are spending on homework and adjust assignments accordingly.

6. Use frequent, regular, and consistent positive reinforcement.
   ■ Remember that any task can be extremely difficult, so praise students sincerely and enthusiastically.
   ■ Identify effective internal and external motivators and use them as rewards.

7. Allow students with learning differences to do written work on a computer, typewriter, or clipboard.
   ■ If students have difficulty composing or writing legibly, typing can be an effective alternative.
   ■ Give students lessons in keyboarding and penmanship.
   ■ Provide students with clipboards they can adjust to comfortable positions for writing.

8. Plan and conduct your lessons in an organized, logical, and sequential manner.
   ■ Begin each class by stating your specific expectations for learning.
   ■ At the beginning of the class, give a *brief* overview of the topic.
   ■ Avoid going off on tangents or getting off the subject significantly, because students with learning differences often have difficulty distinguishing the salient information from related information that is incidental and trivial.
   ■ Indicate important information by changing your voice volume (sometimes higher and sometimes lower) and inflection and slowing the pace.
   ■ End each class with a review session that includes questioning students.

Attention Deficit–Hyperactive Disorder (AD–HD)

For a variety of reasons, more and more students are being diagnosed as having attention deficit–hyperactive disorder. Following is a list of adaptations designed to maximize learning for these students (Frandsen 1993):

1. Keep the classroom as clutter free and calm as possible.
   - AD–HD students require minimal distractions, both visual and auditory, to be able to focus on instruction and learning tasks.
   - Keep classroom decorations to a minimum.
   - Keep bulletin board displays simple and chalkboards uncluttered.
2. Present information to be copied on individual sheets or transparencies to be used at students' desks.
   - AD–HD students become easily distracted while visually tracking information to be copied from the board or overhead.
   - Keep the visual field of material to be copied simple and close at hand.
3. Keep a daily schedule posted and check off each subject or activity before moving on to the next.
   - AD–HD students need help refocusing their attention consistently and regularly.
   - They also need a regular routine or sequence of activities on which they can rely and to which they can become accustomed.
   - Provide students with their own copies of the schedules.
   - When changes must be made, warn students as early as possible.
4. Identify and use consistently some type of signal for getting students' attention.
   - Use an auditory signal (e.g., voice, bell, clapping) along with a visual signal (e.g., lights off, teacher's position, raised hand, overhead transparency) and a kinesthetic signal (e.g., students raise hands, clap, sit, stand, move seats).
   - Reduce outside noise as much as possible.
5. Simplify and clarify instructions while minimizing distractions.
   - Have AD–HD students sit at the front of the classroom.
   - Provide written instructions for AD–HD students as you review them orally.
   - Encourage AD–HD students to repeat instructions.
   - Regularly check levels of understanding by asking specific questions.
6. Make handouts simple, clear, and easy to read.
   - Group similar items together and leave spaces between the groups.
   - Write or type clearly and use a good copier.

■ Provide clear, concrete examples.
■ Color code or underline important words or symbols.
7. Provide taped recordings of instructions, lectures, and class discussions.
■ AD–HD students might need to hear the information repeated several times or more.
■ Homework instructions are especially important to have taped.

SUMMARY

Through Inclusion programs, special-needs learners are mainstreamed into regular classrooms because *all* students benefit from educational and social interaction with students of differing backgrounds, needs, abilities, and talents. In fact, mainstreaming special-needs students with other students parallels the reality of our integrated society. Students will be better prepared for the real world if they learn to value differences and appreciate the contributions of a variety of learners.

To be an effective teacher of content and literacy, you must be able to recognize and plan instruction for the special needs of all your students. When you make careful observations and modify materials and instruction on the basis of your observations, your teaching effectiveness is enhanced significantly. The success of your classroom as a learning community depends on your ability to develop in your students a sense of tolerance, respect, and appreciation for differences.

The special-needs learners addressed in this chapter include gifted and talented (GT) students, students for whom English is a second language (ESL), students with dyslexia and other related learning differences, and students who have difficulty reading and writing. These four types of students with special needs will probably constitute the majority of your students needing special adaptations in content area instruction. However, you will certainly be responsible for planning instruction for other special-needs learners as well. Therefore, you need to find out what kinds of special services and materials are available for your students. You also need to become acquainted with special education faculty, as well as other experts, consultants, and diagnosticians. As a regular classroom teacher, you must seek out the support of your colleagues who are specialists in your students' varying needs.

For several reasons, gifted and talented students can be hard to identify. First, they may exhibit negative behaviors that mask their special abilities. For example, they may be inattentive and disruptive as a result of being bored with and unchallenged by the curriculum. Second, for whatever reason, they may not be achieving to their potential; perhaps they have a learning difference or gaps in their experiential background. Third, they may come from disadvantaged or culturally different communities. Unless teachers are trained to recognize the needs and characteristics of their disadvantaged or culturally different students, they may have difficulty recognizing those who are gifted.

GT students, once identified, need different, not *more* curriculum. Also, they need challenging activities but not frustrating ones. They need to work with a variety of learners including homogeneous groups of other GT students, as well as heterogeneous groups of students with diverse talents, backgrounds, and abilities.

One way to adapt the curriculum to provide different and appropriately challenging activities is through curriculum compacting. In this system, students are pretested, and the content they have already mastered is either eliminated or condensed for review purposes. Then, new content is taught at an accelerated rate in a shorter period of time. The remaining instructional time is spent on enrichment activities and advanced content.

ESL students need to be welcomed into the classroom community with concerted efforts to create a nonthreatening classroom climate in which bilingualism is valued and respected. As the community leader, it is your responsibility to nurture self-esteem, mutual respect, trust, acceptance, and empathy. ESL students need opportunities to develop comfortable working relationships with a wide variety of students by collaborating in pairs and small groups. Adaptive strategies for teaching content should be designed to build and activate background knowledge, develop vocabulary, provide support during reading, incorporate writing activities, and emphasize cooperative learning.

Students who might need special instruction because of dyslexia or a related learning difference can be identified through observation, informal testing, and formal diagnostic testing. Once identified, adaptations need to be made for content area instruction and general classroom procedures. Also, specific adaptations must be made for students with attention deficit–hyperactive disorder (AD–HD).

Two valuable strategies for content area literacy are Listen-Read-Discuss and Learning Centers. Both of these strategies can be quite useful in adapting instruction. They offer a variety of options for serving a wide range of learning styles and special needs.

ENRICHMENT ACTIVITIES

1. After getting permission from a principal and teacher, observe a class of the same students for at least thirty minutes a day, three days in a row. Observe the class for the purpose of identifying special-needs learners and any adaptations made by the teacher for instruction.

Write a brief summary of your observations in terms of any students you suspect may have one or more of the following special needs: gifted and talented, English as a second language, dyslexia or a related learning difference, or difficulty reading and writing. Include in your summary any adaptations the teacher made to address the students' special needs during instruction and any recommendations you would make to the teacher regarding instructional adaptations.

2. Visit a school with a gifted and talented program. Briefly interview the diagnostician to find out how students are identified for the program. Then, interview two students, one who has been identified as gifted and talented and one who has not. If possible, interview the students without knowing which one is which. Last, observe the two students in class for at least thirty minutes. From your conversations with the students, what conclusions might you draw about their potentials for being gifted and talented? Do your conclusions match the diagnostic results? Write a brief summary of your findings by outlining the school's diagnostic process, comparing and contrasting the two students in terms of what you observed, listing your conclusions about their potentials for learning, and indicating the extent to which your observations matched the diagnostic results.

3. After obtaining permission from a principal and teacher, visit a content area classroom that has ESL students. Visit the class at least twice for the purpose of observing two things. Observe the classroom climate in terms of the degrees of involvement and comfort exhibited by the ESL students. Also observe the teacher's role in developing that climate and any instructional adaptations made for the ESL students. Briefly summarize your findings and record constructive feedback in terms of how the classroom climate and content area instruction might be improved for the ESL students.

4. Get permission from a principal and teacher to observe a class that has at least one student diagnosed as having a learning difference (e.g., dyslexia) and at least one student diagnosed as having AD–HD. Take notes on the students' behavior, both on- and off-task, and prepare a brief summary indicating which of your observations support the diagnosis. Include in your summary any instructional adaptations made by the teacher and any others you would recommend.

5. After obtaining permission from a principal and teacher, observe a class for at least three thirty-minute sessions. Watch the students closely and see if you can identify the ones having trouble reading and writing. How well do they hide it? Have they mastered any behaviors designed to hide their poor reading and writing abilities? If so, describe them. Briefly summarize your observations, the stu-

dent characteristics that led you to believe they were having difficulty reading and writing, any cover-up behaviors, any adaptations
made by the teacher or students, and any recommendations you
would make for enhanced learning.

REFERENCES

Carbo, M., R. Dunn, and K. Dunn. (1986). *Teaching students to read through their individual learning styles.* Englewood Cliffs, NJ: Prentice Hall.

Frandsen, B. (1993). *Diversified teaching.* Austin, TX: St. Edward's University.

Kang, Hee-Won. (1994). Helping second language readers learn from content area text through collaboration and support. *Journal of Reading* 37:646–652.

Manzo, A. V., and U. P. Casale. (1985). Listen-read-discuss: A content heuristic. *Journal of Reading* 28:732–734.

Plowman, P. D. (1980). *Teaching the gifted and talented in the social studies classroom.* Washington, DC: National Education Association.

Reis, S. M., and J. S. Renzulli. (1992). Using curriculum compacting to challenge the above-average. *Educational Leadership* 50:51–57.

Romey, W. D., and M. L. Hibert. (1988). *Teaching the gifted and talented in the science classroom.* Washington, DC: National Education Association.

Tarver, S. B., and J. A. Curry. (1992). Gifted students in regular classrooms. In *Children with exceptional needs in regular classrooms.* Edited by L. G. Cohen. Washington, DC: National Education Association.

Tuttle, F. B., Jr. (1983). *What research says to the teacher: Gifted and talented students.* Washington, DC: National Education Association.

West, W. W. (1980). *Teaching the gifted and talented in the English classroom.* Washington, DC: National Education Association.

Wright, J. D. (1983). *Teaching the gifted and talented in the middle school.* Washington, DC: National Education Association.

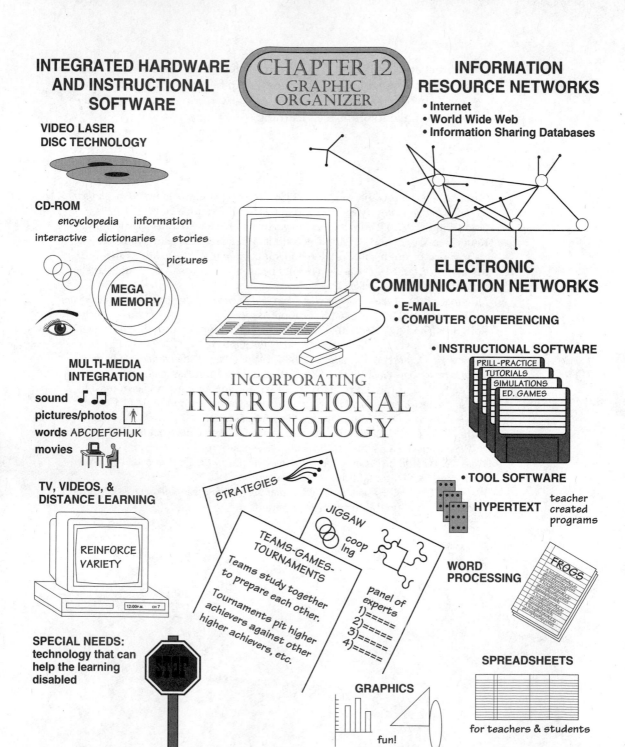

INTEGRATED HARDWARE AND INSTRUCTIONAL SOFTWARE

CHAPTER 12
GRAPHIC ORGANIZER

INFORMATION RESOURCE NETWORKS
- Internet
- World Wide Web
- Information Sharing Databases

VIDEO LASER DISC TECHNOLOGY

CD-ROM

encyclopedia   information

interactive   dictionaries   stories

pictures

MEGA MEMORY

ELECTRONIC COMMUNICATION NETWORKS
- E-MAIL
- COMPUTER CONFERENCING

- **INSTRUCTIONAL SOFTWARE**

PRILL-PRACTICE
TUTORIALS
SIMULATIONS
ED. GAMES

MULTI-MEDIA INTEGRATION

sound ♪ ♫

pictures/photos

words ABCDEFGHIJK

movies

INCORPORATING
INSTRUCTIONAL
TECHNOLOGY

- **TOOL SOFTWARE**

HYPERTEXT   teacher created programs

TV, VIDEOS, & DISTANCE LEARNING

REINFORCE VARIETY

12:00 P.M.   CH 7

STRATEGIES

JIGSAW

coop lng

WORD PROCESSING

FROGS

TEAMS-GAMES-TOURNAMENTS

Teams study together to prepare each other.

Tournaments pit higher achievers against other higher achievers, etc.

panel of experts
1)=====
2)=====
3)=====
4)=====

SPECIAL NEEDS: technology that can help the learning disabled

STOP

GRAPHICS

fun!

SPREADSHEETS

for teachers & students

Incorporating Instructional Technology

To demonstrate mastery of the content, the student will be able to do the following:

PART 1 OBJECTIVES

1. Identify the following strategy, describe its distinguishing features, and assess its significance to teaching content area literacy: Jigsaw.
2. Briefly define the concept of instructional technology and assess its significance to content area learning and literacy.
3. Describe the teacher's role for ensuring the effective use of instructional technology for content area learning and literacy.
4. Briefly define the concept of an information resource network and describe two of the most popular networks.
5. Briefly define the concept of an electronic communications network and distinguish e-mail from electronic dialogues/computer conferences.

PART 2 OBJECTIVES

1. Identify the following strategy, describe its distinguishing features, and assess its significance to teaching content area literacy: Teams-Games-Tournaments (TGT).
2. Distinguish hardware from software and describe the concept of integrated hardware including an example.
3. Define the following terms and assess the role of each in content area literacy and learning: CD-ROM, laser videodisc, LCD, multimedia, and interactive software.
4. Assess the role and importance of television, videos, and distance learning to content area literacy and learning.

PART 1 OBJECTIVES—continued

6. Assess the significance of information resource networks and electronic communication networks in content area learning and literacy development.
7. Briefly describe four types of instructional software and generalize the role of such software in helping students process and evaluate information.
8. Distinguish tool and utility software from instructional software and generalize the role of tool software in helping students communicate information.

PART 2 OBJECTIVES—continued

5. Describe examples of how technology could be used to meet the needs of students with motor or speech impairments, learning disabilities, hearing impairments, and vision impairments.

INTRODUCTION

What is *instructional technology*? It is defined here as any nontextual media (or medium) used for the purpose of teaching content information and/or developing literacy skills. It can include the kinds of media technology that have been common in classrooms for many years such as videos, slide/tape programs, filmstrips, overhead projectors, opaque projectors, and so forth. It also includes the kinds of cutting-edge media technology becoming more and more popular and common in today's classrooms including computers, CD-ROMs, laser videodiscs, multimedia, electronic communication networks, information resource networks, and so forth. These modern and increasingly common forms of instructional technology will be the primary focus of this chapter.

The importance of literacy skills—that is, reading, writing, and thinking—for content area learning has been emphasized throughout this book. The effectiveness of literacy-based strategies has also been a focus. Why, then, should instructional technology be incorporated for content area learning and literacy? Instructional technology can have a crucial impact on content area learning and literacy in several important ways.

First, in terms of content learning, technology offers an exciting and effective set of alternate and supplemental instructional resources. Students today come to school familiar with and experienced in the use and applications of many forms of technology. Thus, using technology as a learning tool in school is a natural extension of the real-life skills they bring to the classroom. Most students can program a VCR, install video games, and play computer games and simulations, among other technological feats. Showing them how to use these skills in taking control of their own learning can be quite motivating. Students encounter technology everywhere and can easily appreciate its importance and impact on life, both in school and out. The motivational effect of instructional technology enhances its effectiveness as a tool for learning content.

Second, technology can offer a wide range of opportunities and experiences to accommodate a variety of students' styles, rates, and preferences for learning. Therefore, technology can be used to individualize instruction. For example, *integrated learning systems* offer thousands of different lessons covering the same basic skills and content. From these lessons, you can prescribe individual learning programs that allow students to learn at their own pace in a nonthreatening environment to build a solid foundation of skills and knowledge (Peck and Dorricott 1994).

For students who prefer artistic modes of communication over more traditional verbal options, instructional technology can open new avenues for learning and communication. Technology-based art forms (e.g., video production, digital photography, computer-based animation, computer graphics, and so on) can nurture artistic expression and have great appeal to a significant number of our diverse student population. When used as instructional devices, these technologies can increase motivation and foster creative problem solving as students assess and compare the many possible ways to communicate their ideas (Peck and Dorricott 1994).

A third way in which instructional technology can have a critical impact on content area learning and literacy involves making content meaningful and relevant. To relate content to the real world, students must be globally aware and have access to resources outside the school. Technological tools allow students to explore the world, learning about other cultures quickly and inexpensively. Such tools can also provide constantly-updated maps and demographic data. Computer-based wire services can bring current events into the classroom as they happen (Peck and Dorricott 1994).

Fourth, the concept of literacy itself relates directly to instructional technology. Technological literacy involves the skills necessary to employ technology as a tool including research and critical thinking. Technology is not a replacement for literacy but rather an enhancement of it. Technological communication of information will probably never replace reading and writing, because the printed word provides an extremely efficient means to store and communicate large amounts of information. However, technological enhancements can certainly boost the effectiveness of the printed word.

More and more, students need to be able to access, evaluate, and communicate information quickly and effectively. Instructional technologies can address these needs by provoking students to raise their own searching questions, debate issues, formulate well-supported opinions, engage in creative problem solving, and test their perspectives and views of reality. Computer technologies allow students to gather information efficiently, evaluate it, and then communicate their thoughts and conclusions (Peck and Dorricott 1994). These processes require the integration of a variety of literacy skills including reading, writing, creating graphic representations, organizing information, and manipulating information.

Increasingly, students must be able to solve complex problems. The higher-level critical thinking processes required for problem solving can only be developed by engaging students in solving actual problems. Students develop these skills when they struggle with questions they have posed for themselves and search out the answers. With appropriate guidance from you, computer applications provide opportunities for students to organize, analyze, interpret, develop, and evaluate their own research. These programs allow students to plan thoroughly what they want to accomplish, quickly test and retest possible solutions, and display their results almost immediately (Peck and Dorricott 1994).

A fifth way in which instructional technology can have a critical impact on content area learning and literacy involves the need for competence with lifelong tools for learning. Today, and especially in the future, students must be competent, confident, and comfortable with the tools of the Information Age. Computers and other forms of technology are a fact of life in most aspects of students' lives. New technologies are being used to convert knowledge bases to digital format and increase the speed, capacity, and reliability of that information's dissemination. Increasingly, familiar technologies such as the telephone, television, and computer are merging to increase available resources and forms of communication (Peck and Dorricott 1994). Technology is here to stay and is increasing in complexity every day. Therefore, familiarity and competence with using technology as a tool for learning is just as important as being able to use reading and writing as lifelong learning tools.

Both as a learning and literacy tool, technology is an important component of instruction in content area literacy. All of the literacy-based strategies and activities discussed in this book can be used with a variety of technological tools. Technology provides opportunities for active learning and lends itself to use by individuals, pairs, small groups, and whole classes. Through instructional technology, individuals can develop and sharpen their independent learning, research, and study skills. They can also strengthen their abilities to work cooperatively with other students. Instructional technology helps teachers meet the individual needs of a variety of students; for example, gifted students can benefit from the challenges offered by technology. In addition, technology can be used to supplement content instruction for poor readers and writers. It can also provide opportunities for students at all skill levels and all levels of language proficiency to practice and develop their literacy skills.

Just as content area literacy supports the various components of the new paradigm of education (see Chapter 1), instructional technology also supports that modern paradigm. Because schools must increase their productivity and efficiency, technology can make the teacher's job easier and more effective. Technology should *re-place* rather than replace the teacher by taking over many of the routine tasks now carried out by teachers. The teacher's role can then be elevated to perform those crucial instructional duties that only a human can accomplish. For example, only teachers can build strong, productive relationships with students. Only teachers can motivate students to love learning. Only teachers can identify and satisfy students' affective needs. Instructional technologies can allow the teacher to do all of this important work involving human interaction, ongoing evaluation, and continuous improvement of the learning environment.

The teacher's role in the use of technology for instruction is absolutely critical to its effectiveness. Technology simply cannot replace good teaching. We have already learned important lessons about the role of the teacher who uses media technology in the classroom. Consider, for example, the use of videos and slide/tape presentations. These forms of instructional technology have been in widespread and common use for many years now. Certainly the quality of the videos or slide/tape programs themselves is an important factor in their effectiveness as instructional media. However, of equal if not greater importance is the manner in which the teacher uses the media.

Unfortunately, many teachers have used (or misused) media in such a way as to reduce or even eliminate its instructional value. These teachers inappropriately attempt to use videos or slide/tape presentations, for example, as a replacement for rather than a supplement or complement to instruction. As a student, you have probably experienced personally a situation at least similar to the following.

At the beginning of class the teacher announces, "Today we're going to watch a video. Be sure and take notes because it will be covered on a test later." The teacher then turns on the VCR and either leaves the room or retreats to her or his desk to grade some papers or complete attendance reports. When the video is over, the teacher turns off the VCR and dismisses class or moves on to the next activity without mentioning the content of the video.

What is wrong with this picture? First of all, after reading the first eleven chapters of this book, you undoubtedly noticed the lack of preparation given students for viewing. Just as building background knowledge, activating schemata, introducing vocabulary, and setting purposes are all important for preparing students to read, they are equally important for preparing students to listen and view nontextual media. Therefore, before turning on the VCR, the teacher should have introduced the subject of the video, related it to the current topic of study, conveyed the value of the information, demonstrated the relevance to the students' lives, introduced key vocabulary, and set specific purposes for listening and viewing. If the teacher is serious about wanting students to learn something from the video, he or she will provide them with some type of listening/ viewing guide to help them identify, record, and think about the most important facts, inferences, conclusions, implications, and so forth.

Another problem with that common scenario is the unspoken message sent by the teacher when he or she ignores the video and uses the time to work on other things. In this case, the teacher is clearly telling the students that the video really is not that important and that her or his paperwork is more important. The teacher is also saying he or she does not really care whether the students pay attention or choose to do something else instead. Finally, the teacher is communicating to the students that this video is really nothing more than something to keep them busy and use time while he or she finishes some paperwork.

If the teacher wants to use a video or some other instructional media/technology effectively, he or she should model for the students appropriate ways to pay attention. As a model, the teacher helps students learn to watch and listen with respect, how to take notes, and how to make a concerted effort to pay attention and learn something. Even if the teacher has seen the video dozens of times, he or she should communicate the importance of the video by watching it and taking notes again, perhaps looking and listening for something new.

Finally, if the video is going to be an effective learning experience, some type of follow-up questioning or discussion of the purposes set for viewing and listening is crucial. Immediately after the video, the teacher should restate the purposes and call on students to respond. Students need to know that the teacher is serious about those purposes and expects them to be fulfilled. Students who do not meet the purposes set may need to experience logical consequences. In other words, they need to learn that if they choose not to pay attention during class time, they are also choosing to give up some of their own free time later. As a result, students should be required to watch the video again on their own time after school or during lunch, study hall, or in-class free time.

A follow-up discussion of the purposes and other information gleaned from the video is essential for helping students sort information, reduce confusion, retain the facts, process the information, relate the information to their own experiences, and internalize key points. Without immediate processing, even for students who pay close attention, the educational value of the video is significantly reduced. Follow-up discussions also give students the opportunity to learn from each other by hearing what others gained from the video, how they interpreted and evaluated the information, and how others related the information to background knowledge and personal experience.

The basic principles of literacy-based instruction apply for all forms of instructional technology presented in this chapter. Instructional technology is a tool for teaching not a replacement for teaching. When using any type of instructional technology, you should prepare students by activating background knowledge, building interest in the topic, and helping them identify the questions that will guide their learning by specifying purposes. While students are working with the technology, you should serve as their model, guide, resource, and consultant. Afterwards, help them make sense of their learning experiences by answering the questions they formulated, identifying new questions to be answered, and evaluating the information in terms of their own prior knowledge and experiences.

As you read about the various types of technology in this chapter, think about ways you might incorporate them into the content area strategies you have learned. Focus on the use of instructional technology as motivational tools, tools for developing literacy, and tools for enhancing content area learning. As a teacher, you must make decisions about how to use these tools effectively. In addition to preparing students for learning about the topic, you should also prime them for learning about instructional media. Help them appreciate its value as a tool for learning. Guide students in the appropriate use of media for achieving their learning goals. Finally, assist them in evaluating the effectiveness of various media for different instructional purposes.

PART 1

STRATEGY: JIGSAW

The Jigsaw, originally designed and described by Aronson, Blaney, Stephan, Sikes, and Snapp (1978), is a cooperative learning strategy that lends itself for use with instructional technology. In the Jigsaw, students are assigned to heterogeneous groups of about four to six members. Each student in the group is assigned a different aspect of the overall project or assignment. Students are then charged with becoming experts on their assigned pieces. To become experts, students temporarily leave their groups to work with "expert groups" consisting of others assigned the same part or topic. After in-depth study, students return to their original groups to teach their group members about their topics or pieces of the assignment. Completion of the assignment or project requires that students put all their individual pieces together, like a jigsaw puzzle. Finally, each student is held accountable for all the pieces by taking individual quizzes over the content. Because every student must depend on her or his team members for information, the key to the Jigsaw strategy is interdependence.

Instructional technology can be used to assist the expert groups in researching and learning about their assigned topics. The Jigsaw was originally designed to split a reading assignment into segments, with each group member reading a different piece of the assignment. However, in addition to reading their assigned piece of the assignment, expert groups can supplement their learning of the content with related information presented with various forms of instructional technology.

The use of technology as a learning enhancement tool for expert groups is especially appropriate for a form of Jigsaw described by Slavin (1986), Jigsaw II. In this variation, all students read the entire assignment, but each student is also assigned a specific topic contained within the assignment. In their expert groups, students solidify and expand their knowledge of their assigned topics. Technological resources provide an excellent means for students to increase their understanding and knowledge about each topic.

Slavin (1986) suggests the following steps in preparing an assignment for use with the Jigsaw II strategy:

1. Select chapters, stories, or other units of content appropriate for two or three lessons. If you want students to read in class, make sure the selections can be read in about thirty minutes. If you want them to read the selections for homework, they can be longer.

2. Make an expert sheet for the unit of content you have selected. This expert sheet should identify four to six topics that are central to the unit. On the sheet, each topic should be represented by one or more questions designed to lead students to key information. Make enough copies for each student to have her or his own expert sheet. This sheet summarizes for them everything they need to know about this unit (i.e., in order to do well on the quiz).

3. Make the quiz you will use for individual assessment at the end of the strategy. You should have an equal number of questions for each topic identified on the expert sheet, making sure you have at least two for each. Multiple-choice tests are recommended for ease of grading. The questions should not be obscure but should require considerable understanding.

4. An optional step is to prepare discussion outlines. A discussion outline for each topic can be used by the students to guide their work

in their expert groups. Each outline should specify the important subtopics that need to be investigated.

5. Assign students to teams heterogeneously, so that each team represents a cross-section of sex, race or ethnicity, and past performance. Consider also personality differences and friendships to develop groups whom you believe can have effective working relationships. Because of all these important considerations, students should *not* be allowed to select their own groups.

Following are Slavin's (1986) recommended procedures for implementing Jigsaw II:

1. Assign students to groups and explain the Jigsaw process to them. A visual representation is sometimes helpful to demonstrate the concept of a puzzle broken into several pieces and put together again. Provide oral and written instructions for the process, explaining how each student will be assigned a topic for which he or she will be responsible for becoming an expert. Then, explain how each expert will be responsible for teaching his or her assigned topic to the rest of the group. Be sure to let students know that they will take a quiz over all of the topics.

2. After being assigned to a group, each student is given a copy of the expert sheet and assigned one of the topics on it. Students then read available materials related to their topics. They can be provided these materials in the classroom or given a library assignment for this part. Students could also be given individual assignments to research their topics using various technological resources. Supervise students carefully and offer consulting when appropriate.

3. After reading and researching individually, the expert groups get together to compare notes and talk about the information they have gathered. Assign a discussion leader and instruct students to use their expert sheets and discussion outlines to guide the process. Each student should take advantage of this opportunity to ensure their information is accurate and complete. They should also use this time to decide how they will teach the information to their group members and plan their presentations for doing so. Encourage students to develop visual aids to enhance the effectiveness of their presentations.

4. At this point, students can supplement their information and solidify their understanding of it. By working through related programs or presentations of information using various forms of instructional technology, students can expand, enhance, and internalize what they have learned. Again, supervise closely and be available for consultation.

5. After becoming experts on their topics, students return to their original groups. Each student then teaches her or his topic to the group. If two students in one group were assigned the same expert topic, they should make a joint presentation. Emphasize to students the importance of both good teaching and good listening in order for all group members to be successful. You might consider offering some type of incentive such as bonus points if everyone in the group achieves a certain score (e.g., eighty or ninety) on the quiz. Finally, give the individual quizzes covering all the topics.

COMPUTER-INTEGRATED INSTRUCTION

Computers are an essential tool for helping students learn to access, acquire, process, evaluate, and communicate information in virtually all content areas. For example, students can access and acquire information through worldwide networks of information resources including databases, libraries, electronic journals, archives, and so on. They can process and evaluate information through instructional software, spreadsheets, and interactive software. Students can report and communicate information using graphics and word processing software. The key to all these applications of technology is the use of computers as a tool. Learning about the computers themselves and how to program them might be an appropriate part of the curriculum in computer science courses. However, in other content areas, students need to learn the many interesting, enjoyable, and exciting applications of computers as tools for content learning and literacy.

Information Resource Networks

Today, people all over the world can communicate through computers connected by telephone lines. When your computer is connected to others, it is said to be *networked* with them. Your computer can be networked with others in your office, classroom, building, campus, city, state, country, and world. Computers are networked for communication purposes, similar to the functions of telephones. When your computer is networked, you can communicate instantly and in writing with everyone from your colleagues on campus to strangers on the other side of the world. As a result, you have instant access to the most up-to-date information related to any content area or topic of study. For these reasons, computer networks are useful for content area learning and literacy because they offer both information resources and a means of communicating that information through reading and writing.

People who use computer networks are called *users*. When they are in the process of communicating, users are said to be *online*. Computers can be connected with regular telephone lines using a *modem*, a device you plug into your computer that allows you to "dial" a number and become connected to a network. Computers can also be connected directly into a network if they are physically close enough to be wired into the system. For example, on a school campus or office complex, you could probably plug your computer directly into the local communication system. If you take your computer home, however, you would need a modem to access the network.

For content area learning and literacy development, information resource networks offer an efficient and effective way to solicit, access, gather, and store information from a wide range of sources. Through computer networks, students have access to literally thousands of information resources all over the world. These resources are available through a labyrinth of networks connected locally, statewide, nationally, and internationally. Networked computers make available a plethora of information from all over the world on almost any topic you can imagine—and many others you could never imagine. Computer networks allow you to examine and compile the most extensive, complete, and up-to-date information possible.

However, the amount of information available to students is so extensive, it can be overwhelming to the novice. Eventually they will become skilled and confident at accessing and acquiring information. Until then, students will need a significant amount of instruction, guidance, and supervision.

First, they need to learn how to narrow the focus of their topics and questions and scan available resources to access the most appropriate ones. They also must learn how to skim information and select only the most relevant. These skills are examples of those students need to learn as they become competent in accessing and gathering information on their own. One of the most important lifelong literacy skills they can develop is the ability to gain access to appropriate resources and collect relevant information independently. Through this process, students will also be learning valuable content in an interdisciplinary context.

The Internet

The benefits of computer networks are so extensive that their popularity and widespread use are increasing at extraordinary and almost incomprehensible rates. On some of the more popular networks, upwards of twenty-five million people are connected, with as many as three million communicating at any given time. One of the most popular networks of information resources is the Internet, which is a worldwide collection of thousands of computer communication networks. The Internet is used to exchange messages, post messages on electronic bulletin boards, inquire about available information, and offer information to others. Although the Internet has no recognized governing structure, there is increasingly widespread agreement among users about standard ways of packaging and sending information (Gilbert 1994).

Although the Internet offers an attractive array of resources, the huge quantity of information can be overwhelming at times. People who do not understand how to use the Internet efficiently can become so over-whelmed that they avoid using it at all. Your efficiency with the Internet will depend not only on your ability to gather and distinguish only the most relevant information but also on your computer hardware and soft-ware. *Hardware* refers to the computer itself, and *software* refers to the pro-grams you install for different uses. The quality and characteristics of your particular computer, its operating system, the telecommunications software you use, and your modem or local area network will influence the extent to which the Internet can be of value to you. Another equally important factor is the type of software tools you have for navigating the Internet (Gilbert 1994). You will need to consult with your school or dis-trict's instructional technology specialist to learn how you and your stu-dents can connect to the Internet with the best possible hardware and soft-ware available to you.

Following are some of the services offered by the Internet:

File Transfer Protocol (FTP):   Often referred to as "anonymous" FTP; pro-vides a quick and reliable way to transfer files of data. Using FTP, you can retrieve documents, files, programs, and other data from archives anywhere on the Internet.

Gopher: A menu-based system to search and retrieve documents; it com-bines features of electronic bulletin boards and fully indexed databases.

UseNetNews: Provides access to news groups, which serve as electronic bulletin boards; allows people all over the world to post messages and receive responses.

Listserv: Allows users to add their names to the mailing distribution list for various interest groups. Users can then create computer conferences on specific topics.

World Wide Web

Another information resource network is rapidly gaining more popularity than the Internet. The World Wide Web (Web) offers even more impressive and well-organized resources than does the Internet. The Web broadens the offerings of the Internet through a networked system of hypermedia documents, which go beyond textual presentation of information to include images, moving images, and sound. Information in hypermedia is accessed through conceptual associations rather than traditional alphabetical indexing. Information in hypermedia is accessed using *browser tools*, which allow you to jump between topics and subtopics using key words. Two of the more widely-used browser tools are *Netscape* and *Mosaic*.

Databases

Information resource networks offer students access to comprehensive and up-to-date databases such as online encyclopedias that are updated quarterly. Also available are information databases for periodicals on many topics. Databases of current events including weather reports are constantly updated and made accessible through the Associated Press newswire.

Electronic Communication Networks

Also called *interactive telecommunications*, electronic communication networks use computers instead of telephones for communicating. Why use computers instead of telephones? First, you might like a written account of the communication or want to communicate the same message to a large number of people at the same time. You might feel more comfortable and confident expressing yourself in writing or comprehend messages better by reading them than by listening to them. You might also want to improve your writing skills by practicing as often as possible. Finally, as discussed in the previous section, you might need to send, receive, and store large amounts of information. Electronic communication networks provide efficient systems for extensive written communication.

Electronic Mail (E-Mail)

E-mail is a computerized system of correspondence that allows individuals to communicate in writing with people all over the world. E-mail addresses are published on most international networks, allowing you to use your computer to contact someone who shares your research interests, for example. You can publish your e-mail address on electronic bulletin boards along with requests for information on a particular topic or specific documents related to the topic. Through e-mail you can request information from a seemingly endless number of sources. You can also share information you have gathered with others who request it. E-mail is an inexpensive and efficient way to communicate with colleagues, friends, pen pals, resource consultants, and anyone else with whom you wish to correspond.

Electronic Dialogues/Computer Conferences

Students can engage in *electronic dialogues*, sometimes called *computer conferences*, with other students in their class, in other classes within their school, and in other schools throughout the country and around the world. These written dialogues or conferences allow students to apply and practice their literacy skills for meaningful and purposeful communication (Moore 1991). In the content area classroom, students can apply their literacy skills in the context of communicating and thinking about (e.g., reflecting on, analyzing, synthesizing, critiquing, questioning) the information gathered. Students can engage in electronic discussions within their classrooms through local area networks (LAN) and all over the world through wide area networks (WAN). Internet conferences and electronic bulletin boards provide excellent opportunities for students interested in particular topics to share information and engage in reflective dialogue.

Electronic dialogues and computer conferences give students the double benefit of participating in class discussions, as well as written communication. In fact, many students who are shy, self-conscious, or otherwise reluctant to participate in a regular class discussion may become eager participants in an electronic discussion.

A computer discussion works in the following way. With electronic conferencing software (e.g., *Aspects* or *Daedalus Interchange*) installed in the computers, participants type the message they want to share. The message is instantly shown on the screen of all the other discussion participants. If the writer wants to direct a comment or question to a specific person, then that person's name should be included in the message. All participants will see the message, but the person to whom it is directed will know that it was addressed specifically to her or him. You might initiate the discussion by having a question or comment on the screen when the students arrive. The students then answer the question or respond to the comment. Then, they begin responding to the other students, in the true form of a discussion (see Chapter 5).

At first, until students have mastered the art of computer conferencing, the electronic discussion can seem rather chaotic and disjointed because students are continuously adding messages to a screen full of scrolling messages. However, once the students learn how to use the different features of the conferencing software, they can keep the discussion more organized and under control. For example, students can stop or even reverse the list of scrolling messages to read ones they missed or reread ones of particular interest. They can also set up "subconferences," so that those interested in a particular subtopic of the discussion can restrict the messages on their screens to those of their subgroup. They can then rejoin the whole-class discussion at any time. Finally, they can save, file, and print a transcript of the discussion (Barker and Kemp 1990).

One particularly effective program for providing structure and coherence in electronic discussions is called Electronic Networks for Interaction (ENFI). This program originated at Gallaudet University, whose students are all deaf. ENFI is a local area network of computers in a classroom or laboratory setting. Students, both in and outside of class, can meet in the ENFI lab to engage in electronic dialogues and discussions (Batson 1993).

Instructional Software

Software refers to computer programs stored on a disk. Instructional software is available for virtually every topic in every content area. Of course, the quality of some software is better than others, so it is important to establish appropriate criteria for evaluation before purchasing it. A number of assessment forms and guides are available, and your school's instructional technology specialist should be able to help you locate the most appropriate ones. Make sure you select software appropriate for your instructional goals, as well as the needs of your students. Instructional software comes in a variety of formats. Some of the most popular and useful formats include drill and practice, tutorials, simulations, and games.

Drill and Practice

This category of software is designed to help students reinforce and internalize previously learned skills, concepts, and information. A certain degree of familiarity with the content is required by students for successful interaction with this type of software (Bullough and Beatty 1991). The use of computers for drill and practice gives students the opportunity to gain experience and confidence with the hardware, i.e., the computer itself, as well as with the content of the software.

Tutorials

Tutorial software puts the computer in the role of teacher and involves the student in a dialogue that gradually increases in complexity. In contrast to drill-and-practice software, which is designed to enhance and reinforce known facts, tutorials are designed to teach new concepts by building on known ones. The tutorial program usually begins with some type of assessment of the students' level of knowledge or ability. Then, as the lesson begins, the nature of the students' responses determines how the program will progress.

If a correct response is given, some type of visual and sometimes audio reinforcement is given before progressing. If the response is only partially correct, additional information is provided the student, who is then given another chance to respond. If the response is totally incorrect, a review sequence is provided before continuing the program.

High-quality tutorial software make use of colorful graphics, helpful prompts, and record-keeping features. Students interact with the computer by manipulating various components on the screen to identify appropriate relationships. At the end of the program, the student's knowledge is evaluated. This information helps you decide if any review or reteaching is necessary.

Simulations

As the name implies, simulation software is designed to represent real-life situations and events. This type of software is highly interactive and involves the student in an essential role in the simulation. Some simulation programs require a significant amount of prior study and learning about the topic. The simulation guides students in integrating and applying the content they have learned in real-world situations or events. For example, simulation programs can give students opportunities to operate nuclear power plants, land airplanes, establish and run small businesses, create and maintain ecosystems, conduct space-flight missions, design and build houses, plan communities, establish world peace, and conduct scientific experiments.

A simulation named *Three Mile Island* presents a nuclear power plant crisis. Students are given complete control and must decide how to handle the situation. They use their knowledge of scientific and mathematical principles in developing strategies for dealing with the crisis. A simulation called *Decisions, Decisions: The Environment* (Tom Snyder Productions) requires students to collect and analyze relevant data before choosing a course of action. Another science-oriented simulation, named *Lunar Greenhouse* (Minnesota Educational Computing Corporation), requires students to control variables for plant growth. A math simulation called *Probability Lab* (Minnesota Educational Computing Corporation) requires students to make hypotheses and test them with simulated coin tosses, dice rolls, card draws, and so forth.

Two other popular simulations are called *Oregon Trail* (Minnesota Educational Computing Corporation) and *Gold Rush* (Minnesota Educational Computing Corporation). In these simulations, students play the roles of pioneers and gold diggers crossing the country. They must first decide what provisions they will take. After setting out on their journey, students are faced with a series of real-life dilemmas and challenges including rivers to cross, broken wagon wheels, spoiled food, inclement weather, mountains, brush fires, hostile Native Americans, among others. The goal is to reach the West Coast without perishing. Anyone who has played these simulations can certainly appreciate the courage and stamina that is the spirit of the American pioneers. A similar simulation, *Wagon Train 1848* (Minnesota Educational Computing Corporation), is designed especially for use with cooperative learning groups.

Literary simulations, also known as interactive fiction or text adventures, allow students to play the roles of various characters. They are given control over the plot and must make decisions about what will happen next. Many different outcomes and endings are possible, and students can make decisions individually or in groups.

Games

Careful review and judicious selection of educational software games can produce excellent opportunities for students to apply knowledge and critical thinking. They require students to develop strategies, assess their effectiveness, and make adjustments accordingly. Computer games can be quite challenging, motivating, and rewarding. They reinforce the concept that learning is an enjoyable and fulfilling part of life. Games also offer opportunities for students to practice collaboration because they work in teams to compete with the computer. Collaborative games require students to work in harmony in order for their strategies to be effective (Bullough and Beatty 1991).

Adventure games.   Adventure games are similar to simulations in that they present real-life challenges and dilemmas. Students are usually given a goal, a set of circumstances, and choices for proceeding. They must evaluate the situation and choose appropriate courses of action. The games allow them to experience the various consequences of their choices.

One of the most popular adventure games is called *Where in the world is Carmen Sandiego?* (Broderbund Software). This game is available in many variations and formats. It puts students in the roles of detectives assigned to track down a notorious master thief who has stolen some priceless national treasure. Students are presented with the circumstances of the disappearance, along with clues related to the thief's whereabouts. To help them interpret the clues—which involve unique characteristics of cities and countries—they are provided a World Almanac and book of facts. Students travel the world in pursuit of clues and check out given clues. In order to capture the thief, they must learn geographical, cultural, and demographic data about various locations around the world.

Arcade games.   These types of instructional games are patterned after familiar arcade games. However, in addition to hand-eye coordination and dexterity, students must rely on their knowledge of the content to win. For example, in a game called *Math Blaster* (Davidson Educational Software), students must shoot down the correct answers to given math problems in order to earn points. Similarly, in a game named *Word Attack* (Davidson Educational Software), students earn points by shooting down words that match given definitions. Another popular arcade game, called *Word Munchers* (Minnesota Educational Computing Corporation) is patterned after the Pac Man arcade game. Students earn points by "munching" words with the same vowel sound as a given word (Bullough and Beatty 1991).

Logic games.   Logic games require the application of analytical reasoning skills. These types of instructional computer games are designed to develop logical thinking and creative problem solving. In a game called *Think Quick* (The Learning Company), students roam through the numerous rooms in a castle by interpreting maps, deciphering codes, designing strategies, managing resources, and making quick decisions as they interact with the computer (Bullough and Beatty 1991).

Role-playing games, a particularly popular type of logic game, are similar to simulations. Students are given identities, characteristics, and resources (e.g., abilities, tools, weapons, money, and so on). They are then posed with a series of challenges and their destiny is determined by the decisions they make. Each decision changes the situation, so that simply mastering a basic set of rules and strategies is not enough. To succeed, students must be constantly thinking, predicting, analyzing, and making logical decisions.

Tool and Utility Software

Tool software is primarily designed to help students process, manipulate, and communicate information accessed and acquired through databases and instructional software. Integrated software packages allow students to move data easily among tool software applications for additional processing. Tool software allows students to create their own products as practical applications of knowledge and authentic documentation of learning.

A variety of communication styles can be served and developed with tool software. For example, word processing programs facilitate all aspects of the writing process including planning, composing drafts, revising, and editing. Hypertext programs encourage creative, nonlinear approaches to compiling and presenting information. Spreadsheet programs facilitate logical organization and mathematical manipulation of information, while graphics programs facilitate the creation of visually oriented representations of information. Using all these types of tools can help students develop a flexible and wide range of critical thinking and communication abilities.

Word Processing
Technology can enhance students' literacy skills by fostering the development of writing, as well as the thinking skills required for the composing process. Word processors, for example, can reduce the phobia often

associated with writing. Because writing on a computer allows easy correction and revision, students often find it easier to be creative and take risks. Adding, deleting, and reorganizing are no longer tedious tasks. Editing and revising can be done almost immediately during the thinking process, as well as after completion of the first draft. Therefore, the processes of drafting, revising, and editing become even more recursive. Also, since difficulty with the fine motor skills required for handwriting usually does not transfer to the keyboard, frustrations are further reduced. The final document produced by a word processor has a polished and professional quality that can give students a greater sense of accomplishment.

Students benefit from mastering keyboarding skills at an early age. Competence with the keyboard makes word processing a much more efficient and valuable tool. Excellent software designed to teach and provide practice in keyboarding skills is available. *Muppet Learning Keys* (Sunburst Communication) can be used to teach keyboarding to primary-age children. Other good keyboarding software recommended by Bullough and Beatty (1991) include *Type!* (Broderbund Software), *Typing Tutor IV* (Simon and Schuster), *Type to Learn* (Sunburst), and *Mavis Beacon Teaches Typing* (Software Toolworks).

Students need to learn the appropriate use of spelling checkers, common features of most word processing software. Spelling checkers can be helpful in catching and correcting misspelled words, as well as learning the correct spellings of words. However, they cannot be used to replace proofreading. Some mistakes involve the misuse of words spelled correctly (e.g., *their* for *they're*); therefore, students must get into the habit of using the spelling checker *and* proofreading their work. A thesaurus is another useful feature of word processing software. It can help students expand their vocabularies and check appropriate uses of words. Because it is so quick and easy to access, students are more likely to take the time to use it.

Programs that include audio instructions and reinforcement can be especially useful for young writers. A number of excellent word processing programs are available for writers of all ages. The following examples of word processing software are recommended by Bullough and Beatty (1991):

1. *Dr. Peet's Talk/Writer* (Hartley Courseware, Inc.) introduces the alphabet and provides opportunities for reinforcing letter names. It then moves on to activities involving the typing of letters, words, and sentences. A speech synthesizer pronounces the letters and words as they are entered.
2. *Talking Text Writer* (Scholastic Software) is another word processing program that provides audio reinforcement of words as they are entered. This program also offers a talking dictionary.

3. *Talking Notebook* (First Byte) provides audio instructions and feedback. The voice can be adjusted for speed, tone, and pitch, so that students can customize the voice to match their compositions. Personalized dictionaries can also be created.

4. *Muppet Slate* (Sunburst Communication) allows students to add pictures and borders to decorate their compositions.

5. *Bank Street Writer* (Scholastic Software), a popular program now in its third edition, includes a spelling checker, thesaurus, pull-down menus (like those used in Macintosh and Windows applications), a student guide, a reference guide, cut-and-paste features, and search-and-replace features.

6. *LogoWriter* (Logo Computer Systems, Inc.) allows students to combine word processing and graphics in a single document. For example, words can be typed anywhere on the screen to label illustrations. Also, several documents (e.g., written by different students) can be linked together into a single document. This capability facilitates collaboration among writers.

7. *GraphicWriter* (DataPak) also has graphics capabilities for illustrating compositions. Black-and-white and color graphics can be positioned any place in the document. In addition, various page formats can be created to arrange graphics and text in different patterns.

8. *MultiScribe* (Scholastic Software) has similar operating features to *GraphicWriter* but is strictly a word processor without the graphic features. A particular advantage of *MultiScribe* is that it displays on the screen features such as underlining exactly as they will appear on the printed page. Another benefit is that you have the choice of using a mouse (a sliding tool for giving commands) or the keyboard itself.

9. *FrEdWriter* (Free Education Writer) is a high-quality, public-domain (i.e., virtually free) software program with a number of useful features. For example, it has built-in "help" features that provide on-the-screen instructions. Also, various functions are accessed using single keys. Another useful feature is called *prompted writing*, which allows you to put prompts on the screen to guide students through the composing process. These prompts appear on the screen but not on the hard copy (i.e., printed page). This program is available for a modest fee (about $20) to cover production, packaging, and postage costs.

10. Integrated word processing software, which include spreadsheets and databases in addition to word processing, are especially useful. Some of the more popular programs include WordPerfect, MicrosoftWorks, and ClarisWorks.

Hypertext

Hypertext software (*Hypercard* for Macintosh computers and *Linkway* for IBM-compatible computers) can be used for two major functions by both teachers and students. The first function involves expressive communication in the form of authoring. It is a tool for writing and developing integrated instructional programs. You can use it to develop your own instructional software customized to your curriculum, teaching style, and student needs. Students can use it as a tool for presenting information they have compiled and processed. Hypertext is a versatile and exciting tool that allows the author to integrate the presentation of text with illustrations, graphics, photographs, sounds, music, voice synthesizing, and live-action video.

The second function of Hypertext involves receptive communication in the form of reading, viewing, and listening. The entire program consists of a stack of "cards." Each card is presented on the screen, one at a time. On each screen, information regarding a particular topic or concept is presented in various forms. The program is interactive in that the learner can select "buttons," which are labeled spaces on the screen, to get more information about certain terms, concepts, and subtopics. When a button is selected, more information is presented in a variety of ways. It might be presented for viewing on another screen or for listening with recorded sounds, music, narration, or synthesized speech. At the learner's discretion, he or she moves on to the next card, thereby controlling the amount of time spent on each topic or concept.

Spreadsheets

Spreadsheets are electronic grids made up of horizontal rows and vertical columns for storing and processing information. Each row and column is labeled. For example, in a grade book spreadsheet, each row might represent all the grades for a particular student, and each column might represent all the grades for a particular assignment. The box created at the intersection of a row and column is called a *cell*. Each cell holds a value, represented by a number. Using the grade book example, each cell would hold a grade on a particular assignment for a particular student.

Formulas can be entered into the spreadsheet program so that calculations between values are made automatically. For example, in a grade book spreadsheet, homework grades can automatically be averaged and computed into the final grade as they are entered. Spreadsheets are especially useful and efficient ways for students to record and make calculations on scientific, mathematical, and statistical data. For example, they can record measurements and other data observed over time and then make calculations to determine changes and draw conclusions from statistical analyses.

A *template* is a spreadsheet format used when the calculations will remain the same, and only the cell values will change. For example, the same spreadsheet template can be used for a grade book for several classes or for a science experiment being replicated. The cell values will change for each class or set of data, but the calculations will remain the same (if, of course, the grading system or data manipulation remains unchanged).

The varied features available for spreadsheet programs make them an attractive tool for recording, storing, and manipulating information. Most spreadsheet programs allow various types of graphs to be generated from the data and calculations. Some spreadsheet programs even have a sorting feature that allows you to sort data in alphabetical or numerical order. The editing, copying, cutting, pasting, and formatting features of spreadsheets make the process of recording and updating data quick and easy. Also, changing the formulas for recalculation of data is a simple process with spreadsheet programs.

Graphics

The quality and quantity of graphics software today and the potential developments for tomorrow are almost mind boggling. Computer graphics is a creative communication tool with almost limitless possibilities. Graphics software can be used for a wide range of communication forms including artistic expression, pictorial representations of information, text illustrations, and multimedia presentations. Some programs are designed only for illustrating and designing graphics. Others, such as desktop publishing programs, integrate graphic capabilities with text-based word processing.

Painting and drawing programs including *MacPaint* (Claris), *MacDraw* (Apple), *MacDraft* (Innovative Data Design), and *Mac3D* (Challenger Software) offer students a wide range of tool options. *MacPaint* allows a free-form approach to creating images in much the same way as an artist painting images on a canvas. The student can choose from various tools and processes such as *paint brush* and *spray paint*, which emulate different types of textures and techniques. *MacDraw* and *MacDraft*, on the other hand, offer more mechanical approaches to creating images. Instead of using the freehand approach, students select drawing instruments and create images using predefined shapes and lines. Drawings are positioned on a grid, and a ruler used to establish different scales. *Mac3D* applies the rules of perspective to transform automatically a two-dimensional image into a three-dimensional image (Bullough and Beatty 1991).

Animation software including *Fantavision* (Broderbund) and *VideoWorks* (Hayden) allow students to develop continuous-action images. Students select beginning and ending figures from the built-in collection of ready-made images, and the computer then automatically fills in the animation necessary to move from the beginning to ending image (Bullough and Beatty 1991).

Printing software such as *The Print Shop* (Broderbund Software) and *Print Magic* (Epyx) can be used to integrate text with graphics for posters and similar visual aids for presenting information. No freehand drawing or lettering ability is needed, because students choose both graphics and letters from a library of stored images. Images for an extensive range of subjects are available, and editing and text layout features allow the student to move the text and images to experiment with a variety of designs (Bullough and Beatty 1991).

Graphing software including *Microsoft Chart* (Microsoft), *AutoGraph* (SVE), *MECC Graphing Primer* (MECC), and *MECC Graph* (MECC) allow students to present numerical data in a wide range of graph formats such as line, circle, bar, and pictograph. Colorful images, often three-dimensional, can be created for highly effective presentation of information. Analysis features allow automatic statistical calculations (means, averages, and percentages) from raw data. Labels, captions, and other text materials can also be added.

Presentation software—*PowerPoint* (Microsoft), *Slide Shop* (Scholastic), and *Presentation Pro* (Strade)—allow students to create color slides, overhead transparencies, posters, handouts, and other visual aids to enhance the effectiveness of oral presentations. A wide variety of type fonts are available, as are various borders, bullets, and special effects for making interesting transitions between slides. *Slide Shop* can be used to copy images onto a video cassette tape for easy presentation and add titles and captions to existing videos. Sound effects, music, and digitized sounds are also available.

Database Programs

For content area instruction, database programs have tremendous utility, particularly in terms of interdisciplinary projects. Files can be set up for a topic of study with *fields*, i.e. categories, set up for the kinds of information to be gathered and stored about the topic (Blanchard and Mason, 1985). For example, the topic of the Ebola virus could be chosen as a springboard for interdisciplinary projects. A file could be established using categories of information that focus on aspects related to different fields, e.g., biology, social studies, and mathematics. The categories for an interdisciplinary study of the Ebola virus might include some of the following:

- dates of discovery and breakthroughs
- scientists and physicians involved
- dates and locations of outbreaks
- length and severity of epidemic periods

- profiles of the international team of epidemiologists involved
- locations of reported cases
- geographic profiles of locations
- numbers of reported cases
- case outcomes
- number of deaths
- length of survival
- reproductive traits of the virus
- bodily targets of attack
- modes and rates of transmission
- symptoms
- prognosis for recovery
- degrees of severity
- mortality rates
- stages of development
- experimental treatments
- results of experimental treatments
- modes of containment
- funding sources for research and containment
- funding needs for research and containment
- involvement and contributions of the Center for Disease Control
- government intervention
- demographic effects
- education programs
- prevention programs

Students could then work collaboratively to compile the information for each database. Compiling the data would involve students in the study and application of information and concepts related to any number of disciplines, including biology, mathematics, statistics, physical geography, cultural geography, sociology, psychology, medical science, demographics, economics, international relations, political science, history, ethics, and social work. The data could then be analyzed and synthesized by teams of students to answer socially-relevant questions such as the following:

- What are the correlations between number of cases, rates of transmission, mortality rates, and community health facilities?
- Based on the locations of outbreak, where should prevention efforts be centered, and what form should those efforts take?
- What are the possible implications to U.S. residents, and what are the most logical responses to the threat?
- To what degree should foreign countries become involved, and what form should that intervention take?
- What are the implications for the U.S. and world economies?

■ How can the citizens of local and international communities support the efforts of the physicians and scientists who are battling the epidemic?

■ From lessons learned with the current outbreak, what steps can and should be taken to prevent future outbreaks?

■ Which forms of experimental treatment and containment should be funded on a priority basis and why?

■ What is the most socially-responsible way to treat the victims in terms of allocating available resources to do the greatest amount of good for the greatest number of people?

■ How does the current viral outbreak compare to and contrast with the one that occurred in the 1970's?

■ Based on lessons learned from the 1970's outbreak, how is this epidemic being handled differently?

■ What effect has the current epidemic had on health care available for the treatment and prevention of other illnesses and diseases?

■ What are the most cost-effective forms of funding for containing the disease?

■ What are the projected demographic effects for the communities involved in the outbreak?

PART 2

STRATEGY: TEAMS-GAMES-TOURNAMENTS (TGT)

The procedures for this cooperative learning strategy were adapted from those originally described by Slavin (1986). Begin by assigning students to heterogeneous teams of four or five students. To ensure a heterogeneous mix, first rank all students in the class according to past performance from lowest to highest achievement. This ranking should be done on paper and in private only for the purpose of assigning teams. Use this ranking list to ensure that each team has one higher-achieving student, one lower-achieving student, and two or three average-achieving students. Team assignments should remain the same for at least several weeks so that students can bond as a team and learn how to work together effectively.

Begin with a class presentation of content. This content could be presented in a variety of ways: in the form of a reading assignment (e.g., using a Directed Reading Activity or other literacy-based strategy) or a lecture followed by a class discussion. Finally, the content could take the form of a technology-based presentation such as a video, film, computer program, or multimedia presentation.

Following presentation of the content, students meet in their teams to study the content and help each other master the content. They should be allowed to study in teams for one or two class periods. Remind students that each member of their teams will compete individually in the tournament, so they need to make sure that every member is well prepared to represent their team in the tournament.

Provide each team with appropriate materials. For example, you could provide study sheets that summarize the content; students could use these study sheets to learn the material and quiz each other. You could also offer practice quizzes that model appropriate types of questions; students then use these to monitor their learning and formulate their own questions to quiz each other over the content. Finally, you could provide students with technology-based materials such as a hypertext program or other type of computer software. Students could then work together at computers to study, quiz each other, and together learn the content.

To begin the tournament, assign students to tournament tables. Students should be assigned to homogeneous groups, so that the higher achievers compete with other higher achievers, lower achievers compete with other lower achievers, and so on. Each table receives three sheets for questions, answers, and scores. The game score sheet should have the students' names listed in the order they will play, the students' team names, and spaces for points earned in each game (see sample game score sheet in Figure 12–1).

The first student begins by reading the first question on the question sheet. If the content is math, students are allowed to use pencil and paper to solve problems. The student to the right of the one answering the question checks her or his response on the answer sheet. If correct, one point is marked for that student on the game score sheet. That student then passes the question sheet to her or his left, and the student with the answer sheet also passes it to the left. The game ends when all of the questions have been answered or a predesignated amount of time has expired. The points are then totaled and recorded on the game score sheet. Additional games can be played during the same class period or at later times as a review of

FIGURE 12–1 Sample Game Score Sheet for Teams-Games-Tournaments

STUDENT	TEAM	GAME 1	GAME 2	GAME 3	TOTAL
Rick E.	Cardinals	12	10	15	37
Lauren P.	Puffins	14	16	10	40
Quita B.	Eagles	17	13	11	41

FIGURE 12–2 Sample Tournament Score Sheet for Teams-Games-Tournaments

TEAM	STUDENT	GAME TOTAL	TEAM TOTAL
Cardinals	Rick E.	37	
	Gifford B.	35	
	Kristen S.	40	112
Puffins	Lauren P.	40	
	Jordan B.	27	
	Kudra E.	25	92
Eagles	Quita B.	41	
	Kyle B.	38	
	Darwin E.	42	121
Pelicans	Edith S.	22	
	Hal F.	27	
	Tonya J.	25	74
Blue Jays	Shannan S.	33	
	Bobby J.	39	
	Margaret M.	29	101

the content. The point totals for each game are recorded on the tournament score sheet (see sample tournament score sheet in Figure 12–2).

The final step in the strategy is team recognition. A class newsletter, chart, or bulletin board can be used to post and celebrate scores. Improvements in scores should be rewarded and celebrated in the same way as winning scores. Team recognition can also take the form of special privileges, prizes, healthy snacks, free reading time, and so forth.

INTEGRATED HARDWARE AND INSTRUCTIONAL SOFTWARE

The term *hardware* is used to refer to computers and other instructional technology devices including interactive video laserdisc players, Compact Disc–Read Only Memory (CD-ROM) drives, and Liquid Crystal Display (LCD) panels. The term *software* is used to refer to the programs inserted into the hardware, enabling it to serve a variety of functions. Instructional, tool, and presentation software can all be enhanced when used with an integrated system of hardware.

For example, videodiscs and CD-ROMs can put literally thousands of images and pieces of information at students' fingertips. Interactive laser videodisc players attached to computers give students a more active role and significantly expand the capabilities for instructional content and presentation. CD-ROM drives attached to computers greatly increase the ability of the software to store and access archived data. LCD panels attached to computers allow you to conduct whole-class or large-group instruction by displaying the computer screen on a projection screen for all to see.

Hardware and software integrated in a variety of ways produce multimedia with almost limitless possibilities. Multimedia technology can combine text, video, audio, photography, animation, graphics, and more for multisensory presentation of information. Through hardware and software integration, multimedia can also be made interactive, moving the student from audience member to active participant.

Interactive Laser Videodiscs

The laser videodisc allows virtually thousands of images together with text and sound to be stored in a format that never wears out. The format also allows easy access of specific components without the linear search required for videotapes. When a videodisc player is attached to a computer and the proper software used, the system becomes interactive. In other words, students can make choices, seek answers, and respond in various ways (Bullough and Beatty 1991).

Teachers can use authoring software to create customized lessons that combine images encoded on the disc with text and sound. Such lessons can be used to introduce information, develop background knowledge, review or reteach selected concepts, reinforce previously learned information, and evaluate learning. The images can be played back in many different combinations including still frame, slow motion, fast motion, and normal speed. Lessons can be programmed so that students can skip familiar areas or get more detailed information and examples for parts they have trouble understanding.

Rock and Cummings (1994) reported the results of a research project on videodisc instruction in science conducted by Optical Data Corporation. The participating schools (eight elementary, three middle, and four high schools) used either *Windows on Science* (K–8 curriculum) or *The Living Textbook* (middle, high school, and college levels). Early in the first year of the research, the teachers' logs reported greater student enthusiasm for science, as well as an apparent increase in the students' self-confidence. In addition to teachers' logs, data were collected from standardized tests, portfolio assessment, and attitude surveys.

Some of the initial results were more dramatic than others. However, the findings suggest that the students who participated in classrooms using videodisc instruction achieved more than students taught using traditional instructional practices in science. Overall, the researchers concluded that videodisc technology has a positive effect on student outcomes (Rock and Cummings 1994).

CD-ROMs and Multimedia

Compact Disc–Read Only Memory (CD-ROM) technology helps make hardware and software multimedia integration more practical by making available to the teacher a multitude of programs, hundreds of which can be stored on a single compact disc. The massive storage capabilities of CD-ROM make it useful in creating a wide range of databases. Also, information in the form of dictionaries, encyclopedias, and almanacs is available on compact discs.

CD-ROM reference materials assist students in organizing and retrieving data efficiently as the amount of information available continues to expand. Using electronic reference sources such as CD-ROMs, students can learn to plan and conduct systematic searches of available data, skim text for relevance, scan for specific information, and retrieve pertinent content. A number of excellent electronic reference resources are available for students to use in doing their own research, putting together their own presentations, and developing their own instructional programs. Two examples of electronic encyclopedias are *Compton's Multimedia Encyclopedia* and *The New Grolier Electronic Encyclopedia*. Each set of encyclopedias (twenty-six volumes and twenty-one volumes, respectively) is contained on a single compact disc. The Grolier CD allows text retrieval only; it does not incorporate pictures or sound. Because its readability is challenging, it may be more appropriate for secondary school students. The Compton CD, on the other hand, incorporates both text and picture retrieval, in addition to sound and graphic features. For example, students can listen to the music of famous composers, see motion pictures of erupting volcanoes, and observe through animation the working of the human heart. Also, using hypertext features, students can highlight difficult words for voice pronunciations and dictionary entries (Melnick 1991).

Another example of electronic reference materials is the *Microsoft Bookshelf, 1993 Multimedia Edition* (Microsoft), which includes the following reference books: *The American Heritage Dictionary, 2nd College Edition; Bartlett's Familiar Quotations, 15th Edition; The Concise Columbia Encyclopedia of Quotations; The Concise Columbia Encyclopedia, 2nd Edition; The Hammond Atlas; Roget's II Electronic Thesaurus;* and the *World Almanac and Book of Facts, 1993*. All of these books are enhanced with full-motion video and sound. Also, all seven books are linked together in a single index to simplify searching for information on a particular topic.

As defined by Kanning (1994), the term *multimedia* refers to the use of more than one medium to communicate information. Multimedia presentations may include video, sound effects, music, synthesized speech, illustrations, graphics, still photography, animation, and text in almost any combination. Technological advances have also made possible various forms of *interactive* multimedia.

An example of multimedia is the resource developed by Kanning (1994) for middle school math teachers: *Interactions: Real Math—Real Careers*. Using interactive laser videodisc, the program connects math topics to specific career applications involving high-interest activities such as protecting endangered species, managing water resources, and planning a trip to Mars. You can see how this program could be used for interdisciplinary instruction (e.g., math and science, or math, science, and social studies) as well.

Another example of multimedia described by Kanning (1994) involves the use of video footage, scanned maps, and graphs generated from spreadsheet programs used for instructional presentations in history. Using a multimedia authoring package, *Authorware Professional,* the history teacher created a presentation about life during the Great Depression. The presentation uses graphs to show the falling Gross National Product figures and the rising unemployment rates. Also during the presentation, questions are displayed for all to see, using an LCD projection panel. In addition, students can use multimedia to enhance their presentations. For example, they can show parts of a television documentary recorded on laserdisc.

A third example of multimedia described by Kanning (1994) involves a middle school science teacher. Using a multimedia authoring package, *NIH Image*, the teacher created dozens of activities that require students to process various images. For example, in one activity, students search for sulphur on Io, one of Jupiter's moons, using images from NASA's CD-ROM series. These types of activities further the goal of developing science knowledge while also developing scientific observation skills.

The students also can *create* multimedia presentations of science knowledge. For example, using hypertext, students develop multimedia reports on topics of their choice. The presentations can include scanned images, student-drawn illustrations, text, sound effects, speech, music, and video or film clips. One example of such a presentation, described by Kanning (1994), involved a group of students studying plate tectonics. They researched their topic in encyclopedias, books, and scientific databases on CD-ROM. While conducting their research, they collected suitable images from the various sources. To illustrate the motion of the plates, they created clay models of the Earth's plates, filmed the models using a portable video recorder, digitized the images, loaded them into the computer, and colorized them. They incorporated about 20 frames of the footage into their presentation.

Still another example of multimedia described by Kanning (1994) involves first- and second-grade science classes and a *HyperCard* stack produced by the Smithsonian Institution. The program, called *Dino Hunt*, leads students through an archaeological dig with the goal of identifying a dinosaur bone. Instead of supplying answers, the program gives clues, and students investigate them on maps and in books. Intermediate-grade students (i.e., fourth through sixth grades) can begin learning to create their own hypertext programs. You could develop a "skeleton" program that students can complete by adding definitions, filling in specific information, and providing examples (Kanning 1994).

The Public Broadcasting Service has published an excellent interactive multimedia resource called *Eyes on the Prize*. It consists of video segments, lesson plans, and an extensive archive of photos, maps, graphs, biographies, documents, and music. This program brings to life America's civil rights history and can serve as a resource for both you and your students.

TELEVISION, VIDEOS, AND DISTANCE LEARNING

In spite of increasing numbers of "trash T.V." programming on network television, a number of excellent educational programs and videos are available through the major cable networks and the Public Broadcasting System (PBS). For example, Ken Burns' Civil War series, now available from PBS on videocassette, is an exceptional nine-part documentary. Using actual photographs, period music, narration by actors representing major historical figures, actual letters and notes from the Civil War era, and interviews by historians, the program gives viewers a fascinating and often painfully realistic view of the war including the events leading up to it, the holocaust of the battle fields, and the tragic aftermath. PBS offers many excellent videos available on a variety of topics including the Great Depression, African-American studies, Latin American studies, Native American studies, ethics and values, government and politics, health sciences, history, the environment, math and technology, physical sciences, biological sciences, and earth sciences.

The Discovery Channel offers excellent programs on science and nature, many of which are sponsored by the National Geographic Society. Public Access television provides many high-quality programs focused on topics and issues of local concern including city council meetings, school board meetings, and public hearings. C-Span airs national legislative proceedings, allowing the public to see firsthand their government in action.

As with all forms of instructional technology, videos, television programs, and distance learning presentations should be incorporated into carefully planned lessons designed for maximum content area learning and literacy development. Specifically, they need some type of written guide to clarify their purposes for listening and viewing. Chapter 5 described a variety of study guides for helping students get the most out of their assigned readings. That chapter also described and presented an example of a listening guide to accompany books, chapters, or passages on audiotape for learners who have difficulty reading. The listening guide format can also be used to help students of all ages and ability levels get the most out of television programs, videos, and distance learning presentations.

Listening/viewing guides can specify learning objectives so that students know exactly what they are supposed to glean from the experience. Such guides can also provide questions and statements designed to help students make sense of the information by relating it to prior learning, background knowledge, and relevant real-life experiences. In addition to helping students focus their attention on salient points and relationships between concepts, listening/viewing guides can help them monitor their understanding during the presentation and evaluate their learning afterwards. Figure 12–3 provides an example of a listening/viewing guide that can be used to enhance learning with television programs, videos, and distance learning presentations.

Distance learning technologies use video and audio to transmit instructional presentations to students in other—sometimes far away—locations. They allow students across the country access to a greater number of quality educational presentations, some of which are interactive. Distance learning is important for making enriched and diverse learning experiences accessible to all students, especially in remote areas with small student populations where course offerings are limited (Peck and Dorricott 1994).

INSTRUCTIONAL TECHNOLOGY FOR SPECIAL-NEEDS LEARNERS

Technology facilitates expressive communication for students with motor or speech impairments. Portable laptop computers with speech synthesizers and specialized word processing programs can help these students overcome obstacles to composing, writing, and speaking. Word prediction and abbreviation expansion features can help students circumvent the fine-motor and spelling demands of writing. The word prediction feature works by producing a list of words that begin with the letter just typed. The student can then choose an appropriate word and insert it

---

FIGURE 12–3 Listening/Viewing Guide

Instructions:

As you listen to and watch the video about Mexico, think about the following questions and take notes in the space provided.

1. When and why did the Spanish explorers invade Mexico and make the Aztec people their slaves?

2. Identify some of the traditions, customs, and folkways of the people of modern Mexico that can be traced to their Aztec ancestry.

3. Identify some of the traditions, customs, and folkways of the people of modern Mexico that can be traced to their Spanish ancestry.

4. When and how did the Mexican people eventually gain their independence from Spain?

5. How do the Mexican people celebrate their independence day?

6. Why do Americans celebrate Mexican Independence Day and why do Mexican-Americans celebrate the Fourth of July?

---

with a single keystroke. The abbreviation expansion feature works by encoding messages that can then be retrieved with a simple keystroke combination. Speech feedback helps the students monitor and edit their writing (Zorfass, Corley, and Remz 1994).

Also, special keyboard settings can accommodate slower key releases to avoid the problem of repeating letters. Plastic keyguards placed over the keyboard enable students with limited arm or hand dexterity to access individual keys with greater precision. Even students without use of the arms or hands can make selections from the keyboard using headsticks, mouthsticks, or customized hand-held pointers. Alternate keyboards of various sizes and configurations can help students who have reduced fine-motor ability or limited range of movement.

For students with learning disabilities, word processing, spelling checkers, grammar checkers, and speech synthesizers can ease the physical burdens of writing. Sustained writing projects such as research reports can be facilitated with software like *Search Organizer* (Education Development Center, Inc.). This program is designed to support middle school students as they work through a systematic process of identifying a research question, developing a search plan, gathering and integrating information, and writing the report (Zorfass, Corley, and Remz 1994).

Instructional technology helps students with hearing impairments appreciate the use of written language as a tool that allows communication with a variety of audiences for different purposes. For example, by using electronic mail (e-mail), deaf students have the opportunity to practice reading and writing for specific and meaningful communication purposes. Students can communicate with each other in the same class, in different classes within the same school, in different schools within the same city, or in different cities, states, and countries. Technology can also be used to help students who use American Sign Language to become writers of English.

Zorfass, Corley, and Remz (1994) identify three ways in which technology can assist students with vision impairments. First, it offers an alternate means of text input. Students can use either a traditional keyboard with standard touch-typing technique or a Braille keyboard that enables them to input Braille text. Electronic devices are also available for visually impaired students to input Braille notes. They can listen to these notes later as synthesized speech, download them to a computer file, and eventually print them out in either Braille or text.

Second, technology helps students monitor the text while writing. For low-vision students, hardware- or software-based text enlargers can be used to facilitate them in monitoring their own writing. However, text enlargers obviously limit the amount of text that can be viewed at one time. Word processing programs with speech feedback enable students to hear words as they are entered. Screen-reading programs allow students to listen to their running text after it has been entered. Also, a Braille display device can be attached to a computer to translate the print displayed on the monitor into Braille. However, such devices require the student to juggle two very different motor activities, i.e., keyboarding and Braille reading, which can interrupt the writing process.

Third, technology provides ready access to written products in print or Braille. For example, a Braille translation program can be used to print work on a Braille printer, as well as in standard print format. Braille copies are important for allowing students to make permanent written records for themselves.

Most visually impaired students have limited experience with printed text. As a result, they can have particular difficulty with spelling and text-based conventions in grammar and punctuation. Therefore, word processing programs with spelling and grammar checkers can be helpful.

SUMMARY

Instructional technology can have a crucial impact on content area learning and literacy. It offers exciting and effective alternate and supplemental instructional resources. It can offer different opportunities and experiences to accommodate a wide range of students' styles, rates, and preferences for learning. For example, for students who prefer artistic modes of communication over more traditional verbal options, instructional technology can open new avenues for learning and communication.

Instructional technology impacts content area learning and literacy in terms of making content more meaningful and relevant. Technology connects students to local and worldwide communities. For example, information resource networks such as the Internet and World Wide Web allow students to explore the world and make real-life applications quickly and inexpensively. In addition, electronic communication networks including e-mail and computer conferencing encourage students to engage in written dialogues and discussions with each other and with other people around the world.

Technological literacy is an important part of content area literacy. It involves the skills necessary, including research and critical thinking, to employ technology as a tool. Technology is not a replacement for literacy but rather an enhancement of it. More and more, students need to be able to access, evaluate, and communicate information quickly and effectively. These processes require the integration of a variety of literacy skills. Instructional technologies engage students in the process of solving complex problems. Students develop higher-level critical thinking skills when they struggle with and research questions they have posed for themselves.

Literacy-based strategies and cooperative learning activities including the Jigsaw and Teams-Games-Tournaments can be used with a variety of technological tools. Technology provides opportunities for active learning and lends itself to use by individuals, pairs, small groups, and whole classes. Using various forms of instructional software such as tutorials, simulations, and games, students can develop and sharpen their independent learning, research, and study skills. They can also strengthen their abilities to work cooperatively with other students. Instructional technology helps you meet the individual needs of a wide range of students from the gifted to the learning disabled. Tool software provides opportunities for students at all levels of skill and language proficiency to practice and develop their literacy skills.

Just as content area literacy supports the various components of the new paradigm of education (discussed in Chapter 1), instructional technology also supports that modern paradigm. Because schools must increase their productivity and efficiency, technology can make the teacher's job easier and more effective. For example, massive amounts of information can be made available to students in the convenient forms of CD-ROMs and laser videodiscs. Also, integrated hardware, interactive software, and multimedia can involve students more actively in learning and applying knowledge. Finally, the use of high-quality television programs and videos can make effective use of a medium that is both familiar and motivating to students.

ENRICHMENT ACTIVITIES

Complete these activities with a cooperative learning group of two to four students. Divide each activity so that each person in the group is assigned a specific task or role and is held accountable for her or his assignment.

1. Choose a unit topic for a particular grade level and content area. Then, develop a bibliography of available instructional software (including drill and practice, tutorials, simulations, and games), CD-ROMs, laser videodiscs, hypertext programs, multimedia programs, videos, and television programs. The following resources should help you get started: librarians, computer databases, instructional technology specialists, catalogues, educational technology stores, publishing companies, and media specialists.

2. Use the same or choose another unit topic for a particular grade level and content area. Using a computer with access to worldwide information resources such as the Internet, conduct a search for information related to that topic. Make sure you narrow your topic sufficiently to exclude all but the most germane information. Print a summary of your research.

3. Plan a set of Learning Centers for a unit topic you identify for a particular grade level and content area. Incorporate some form of instructional technology into each center. Also, provide specific instructions appropriate for the grade level you select at each center. Finally, give instructions for students to guide them in checking their own work. Make at least one of the centers a cooperative

learning activity in which you structure the task for individual accountability and positive interdependence.

4. Design a series of three enrichment activities for gifted students in a particular content area grade level. Use a different form of instructional technology for each activity, allowing students to make some choices for self-directed learning in each. Make at least one of the activities a cooperative learning activity in which you structure the task for individual accountability and positive interdependence.

5. Design a checklist of available instructional technologies. After obtaining permission from school administrators, visit a local school. Using your checklist, develop an inventory of the types of instructional technology available. In your inventory, identify each type, how many are available, where they are kept, who has access to them, who actually uses them, and how many students are served by them. Draw some conclusions from your observations. For example, is more technology needed? If so, how much and what kinds? Is it being used properly and efficiently? If not, how could it be used differently?

REFERENCES

Aronson, E., N. Blaney, C. Stephan, J. Sikes, and M. Snapp. (1978). *The jigsaw classroom.* Beverly Hills, CA: Sage.

Barker, T. T., and F. O. Kemp. (1990). Network theory: A postmodern pedagogy for the writing classroom. In *Computers and community: Teaching composition in the 21st century.* Edited by C. Handa. Portsmouth, NH: Boynton/Cook.

Batson, T. (1993). The origins of ENFI. In *Network-based classrooms: Promises and realities.* Edited by B. Bruce, J. K. Peyton, and T. Batson. New York: Cambridge University Press.

Bullough, R. V., Sr., and L. F. Beatty. (1991). *Classroom applications of microcomputers,* 2d ed. New York: Merrill.

Edinger, M. (1994). Empowering young writers with technology. *Educational Leadership* 51:58–60.

Gilbert, S. W. (1994). *Welcome to the Internet: Nightmare or paradise?* AAHE Bulletin 7:3–4.

Kanning, R. G. (1994). What multimedia can do in our classrooms. *Educational Leadership* 51:40–44.

Melnick, S. A. (1991). Electronic encyclopedias on compact disk. *The Reading Teacher* 44:432–434.

Moore, M. A. (1991). Electronic dialoguing: An avenue to literacy. *The Reading Teacher* 45:280–286.

Peck, K. L., and D. Dorricott. (1994). Why use technology? *Educational Leadership* 51:11–14.

Rock, H. M., and A. Cummings. (1994). Can videodiscs improve student outcomes? *Educational Leadership* 51:46–50.

Slavin, R. E. (1986). *Using student team learning*, 3d ed. Baltimore, MD: Johns Hopkins University, Center for Research on Elementary and Middle Schools.

Zorfass, J., P. Corley, and A. Remz. (1994). Helping students with disabilities become writers. *Educational Leadership* 51:62–68.

Study Strategies for All Learners and Content Areas

PREDICT, ORGANIZE, REHEARSE, PRACTICE, EVALUATE (PORPE)

This study strategy, developed by Simpson (1986), has many advantages for both students and teachers. For example, PORPE actively involves students in planning, monitoring, and evaluating their own learning. It also engages students in the activities of good readers, such as defining tasks, setting purposes, identifying key ideas, reorganizing information using their own words and schema, self-questioning, and self-testing. PORPE makes explicit for students the processes involved in preparing for essay exams. It demands that students focus on content and its relation to themselves to see whether they are learning. Finally, it can be taught by any content area teacher without jeopardizing the time necessary for learning content.

In the first step, students **predict** potential essay questions that will guide their study processes after they read the text. Simpson (1986) recommends direct instruction and modeling of the process of developing essay questions. First, introduce the language used for writing essay questions, e.g., *explain, criticize, compare,* and *contrast.* Second, model the process of predicting essay questions concerning the important aspects of a given body of information. Third, help students start composing their own questions by giving them stems for potential questions. Finally, have students develop their own questions and share and discuss the plausibility of them with classmates in pairs or small groups.

In the second step, students **organize** the key information necessary for answering the predicted essay questions. This process requires students to summarize and synthesize the material. Then, they outline their answers either in conventional form or as a graphic organizer. Simpson (1986) also recommends direct instruction and modeling for this step.

In the third step, students engage in a **rehearsal** designed to program key ideas, examples, and organization into their long-term memories. This step is characterized by oral recitation and self-testing. Once the information is committed to memory, the slow, continual process is emphasized as students continue to test themselves several times over a period of days.

Fourth, students **practice** by writing out in detail what they learned during the rehearsal process. Again Simpson (1986) suggests that you model the process of composing effective essay answers. In doing so, stress the following steps: (1) outline or map the answer quickly before writing; (2) in the opening statement of the answer, rephrase the question or take a position; (3) include transitional words (e.g., *first, on the other hand*) to make the structure of the answer obvious; (4) include examples for each major point; (5) after completion, compare the outline to the written answer and proofread it.

The fifth step requires that students **evaluate** the quality of the answers to their predicted essay questions. The goal in this step is for students to appreciate writing as a way to monitor and reinforce their learning. Once again, Simpson (1986) recommends direct instruction and the use of a checklist of evaluation criteria for this process. Tierney, Readence, and Dishner (1990) suggest the following questions to help guide students' evaluations: (1) Is the question directly answered? (2) Does the introductory sentence rephrase the question or take a position? (3) Are the major points organized in a way that makes them obvious to the reader? (4) Are appropriate examples used to prove and clarify each point? (5) Are clear transitional cues provided to the reader? (6) Does the content make sense?

OVERVIEW, ASK, READ, WRITE, EVALUATE, TEST (OARWET)

This strategy was described by Maxwell and Norman (1980) as an organized approach to study reading. You will recognize the steps as variations of SQ3R. As you read about OARWET, think about the key similarities and differences between it and SQ3R.

The first step is the **overview,** which is essentially the same as the survey step of SQ3R. Students are directed to read the title and subheadings, as well as look at pictures, maps, graphs, and charts. They are then instructed to read the first few paragraphs to locate the topic sentence that states the main theme of the chapter. Last, they are directed to read the summary paragraph at the end.

The second step is to **ask,** which is similar to the questioning segment of SQ3R. If questions are provided by the text, students read them immediately after the overview. If questions are not provided, students are instructed to formulate their own from the subheadings.

The third step is to **read.** Again, this step is essentially the same as the third step of SQ3R. Students are directed to read for the purpose of looking for information that will answer the questions. From the overview, it is determined that the author considers this information important.

The fourth step is to **write,** a step that parallels the recite portion of SQ3R. Students are instructed to take notes, summarize, paraphrase, or outline; they should also write answers to the questions.

The fifth step is to **evaluate.** In this step, students ask themselves questions such as the following: What is the significance of this information? Does it make sense? How does it relate to my background knowledge and experience? What are the implications and relevance? Answering such questions requires students to process and internalize the information. By processing it, they can more easily assess their level of learning.

The sixth step is to **test.** Here, students evaluate how well they met their purposes for reading. They answer the questions out loud, rereading if necessary to clarify and complete information. Students use the questions for a self-assessment of learning.

PREVIEW, QUESTION, READ, REFLECT, RECITE, REVIEW (PQ4R)

This effective variation of SQ3R was developed by Thomas and Robinson (1972). The **preview** step parallels the survey step of SQ3R. The **question** and **read** steps are essentially the same as those in SQ3R.

After reading, students are instructed to **reflect** on the material and how well they understood it. At this point, they should reread as necessary. Then, students should identify the important parts to remember, as well as the parts that are most meaningful to them personally. Then, the **recite** and **review** steps are carried out in the same way as the same steps in SQ3R.

PREVIEW, ASK QUESTIONS, READ, SUMMARIZE (PARS)

Another alternative to SQ3R was suggested by Smith and Elliott (1979). The steps that direct students to **preview, ask questions,** and **read** are similar to the survey, question, and read steps of SQ3R. After reading, students are instructed to **summarize** by writing a paragraph that pulls together the key points of the information read.

PREVIEW, STUDY, CHECK (PSC)

Still another modification of SQ3R was developed by Orlando (1980). Before reading, students **preview** (survey) to get an overview of the content. While reading, they are directed to **study** short sections at a time, stopping to write short summaries and check the accuracy of their summaries after reading each section. After reading, they **check** by reviewing their entire set of summaries.

SURVEY, QUESTION, READ, RECORD, RECITE, REFLECT (SQ4R)

This strategy was originated by Pauk (1984) as an alternative to SQ3R, which deemphasizes the survey step in favor of spending more time recording, reciting, and reflecting. The first three steps, **survey, question,** and **read,** are basically the same as those in SQ3R. The only exception is that the survey is designed to provide a quick overview before setting purposes for reading.

After reading, students are instructed to **record** important information. They are encouraged to be selective and write concise notes that can be used as cues for review. Then, they **recite** by recalling information aloud, using their notes as cues. Last, they **reflect** by doing a critical analysis of the information and thinking about how the information might be useful to them.

PURPOSE, ADAPTABILITY OF RATE, NEED TO QUESTION, OVERVIEW, READ AND RELATE, ANNOTATE, MEMORIZE, ASSESS (PANORAMA)

This strategy, developed by Edwards (1973), is an extended version of SQ3R. In the first stage, students prepare for reading by first identifying their **purpose** for reading. Second, they consider **adaptability** of rate by deciding on an appropriate rate for reading according to the difficulty of the material. Third, students recognize the **need** to question by converting subheadings into questions to be answered by reading.

In the second stage, students gain an **overview** of the material by surveying it and noticing how it is organized. Next, they **read** and **relate** by answering the questions they developed. At this point, they also locate the author's main point along with supporting ideas and facts. They then **annotate** by making relevant and appropriate notes on the main ideas and supporting information.

In the final stage, after reading, students **memorize** important information by outlining it on note cards. They also use acronyms and other mnemonic aids to help them memorize the major points. Finally, they **assess** their learning by self-testing to evaluate how well they have understood and recalled the material.

THINK, THINK, SKIM, STUDY, THINK (TTSST)

Crawley and Mountain (1988, 172) describe this strategy as a way to "help students arouse their interest in, and think about, the assignment being read." It is specially designed to generate active learning.

Before reading, students are instructed to **think** about what the teacher said about the topic when the assignment was given. Next, they **think** about the topic in relation to prior learning and the broader and narrower topics in the table of contents. Then, immediately before reading, students **skim** the assignment to locate the main ideas and develop an interest in the topic.

While reading, students **study** in detail. In this step, they locate meanings of unknown vocabulary and take notes by paraphrasing the information in their own words. Putting the information into their own words helps students assess their understanding.

After reading, students are directed to **think** about what they read by reviewing their notes. During this step, they should also draw their own conclusions and identify implications of the information. This final step helps students react to what they read and become more actively involved in the learning process.

CONCENTRATE, READ, REMEMBER (C2R)

This study strategy, developed by Moore (1981), encourages students to consider their own learning styles and preferences to personalize the strategy. In the first step, students **concentrate** by first making decisions based on factors such as where, when, and with whom they study best. Then, if they lose concentration, they are encouraged to try some of the following solutions:

1. Select an area that you can designate for studying only. If you use the kitchen or dining room table, use a different chair for studying.
2. Keep your work area free from distracting clutter.
3. Keep only materials from the subject you are studying on your desk or work area.
4. Alter your reading rate faster or slower to determine an appropriate rate to maintain concentration.
5. Ask yourself questions and look for answers while you read.
6. Stop frequently, after each section or page, to recite key points.
7. While studying, make a list of extraneous thoughts that interrupt your concentration. Then, ponder the list after you have finished studying.
8. Reward yourself after a successful study session.
9. Break the habit of allowing your mind to wander by learning to recognize it quickly and doing something about it.

In the second step, students **read** with a purpose in mind. They are also instructed to look for organizational patterns and reminded to adjust their rate according to their purpose and the difficulty of the material. If students have trouble identifying what is important, they are directed to try some of the following solutions:

1. Ask for assistance from the teacher or a competent classmate about what you are expected to learn.
2. Survey the assignment, looking for main ideas.
3. Identify similarities between lecture notes and the reading assignment.
4. Read the preface, introduction, and summary for ideas about the book's thesis.
5. Identify key words that might give clues to the main ideas.
6. Look for organizational patterns (e.g., cause/effect, chronological sequencing, reasons, examples, and compare/contrast).
7. Formulate questions from the headings and subheadings; then, read to locate answers to the questions.

After reading, students **remember** the material by developing and improving their memories. They organize the material into manageable and meaningful units, use association techniques, and develop plans for reviewing on a regular basis.

PREPLAN, LIST, ACTIVATE, EVALUATE (PLAE)

This strategy was developed by Simpson and Nist (1984) as a method for assisting students in consciously selecting the strategies they use. The underlying principle of this strategy is that good readers have mastered a variety of strategies and know how to select strategies appropriately in response to the demands of the task and materials. As a content area teacher, you can use this strategy to guide your students through the process of analyzing the demands of the task and materials and then selecting appropriate strategies.

In the first step, students **preplan** by examining the task and the difficulty of the material. They also consider their background knowledge and determine their purpose, i.e., exactly what is to be accomplished. In the second step, students **list** strategies they believe might be appropriate for accomplishing the task. Third, they select one of the strategies they listed and **activate** it by using the strategy to complete the assignment for the identified purposes. Finally, they **evaluate** the appropriateness of the strategy according to how well the purposes were achieved. If the purposes were not achieved, students identify strategies that might have been more effective.

SURVEY, QUESTION, REREAD, QUESTION, COMPUTE, QUESTION (SQRQCQ)

This study strategy was specially designed by Fay (1965) to assist students in reading and learning mathematics. In the first step, students **survey** the problem quickly to gain a general understanding of it. Second, they formulate a **question** that focuses on the information the problem is seeking. Third, students **reread** the problem to identify relevant facts and their relationships. Students formulate another **question** that focuses on the process of how the problem should be solved in the fourth step. Fifth, students **compute** to solve the problem. Finally, they formulate and answer another **question** designed to check the accuracy of the answer.

PREVIEW, QUESTION, READ, SUMMARIZE, TEST (PQRST)

Another strategy recommended by Fay (1965) is PQRST, another variation of SQ3R. This strategy is recommended as especially appropriate for science content. The **preview** step involves a rapid skimming of the whole selection. In the **question** step, students raise questions in terms of the study purposes. They then **read** the selection, keeping the questions in mind. In the next step, students **summarize** and organize the information. Finally, they **test** themselves by checking their summaries against the selection.

EXPLORE, VOCABULARY, ORAL READING, KEY IDEAS, EVALUATE, RECAPITULATE (EVOKER)

This strategy was designed by Pauk (1963) to assist students in reading literature including imaginative prose, poetry, and drama. In the first step, students **explore** by reading the entire selection from beginning to end without stopping. This step is designed to give students the "big picture" of the author's message.

In the second step, students record key **vocabulary** in the selection. They look up unfamiliar words and familiarize themselves with names, events, and places. The third step is **oral** reading of the selection with appropriate expression. Fourth, students locate **key** ideas and determine the author's organization. The fifth step is to **evaluate** by analyzing the key words and ideas; students note how the key words help develop mood and shades of meaning. Finally, students **recapitulate** by rereading to place the individual parts into the context of the selection.

REFERENCES

Crawley, S. J., and L. H. Mountain. (1988). *Strategies for guiding content reading.* Needham Heights, MA: Allyn & Bacon.

Edwards, P. (1973). Panorama: A study technique. *Journal of Reading* 17:132–153.

Fay, L. (1965). Reading study skills: Math and science. In *Reading and inquiry.* Edited by J. A. Figurel. Newark, DE: International Reading Association.

Maxwell, H., and E. Norman. (1980). *Successful reading,* 3d ed. New York: Holt, Rinehart and Winston.

Moore, M. A. (1981). C2R: Concentrate, read, remember. *Journal of Reading* 24:337–339.

Orlando, V. P. (1980). Training students to use a modified version of SQ3R: An instructional strategy. *Reading World* 20:65–70.

Pauk, W. (1963). On scholarship: Advice to high school students. *The Reading Teacher* 17:73–78.

———. (1984). The new SQ3R. *Reading World* 23:274–275.

Simpson, M. L. (1986). PORPE: A writing strategy for studying and learning in the content areas. *Journal of Reading* 29: 407–414.

Simpson, M. L., and S. L. Nist. (1984). PLAE: A model for planning successful independent learning. *Journal of Reading* 28:218–223.

Smith, R., and P. G. Elliot. (1979). *Reading activities for middle and secondary schools.* New York: Holt, Rinehart and Winston.

Thomas, E. L., and H. A. Robinson (1972). *Improving reading in every class: A sourcebook for teachers.* Boston: Allyn & Bacon.

Tierney, R. J., J. E. Readence, and E. K. Dishner. (1990). *Reading strategies and practices: A compendium,* 3d ed. Needham Heights, MA: Allyn & Bacon.

Procedures for Calculating Reading Rate

1. Calculate the average words per page in the book.
    a. Select a full page of print (e.g., not the beginning or end of a chapter).
    b. Count the number of words in three full lines of print.
    c. Divide by three to get the average number of words per line.
    d. Count the number of lines on the page.
    e. Subtract two to compensate for short lines.
    f. Multiply the number of lines by the number of words per line.
    g. Record this number, so you can reuse it each time you calculate your rate for this particular book.
2. Read for a predetermined time, usually between five and twenty minutes.
3. Count the number of pages you read in that time.
4. Multiply the number of pages by the number of words per page (calculated in the first step).
5. Divide by the number of minutes.
6. Record your rate, along with the date, and a general rating of your level of comprehension (e.g., poor, fair, adequate, good, excellent).

A P P E N D I X C

A Process and Format for Writing Lesson Plans

STEP 1: OBJECTIVES AND MATERIALS

First, identify the content objectives that summarize the content or information you expect the students to know by the end of the lesson. Write the objectives in the form of behavioral/performance objectives (i.e., what students will do at the end of the lesson to demonstrate learning, not what they will do during the lesson to accomplish learning). For example, you could use the stem "Students will demonstrate learning by," followed by a verb appropriate for the level of thinking (according to Bloom's Taxonomy) you intend to tap and develop. Here are some examples:

knowledge

cite	label	name	reproduce
define	list	quote	pronounce
identify	match	recite	state
tell	recall	remember	repeat
recognize	describe	memorize	locate
draw	write	select	

comprehension

alter	discover	manage	relate
change	explain	rephrase	substitute
convert	give examples	represent	summarize
depict	restate	translate	describe
illustrate	reword	vary	interpret
paraphrase	transform	review	generalize

| infer | match | express | defend |
| predict | distinguish | compare | extend |

application

apply	discover	manage	relate
classify	employ	predict	show
compute	evidence	prepare	solve
demonstrate	manifest	present	utilize
direct	practice	use	illustrate
report	change	choose	interpret
draw	model	modify	sketch
paint	dramatize	collect	discover
produce	make		

analysis

ascertain	diagnose	distinguish	outline
analyze	diagram	divide	reduce
associate	differentiate	examine	separate
conclude	discriminate	find	determine
designate	dissect	infer	investigate
compare	contrast	survey	organize
separate	categorize	classify	construct
research	subdivide	point out	

synthesis

combine	devise	originate	revise
compile	expand	plan	rewrite
compose	extend	pose	synthesize
conceive	generalize	propose	theorize
create	integrate	project	write
design	invent	rearrange	develop
modify	construct	imagine	produce
role play	hypothesize	add to	formulate
organize			

evaluation

appraise	conclude	critique	judge
assess	contrast	deduce	weigh
compare	criticize	evaluate	decide
select	justify	debate	verify
recommend	solve	summarize	relate
consider			

The reading materials that will be used in the lesson should be listed at the beginning of the lesson plan along with the objectives. First, if a textbook will be used, identify it and specify the reading assignments. Then, list other reading materials to be used either in the lesson itself or as enrichment at the end of the lesson. These materials could include children's or adolescent literature including fiction and nonfiction, as well as magazines, newspapers, journals, pamphlets, and technical reports. A list of resource books for bibliographies of children and adolescent literature, some of which are organized by topic, is provided in Appendix L. Your school or public librarian can direct you to these reference materials. Keep in mind the importance of exposing students to a wide range of reading materials; doing so can improve attitudes toward reading and learning by generating interest in and curiosities about a variety of topics and information sources.

You should also include on your lesson plan any other instructional materials you use including instructional technology. Your librarian can help you locate resource books for instructional materials such as video- and audiotapes, slides, computer software, video discs, and television programs. You should include as varied an array of information sources as possible. Texts and reading materials should be selected using information gained about students' reading abilities and interests. This information can be obtained easily using informal teacher-made or commercial inventories. Some examples of informal inventories are described in Chapters 7 and 9.

STEP 2: INTRODUCTION AND VALUE

The next step involves planning an attention-grabbing introduction. Each lesson should begin with an introduction designed to focus the students' attention by getting them involved on a personal level immediately. The introduction should motivate students internally by showing the lesson's specific value or relevance to the world of today and, more importantly, to their own personal lives. In this segment, you should provide meaningful examples and ask questions about the students' personal knowledge and experiences with regard to the topic or some aspect of it. For example, in introducing a math lesson on fractions, you might ask: "Has anyone ever shared a pizza with friends or family members? How did you make sure everyone got an equal portion? If the pizza were not already cut, how would you know how many pieces to cut? Tell us how you have done it or would do it."

Finally, you must clearly relate the introduction to the topic and activities of the day's lesson. In other words, students must be able to see how your attention-grabbing introduction is relevant to the rest of the lesson. At this point, you must provide a clear link between the introduction and the lesson itself by communicating your expectations of students, i.e., what you expect them to do and learn. Do not assume that your students will infer what your introductory activity, questions, or discussion have to do with the topic and objectives of the lesson. You must state directly to your students the connection between the introduction and the lesson. For example, in the same math lesson, you might conclude the pizza discussion with the following statements. "Well, today we are going to learn about fractions. We will learn how to use fractions in different ways. For example, we can use fractions to decide how to share a pizza, money, or a six-pack of cola. You will see that fractions are very important for helping you determine your fair share to make sure you never get cheated or cheat others."

STEP 3: STRATEGY AND PROCEDURES

The next step involves deciding on an appropriate content area literacy strategy (or strategies) and listing the procedures for implementation. Simply copying the steps of the strategy is not sufficient. You need to describe fairly specifically how each step will be implemented in this particular lesson and reading assignment, providing enough detail to enable you and others to visualize exactly how it will take place. For example, simply saying that you will have the students survey the chapter is not enough. Will you do this with them as a whole class or will they do it with partners or in small groups? What instructions will you give them for surveying? How will you assess to ensure students got an accurate overview of the chapter? Your procedures should also identify any vocabulary you will introduce and present the words in the context of sentences. Make sure you identify the general and specific purposes for reading you will establish. Additionally, you should specify the point at which you will ask any questions in your procedures.

STEP 4: QUESTIONS AND ASSESSMENT

The next step is to write comprehension questions from all levels of thought, ensuring you require students to think critically. In other words, ask questions that not only require students to recall facts and concepts but also make inferences, draw conclusions, make value judgments, and apply the information to a new situation. (Levels of questioning are discussed in detail in Chapter 5.) You need to formulate questions as part of the lesson-planning process to ensure a variety of quality questions that require higher-level thinking. If questions are taken directly from the teacher's manual, be selective and use only the best and most appropriate questions for your objectives. In your procedures section, specify at what point in the lesson the questions will be asked. Use as many questions as necessary to adequately check comprehension and assess attainment of objectives. You might need to supplement the questions with other means of assessing whether students achieved your stated objectives (e.g., quiz, writing activity, cooperative learning project, oral question and answer session, or in-class discussion.)

STEP 5: CLOSE AND ENRICHMENT

The last step is to plan an appropriate close to your lesson. Each lesson should end with a close that somehow reviews and ties it all together. The comprehension questions and evaluation activity should not serve as a close to the lesson. Leave students with a summary of main ideas learned in that lesson, along with the value and relevance of that information. You may provide the summary and value, or you may ask the students to contribute.

At the end of your lesson plan, identify at least one enrichment activity, that allows students to reflect on and process the information learned, relating it to prior learning and applying it to new situations. Enrichment activities should involve a variety of communication skills (e.g., using a cooperative learning discussion or writing assignment to relate the information to current events).

If not done earlier in the lesson, the enrichment activities should also incorporate fiction and nonfiction literature related to the topic of the lesson. Enrichment activities with a variety of literature give students opportunities to get acquainted with exciting alternatives to the textbook. This exposure to varied reading materials is important for stimulating interest and curiosity in content area topics, as well as for improving attitudes toward reading and learning.

For enrichment through literature, offer a variety of fiction and nonfiction books related to the topic. Give students a specific task that requires them to at least skim through the books, read selected parts, and discuss what they liked or found interesting about them. The exact nature of the task will depend on the amount of time available for enrichment. Students can work with partners or in small groups to share books so you do not have to provide an entire class set for every lesson. The important thing to remember about enrichment activities with literature is that many students do not know how to skim books to get an overview of them. Skimming is a skill that will have to be modeled and directly taught. Students will need specific instructions to follow in skimming the books and then again in sharing what they discovered. The books and other materials used for enrichment should be kept in a room library, so students can spend time later perusing and reading them when they finish other work or have projects to research.

LESSON PLAN FORMAT

Name of teacher(s) _____ **Date** _____

Grade level(s) _____ **Content area(s)** _____

Strategy(ies) _____

    I.   **Content Objectives** (See Step 1 in process.)

   II.   **Materials** (See Step 1 in process.)

  III.   **Introduction and Value** (See Step 2 in process.)

  IV.   **Procedures** (See Step 3 in process.)

   V.   **Comprehension Questions and Assessment** (See Step 4 in process.)

  VI.   **Close and Enrichment** (See Step 5 in process.)

Sample Lesson Plans

Strategy: Graphic Organizer
Primary Content Area: Algebra
Grade Level(s): 9–10

CONTENT OBJECTIVES

Students will demonstrate learning by

1. graphing ordered pairs of numbers.
2. determining a solution for an equation with two variables.
3. assessing the relationships between a linear equation, a set of ordered pairs of numbers, and a set of points on a coordinate plane.
4. defining and applying the following terms: abscissa, coordinate system, coordinates, graph, ordered pair, ordinate, origin, plot, quadrant, x-axis, y-axis.

TEXT ALTERNATIVES/SUPPLEMENTS

1. *High Performance Computer Architecture* by Harold Stone
2. *Principles of Economics* by Roy Ruffin
3. *Modern High School Physics* by Columbia University Teacher's College

4. *Mathematics: A System of Doing Mathematics by Computer* by Stephen Wolfram
5. *Environmental Geologic Atlas with the Texas Coastal Zone* by University of Texas at Austin Bureau of Economic Geology
6. *Make It Graphic! Drawing Graphs for Science and Social Studies Projects* by Eve Stwertka and Albert Stwertka
7. *Graph Games* by Frédérique and Papy
8. *The I Hate Mathematics! Book* by Marilyn Burns
9. *The Sneaky Square and 113 Other Math Activities for Kids* by Richard M. Sharp and Seymour Metzner

INTRODUCTION, VALUE, AND EXPECTATIONS

1. The teacher has the game Battleship set up at the front of the room before the class enters. Without any explanation, the teacher asks for two volunteers to play the game. Play continues for two to three minutes. The teacher thanks the students; they return to their seats.
2. The teacher explains that grids and coordinate systems are encountered/used in many areas of life, both in games and occupations. The teacher then cites examples including: a hurricane-tracking chart, road atlas, map with latitude and longitude lines, architecture, interior design, physics, business, and computer programming.
3. The teacher explains that coordinate systems are the foundation for understanding linear equations. Linear equations are also important for understanding and demonstrating concepts such as correlations between variables. Research in all fields depends heavily on the concept of correlations, i.e., predictions of unknown effects based on known effects. In medical science, for example, the correlation between the variables of birth weight and life expectancy play a critical role in designing prenatal care programs. Examining correlations is an important part of understanding every aspect of our lives and world. Correlations are crucial for helping us make effective decisions and plans based on what is already known. Without correlations, life would be nothing more than random acts and arbitrary decision making.
4. "In this lesson, we will begin our unit on linear equations. You will learn some of the vocabulary you need to understand linear equations. You also will learn how to graph ordered pairs and find the solution of an equation with two variables. In our next lesson, you will learn how to apply linear equations to determine and demonstrate correlations."

PROCEDURES

Prereading

1. The teacher pronounces the vocabulary words in the context of sentences, while pointing to them on the board.
2. The teacher explains the importance of this vocabulary for understanding the rest of the unit and that most of the words are familiar because they have been covered in the previous unit on real numbers.
3. The teacher draws a Graphic Organizer (with blanks) on the board; the Graphic Organizer demonstrates the relationships among the vocabulary words and between them and the overall topic.
4. The teacher asks students to guess what might go in the blanks. The teacher writes some of the student responses.

During Reading

5. Students are instructed to check the accuracy of the vocabulary Graphic Organizer during reading.
6. The teacher hands each student a Graphic Organizer that provides a visual representation of the steps for solving linear equations; blanks are placed in key positions.
7. The teacher divides students in groups of three (leader, reader, and checker). The teacher tells students to read the text and complete the Graphic Organizers.
8. The teacher walks around the room, monitoring and helping if necessary.

Postreading

9. Each group discusses the accuracy of the vocabulary Graphic Organizer and suggests changes to the whole class if appropriate.
10. The teacher selects a member of each group at random to explain the group's Graphic Organizer for the steps in completing linear equations.
11. The teacher writes the correct answers on the board and explains relationships among the steps and between the steps and vocabulary.
12. After demonstrating representative problems on the board by following the steps outlined on the Graphic Organizer, the teacher assigns problems.
13. Students begin working on the problems in their groups.
14. At the end of class, the teacher asks the comprehension questions.
15. The teacher explains the enrichment activity.
16. Students finish the problems for homework. They are checked and discussed within their groups the next day before submitting them.

QUESTIONS AND ASSESSMENT

Literal
1. What is the difference between the abscissa and the ordinate?
2. When plotting a point, where do you start?

Interpretive
1. What do all solutions of a linear equation have in common?
2. What would happen to a graph if the units on the horizontal axis were doubled?
3. How many solutions does an equation with two variables have?
4. How do you determine whether a given ordered pair is a solution for a given equation?

Applied
1. How could you use linear equations to propose solutions for the high school dropout problem?
2. How would you design a linear equation to examine the correlation between dropping out of school and earning potential?

CLOSE AND ENRICHMENT

1. The teacher asks students for more examples of using or encountering coordinate systems.
2. The teacher explains the background knowledge students now have for studying linear equations and applying them in practical research.
3. For extra credit, students may write a short (one-half to one page) paper on the use of grids/coordinate systems in the real world or in other disciplines and the use of linear equations for research. Students may use the enrichment materials or may select other sources (subject to the teacher's approval). The paper will count as an extra homework grade. The teacher will display the papers on a bulletin board.

Strategy: LEA
Primary Content Area: Social Studies
Grade Level(s): 5

CONTENT OBJECTIVES

Students will demonstrate learning by

1. examining different perspectives presented in books about Columbus.
2. defining and demonstrating the concept of historical relativity.

TEXT ALTERNATIVES/SUPPLEMENTS

1. *Christopher Columbus, Great Explorer* by David Adler
2. *Pedro's Journal* by Pam Conrad
3. *The Columbus Story* by Alice Daigliesh
4. *Westward with Columbus* by John Dyson
5. *Where Do You Think You're Going, Christopher Columbus?* by Jean Fritz
6. *The First Americans* by Joy Hakim
7. *Christopher Columbus* by Stephen Krensky
8. *Christopher Columbus* by Ann McGovern
9. *I Sailed with Columbus* by Susan Martin
10. *Discovering Christopher Columbus: How History Is Invented* by Kathy Pelta
11. *I, Columbus, My Journal* by Peter Roop and Connie Roop
12. *Christopher Columbus: The Great Adventure and How We Know about It* by Delno West and Jean West
13. *Christopher Columbus* by Piero Ventura
14. *I, Columbus* by Lisl Weil
15. *Encounter* by Jane Yolen
16. *Christopher Columbus: How He Did It* by Charlotte Yue

INTRODUCTION, VALUE, AND EXPECTATIONS

1. "Close your eyes and imagine this scene: Here in our classroom we are working together in groups to do research on the problem of homeless children and ways we might solve that problem. Suddenly we hear a loud noise and look up to see a huge military helicopter full of soldiers with guns landing on our school playground. The soldiers jump out of the helicopter and run into the school building.

They don't speak a language we understand, but by pointing their guns, they force us to leave the building and stand outside while they go through the building and take everything valuable. They take all our backpacks, purses, computers, calculators, books, VCRs, televisions, *everything!* Then they force us to carry everything and load it in the helicopter. Several of the soldiers take off with the helicopter and our possessions. The remaining soldiers force us to walk to the nearest neighborhood where they evacuate people from their houses. Each soldier takes several of us and goes into a house where we are forced to work for them as servants."

2. "What would you think was happening? How would you feel? What would you do? Would you try to be nice to the soldiers so they in turn would be nice and let you go? Would you try to escape? Where would you go? Could you help the others? How? Why do you think the soldiers would do this? Could you stop them? How?"

3. "This terrible situation sounds like something out of a fiction story or a fantasy movie. Unfortunately, this and situations like it have happened to people over and over again, throughout history and all over the world. If it happened in the past or in other places around the world, though, why should we care? Why would we want to know what happened in historical events? It's over now, why would we be interested? Why would we want to know how it started and how it ended? The most important reason we want to know what happened in the past is so that we know how to prevent such terrible tragedies from happening to us or anyone ever again. There are many, many reasons for studying history."

4. "Why study history? Historical events provide essential information we need for making informed judgments and wise decisions. Every day, in our personal lives, as citizens in our local community, and as members of our world community, we make important choices. These choices affect not only our own lives but also every other living thing on Earth. All the problems, issues, questions, and challenges facing the world today have been addressed in some fashion in the past. Perhaps the context was different, but people in the past have been faced with having to make similar choices and decisions. If, on the other hand, we are ignorant of their struggles and victories, then we are unable to learn from their mistakes and successes. With that vital information, we have a much better chance of making good choices that lead to better lives for us, our community, and our environment."

5. "Consider, for example, this question: Should we spend our classroom money on a new computer or on a classroom library? One way to decide would be to flip a coin; then after the money was

spent, we could look back and decide whether we think we made the right decision. Perhaps a better way would be to ask the other teachers what their classes have done in the past. From those who bought computers, we could find out how they used them and how well they liked them. From those who bought books for their classroom library, we could find out what kinds they bought, how they used them, and how well they liked them. Using this information, we could make an informed decision that is more likely to suit our needs."

6. "Consider also this example on a much larger scale: Every day the news reports tell us about the civil war in Bosnia and how other countries have been sending troops and supplies to protect human rights and prevent suffering. However, the United States has not yet decided whether or how to intervene. We have not forgotten the painful yet valuable lessons we learned from the Vietnam War. If we use those lessons to make an informed decision about our role in Bosnia, perhaps we can save the lives of young Americans who would be sent to fight. Consequently, knowing what happened in Vietnam and how we got involved can help us prevent another situation that might result in some of you being sent to war when you turn eighteen."

7. "When studying history, an important thing to consider is the fact that we never really get the whole story. We know the things that were written down and that are still around to be read and studied. For example, we know about Leif Ericson because someone wrote down the saga of his voyage hundreds of years after he was dead. Some other equally brave adventurer might have gone to a different part of America, but we just don't have his or her story written down."

8. "Also, when a story is written down, the person writing it must write it in such a way that the best or worst parts are remembered, depending on his or her opinion. For example, if my sister and I are fighting over a toy and my mom comes in to see what is going on, I would have a difficult time giving an absolutely honest account of what happened. I would probably try to describe it in such a way that showed I was doing the right thing under the circumstances."

9. "We have thousands of books written about Christopher Columbus, and most present him as a brave man with a new vision that the world was round. This is probably true, but what we often don't hear is how he was also very eager for gold; nor do we hear that because the Native Americans he found were not Christians, he and his men did not consider them to be totally human, but rather more like animals. Therefore, they felt it acceptable to sell the Native Americans into slavery to make a profit."

PROCEDURES

1. "I am going to read you a book I found that presents a different view of Columbus's great discovery. While I'm reading, think about how this view is different from what you already know about Columbus and whether this view is also likely to be true. Then, think about whether this new view changes your ideas about Columbus."

2. Read *Encounter*. Lead discussion with questions from the list that follows.

3. After discussion, put students into cooperative learning groups (recorder, checker for agreement, and presenter to read summary to the class).

4. Each group writes its own summary, using at least one sentence from each group member to explain whether and how this book changed their views on Columbus.

5. Recorder takes dictation using the exact words of the students. Students can talk about how they want to phrase sentences before they are written, but it must be in the student's own language.

6. When each group is ready, summaries are read to the class.

7. Any discrepancies are discussed, and solutions are proposed; the comprehension questions are asked at this point.

8. Teacher asks for a good way to summarize this presentation. In other words, what does this lesson on Columbus teach us about studying history? (For example, history is what the people writing it want you to know; also, watch out for incomplete or one-sided versions.)

QUESTIONS AND ASSESSMENT

Literal

1. How did the Native American boy describe Columbus and his men?
2. What fears led the boy to try to warn his family about the strangers?

Interpretive

1. The natives treated the visitors with respect and generously shared gifts with them. Do you think the Spanish were, in turn, fair with the natives? What makes you think that?

2. We know that many of these people soon died from new diseases brought by the Europeans and from the hard work they were forced to perform in the gold mines. Does this information fit with the brave and good image we often have of Columbus? Explain.

3. How was this story different from other stories you've heard about Columbus's discovery of America?

Applied

1. How did this book make you feel about Columbus?
2. Can you imagine being a Native American who saw the three ships? What would you do if large trucks full of armed soldiers who looked strange and spoke an unknown language stopped in your neighborhood? Would you be friendly and welcome them or would you hide in your house? Why?

CLOSE AND ENRICHMENT

1. "Turn to your group members and thank them for working with you."
2. Have students explain in their own words the concepts of historical relativism.
3. "We have about twenty books about Columbus in our classroom library. Take any two and compare the pictures and descriptions of Columbus and his men; note the date of publication. What are the differences and similarities between them?"
4. Have students write a paragraph about how we could use the information we learned from the story of Columbus to help us make our lives better and our world a better place.

Strategy: KWL
Primary Content Area: World Geography
Grade Level(s): 9

CONTENT OBJECTIVES

Students will demonstrate learning by

1. comparing physical regions of Africa.
2. associating the wildlife of Africa with the regions in which they are found.
3. constructing a map of the physical regions of Africa to include African wildlife.

TEXT ALTERNATIVES/SUPPLEMENTS

1. *A is for Africa* by Ifeoma Onvefulu
2. *American Animal Tales* by Rogerio Andrade Barbosa
3. *Bringing the Rain to Kapiti Plain* by Verna Aardema
4. *Why Mosquitos Buzz in People's Ears* by Verna Aardema
5. *Rain Forest Secrets* by Arthur Dorros
6. *Africa Is Not a Country: It's a Continent!* by Dr. Arthur Lewin
7. *Hammond Comparative World Atlas*

INTRODUCTION, VALUE, AND EXPECTATIONS

1. "How many of you heard about the bombing of the federal building in Oklahoma? Have you discussed this tragedy at home, with friends, or in other classes? How did this terrible event make you feel? Do you feel any less safe now than you did before the bombing? Why or why not? Why do you think most people who live in the United States feel more secure than people in other countries such as Lebanon, Israel, or Iraq?"

2. "One reason we in the United States probably feel more secure has to do with our geographical location. With the exception of Canada and Mexico, we are fairly isolated geographically from the rest of the world. As a result, foreign terrorists have a more difficult time operating in our country than they do in their own or neighboring countries. The security we have traditionally felt in this country because of geographical isolation is threatened when we are faced with the possibility of terrorist acts by our own citizens."

3. "Why study geography? This concept of security related to geographical location is but one example of how geography affects people's lives, traditions, beliefs, and cultures. People are, in large measure, shaped by their environment. They must adapt and develop lifestyles that are compatible with their geographical surroundings. The more we know about people around the world and the better we understand them, the easier it will be to make informed choices and decisions that affect everyone. As technology advances, we in the United States are becoming less and less isolated. We are members of a global community, and what we do affects others just as what people do in the rest of the world influences us. For example, the civil war in the African country of Rwanda led to our decision to send U.S. troops and money on a humanitarian mission. Why would we want to help make things better in Rwanda? How would peace in Rwanda ultimately help us?"

4. "Let's consider a familiar example of how geography influences people's lives: How many of you have traveled to different regions of Texas or to other states? What regions or states are those? How do the land and climate differ in these regions of Texas and in other states? (For example, the climate and land are dry and flat in northern Texas; warm and semitropical in the Rio Grande Valley of southern Texas; mountainous in western Texas; and so on.) What are the distinctions between ways people live and earn money in those various regions? What role does geography play in those differences? What types of animals do you associate with those various regions or states? How do they affect the lives of the people who live there?"

5. "Now let's consider a less familiar but equally important example: Have any of you ever been to any countries in Africa? What do you know about the land in the various countries in Africa? The regions in Africa differ greatly, much like the regions of Texas, or even the United States in general. What kinds of animals do you associate with Africa? How do you think the geography of the various countries of Africa has affected the people who live there? Do you think that most Africans consider themselves safe and secure? In which countries do you think they feel more secure or less secure? Why? How might the people and events in various African countries affect the quality of our lives here in the United States?"

6. "Today we are going to learn about and compare the various regions in Africa and the animals that live in these regions. It is very important that you pay attention to the information we learn about Africa, because next week we are going to plan imaginary trips to Africa. Each of you will choose a different country in Africa that you wish to visit. From your imaginary visit you will learn about the geography, people, and animals of that country, as well as how conditions in that country could affect our lives in the United States and others all over the world."

PROCEDURES

1. The teacher will begin the lesson on Africa with a Read-Aloud, reading the students *A is for Africa*, a book that is very interesting and has wonderful pictures. The teacher then sets the purpose for listening by instructing students to pay close attention to the pictures, especially the landforms and animals in them.

2. The teacher uses a KWL to introduce the students to the regions of Africa, providing each student with a KWL form and explaining the

strategy to them. He or she completes a KWL on the board as a class model.

3. To begin the process, the teacher asks students what they know about various regions in Africa: names of deserts, rivers, oceans surrounding Africa? countries in Africa? types of animals students associate with Africa? where they would expect to find these types of animals (i.e., in what type of climates or regions)? The teacher and students will then form such categories as deserts, plains, rain forests, coastal regions, and animals for expected information in the reading.

4. To set the purpose for reading and to generate questions, the teacher guides the students in the questioning process, asking them to decide which regions most interest them. The teacher also asks students to think about what it would be like to live in these various regions and how the people who live in these regions have adapted to the unique conditions of their environments. The teacher then explains to the students that they will be constructing a map of Africa to show these regions, so they need to pay close attention to the maps they will be given.

5. During and after reading, students take notes on what they learned about the different geographical regions of Africa. Using the comprehension questions, the teacher guides the students as they share what they learned with the rest of the class. He or she explains how to use other resources to locate unanswered questions and plans an activity in which students will be given a blank map of Africa. They will color and label the regions of Africa, using a map in the text for guidance. After students have constructed their maps, the teacher gives them a handout of African animals that are labeled by regions. Students will then add this information to their maps.

QUESTIONS AND ASSESSMENT

Literal
1. What are the geographical regions of Africa?
2. Where are these geographical regions located on your map?
3. What type of land forms are characteristic of each geographical region?
4. What types of animals are found in the various geographical regions of Africa?

Interpretive

1. How do the geographical regions of Africa compare and contrast with one another?
2. How are the geographical regions of Africa similar to and different from the regions of Texas? of the United States?
3. What geographical features influence African literature? How is this influence expressed through animal fables?
4. Predict where specific animals live in Africa using your background knowledge of animals along with the textual information provided.

Applied

1. In which geographical region would you most like to live? Why?
2. In which geographical region would you least like to live? Why?
3. How might the people and animals in each African region somehow influence our lives in the United States and other countries throughout the world?
4. How might we influence the lives of the people and animals in each region of Africa?
5. Why should you care what life is like in Africa?

CLOSE AND ENRICHMENT

1. To close the lesson, the teacher has students review their KWL forms, focusing on what they learned about each region. He or she also reviews a map of Africa with the students, including the major landforms such as deserts and rivers.
2. Using the applied-level questions, the teacher asks students to assess the significance of what they learned.
3. After reminding students of the imaginary trips, the teacher asks them if they have any ideas about where they would like to go.
4. Finally, the teacher reads aloud short stories from *African Animal Tales*, asking students to listen to these stories for the purpose of evaluating how the regions and animals of Africa influence fables. The class then has a short discussion about these stories in preparation for the enrichment activity.
5. After reading some fables from *African Animal Tales*, the teacher puts students into groups and supplies each group with a fiction story about Africa or different African animals. Students read or at least skim the books for the purpose of identifying elements of African influence.

Strategy: GRP
Primary Content Area: Biology
Grade Level(s): 9

CONTENT OBJECTIVES

Students will demonstrate learning by

1. creating a new planet using various components of the earth's ecosystem.
2. designing the plant life for their new planet based on evolutionary trends in plants on earth and their adaptations to life on land.

TEXT ALTERNATIVES/SUPPLEMENTS

1. *Taking Sides* by Theodore Goldfarb
2. *Life* by Ricki Lewis
3. *The Global Environment* by Penelope ReVelle
4. *The Nature of Life* by John Postlethwait and Janet Hopson
5. *Exploring the Atmosphere* by G. M. B. Dobson
6. *Atmosphere, Weather, and Climate* by R. G. Barry and R. J. Chorley

INTRODUCTION, VALUE, AND EXPECTATIONS

1. "What is required for human beings to live? Air, water, and food, of course; anything else? Shelter, clothing, companionship? We can continue adding things that improve the quality of life, but the quality of our lives is irrelevant without the basic requirements we get from our environment: air, water, and food. It's very easy to take these things for granted. Perhaps food is the requirement we take for granted least, because it is the most difficult to obtain. Why is it harder to get food than air or water? We all know the feeling of hunger, especially when a supply of food isn't readily available. The discomfort grows and grows. If it is not provided for us, we have to use our wits to obtain food or money to buy food. What if there were no food to buy? What if you went to the grocery store and the shelves, produce bins, and freezers were all empty? Where would you get food? What if the soil became so poisoned with pesticides and herbicides that it would no longer grow plants? Could we still eat meat? No, because most of the animals we eat survive on plants.

The carnivorous animals would die from eating animals poisoned by contaminated plants. Our very survival depends heavily on the earth's food supply."

2. "What about water? What does the tap water in our city taste like? Can you taste any minerals? Can you taste chlorine? Here are two paper cups for each of you. One of them contains city water from the faucet; the other contains bottled water from an underground spring. Taste them. Do they taste the same or different? How would you describe the taste? More and more cities are having to resort to pouring more and more chlorine into the city's water supply to disinfect it. In some cities, it's almost like drinking swimming pool water. Besides having an unpleasant taste, does chlorine have any harmful effects? If so, what are they? Why should we be concerned about how much chlorine is added to our water supply? Can we prevent the contamination of our water supplies, so that chlorine additives can be reduced or even eliminated? If so, how? It's very easy to take water for granted when all we have to do is turn on a faucet to get it, in many places all over the world, the water coming out of the faucets is unfit for drinking. It is so contaminated that it can cause violent illness, even death. What people do here and all over the world will ultimately affect everyone's water supplies. This topic is one that is of concern to all of us."

3. "What about air? Have you ever been walking or standing on a sidewalk and smelled the exhaust fumes of cars, buses, and trucks? What does it smell like? It smells bad, but can it hurt you? It looks bad because it causes a hazy smog to cover the city, but is it harmful in any way? Air is easier to get than food and water, but is our air supply in danger? Is it possible that the air quality could become so poor that we could be poisoned just by breathing? In many cities, the air has become so polluted with poisonous chemical fumes, people are in danger of becoming sick or even dying. Are we sentencing ourselves to die in the gas chamber by continuing to allow pollutants to be pumped into the air?"

4. "Of course, it costs money to clean our air, water, and soil and even more money to keep it clean. Is it worth it? Many business people, politicians, and even citizens say it isn't. They believe that it is better to make more money now and live lives of luxury as long as possible rather than investing in the future of the earth's supply of air, water, and soil. In fact, Congress has just passed legislation that would limit the ability of the Environmental Protection Agency (EPA) to ensure businesses and industries do not pollute our air, water, and soil. The majority of the Congressional representatives apparently decided against spending money to prevent pollution. In

addition to their goal of cutting spending, they were also under pressure from the very businesses and industries being regulated. They wanted Congress to ease the restrictions placed on them by the EPA so that they could make more money. It is much cheaper to empty pollutants into the environments than to dispose of them safely; they can make much more money if they are allowed to contaminate the environment. They also say that environmental protection regulations could make them lose so much money that they would be in danger of going out of business. That, in turn, would result in more and more people being out of work. What do you think? Is it worth it? Maybe these business people and politicians look at the situation this way: The basic requirements for life will probably be available, although with varying levels of contamination, for the rest or our lives. Why should we care what happens to the people left on earth after we die? As long as there's enough for us to live on, perhaps we just shouldn't worry about it. If keeping our air, water, and soil clean means putting people out of work, then what choice do we have?"

5. "However, consider this. What if our grandparents and great-grandparents had decided to make money for luxurious living at the expense of contaminating our air, water, and soil? Unfortunately, many of them did, and that's why pollution is such a problem today. If they had poisoned the earth even more, though, we would be faced with the prospect of dying at an even younger age, perhaps as children. Is that death sentence what we want to give future generations, including our children and grandchildren?"

6. "What can we do? Well, first, we must become informed. With knowledge and education about our environment, how it has been damaged, and ways it can be restored and protected, we may be able to create viable alternatives. Perhaps we could deal with the unemployment problem by creating new jobs designed to clean up and protect the environment. Such solutions are possible only if we first learn about the biological principles at work in our ecosystem. We have to learn about the earth's environment first. Then, we can address the problems and threats posed against it."

7. "The result of ignorance about our environment and delicate ecosystem is obvious. People who choose not to learn about biology and our requirements for life on earth are destined to destroy it for the rest of us. It's very easy for them to pretend that nothing is wrong and that making money is an end to justify all means, even if it means polluting our world beyond repair. The choice is yours and mine, just as it is theirs. I'm choosing to learn this essential information about biology right along with you. The information is

constantly changing as our environment changes as a result of the destruction committed by humans. We must continually update our knowledge so that our choices are informed ones. We must constantly pay attention to the decisions being made by our government and business leaders. We live in a democracy, so our opinions matter and can make a difference if we choose to participate in the decision-making process."

8. "To learn about our earth's ecosystem, we are going to begin a major project today. We will be working on this project over the course of the next week in cooperative learning groups. Each group is going to create its own planet by choosing different parts of the earth's ecosystem related to its atmosphere, weather, geological configurations and formations, organisms, lifecycles, and ecology. Each group will have a meteorologist, geologist, biologist, and ecologist."

PROCEDURES

1. "Today you are going to begin working in your groups to collect information about plants to use in creating your planets. What do you already know about plants? What do they provide for us? What is their role in the ecosystem? Have plants always been as they are now? If not, how have they changed?"

2. "In your groups, each person has been provided a different passage about plants. Your purpose for reading is to remember everything you can to share with your group members. At this point, read straight through the passage only once."

3. "When you finish, close the book and start writing everything you can remember without looking back. When you can't remember any more, you may open the book to check your recall. Reread for the purpose of making sure you made notes of the most important points and information to share with your group members. Make corrections, additions, and deletions if necessary."

4. "When you and at least one other group member have finished, share your notes with each other. Combine the information and organize it into categories. After you have compared notes and shared information with everyone in your group, integrate all the information into a single outline or Graphic Organizer. You will use this summary of information as a resource for planning the plant life on your planet."

QUESTIONS AND ASSESSMENT

Literal
1. What are the six adaptations to life on land that plants have made?
2. What is the main point of the concept of evolutionary trends in plants?

Interpretive
1. How do aquatic plants take in water as compared with land plants?
2. What are two different ways that plants have evolved?
3. What would happen if land plants did not evolve vascular tissue?
4. What effects has the evolution of plants had on other life forms?

Applied
1. What are some ways that plants improve the quality of your life either directly or indirectly?
2. What can you do as an individual to prevent the contamination of plant life in our community?

CLOSE AND ENRICHMENT

1. The teacher asks the literal and interpretive comprehension questions at this point to verify students' understanding of the key concepts. Students use these concepts in making decisions about which plants to include on their planets.
2. "In your groups, examine your plant outlines or Graphic Organizers to identify some of the types of plant life you want to have on your planet. Make sure you select ones that are compatible and that can support one another. Make a list of plants you choose, along with brief explanations for choosing them; explain your choices in terms of the evolutionary concepts you learned today.
3. The teacher asks the applied-level questions to start a class discussion on the relevance to our everyday lives of the biological facts learned today about plants.

Strategy: SQ3R
Primary Content Area: Geometry
Grade Level(s): 6

CONTENT OBJECTIVES

Students will demonstrate learning by

1. designing a paper model of a pyramid.
2. identifying the properties of points, lines, rays, angles, segments, and planes and their importance to the design of pyramids.

TEXT ALTERNATIVES/SUPPLEMENTS

1. *Shapes* by Richard Allington
2. *Finding Out about Shapes* by Maye Freeman
3. *Angles Are Easy as Pie* by Robert Froman
4. *Dancing Curves: A Dynamic Demonstration of Geometric Principles* by Merwin Lyng
5. *The Pyramids* by John Weeks

INTRODUCTION, VALUE, AND EXPECTATIONS

1. The teacher asks the students to look around the classroom and describe the different shapes they see. Examples might include rectangular desk tops, circular flower pots, or straight-edged corners of the walls. The teacher records their responses on the board. The teacher then encourages students to think about the buildings in the downtown area and describe their appearances, asking students to propose reasons for the various designs and geometric shapes of buildings.
2. At this point, the teacher relates today's lesson to the previous lesson on Egyptian monuments and pyramids. The teacher reminds students that the Egyptians were able to build such structures through the use of geometry. Learning about geometry is important because it helps us understand an object's relationship in space. Geometric principles provide the foundation for all architectural structures. The fact that Egyptians used such principles before the advent of the technological age shows the ingenious workings of the human mind. Without geometric principles, the houses that you live in, the bridges across the river in the city, and even architectural wonders like the new shopping mall would not have been possible.

3. To relate the introduction to today's lesson the teacher says, "Not only is geometry all around us, it serves many valuable functions for us. Today, we are going to learn about the basic properties of geometry. These basic properties are important for helping you understand, design, and create new models and structures for practical uses, as well as to fix and renovate old ones that are no longer functional or are no longer meeting our needs."

PROCEDURES

1. The teacher guides students through the steps of an SQ3R. Before reading, the teacher models for and instructs students to survey the assignment by reading the title and looking at the graphic aids.
2. From this overview, the teacher guides students in formulating and recording questions to serve as their purposes for reading. If they have difficulty formulating questions, the teacher demonstrates the process for them using a think-aloud. For example, say "Hmmm . . . the title is *Geometry: Theme-Dance and the Fine Arts.* The picture shows ballet dancers moving through space. I wonder what types of geometric ideas they are presenting," or "The graphic aid on page 162 shows many triangles. What kinds of triangles are used in this design?"
3. The students then read while keeping their questions in mind. They answer their questions as they read by taking notes about what they learned.
4. After reading, students get together in groups to compare and share answers, ensuring that their purposes for reading have been met. They should also make sure that they have identified any other information they think is important or interesting.
5. Students review what they learned by assessing and reflecting on it. The teacher will guide this process with the comprehension questions. If there are knowledge gaps or unanswered questions, students reread the assignment and the teacher helps them clarify important concepts.
6. Finally, students demonstrate what they have learned about geometric principles and properties by using them to create their own pyramids out of paper.

QUESTIONS AND ASSESSMENT

Literal
1. What are points, lines, and planes?
2. What are segments, rays, and angles?

Interpretive
1. Describe the geometric properties that can be found in pyramids.
2. Describe the classroom in terms of geometric properties.

Applied
1. Describe some everyday objects that suggest lines, points, and planes.
2. Design a model of your own creation (e.g., doghouse, mansion, cabin, tower, house, warehouse, indoor pool, office building, factory) using geometric principles.

CLOSE AND ENRICHMENT

1. To close the lesson, the teacher asks students to summarize the main ideas of the assignment. Students state the properties of lines, points, planes, angles, rays, and segments.
2. As an enrichment activity, the teacher gives the students a handout outlining procedures for constructing geometric shapes. The students use the shapes in designing and constructing models of their own creation. The supplemental books are used as a reference, and the students research additional shapes found in various structures in their communities.

Strategy: REAP
Primary Content Area: Science
Grade Level(s): 3

CONTENT OBJECTIVES

Students will demonstrate learning by

1. summarizing the process of how thunderstorms form.
2. explaining what causes lightning.
3. identifying ways to keep safe during a storm.

TEXT ALTERNATIVES/SUPPLEMENTS

1. *Weatherwise* by Jonathan Kahl
2. *Lightning* by Stephen Kramer

3. *Science Today* by Mark Pettigrew
4. *Storms* by Seymour Simon
5. *Weather* by Imeld Updegraff and Robert Updegraff
6. *What Will the Weather Be Like Today?* by Paul Rogers

INTRODUCTION, VALUE, AND EXPECTATIONS

1. "When was the last thunderstorm you remember? Where were you? How hard did it rain? Was there lightning and thunder? How long did the storm last? Were you scared? Can thunderstorms be dangerous? Is it dangerous to be in water outdoors during a thunderstorm? Why or why not? My dogs are really scared of lightning. Do you have any pets that get scared during thunderstorms? What do they do? Why do you think they are scared?"

2. "Today we're going to learn how thunderstorms form, what causes lightning, and how to keep safe during storms. We have already learned how water vapor creates clouds, snow, and rain. We have also learned how moving air creates the wind and weather patterns all around us. Today we will be learning about the different types of clouds that produce storms with high winds, heavy rains, and lightning."

PROCEDURES

1. The teacher introduces vocabulary on the overhead:
   thunderheads   towering clouds that often cause thunderstorms; also called cumulonimbus clouds.
   electrons   the tiny parts of atoms that rush through the air during a lightning strike.

2. He or she then puts students into cooperative learning groups and assigns roles: speaker, reader, and writer.

3. Each group reads a page from a different book on storms. They discuss the ideas and information, putting it into their own words. The teacher explains the concept of summary annotation and has each group write an annotation of the author's ideas by summarizing and translating them into their own language. Model the process by reading aloud a sample paragraph displayed on the overhead. Then, do a think-aloud to demonstrate how to pull out key points, summarize them, and reword them into an annotation (e.g., "Cool air replaces warm air in the sky, which causes cumulous clouds to form. It rains when water in the clouds gets too heavy.").

4. Students work in groups to read, take notes, discuss the information, and develop their summary annotations. Each group is given an overhead transparency and marker for recording its annotation.
5. One student from each group displays the group's annotation and reads it aloud to the rest of the class. Then another group member reads the original passage from the book while the rest of the class ponders and evaluates the displayed annotation according to these questions: Does it make sense? Is it accurate? Is the language simple and understandable? Is it complete, but not too long?
6. The teacher and class members suggest improvements for the annotation. Finally, the group checks for understanding by asking the rest of the class questions about their annotation. The teacher interjects the comprehension questions at this point. The process continues until all groups have presented their annotations.

QUESTIONS AND ASSESSMENT

Literal
1. What causes lightning to occur?
2. What color are storm clouds?

Interpretive
1. How can people keep safe during a thunderstorm?
2. How large can thunderstorms get?
3. What causes thunder?
4. Under what conditions are thunderstorms likely to occur?

Applied
1. Should you plan to go on an outdoor picnic if you see thunderheads in the sky? Why or why not?
2. Why isn't it safe for someone or something to be the tallest object around a storm?
3. If you are caught outdoors during a thunderstorm, where is the best place to seek shelter? Under a tree, a bridge, building? Why or why not?
4. Is it safe to swim outdoors during a thunderstorm? Why or why not?

CLOSE AND ENRICHMENT

1. The teacher reads aloud the story *What Will the Weather Be Like Today?* by Paul Rogers. Students listen to identify which types of weather they have studied.

2. In groups, students create a list of safety "do's and don'ts" for people and pets during thunderstorms.

3. The teacher reads aloud page 18 from *Lightning* and page 19 from *Weather*. Students write a journal entry about a time when they were in a thunderstorm, describing what they saw and how they felt during the storm.

Strategy: DRA
Primary Content Area: Art
Grade Level(s): 1–3

CONTENT OBJECTIVES

Students will demonstrate learning by

1. creating a pinch pot from clay.
2. creating designs on the pot using objects or tools.

TEXT ALTERNATIVES/SUPPLEMENTS

1. *Origins of Modern Sculpture: Pioneers and Premises* by Albert E. Elsen
2. *Masterpieces* of Art by Charles Wentinck
3. *Art* by Fredrick Hartt
4. *The Sculpture of Picasso* by R. Penrose
5. *Picasso* by J. Sabartes and W. Boeck

INTRODUCTION, VALUE, AND EXPECTATIONS

1. The teacher shows students slides of a variety of types of pinch pots, asking if anyone knows what they are or how they were made. As the teacher passes around examples for the students to touch and describe, he or she asks them whether they are pieces of art for practical use (like for cooking), decoration, or both.

2. The teacher asks students if they have any idea about how, when, and why art actually began, explaining that we have evidence that even the earliest humans created art in a variety of ways for a variety of reasons. Some art was created to tell a story; some was created

for enjoyment; some was created for practical use. For example, the pinch pot was used as a container.

3. The teacher then explains that many pieces of art we have found were made by people thousands and thousands of years ago. This art tells a very interesting story about the people who made it including how they lived, what they were like, what they thought about, what was important to them, and what made them happy. From that art we have learned that creating art is a very important part of being human. The study of past human life from the art and other objects they left behind is called *archaeology*, and the scientists who study it are called *archaeologists*.

4. The teacher encourages students to imagine for a minute that a thousand years have passed and that archaeologists have just discovered the ruins of their school. He or she asks them to suggest what might be found and how it might compare to things made in that future time and what the archaeologists might learn about us from the things they would find in the classroom.

5. Finally, the teacher tells students that they are going to learn about a form of art that began in ancient times and is still done today, encouraging them to guess what that might be based on the examples they examined earlier. After learning about this form of art, the teacher and students together will show what they have learned by making their own pinch pots.

PROCEDURES

1. The teacher displays the following sentences to provide context for the new vocabulary. As each word is introduced in the sentence, the students talk about it using their own words and experiences.
    Ceramics is the art of making objects from clay.
    A piece of clay is dried to a *leather-hard* feel before being cooked.
    The process of cooking clay to harden it permanently is called *firing*.
    Before firing, clay objects are called *greenware*.
    The oven used to fire clay is called a *kiln*.

2. The teacher develops background knowledge by showing some examples of pinch pots with designs etched into the clay and asking students to guess what kinds of objects or tools might be used to create such designs. The teacher then shows them some examples of such tools. Explaining that pinch pots are hand-formed instead of "thrown" on a potter's wheel, the teacher introduces briefly the process of working with clay.

3. He or she tells students that they are going to read to find out the steps to follow in making pinch pots. Students then read a one-page summary of "Steps in Creating a Pinch Pot."

4. Students read silently while the teacher reads it aloud to them, or they read with a partner using Radio Reading (i.e., the listener doesn't have a written copy, but checks the reader's accuracy by repeating the message).

5. After reading, the teacher checks to see that the purposes for reading have been met. While demonstrating the procedures, he or she calls on individuals randomly to repeat orally each step to be followed in making the pinch pots. Then, the teacher asks the literal and interpretive comprehension questions.

6. The teacher checks the students' understanding of the process by monitoring their work. As they begin working with the clay, he or she checks for rounded forms, stable bases, and well-designed decorative textures. When they finish their piece, students should etch their initials on the bottom and place it on the shelf for air drying.

QUESTIONS AND ASSESSMENT

Literal

1. Has anyone ever worked with ceramic clay before? Tell us about it.
2. Has anyone ever made a pinch pot? Tell us about it.
3. What is a pinch pot?
4. What are the steps to be followed in making a pinch pot?
5. How will you form the clay?

Interpretive

1. Why is it called a "pinch pot"?
2. What are some practical uses for pinch pots?
3. How is a pinch pot different from a salad bowl?
4. What are some ways to create different textures on the pots?
5. What is the purpose of air drying?
6. What are some of the basic shapes a pinch pot could be?
7. What are some of the different finishes that could be used on the edges?
8. Why is it important to smooth the walls of the pots?

Applied

1. Do you think pinch pots should be used for decoration only or as containers also? Why?
2. What does the kind of design you created on your pinch pot tell us about you?

CLOSE AND ENRICHMENT

1. The teacher uses the applied-level questions to lead a discussion about the value of pinch pots as art and as objects for practical uses. Students then think of different kinds of things they could store in their pinch pots (e.g., buttons, beads, jewelry, water for artwork, and so on). Finally, they share with the class their ideas for what they're going to do with their pinch pots when they take them home (e.g., give them as gifts, decorate shelves, keep small objects from getting lost, and so on).
2. Using the supplemental books, the teacher helps students explore the numerous variations in shape, size, and textured decoration. They investigate and report on pots and the methods used by one or more Native American cultures such as the Hopi or Pueblos. Finally, students compare and contrast pinch pots with other types of clay sculptures.

Strategy: DR-TA
Primary Content Area: Algebra
Grade Level(s): 9–10

CONTENT OBJECTIVES

Students will demonstrate learning by

1. graphing linear equations using tables of ordered pairs.
2. graphing linear equations from their x- and y-intercepts.
3. defining and applying the following terms: *linear equation, standard form, x-intercept, y-intercept.*

TEXT ALTERNATIVES/SUPPLEMENTS

1. *A Game of Functions* by Robert Froman
2. *The King's Chessboard* by David Birch
3. *Number Mysteries* by Cyril Hayes and Dympna Hayes
4. *MatheMagic: Magic, Puzzles, and Games with Numbers* by Royal Vale Heath
5. *Logic for Space Age Kids* by Lyn McClure Butrick

6. *Probability* by Charles F. Linn
7. *Do You Wanna Bet? Your Chance to Find Out about Probability* by Jean Cushman
8. *Socrates and the Three Pigs* by Tuyosi Mori
9. *Winning with Number: A Kid's Guide to Statistics* by Manfred G. Riedel

INTRODUCTION, VALUE, AND EXPECTATIONS

1. "Have you ever considered that certain information has predictable, continuing relationships? For example, the salary of a professional basketball player and the number of baskets he makes per game are usually related. Also, the taste of a restaurant's pizza and the number of pizzas the restaurant sells is generally predictable—the better the pizza tastes, the more pizzas people will buy. Using information we know to make predictions about things we don't know is a valuable use of linear equations. When we know how to apply linear equations, we can make better use of our knowledge. The things we know can then serve as tools for helping us figure out things we don't know, but want to know. For example, let's say that I decide to ask my parents for more allowance each week, but they don't think I need more money. I can show them mathematical predictions of my budgetary needs based on a combination of last year's expenses along with this year's expected spending increases (e.g., inflation). Using my mathematical skills, I can present a well-documented proposal for an increased allowance. How could they refuse?"

2. "Now that you have learned how to graph ordered pairs, we are ready to begin studying linear equations. In today's lesson you will learn the definition of a linear equation in terms of appropriate applications, as well as two ways to graph linear equations. We will graph linear equations by making tables of ordered pairs and by plotting x- and y-intercepts."

PROCEDURES

1. The teacher explains the mechanics of the DR-TA: the class will study the material together by predicting what it will cover, reading it, and then comparing their predictions with the information presented.
2. The teacher divides the class into groups of four members (leader, reader, recorder, and speaker).
3. The teacher tells the class that the title of the day's lesson is "Graphs of Linear Equations." The teacher asks the class to predict what they will learn.

4. The teacher records predictions on the board and leads a guided discussion.
5. The teacher instructs the class to open their text and read the first section in their groups to check the accuracy of their predictions.
6. The teacher monitors the reading and helps groups if needed.
7. The teacher tells the groups to write notes on whether their predictions turned out to be accurate; if not, they should note whether the predictions were at least logical and reasonable. Then, students make new predictions for reading the next section.
8. The teacher asks the speaker of each group to comment on the group's notes and new predictions; using open-ended questions, the teacher leads a brief discussion of each group's reflections.
9. After all groups have shared their reflections, the teacher asks the appropriate literal and interpretive comprehension questions.
10. Steps 5–9 are repeated for the remaining sections in the chapter.
11. After all remaining sections have been discussed, the teacher asks the applied comprehension questions.
12. The teacher assigns each group a set of problems requiring practical applications of linear equations. Students begin work on the problems in their groups and finish them for homework. The following day students compare and discuss results in their groups before submitting them.

QUESTIONS AND ASSESSMENT

Literal
1. What is a linear equation?
2. What is standard form?
3. In standard form, what types of numbers must A, B, and C be?

Interpretive
1. Why is the first step in solving an equation to solve for y?
2. When graphing a linear equation, why is it helpful to write the equation in standard form?
3. When graphing a linear equation, what does it mean if a line cannot be drawn through all the plotted points?
4. If an equation is in standard form, can both A and B be zero?

Applied
1. What kinds of everyday questions and problems might be answered or solved using linear equations?
2. Design a real-life practical problem that could be solved using linear equations.

CLOSE AND ENRICHMENT

1. Using a practical example, the teacher reviews the procedures for solving linear equations.
2. Each student turns to a partner and explains the procedures using a sample problem.
3. Using the textbook alternatives and supplements, students design a mini-quiz by composing five problems for linear equations similar to those presented in the text. The students create a separate key that shows the problems and solutions clearly.
4. After reviewing the mini-quiz, the teacher places copies of it in a notebook at the back of the room. For extra credit, students may complete one or more of the quizzes. They can check their own work using the key.

Strategy: ReQuest/InQuest
Primary Content Area: Health/Physical Education
Grade Level(s): 2

CONTENT OBJECTIVES

Students will demonstrate learning by

1. locating the different muscles in the body.
2. matching different muscles with the activities they perform.

TEXT ALTERNATIVES/SUPPLEMENTS

1. *You Can't Make a Move without Your Muscles* by Paul Showers
2. *The Muscular System: How Living Creatures Move* by Alvin Silverstein and Virginia Silverstein
3. *The Magic School Bus: Inside the Human Body* by Jeanne Cole
4. *The Human Body* by Jonathan Miller
5. *Look Inside Your Body* by Gina Ingoglia
6. *Nailhead and Potato Eyes* by Cynthia Basil
7. *My Body Is Where I Live* by Dorothy Chapman

INTRODUCTION, VALUE, AND EXPECTATIONS

1. The teacher shows a video of people suffering from Lou Gehrig's disease, multiple sclerosis, and muscular dystrophy, asking students if they know anyone with one of these or a similar disease. Students will be asked to describe the effects based on personal experiences or the video. Finally, they will generalize what physical effects all of these disorders have in common—they all affect the strength, coordination, flexibility, and control of the muscles.

2. The teacher explains to students the importance of taking good care of their muscles. Muscular health relates directly to the types of food they eat and the exercise they get. The teacher explains how important it is to understand what they need to do to keep their muscles strong, conditioned, and flexible. Without good nutrition and regular exercise, muscles will get too weak, small, and tight for coordinated, strong, and complete movements with full range of motion. In other words, poor nutrition and lack of exercise can have the same negative results as the debilitating diseases discussed earlier.

3. The teacher tells the students that he or she has good news: today they will learn how to take care of their muscles so that they can prevent muscle weakness, deterioration, and stiffness.

PROCEDURES

1. The teacher introduces the strategy by explaining that the purpose is to help students understand what they read by asking themselves good questions.

2. Students are assigned partners for reading. They read for the purpose of forming at least two good questions. Students then put themselves in the place of the teacher and make up questions a teacher might use to find out how well the students understood what they read. They should write down their questions. The teacher gives the students strips of paper for recording their questions, so the questions can be hung on the wall.

3. After reading, the teacher models for students the process of taking turns asking and answering each other's questions. First, the teacher calls on a student to ask him or her a question. After answering it, the teacher asks a question. That student can either answer it or call on another student to respond.

4. After several such exchanges, the teacher instructs students to join another pair and take turns asking and answering each other's

questions. After giving students strips of paper for recording the answers, they again hang the strips on the wall.

5. The teacher monitors the students as they ask and answer each other's questions; the quality of their questions tell the teacher how well they understood the material.

6. After all the students' questions and responses have been posted on the wall, the teacher asks the literal and interpretive questions that follow (if they have not already been addressed by the students).

QUESTIONS AND ASSESSMENT

Literal
1. How do your muscles work?
2. What happens if your muscles do not work?
3. What muscles work even when we are asleep?

Interpretive
1. How can we keep our muscles healthy?
2. Which muscles do we use for moving?

Applied
1. Does the food we eat make a difference in how our muscles work? If so, explain the difference.
2. What kinds of foods must we eat regularly to keep our muscles healthy?
3. What kinds of exercise are required to keep our muscles healthy?
4. How often and how regularly must we exercise to keep our muscles healthy?
5. What is the importance of stretching exercises and weight training in maintaining healthy muscles?

CLOSE AND ENRICHMENT

1. The teacher closes the lesson by leading a discussion of the significance of the information students learned, using the applied-level questions to lead the discussion.
2. Students choose a book and read a section of it. They then summarize for a partner what they read and why that information is important to their own lives.
3. The students critically review the book they read; they tell their classmates whether they would recommend it and why or why not.

Strategy: QAR
Primary Content Area: History
Grade Level(s): 12

CONTENT OBJECTIVES

Students will demonstrate learning by

1. summarizing key events and situations leading to the Vietnam War.
2. describing the major public opinion of Americans about the Vietnam War.
3. suggesting reasons for that general public opinion.
4. describing the major public opinion of Americans about the Persian Gulf War.
5. proposing an explanation for the differences in American public opinion toward the Persian Gulf War and the Vietnam War.
6. assessing the role and potential role of the United States as a "world police oficer."

TEXT ALTERNATIVES/SUPPLEMENTS

1. *Angel Child, Dragon Child* by Michele Maria Surat
2. *Lee Ann: The Story of a Vietnamese-American Girl* by Tricia Brown
3. *The Wall* by Eve Bunting
4. *An Album of the Vietnam War* by Don Lawson
5. *Always to Remember: The Story of the Vietnam Veterans Memorial* by Brent Ashabranner
6. *America and Vietnam: The Elephant and the Tiger* by Albert Marrin
7. *And One for All* by Theresa Nelson
8. *The Best of Friends* by Margaret I. Rostkowski
9. *Charlie Pippin* by Candy Dawson Boyd
10. *December Stillness* by Mary Downing Hahn
11. *Fallen Angels* by Walter Dean Myers
12. *Little Brother* by Allan Baillie
13. *My Name Is San Ho* by Jayne Pettit
14. *Park's Quest* by Katherine Paterson
15. *To Stand Against the Wind* by Ann Nolan Clark
16. *The Story of the Persian Gulf War* by Leila Merrell Foster
17. *War in the Persian Gulf* by Fred Bratman
18. *The War Began at Supper: Letters to Miss Loria* by Patricia Reilly Giff
19. *Desert Shield: Fact Book* by Frank Chadwick

INTRODUCTION, VALUE, AND EXPECTATIONS

1. The teacher and several students enact a skit about an American soldier coming home from the Vietnam War (negative homecoming) and another about a soldier coming home from the Persian Gulf War (a hero's welcome).

2. The teacher then asks these questions: Did anyone have a relative or friend who served in the Gulf War? If so, how did you feel about their involvement? Were you proud or disappointed? Did anyone have a relative or friend in Vietnam? If so, how did you feel about their involvement? Were you proud or disappointed? How would you like to be treated upon return from fighting for your country?

3. "Today we are going to compare the attitudes of the United States people to Vietnam War veterans and to Desert Storm veterans. By the end of class, you will be able to explain why the Vietnam War and its veterans became so unpopular, and why the Gulf War and its veterans were so much more appreciated."

4. The teacher leads a discussion about why it is so important to understand the different experiences of these two groups of soldiers. Students describe how they might be more sensitive to the needs and problems of Vietnam War veterans. They also propose ways to work proactively to show veterans a different public opinion from the one they encountered upon their return.

5. Finally, the teacher leads students in a discussion of the value of learning the facts surrounding those two wars, understanding their similarities and differences, and most importantly, the lessons learned from both. Students propose ways this information could be valuable today and in the future. They provide examples of the places all over the world engaged in armed conflict presently, and how these places are potential battlegrounds for U.S. soldiers. The teacher reminds students that if the U.S. becomes engaged in one or more significant wars, the draft could be reinstated, putting each of them in the same situation faced by Vietnam or Desert Storm veterans. Therefore, they all need to be informed, pay attention to national and world affairs, and actively participate as citizens in our democratic process. We remind them that they can make a difference, as individuals, but only if they are informed and active participants in our democracy.

PROCEDURES

1. Students are instructed to read for the purpose of comparing and contrasting the public perceptions of the Vietnam and Persian Gulf Wars. They are further instructed to read for the purpose of understanding the U.S. government's commitment in both conflicts. Finally, students read for the purpose of determining the outcomes of both conflicts.
2. The teacher distributes to students a study guide with questions from all three levels (literal, interpretive, and applied). As they read, they answer each question and note its location(s).
3. After reading, students work in cooperative learning groups to categorize each question, based on the location of its answer, as either "in the book" or "in my head." They then label each "in the book" question as either "right there" or "think and search." Finally, they label each "in my head" question as either "author and me" or "on my own."
4. Group representatives share with the class their labels for each question, along with an explanation of how each label reflects the location(s) of the answer. Differences are discussed and consensus reached, if possible. As long as a satisfactory explanation can be provided, the label may stand, even if different from the majority.
5. Finally, the teacher leads a discussion of the answers to the questions, focusing on the purposes set for reading. Students reread as necessary for clarification of misconceptions, inaccuracies, and misunderstandings.

QUESTIONS AND ASSESSMENT

Literal ("Right There" and "Think and Search")
1. What were the circumstances surrounding U.S. involvement in each war?
2. What was the outcome of each war?
3. What was the major public perception of the veterans of each war?

Interpretive ("Think and Search" and "Author and Me")
1. Why was public opinion generally negative for veterans of the Vietnam War and positive for veterans of the Gulf War?
2. How did the outcome of each war influence public perception?

Applied ("On My Own")

1. What lessons can we learn from each war to help us in making decisions about whether and to what extent to enter armed conflicts in the future?
2. Based on these lessons learned, what is your opinion about what the U.S. involvement should be in each of the following current armed conflicts and civil wars:

   Croatia/Bosnia-Herzegovina
   Rwanda
   China/Taiwan
   China/Tibet
   Russia/Chechnya
   Myanmar (Burma)
   Haiti
   Guatemala

CLOSE AND ENRICHMENT

1. The teacher reviews the basic history of the Vietnam and Gulf Wars, the public perception of each war, and the public response to the veterans of each war.
2. He or she leads a class discussion using the applied-level questions.
3. Students write a journal entry summarizing their personal thoughts, reflections, and feelings toward each war.
4. Students write a position paper about the potential U.S. role of police officer of the world; the paper should address these questions: Should the United States ever get involved in foreign armed conflict? If so, under what circumstances? If not, why? What policies should we adopt to ensure that we do not repeat mistakes made in previous armed conflicts, particularly in Vietnam?

APPENDIX E

Classroom Management

A classroom management system that includes an effective system of discipline is crucial to the success of content area instruction. Without an effective classroom management system, the strategies for content area learning and literacy cannot be applied effectively. Developing an effective system requires concentrated effort and planning but is well worth the necessary time and energy. Both your students and you will be happier, and you will foster a supportive learning community if you develop and implement an effective classroom management plan. Your plan should reflect the philosophies, beliefs, and goals you outlined in your Mission Statement for Chapter 1.

The "basics" for classroom management as a context for content area literacy and learning include the following:

- You *must* make personal connections with your students. As quickly as possible, learn their names and something positive and special about them as individuals. Express interest in their lives, show them you care about and like them as they are, even with the faults and failings that make them human.
- Set strict limits with predetermined rewards and consequences. Then, always reward students when they earn it and administer consequences *consistently*, after only one or two warnings.
- When they have broken a rule, do not ignore it and hope students will stop. Immediately address the infraction with an authoritative tone of voice and facial expression. Look them intently in the eye and tell them specifically and exactly what behavior you expect (rather than what you want them to *stop* doing).
- *Never* embarrass students. Always speak to them privately. Public humiliation almost always does more harm than good in the long run.

■ Respond to anger and defiance with calm acceptance, a caring attitude, and a compassionate tone. Don't let students bait you into an angry or sarcastic response. Instead, model for them ways to avoid verbal attacks and express anger and frustration appropriately.

■ Use "I" messages instead of "you" messages. For example, avoid saying things like "You are interrupting!" or "You are making me angry!" Instead, say "I feel a lack of respect when you interrupt me" or "I feel very angry when you show me disrespect."

This appendix is designed to provide you with additional background knowledge, critical components, and helpful guidelines for developing your own classroom management system. All of the information on classroom management and discipline presented in the remainder of this appendix is recommended by Charles (1992), who first summarizes eight major models of discipline, then outlines a series of steps for helping teachers develop personal systems of discipline. His book, *Building Classroom Discipline,* is an excellent resource for investigating and choosing from a variety of effective classroom management systems and discipline strategies.

MANAGING CLASSROOM ROUTINES

Charles (1992) recommends putting in place specific procedures for daily routines so that students know exactly what to do and have a predetermined plan to follow. First, develop procedures for your opening and closing activities. To avoid wasting valuable time as students arrive and get settled, establish routine procedures that get them to work immediately. For example, an opening assignment can be put on the board every day, or students can begin each class by writing in their journals, reading library books silently, doing math or vocabulary exercises, or playing with educational games while roll is taken. Routines should also be established for replacing materials and filing and turning in work at the end of the day.

Class time is often wasted by distributing and replacing materials. If materials are to be dispersed, several students should be preassigned the role on a rotating basis, and their names posted so they know to begin their task as soon as they arrive. If students are to get their own materials, the materials should be easily accessible, and the students should have predetermined routines for picking them up as they arrive. Procedures for replacing the materials at the end of class should be just as specific. Pencil sharpening should be limited to before class or with permission.

Turning in completed work is another daily routine that can cause disruption and wasted time if procedures are not established. Rather than putting work directly into the hands of the teacher, a more efficient routine would be to have students leave it in a file box or basket, on a corner of the desk, or on a shelf. Then, you can collect the work later.

An additional way to manage your classroom routines efficiently is to use students as assistants. Having students take responsibility for daily routines not only helps the teacher but also improves the students' attitudes. Duties for student assistants might even include grading papers, keeping records, typing, duplicating, and taking roll. Other tasks can be accomplished by having student assistants take on roles such as lights monitor, table leader, messenger, line monitor, plant and pet caretakers, materials monitor, and audiovisual assistants.

Routine procedures should also be established and consistently followed for helping students while they work. Charles (1992) makes the following suggestions, taken from the Fredric Jones model of discipline. First, make sure students have clear directions for what they are supposed to do and how they are supposed to accomplish the task. Second, provide a written model or set of directions to which students may refer while they work. Third, monitor the students by circulating to check progress and catch errors. Fourth, when students ask for assistance, give them direct help and then move away quickly, preferably in less than twenty seconds. Prevent students from becoming psychologically dependent on you and positively reinforce those who work well independently. Fifth, do not give in to the temptation to reteach students or take them through tutorials on an individual basis. If several students are having the same difficulty, consider reteaching the concepts to a small group or even to the whole class.

PREVENTIVE DISCIPLINE

Effective classroom management involves a system of discipline composed of three parts: preventive, supportive, and corrective. The first part, preventive discipline, relates to the things you do to reduce the likelihood of behavioral problems.

First, make learning as worthwhile and enjoyable as possible. Clearly communicate the value and relevance of the learning. Make a concerted effort to plan lessons that will be fun and interesting. Second, take charge of your classroom by maintaining ultimate authority. Be pleasant and helpful and ask for student input but always make the final decisions.

Third, you and your students should develop a set of class rules together. The rules should be short, clear, stated in the positive (i.e. what they should rather than what they should not do), and no more than about five in number. After discussing each rule thoroughly with the class, post the rules for all to see. Refer to and review them often.

Fourth, emphasize good manners and the "golden rule." Communicate clearly from the start that because you care about your students, you expect nothing less than the highest standards of behavior and manners. Emphasize your expectations that they never be sarcastic or cruel to you or their classmates. Most importantly, be the best model you can by showing concern, good manners, courtesy, and helpfulness. Discuss these considerate behaviors frequently and call attention to improvements made in this area.

SUPPORTIVE DISCIPLINE

Supportive discipline includes techniques for helping students maintain self-control when they somehow get off track without intending to misbehave. First, use signals to get students' attention in a subtle fashion. For example, learn to catch their eyes and use head shakes, frowns, and hand signals. Then, once you have their attention, redirect them appropriately.

Second, when signals are not effective, try using physical proximity. Simply move nearer the students until you redirect their attention back to task. You might also ask the student to move nearer to you.

Third, show interest in their work. Move alongside students, look at their work, ask questions cheerfully, or make positive comments about it. Sometimes you might give them a challenge: "You've done a lot of work here, but I'll bet you can't get two more done before it's time to stop."

Fourth, learn to spot students who are having difficulties. Then, offer assistance by providing hints, clues, or direct suggestions. You might need to restructure the task by making it more exciting or less challenging so they can be successful.

Fifth, interject humor into lessons that students perceive as tedious or tiring. Humor is uplifting and provides a welcome respite from tension. Sometimes a momentary break is all that is needed. You should be careful, however, that the humor does not degenerate into inappropriate horseplay and joking that ruins the lesson before work is completed.

Sixth, remove distracting nonschool objects such as toys, comics, rubber bands, animals, and notes, which can divert students' attention from the lesson. If students do not put them away after being asked, take possession of them without making a fuss about it. Then return the items at the end of the class or day along with strong reminders about leaving them at home or in their lockers.

Seventh, reinforce good behavior in an appropriate and timely manner. Preferably, positive reinforcement should be done informally with nods, smiles, and kind words such as "Thanks," "Good," and "Keep up the good work." Compliment students when they show good effort but avoid singling out older students for praise in front of their peers, because it can be embarrassing. Reinforce them as part of a group as much as possible or praise them quietly in private.

Eighth, directly request good behavior with suggestions, hints, and "I" messages when you notice students drifting toward misbehavior. At the same time, show them that you understand when a situation is difficult: "You have worked awfully hard, and I know we are all getting tired. But, please give me a few more minutes of your attention and we will be able to finish."

CORRECTIVE DISCIPLINE

Corrective discipline is designed to address misbehavior that must be stopped and redirected. The corrective techniques should be neither intimidating nor harsh but only what is necessary to stop the misbehavior and redirect it in a positive fashion. First, be assertive about insisting on two basic rights in the classroom. One is your right to teach without disruptions, and the other is the students' right to learn. Explain what rights are and what these rights mean. During your explanation, give hypothetical examples of violations. Then, when a student misbehaves, reassert the rights.

Second, stop the misbehavior quickly rather than ignoring it and hoping it will go away. If the behavior is a gross violation of rules (like fighting or loud swearing), you must stop it immediately and with a forceful tone of voice. For example, "Johnny, bad language is not used in this class!" or "Mary, sit down at once!" Milder misbehavior can be stopped by putting names on the board as a warning, as advocated by the assertive discipline model.

Third, implement the predetermined consequences of the misbehavior. Because the class helped you establish the rules and you have thoroughly discussed them, your students understand that if they choose to break the rules, they automatically choose the consequences that accompany the misbehavior. You need not get visibly upset but calmly say something such as "Linda, you are not living up to our agreed-upon rules, so you will have to move away from your group and complete your work by yourself."

Fourth, *always* follow through consistently. Make sure that you implement those consequences the same way for everyone every day. Showing inconsistency by being firm one day and lax the next confuses students and encourages them to test you. Also, do not let students talk you out of the predetermined consequences; if you do, they will surely test you again.

Fifth, redirect misbehavior in positive directions. For example, ask students who have misbehaved to return to work as agreed. Then, talk with them later about their behavior. Also, ask them how you can help them get the most out of school without interfering with others' learning.

DEVELOPING A CLASSROOM MANAGEMENT SYSTEM

Because your classroom management system will reflect your individual philosophies and values as a teacher, you should develop a personalized system of classroom management. Your system should include managing daily routines and discipline. Your system should be effective in meeting your own needs, as well as the needs of your students. The following is a process adapted from the seventeen-step process outlined by Charles (1992).

1. Make a list of your own traits and needs. Envision behavior limits within your level of tolerance. Consider such matters as talk, movement, noise, self-control, beginning and completing work, and personal manners. If you have a particular need (such as quiet and order) or a pet peeve, be honest about it and ask for the students' cooperation.

2. Make a tentative list of what you want to do for preventive, supportive, and corrective discipline.

3. Discuss discipline with your students on the first day of classes. Ask students their preferences for a learning environment. Share with them your needs and explore procedures that would meet both your needs and theirs. Show the students that you are flexible and willing to make compromises but retain the ultimate decision-making authority to ensure the students' best interests.

4. You and your students contribute rules for managing behavior in your classroom. In addition to formulating rules, make a list of positive consequences (rewards, praise, or positive reinforcement) and negative consequences (punishment, loss of privileges, or isolation). Record the rules and consequences for all to see. Then, discuss them for clarification and agreement.

5. Next write a revised, complete list of what you intend to do for preventive, supportive, and corrective discipline.

6. Prepare a list of ideas for ways you can build a positive classroom climate that will help students maintain self-control while also allowing for personality differences. Discuss these ideas with your students.

7. Establish a support system of administrators, fellow teachers, and parents. Share your discipline plan with your principal and ask for

his or her support. Then share it with one or more colleagues and ask them if you can turn to them for help or advice if necessary. Also, write a description of your system to share with parents and ask for their support in providing the best possible education for their children.

8. Put your system into effect. During the first week, assess it in terms of how well it contributes to a positive, enjoyable classroom climate, its ease of operation and implementation, and how effective it is in controlling behavior.

9. Discuss your assessment with the students and ask for their input in consideration of making changes. Modify your system if necessary, making sure the students are involved and understand the need for the changes.

10. Enliven your curriculum by ensuring it is worthwhile and interesting. Include topics of special interest to you or your students. Also, include topics about which you are particularly knowledgeable or enthusiastic.

11. Establish and write classroom procedures for smooth and efficient daily routines.

12. Be the best possible model you can be for your students by acting as you want them to act and speaking as you want them to speak.

13. Interact with your students on a personal level. Talk with them. Listen to them. Show interest in and acknowledge their problems and victories.

14. When students misbehave, discuss the problem with them and ask for their suggestions about how you might help.

15. Engage in a process of continuous self-reflection, consideration of student input, and improvement of the system. Keep faith in your system even during difficult times when students do not seem to appreciate your efforts. Remain secure in the knowledge that your commitment to your classroom management system and its continuous improvement will result in a quality learning environment for your students.

REFERENCES

Charles, C. M. (1992). *Building classroom discipline*, 4th ed. White Plains, NY: Longman.

APPENDIX F

Grouping Techniques for Effective Cooperative Learning

HETEROGENEOUS GROUPS

Heterogeneous groups are made up of students of mixed abilities, talents, backgrounds, learning styles, and so forth. The premise behind heterogeneous grouping is that synergy (the combined abilities, talents, experiences, and learning styles) will result in greater learning for all. The process of working with heterogeneous group members not only increases learning but also enhances social skills, develops appreciation for diversity, and prepares students to be effective collaborators.

Wood (1992) describes a heterogeneous grouping system called the *buddy system*, which was originally developed by Daniel Fader (1976). In this system, the class roster is divided into three groups by ability (high, middle, and low) using previous test performance, standardized test scores, and so on. Then, rank the students within each group from highest to lowest. Next, form a group of three by taking the top student from each of the three groups; form another group by taking the second highest student from each group and continue in that fashion until all the groups are formed. The result is heterogeneous groups of three in which the disparity of ability is minimized.

HETEROGENEOUS PAIRS

By matching a more-able student with a less-able student, you establish a peer tutoring situation. Be careful about matching personalities to

638

ensure effective collaboration. Heterogeneous pairs can be created on a short-term basis, e.g., one class period only, when one student is having trouble understanding or mastering a concept. Students sometimes understand explanations provided by their classmates better than those offered by adults. Heterogeneous pairs can also be formed on a long-term basis, so that students can develop effective working relationships. The less able students then have someone they can trust, feel comfortable with, and rely on to answer questions, offer explanations, and provide assistance when necessary.

Wood (1992) calls heterogeneous pairs "tutorial grouping." She suggests this type of grouping to provide assistance for learning disabled or educable mentally handicapped students. She also suggests that the students being paired should be academically compatible in terms of needs and abilities so that both students can learn from the experience. However, one student should be at least slightly more proficient in order to provide the tutorial effect.

HOMOGENEOUS GROUPS

At times, students should be given opportunities to work with other students of similar abilities. Students working in homogeneous groups often can challenge each other to reach toward higher levels of thinking and achievement in a way that might not happen with heterogeneous groups. When you group students with similar abilities, you can more effectively address the needs of those particular students. For example, if you have three groups, you can work with each group for part of the class period while the other two groups work individually at Learning Centers or on cooperative learning activities.

Wood (1992) calls this type of grouping "ability grouping." She wisely cautions against overuse of ability grouping, because your classroom learning community can become segregated. All students know which group is the highest ability group and which is the lowest ability group. Use homogeneous groups sparingly and cautiously to avoid the development of a "caste system," which can be detrimental to a productive and cooperative classroom climate. However, at times, homogeneous groups are quite appropriate and effective. For example, you could divide students for brief periods of small-group instruction and demonstrations, which might be especially useful in a math or science class.

HOMOGENEOUS PAIRS

For reasons similar to those for using homogeneous grouping, students will sometimes benefit from working with a partner of similar abilities.

The competition and collaboration between the two can lead to increased production and higher-level learning. However, you want to avoid the "blind leading the blind" situation by making sure that the activities and projects you assign are appropriate for their abilities. Activities should be challenging but not frustrating. Students should put their heads together to complete the task successfully.

Wood (1992) describes a system called "dyadic learning," which was originally developed for use with college students by Larson and Dansereau (1986). Homogeneous pairs would work nicely in this system, in which students read and study their content area material together. They begin by reading two pages silently. One partner, the "recaller," orally summarizes from memory what was read; the other partner, the "listener/facilitator," makes corrections, clarifications, and elaborations. After reading the next two pages, the partners switch roles. The process continues in this fashion until the assignment is complete.

RESEARCH GROUPS

In research groups, students work together to research the same topic and present their findings. Generally, homogeneous groups work best for research projects, especially to avoid the tendency for most of the work to fall on the most able students' shoulders. However, if the project is carefully structured, heterogeneous groups can also work nicely. You might want to establish heterogeneous groups for research projects when you have students of varying abilities interested in researching the same topic. You can divide the task so that the students research different aspects of the same topic and use different approaches as appropriate for their abilities.

Wood (1992) suggests using research groups either before, during, or after a thematic unit of study on topics that are either self-selected or assigned by you. She also suggests using research groups in science classes, in which each group conducts a variation of the same experiment. For heterogeneous research groups, establish subgroups and subtasks so that students of varying abilities can help each other without becoming overloaded with responsibility for the whole group.

REAL-WORLD GROUPS

In the real world, we generally are assigned to work together with a random assortment of people who may have diverse backgrounds, abilities, talents, interests, and personalities. For example, when assigned to work on a committee, someone might need to develop a working relationship with a diverse group of people. Committees are not chosen because of similar IQs, college degrees, fields of study, or personal relationships.

Usually, people are grouped to represent diverse interests, experiences, and programs. Although this diversity is a significant plus, it can also cause difficulties in the process of developing working relationships. For example, if a person is assigned to work on a committee with someone who has a different organization style, that person might become frustrated at the lack of a structured agenda or if another committee member has less knowledge about and expertise in the topic of the committee assignment. However, one cannot change committees simply because he or she feels that the other people on the committee are not as smart or organized.

In the real world, we must learn to make adjustments and overcome petty annoyances. We must also learn to look beyond initial impressions of our cohorts in search of special talents, experiences, and knowledge that might be advantageous to the task at hand. The ability to collaborate is a valuable skill in the world now and in the future. Students need to be able to find value in the differences of their coworkers and apply those differences to enhance the process of collaboration.

Therefore, at times, students should be grouped randomly, with possibly nothing in common but the task at hand. They must then be guided in the processes of becoming acquainted, building a team, organizing a plan, dividing the task, developing roles, and identifying leaders. They should be able to collaborate successfully with any classmates randomly assigned to their group.

Wood (1992) suggests that random grouping is valuable for expediency in establishing groups and physically moving students into groups. For example, if you decide in the middle of a lesson to spend some time reviewing a particular concept, you could quickly assign groups by numbering students. Also, sometimes you may not have enough class time available for students to move their desks across the room or even get up with their materials and move across the room. In such cases, you could tell students to pair up with the people sitting next to them or form a threesome or foursome with those sitting nearby.

FRIENDSHIP GROUPS

Sometimes, allowing students to work with their friends can be very motivating. When students are allowed to work with their friends on occasion, they are reminded that learning activities can be fun and exciting.

However, you must monitor the groups closely to make sure that they stay focused. You will have to expect and accept that students will probably do more talking and be more animated when working with their friends. As long as they are making good progress on the task, a higher-than-usual noise level probably means that they are having a good time while learning.

Wood (1992) suggests using social grouping as a reward for good work on previous tasks and motivators for upcoming tasks. Students should be reminded that they will be allowed to work with others of their choice as long as they get their work done and are not too loud. Then, if any students abuse the privilege, they can be reassigned.

BASE GROUPS

Base groups are long-term groups whose members meet regularly at the beginning of class. Base groups can work on academic projects, but their primary function is to provide social and emotional support for members. Group members check in with each other, discuss progress on projects, share successes and failures, offer solutions to problems, express interest in each other's work, share books and other materials, study for tests, and so forth. The base group was suggested by Johnson, Johnson, and Holubec (1991) as a kind of support group that emphasizes the classroom as a supportive learning community.

INTEREST GROUPS

Working together with others who share your interests can be a very motivating and rewarding experience. When students are interested in the same topic, their enthusiasm can be contagious and their shared learning inspiring. Wood (1992) suggests giving students lists of topics and having them choose the ones of interest to them. Students can also be allowed to suggest their own topics related to the thematic unit. Once the groups are formed from this information, students can either create their own projects or you can offer suggestions or have projects ready to assign.

SKILL-NEEDS GROUPS

One of the most effective ways to individualize instruction is through the use of skill-needs groups. In these groups, students of similar needs in terms of literacy skills work together for special instruction by you, the teacher, and then work together on reinforcement activities. For example, students who need to develop questioning skills can be grouped together for some direct instruction and modeling by you on how to formulate good questions. Then, the group can work together on a task requiring them to formulate and ask each other questions at various levels. Other possible skill needs include word recognition, concept development, summarizing, annotating, metacognition, previewing, setting purposes for reading, rate flexibility, skimming, scanning, making inferences, drawing conclusions, paraphrasing, library research, and use of textbook study aids. Wood (1992) suggests using content inventories (see Content Area Reading Inventory in Chapter 9), pre- and posttests, and chapter or unit tests to identify students' needs for grouping. You can also identify skill needs through observation and analysis of errors on assignments.

CONTENT-NEEDS GROUPS

Content-needs groups are similar to skill-needs groups except that instead of grouping students according to needs in literacy skills, they are grouped according to levels and area of content mastery. Wood's (1992) suggestion of using content inventories (see Content Area Reading Inventory in Chapter 9), pre- and posttests, and chapter or unit tests to identify students' needs for grouping would be especially useful for content-needs grouping. For example, students who need review or reteaching on particular concepts can be grouped together for instruction, so that the students who have already mastered the concept can progress to new content.

Wood (1992) describes a technique called associational dialogue that would be appropriate for use with content-needs groups. In this technique, you give students a list of the key concepts to be discussed. The students are then instructed to take notes from their textbooks and lecture notes on separate sheets of paper by organizing important details in clusters around the major concepts. Then on their own, students study the material by reciting the content related to each of the key concepts on the teacher-made list until they can associate the appropriate information with each concept. In class, the students work in pairs in an "associational dialogue" to discuss in their own words each concept on the list. As partners listen, they can contribute information and ask for clarification. Finally, discuss the concepts by eliciting and elaborating on responses from the students.

REFERENCES

Fader, D. (1976). *The new hooked on books*. New York: Berkley Publishing.

Johnson, D. W., R. T. Johnson, and E. Holubec. (1991). *Cooperation in the classroom*. Edina, MN: Interaction Book Company.

Larson, C. O., and D. F. Dansereau. (1986). Cooperative learning in dyads. *Journal of Reading* 29:516–520.

Wood, K. D. (1992). Fostering cooperative learning in middle and secondary level classrooms. In *Reading in the content areas: Improving classroom instruction*. Edited by E. K. Dishner, T.W. Bean, J. E. Readence, and D. W. Moore. Dubuque, IA: Kendall/Hunt Publishing Company.

Sample Study Guides

TEXT PATTERN GUIDE

High School English Literature

The Rocking Horse Winner

Directions: Match the cause to the effect from the story *The Rocking Horse Winner* by D. H. Lawrence.

Causes

_____ 1. Paul felt as if the house were whispering, "There must be more money."

_____ 2. Paul had not found a winner for the Grand National race or the Lincoln race.

_____ 3. Paul rode his horse very hard to find a winner in the Derby.

_____ 4. Paul's mother said it was better to be born lucky than to be born rich.

_____ 5. Paul's mother had married an unlucky man.

_____ 6. Paul's father and mother had very expensive tastes.

Effects

a. Paul rode his rocking horse so hard to find a winner for the Derby that he put himself in a coma.

b. Paul rode very hard to find a winner for the Derby.

c. Paul's mother was no longer lucky.

d. Paul rode his rocking horse to find winners of horse races so that his mother could have more money.

e. The house always seemed to whisper, "There must be more money."

f. Paul told his mother that he was lucky.

TEXT PATTERN GUIDE

Third-Grade Social Studies

Mexico, the Community

Directions: Read the passage, "Mexico, the Community," and as you read, write down three important points relating to each of the following topics.

1. Mexico City
   a.
   b.
   c.
2. Celebrations of Mexico
   a.
   b.
   c.
3. Mexico flag
   a.
   b.
   c.
4. Conflicts of Mexico
   a.
   b.
   c.

Directions: From the information provided, we can begin to note a connection between various events in history. In this section, we will be examining the causes (why something happened) and the effects (what happened) of historical events. Match each cause in the left-hand column with the effects from the right-hand column, putting the letter of the effect on the appropriate line.

Examples

Causes

_____ 1. The Mexican flag has a symbol called a coat of arms.
_____ 2. The Mexican flag has a snake and an eagle on it.

Effects

a. This reminds the Mexican citizens of their home and the story of the cactus, eagle, and a snake.
b. This reminds the Mexican citizens of the Aztec Indians of long ago.

Examples

Causes

Effects

_____ **3.** The Mexican citizens live, work, and play in communities and cities in Mexico.

_____ **4.** Mexico City is more that six hundred years old.

_____ **5.** The National Palace is a huge Spanish government building standing in Mexico today.

_____ **6.** The soldiers came from Spain and fought the Aztecs, destroying their city.

_____ **7.** A priest in Mexico called for the people to rise up against the Spanish king.

_____ **8.** Texans share some holidays with Mexico.

_____ **9.** Texans defeated Mexico in 1836.

_____ **10.** The war of 1836 was a war that the people of San Antonio, Texas fought for their freedom.

c. Mexico is a mix of the old and new.

d. Mexico has an interesting history.

e. Many Aztec buildings were buried under Mexico City after the Spanish invasion.

f. May 5th Texans remember Mexico's victory over France in 1862.

g. The president works in an old building surrounded by new, modern buildings.

h. The fight for freedom began in 1821, and Mexico won its freedom.

i. "REMEMBER THE ALAMO!" was the battle cry from this famous fight.

j. The Lone Star flag was raised for the first time.

TEXT PATTERN GUIDE

First-Grade Science

I. Autumn

Directions: Check the sentences that describe events that happen in autumn.

_____ **1.** The leaves change colors.
_____ **2.** Snow falls from the sky.
_____ **3.** Thanksgiving.
_____ **4.** School is out.
_____ **5.** Birds fly south.

II. Winter

Directions: Check the sentences that describe events that happen in winter.

_____ **1.** It is hot.
_____ **2.** Christmas and Hanukkah
_____ **3.** Snow falls from the sky.
_____ **4.** It is very cold.
_____ **5.** The leaves change colors.

TEXT PATTERN GUIDE

Second-Grade Science

Directions: Place a line connecting the statement in the cause column that correctly belongs with the statement in the effects column.

Causes

1. Warm air is forced up by a block of cold air.
2. Breathe on a cold day.
3. Water vapor is in the air.
4. Air is moving.
5. Water boils.
6. A cloud full of water vapor is cooled.
7. Lightning heats up the air quickly.
8. The sun is behind you and the rain is in front of you.
9. The earth is tilted toward the sun.
10. The earth is tilted away from the sun.

Effects

1. Dew forms.
2. Clouds form.
3. Water vapor in your breath cools and turns into water.
4. Steam forms.
5. The weather turns cooler.
6. The weather turns hot.
7. You see a rainbow.
8. Wind forms.
9. You see a rainbow.
10. We get rain or snow.

TEXT PATTERN GUIDE

High School Math

Directions: Our text presents much of its material in an "if-then" format. We learn that *if* a specific condition or cause exists, *then* a corresponding specific outcome or effect must be true.

   Read pages 384–390 in Chapter 9. Then, read each statement in the *if* column. Determine the *then* statement that best defines the outcome precipitated by the *if* statement and write its letter in the blank. The *then* statements may be used more than once.

If

1. If a line slants up to the right,
2. If two points of a line are known,
3. If a line contains the points (0,6) and (–5,6),
4. If a line has no slope,
5. If a line slants down to the right,
6. If one point of a line and its slope are known,
7. If a line contains the points (7, –1) and (7,12),
8. If the slope of a line is zero,

Then

a. then it is a verticle line.
b. then it has a negative slope.
c. then the slope can be calculated.
d. then the line can be graphed.
e. then it has a positive slope.
f. then it is a horizontal line.

THREE-LEVEL GUIDE

High School Geography and History

Objectives: The student will comprehend how:

∎ geography has greatly affected history.
∎ maps have helped us understand history.
∎ people have influenced their environment throughout history.
    a. Interrupted
    b. Mercator
    c. Eckert

Level I

Directions: First read the statements, then read the selection. As you read, put a check next to the statements that agree with what the author says. Sometimes the author's exact words are used, and sometimes other words are used.

Section 1

____ **1.** Mountainous regions do not encourage dense population.
____ **2.** People and trade do not mix well with mountains.
____ **3.** Deserts and tundra have proven to be inhospitable to people.
____ **4.** One ally of people has been the rain forest.
____ **5.** Oceans have played great importance in the decision of where to live.
____ **6.** Islands are stepping stones from one civilization to another.

Section 2

____ **1.** Maps help us understand history.
____ **2.** Projections make something in geography more understandable.
____ **3.** Maps vary not only according to projections, but also as to the kind of information shown on them.
____ **4.** Most maps used in the study of history show political boundaries.
____ **5.** Resources or products are sometimes shown on maps used in history.
____ **6.** Climate maps are used to show the history of a continent's weather.

Section 3

____ **1.** People and nations sometimes, almost miraculously rise above the limiting effects of their environment.
____ **2.** The Atlantic Ocean is a much less effective defense barrier today.

_____ **3.** It was not soil alone, but also rainfall, planting, and water transportation that stimulated development of the north-central United States and south-central Canada as the "bread-basket" of the world.

Level II

Directions: Check the statement that tells what the author means. Be able to find information in the selection that shows you are right.

Section 1

_____ **1.** The valleys of mountainous regions are themselves redeeming qualities for humans.

_____ **2.** Nomads are inhospitable people.

_____ **3.** People naturally move to lowlands and plains regardless of their continent.

_____ **4.** Oceans and seas, while originally hindering development of civilization, have now become allies.

_____ **5.** Rivers are the least important connection to the rise of many civilizations.

Section 2

_____ **1.** A map projection is a way of showing the spherical earth on a flat paper.

_____ **2.** A Mercator map looks as if it were made by placing a light source at the center of a transparent globe and curling a paper cylinder around the globe touching it at the equator.

_____ **3.** An Eckert projection is commonly used in textbooks because it gives a clearer picture of the shapes and sizes of the continents.

_____ **4.** In an Interrupted projection, the ocean and land areas are split or broken up.

Section 3

_____ **1.** Shopping malls are an example of people controlling their environment.

_____ **2.** Deserts can become useful to humans in some ways, either industrially or strategically.

_____ **3.** A country neighboring a neutral country may still be involved in war.

_____ **4.** Hitler, as a war leader, can be considered as important as the facts of environment.

Level III

Section 1
Directions: Check the statements that use ideas from the reading selection and your own experiences. Be able to support your answers from the passage.

_____ **1.** Rome was not built in a day.
_____ **2.** The correct tools are needed to do a job correctly.
_____ **3.** Better safe than sorry.
_____ **4.** Life would be boring if everyone and everything were the same.
_____ **5.** As one increases options, one increases the need for making decisions.

Section 2
Directions: The following activity will help you find distortions of the three maps in this lesson. Fill in the chart on this paper. Answer by placing *yes* or *no* in the space for each statement. Remember that on a globe, the answers to these five statements always are *yes*. Whenever you write *no* on the chart, you have discovered a source of distortion on that map.

	Mercator	**Interrupted**	**Eckert**
1. All meridians are the same length.			
2. All lines of latitude are parallel.			
3. Parallels decrease in length from the Equator to the poles.			
4. Distances between any two parallels are equal.			
5. All parallels and meridians meet at right angles.			

Section 3
Directions: Same as for Section 1.

_____ **1.** A decision we make can change our environment.
_____ **2.** A mailman's motto, "rain, snow, sleet," for example, can affect people in their environment.

THREE-LEVEL GUIDE

High School English Literature

"The Storm" by McKnight Malmar

Check the items that explicitly represent some of the important details and actions in the short story.

____ 1. The husband was expecting his wife to be home.

____ 2. The wife found white envelopes addressed to her husband on more than one occasion.

____ 3. The woman saw a dead body as she ran toward the wood pile in the cellar.

If you think any of the statements are reasonable inferences and conclusions, put a check on the line provided. Be prepared to support your answer.

____ 1. The wife may not have felt so lonely if she had had a good marriage.

____ 2. The wife's insecurity, fear, loneliness, and immaturity caused her to imagine the intruder.

____ 3. The husband killed the woman, because he had the lion ring on his little finger.

To apply what you read means to take information and ideas from what you have read and connect it to what you already know. Place a check in the blanks next to the statements you feel are true.

____ 1. At some point, everyone's imagination can run away with him or her.

____ 2. Many events are coincidental and can make a person believe something that may not be true.

THREE-LEVEL GUIDE

Second-Grade Science

I. Literal Level

Directions: Check the items you think are true after reading pages 18–25.

1. ____ The weather never changes.
2. ____ There are different parts that make up the atmosphere.
3. ____ The atmosphere is like a blanket.
4. ____ Moving air is called wind.

II. Interpretive Level

Directions: Check the items you think make sense after reading pages 18–25.

1. ____ The atmosphere really protects us.
2. ____ Wind is constantly there even if we cannot feel it.
3. ____ It rains and snows more often on mountains.
4. ____ More than one type of cloud can produce rain.

III. Applied Level

Directions: Check the items you agree with after reading pages 18–25.

1. ____ The atmosphere is important in determining our weather.
2. ____ All clouds are alike and still different.
3. ____ Some clouds can tell you what kind of weather is near.
4. ____ The rain maker on Mopac is not a part of the weather.

THREE-LEVEL GUIDE

First-Grade Science

I. Literal Level

Directions: Check the items you think are true after having *Seasons* read to you.

_____ **1.** Summer comes after spring.
_____ **2.** It rains most in the spring.
_____ **3.** It is very cold in the summer.

II. Interpretive Level

Directions: Check the items you think make sense based on *Seasons*.

_____ **1.** Leaves changing color, days getting shorter, and school starting are all signs that summer is ending.
_____ **2.** Spring lasts for three months, has windy days good for flying kites and many blooming flowers.
_____ **3.** Spring comes after winter bringing snowy days and frozen ponds.

III. Applied Level

Directions: Check the items you think make sense based on the ideas in *Seasons*.

_____ **1.** Summer is the best season for sleeping late, playing outside and going on vacations.
_____ **2.** Spring time is the best time to fly kites and pick flowers.
_____ **3.** Spring and summer are good seasons to ice skate and build snowmen.

THREE-LEVEL GUIDE

High School Math

Problem: On the warm, sunny Monday morning of July 5, 1993, Joe Ellery needed to take down the July 4th decorations that were strung across the main street of Austin, Texas. The banners ran from the top of the hotel, parallel, to the top of Joe's store. Joe remembered a friend once figured the height of the hotel to be _____ and the distance from the hotel to Joe's store to be _____. As Joe stood in front of his store looking at the top of the hotel across the street, he wondered what the distance was between where he stood and the top of the hotel? Solve the problem for Joe.

I. Facts of the Problem

Directions: Read word problem above. Under column **A**, check those statements that contain important facts of the problem. Look back at the problem to check your answers. Under column **B**, check those statements you think will help you solve the problem.

A (Facts)	B (Will help)	
_____	_____	Joe owns a restaurant that is very popular.
_____	_____	It was sunny and warm on July 5th.
_____	_____	The hotel was ____ high.
_____	_____	Joe's store was as high as the hotel.
_____	_____	Distance from hotel to store.
_____	_____	Joe studied Algebra II every day.
_____	_____	Austin, Texas celebrates on July 4th.

II. Math Ideas

Directions: Check the statements that contain math ideas about this problem. Look back to column **B** of Part I to prove your answers. (You may change your answers in Part I if you wish.)

_____ product of binomials with radicals

_____ pythagorean theorem

_____ simplifying expressions with radicals

_____ solving equations containing radicals

_____ finding decimal representations of real numbers

_____ quotients of binomials with radicals

III. Numbers

Directions: Following are possible ways of getting an answer. Check those that will work in this problem. Look back to column **B** of Part I and Part II to prove your answers. (You may change some of your answers in Parts I and II if you wish.)

_____ $a^2 + b^2 = c^2$

_____ $\left(\sqrt{7}\right)^2 = 7$

_____ $c = \sqrt{a^2 + b^2}$

_____ $\sqrt{12} = \sqrt{4 \cdot 3} = 2\sqrt{3}$

_____ $\left(\sqrt{11} - 3\right)\left(\sqrt{11} + 3\right) = 8$

APPENDIX H

Purposeful Oral Reading Activities

RADIO READING

This strategy was designed by Searfoss (1975) to give students the opportunity to practice communicating a message accurately through oral reading, summarizing a message read orally, and developing listening comprehension. The name, radio reading, is derived from the analogy of a radio announcer reading aloud to a listening audience whose members do not have the script in front of them. The reader's job is to communicate accurately a message by reading it orally. The listener's job is first to discuss and restate the message, then evaluate whether the passage was accurately and clearly communicated. Because the listeners do not have copies of the passage, they cannot correct word recognition errors. Therefore, as long as the reader communicates the message accurately, word pronunciation does not have to be perfect. As a result, this strategy provides the reader a safe atmosphere to practice oral reading with an emphasis on word meaning rather than word calling.

Radio reading is implemented in four basic steps (Searfoss 1975). First, the teacher selects materials that are challenging but not frustrating and of a reasonable length—a paragraph or two for lower grades and up to a page for upper grades. When explaining the procedure to students, emphasis should be placed on the responsibility of the reader to communicate a clear message and on the listeners to listen carefully for the purpose of being able to summarize the message accurately. Students should be placed in pairs or small groups for this strategy.

Second, as the message is being communicated (i.e., read orally), the reader is allowed to make minor wording changes as long as the meaning of the message remains accurate and clear. The reader should ask for assistance with words if he or she decides help is needed; otherwise, you and the other listeners should refrain from prompting or word recognition coaching. If the reader asks for assistance with a word, he or she should be told the word immediately and allowed to continue without interruption.

Third, after the message has been read orally, the listeners discuss the content by restating and summarizing it. The listeners should ask the reader to reread parts as necessary to check for accuracy.

Finally, if the listeners give conflicting or inaccurate information, the reader should reread the parts necessary to allow the listeners to make corrections. Continue with a new reader by repeating the steps.

PAIRED READING

Paired reading is another strategy that gives students practice in meaningful oral reading in a nonthreatening atmosphere. It also frees you to individualize instruction. Paired reading is based on the concept of peer tutoring; two students of differing oral reading abilities are paired, so that better readers can serve as peer models for students with poorer fluency. However, avoid pairing a younger, more competent reader with an older, less competent reader. Students should read materials suited to their abilities (Tierney, Readence, and Dishner 1990).

In paired reading, students sit next to each other and share only one set of materials. The listener follows along silently while the reader reads orally. When the less competent reader is reading orally, the more competent one should refrain from prompting unless he or she is asked for assistance. The readers monitor their comprehension by discussing and retelling the content; readers summarize the content after it is read orally. Readers should continually ask themselves, "Does that make sense?" (Tierney, Readence, and Dishner 1990). Readers should change roles every ten to fifteen minutes for lower grades and twenty to thirty minutes for upper grades.

ECHO READING

Echo reading was originally termed the "neurological impress method" and designed as a remediation technique for poor readers (Heckelman

1969). However, another more recently designed oral reading strategy is also known as echo reading (Frandsen 1993). This strategy may be used with the whole class for lower grades; for upper grades, pairs or small groups should be used.

In this strategy, after setting a purpose for reading, read one sentence orally, modeling proper oral fluency and expression, while students repeat or "echo read" the same sentence immediately. When the whole class is involved, groups may be formed; each group then takes a turn echo reading. If pairs or small groups are used, the assigned oral reader should provide a good model of oral reading. After reading a segment of the assignment, students should stop and ensure that the purposes set for reading have been achieved. Especially in the upper grades, this strategy should only be used for brief portions of the assignment. It should be alternated or supplemented with other oral or silent reading strategies.

CHORAL READING

This oral reading strategy is especially useful for literature classes. It provides students the opportunity to share not only the meaning but also the aesthetic value of creative works of literature, especially poetry and drama. However, it can be used as an oral reading strategy for almost any content area, because it stresses the importance of proper rhythm, tone, phrasing, enunciation, and expression in conveying meaning. Teacher modeling with a variety of materials is an important part of choral reading.

Casting for choral and repeated reading can be organized in a variety of ways. First, a whole group or class reads together in unison. Second, one student or group begins, and then another student or group joins in, continuing for a cumulative crescendo effect. Third, different parts are assigned to different students or groups for dialogue. Finally, different students or groups are assigned a refrain.

ORAL CLOZE

The concept behind the oral cloze strategy (Frandsen 1993) is closure or completion. The unusual spelling is derived from the pronunciation of *closure*. The cloze procedure is widely used as a way to help teachers determine whether students can comprehend a given text. This procedure is described more fully in Chapter 9. Nonassessment types of cloze activities typically consist of fill-in-the-blank activities designed to give students practice in attending to meaning by using context clues to fill in the blanks (see Chapter 8).

Oral cloze requires students to pay attention to what is being read and be prepared to provide the next word when the oral reader gives a signal. Meaning is emphasized because, as long as a word makes sense and fits the author's intended message, whatever word the student provides is accepted. Like echo reading, this strategy should only be used for brief portions of an assignment, especially in upper grades.

In this strategy, begin reading aloud while walking around the room; students follow along in their texts. At some point, stop reading and either call on a student or tap a student on the shoulder. The designated student then suggests the next word. Continue reading while students follow along in their books in order to be ready with the next word.

The idea behind oral cloze is that for strategies that rely on an oral reading model to be effective, students must follow along silently while listening. A variation of oral cloze is for you, the teacher, to stop and tell all the students to say the next word silently to themselves before calling on someone. This variation gives the students a chance to think about and possibly decode the next word if it is not known by sight.

REFERENCES

Frandsen, B. (1993). *Diversified teaching: An anthology of strategies.* Austin, TX: St. Edward's University.

Heckelman, R. G. (1969). A neurological-impress method of remedial-reading instruction. *Academic Therapy* 4:277–282.

Searfoss, L. W. (1975). Radio reading. *The Reading Teacher* 29:295–296.

Tierney, R. J., J. E., Readence, and E. K. Dishner. (1990). *Reading strategies and practices: A compendium,* 3d ed. Needham Heights, MA: Allyn & Bacon.

Examples of Children's and Adolescent Literature Appropriate for Various Content Areas and Topics

SOCIAL STUDIES

- *A Picture Book of Abraham Lincoln* by David A. Adler
- *A Picture Book of George Washington* by David A. Adler
- *A Picture Book of Martin Luther King, Jr.* by David A. Adler
- *Alexander, Who Used to Be Rich Last Sunday* by Judith Viorst
- *Antler, Bear, Canoe: A Northwoods Alphabet Year* by B. Bowen
- *Before Columbus* by Muriel Batherman
- *Ben and Me* by Robert Lawson
- *Black Heroes of the American Revolution* by Burke Davis
- *Bringing the Rain to Kapiti Plain* by Verna Aardema
- *Chinese New Year* by Tricia Brown
- *Christmas Time* by Gail Gibbons
- *Encounter* by Jane Yolen (tells the story of the "discovery" of America from a young Native American boy's perspective)
- *Extraordinary Black Americans from Colonial to Contemporary Times* by Susan Altman
- *Family Farm* by Thomas Locker

- *Fawn* by Robert Newton Peck (tells the story of the British attack on Fort Ticonderoga in 1758 from a young Mohawk boy's perspective)
- *First Came the Indians* by M. J. Wheeler
- *Hannah's Farm* by Michael McCurdy
- *Hanukkah* by Miriam Nerlove
- *I Like Me!* by Nancy Carlson
- *If I Were in Charge of the World* by Judith Viorst
- *If You Grew Up with George Washington* by Ruth Belov Gross
- *Johnny Tremain* by Esther Forbes (Revolutionary War)
- *Knots on a Counting Rope* by Bill Martin, Jr., and John Archambault (Native Americans)
- *Little House on the Prairie* by Laura Ingalls Wilder
- *Log Cabin in the Woods* by Joanne Landers Henry
- *Of Quarks, Quasars, and Other Quirks: Quizzical Poems for the Supersonic Age* by Sara Brewton, John E. Brewton, and John Blackburn ("a collection of spoofs on modern life and scientific progress, including credit card overuse, TV mania, computer craziness, and transplants") (Cline and McBride 1983)
- *Pets without Homes* by Caroline Arnold
- *Squanto and the First Thanksgiving* by Joyce Kessel
- *Thanksgiving Day* by Gail Gibbons
- *The Alamo* by Leonard Everett Fisher
- *The Battle of Gettysburg* by Neil Johnson
- *The Double Life of Pocahontas* by Jean Fritz
- *The Greek Treasure* by Irving Stone
- *The Legend of the Indian Paintbrush* by Tomie de Paola
- *The Many Lives of Benjamin Franklin* by Aliki
- *The Relatives Came* by Cynthia Rylant
- *The Story of the Statue of Liberty* by Betsy Maestro and Giulio Maestro
- *What is the Sign for Friend?* by Judith Greenberg
- *Your Family, My Family* by Joan Drescher

MATH (MOTIVATIONAL)

- *Anno's Hat Tricks* by Akihiro Nozaki
- *Anno's Math Games* by Mitsumasa Anno
- *Anno's Math Games II* by Mitsumasa Anno
- *Anno's Math Games III* by Mitsumasa Anno
- *Asimov's Mysteries* by Isaac Asimov

- *Calculator Game Book for Kids of All Ages* by Arlene Hartman
- *Exploring Technology* by Computer Society Press
- *Getting Started in Problem Solving* by Michael Ecker
- *Guinness Game Book* by Norris McWhirter and Norvin Pallas
- *Knotted Doughnuts and Other Mathematical Entertainments* by Martin Gardner
- *Let's Experiment* by Martin Keen
- *Let's Explore Mathematics* by Leonard March
- *Math for Everyone* by Janice Van Cleare
- *Mathematical Puzzles* by Martin Gardner
- *Mathematics Encyclopedia* by Leslie Foster
- *Mathematics for Pleasure* by Oswald Jacoby and William Benson
- *Metric Puzzles* by Peggy Adler and Irving Adler
- *More New Ways in Math* by Arthur Jonas
- *The "I Hate Mathematics!" Book* by Marilyn Burns
- *The Math Menagerie* by Robert R. Kadesch
- *Newton at the Bat: The Science in Sports* by Eric W. Schrier and William F. Allman (editors)
- *Quick and Easy Math* by Isaac Asimov
- *Science Fun* by James Hyer and Mildred Hyer
- *The Complete Book of Finger Math* by Edwin Lieberthal
- *The Joy of Mathematics* by Theoni Pappas
- *Unexpected Hanging and Other Mathematical Diversions* by Martin Gardner

MATH AND SCIENCE (CAREERS)

- *A Guide to Computer Careers* by D. D. Spencer
- *Career Choices for Students of Mathematics* by Career Associates
- *Careers in Environmental Protection* by Reed Millard and Science Book Associates Editors
- *High Tech Career Strategies for Women* by J. R. Goldberg
- *Nontraditional Careers for Women* by Sarah Splaver
- *The American Almanac of Jobs and Salaries* by John Wright
- *The Computer Careers Handbook* by Connie Winkler
- *What Can I Do with a Major in . . . ?* by Lawrence Malnig
- *What Can She Be? A Geologist* by Gloria Goldreich and Ester Goldreich
- *Women in Medicine* by Sandra L. Chaff (editor)

MATH AND SCIENCE (MAKING ABSTRACT CONCEPTS MORE CONCRETE)

- *Anno's Mysterious Multiplying Jar* by Masaichiro Anno and Mitsumasa Anno
- *Anno's Sundial* by Mitsumasa Anno
- *How Many, How Much: A Funny Number* by Steven Chapman
- *How Much Is a Million?* by David Schwartz
- *Less Than Nothing Is Really Something* by Robert Froman
- *Let's Find Out about Subtraction* by David Whitney
- *Let's Go Metric* by Frank Donovan
- *Metric Can Be Fun* by Munro Leaf
- *Metric Measure* by Herbert Zim and James Skelly
- *Square the Number* by Mattie Mae Woodruff
- *Tell Me About Measures* by Alain Gree
- *The Easy Book of Division* by David Whitney
- *The Modern Way to Measure* by Miriam Schlein
- *Think Metric!* by Franklyn Branley

MATH AND SCIENCE (PRACTICAL APPLICATIONS)

- *A Desert Year* by C. Lerner
- *A River Ran Wild: An Environmental History* by L. Cherry
- *A Tree in a Forest* by J. Thornhill
- *A Water Snake's Year* by Doris Gove
- *ABZ's of Economics* by Susan Lee
- *Amazing Wolves, Dogs and Foxes* by Mary Ling
- *Bless the Beasts and the Children* by Glendon Swarthout
- *Bringing Back the Animals* by Teresa Kennedy
- *Chaos* by James Gleick
- *Charles Darwin and Evolution* by S. Parker
- *Come Back, Salmon* by M. Cone
- *Contemporary Economics* by Milton Spencer
- *Cosmos* by Carl Sagan
- *Economics: The Science of Common Sense* by Elbert Bowden
- *Exploring the Everyday World* by Margaret Bartlett
- *Heart to the Hawks* by Don Moser
- *Ideas and Information* by Arno Penzias
- *Incident at Hawk's Hill* by Allan W. Eckert
- *Invitation to Economics* by Lawrence Wolken
- *Junior Science Book of Volcanoes* by Patricia Lauber

- *Let a River Be* by Betty Sue Cummings
- *Misplaced Animals, Plants, and Other Living Creatures* by Alice Hopf
- *Mother Earth* by Nancy Luenn
- *Mountains and Volcanoes* by Kay Ware
- *Mustangs: A Return to the Wild* by Hope Ryden
- *New Earth Book: Our Changing Planet* by Melvin Berger
- *Never Cry Wolf* by Farley Mowat
- *Orphan, the Story of a Baby Woodchuck* by Faith McNulty
- *Pond Life: A Close-Up Look at the Natural World of a Pond* by B. Taylor
- *Rabbits: See How They Grow* by Barrie Watts
- *Rainforest Animals* by M. Chinery
- *Secrets of a Wildlife Watcher* by Jim Arnosky
- *Silent Spring* by Rachel Carson
- *Since Silent Spring* by Frank Graham
- *Small and Furry Animals* by Gill Tomblin
- *Solo: The Story of the African Wild Dog* by Hugo Van Lawick
- *Squirrel Watching* by Miriam Schlein
- *Swanfall: Journey of the Tundra Swans* by Tom Horton
- *The Animal Atlas* by David Lambert
- *The Big Tree* by B. Hiscock
- *The Gift of the Tree* by A. Tresselt
- *Geological Disasters: Earthquakes and Volcanoes* by Thomas Aylesworth
- *The Great Barrier Reef: A Living Laboratory* by R. Johnson
- *The Grizzly* by Annabel Johnson and Edgar Johnson
- *Historical Catastrophes: Earthquakes* by Billye Brown
- *Historical Catastrophes: Hurricanes and Tornadoes* by Billye Brown
- *The Illustrated World of Oceans* by S. Wells
- *The Making of the Atomic Bomb* by Richard Rhodes
- *The Space Shuttle Operator's Manual* by Mark Kerry Joels
- *The Space Shuttle Story* by Luke Begarnie
- *The Story of the Earth* by William Matthews
- *The Visual Dictionary of Animals* by Doris Kindersley
- *Thinking Economically* by Maurice Levi
- *Tiger with Wings: The Great Horned Owl* by Barbara Esbensen
- *Will We Miss Them? Endangered Species* by A. Wright

MATH AND SCIENCE (BIOGRAPHIES OF FAMOUS MATHEMATICIANS AND SCIENTISTS)

- *A Passion to Know: 20 Profiles in Science* by Allen Hammond
- *Amelia Earhart: A Discovery Book* by John Parlin

▌ *Americans in Space* by American Heritage Junior Library
▌ *Biographical Encyclopedia of Science and Technology* by Isaac Asimov
▌ *Carl Friedrich Gauss* by William L. Schaaf
▌ *Famous Mathematicians* by Frances B. Stonaker
▌ *Famous Men of Science* by Sarah K. Bolton
▌ *Pioneers in Science* by Frank Siedel
▌ *Seven Black American Scientists* by Robert C. Hayden
▌ *Women in Mathematics* by Lynn M. Osen

COMPUTER SCIENCE

▌ *Computers and Mathematics* by Carol Gourley
▌ *Computers and Small Fries* by Mario Pagnoni
▌ *Computing before Computers* by William Aspray
▌ *Database Step by Step* by Mark L. Gillenson
▌ *Developing Computer Skills* by Marily N. Suydam and Robert E. Reys
▌ *Giving Man Western Culture in the Computer Age* by J. David Botter
▌ *How to Model It?* by Anthony M. Starfield
▌ *History of Programming Language* by Richard L. Wexelblat
▌ *Ideas and Information* by Arno Penzias
▌ *Machines That Think* by Isaac Asimov
▌ *Parents and Computer Books* by M. David Stone
▌ *Technology 2001* by Derek Leebart
▌ *The Big Byte* by Peter Ognibene
▌ *The Computer Impact* by Irene Travis
▌ *The Cult of Information* by Theodore Rosnak
▌ *The High Ghost and High Tech* by Lenny Siegel and John Markoff
▌ *The Making of the Micro* by Christopher Evans
▌ *The Quest for Artificial Intelligence* by Dorothy Patent
▌ *Young Children and Microcomputers* by Patricia Campbell and Greta Fein

SCIENCE FICTION

▌ *A Wrinkle in Time* by Madeline L'Engle
▌ *Brave New World* by Aldous Huxley
▌ *Deadeye Dick* by Kurt Vonnegut, Jr.
▌ *Dune* by Frank Hebert
▌ *Earth in Transit* by Sheila Schwartz
▌ *Foundations* by Isaac Asimov

- *Future Stuff* by Malcolm Abrams
- *Level 7* by Mordecai Roshwald
- *More Soviet Science Fiction* by Isaac Asimov
- *1984* by George Orwell
- *On the Beach* by Nevil Shute
- *Player Piano* by Kurt Vonnegut, Jr.
- *Rama II* by Arthur C. Clarke
- *Robots of Dawn* by Isaac Asimov
- *The Fall of Hyperion* by Dan Simmon
- *The Population Bomb* by Paul Ehrlich
- *The Restaurant at the End of the Universe* by Douglas Adams
- *The Sirens of Titan* by Kurt Vonnegut, Jr.
- *The Space Merchants* by Frederik Pohl and C. M. Kornbluth
- *The Time Machine* by H. G. Wells
- *This Perfect Day* by Ira Levin
- *20,000 Leagues Under the Sea* by Jules Verne
- *When Harlie Was One* by David Gerrold
- *Where Do We Go From Here?* by Isaac Asimov
- *Z for Zachariah* by Robert C. O'Brien

ART (THEMATIC UNITS; LAUGHLIN AND STREET 1992)

- *Alexander and the Terrible, Horrible, No Good, Very Bad Day* by Judith Viorst
- *Alexander and the Wind-Up Mouse* by Leo Lionni
- *Circles, Triangles and Squares* by Tana Hoban
- *Diego Rodriguez de Selva y Velasques* by Ernest Raboff
- *Dots, Spots, Speckles, and Stripes* by Tana Hoban
- *Inspirations: Stories about Women Artists* by Leslie Sills
- *Jumanji* by Chris Van Allsburg
- *Owl Moon* by Jane Yolen
- *Pablo Picasso* by Ernest Raboff
- *Pattern* by Henry Pluckrose
- *Shadows and Reflections* by Tana Hoban
- *Shapes* by John J. Reiss
- *Sky Songs* by Myra Cohn Livingston
- *The Girl Who Loved Wild Horses* by Paul Goble
- *The Mixed-Up Chameleon* by Eric Carle
- *The Paint-Box Sea* by Doris Herold Lund
- *The Turn about, Think about, Look about Book* by Beau Gardner
- *The Wing on a Flea* by Ed Emberley

■ *Topsy-Turvies: Pictures to Stretch the Imagination* by Mitsumasa Anno
■ *Two Bad Ants* by Chris Van Allsburg
■ *Up and down on the Merry-Go-Round* by Bill Martin, Jr. and John Archambault
■ *Vincent Van Gogh* by Ernest Raboff
■ *When Clay Sings* by Byrd Baylor

MUSIC (THEMATIC UNITS; LAUGHLIN AND STREET 1992)

■ *Arroz Con Leche: Popular Songs and Rhymes from Latin America* illustrated by Lulu Delacre
■ *Brass* by Dee Lillegard
■ *Chicka Chicka Boom Boom* by Bill Martin, Jr., and John Archambault
■ *Dance Away* by George Shannon
■ *Drummer Hoff* by Barbara Emberley
■ *Duke Ellington: King of Jazz* by Elizabeth Rider Montgomery
■ *Frog Went A-Courtin'* by John Langstaff
■ *Great Composers* by Piero Ventura
■ *I Am Phoenix: Poems for Two Voices* by Paul Fleischman
■ *I Know an Old Lady* by Glen Rounds
■ *Louis Armstrong* by Genie Iverson
■ *Ludwig van Beethoven: Musical Pioneer* by Carol Greene
■ *Mozart: Scenes from the Childhood of the Great Composer* by Catherine Brighton
■ *Musical Max* by Robert Kraus
■ *Orchestranimals* by Vlasta van Kampen and Irene C. Eugen
■ *Over the River and through the Wood* by Lydia Maria Child
■ *Peter and the Wolf* by Sergei Prokofiev
■ *Percussion* by Dee Lillegard
■ *Silent Night* by Joseph Mohr
■ *Strings* by Dee Lillegard
■ *Swan Lake* by Margot Fonteyn
■ *The Bremen Town Musicians* by Grimm Brothers
■ *The Complete Story of the Three Blind Mice* by John W. Ivimey
■ *The Magic Flute: The Story of Mozart's Opera* by Francesca Crespi
■ *The Marvelous Music Machine* by Mary Blocksma
■ *The Sorcerer's Apprentice* by Robin Muller
■ *The Thirteen Days of Halloween* by Carol Greene
■ *Wheels on the Bus* by Paul O. Zelinsky
■ *Where the Sidewalk Ends* by Shel Silverstein
■ *Woodwinds* by Dee Lillegard

HEALTH AND PHYSICAL EDUCATION (INCLUDING SOME RECOMMENDED BY CARTER AND ABRAHAMSON 1988)

- *Advice for Life: A Woman's Guide to AIDS Risks and Prevention* by Chris Norwood
- *Afraid to Ask: A Book for Families to Share about Cancer* by Judylaine Fine
- *Being Born* by Sheila Kitzinger
- *Discovering the Human Body* by Bernard Knight
- *Germs Make Me Sick!* by Melvin Berger
- *Learning about Sex: A Contemporary Guide for Young Adults* by Gary F. Kelly
- *Muscles to Machines* by Neil Ardley
- *People, Love, Sex, and Families: Answers to Questions That Preteens Ask* by Eric W. Johnson
- *Recovering from Rape* by Linda E. Ledray
- *Safe, Strong, and Streetwise* by Helen Benedict
- *Teen Pregnancy* by Sonia Bowe-Gutman
- *The Nutritional Ages of Women: A Lifetime Guide to Eating Right for Health, Beauty, and Well-Being* by Patricia Long
- *The Skeleton Book* by Madeleine Livaudais and Robert Dunne
- *The Truth about AIDS: Evolution of an Epidemic* by Ann Guidici Fettner and William A. Check
- *Time—Atlas of the Body* by Claire Rayner
- *Your Skeleton and Skin* by Ray Broekel
- *What Happens to a Hamburger* by Paul Showers
- *Why Does My Nose Run? (And Other Questions Kids Ask about Their Bodies)* by Joanne Settel and Nancy Baggett

SPORTS AND RECREATION (CARTER AND ABRAHAMSON 1988)

- *The Armchair Book of Baseball* by John Thorn (editor)
- *Bird on Basketball: How-To Strategies from the Great Celtics Champion* by Larry Bird (with John Bischoff)
- *Careers in Sports* by Bob McGonagle and Marquita McGonagle
- *Careers in the Sports Industry* by Barbara Fenton and D. X. Fenton
- *The Contender* by Robert Lipsyte
- *Courting Fame: The Perilous Road to Women's Tennis Stardom* by Karen Stabiner

- *Drugged Athletes: The Crisis in American Sports* by Jonathan Harris
- *Encyclopedia of Modern Bodybuilding* by Arnold Schwarzenegger (with Bill Dobbins)
- *Endurance: The Events, the Athletes, the Attitude* by Albert C. Gross
- *Giant Steps* by Kareem Abdul-Jabbar and Peter Knobler
- *Guinness Sports Record Book* by Norris McWhirter
- *Jackie Robinson: A Life Remembered* by Maury Allen
- *Martina* by Martina Navratilova (with Geoge Vecsey)
- *Mary Lou: Creating an Olympic Champion* by Mary Lou Retton and Bela Karolyi (with John Powers)
- *Olympic Controversies* by Harvey Frommer
- *Running Loose* by Chris Crutcher
- *She's on First* by Barbara Gregorich
- *Stressing and Unstressing in a Tent* by Stuart L. Burns
- *The Athlete Within: A Personal Guide to Total Fitness* by Harvey B. Simon and Steven R. Levisohn
- *The Mystic Arts of the Ninja: Hypnotism, Invisibility, and Weaponry* by Stephen K. Hayes
- *Winning Kicker* by Thomas Dygard

REFERENCES

Carter, B. C., and R. F. Abrahamson. (1988). *Books for you: A booklist for senior high students,* 5th ed. Phoenix: Oryx Press.

Cline, R. K. J., and W. McBride. (1993). *A guide to literature for young adults: Background, selection, and use.* Glenview, IL: Scott, Foresman and Company.

Laughlin, M. K., and T. P. Street. (1992). *Literature-based art and music.* Phoenix: Oryx Press.

Commonly Used Prefixes, Suffixes, Rimes (Phonograms), and Affixes and Roots Derived from Greek and Latin

COMMONLY USED PREFIXES

Prefix	Meaning	Example
a=	on, toward	aboard
ab=	away, from	abduct
ambi=	both	ambivalent
ante=	before	antechamber
anti=	against	antidote
aqua=	water, liquid	aquarium
audio=	sound	audiometer
auto=	self	automatic
baro=	weight	barometer
cata=	down	catastrophe
chrono=	time	chronological
circum=	around	circumference
co=	together	cooperate

Prefix	Meaning	Example
col=	with	collide
com=	with	commune
con=	with	continue
contra=	against	contraband
de=	down	demote
di=	two	divide
dis=	separate, reverse	disapprove
ecto=	outer	ectoplasm
endo=	inner	endoderm
epi=	over, above	epidermis
eu=	good, well	eulogy
extra=	outside, beyond	extracurricular
hemi=	half	hemisphere
hemo=	blood	hemostats
hyper=	over, above	hyperactive
hypo=	below	hypoglycemic
il=	not	illegal
im=	not	immeasurable
in=	in or not	inept
inter=	between, among	interstate
intra=	within	intrastate
intro=	inside	introduction
ir=	not	irresponsible
lacto=	milk	lactose
litho=	stone	lithograph
macro=	large	macroeconomics
mal=	bad	malevolent
micro=	small	microscopic
mis=	wrong	misinterpret
multi=	many	multiply
neo=	new	neonatal
non=	not	nonsense
octo=	eight	octagon
over=	above	overkill
pan=	all	panorama
para=	beside	paramilitary
patho=	disease	pathology
per=	through	permeable
photo=	light	photosynthesis
post=	after	postwar
pre=	before	premeditate

Prefix	Meaning	Example
pro=	in favor of	promote
pseudo=	false	pseudonym
re=	again	repeat
semi=	half or partially	semicircle
sub=	below or under	submarine
super=	above or over	superhighway
syn=	with	synonym
trans=	across	transport
ultra=	beyond	ultrasound
un=	not	unsure
under=	below	understatement
zoo=	animals	zoology

COMMONLY USED SUFFIXES

Suffix	Meaning	Example
=able	capable of	marketable
=acean	organism	crustacean
=acity	quality, state of	veracity
=age	result	wreckage
=an	belonging to	American
=ance	state of	contrivance
=ant	causing, being	redundant
=arch	ruler, leadership	monarch
=archy	rule, government	anarchy
=arium	place	terrarium
=cade	procession	arcade
=chrome	color	momochrome
=cide	killer	pesticide
=coccus	microorganism	streptococcus
=cracy	government	democracy
=cy	state of being	normalcy
=ectomy	removal of	tonsillectomy
=ed	having	marked
=eer	one concerned with	engineer
=en	consisting of	molten
=ence	state of	independence
=ent	state of	benevolent
=er	doer, performer	rider

Suffix	Meaning	Example
=ese	relating	Chinese
=est	most	hardest
=fuge	driving away from	refuge
=ful	full of	hopeful
=fy	form, make	terrify
=hood	condition	childhood
=ia	disease	malaria
=ial	pertaining to	congenial
=ian	of	grammerian
=iatric	medical treatment	pediatric
=ible	capable of	forcible
=ic	pertaining to	ethnic
=ine	resembling	canine
=ion	act, process	vocation
=ish	of, like	childish
=ism	system	socialism
=ist	doer, agent	receptionist
=ite	native, follower	socialite
=itis	inflammation	tonsillitis
=ity	condition, degree	paucity
=ive	tending toward	relative
=ize	cause	victimize
=lepsy	fit, seizure	narcolepsy
=less	without	hopeless
=let	small	tablet
=like	resembling	childlike
=ly	characterized by	comely
=ment	state of	resentment
=meter	measuring device	odometer
=most	most	uppermost
=ness	state of	goodness
=onomy	body of knowledge	astronomy
=oid	resembling	ellipsoid
=opsy	examining	autopsy
=or	performer	editor
=ory	place for, used as	rectory
=osis	abnormal condition	neurosis
=ous	full of	porous
=phony	sound	caucophony
=proof	able to resist	waterproof
=ship	state, condition	township

Suffix	Meaning	Example
=sion	state of	confusion
=some	characterized by	fearsome
=sphere	spherical	biosphere
=ster	one who is	youngster
=tion	state of	modernization
=tomy	cutting	appendectomy
=tude	state of being	attitude
=ule	small	miniscule
=ure	act, process	erasure
=vorous	eating, feeding	herbivorous
=ward	direction	toward
=wide	extent	citywide
=work	product, production	handiwork
=zoan	member of group	protozoan

COMMONLY USED RIMES (PHONOGRAMS)

Rime	Rhyming words formed by blending the onset and rime
ace	ace, brace, grace, lace, pace, place, race, space, trace
ack	back, black, crack, jack, lack, pack, quack, rack, stack, shack
ag	bag, brag, crag, gag, hag, jag, lag, mag, nag, rag, sag, shag, snag, stag, tag, wag
ail	ail, fail, frail, hail, jail, mail, pail, quail, rail, sail, snail
ain	brain, chain, drain, gain, grain, lain, main, pain, plain, rain, sprain, stain, train
ake	bake, brake, cake, flake, lake, make, rake, shake, snake, stake, take, wake, mistake
ale	ale, bale, gale, male, pale, sale, scale, stale, tale, whale
ame	blame, came, dame, flame, game, lame, name, same, shame, tame
an	an, bran, can, fan, man, pan, plan, ran, span, tan, than
ank	bank, blank, crank, frank, plank, rank, sank, spank, tank, thank, drank
ap	cap, chap, clap, gap, lap, map, nap, sap, snap, scrap, tap, trap, wrap
ar	bar, car, char, far, gar, jar, mar, par, spar, star, war
ash	ash, cash, clash, crash, dash, flash, gash, gnash, hash, mash, rash, sash, smash, splash, trash
ate	ate, date, gate, hate, late, mate, plate, rate, skate, slate, state

Rime	Rhyming words formed by blending the onset and rime
aw	caw, claw, draw, flaw, gnaw, jaw, law, paw, raw, slaw, squaw, straw, taw, thaw
ay	bay, bray, clay, day, dray, gay, fray, hay, jay, lay, may, pay, play, ray, say, spray, stay, tray, sway
each	each, beach, bleach, peach, preach, reach, teach
eal	deal, heal, meal, seal, squeal, steal, veal
eam	beam, dream, gleam, scream, steam, stream, team
ear	ear, clear, dear, fear, hear, near, rear, smear, spear
eat	eat, beat, cheat, heat, meat, neat, peat, seat, treat, wheat
ee	bee, fee, flee, glee, see, spree, tee, thee, tree, wee
eed	bleed, deed, feed, need, seed, speed, tweed, weed
eel	eel, feel, heel, kneel, peel, reel, steel, wheel
eep	creep, deep, keep, peep, sheep, sleep, sweep, weep
eeze	breeze, freeze, sneeze, squeeze, wheeze
ell	bell, cell, fell, hell, sell, shell, smell, spell, tell, well, yell, swell
end	end, bend, blend, lend, mend, send, spend, tend
ent	bent, cent, dent, lent, vent, scent, spent, tent, went, rent
ess	bless, chess, dress, guess, less, mess, press
est	best, blest, chest, guest, nest, pest, rest, test, vest, west
et	bet, get, jet, met, net, pet, set, wet, yet
ew	brew, chew, crew, dew, drew, flew, grew, new, screw, slew, stew
ew	few, hew, mew, pew, spew, yew
ice	ice, dice, lice, nice, price, rice, slice, spice, twice
ick	brick, chick, click, kick, lick, nick, pick, quick, sick, stick, thick, trick, wick
ide	bride, glide, guide, hide, pride, ride, side, slide, tide, wide
ight	bright, fight, flight, fright, height, light, might, night
ike	hike, like, pike, spike, strike, alike
ill	ill, bill, chill, dill, drill, frill, fill, grill, hill, kill
im	brim, dim, grim, him, prim, rim, slim, trim, vim, whim
ime	chime, crime, dime, grime, lime, prime, time
in	in, bin, chin, din, fin, gin, grin, pin, sin, skin, spin, thin, tin, twin, win
ine	dine, fine, line, mine, nine, pine, shine, spine, swine, tine, twine, vine, whine, wine
ing	bring, cling, ding, king, ping, ring, sing, sling, spring, sting, string, swing, thing, wing, wring
ink	ink, blink, brink, drink, kink, link, shrink, sink, think, wink
int	flint, glint, hint, lint, mint, print, splint, squint, tint
ip	chip, clip, dip, drip, flip, grip, hip, lip, nip, rip, ship, sip, skip, slip, snip, strip, tip, trip, whip

Rime	Rhyming words formed by blending the onset and rime
it	bit, fit, grit, hit, kit, lit, mit, pit, quit, sit, slit, spit, wit, knit
ive	dive, five, hive, live, strive, thrive, arrive
oat	oat, boat, coat, float, gloat, goat, throat
ock	block, clock, crock, dock, flock, frock, knock, lock, rock, shock, smock, sock, stock
oil	oil, boil, broil, coil, foil, soil, spoil, toil
oke	broke, choke, coke, joke, poke, smoke, spoke, stroke, awoke
old	bold, cold, fold, gold, hold, mold, sold, told
one	bone, cone, lone, stone, throne, tone, zone, alone
ong	along, gong, long, prong, song, strong, wrong
ool	cool, drool, fool, pool, school, spool, tool
oop	coop, droop, hoop, loop, scoop, stoop, swoop, troop
op	chop, crop, drop, flop, hop, lop, mop, pop, prop, shop, slop, sop, stop, top
ore	bore, core, fore, score, shore, snore, sore, store, swore, tore, wore
ot	blot, cot, dot, got, hot, jot, knot, lot, not, pot, plot, rot, shot, trot, tot
ought	ought, bought, brought, fought, sought, thought, wrought
ound	bound, found, ground, hound, mound, pound, round, sound, wound
out	about, bout, clout, devout, lout, pout, rout, shout, snout, stout, tout, trout, without
ow	blow, bow, crow, flow, glow, grow, know, low, mow, row, show, slow, snow, stow, throw
ow	bow, brow, cow, how, now, plow, prow, row, scow, sow, vow, allow
ub	club, cub, grub, hub, scrub, shrub, stub, tub
uck	chuck, cluck, duck, luck, puck, stuck, shuck, suck, truck, tuck
udge	budge, grudge, judge, nudge, smudge
uff	bluff, cuff, gruff, snuff, stuff, puff
ug	bug, drug, dug, hug, jug, mug, pug, plug, rug, snug, tug
um	drum, gum, hum, plum, rum, scum, slum, strum, sum
umble	bumble, fumble, humble, jumble, mumble, rumble, stumble, tumble
ump	bump, dump, hump, jump, lump, plump, rump, slump, stump, thump, trump
un	bun, dun, fun, gun, nun, pun, run, spun, stun, sun
unch	bunch, crunch, hunch, lunch, munch, punch, scrunch
ung	clung, flung, hung, lung, rung, slung, sprung, strung, sung, swung, stung

Rime	Rhyming words formed by blending the onset and rime
unk	bunk, chunk, drunk, hunk, junk, punk, shrunk, skunk, spunk, sunk, trunk
unt	blunt, bunt, grunt, hunt, punt, runt, stunt
urn	urn, burn, churn, turn, return
ust	bust, crust, dust, just, lust, must, rust, trust

COMMONLY USED AFFIXES AND ROOTS DERIVED FROM GREEK AND LATIN

Affix or root word	Meaning	Example
anima	mind, breath, soul, spirit	animate
anthropos	mankind	anthropology
archae	ancient	archaeology
act	to do, drive	action
amb	to walk, go about	ambulatory
ast	star	astronaut
aud	to hear	audible
bene	well	benevolent
bi	two	bicycle
bios	life	biology
card	heart	cardiac
carn	flesh	incarnate
caust	to burn	caustic
cyclos	wheel or circle	lifecycle
deci	one-tenth	decibel
deme	people	demographics
derm	skin	dermatologist
dic	to say	dictate
deka	ten	dekagram
doct	to teach	doctrine
duc	to lead	induction
entomon	insect	entomology
equ	equal	equity
ethnos	race	ethnic
fac	to do or make	factory
feder	league, treaty	federation
gamos	marriage	bigamy
geo	earth	geography
gnost	knowledge, judgment	agnostic
grad	to go, step	graduate

Affix or root word	Meaning	Example
gram	to write	telegram
graph	to write	biography
logos	study, science, discourse	geology
kilo	one thousand	kilometer
kine	to move, motion	kinesthesiology
lateris	side	bilateral
magnus	large	magnitude
mania	derangement	maniac
milli	one-thousandth	millimeter
monos	one	monogamy
morph	shape, form	amorphous
mut	to change	mutate
narc	numbness, stupor	narcotics
neur	nerve	neurology
oculus	eye	binoculars
ornis	bird	ornithology
ped	feet	biped
pend	to hang, hanging	pending
phil	to love	philanthropy
photo	light	photosynthesis
podos	foot	podiatrist
poly	many	polyglot
port	to carry	transportation
psyche	soul or mind	psychology
pyro	fire	pyromania
rupt	to break	interrupt
scope	to see, watch	microscope
sectus	cut	dissect
spec	to look	inspector
tech	art, craft, skill	technical
theos	god	theology
tri	three	triple
unus	one	unison
viv	to live	survive
voc	voice, call	vocal
volens	wishing	volunteer

APPENDIX K

Test Construction

The information in this appendix is taken from a test construction manual developed by William Taylor for staff development at Oakton Community College (1987) and presented by him at a faculty development workshop for St. Edward's University in March, 1990. This information is designed to help you construct tests that are effective as both teaching and assessment tools. Use this information to help you design tests that reflect the content and literacy (including thinking) skills you want to communicate as important in your discipline. The tendency of most teachers is to test at the literal recall level of thought. Be careful to avoid overuse of this type of question unless that is the type of thinking you wish to emphasize as important to your discipline.

GENERAL GUIDELINES

1. Develop test questions throughout the semester, rather than waiting until just before the exam, because writing good, reliable test items is difficult and time consuming. Also, if you write a question or two after each class, the test will represent more closely your objectives and instruction.
2. Have a clear understanding of the purpose of the test by responding to questions such as these: Are you assessing literacy skills, content, or both? What levels of competency do you expect? Do

your students need to apply and understand the information they have learned, or is it enough for them to recognize, memorize, and recall the content?

3. Make sure that the test parallels your instruction by developing a test blueprint that supports your curriculum. Consider questions such as the following: What is the need for a test at this point? What type of test will do the best job of assessing this particular information?

4. If the test is designed to assess a critical body of knowledge, make sure the test questions do so as well. Avoid the common teacher trap of testing insignificant material that was not emphasized in class and assignments. If you focus on certain critical material, then make sure your test covers that material.

5. Ensure that your test questions assess achievement beyond the superficial and obvious.

6. Do not write questions on inconsequential details just to "catch" students.

7. Avoid the use of *all, always, never, only, no, none,* and so on, because it takes only one exception to give away the answer.

8. Be careful not to use controversial or evaluative words such as *important, excellent,* or *major reason,* which may be interpreted as a matter of judgment. If you have to use such a term, use a disclaimer such as, "According to the text. . ."

9. Do not try to put too much information into a single question; make sure each contains only one idea.

10. Do not make ambiguous references (e.g., do not assume students will know what is meant by *the war*).

11. Be careful about the vocabulary you use in the test items. We tend to write at a higher level than we speak: be sure to use language that comes close to the language used during instruction. Maintain a simple readability level while retaining concept difficulty.

12. *If* you are assessing material you consider so basic that you want to be sure everyone knows it, it is acceptable to include a question that everyone may be expected to get correct.

13. Begin the test with easy questions and progress to more difficult ones.

TRUE/FALSE STATEMENTS

In deciding whether to use true/false statements as test items, consider the following strengths and weaknesses in terms of your specific assessment purposes. When facts and definitions are important, true/false questions may be the best way to assess them. However, keep in mind that true/false tests tend to be overused and poorly constructed. If you decide to use them, construct the statements according to the guidelines provided.

Strengths

+ permit a wide sampling of content
+ assess learning of facts and definitions well
+ relatively easy to prepare, because each item comes directly from the content
+ offer the opportunity to cover more content with test items, because students can respond to many in a limited time
+ usable with students who have reading problems
+ quick and easy objective scoring

Limitations

− may not give a true estimate of the student's knowledge, because 50 percent could be answered correctly by chance
− prone to ambiguity and misrepresentation
− tend to emphasize trivial details
− give little diagnostic information (i.e., students' strengths and weaknesses)
− generally considered by students to be tricky
− tend to be either extremely easy or extremely difficult

Guidelines

1. Use positively stated, simple, declarative sentences. If more than one clause is used, both should be true or false. (Avoid the use of negatively stated sentences, e.g., China is *not* a member of the United Nations).
2. Vary the length of both true and false statements. Be careful to avoid the tendency to make true statements longer than false ones.
3. Determining whether a statement is true or false should not involve trivia or trick phrases.
4. Include randomly interspersed, roughly equal numbers of true and false questions.
5. Because timed true/false tests are more reliable, set a deadline for the entire test or the true/false portion.
6. Be sure to have a manageable number of statements for the time allotted. Generally speaking, a student should be able to respond to three well-constructed true/false statements in about two minutes.

MATCHING EXERCISES

In deciding whether to use matching exercises as test items, consider the following strengths and weaknesses in terms of your specific assessment purposes. When associations and relationships within a single topic are important, well-constructed matching exercises may be the most efficient way to assess them. If you decide to use matching exercises, construct the statements according to the guidelines provided.

Strengths

+ especially suitable for *who, what, when,* and *where* questions
+ efficient for testing several relationships within a topic
+ have a compact format that allows coverage of much material in a small space
+ assess the ability to make associations and identify relationships
+ have quick and easy objective scoring
+ can include more responses than stimuli to reduce the problem of guessing

Limitations

– seldom appropriate to measure beyond recognition of basic factual knowledge
– usually poor for diagnosing student strengths and weaknesses
– difficult to construct
– have reduced flexibility, which often results in overemphasis on one topic
– tend to focus on trivial facts
– susceptible to irrelevant clues (e.g., using process of elimination)
– appropriate in only a limited number of situations

Guidelines

1. Include only homogeneous information related to one concept or topic in a single matching exercise (e. g., inventions and inventors). Giving a title to each column will help you exclude nongermane material.
2. Keep items brief in wording, using one-word responses if possible.
3. Use no more than twelve items.
4. Use more responses than stimuli. A good ratio is 7:5.
5. It is possible to have items on the second list used more than once.
6. One column or the other should be in some kind of order to aid students in locating the correct answer efficiently.

7. Make responses agree grammatically.
8. Keep the entire set of items on one page.
9. Procedures should allow students to indicate the answer by letter or number, not by drawing lines.

MULTIPLE-CHOICE QUESTIONS

Multiple-choice questions contain a stem, which is usually a question or incomplete sentence, and a list of alternatives. One of the alternatives is the answer, and the others serve as distractors. Because multiple-choice questions are highly versatile and objective, they may be the best all-around type of question. When deciding whether to use multiple-choice questions as test items, consider the following strengths and weaknesses in terms of your specific assessment purposes. If you decide to use them, construct the statements according to the guidelines provided.

Strengths

+ allow assessment of a wide range of content at various levels of thinking
+ can control the level of difficulty by the distractors used
+ can be written to assess students' abilities to integrate information from several sources when formulating an answer
+ can be used to assess students' levels of understanding and abilities to apply learning
+ useful for obtaining diagnostic feedback, if the incorrect alternatives are constructed to include common errors
+ have quick and easy objective scoring
+ can provide an excellent basis for posttest discussion, especially if the discussion includes why the incorrect responses were wrong, as well as why the correct responses were right

Limitations

− difficult and time consuming to construct well
− may not be appropriate when identifying four or five plausible distractors is difficult
− may have longer response time than for other types of objective questions, thereby reducing the amount of materials that can be tested
− open to misinterpretation by students who read more into the question than is there
− may appear too discriminative (picky) to students, especially when the alternatives are well constructed

Guidelines

1. Do not assume that questions provided by the publisher are well constructed.
2. Write the stem to present a single, specific problem that is meaningful in itself. The student should be able to discern the issue without having to read all the options.
3. Put as many words in the stem and as few words as possible in the alternatives to save reading time. Do not be afraid to give necessary information to set the stage in the stem.
4. Make the correct answer and the distractors about equal in length. (Do not make the correct answer *always* longer or shorter.)
5. Alternatives should be homogeneous and parallel while also being clearly distinct from one another.
6. Distractors should represent common student mistakes. Make them plausible and attractive to students who have not mastered the content. If an alternative is never chosen, it might as well not be included.
7. To increase the difficulty of a question, make its distractors similar to the correct answer.
8. Make all choices agree grammatically, and ensure that the wording in the stem does not point to the correct answer. For example:
   The drug codeine is an:
   a. alkaloid
   b. carotenoid
   c. steroid
   d. tarrin
   e. terpine

   The stem should read: The drug codeine is a(n):

9. Use four or five alternatives. If you cannot think of enough good distractors, consider using another type of question.
10. Start each choice with a new line to make reading easier.
11. Never use *all of the above* and use *none of the above* sparingly, because it can turn a multiple-choice question into a true/false question.
12. Randomly vary the position of the correct answer.
13. If you use a negative, call attention to it by capitalizing or underlining it.
14. Be careful about using a series of questions that build on an earlier question. If the student gets the first question wrong he or she will likely get them all wrong.

15. It is possible to use the multiple-choice format for definitions and matching questions. For example:

Use the five lettered statements that follow to answer questions 1–4. Each may be used once, more than once, or not at all.

a. radiator
b. air conditioner
c. carburetor
d. transmission
e. alternator
   (1) Responsible for cooling the engine: _____
   (2) Mixes a vaporized gasoline/air combination: _____
   (3) Must be filled with a solution that will prevent freezing and/or boiling over: _____
   (4) Called a gearbox in some literature: _____

16. Questions can be constructed that have several sets of choices. For example:

(1) A person may be poisoned by inhaling carbon monoxide because carbon monoxide:
   1. dissolves delicate lung tissue
   2. combines with hemoglobin more readily than oxygen
   3. stimulates the heart excessively
   4. reduces the amount of oxygen in the lungs
   5. ties up the hemoglobin so oxygen cannot attach itself

Of the above statements:
a. all are false
b. all are true
c. only 2 and 5 are ture
d. only 1 and 4 are true
e. only 2 is true
(The correct answer is C.)

SHORT-ANSWER (FILL-IN-THE-BLANK) QUESTIONS

Short-answer questions are sometimes called "fill-in-the-blank" or "completion" questions. Rather than requiring that students simply recognize the right answer (as in true/false, matching, and multiple choice), they require students to produce their own answers. Responses usually take the form of a word, phrase, sentence, or symbol. Short-answer questions primarily test lower-level thinking skills. When deciding whether to use short-answer questions as test items, consider the following strengths and weaknesses in terms of your specific assessment purposes. If you decide to use them, construct the statements according to the guidelines provided.

Strengths

+ brevity allows for a wide sampling of content
+ test construction is easier than when distractors are needed
+ minimize guessing
+ easy to prepare
+ use vocabulary or phrasing exactly as presented in instruction or readings
+ good for strictly factual information in which a specific word or expression is important to know
+ test math and science problem-solving skills well

Limitations

− reduce objectivity in scoring unless only one word or expression is correct
− tend to test only rote, repetitive responses, often using the words of the text
− may be ambiguous, without sufficient context
− generally limited to testing lower-level thinking
− may discourage students because the task is so precise and often difficult
− encourage a fragmented study style because memorization of bits and pieces results in higher scores

Guidelines

1. Make sure there is only one correct answer.
2. Try not to have a long phrase as the answer.
3. Delete only key words from statements, not trivial ones.
4. Place blanks toward the end rather than at the beginning of the statement.
5. Regardless of the length of the correct answer, provide the same line length for all answers.
6. Make yourself an answer key before giving the test. Indicate acceptable variations and guidelines for allowing partial credit.

ESSAY QUESTIONS

Essay questions consist of a sentence or set of sentences that describe a situation, pose a problem, or ask a question; background information may be provided. The student's task is to respond by writing an essay, two types of which are possible. The first type is the broad long-answer or extended-response item, which assesses students' writing skills and abilities to retrieve and organize ideas in a limited period of time. The second type is the short-answer or limited-response item, which assesses students' content mastery by asking a narrow question. When deciding whether to use short-answer essay questions as test items, consider the following strengths and weaknesses in terms of your specific assessment purposes. Essay questions are appropriate when you want to require original or creative thinking and assess writing ability. If you decide to use them, construct the tests according to the guidelines provided.

Strengths

+ give greater freedom for students to express what they know
+ encourage students to strive toward understanding a concept as an integrated whole
+ allow expression of both breadth and depth of learning
+ encourage originality, creativity, and divergent thinking
+ can be less time consuming to prepare than any other item type
+ can be used to assess higher-level thinking skills: analysis, synthesis, evaluation

Limitations

- permit only a limited sampling of learning because of the time required for students to respond
- not appropriate for all subject matter
- provide students more opportunity for bluffing, rambling, and snowing
- very difficult and time consuming to grade
- subject to biased and unreliable scoring
- permit ratings influenced more by organizational style, grammar, and neatness than by content of response; as a result, poor writers who may have mastered the content are penalized
- can have low reliability of scores because of subjectivity

Guidelines

1. Allow yourself enough time to construct a good essay test.
2. If an objective question can be used to test the same skills or concepts, do not use an essay question.
3. Define the problem or issue completely, specifically, and in as much detail as necessary. It is better for your students to read longer directions and write a shorter, more focused answer.
4. Frame the questions carefully. Use *compare, contrast,* and *defend* rather than vague phrases such as *discuss, explain,* or *tell all you know.*

Vague directions allow for too much leeway and make it hard to draw fair comparisons among students.

5. For a better sampling of content, use more questions requiring shorter answers rather than fewer questions requiring longer answers.

6. Before giving the test, write model answers of the quality you expect from your students. Then decide if the question might be too difficult or too easy. Also get a sense of how long it will take to answer the question, making allowances for thinking time. Set the number of questions accordingly.

7. Find some way to ensure that you do not know whose test you are grading.

8. Use your model answer as a guide as you grade the answers.

9. Grade all the first questions and then all the second questions, and so on, to foster consistency in grading.

REFERENCES

Taylor, W. (1987). *Test construction manual.* Oakton, IL: Oakton Community College.

APPENDIX L

Resource Books for Teachers

CHILDREN'S AND YOUNG ADULT LITERATURE

Carlsen, G. R. (1980). *Books and the teenage reader: A guide for teachers, librarians, and parents.* New York: Bantam Books.

Carter, B. C., and R. F. Abrahamson. (1988). *Books for you: A booklist for senior high students*, 5th ed. Phoenix: Oryx Press.

———. (1990). *From delight to wisdom: Nonfiction for young adults.* Phoenix: Oryx Press.

Christensen, J. (Ed.). (1983). *Your reading: A booklist for junior high students.* Urbana, IL: National Council of Teachers of English.

Cline, R. K. J., and K. J. Hartman. (1990). Practical ideas for linking novels with students' writing. *The ALAN Review* 17:38–41.

Cline, R. K. J., and W. McBride. (1983). *A guide to literature for young adults: Background, selection, and use.* Glenview, IL: Scott, Foresman and Company.

Cohen, L. G. (Ed.). (1992). *Children with exceptional needs in regular classrooms.*

Donelson, K. L., and A. P. Nielsen. (1989). *Literature for today's young adults*, 3d ed. Glenview, IL: Scott, Foresman and Company.

Field, E. W. (Ed.). (1969). *Horn book reflections on children's books and reading: Selected from eighteen years of the Horn Book Magazine.* Boston: Horn Book.

Freeman, E., and D. G. Person. (Eds.). (1992). *Using nonfiction trade books in the elementary classroom: From ants to zeppelins.* Urbana, IL: National Council of Teachers of English.

Gillespie, J. T. (Ed.). (1985). *The junior high paperback collection.* Chicago: American Library Association.

———. (Ed.). (1986). *The senior high paperback collection.* Chicago: American Library Association.

Heimberger, M. J. (1980). *Teaching the gifted and talented in the elementary classroom.*

International Reading Association. (1991). *Kids' favorite books: Children's choices 1989–1991.* Newark, DE: International Reading Association.

———. (1992). *Teens' favorite books: Young adults' choices 1987-1992.* Newark, DE: International Reading Association.

———. (1994). *Teachers' favorite books for kids: Teachers' choices 1989-1993.* Newark, DE: International Reading Association.

Jett-Simpson, M. (Ed.). (1989). *Adventuring with books: A booklist for pre-K–grade 6,* 9th ed. Urbana, IL: National Council of Teachers of English.

Kennemer, P. K. (1993). *Using literature to teach middle grades about war.* Phoenix: Oryx Press.

Kobrin, B. (1988). *Eyeopeners.* New York: Viking Press.

Lamme, L. L., S. L. Krogh, and K. A. Yachmetz. (1992). *Literature-based moral education.* Phoenix: Oryx Press.

Laughlin, M. K., and P. P. Kardeleff. (1991). *Literature-based social studies: Children's books and activities to enrich the K–5 curriculum.* Phoenix: Oryx Press.

Laughlin, M. K., and T. P. Street. (1992). *Literature-based art and music.* Phoenix: Oryx Press.

McBride, W. G. (Ed.). (1990). *High interest–easy reading: A booklist for junior and senior high school students,* 6th ed. Urbana, IL: National Council of Teachers of English.

Plowman, P. D. (1980). *Teaching the gifted and talented in the social studies classroom.*

Reed, A. J. S. (1988). *Comics to classics: A parents' guide to books for teens and preteens.* Newark, DE: International Reading Association.

Romey, W. D., and M. L. Hibert. (1988). *Teaching the gifted and talented in the science classroom.*

Roser, N., and M. Frith. (1983). *Children's choices: Teaching with books children like.* Newark, DE: International Reading Association.

Roser, N., and M. G. Martinez. (Eds.). (1995). *Book talk and beyond: Children and teachers respond to literature.* Newark, DE: International Reading Association.

Ryder, R. J., B. B. Graves, and M. F. Graves. (1989). *Easy reading: Book series and periodicals for less able readers,* 2d ed. Newark, DE: International Reading Association.

Thiessen, D., and M. Matthias. (Eds.). (1993). *The wonderful world of mathematics: A critically annotated list of children's books in mathematics.* Reston, VA: National Council of Teachers of Mathematics.

Tunnel, M., and R. Ammon. (Eds.). (1993). *The story of ourselves: Teaching history through children's literature.* Portsmouth, NH: Heinemann Boyton/Cook.

Tuttle, F. B., Jr. (1983). *What research says to the teacher: Gifted and talented students.*

Tuttle, F. B., Jr., L. A. Becker, and J. A. Sousa. (1988). *Program design and development for gifted and talented students,* 3d ed.

———. (1988). *Characteristics and identification of gifted and talented students,* 3d ed.

West, W. W. (1980). *Teaching the gifted and talented in the English classroom.*

Wright, J. D. (1983). *Teaching the gifted and talented in the middle school.*

INFORMAL READING INVENTORIES

Bader, L. A. (1983). *Bader reading and language inventory.* New York: Macmillan.

Burns, P. C., and B. D. Roe. (1993). *Informal reading inventory,* 4th ed. Boston: Houghton Mifflin.

Ekwall, E. E., and J. L. Shanker. (1993). *Ekwall/Shanker reading inventory,* 3d ed. Needham Heights, MA: Allyn & Bacon.

Flynt, E. S., and R. B. Cooter, Jr. (1993). *Reading inventory for the classroom.* Scottsdale, AZ: Gorsuch Scarisbrick.

Fry, E. B. (1981). *Reading diagnosis: Informal reading inventories.* Providence, R. I.: Jamestown.

Jacobs, H. G., and L. W. Searfoss. (1979). *Diagnostic reading inventory,* 2d ed. Dubuque, IA: Kendall/Hunt Publishing Company.

Johns, J. L. (1981). *Advanced reading inventory: Grades seven through college.* Dubuque, IA: Wm. C. Brown.

———. (1985). *Basic reading inventory,* 3d ed. Dubuque, IA: Kendall/Hunt Publishing Company.

Leslie, L., and J. Caldwell. (1990). *Qualitative reading inventory.* Glenview, IL: Scott, Foresman and Company.

Rakes, T. A., J. S. Choate, and G. L. Waller. (1983). *Individual evaluation procedures in reading.* Englewood Cliffs, NJ: Prentice Hall.

Rinsky, L. A., and E. de Fossard. (1980). *Contemporary classroom reading inventory.* Scottsdale, AZ: Gorsuch Scarisbrick.

Scott, J., and S. McCleary. (1993). *Diagnostic reading inventory for primary and intermediate grades.* Akron, OH: Scott & McCleary.

Silvaroli, N. J. (1990). *Classroom reading inventory,* 6th ed. Dubuque, IA: Wm. C. Brown.

Woods, M. L., and A. J. Moe. (1989). *Analytical reading inventory,* 4th ed. Columbus, OH: Merrill.

INSTRUCTIONAL TECHNOLOGY

The following books are either published or distributed by the International Society for Technology in Education (ISTE 1-800-336-5191):

Angell, D., and B. Helsop. (1994). *The elements of e-mail style—Communicate effectively via electronic mail.* Reading, MA: Addison-Wesley.

Armstrong, S. (1995). *Telecommunication in the classroom,* 2d ed. Eugene, OR: ISTE.

Barron, A. E., and G. W. Orwig. (1993). *New technologies for education—A beginner's guide.* Englewood, CO: Libraries Unlimited.

Beaver, J. F. (1994). *Problem solving across the cirruculum—Improving students' problem solving skills using off-computer and on-computer activities.* Eugene, OR: ISTE.

Beekman, G. (1994). *Computer currents—Navigating tomorrow's technology.* Redwood City, CA: Benjamin Cummings.

Boone, R. (Ed.). (1991). *Teaching process writing with computers.* Eugene, OR: ISTE.

Butler, M. (1994). *How to use the Internet.* Emeryville, CA: Ziff-Davis.

California Model Technology Schools Project—Montery. (1992). *Destination: tomorrow—An atlas for technology tool use in education.* Montery Peninsula Unified School District.

Cannings, T. R., and L. Finkle. (Ed.). (1993). *The technology age classroom.* Wilsonville, OR: Franklin Beedle and Associates.

Eddings, J. (1994). *How the Internet works.* Emeryville, CA: Ziff-Davis Press.

Ellsworth, J. H. (1994). *Education on the Internet—A hands-on book of ideas, resources, projects and advice.* Indianapolis, IN: Sams Publications.

Fraase, M. (1993). *The Mac Internet tour guide—Cruising the Internet the easy way.* Chapel Hill, NC: Ventana Press.

———. (1994). *The PC Internet tour guide—Cruising the Internet the easy way.* Chapel Hill, NC: Ventana Press.

———. (1995). *The Windows Internet tour guide—Cruising the Internet the easy way,* 2d ed. Chapel Hill, NC: Ventana Press.

Harris, J. (1994). *Way of the ferret—Finding educational resources on the Internet.* Eugene, OR: ISTE.

Kehoe, B. (1994). *Zen and the art of the Internet—A beginner's guide.* Englewood Cliffs, NJ: PTR Prentice Hall.

Kuntz, M. (1993). *Kermit learns how computers work—Starring Jim Henson's Muppets.* Rocklin, CA: Prima Publishing.

LaQuey, T., and J. C. Ryer. (1993). *The Internet companion—A beginner's guide to global networking,* 2d ed. Reading, MA: Addison-Wesley.

Male, M. (1994). Technology for inclusion—Meeting the special needs of all students, 2d ed. Needham Heights, MA: Allyn & Bacon.

Marshall, G. (1995). *Travelers through time and space—Multicultural activities for the computer classroom.* Eugene, OR: ISTE.

McCain, T. D. E., and M. Ekelund. (1993). *Computer networking for educators.* Eugene, OR: ISTE.

Means, B. (Ed.). (1994). *Technology and education reform.* San Francisco: Jossey-Bass.

Moursund, D. (1995). *Increasing your expertise as a problem solve—Some roles of computers.* Eugene, OR: ISTE.

———. (1993). *Problem solving models for computer literacy—Getting smarter at solving problems.* Eugene, OR: ISTE.

Muir, M. (1995). *Kindling the fire—Integrating the hypercard into the classroom.* Eugene, OR: ISTE.

National Research Council. (1994). *Realizing the information future—The Internet and beyond.* Washington, DC: National Academy Press.

Perrson, E. (1993). *Net power—Resource guide to online computer services.* Lancaster, PA: Fox Chapel.

Pollak, R. (Ed.). (1994). *1995 multimedia and videodisc compendium for education and training.* St. Paul, MN: Emerging Technology Consultants.

Poole, B. J. (1995). *Education for an information age—Teaching in the computerized classroom.* Dubuque, IA: Wm. C. Brown.

Ryba, K., and B. Anderson. (1993). *Learning with computers: Effective teaching strategies.* Eugene, OR: ISTE.

Semrau, P., and B. A. Boyer. (1994). *Using interactive video in education.* Needham Heights, MA: Allyn & Bacon.

Senn, P. Breivik, and J. A. Senn. (1994). *Information literacy—Educating children for the 21st century.* New York: Scholastic, Inc.

Thornburg, D. D. (1994). *Education in the communication age.* San Carlos, CA: David Thornburg and Starsong Publications.

———. (1991). *Education, technology, and paradigms of change for the 21st century.* San Carlos, CA: David Thornburg and Starsong Publications.

Turner, S., and M. Land. (1994). *HyperCard—A tool for learning.* Belmont, CA: Wadsworth.

Wiebe, J. (1993). *Computer tools and problem solving mathematics.* Wilsonville, OR: Franklin Beedle and Associates.

Willing, K. R., and S. Girard. (1991). *Learning together—Computer integrated classrooms.* Portsmouth, NH: Heinemann.

Yoder, S. (1993). *LinkWay scripting—An introduction.* Eugene, OR: ISTE.

Yoder, S., G. Bull, and J. Harris. (1992). *LinkWay for educators—An introduction.* Eugene, OR: ISTE.

MISCELLANEOUS

Adams, M. J. (1994). *Beginning to read: Thinking and learning about print.* Cambridge, MA: MIT Press.

Adler, M. J., and C. Van Doren. (1972). *How to read a book: The classic guide to intelligent reading.* New York: Simon and Schuster.

American Association of University Women and the Wellesley College Center for Research on Women. (1992). *The AAUW report: How schools shortchange girls.* Washington, DC: AAUW Educational Fund.

Bonstingl, J. J. (1992). *Schools of quality: An introduction to total quality management in education.* Alexandria, VA: Association for Supervision and Curriculum Development.

Carbo, M., R. Dunn, and K. Dunn. (1986). *Teaching students to read through their individual learning styles.* Englewood Cliffs, NJ: Prentice Hall.

Chall, J. (1983). *Learning to read: The great debate.* New York: McGraw-Hill.

Charles, C. M. (1992). *Building classroom discipline,* 4th ed. White Plains, NY: Longman Publishing Co.

Curwin, R. L., and A. N. Mendeler. (1988). *Discipline with dignity.* Alexandria, VA: Association for Supervision and Curriculum Development.

Fiske, E. B. (1991). *Smart schools, smart kids.* New York: Touchstone.

Frandsen, B. (1994). *Diversified teaching: An anthology of strategies.* Austin, TX: St. Edward's University.

———. (1995). *Managing the cooperative classroom.* Austin, TX: St. Edward's University.

Gardner, H. (1993). *Frames of mind: The theory of multiple intelligences.* New York: Basic Books.

———. (1993). *Creating minds.* New York: Basic Books.

Glasser, W. (1992). *The quality school.* New York: HarperCollins.

Johnson, D. W., R. T. Johnson, and E. J. Holubec. (1991). *Cooperation in the classroom.* Edina, MN: Interaction Book Company.

Spaneberg-Urbshat, K., and R. Pritchard. (Eds.). (1994). *Kids come in all languages: Reading instruction for ESL students.* Newark, DE: International Reading Association.

Tierney, R. J. , J. E. Readence, and E. K. Dishner. (1995). *Reading strategies and practices,* 4th ed. Needham Heights, MA: Allyn & Bacon.

Trealease, J. (1989). *The new read-aloud handbook.* New York: Penguin Books.

MULTICULTURAL LITERATURE GUIDES

Banfield, B. (1985). Books on African-American themes: A recommended booklist. *Interracial Books for Children Bulletin* 16:4–8.

Corson, C. M. (1987). YA Afro-American fiction: An update for teachers. *English Journal* 76:24–27.

Duff, O. B., and H. J. Tongchinsub. (1990). Expanding the secondary literature curriculum: Annotated bibliographies of American Indian, Asian American, and Hispanic American literature. *English Education* 22:220–240.

Frankson, M. S. (1990). Chicano literature for young adults: An annotated bibliography. *English Journal* 79:30–38.

Miller-Lachmann, L. (1992). Our family, our friends, our world: An annotated guide to significant multicultural books for children and teenagers. New Providence, NJ: R. R. Bowker.

Tarry-Stevens, Patricia. (1990). The Hispanic in young adult literature. *The ALAN Review* 31:1–3.

Glossary

These terms have been defined for the purposes of this textbook.

adaptability of rate ability to alter one's reading speed to accommodate differences in purpose, text difficulty, subject difficulty, and desired level of comprehension.

affixes meaningful groups of letters added to a root word, i.e., prefixes and suffixes.

age equivalency score standardized test result that states a student's performance in terms of a comparable performance of students in a particular age group of the test-norming population (e.g., a student with an age equivalency score of 10.0 performed approximately as well as did the ten-year-olds in the norming population; so, if the student were younger than ten, according to that particular score, he or she performed at an above-average level).

analytic learning style often characterized by preferences for auditory learning, traditional outlining, attention to detail, recall of facts and dates, breaking a whole into its component parts, sequential and logical thinking, rational-based decisions, routine procedures, careful planning and organization, and punctuality.

annotation notes or comments made for a particular purpose, usually in response to something read; the notes can take various forms (e.g., summaries, questions, critiques, paraphrases, highlights).

Anticipation Guide strategy involving a set of about five to ten nonfactual statements that are open to differences of opinion, interpretation, and perspective; before reading, students respond by agreeing or disagreeing with each, then they read for the purpose of deciding whether the author would agree or disagree with each statement; this strategy is designed to be motivational by stimulating background knowledge and encouraging expression of personal opinions.

Attention Deficit–Hyperactive Disorder (AD–HD) broadly defined learning disability that interferes with a student's ability to concentrate on a task, pay attention to instruction, and remain physically calm for any significant amount of time.

attitude survey series of statements to which students respond to indicate to the teacher the degree of positive or negative feelings they have toward particular content areas (e.g., history, math, science, literature) and/or literacy skills (e.g., reading, writing, speaking, listening, critical thinking).

authentic assessment evaluation that focuses on documenting the learning process by collecting representative samples of student work at various stages of completion; also, the work itself is characterized by an emphasis on real-life applications of knowledge and literacy.

Barrett's Taxonomy hierarchy of categories designed to distinguish various levels of reading comprehension including literal, inferential, evaluative, and appreciative; often used by teachers to ensure the planning of questions and activities designed to develop comprehension at all levels, particularly the higher ones.

behavior management refers to the actions and language used by teachers and parents for the purpose of positively shaping the actions and language of children and young adults.

bibliotherapy process of addressing one's problems by reading about the factual or realistic problems of people or characters.

Bloom's Taxonomy hierarchy of categories used to distinguish various levels of thinking including knowledge, comprehension, application, analysis, synthesis and evaluation; often used by teachers to ensure the planning of questions and activities designed to develop comprehension at all levels, particularly the higher ones.

CD-ROM stands for "compact disc–read only memory"; a multimedia storage device resembling music CDs; in addition to music, narration, speeches, and other audio forms of presentation, they also can contain photographs, illustrations, animation, videos, and other forms of visual presentation.

classroom management refers to a carefully planned system designed by the teacher and students to establish classroom rules and routines, positive reinforcement, and consequences; the plan should reflect the teacher's and students' values and philosophies of teaching and learning; it should also be consistently implemented, regularly assessed for effectiveness, and revised as necessary.

closure refers to a thinking process involving a natural tendency to fill gaps as necessary for reaching completion, particularly in language (e.g., the urge to complete another person's unfinished sentence or to supply a word when the speaker is unable to think of an appropriate one).

cloze term whose meaning is derived from the word *closure*, and whose spelling (i.e., with a *z*) reflects the pronunciation of the *s* in *closure*; it is used to describe fill-in-the-blank activities designed for particular purposes.

Cloze Procedure fill-in-the-blank activity designed to help students learn to use context clues (i.e., surrounding word meanings) as a tool in word recognition (i.e., decoding word pronunciations) and concept development (i.e., unlocking word meanings).

Cloze Test or Inventory fill-in-the-blank activity designed as a quick measure of the suitability of a piece of reading material (e.g., book, chapter, article, passage) in terms of a student's reading ability and background knowledge on the topic.

collateral reading materials variety of reading materials used as supplements, complements, or alternatives to the textbook.

concept development refers to both the act of and skill related to unlocking and learning word meanings.

conceptual density number of new or difficult ideas and information introduced in a particular reading passage, lesson, unit, or subject area.

content refers to information and knowledge that is generally related to one or more subject areas.

content acquisition process of understanding and internalizing information and knowledge; it can be accomplished through a variety and combination of means including reading, listening, writing, and speaking.

content area refers to a subject area such as science, social studies, literature, math, art, or physical education.

content area literacy use of reading, writing, and critical thinking as tools for gaining knowledge and information.

Content Area Reading Inventory (CARI) informal (not standardized) diagnostic test designed to be given on a group basis (for efficiency); it gives the teacher extensive and detailed information about students' reading abilities, background knowledge, vocabularies, and study skills in one or more subjects.

context clues overall or surrounding meaning provided by a passage, paragraph, sentence, and/or phrase to determine the pronunciation or meaning of unknown words or familiar words in unknown settings.

Control Theory classroom management philosophy aimed at motivating rather than coercing students; it is based on the notion that students will become willing participants if they are given the responsibility for making their own choices, enjoying the rewards, and living with the logical and natural consequences.

cooperative learning carefully structured learning activities in which students are held accountable for their individual contributions, participation, and learning ("no free rides"); students are also provided incentives to work as a team in teaching and learning from each other ("helping you helps me").

Cooperative Reading Teams heterogeneous (i.e., of differing abilities) groups of students who share a common interest in a particular topic; they collaborate on a research project carefully structured by the teacher to focus on specific purposes and questions related to content learning.

corrective discipline designed to stop and redirect inappropriate and unacceptable behavior in ways that are neither harsh nor intimidating.

criterion-referenced test evaluation instrument that measures a student's performance relative to her or his previous performance or to a predetermined set of mastery levels.

critical annotation notes or comments of a personal nature, consisting of the reader's overall impressions and reactions; it can address the extent to which the author's message, position, or point of view is interesting, important, valuable, questionable, viable, practical, confusing, and so forth.

critical thinking includes such higher-level processes as evaluating, applying, analyzing, synthesizing, making value judgments, problem-solving, categorizing, comparing, contrasting, and so forth.

curriculum compacting process of adapting a curriculum to serve the needs of students who are gifted and/or talented in a particular area; they are given the opportunity to replace parts of the curriculum they have already mastered with enrichment activities designed to cultivate content learning and strengthen literacy skills, as well as challenge, motivate, and inspire them as lifelong leaders and learners.

debate listening paying attention for the purpose of responding to the speaker's message as it relates to predetermined questions, issues, or positions.

decoding process of interpreting written symbols into spoken or signed language, e.g., pronouncing words either orally or silently.

deductive teaching refers to an instructional method that begins by presenting and explaining information or concepts to be learned, followed by examples and supervised practice in applying the information or concepts (the traditional lecture approach is a form of deductive teaching).

dialogue journal ongoing written conversation between a student and teacher (involving at least weekly exchanges of messages); it serves as a method of feedback for both the student and teacher.

dictionary usage for concept development skill generally used to supplement context clues for unlocking word meanings; it involves specific subskills that must be taught directly and practiced under supervision (e.g., alphabetizing, guide words, multiple meanings, and so forth).

dictionary usage for word recognition decoding skill that should be used as a last resort, i.e., after the reader has tried all other decoding skills; it involves specific subskills that must be directly taught and practiced under supervision (e.g., alphabetizing, guide words, pronunciation keys, and so forth).

discussion conversational interaction between the teacher and students or between students and students for the purpose of allowing students to explore their own and listen to each other's ideas, perceptions, interpretations, and opinions; the interaction is characterized by minimal teacher participation, i.e., only as much as necessary to provide focus and guidance.

distance learning classroom situations using television, videos, and teleconferencing to present content.

dyslexia any congenital disorder generally manifested by difficulty in reading, writing, and/or spelling in spite of normal conditions in classroom instruction, intellectual potential, and sociocultural opportunity.

electronic communication network computerized alternative to the telephone that allows instantaneous connections; provides a forum for dialogue and information exchange through computers linked to a centralized system called an information server.

electronic dialogues/computer conferences instantaneous written communication between and among individuals and groups within the same or different classes, schools, cities, states, and countries.

e-mail computerized system of correspondence that allows individuals to communicate in writing with people all over the world.

empathic listening paying attention for the purpose of completely understanding a message through a process of vicariously sharing the speaker's or author's experience; empathy implies full understanding without agreement or disagreement.

enrichment activities designed to help students process and internalize content, as well as strengthen literacy skills in meaningful ways using a variety of supplemental reading and multimedia materials.

excluding concept development activity (i.e., designed to teach word meanings) that involves identifying words that do not belong with others in a group.

extrinsic motivation sense of desire or determination that originates externally or outside the student, e.g., grades, food, and free time; overuse of external rewards can undermine the development of intrinsic motivation (desire from within, e.g., curiosity).

formal tests standardized, commercially published assessment instruments developed according to systematic procedures and characterized by very specific guidelines for administration, scoring, and interpretation.

gender bias   term describing the unequal treatment of boys and girls in the classroom; most often, teachers (although unwittingly and in very subtle ways) give boys preferential treatment in terms of more and better-quality instructional time.

gifted and talented   children and youth who are identified as having high performance potential in areas that include intellectual achievement, creativity, academic achievement in specific content areas (subjects), and leadership.

global learning style   often characterized by preferences for visual learning, graphic outlines (e.g., mapping, webbing, diagramming), attention to main ideas, getting the big picture, combining component parts into a meaningful whole, random and creative thought, impulsive decisions, change from routine, action over planning, and brainstorming.

grade equivalency score   standardized test result that states a student's performance in terms of a comparable performance of students in a particular grade level of the test norming population (e.g., a student with a grade equivalency score of 4.8 performed approximately as well as did the students in their eighth month of fourth grade; so, if the student were in the sixth grade, according to that particular score, he or she performed at a below-average level).

graphics software   programs that serve as a tool to facilitate the creation of visually oriented representations of information; allow the integration of visual components with written text and can include artistic expression, pictorial representations, photographs, text illustrations, and multimedia presentations.

Herber's Taxonomy   hierarchy of categories designed to distinguish various levels of reading comprehension including literal, interpretive, and applied; often used by teachers to ensure the planning of questions and activities that develop comprehension at all levels, particularly the higher ones.

heterogeneous grouping   assigning students of mixed abilities to work together.

heuristic annotation   notes or comments resulting from a process in which the reader discriminates and synthesizes the ideas of the author, translates them into her or his own language, and puts them in writing.

historical fiction   original stories whose characters and plots are based on real people and actual events; they are designed to recreate past events in a narrative fashion, allowing readers to "be there now" and vicariously experience events of long ago.

holistic scoring   form of writing assessment based on the overall impression of the work; instead of being evaluated separately, content and form are considered in terms of how effectively they integrate as a whole; although emphasis is placed on the message itelf, excessive errors in mechanics can reduce the effectiveness of its communication.

homogeneous grouping   assigning students of the same or similar abilities to work together.

hypertext   software that allows the author to integrate the presentation of text with illustrations, graphics, photographs, sounds, music, voice synthesizing, and live action.

implying concept development activity (i.e., designed to teach word meanings) that involves making analogies.

inclusion educational program design in which learners with special needs remain in the regular classroom; specially trained teachers work with the classroom teachers, both in planning and classroom instruction, to make modifications for effective content learning and literacy development; it is based on the notion that all children benefit from full and meaningful interaction with children of varied learning abilities and characteristics.

individual accountability characteristic of cooperative learning (distinguishing it from traditional group work) resulting from a structure that is carefully planned by the teacher to ensure that every student in a group participates equitably and meets the learning objectives.

individualized instruction educational plan designed to address the unique and varied needs of all students.

inductive teaching instructional method in which students are led to discover information and concepts for themselves, rather than having the information provided or the concepts defined for them; it is based on the notion that many people learn more effectively when they uncover information for themselves as needed for practical application (inquiry and discovery methods are forms of deductive teaching).

Informal Reading Inventory (IRI) diagnostic test administered for the purpose of gathering detailed information about a student's reading abilities including both strengths and weaknesses; because it must be administered in a one-on-one setting, it is generally used by classroom teachers only with students they identify as having difficulty reading.

informal tests assessment instruments that are not standardized; they can be either commercially or teacher-made and are usually designed to diagnose strengths and weaknesses or to measure mastery of content (information) and literacy skills.

information resource networks systems of connections between computers designed to give and receive information all over the world and on virtually any topic.

Instructional Framework flexible structure for lesson planning; its three parts are preparation (before), guidance (during), and independence (after).

instructional software computer programs stored on a disk and used to enhance or complement classroom instruction; includes software for drill and practice, tutorials, simulations, and games.

instructional technology any nontextual media (or medium) used for the purpose of teaching content information and/or developing literacy skills.

intention annotation notes or comments that identify the author's reasons for writing and are based on what the author reveals in the text, as well as what the reader knows about the author.

interdisciplinary describes learning activities that integrate more than one content area.

interdisciplinary themes topics of study around which instruction focusing on several content areas is planned.

interest inventory questionnaire or checklist completed by students to give the teacher useful planning information about their interests.

intrinsic motivation   sense of desire or determination that originates internally or within the student; for example, reading to satisfy natural curiosities or to acquire knowledge for its own sake.

joining   concept development activity (i.e., designed to teach word meanings) that involves grouping words together according to categories.

LCD panel   liquid crystal display panel; a device that is connected to a computer and placed on top of an overhead projector; instead of projecting a transparency it projects the computer screen, thereby allowing the teacher to use a computer instead of the chalkboard or overhead projector.

Learning Center   specific area in a classroom created for self-contained independent and small-group activities; detailed instructions must be provided, and the activities must be self-checking.

learning log   type of journal that emphasizes writing as a tool for learning and as a means for keeping written records of content learned.

learning styles   preferences for certain methods and combinations of methods (e.g., visual and auditory) for acquiring knowledge, varying widely among individuals.

literacy-based strategies   lesson plans designed to improve content area learning using reading, writing, and critical thinking.

Marginal Gloss   type of study guide providing notes to the reader in the margins of the text; the notes are designed to emphasize important concepts, define

technical terms, provide examples, ask higher-level questions, and so forth.

Maze Activity   variation of the Cloze Procedure in that it uses a multiple-choice format; it is a fill-in-the-blank activity designed to help students learn to use context clues (i.e., surrounding word meanings) as a tool in word recognition (i.e., decoding word pronunciations) and concept development (i.e., unlocking word meanings).

metacognition   refers to an awareness of one's thinking and learning processes, particularly in terms of their effectiveness, as one is engaged in a learning activity.

mini-lesson   brief meeting of the whole class (five to ten minutes) before or during an instructional activity for the purpose of clarifying or teaching specific concepts essential to the effectiveness of the overall activity.

modeling   act of demonstrating a strategy, activity, or procedure, usually performed by the teacher or capable student peers.

motivation annotation   notes or comments that interpret the author's motives, biases, and perspectives.

multimedia   technology that combines one or more of the following for multisensory presentation of information: text, video, audio, photography, animation, and graphics.

multiple intelligences   concept that every learner has unique areas of strength ranging from physical to musical to academic to artistic.

nonfiction narrative   type of literature that provides an interesting account, including dialogue, of actual events; such literature is usually based on the recollections, recordings, and written accounts of the actual participants.

norming population   large group of students (usually several thousand) who participate nationwide in a testing project designed to develop standards (or norms) with which to compare individual performances.

norm-referenced test   formal assessment instrument used to compare the performance of a student with that of similar students who participated in the standardization procedures.

onset(s)   initial consonant sound(s) that precede(s) the vowel sound in a word or syllable.

percentile score   indicator of how well a student performed relative to other students in the norming population.

phonemes   speech sounds that are blended together to form syllables and words.

phonics   use of sound-to-symbol relationships to decode words.

phonograms   word families that produce rhyming words (e.g., *ain, eed, oil, ent, air, old,* and so forth).

portfolio   collection of work samples that document a student's progress in the development of literacy skills and content learning; portfolios are the primary means of authentic assessment.

positive interdependence   characteristic of cooperative learning (distinguishing it from traditional group work) resulting from a structure that is carefully planned by the teacher to ensure that group members have an incentive to help each other and work together, i.e., the success of the group depends on the success of each member and vice versa.

positive reinforcement   use of praise and rewards to encourage and develop appropriate behavior.

question annotation   notes or comments that reformulate key ideas from the text into interrogative form.

raw score   number of correct responses on a test.

readability   characteristic of reading materials that indicates how well given materials can probably be read by certain students; relevant factors include those related to the text (e.g., sentence length, vocabulary difficulty, style, organization, study aids, and so forth) and those related to the student (e.g., interests, background knowledge, reading ability, vocabulary knowledge, and so forth).

readability formula   algorithm used to measure the linguistic complexity of a reading passage, usually in terms of sentence and word length.

Read-aloud   strategy in which the teacher reads out loud to the students for the purpose of sharing a variety of content-related literature in the classroom.

reader-based interpretation   translation of the author's message that emphasizes the reader's reactions and responses to the text through higher-level thinking.

realistic fiction   type of literature that portrays characters who are believable as real-life people and events that are believable as real-life occurrences.

recitation   act of demonstrating information memorized through a turn-taking session of literal-level questions and answers.

remediation   program of reteaching in the same manner, except more slowly for learners who missed or failed to master information or skills.

report writing process involved in producing a written summary and/or analysis of information related to a specific topic or issue; the process includes topic selection, planning, researching, organizing, composing, editing, and revising.

rime vowel and any consonant sound(s) that follow(s) the initial consonant sound(s) in a word or syllable.

round-robin oral reading overused classroom activity involving students taking turns reading out loud for little or no apparent purpose toward comprehension; its many disadvantages include the embarrassment of poor readers, the boredom of good readers, little attention given to the content, reinforcement of the misconception that reading is a performance in decoding rather than a process of understanding, no reinforcement of good silent reading habits, and an overall inefficient and ineffective use of learning time.

rubric set of assessment criteria that specifies the required characteristics for each level of quality, usually identified by a letter or number grade.

saccadic movements choppy movements of the eyes as they move across lines of print during reading, stopping to focus for only a split second at a time.

scaffolding reading comprehension support provided by the teacher or study guides to help students construct knowledge from the text; it is based on the notion that as students acquire skills and strategies for constructing knowledge on their own, the support is slowly taken away.

scaled scores results of a subtest reported as a number on a continuum with equal intervals, making possible comparisons across grade levels.

schema framework of knowledge, background information, and experiences each learner brings to the classroom; this framework provides the "hooks" upon which new knowledge is stored.

schemata mental categories and frameworks necessary for processing, integrating, and internalizing new knowledge.

selecting concept development activity (i.e., designed to teach word meanings) that involves the identification of appropriate synonyms.

sight words those words recognized immediately upon being encountered by the reader; often sight words must be visually memorized because they do not follow sound-to-symbol patterns.

simulations computer programs designed to represent actual or possible real-life situations and events in which the student is involved.

special-needs learners students for whom instruction must be adapted in some way to facilitate maximal performance; includes a wide variety of unique challenges, e.g., gifted and talented, learning disabled, visually-impaired, hearing-impaired, and physically-impaired.

spreadsheets electronic grids made up of horizontal rows and vertical columns for storing and processing information and data on computers.

stanine scores test results converted on an evenly spaced scale, resulting in the converted and raw scores having the same relationship; stanines consist of single-digit scores, ranging from 1 to 9, with 1 to 3 representing below-average performances, 4 to 6 representing average performances, and 7 to 9 representing above-average performances; this type of score can be compared across tests and subtests.

structural analysis word recognition (decoding) skill that involves breaking a word into component parts such as syllables, prefixes, and suffixes.

summary annotation notes or comments in which the reader condenses the author's ideas into his or her own words.

Sustained Silent Reading (SSR) strategy that provides students with regular opportunities for reading nontextbook materials including fiction and nonfiction literature and periodicals.

syllabication process of dividing a word into individual units for help in decoding and concept development.

synergy concept that the combined effort and achievement of all group members is greater than that of any individual.

technical writing process involved in producing reports that require specialized knowledge such as scientific papers or laboratory reports.

text-based interpretations translation of the author's message that integrates textual information with the reader's background knowledge.

Text-Pattern Guide scaffolding (support) strategy designed to enhance reading effectiveness by helping students identify major patterns of text organization, e.g., chronological order, reasons, examples, cause-effect, compare-contrast, problem-solution, description, spatial order, and so forth.

thematic unit set of lesson plans all related to a selected topic.

thesis annotation notes or comments involving identification of the overall theme and author's point of view.

Think-Pair-Share three-step cooperative learning activity: individually pondering a question, forming a partnership to exchange ideas, and, finally, forming a quad to discuss those ideas.

Think Sheet strategy that capitalizes on students' own interests, prior knowledge, and curiosities by using a system for helping them formulate and answer their own questions from trade books.

Three-Level Guide study guide based on the literal, interpretive, and applied levels of comprehension; it includes support for developing the reader's comprehension at all three levels.

Total Quality originally a business management concept; when applied to education, it emphasizes teaching and learning as ongoing processes for continuous improvement, capitalizing on the principles of synergy, self-evaluation, and leadership.

trade books fiction and nonfiction books intended for sale in general bookstores and typically found in libraries; they are clearly distinguishable from textbooks.

tutorials software that puts the computer in the role of teacher to introduce new concepts by building upon known ones; the programs usually begin with some type of assessment of the students' levels of knowledge or ability; then, the nature of the students' responses determines how the program will progress.

visual configuration overall shape of a particular word; the concept is important for helping students memorize sight words.

word recognition act of decoding and pronouncing written words orally or silently.

Writing Guides type of scaffolding, similar to study guides, that helps students construct meaning by leading them through the steps involved in completing a particular writing task.

writing-to-learn activities designed to enhance learning and help students monitor their own understanding and processing of new information.

Writing Workshop in the content area classroom, it involves time set aside each day for students to write with the deliberate purpose of reflecting on and personalizing the content under study.

Subject Index

Author and Title Index